THE POLITICS OF NUCLEAR ENERGY
IN WESTERN EUROPE

The Politics of Nuclear Energy in Western Europe

Edited by
WOLFGANG C. MÜLLER and
PAUL W. THURNER

UNIVERSITY PRESS

OXFORD
UNIVERSITY PRESS

Great Clarendon Street, Oxford, OX2 6DP,
United Kingdom

Oxford University Press is a department of the University of Oxford.
It furthers the University's objective of excellence in research, scholarship,
and education by publishing worldwide. Oxford is a registered trade mark of
Oxford University Press in the UK and in certain other countries

© Oxford University Press 2017

The moral rights of the authors have been asserted

First Edition published in 2017

Impression: 1

All rights reserved. No part of this publication may be reproduced, stored in
a retrieval system, or transmitted, in any form or by any means, without the
prior permission in writing of Oxford University Press, or as expressly permitted
by law, by licence or under terms agreed with the appropriate reprographics
rights organization. Enquiries concerning reproduction outside the scope of the
above should be sent to the Rights Department, Oxford University Press, at the
address above

You must not circulate this work in any other form
and you must impose this same condition on any acquirer

Published in the United States of America by Oxford University press
198 Madison Avenue, New York, NY 10016, United States of America

British Library Cataloguing in Publication Data

Data available

Library of Congress Control Number: 2016955292

ISBN 978-0-19-874703-1

Printed and bound by
CPI Group (UK) Ltd, Croydon, CR0 4YY

Links to third party websites are provided by Oxford in good faith and
for information only. Oxford disclaims any responsibility for the materials
contained in any third party website referenced in this work.

Acknowledgements

We are grateful to the MZES, the Mannheimer Zentrum für Europäische Sozialforschung (Mannheim Centre for European Social Research), for including our project in its research programme and financing a first workshop. We are also indebted to the Lorenz-von-Stein-Gesellschaft for supporting this meeting. We are most grateful to the Fritz Thyssen Stiftung for providing a grant for the Project 'Phasing-out and Phasing-in: The Comparative Politics and Policies of Nuclear Energy in Europe' (Az. 20.08.0.126) that has allowed the financing of several follow-up workshops by the book's authors and research assistance for the project. Our greatest debt is with the contributors to the book. Highly valuable research assistance has been provided by Michael Imre, Theresa Kernecker, Ingrid Mauerer, and Mirjam Selzer. Finally, we are very grateful to the reviewers for Oxford University Press for their valuable comments and suggestions and to Dominic Byatt for ably guiding our project through different stages, Jane Robson for careful copy-editing, and Subramaniam Vengatakrishnan for steering the production process.

Contents

List of Figures	ix
List of Tables	xiii
List of Contributors	xv

1. Nuclear Energy in Western Europe: Revival or Rejection? An Introduction — *Wolfgang C. Müller and Paul W. Thurner* — 1

2. Understanding Policy Reversals and Policy Stability — *Wolfgang C. Müller and Paul W. Thurner* — 21

3. Comparative Policy Indicators on Nuclear Energy — *Paul W. Thurner and Wolfgang C. Müller* — 47

4. The Conflict over Nuclear Energy: Public Opinion, Protest Movements, and Green Parties in Comparative Perspective — *Paul W. Thurner, Sylvain Brouard, Martin Dolezal, Isabelle Guinaudeau, Swen Hutter, and Wolfgang C. Müller* — 65

5. Austria: Rejecting Nuclear Energy—From Party Competition Accident to State Doctrine — *Wolfgang C. Müller* — 98

6. Nuclear Politics in France: High-Profile Policy and Low-Salience Politics — *Sylvain Brouard and Isabelle Guinaudeau* — 125

7. Germany: Party System Change and Policy Reversals — *Paul W. Thurner* — 157

8. Why Italian Nuclear Energy Policy Failed Twice — *Fabio Franchino* — 183

9. Nuclear Power and Politics in the Netherlands — *Kees Aarts and Maarten Arentsen* — 215

10. The Will of the People? Swedish Nuclear Power Policy — *Sören Holmberg and Per Hedberg* — 235

11. Switzerland — *Hanspeter Kriesi* — 259

12. Conclusion: Explaining Nuclear Policy Reversals *Wolfgang C. Müller, Paul W. Thurner, and Christian Schulze*	286
Appendix: Other European Countries—An Analytical Reconstruction *Paul W. Thurner, Wolfgang C. Müller, and Christian Schulze*	324
Appendix: Policy Scales for a Country's Nuclear Energy Policy	361
Index	365

List of Figures

3.1. Role of Nuclear Energy in 2013 in Comparison—Gross Inland Energy Consumption	50
3.2. Role of Nuclear Energy in 2013 in Comparison—Absolute Electricity Production (TW.h) and Shares in Domestic Electricity Production (%)	51
3.3. Annual Number of NPPs in Construction and in Commercial Operation in the EU-28 Plus Switzerland 1960–2014	53
3.4. Nuclear Electricity Capacity in Construction and in Commercial Operation in the EU-28 Plus Switzerland 1960–2014	54
3.5. Mean Import Dependency 1990–2013	55
3.6. Mean Share of Nuclear Energy in Gross Inland Consumption 1990–2013	57
3.7. Mean Nuclear Energy Contribution to Electricity Generation 1990–2013	58
3.8. Scatterplot: Nuclear Electricity Generation (%) and Import Dependency (%)	59
3.9. Scatterplot: Nuclear Electricity Generation (%) and Import Dependency (%)	59
3.10. Scatterplot: Nuclear Energy Contribution to Gross Inland Consumption (%) and Import Dependency (%)	60
4.1. Public Opinion Trends in Selected Countries: Opposition to Nuclear Energy (1978–2011)	70
4.2. Import Dependency and Proportion of Anti-Nuclear Attitudes (2008)	74
4.3. Share of Domesticly Produced Nuclear Energy in Gross Inland Consumption and Proportion of Anti-Nuclear Attitudes (2008)	74
4.4. Protest Participants by Country, 1975 to 2011	77
4.5. Protest Events by Country, 1975 to 2011	78
4.6. Green Parties' Electoral Performance: 1975–2014 (Votes)	88
4.7. (a–c). Disproportionality and Green Party Shares in Three Different Elections	91
5.1. Nuclear Energy Policy Development in Austria, 1945–2013	100
6.1. Sources of French Electricity Production 1960–2012	126
6.2. Number of Statutes Regarding Nuclear Energy Issue	132
6.3. Attention to Nuclear Energy, Farmers and Culture in French Party Manifestos (% of words)	136
6.4. French Party Stances on a Pro-Nuclear–Anti-Nuclear Energy Scale	137
6.5. Level of Support to Nuclear Energy in France 1975–2013	140
6.6. Media Attention to Nuclear Energy in France 1977–2012	143
6.7. Level of Nuclear Support among Party-Leaners in France, 1980–2005	145
6.8. Level of Inconsistency between Policy Attitudes and Partisan Leaning of French Voters, 1982, 1994, 2002, and 2012	147
6.A1. Nuclear Energy Policy Development in France, 1945–2013	153
7.1. Nuclear Energy Policy Development in Germany, 1945–2013	161

List of Figures

7.2.	Public Expenditures for R&D in Nuclear Energy: Percentages of Budget Changes (Adjusted for Prices) 1974–2014	162
7.3.	Development of Attitudes towards Nuclear Energy	174
7.4.	Share of 'Inconsistent Voters' 1977–2011	175
7.5.	Parties' Position-Taking in German Electoral Manifestos	176
7.6.	Share (%) Nuclear Energy in Electoral Manifestos	178
8.1.	Gross Electricity Production and Capacity from Nuclear Energy, 1963–1989	184
8.2.	Attitudes towards Nuclear Energy, 1978–2008	196
8.3.	Ideological Distribution of Opponents of Nuclear Energy, 1978–2008	197
8.4.	Attitudes towards Nuclear Energy, 2000s	201
8.5.	Attitudes toward Nuclear Energy and Ideology	202
8.6.	Attitudes towards Nuclear Energy and Partisanship, 2009	202
8.A1.	Nuclear Energy Policy Development in Italy, 1945–2013	212
8.A2.	Parties' Position-Taking in Italian Electoral Manifestos	213
8.A3.	Nuclear Energy Salience in Party Electoral Manifestos (%)	213
9.1.	Nuclear Energy Policy Development in the Netherlands 1945–2013	220
9.2.	Mean Respondent Position on Nuclear Power Plants and Perceived Party Positions	226
9.3a.	Voting Behaviour by Position on Nuclear Power Plants, 1977	228
9.3b.	Voting Behaviour by Position on Nuclear Power Plants, 1989	229
9.3c.	Voting Behaviour by Position on Nuclear Power Plants, 1998	229
9.3d.	Voting Behaviour by Position on Nuclear Power Plants, 2012	230
9.4.	Mean Position on Nuclear Power Plants of Voters of Various Parties	231
9.5.	Voters and Perceived Party Positions on Nuclear Power Plants for Four Parties	232
10.1.	Nuclear Energy Policy Development in Sweden, 1945–2013	238
10.2.	Swedish Opinion on Nuclear Power 1976–2014 (%)	247
10.3.	Swedes on the Use of Nuclear Power as an Energy Source (%)	248
10.4.	Percentage in Favour of Nuclear Power among Voters for Different Swedish Parties 1979–2014	249
10.5.	Percentage in Favour of Using Nuclear Power among Swedes with Different Party Sympathies	250
10.6.	Policy Representation in Sweden—Attitudes on Nuclear Power among Members of Parliament and Eligible Voters in 1985–2014 (%)	253
11.1.	Nuclear Energy Policy Development in Switzerland, 1945–2013	261
11.2.	Development of the Mobilization by the Anti-Nuclear Movement in Switzerland	265
11.3.	Party Scales	272
11.4.	Overall Salience of Major Groups of Actors by Period: Percentages of All Mentions in the Press	277
11.5.	Overall Use of Frames by the Three Major Groups of Actors: Percentages	278
11.6.	Development of Public Opinion on Nuclear Energy: Percentage of People Against	279

List of Figures

11.7.	Level of Policy-Specific Awareness in the Three Votes on Nuclear Energy (%)	281
11.8.	Difference in Vote Shares 2003–1990, by Level of Awareness (%)	282
12.1.	Attitudes towards Nuclear Energy in the first Eurobarometer Available	300
12.2.	Public Opinion Trends in Selected Countries: Opposition to Nuclear Energy (1978–2011) (Group 2)	301
12.3.	Public Opinion Trends in Selected Countries: Opposition to Nuclear Energy (1978–2011) (Group 4)	310
12.A1.	Nuclear Energy Policy Development in Denmark, 1945–2013	326
12.A2.	Nuclear Energy Policy Development in Ireland, 1945–2013	328
12.A3.	Nuclear Energy Policy Development in Luxembourg, 1945–2013	330
12.A4.	Nuclear Energy Policy Development in Norway, 1945–2013	332
12.A5.	Nuclear Energy Policy Development in Portugal, 1945–2013	334
12.A6.	Nuclear Energy Policy Development in Greece, 1945–2013	336
12.A7.	Nuclear Energy Policy Development in Belgium, 1945–2013	338
12.A8.	Attitudes on Nuclear Energy among Belgian Party Voters in 1978 (First Available EB)	340
12.A9.	Attitudes on Nuclear Energy among Belgian Party Voters in 1996	341
12.A10.	Nuclear Energy Policy Development in Spain, 1945–2013	344
12.A11.	Attitudes on Nuclear Energy among Spanish Party Voters in 1986	345
12.A12.	Attitudes on Nuclear Energy among Spanish Party Voters in 1996	346
12.A13.	Nuclear Energy Policy Development in Finland, 1945–2013	348
12.A14.	Attitudes on Nuclear Energy among Finnish Party Voters in 1996	351
12.A15.	Nuclear Energy Policy Development in Britain, 1945–2013	353
12.A16.	Attitudes on Nuclear Energy among British Party Voters in 1978	354
12.A17.	Attitudes on Nuclear Energy among British Party Voters in 1996	355

List of Tables

3.1. Nuclear Power Plants in the EU, in Operation and under Construction, 2015	52
3.2. Nuclear Power Plants Removed from the Grid in Eastern European EU Accession States	53
3.A1. Share of Nuclear Energy in Gross Inland Consumption (1990–2013)	61
3.A2. Electricity Generation by Origin: Nuclear 1990–2013 (%)	62
3.A3. Energy Dependency 1990–2013 (%)	63
4.1. Approval and Rejection of Nuclear Energy in Twenty-Seven European Countries (2008)	72
4.2. Approval and Rejection of Nuclear Energy in Twelve European Countries Just Before Fukushima (2011)	73
4.3. Mobilization Levels by Country and Time Period	79
4.4. Three Major Thresholds in the Development of Green Parties on the National Level	86
5.1. Party Sympathy and Policy Preferences over the Nuclear Power Station at Zwentendorf in Referendum Run-Up and Referendum Voting, January to November 1978	108
5.2. Referendum Voting Behaviour of Party Sympathizers	109
5.3. Eligibility of Pro-Nuclear Party (June–September 1978)	110
5.4. Voters' Motives in the 1979 General Election	110
5.5. Post-Referendum Attitudes on Nuclear Power (Vote Intention in Referendum Today)	114
5.6. Post-Chernobyl Attitudes towards Nuclear Energy in Austria	115
6.A1. Main Events of the Nuclear French Policy	154
8.A1. Raw Data for a Nuclear Energy Policy Scale	207
9.1. Chernobyl and Public Opinion on Operational Nuclear Power Plants. Responses to Question Item: 'Close Existing Nuclear Plants?'	227
11.1. Energy Policy Milestones in Switzerland	263
12.1. Observation Window and Number of Cabinets until 2013	313
12.2. Overview of Minor and Major Nuclear Energy (NE) Policy Reversals in Western Europe 1945–2013	314
12.3. Operationalization of the Variables	316
12.4. Fixed Effects Logit Model of Nuclear Policy Reversals (Against Nuclear Energy) in Western Europe 1945–2013	317
A.1. Pro-Nuclear Decisions	361
A.2. Anti-Nuclear Decisions 1	362
A.3. Anti-Nuclear Decisions 2	362
A.4. Position-Taking on Nuclear Energy in Party Manifestos	363

List of Contributors

Kees Aarts is a professor of Political Institutions and Behavior at the University of Groningen, the Netherlands.

Maarten Arentsen is an associate professor at the Department of Governance and Technology for Sustainability, University of Twente, the Netherlands.

Sylvain Brouard is Senior Research Fellow FNSP at CEVIPOF, Sciences Po, France.

Martin Dolezal is a researcher in political science at the Department of Government, University of Vienna, Austria.

Fabio Franchino is a professor in political science at the University of Milan, Italy.

Isabelle Guinaudeau is an associate CNRS researcher at the Centre Emile Durkheim, Institut d'Etudes Politiques de Bordeaux, France.

Per Hedberg is deputy chief analyst at the SOM (Society Opinion Media) Institute, University of Gothenburg, Sweden.

Sören Holmberg is a professor emeritus in political science at the University of Gothenburg, Sweden.

Swen Hutter is a post-doctoral research fellow at the European University Institute in Florence, Italy.

Hanspeter Kriesi is a professor in Comparative Politics (Stein Rokkan Chair) at the European University Institute, Italy.

Wolfgang C. Müller is professor of Democratic Governance at the Department of Government, University of Vienna, Austria.

Christian Schulze holds an MA in political science and is currently a business consultant.

Paul W. Thurner is a professor of Empirical Political Research and Policy Analysis at the University of Munich (LMU), Germany.

1

Nuclear Energy in Western Europe

Revival or Rejection? An Introduction

Wolfgang C. Müller and Paul W. Thurner

1.1 INTRODUCTION: THE NUCLEAR ENERGY PUZZLE

Ever since mankind has begun to untie the power of atoms, this has been accompanied by both fascination and fright. Madame Curie won the Nobel Prize for her path-breaking work on radiation, but died from radioactive contamination. The horror of Hiroshima and Nagasaki gave way to the hope that the prospects of mutual destruction from a nuclear war would not just prevent such wars, but also conventional ones between nuclear countries and their allies. Indeed, the threat of 'mutually assured destruction' (MAD) helped maintain the largely peaceful coexistence of ideologically hostile superpowers over decades. Finally, the great hopes initially placed in the peaceful use of nuclear energy soon were balanced by fears of nuclear accidents that would kill large numbers of people and render vast territories uninhabitable, the looming dangers of atomic terrorism (Allison 2005; Levi 2009), and the emergence of intrusive government and severely constrained civil rights to counter such threats (the 'atomic state'—see Jungk 1977). The nuclear accidents of Chernobyl and Fukushima Daiichi (from now on Fukushima) have underlined that such dangers do not exist only theoretically, but are all too real.

Due to such diverse and conflicting perceptions, civil nuclear power has become a highly divisive political issue at least since the early 1970s. As such, it tended to trigger strong rather than lukewarm feelings among citizens. At the same time, the long-time horizons of all kinds of nuclear programmes and their high costs increase the stakes of decision-makers with rather short-term re-election perspectives (cf. Jacobs 2011; Jacobs and Matthews 2012; Felder 2013). Interestingly, different nations have responded very differently to these challenges. If we look only at the outcomes of the decision-making processes on nuclear energy, it is clear that some countries have opted for the use of nuclear energy and have upheld their decisions. At the other extreme of the continuum, we find countries that have consistently refrained from adopting nuclear energy. Yet many countries place themselves in between these two poles, making opposite decisions on the use of nuclear energy at different points in time, thus leading to various phasing-in and phasing-out periods.

The present volume seeks to understand why nations have made such different decisions on nuclear energy and why some of the decisions were upheld and others reversed. We are particularly interested in policy reversals. The high costs of entry and the enormous sunk costs of a sizeable nuclear energy programme make such reversals rare but very important decisions. In studying these decisions we are particularly interested in the *political* factors driving them. Despite the unique aspects of the nuclear energy issue these processes highlight how different political systems work. Of course, we recognize that other factors also weigh in. Think of the power of technological progress that provides for the world-wide application of new technologies, with only socio-economic factors determining when a country is ready for them. Clearly, this is not the case with nuclear energy, as some of the most developed rich countries do without and others, including the European powerhouse of technology, Germany, have just decided to abandon nuclear energy. Or consider the endowment with natural resources—such as oil and gas. Clearly, there are countries that can easily afford to remain non-nuclear (think of oil-rich Saudi-Arabia or oil- and hydro-electric-power-rich Norway). Yet even countries with large endowments of traditional energy sources such as coal have chosen to go nuclear. Most Western European countries are vast net-importers of energy. Still, some choose to include nuclear power in their energy mix, while others do not. Even countries highly dependent on imports of all kinds of fossil energy resources have opted to abandon (e.g. Italy since 1990) or not to choose the nuclear path (e.g. Portugal). In short, the different fate of nuclear energy in countries that share similar conditions of technological development, economy, and natural energy endowments suggests that these factors, while important, cannot fully explain the different outcomes in terms of energy policy choices. We explore this topic more systematically in Chapter 3.

As a rule, countries do make a series of explicit political decisions on nuclear energy. Given its characteristics—from the requirement of costly long-term programmes to difficulty in social acceptance—this form of energy is arguably the most politicized one. We are particularly interested in public opinion dynamics and their impact on political decision-making. Yet, in modern democracies the people's will is mediated and formed by political parties (Dalton et al. 2011). In articulating policy preferences and making public policy decisions, parties interact with the electorate, but also with each other. Theories of the policy process (see Sabatier 2007) tell us that even in democracies there is no guarantee that public opinion and policy outcomes match. In this volume we seek to understand how public opinion on nuclear energy, party affiliations of voters, inter-party competition, and the party composition of government interact to produce public policy on nuclear energy.

In the bulk of this volume we concentrate on countries of Western Europe that in many ways are similar cases, but at the same time provide examples for the entire range of decisions on nuclear power. The intensive part of our research design allows for in-depth analyses of political processes and the dynamic interplay of factors in individual countries. In the comparative chapters we bring in additional countries that are also diverse in terms of their economic and political background conditions.

The present chapter proceeds as follows. We will present a short history of nuclear energy with particular emphasis on the most recent period that has rarely been subjected to systematic political science analyses. We identify two contradicting trends: first, a world-wide revival of nuclear energy setting in during the late 1990s after years of relative neglect, followed by quite heterogeneous reactions to the Fukushima catastrophe. While the catalyst effect of the nuclear power disasters seems to be easy to observe, the actual political processes that lead to key public policy decisions are often complex and worth studying. This is what we do in the case studies that follow (Chapters 5 to 11). In this chapter we briefly map the factors that are common inputs to the politics and policies of nuclear energy in individual countries. After that, we provide an overview of the following chapters.

1.2 THE RETURN OF NUCLEAR ENERGY TO THE POLITICAL AGENDA

Nuclear energy was part of the post-Second World War consensus of economic growth and of an almost unlimited belief in technological progress (Cooke 2009; Mahaffey 2009). In the words of President Eisenhower, nuclear energy would 'provide abundant electrical energy in the power-starved areas of the world'.[1] This resulted in large-scale planning and building of nuclear power capacity in many industrialized countries from the 1950s. The world's first atomic reactors for electricity production were connected to the grid in 1954 both in the Soviet Union (Obninsk) and the West (Sellafield, UK). From there, nuclear energy rapidly expanded: by 1960 fifteen reactors were in operation, 84 by 1970, 245 by 1980, and 416 by 1990 (IAEA 2011: 21). The total capacity increased at an even greater pace, from 1087 MW(e) in 1960 to 318,253 MW(e) in 1990 (IAEA 2011: 21).

Notwithstanding some early protests against nuclear energy, the issue became the subject of massive citizen protests in the 1970s (e.g. Kitschelt 1980, 1986a, 1986b; Nelkin and Pollak 1981; Rootes 2007; Rucht 1994). As a consequence, the nuclear power industry began to suffer stagnation and decline. In the words of the World Nuclear Organization, a lobby group, 'Few new reactors were ordered, the number coming on line from mid 1980s little more than matched retirements, though capacity increased by nearly one third and output increased 60% due to capacity plus improved load factors. The share of nuclear world electricity (production) from mid 1980s was fairly constant at 16–17%. Many reactor orders from the 1970s were cancelled'.[2]

From the late 1990s, however, the same source reports a 'nuclear renaissance'. The first third-generation reactor (characterized by significantly increased projected lifetime and safety standards) was commissioned by Japan in the late 1990s and other orders followed (for instance by Finland in 2004). Other observers see a 'renaissance' from the mid-2000s (WEC 2012: 8).[3] Consequently, in the

---

[1] Dwight D. Eisenhower, 'Atoms for Peace', address to the 470th Plenary Meeting of the United Nations General Assembly, 8 Dec. 1953.
[2] <http://www.world-nuclear.org/info/inf54.html>.
[3] Schneider and Froggatt (2012: 20) take issue with the 'renaissance' interpretation. Emphasizing the declining market share of nuclear energy (cf. WEC 2012: 8), they talk about a 'survival strategy' that 'was sold to the world as revival'.

half-decade ending in 2010, fifty new nuclear power stations went under construction world-wide—more than in the fifteen years before. Comparing IAEA technical reports, it becomes obvious that the number of construction starts increased dramatically from 2006 ($n = 3$) to 2010 ($n = 16$). Moreover, a series of countries, including Poland, Turkey, Kenia, Namibia, Vietnam, and Indonesia, announced that they would go nuclear.

Major efforts have gone into developing so-called Generation IV reactors to be ready by 2030. On 12 March 2011, the day when the Fukushima tragedy began to unfold, a total of thirty countries ran 442 nuclear power reactors with a total capacity of 379,001 MWe (megawatts). Sixty-five reactors were under construction (with a planned capacity of 62,862 MWe) and 159 (amounting to 178,123 MWe) were planned (WEC 2012: 10–11).

Behind this macro picture of the development of the global nuclear energy sector there were many individual decisions taken at firm and country levels. The stagnation and decline period resulted from several countries' explicit decisions to abstain from nuclear energy despite earlier plans of 'going nuclear', or to abandon it although already in use. The same effects result from the decisions to cut back or postpone agreed nuclear investment programmes up to the point when such decisions implicitly mean that the nuclear industry will be phased out by the existing capacities reaching their projected decommissioning date. Likewise, the more recent trend of nuclear energy revival roots in individual firm and country decisions to 'go nuclear' for the first time, to revive dormant plans for nuclear expansion, or to reverse an earlier phase-out decision. In a globalized world with important centres of regional integration the nuclear energy topic also has an international dimension. We briefly review the developments that are most important in this nuclear energy revival, beginning with supra-national attempts.

Technological development is the key objective of the Generation IV International Forum (GIF) that was established in 2001 and brings together the most important economies (including Argentina, Brazil, Canada, China, France, Japan, Russia, the United Kingdom, the United States, and Euratom). Whereas one of the GIF concerns is achieving higher standards of nuclear safety, the G8 summit in St Petersburg in 2006 was mainly concerned with 'global energy security'. While recognizing differences in opinion among the G8 members, the summit identified the further development of nuclear energy as contributing to 'global energy security, simultaneously reducing harmful air pollution and addressing the climate change challenge'.[4] In 2007 the United States Department of Energy released the 'Global Nuclear Energy Plan' that promoted the 'peaceful use of nuclear energy' in the US and elsewhere. Another important development at the international level was the Global Nuclear Energy Partnership initiative of the George W. Bush administration. Founding members in 2007 were the USA, China, France, Japan, and Russia. This initiative was renamed the International Framework for Nuclear Energy Cooperation in 2010 and is now comprised of twenty-five countries[5] and

---

[4] G8 Summit 2006, Global Energy Security, St Petersburg, 17 July 2006, point 29.
[5] The International Framework for Nuclear Energy Cooperation countries are Armenia, Australia, Bulgaria, Canada, China, Estonia, France, Ghana, Hungary, Italy, Japan, Jordan, Kazakhstan, Republic of Korea, Lithuania, Morocco, Oman, Poland, Romania, Russia, Senegal, Slovenia, Ukraine, the United Kingdom, and the United States.

the IAEA, GIF, and Euratom as permanent observers. The main objective of this platform is the development of nuclear energy technologies and infrastructures while at the same time guaranteeing non-proliferation and nuclear safety.

In addition to these global initiatives, some regional ones provide cross-national support in the use of nuclear energy. One is the Forum for Nuclear Cooperation in Asia, initiated already in 1990 and consisting of Australia, Bangladesh, China, Indonesia, Japan, Kazakhstan, Korea, Malaysia, Mongolia, the Philippines, Thailand, and Vietnam. Note that at the very centre of European integration is the Euratom treaty (it was one of the three founding treaties in the 1950s of what is now the EU). Thus, nuclear energy has continuously been part of EU policy-making.

Here we refer to several more recent EU initiatives. The European Council meeting of March 2007 adopted a comprehensive energy action plan—'An Energy Policy for Europe'—for the period 2007–9 (European Council 2007). It identified nuclear energy as 'one of the cheapest sources of low carbon energy that is presently produced in the EU'. Nuclear energy was also considered as having 'relatively stable costs' and being based on 'on sources that are sufficient for many decades and widely distributed around the globe'. While explicitly recognizing the member states' freedom of choice with regard to the use of nuclear energy, the Commission also launched a best-practice 'Nuclear Illustrative Programme' and a EU Network of Energy Security Correspondents (NESCO, endorsed by the European Council in December 2006) in 2007. Although the EU seems to have somewhat dampened its promotion of nuclear energy in the aftermath of Fukushima and related decisions by member states to abandon it, the 'EU Energy Roadmap 2050' (December 2011) still maintains that nuclear energy will continue to play a necessary role in the EU power generation mix as contributing to 'lower system costs and electricity prices' and as a 'large scale low-carbon option' to fight climate change (COM 2011 8852, 8, 13). In its climate and energy policy framework 2020–30 from 2014 the EU Commission listed nuclear energy as one of several strategies individual countries may use (COM 2014 15, 11). At the same time, the EU emphasizes waste and safety concerns, aiming at completing the legal framework for nuclear energy to include training, certification, licensing, and civil liabilities.

Such multi-national initiatives to advance nuclear energy are paralleled by national ones. To contextualize the European story, we refer only to the most significant developments here. In the US, the 2005 Energy Policy Act provided incentives for establishing new-generation power reactors. In 2006 President George W. Bush launched the 'Advanced Energy Initiative'. It aimed at providing the United States with 'affordable energy' and to lessen its addiction to oil by investment in research. Next to research in renewable forms of energy, Bush mentioned 'clean, safe nuclear energy'.[6]

Despite all their differences, President Bush's successor, President Barack Obama, maintained the positive view of nuclear energy. In his 2010 Presidential Address he made nuclear energy part and parcel of a grand strategy designed to combine economic growth with fighting climate change, saying 'to create more of

---

[6] State of the Union Address by the President, 31 Jan. 2006.

these clean energy jobs, we need more production, more efficiency, more incentives. That means building a new generation of safe, clean nuclear power plants in this country' (28 January 2010). In his 2011 State of the Union Address Obama repeated his commitment to clean energy sources—including nuclear energy—and set the goal of producing 80 per cent of the US electricity demand from these sources by 2035 (25 January 2011). In 2012, the US Nuclear Regulatory Commission decided positively on the licences for a total of four new nuclear power reactors at already existing sites in Georgia and South Carolina, respectively. These plants would be connected to the grid between 2015 and 2020. The US government supports these projects with substantial federal loan guarantees while South Carolina has been allowed to burden customers with the nuclear investments early on—a model that seems unlikely to be widely adopted in other US states (Schneider and Froggatt 2015: 111–12).

Even the most ambitious plans of European and American countries are dwarfed by those of China, India, Russia, pre-Fukushima Japan, and South Korea (see e.g. Kim and Chang 2012; Mallah 2011; Yi-chong 2010, 2011; Zhou et al. 2011). Pre-Fukushima China alone planed a six-fold increase in nuclear power capacity by 2020. In 2010 China connected two reactors to the grid, started the construction of ten more, and had forty-two more planned (IAEA 2011: 24–6). Many of these are of the latest Western design. Altogether, the IAEA (2011) reported the connection to the grid of five new reactors and sixteen more under construction in China in 2010. These brought the number of reactors under construction world-wide to a total of sixty-seven in the year before Fukushima. Moreover, the IAEA reported plans for the construction of 120 additional reactors as known by the end of 2010. China appears largely untroubled by the Fukushima accident. After a brief slowdown following the nuclear disaster in Japan it basically continued with its ambitious nuclear programme in its five-year plan accepted by the People's Congress in 2011, though more attention seems to be given to safety concerns.

Japan adopted in its 2005 'Framework for Nuclear Energy Policy', the plan of maintaining the share of 30 per cent of its electricity to be based on nuclear energy and possibly even increasing it to 40 per cent until after 2030. Less than a year before the Fukushima disaster the plan was revised and made even more ambitious, with a 53 per cent nuclear energy share by 2030 (Hayashi and Hughes 2013). Additionally, the plan scheduled the commercial operation of fast-breeder reactors starting in 2050. It is obvious that large amounts of R&D investments were committed to realizing these plans.

Understandably, the Fukushima catastrophe led to immediate policy reaction in Japan. Its nuclear power plants were gradually shut down for safety inspection. By May 2012 this process was completed, with no nuclear plant producing electricity. Prime Minister Naoto Kan, who had presided over the above-mentioned expansion strategy, and his successor, Yoshihiko Noda, hesitated to allow them to go online again after the inspection was completed. They also tried to set Japan on a path to make it less dependent on nuclear energy or even to a long-term phase-out. A policy review resulted in alternative plans allowing for nuclear energy shares between 0 and 25 per cent (Hayashi and Hughes 2013). These plans were met with scepticism early on, as nuclear energy policy would be locked in and supported by a powerful network of vested interests (e.g. Takubo 2011; Vivoda 2012). Despite Japan's electorate remaining quite sceptical about nuclear energy after Fukushima, the new LDP government under Prime Minister Shinzo Abe, assuming office after a landslide victory in the election of December 2012, decided to switch on the inspected nuclear plants. The first reactor was restarted in August 2015. Before that, in 2014, his government granted permission to complete the construction of three nuclear power plants that had been stopped after the Fukushima accident. As a consequence of the accident and the inspection, Japan's fleet of nuclear power plants was substantially reduced (Schneider and Froggatt 2015: 173). Japan's Fourth Basic Energy Plan from 2014 does not aim to phase out nuclear energy but aims for a more balanced energy mix (with nuclear energy accounting for 20–2 per cent of energy generation, compared to 22–4 per cent to be contributed by renewable energy until 2030).[7]

In Europe the enthusiasm for nuclear energy has been particularly strong in the new member states of the EU (Verse 2012). It is symptomatic that the Commission-initiated European Nuclear Energy Forum (ENEF), a network for discussions among the stakeholders in the atomic energy sector founded in 2007, holds its annual plenary meetings in Bratislava and Prague. With the exception of Poland, all the new EU member states inherited nuclear energy in some form from the communist era. EU accession meant that power plants considered particularly unsafe had to be closed down (Kozloduy 1–4 in Bulgaria, Bohunice 1 and 2 in Slovakia, Ignalia in Lithuania) and ongoing planning and building processes had to be cancelled or adapted to Western standards. This did not dissuade these countries from betting on nuclear energy, however. Even without the defunct power stations, the contribution of nuclear energy to electricity generation is larger in the new EU member states than in the old ones and the countries have worked to further increase it by the building of new nuclear power capacity. Many of these projects are conducted with the know-how and capital of Western companies. Romania, a nuclear latecomer among these states, completed and connected to the grid the Cernavoda 1 and 2 reactors in 1996 and 2007, respectively (Heffron 2012). With the help of foreign investors, most recently China, Romania is further expanding its nuclear energy capacity (Schneider and Froggatt 2015: 162–3). Lithuania, Latvia, and Estonia are building a new joint nuclear plant close to the now defunct Ignalina power station (projected to go to the grid by 2020). The project met considerable resistance and was even rejected by a consultative referendum but nevertheless was followed through. The Ukraine crisis has been helpful in rallying all-party support behind the project as part of a strategy to substitute energy imports from Russia (Schneider and Froggatt 2015: 48–9). Initially, Poland had also been part of the Ignalina consortium but withdrew from the project in 2011 to concentrate on the development of plans for two nuclear power plants on its own territory. However, the plan ran into difficulties. Although the government remains committed in principle to this path, it is currently not specific enough to be included in the latest IAEA (2015) list of planned projects. The Czech Republic originally had plans to build eighteen new nuclear reactors. However, these grand plans had to be scaled down. Two reactors were added to the Temelin site and went into production in 2000 and 2003, respectively. In addition, the Dukovany power plant was upgraded, its capacity

---

[7] 'Plan sets out Japan's Energy Mix for 2030', *World Nuclear News*, 3 June 2015.

expanded, one lifetime extension granted (until 2025), while a second one (until 2035) is currently under discussion. Plans to add two more reactors to the Temelin site, however, failed due to lack of profitability (Schneider and Froggatt 2015: 161). Slovakia is already constructing two more reactors in Bohunice (to be completed until 2017) and plans for two more in Mochovce by 2025. Slovenia plans for the lifetime extension of its only nuclear power station and the building of a new reactor there. Hungary decided in 2009 to add two more blocks to its Paks nuclear power plant. In 2014 it turned to the Russian government and nuclear industry to finance and realize this plan (Schneider and Froggatt 2015: 161). The nuclear energy expansion path was most bumpy in Bulgaria. It began building a new nuclear power plant at Belene but terminated construction for economic reasons in 2012. An attempt to revive the project via referendum failed in 2013 because participation remained below the quorum. The Fukushima disaster of 2011 did not exercise great influence on this referendum. Other attempts at reviving this project with the help of foreign investors also came to nothing for economic reasons. In any case, the Fukushima accident could not derail the nuclear expansion path in the central eastern EU member states. Nuclear energy is not only important in these countries; with the exception of Lithuania (which voted 'no' in a consultative referendum on the planned nuclear power plant in 2012), it also enjoys a great amount of societal acceptance (see Chapter 4). Yet other factors, in particular concerns about the returns on investment, have increasingly been visible.

The situation is different in Western Europe. Even before Fukushima the countries differed in their willingness to join the international trend of rejuvenating nuclear energy and those who did differed in form, timing, and scope of their attempts. France, the country most committed to nuclear energy, after a fifteen-year pause announced a major investment programme in nuclear energy in 2009 (see Chapter 6). After the Fukushima accident the French nuclear industry and the conservative government under President Nicolas Sarkozy quickly returned to 'business as usual'. However, nuclear energy was challenged by the opposition, and became an issue in the 2012 presidential and parliamentary elections. As the left won the election, nuclear energy was reviewed by President François Hollande and his governments under Prime Ministers Jean-Marc Ayrault and Manuel Valls (Schneider 2013b; Chapter 6 this volume), a process that was concluded in 2015. The left majority set a nuclear power capacity cap at the present level of 63.2 GWe and the target of reducing nuclear energy's contribution to total electricity supply at 50 per cent by 2025 (currently 75 per cent).[8] Finland, which has operated nuclear power plants since the 1970s but had rejected the building of new nuclear power capacity in 1993, decided to build a fifth nuclear power plant in 2002 and two more in 2011 (shortly after the Fukushima accident). The UK, which for many years seemed to have opted for a quiet death of its nuclear sector by not replacing power stations that had reached the end of their lifetime, changed course in 2008. A White Paper ('Meeting the Energy Challenge') of the Labour government under Tony Blair reopened the nuclear energy option. In October

---

[8] World Nuclear Association, 'Nuclear Power in France', Sept. 2015; Schneider and Froggatt 2015: 147–8; *FAZ*, 22 July 2015.

2010 the British government (then the Conservative-Liberal Coalition under David Cameron) eventually gave the green light for the construction of up to eight new nuclear power plants. These plans still hold after Fukushima. Important steps have also been taken to realize the first reactor project (Hinkley Point, planned to be operational in 2025). However, these plans also met difficulties that had not been foreseen such as the British government's financial support (approved by the EU Commission) being fought at the European Court of Justice, difficulties in attracting private investors, and the builder Areva running into severe economic troubles. In Sweden, parliament decided to authorize the building of ten new reactors as replacement (but capacity-increasing) investment on existing sites in 2010 (Chapter 10). Yet the new Red-Green government's policy and the current market conditions (which make a return on investment unlikely) suggest that a renewal of the Swedish reactor fleet will not happen in the near future. The governments of Belgium and Germany pursued less far-reaching strategies and opted for the lifetime extension of existing nuclear power plants in 2009 and 2011, respectively (Chapters 7 and 12). While the German decision was revised after the Fukushima disaster and the country reset on the phasing-out track, the Belgian parliament ratified lifetime extensions while remaining formally committed to long-term phasing-out.

Processes similar to those in France, Britain, Finland, and Sweden seemed to be unfolding in Switzerland and the Netherlands. In Switzerland the atomic industry asked for the authorization to build three new nuclear power plants in 2008 (Chapter 11). No decision was made before the Fukushima accident in 2011 and Switzerland since then has decided to phase out nuclear energy. In the Netherlands an application to expand the Borssele nuclear power plant was filed in 2009 but withdrawn after the accident (Chapter 9). Italy, having phased out nuclear energy already in the 1980s, aimed for a return to nuclear energy under the last Berlusconi government and put the issue to referendum in 2011. With the Fukushima disaster intervening, nuclear power received a landslide rejection (Chapter 8).

Spain held a political debate on expanding its existing nuclear energy production that remained inconclusive until the game-changing Fukushima disaster when it died off. Finally, the nuclear revival dynamics also encouraged Greece and Portugal, which have not yet invested in this technology, to register their interest with the IAEA on introducing nuclear energy (Jewell 2011). Currently, no further action seems to have been taken.

Overall, the Fukushima disaster slowed down but did not derail the process of nuclear build-up in those countries that have mostly accounted for the global 'revival' of this technology, although Japan is no longer a nuclear expansion country. As a result of safety inspections, the decommissioning of particular problematic reactors, and policy change in some countries, nuclear energy production shrunk.

More than four years after the Fukushima accident, on 1 July 2015 the world total was 391 running commercial reactors in thirty countries with a total capacity of c.337,000 MWe (fifty-one reactors and 42 MWe down from pre-Fukushima levels). According to Schneider and Froggatt's cautious calculating, sixty-two reactors were under construction in 2015 in fourteen countries, with China (twenty-four reactors), Russia (eight), and India (six) in the lead. EU Europe accounts for four reactors under construction (one each in Finland and France and two in Slovakia) (Schneider and Froggatt 2015: 30–1). While all these figures are very close to pre-Fukushima levels, the number of reactors planned as of 31 December 2014 is substantially reduced. The IAEA (2015: 25–7) reported a world total of ninety-six, none of which in EU Europe (sixty-three down compared to pre-Fukushima status).

In sum, we observe a new bifurcation of nuclear energy policy after the Fukushima accident in 2011. More specifically, we see that non-democratic countries and the countries with doubtful democratic credentials already on the nuclear track have maintained their course of introducing or expanding nuclear energy. Yet fully democratic countries display very different patterns. Most of them remained unaffected by the disaster at the policy-making level. Solidly pro-nuclear countries—the US, Canada, France, Finland, and the new EU member states—basically remained on their course, as did those which ardently reject atomic power—such as Austria, Denmark, Norway, and New Zealand. However, the response was mixed among the remaining countries. Britain and Sweden maintained their new pre-nuclear course. Italy aborted a reversal attempt by referendum. Germany and Switzerland turned away from nuclear energy despite the opposite decisions they had made only shortly before. In a more long-term perspective, we find such policy reversals also in some of the countries that did not change course after Fukushima, including Austria, Finland, and even France. Yet as reported France introduced a more major change in 2015 by putting a cap on the number of reactors and defining a target level of the nuclear energy share in electricity supply well below the present one. This decision was politically contested and hence may not survive a change in government. By itself it will also have only limited short-term effects yet the French nuclear energy sector is currently facing multiple problems that collectively may lead to its massive decline.

This short review suggests that it is the specific democratic linkage between civil society and politicians rather than technical or economic factors that determine nuclear energy policy. Therefore, we ought to look at actor preferences, actor constellations, and the specifics of institutions to unravel the puzzle of why especially democratic countries differ so much in their nuclear energy policy despite similar background conditions. This is what we attempt to do in the present volume.

1.3 INTERNATIONAL DRIVERS OF NUCLEAR ENERGY POLICY

Our brief review of nuclear energy history has revealed some broad international trends: early enthusiasm for nuclear power as a kind of energy panacea, stagnation and decline setting in in the late 1970s, culminating in the aftermath of the 1986 Chernobyl disaster, then, beginning in the late 1990s/early 2000s, a nuclear energy renaissance, and most recently a bifurcation of industrial nations, with some abruptly ending the revival of nuclear power while others continue on the nuclear path. While the extant literature on the history and politics of nuclear energy has given much attention to the early periods (Flam 1994; Jasper 1990; Joppke 1993; Kitschelt 1980, 1982, 1983, 1986a, 1986b; Nelkin and Pollak 1981), the recent renaissance of nuclear energy and post-Fukushima decisions remain to be analysed thoroughly.[9] For that purpose, the following section highlights the factors that affect all nations in a similar way. We turn to the more divisive factors in the next chapter.

We have already come across a few of the arguments that are made to motivate the renaissance of nuclear energy. The hunger for more energy is at the heart of this process. Political decision-makers and investors have also found other energy forms problematic for various reasons. We briefly review the most important arguments.

- Economic Competitiveness: Volatile and rising energy prices constitute a threat to economic growth.[10] More specifically, they undermine the viability of energy-intensive industrial sectors in countries that lack access to relatively cheap energy sources. Nuclear energy is considered as a solution to these problems. On the one hand, its price is considered to be relatively stable. On the other hand, the actual use of nuclear energy over the post-war period indicates that important cost factors could be rolled over to the public purse and/or become effectively postponed or absorbed (in particular the costs for nuclear waste disposal and accidents). Commercial plans for using nuclear energy typically rest on the assumption that this business model will be maintained.

- CO_2 Reduction: The use of all forms of carbon-based energy production conflicts with the goal of fighting climate change via the reduction of CO_2 emissions. International obligations, beginning with the Kyoto goals, have considerably reduced the room for manoeuvre of individual countries. Consequently, low-carbon nuclear energy seems attractive (e.g. Elliot 2007; Menyah and Wolde-Rufael 2010), at least as 'bridge technology' until the socially more acceptable new renewable energies—small hydro-electric power, biomass, wind, solar, and geothermal power—can replace it.

- Security of Energy Supply: The concern for energy security has become more prominent.[11] Even before the 2011 upheavals during the Arab Spring, the Middle East, home of the world's greatest oil reserves and most important producers and exporters, had been considered a powder keg. The most important oil exporter in the Americas, Venezuela, though critically dependent on income from these exports, had become increasingly unpredictable under the Chávez-Maduro regime. Finally, the temporary breakdown of Western European gas supply from Russia over this country's

---

[9] See, however, Netzer and Steinhilber (2011), Schneider et al. (2011), Elliot (2013), and Schneider and Froggatt (2015). These studies, however, have a very different focus than ours. The study of Sovacool and Valentine (2012) is more similar but has a different geographical focus (with only one country study overlapping) than the present volume.

[10] Between Jan. 2002 and July 2008 the world market price of a barrel of oil climbed from $18.68 to $145 (Maloney 2010: 37). After a 75% decline at the beginning of 2009, early autumn 2007 prices were reached again in early 2010 (von Hippel et al. 2011: 75).

[11] See e.g. Bahgat (2011), Crane et al. (2009), Findlay (2010), Lévêque (2010), Maloney (2010), Marquina (2008), Pascual and Zambetakis (2010), and Youngs (2009).

conflict with Ukraine in the winter of 2008/9 and increasing concern that Russia might abuse its power to hold back energy supply for political reasons have made dependence on this supplier more problematic. These concerns were further fuelled by the Ukraine crisis unfolding since 2014 that led to sanctions of the USA and EU against Russia and caused talk of a 'new cold war'. Alternative supply avenues explored by Western firms with the active encouragement of the EU in the Caucasus region have yet to materialize. In this context, a diversification of energy supply is attractive for Western countries in general and European ones in particular. Nuclear energy then emerges as one component of an energy mix that can reduce such supply risks. This, of course, is not the case when EU member states rely on integrated packages of credit provision, nuclear technology, and fuel supply offered by Russia against which the EU explicitly warns[12] (a strategy followed by Hungary and Slovakia).

- Technological Progress: This has led to a new generation of nuclear power stations (generation III) promising higher safety standards than their predecessors. Likewise, advances in developing even more efficient and less waste-producing generation IV reactors indicate that this technology still has a future. New technology is important as such, but it may also help political actors to justify policy reversals.

- International Learning: This is a genuinely political aspect. To begin with, only few nations would have the capacity to employ nuclear energy without relying on international cooperation, not to say doing so in a cost-efficient manner. For these reasons and for safety concerns, international cooperation has taken a prominent role in developing and spreading nuclear energy since the 1950s. Think of the missions and accomplishments of organizations such as the World Nuclear Association, International Atomic Energy Agency (IAEA), Euratom, and the World Association of Nuclear Operators (WANO). While all these organizations have been in place for a long time, our brief review of the activities of new international forums and initiatives in the ongoing attempts at rejuvenating nuclear energy indicates that such international influences have intensified since the 1990s.

We should not underestimate the extent to which countries learn from each other, in particular when they share similar conditions in terms of economic and technological development, natural endowments, and political liberty. We could expect that a revival of nuclear energy in some countries would increase the chances of nuclear energy in structurally similar countries. The presence of 'nuclear frontrunners' signals to political decision-makers that turning (again) to nuclear energy is technically feasible, economically efficient, and potentially viable politically. Such an example may also lead politicians and citizens to not grant other nations competitive advantages (from guaranteed supply and stable prices of energy). Conversely, we expect that, by turning away from nuclear energy, countries will undermine the viability of nuclear energy in those that are structurally similar. In that vein, the German phase-out decision under a conservative and economically successful government in 2011 might turn out to

---

[12] See EU Commission, *European Energy Security Strategy*, COM (2014) 330, 16.

be particularly important in giving credibility to the viability of a non-nuclear energy strategy. If the largest and most industrialized European economy that hitherto has relied to a considerable extent on nuclear power and also is an important producer of relevant technology can shift away from nuclear energy, it should be feasible for other countries, too.

Finally, international learning also applies to the political strategies and tactics of domestic actors in nuclear energy decision-making. Clearly, the national anti-nuclear movements have learned from each other how to set the public agenda and mobilize against the relevant projects. Similarly, since the 1976 Swedish elections, political parties observe what similar parties or parties in similar situation in other countries do when the nuclear energy issue is on the agenda and what effects their decisions have on these parties' electoral and office ambitions.

- Events: The history of nuclear energy has been significantly influenced by the occurrence of nuclear accidents. Three stand out: Harrisburg (Three Mile Island) in 1979, Chernobyl in 1986, and Fukushima in 2011. Each of these accidents constituted a significant challenge to nuclear energy and they thus signify instances where policies were 'their own worst enemies' (Hood 1994: 13), producing 'negative feedback' (Weaver 2010). Most obviously, each event drew attention to the issue. Each accident also provided new information on the problems arising from the interaction of this technology with its natural and human environment. This, in turn, led to a challenge of dominant interpretations and evaluations by both citizens and political decision-makers. Indeed, we can observe considerable citizen mobilization, political repositioning of political actors, and direct impact on policy outcomes resulting from these accidents. Yet each of these accidents had individual characteristics that may limit their impact (see Chapter 2).

1.4 OBSTACLES TO THE REVIVAL OF NUCLEAR ENERGY

The case for nuclear energy is all but universally made and the claims made in its favour remain contested. A study of the Global Public Policy Institute has put it into a nutshell: 'when cost, safety and accidents, fuel scarcity, environmental insults, and insecurity are taken into consideration, it becomes close to impossible to build a credible case for nuclear energy in a carbon-constrained, post-Copenhagen world' (Sovacool 2010: 19). This conclusion is based also on the arguments that 'new nuclear plants are excessively capital intensive, take years to build, are prone to cost overruns, and are economically competitive only when significantly subsidized'.

While some such problems will only emerge in the long run and may be pushed aside by decision-makers who think in electoral cycles, others also have a more short-term dimension and thus may be obstacles to a renaissance of nuclear energy. One is economic. Given the lack of recent experience of building nuclear power capacity, estimates of investment costs made early in the nuclear renaissance period were based on much guesswork and turned out overly optimistic (Kidd 2013). Indeed, in the US the financial incentives for investment in new nuclear power introduced by federal legislation have not proven strong enough to attract private capital in most of the country. Only in states that back up federal incentives by their own programmes and that have not fully liberalized their electricity markets (and thus allow for upfront loading-down of investment costs on consumers) is new nuclear capacity being developed currently (IAEA 2012: 16; Bradford 2013). Indeed, from the history of nuclear energy the evidence is overwhelming that projected costs and time horizons for the building of power stations are routinely overshot very substantially (Cooper 2012; Sovacool 2012; Schneider and Froggatt 2012: 12–14; Thurner et al. 2014; Csereklyei et al. 2016). Increased post-Fukushima safety concerns have further driven up the costs of both building new nuclear power capacity and maintaining the fleet of existing units (Cooper 2012; Schneider 2013a: 24). At the same time, the shale gas boom in the US provides an ever-increasing flow of energy at prices much below the production costs of nuclear energy (Levi 2012; Felder 2013). Consequently, the number of licences for new nuclear units issued in the US has remained small and much below government intentions (Bradford 2013; Lovins 2013).

Outside the US for the time being, nuclear energy seems to be 'safe from the threat of a burgeoning natural gas industry' (Levi 2012: 55) but the other economic factors also apply. In Britain, precedence is given to a competitive energy market over encouraging nuclear power, and dim projections have been made about the commercial viability of this form of energy (Thomas 2010; Heffron 2013). Major firms in the nuclear energy sector find themselves in economic difficulties and unattractive for capital in search of investment (Schneider and Froggatt 2012, 2015). Where the disciplining forces of the market economy are less relevant in governing the energy sector, however, cost factors will be less decisive. For instance, the large majority of the sixty-two reactors under construction in 2012 was financed by governments or private–public cooperation (IAEA 2012: 16). Another mechanism that could potentially intervene in favour of nuclear energy would be an emission-based carbon tax that has been discussed in the context of the fight against global warming. In short, to some extent the economics of nuclear energy can be influenced by political decisions. To the extent that these decisions require international coordination (to avoid competitive disadvantages), however, politicians seem severely constrained.

Another concern is that there are doubts about the availability of nuclear fuel (high-quality uranium) in large enough quantities to allow nuclear expansion. According to facts provided by the IAEA, reasonably assured uranium resources can maintain the current production for more than half a century, but this time would shrink when large-scale additions were made to today's fleet of reactors (IAEA 2012: 1; Sovacool 2012: 85–91; Guidolin and Guseo 2012; Dittmar 2012). Even today uranium consumption exceeds current production and can be satisfied only by recycling material from civilian and military use. Although history tells that most estimates of world reserves of raw materials have been revised upwards constantly, the most rewarding sources may already have been tapped and largely exploited while developing new ones will be more costly and risky.

Another problem identified by some authors is a scarcity of qualified personnel both at the side of nuclear producers and government oversight (e.g. Ahearne 2011: 575). While some Western countries have recognized the potential shortage and taken measures, in a global perspective this problem is not yet sufficiently addressed (IAEA 2012: 4; cf. Heffron 2013: 607).

Long-term concerns include costs that have been rolled over to the public purse since the early days of nuclear energy, such as basic research, waste disposal, and risk assurance. There are also far less optimistic perspectives on the potential contribution of nuclear energy to fighting global warming once its long-term carbon imprint is considered (Sovacool 2008, 2012). While decision-makers may shy away from considering these costs, their competitors and parts of the electorate may not.

Other concerns related to global nuclear power expansion are further removed from national decision-making on nuclear energy in Western Europe. One is that civilian nuclear power programmes may shield military programmes and thus allow for the further proliferation of nuclear weapons (Fuhrmann 2012; Stulberg and Fuhrmann 2013). International conflict regions and rogue regimes are particularly prone to such abuse (Solingen 2007). These concerns constitute a disincentive to promote nuclear energy on a global scale or to design programmes providing material inputs to the production of nuclear energy that substitute the development of national nuclear know-how that might be abused for military purposes. The various international programmes going back to an initiative of the US Bush administration constitute prominent examples of the latter approach. Although of great importance to global security, these concerns are likely to have a minimal impact on the decisions of European democracies about their own engagement with nuclear energy.

We do not want to engage in the debate about the contested claims on the benefits of nuclear energy in the present volume. For us it is only important to note that the factual claims behind the revival of nuclear energy remain as contested as many of those employed earlier in the nuclear energy debate. Against this background genuine political factors such as agenda setting and framing become even more important. Process outcomes thus may depend more on the timing of decisions (Pierson 2004) and actors' strategies and skills (which, of course are always important) than is the case in many other contexts.

1.5 THE PLAN OF THE BOOK

Our brief narrative of the fate of nuclear energy has revealed a substantial number of full or partial policy reversals. Even many countries that have never gone nuclear were once on the track of introducing nuclear energy. How can we explain nuclear energy-related policy decisions in the individual countries and the differences between them? Potentially, there are many factors that are likely to exercise influence on the fate of nuclear energy in democracies. We are faced with the 'many variables, few cases' problem that is notorious in comparative politics. In this volume we follow a two-track strategy to cope with the resulting challenge: conducting case studies and comparative analyses.

Three comparative chapters follow this one. In Chapter 2 we discuss various approaches to understanding policy reversals and their suitability for our purpose. We then present our analytical framework and guiding hypotheses. Chapter 3 provides a more thorough account of the energy background and policies in selected countries. Chapter 4 maps the protest behaviour directed against nuclear energy from the mid-1970s through 2011, records party political manifestation of this process in the form of Green parties, and more generally voter scepticism about nuclear energy. Both chapters are of descriptive nature and help set the stage for our case studies and comparative analyses of political decision-making processes. We then present seven in-depth analyses of how single countries have dealt with the nuclear energy issue.

Case studies are the most intensive research design (Gerring 2007). They allow for detailed configurative analysis and the capturing of the dynamics of political decision-making processes. Although the case studies in this book use quantitative data to a great extent, the thrust of their argument comes from the qualitative analysis. In particular they show how the many relevant factors that impinge on the relevant decisions lead to varying policy outcomes in different contexts.

Our study focuses on Western Europe as a set of 'most similar' cases that display the most interesting within-case variation. Our selection of cases for country studies is driven by the concept of policy reversal, that is, the volume focuses especially on those countries with multi-party systems that have decided for a complete phasing-out of nuclear energy or at least partial moratoria at some point in time (Austria, Germany, Italy, Netherlands, Sweden, and Switzerland). The volume also includes a case study of France that has upheld nuclear energy continuously but has a history of nuclear energy contestation and partial reversals of relevant parts of its nuclear energy programme. As mentioned above, even the phasing-out countries differ considerably with regard to the fate of nuclear energy. Thus, we avoid selection bias resulting from case selection along the dependent variable even among country chapters.[13] In the comparative chapters we go beyond the countries studied individually and include in our systematic analyses other countries from Western Europe: Belgium, Denmark, Finland, Greece, Ireland, Luxembourg, Norway, Portugal, Spain, and the UK. These countries either employ nuclear energy or at some point were seriously planning for its use. For these countries we include short analytic stories of their decision-making on nuclear energy in the final chapter and we include them in its comparative-configurative and quantitative analyses. Whenever possible, we locate the Western European cases within a larger universe of countries (in particular in Chapter 3).

Placing the country studies in the wider West European context, Chapter 12 discusses the relevance of the various explanatory factors introduced in Chapters 2, 3 and 4. It highlights how public opinion on nuclear energy, party affiliations of voters, inter-party competition, and the party composition of government interact to produce public policy on nuclear energy. As we are interested in policy decisions that are contested within the countries we analytically move from the country level to the level of individual governments. We also discuss the extent to which our approach and findings can be generalized beyond the politics and policies of nuclear energy. Finally, we return to our policy area and briefly discuss the future of nuclear energy in Western Europe.

---

[13] King et al. (1994: 129) formulate the following 'basic and obvious rule': 'selection should allow for the possibility of at least some variation on the dependent variable'.

REFERENCES

Ahearne, John F. (2011). 'Prospects for Nuclear Energy.' *Energy Economics*, 33: 572–80.
Allison, Graham (2005). *Nuclear Terrorism: The Ultimate Preventable Catastrophe*. New York: Holt.
Bahgat, Gawdat (2011). *Energy Security: An Interdisciplinary Approach*. Chichester: Wiley.
Bradford, Peter A. (2013). 'How to Close the US Nuclear Industry: Do Nothing.' *Bulletin of the Atomic Scientists*, 69(2): 12–21.
Cooke, Stephanie (2009). *In Mortal Hands: A Cautionary History of the Nuclear Age*. New York: Bloomsbury.
Cooper, Mark (2012). 'Nuclear Safety and Affordable Reactors: Can we Have Both?' *Bulletin of the Atomic Scientists*, 64(4): 61–72.
Crane, Keith, Andreas Goldthau, Michael Toman, Thomas Light, Stuart E. Johnson, Alireza Nader, Angel Rabasa, and Harun Dogo (2009). *Imported Oil and U.S. National Security*. Santa Monica, CA: RAND Corporation.
Csereklyei, Zsuzsanna, Paul W. Thurner, Alexander Bauer, and Helmut Küchenhoff (2016). 'Pressure of Economic Growth and Oil Prices, and the Benefits of Reactor Standardization: Duration of Nuclear Power Plant Construction Revisited.' *Energy Policy*, 91: 49–59.
Dalton, Russel J., David M. Farrell, and Ian McAllister (2011). *Political Parties and Democratic Linkage*. Oxford: Oxford University Press.
Dittmar, Michael (2012). 'Nuclear Energy: Status and Future Limitations.' *Energy*, 37: 35–40.
Elliot, David (ed.) (2007). *Nuclear or Not? Does Nuclear Power Have a Place in a Sustainable Energy Future?* Basingstoke: Palgrave Macmillan.
Elliot, David (2013). *Fukushima: Impacts and Implications*. Basingstoke: Palgrave Macmillan.
European Council (2007). 'European Council Action Plan (2007–2009). Energy Policy for Europe (EPE)', *Presidency Conclusions*. Brussels: European Council, 8–9 Mar., 16–23. http://www.consilium.europa.eu/ueDocs/cms_Data/docs/pressData/en/ec/93135.pdf.
Felder, Frank A. (2013). 'Nuclear Power in the Second Obama Administration.' *Electricity Journal*, 26(2): 25–31.
Findlay, Trevor (2010). *Nuclear Energy and Global Governance: Ensuring Safety, Security and Nonproliferation*. Abingdon: Routledge.
Flam, Helena (ed.) (1994). *States and Anti-Nuclear Movements*. Edinburgh: Edinburgh University Press.
Fuhrmann, Matthew (2012). *Atomic Assistance: How 'Atoms for Peace' Programs Cause Nuclear Insecurity*. Ithaca, NY: Cornell University Press.
Gerring, John (2007). *Case Study Research: Principles and Practice*. Cambridge: Cambridge University Press.
Guidolin, Mariangela, and Renato Guseo (2012). 'A Nuclear Power Renaissance?' *Technological Forecasting and Social Change*, 79: 1746–60.
Hayashi, Masatsugu, and Larry Hughes (2013). 'The Policy Responses to the Fukushima Nuclear Accident and their Effect on Japanese Energy Security.' *Energy Policy*, 59: 86–101.
Heffron, Raphael James (2012). 'Romanian Nuclear New Build: Progress Amidst Turbulence 1990–2010.' *Progress in Nuclear Energy*, 56: 43–60.
Heffron, Raphael James (2013). 'The Application of Contrast Explanations to Energy Policy Research: UK Nuclear Energy Policy 2002–2012.' *Energy Policy*, 55: 602–16.
Hood, Christopher (1994). *Explaining Economic Policy Reversals*. Buckingham: Open University Press.
International Atomic Energy Agency (2011). *Nuclear Power Reactors in the World*. 2011 edn. Vienna: IAEA.

International Atomic Energy Agency (2012). *International Status and Prospects for Nuclear Power 2012: Report by the Director General*. GOV/INF/2012/12-GC(56)/INF/6. Vienna: IAEA.

International Atomic Energy Agency (2015). *Nuclear Power Reactors in the World*. 2015 edn. Vienna: IAEA.

Jacobs, Alan M. (2011). *Governing for the Long Term: Democracy and the Politics of Investment*. Cambridge: Cambridge University Press.

Jacobs, Alan M., and J. Scott Matthews (2012). 'Why do Citizens Discount the Future? Public Opinion and the Timing of Policy Consequences.' *British Journal of Political Science*, 42(4): 903–35.

Jasper, James M. (1990). *Nuclear Politics: Energy and the State in the United States, Sweden, and France*. Princeton: Princeton University Press.

Jewell, Jessica (2011). 'Ready for Nuclear Energy? An Assessment of Capacities and Motivations for Launching New National Nuclear Power Programs.' *Energy Policy*, 39: 1041–55.

Joppke, Christian (1993). *Mobilizing Against Nuclear Energy: A Comparison of Germany and the United States*. Berkeley, CA: University of California Press.

Jungk, Robert (1977). *Der Atomstaat*. Reinbek bei Hamburg: Rororo.

Kidd, Stephen W. (2013). 'Nuclear Power: Economics and Public Acceptance.' *Energy Strategy Reviews*, 1: 277–81.

Kim, Yong-Min, and Sunyoung Chang (2012). 'The Comprehensive Nuclear Promotion Plan of the Republic of Korea.' *Progress in Nuclear Energy*, 58: 58–63.

King, Gary, Robert O. Keohane, and Sidney Verba (1994). *Designing Social Inquiry: Scientific Inference in Qualitative Research*. Princeton: Princeton University Press.

Kitschelt, Herbert P. (1980). *Kernenergiepolitik: Arena eines gesellschaftlichen Konflikts*. Frankfurt am Main: Campus.

Kitschelt, Herbert P. (1982). 'Structures and Sequences of Nuclear Policy Making.' *Political Power and Social Theory*, 3: 271–308.

Kitschelt, Herbert P. (1983). *Politik und Energie: Eine vergleichende Untersuchung zur Energie-Technologiepolitik in den U.S.A., der Bundesrepublik, Frankreich und Schweden*. Frankfurt am Main: Campus.

Kitschelt, Herbert P. (1986a). 'Political Opportunity Structures and Political Protest: Anti-Nuclear Movements in Four Democracies.' *British Journal of Political Science*, 16(1): 57–85.

Kitschelt, Herbert P. (1986b). 'Four Theories of Public Policy-Making and Fast Breeder Reactor Development in France, the United States, and West Germany.' *International Organization*, 40(1): 65–104.

Lévêque, Françoise (ed.) (2010). *Security of Energy Supply in Europe: Natural Gas, Nuclear and Hydrogen*. Cheltenham: Edward Elgar.

Levi, Michael (2009). *On Nuclear Terrorism*. Cambridge, MA: Harvard University Press.

Levi, Michael (2012). 'Splitting Rock vs. Splitting Atoms: What Shale Gas Means for Nuclear Power.' *Bulletin of the Atomic Scientists*, 68(4): 52–60.

Lovins, Amory B. (2013). 'The Economics of a US Civilian Nuclear Phase Out.' *Bulletin of the Atomic Scientists*, 69(2): 44–65.

Mahaffey, James (2009). *Atomic Awakening: A New Look at the History and Future of Nuclear Power*. New York: Pegasus Books.

Mallah, Subhash (2011). 'Nuclear Energy Option for Energy Security and Sustainable Development in India.' *Annals of Nuclear Energy*, 38: 331–6.

Maloney, Suzanne (2010). 'Energy Security in the Persian Gulf', in Carlos Pascual and Jonathan Elkind (eds), *Energy Security: Economics, Politics, Strategies, and Implications*. Washington, DC: Brookings Institution Press, 37–58.

Marquina, Antonio (ed.) (2008). *Energy Security: Visions from Asia and Europe*. Basingstoke: Palgrave Macmillan.
Menyah, Kojo, and Yemane Wolde-Rufael (2010). 'CO_2 Emissions, Nuclear Energy and Economic Growth in the US.' *Energy Policy*, 38: 2911–15.
Nelkin, Dorothy, and Michael Pollak (1981). *The Atom Besieged: Extra-Parliamentary Dissent in France and Germany*. Cambridge, MA: MIT Press.
Netzer, Nina, and Jochen Steinhilber (eds) (2011). *The End of Nuclear Energy? International Perspectives After Fukushima*. Bonn: Friedrich Ebert Stiftung.
Pascual, Carlos, and Evie Zambetakis (2010). 'The Geopolitics of Energy', in Carlos Pascual and Jonathan Elkind (eds), *Energy Security. Economics, Politics, Strategies, and Implications*. Washington, DC: Brookings Institution Press, 9–35.
Pierson, Paul (2004). *Politics in Time: History, Institutions, and Social Analysis*. Princeton: Princeton University Press.
Rootes, Christopher (ed.) (2007). *Environmental Protest in Western Europe*. 2nd edn. Oxford: Oxford University Press.
Rucht, Dieter (1994). *Modernisierung und neue soziale Bewegungen*. Frankfurt am Main: Campus.
Sabatier, Paul (ed.) (2007). *Theories of the Policy Process*. 2nd edn. Boulder, CO: Westview.
Schneider, Mycle (2013a). 'Nuclear Power and the French Energy Transition: It's the Economics, Stupid!' *Bulletin of the Atomic Scientists*, 69(1): 18–26.
Schneider, Mycle (2013b). 'France's Great Energy Debate.' *Bulletin of the Atomic Scientists*, 69(1): 27–35.
Schneider, Mycle, and Antony Froggatt (2012). '2011–2013 World Nuclear Industry Status Report.' *Bulletin of the Atomic Scientists*, 68(5): 8–22.
Schneider, Mycle, and Antony Froggatt (2015). *The World Nuclear Industry Status Report 2015*. Paris: Mycle Schneider Consulting.
Schneider, Mycle, Antony Froggatt, and Steve Thomas (2011). *Nuclear Power in a Post-Fukushima World: 25 Years After the Chernobyl Accident*. The World Nuclear Industry Status Report 2010–2011. Paris: Worldwatch Institute.
Solingen, Etel (2007). *Nuclear Logics: Contrasting Patterns in East Asia and the Middle East*. Princeton: Princeton University Press.
Sovacool, Benjamin K. (2008). 'Valuing the Greenhouse Gas Emissions from Nuclear Power: A Critical Survey.' *Energy Policy*, 36: 2950–63.
Sovacool, Benjamin K. (2010). *Questioning a Nuclear Renaissance*. GPPI Policy Paper, 8. Berlin: Global Public Policy Institute.
Sovacool, Benjamin K. (2012). *Contesting the Future of Nuclear Power: A Critical Global Assessment of Atomic Energy*. Singapore: World Scientific.
Sovacool, Benjamin K., and Scott Victor Valentine (2012). *The National Politics of Nuclear Power: Economics, Security, and Governance*. London: Routledge.
Stulberg, Adam N., and Matthew Fuhrmann (eds) (2013). *The Nuclear Renaissance and International Security*. Palo Alto, CA: Stanford University Press.
Takubo, Masa (2011). 'Nuclear or Not? The Complex and Uncertain Politics of Japan's Post-Fukushima Energy Policy.' *Bulletin of the Atomic Scientists*, 67(5): 19–26.
Thomas, Steve (2010). 'Competitive Energy Markets and Nuclear Power: Can we Have Both, do we Want Either?' *Energy Policy*, 38: 4903–8.
Thurner, Paul W., Laura Mittermeier, and Helmut Küchenhoff (2014). 'How Long does it Take to Build a Nuclear Power Plant? A Non-Parametric Event History Approach with P-splines.' *Energy Policy*, 70: 163–71.
Verse, Björn (2012). *Die Kernenergiepolitik in Ost- und Mittelosteuropa: Eine vergleichende Analyse*. Munich: BA thesis LMU Munich.

Vivoda, Vlado (2012). 'Japan's Energy Security Predicament Post-Fukushima.' *Energy Policy*, 46: 135–43.

von Hippel, David F., Suzuki, Tatsujiro, and Williams, James H. (2011). 'Evaluating the Energy Security Impacts of Energy Policies', in Benjamin K. Sovacool (ed.), *The Routledge Handbook of Energy Security*. London: Routledge, 74–95.

WEC World Energy Council (2012). *World Energy Perspective: Nuclear Energy One Year After Fukushima*. London: World Energy Council.

Weaver, R. Kent (2010). 'Paths and Forks or Chutes and Ladders? Negative Feedbacks and Policy Regime Change.' *Journal of Public Policy*, 30(2): 137–62.

Yi-chong, Xu (2010). *The Politics of Nuclear Energy in China*. Basingstoke: Palgrave Macmillan.

Yi-chong, Xu (ed.) (2011). *Nuclear Energy Development in Asia: Problems and Prospects*. Basingstoke: Palgrave Macmillan.

Youngs, Richard (2009). *Energy Security. Europe's New Foreign Policy Challenge*. London: Routledge.

Zhou, Yun, Christhian Rengiof, Peipei Chen, and Jonathan Hinze (2011). 'Is China Ready for its Nuclear Power Expansion?' *Energy Policy*, 39: 771–81.

2

Understanding Policy Reversals and Policy Stability

Wolfgang C. Müller and Paul W. Thurner

In this chapter we discuss domestic politics and other situational factors that exercise influence on nuclear energy policy. We aim to identify conditions that render policy change more likely and to disentangle how various factors may impact on the direction and level of nuclear energy policy. First, we briefly review the relevant literature. We then discuss our dependent variable: nuclear energy policy reversals. In so doing, we highlight different dimensions and the degrees to which a given nuclear energy policy can be fully or partially reversed. Next, we discuss the independent variables that might exert influence on policy decisions and the variation of which might account for policy reversals.

2.1 THE STORY SO FAR: EXPLAINING NUCLEAR ENERGY POLICY

The question whether, why, and to what degree countries choose to go nuclear or to refrain from doing so, has mainly been treated in qualitative single and multiple case studies. Only recently, have quantitative approaches been applied to this research question to establish generalizable patterns and to control multivariately for competing hypotheses (Fuhrmann 2012; Gourley and Stulberg 2013; Csereklyei 2013).

Taking the beginning of nuclear power reactor construction in 129 countries in the 1965 to 2000 period as a binary dependent variable, Fuhrmann (2012) finds nuclear power expansion related to growing energy demands and energy security concerns, but not to ambitions for nuclear weapons. He also finds that nuclear accidents have a dampening effect on nuclear power expansion in democracies (Fuhrmann 2012). Gourley and Stulberg (2013) include 150 countries in the 1950–2001 period and follow Fuhrmann in taking the year construction begins as the dependent variable. From their findings, and similar to Fuhrmann, they remain sceptical about a military connection to civilian nuclear expansion but support the energy security motive, in particular for the most recent years. Probing into the relevance of economic factors, they find nuclear power expansion to be more likely in larger countries, more self-contained than in open economies and in periods of rapid growth. They do not detect a statistical relationship between regime type (i.e. democracy or non-democracy) and the building of nuclear power stations. Finally, Gourley and Stulberg (2013) find statistical support for a retarding effect of nuclear accidents on the beginning of new reactor projects, but remain sceptical about a substantive relationship between the two.

In her study of thirty-one countries that have employed nuclear energy in the 1965–2009 period, Csereklyei (2013) used the amount of construction commencements in MW(e) capacity in a given year as the dependent variable. She identifies a positive relationship between nuclear power expansion and primary energy consumption in the past five decades, and a dampening effect of the Chernobyl accident.

While we can learn much about the commonalities of a large set of countries and globally relevant factors from such quantitative studies, they have their limitations when it comes to understanding the nuances and sequences of nuclear energy policy-making in individual countries or in world regions. It thus constitutes a valuable complement to the research agenda we pursue in this volume. As Gourley and Stulberg note, the countries in each of the categories constituting the 'nuclear energy club' are a 'mixed bag'. In sketching out future research, they recognize, for instance, a 'need for delving deeper into understanding how states make trade-offs among options for reducing energy deficits' (2013: 36). They also acknowledge that political factors 'vary greatly across democratic regimes' and they provide a few examples that suggest it might be important to account for these differences (2013: 37). Similarly, Christopher Way (2013: 166–70) relates the non-findings of political factors to the research strategy chosen in these studies and makes a plea for unpacking the regime type and opening the state's 'black box'.

In their study of the eight major countries (the US, France, Japan, Russia, South Korea, Canada, China, and India) that together host almost three-quarters of the world's nuclear reactors, Sovacool and Valentine aim to 'explain why nations choose to accept the risks associated with nuclear power and support the development of nuclear power programs' (2012: 1). They claim that six bundles of factors can explain the use of nuclear power: national security concerns (from energy security to military nuclear ambitions), the predominance of a technocratic ideology, economic interventionism (from economic planning to providing specific incentives for nuclear energy), a centrally coordinated energy stakeholder network, subordination of opposition to political authority, and the 'social peripheralization' of nuclear energy's opponents. Their categories are sufficiently broad to cover a wide range of political, economic, social, and technological factors. Those related to politics include, for instance, 'the ability to maintain a commitment to nuclear power through strong majority government, dictatorship, genuine consensus across party lines or a government that has lengthy tenure (whether this is through a democratic majority, extended periods in power, or absolute political authority)', 'a "closed" political system that limits access to discussions and decisions about nuclear power', 'low levels of civic activism', 'a mimetic and complacent media that avoids critical perspectives', and the 'ability and desire to externalize many of the costs and damages from nuclear power to future generations, undesirable parts of the country, other countries, or political powerless communities' (Sovacool and Valentine 2012: 14). These authors conclude that their six drivers of nuclear power 'must exist simultaneously to induce uninterrupted development' (2012: 235). All these conditions seem indeed very likely to allow policy-makers to engage in the development and implementation of nuclear power programmes as they advantage any high-risk long-term strategy. At the same time, the independent variables are specified in functional terms (i.e. from the perspective of claimed effects on the dependent variable) to allow lumping together different mechanisms in very different systems. Our task in this book is very different: to identify defined actor constellations more precisely, and institutional and situational factors that bring about nuclear energy policy change in a set of similar systems.

Closest to the present study are the studies of Kitschelt (1986) and Midttun and Rucht (1994). Kitschelt's path-breaking study focused on the strategies of anti-nuclear power movements in three of our countries—France, Germany, Sweden— and the United States and their impact on nuclear energy policy. He theorized that movement strategies and policy outcomes result from the particular combination of the political systems' input and output structures. With respect to the input side, he distinguished 'open' and 'closed' systems. Open ones are characterized by the following features: many political parties, stronger 'centrifugal' tendencies, a higher degree of parliamentary independence from the government, pluralist systems of interest representation, and 'mechanisms' that allow new demands to 'find their way into the processes of forming policy compromises and consensus' (Kitschelt 1986: 63). With regard to the systems' output structures ('state capacities'), Kitschelt expected nuclear power to fare better when the state apparatus is centralized, the political control of the economy stronger, and judicial activism weak.

Building on the political economy approach to understanding the development of the nuclear energy sector (e.g. Campbell 1988) and Kitschelt's (1986) theoretical framework for analysis, Midttun and Rucht (1994) further elaborated the political economy and political structure dimensions and added the political process dimension to the explanatory variables. In contrast to the two other dimensions, the process dimension contains factors that are likely to show short-term variation. These are the degree of elite consensus on the issue of nuclear energy, public attitudes to it, protest events, and the use of referendums. In this book, we follow Midttun and Rucht (1994) in paying tribute to all three of these dimensions. We are even more interested in the political process dimension on which we further elaborate.

When the studies of Kitschelt (1986) and Midttun and Rucht (1994) concluded, nuclear energy was a newly politicized issue. The traditional elite consensus and mass acquiescence on nuclear energy could only be undermined by issue entrepreneurship from new political actors. Early studies thus focused largely on system openness—the possibility of the new actors confronting the traditional elites with their concerns and mobilizing supportive public opinion. Green parties, the archetypical party political manifestations of anti-nuclear concerns, were still struggling to establish themselves as permanent players in the parliamentary party systems at the time. The pioneering studies on nuclear power politics therefore chose to highlight movement politics and movements' access to the political decision-making arena. Since then, the traditional elite consensus on nuclear energy has waned and Green parties have become permanent additions to the parliamentary party systems in many but not all countries. Over the years, nuclear energy has become more of a 'normal' issue on which political parties compete. Although movement politics and protest behaviour remain more important here than in most other issue domains, analysing the politics of nuclear power today requires a focus shift towards a party democracy and party government perspective.

At the same time, upon the conclusion of the pioneering studies, the outcome variation was limited. Although Kitschelt's four empirical cases varied considerably with regard to their investment in nuclear energy and their adherence to the original plans, none of them had gone through a full reversal of nuclear energy policy. At the end of his observation period, even Sweden, which had decided to abandon nuclear energy in the long run, had a sizeable nuclear energy production. The phase-out decision remained very vulnerable to reversals, as subsequent developments have demonstrated. Midttun and Rucht (1994) had eight cases in their sample that showed a greater range in nuclear policy outcomes, including Norway which never went beyond planning, Austria which never connected its only nuclear power plant to the grid, and Italy which brought nuclear energy production to a sudden end in 1987 (see Andersen and Midttun 1994; Preglau 1994; Müller, this volume; Diani 1994; Franchino, this volume). As Chapter 1 has argued, the world of energy politics has changed considerably since the end of these studies' observation periods in terms of 'nuclear renaissance' and 'nuclear decline'. Some countries have reconfirmed their rejection of nuclear energy without wavering while some have worked towards nuclear rejuvenation without bringing the policy process to a conclusion. Others failed in attempts at policy reversal while still others have succeeded. One country—Germany—has gone back and forth on nuclear energy. At the time of writing, it is still unclear whether the UK and Spain will actively re-enter the nuclear path after (de facto) moratoria. In sum, we have many more instances of nuclear energy policy-making processes and a greater range of outcomes given this long time period. Before we lay out how we are going to address that variety of outcomes in this book, we briefly discuss in the next section the dimensions of nuclear energy policy change available to political decision-makers.

2.2 OUR DEPENDENT VARIABLE: NUCLEAR ENERGY POLICY REVERSALS

In this book we want to contribute to understanding the conditions under which European multiparty democracies substantively change the course of their nuclear energy policies. First, we have to clarify the dependent variable: policy reversal. A policy reversal is a change in the *direction* of a policy. The hard core of the nuclear energy issue, of course, encompasses saying 'yes' or 'no' to nuclear energy, allowing or outlawing its use, and actually employing it or not. In Peter Hall's (1993) classification, that kind of policy change would be of 'third order' nature (i.e. the most fundamental). Ardent adversaries of nuclear energy are not willing to accept anything less than a clear 'no' to all of these questions. Yet not all nuclear energy sceptics are equally demanding and willing to live with the costs implied by abandoning nuclear energy (if it is already in place) or to prioritize a non-nuclear energy production over other goals such as economic growth, security of energy supply, and reduction of CO_2 emissions that are claimed to benefit from using nuclear energy (see Chapter 1). Political actors may thus aim to win acceptance or acquiescence for a policy that settles somewhere between a sizeable all-stage nuclear energy programme and a state of the world where nuclear energy is not employed, its use outlawed and where the actors allow for almost no gap between making these decisions and full compliance. Policy reversal thus can also mean more limited change (e.g. abandoning those parts of the programme that have caused most controversy). In Hall's (1993) categories these would be of 'second order' nature. We do not, however, consider 'first order' changes as policy reversals. Such changes are much more limited in their nature and result from the pragmatic adaptation of programmes. An example would be the adaptation of building programmes of nuclear energy plants to revised forecasts of electricity demand. We can think of at least five analytical distinct but empirically overlapping dimensions that may allow second order variations in nuclear energy policy.

- Comprehensiveness of Nuclear Energy Programmes: As already mentioned, a nuclear energy programme allows for some variation between a fully developed nuclear production chain and a rudimentary one. Countries can commercially produce nuclear energy, for instance, without accompanying technologies considered particularly dangerous (such as fast-breeder reactors and reprocessing facilities).
- Magnitude of Nuclear Energy Programmes: A nuclear energy programme may involve an arbitrary number of power stations, capacities, and outputs. Of course, principled opponents of nuclear energy consider even a single nuclear power station one too many. However, 'not in my backyard' opponents may be pacified by fewer power stations located in remote areas (which, admittedly, is easier in large and not densely populated countries).
- Quality of Nuclear Energy Programme: A nuclear energy programme may maximize either economic returns (implying the maximization of reactor hours) or nuclear safety (implying the use of state-of-the-art technology in as many reactors as technically possible). The most obvious indicators would be the safety standards applied, the time and costs taken for upgrades of older plants, and the number of years a reactor remains in operation. While these might be more relevant in some countries not covered in our study, other quality indicators may be found in the independence, transparency, and credibility of national oversight of nuclear energy programmes. Again, sceptics (rather than principled opponents) of nuclear energy may prefer or be acquiescent to a high-quality nuclear energy programme over its short-term alternatives.

While the first three dimensions relate to the substance of nuclear energy programmes, the remaining two are related to the process of nuclear energy politics and policy.

- Procedural Measures: Nuclear energy policy can also be changed not in substance but in terms of the procedure. The government may, for instance, delegate security matters to independent experts (rather than government agencies) or make changes in the relevant jurisdictions (e.g. by centralization or decentralization). They additionally might change the process of making authoritative decisions on nuclear energy issues (e.g. requiring legislation rather than governmental decrees or administrative decisions, qualified rather than simple majorities in legislation, or employing inquiries, public debates, or even the referendum device). Typically, such changes of the decision-making mode are strategic. The intention may be, for instance, to speed up the process, to buy legitimacy, or to neutralize a politically 'hot' issue in order to avoid electoral fallout. Although the short-term intentions behind such moves are often easy to understand for the experts at the time, observers in other countries and in later periods may fail to catch the rationale. Finally, the strategy may not always play out as intended. Hence, the long-term consequences may be quite different from original intent. It is thus complicated to qualify such moves as pro- or anti-nuclear in general terms because decision-makers often disguise their intentions.

- Time-Related Changes: Nuclear energy policy can vary in terms of time in many ways. With regard to the main issue, whether to use nuclear energy or not, it allows for variation by gradual nuclear power phase-in and phase-out programmes and by establishing deadlines and time-out periods. For technological and financial reasons, the build-up of nuclear power programmes typically follows a gradual logic. The same forces plus supply security considerations are at work when nuclear energy is gradually phased out rather than quickly abandoned. In order to work, transitions have to be 'orderly'. Nevertheless, unintended consequences and feedback processes loom large here due to the complexity of energy infrastructures in modern societies. Stretching the implementation of a policy over time, however, also provides ample chances for controlled re-reversals. This is even more the case if only an end-date for abandoning nuclear energy is set in the far future. Cutting back or stretching over time interim periods may have larger implications for a country's overall nuclear energy path. Time-out periods during which, for instance, no further reactor is built or commissioned, construction is stopped, or reactors are temporarily switched off, may be called to conduct further studies or to advance security standards. The motives behind such time-outs may be honest (such as to avoid violent conflict or to minimize the risk of accidents). Yet they may also have a hidden purpose such as to break the momentum of an anti-nuclear movement or to decouple nuclear energy policy decisions from other events (such as scheduled elections, government formations, or nuclear accidents).

Nuclear energy policy thus has several potentially relevant dimensions with many different choices in each of them. In Hall's categories, moving from one of them to another one would constitute 'second order' (i.e. instrument-related) or 'first order' (i.e. purely adaptive) policy changes. The country chapters pay tribute to this complexity in their accounts of policy development. At the same time it is useful to have a more aggregated measure of nuclear energy policy. In our project we have therefore developed a nuclear energy policy scale that allows mapping national policies (Appendix A).[1] Pro-nuclear energy decisions follow a common logic in going through different stages. Initially, all countries are in what can be dubbed 'state of nature' with no nuclear energy policy. Early stages include the establishment of preconditions (such as scientific, administrative, or industrial structures devoted to the development of nuclear energy or building research reactors), followed by the decision to 'go nuclear', i.e. the actual construction of the first commercial reactor, its connection to the grid, and further expansion of nuclear energy capacity. Once that stage has been reached, it is most useful to employ indicators such as the number of nuclear power reactors or capacity in megawatts (MW) to capture different degrees of commitment to nuclear power. Our scale also captures policy decisions that freeze, downsize, or abandon nuclear energy. Again, such stages of policy development are best seen in conjunction with indicators on the capacity of nuclear power stations in operation and their contribution to total energy and to electricity production. The nuclear energy policy scale is used in the country chapters (when the nuclear energy trajectory was complex and the scale thus had heuristic value) and in the concluding chapter.

Political decisions are at the heart of all policy changes. Therefore, our main strategy in measuring our dependent variable is focusing on the enacted policy. It may take the form of law or executive decisions. Yet there is often a time gap between a policy decision and its implementation. In the case of nuclear energy, experience tells that this time gap has a huge variance ranging from a few months to decades. Such gaps provide ample opportunity for political actors—the losers of political battles may use them to work towards the revision of the disliked decision. Returning to the pre-decision status quo or something close to it is certainly easier before accomplished facts (such as nuclear facilities switched on or dismantled, respectively). We therefore throughout the volume employ a second measure shedding light on the status quo of nuclear energy policy: the contribution of nuclear energy to electricity production.

2.3 A FRAMEWORK FOR ANALYSING NUCLEAR ENERGY POLICY CHANGE IN EU MEMBER STATES

Once we have mapped nuclear policy change, we of course want to understand which factors make such change likely. In the remainder of this chapter we outline our approach. In the process we formulate several hypotheses that we expect to hold under otherwise equal conditions. All our hypotheses are formulated bivariately. Evidently, as happens most of the time in social science settings, the hypothesized impact is never unconditional and additive. Therefore, this is a deliberate simplification. Any political scientist trained and experienced with the formation of hypotheses knows about the conditionality of causalities. Here we

---

[1] A first such scale has been developed by Sören Homberg and Per Hedlund. Building on their work the present scale has been mainly developed by the editors and Sylvain Brouard with inputs from all members of the research group.

provide several examples for such conditionalities. These will be discussed in more detail in the country chapters and in the concluding chapter.

2.3.1 Policy Dynamics and Public Opinion

According to democratic theory, the unique quality of democracies is that citizens live under laws they have given themselves—or at least under laws that the majority of citizens can agree with (Dahl 2000). Citizen preferences thus take a prominent place in both the motivation of political actors and in our analyses. Yet the relationship between public opinion and political decisions is complex in modern democracies as these are based on political representation and vary in their use of direct democracy as a corrective to decision-making through the representative channel (e.g. Strøm et al. 2003: 689–93). Hence, in most cases not citizens but political representatives decide on public policy. While there is little on what theorists of democratic representation can agree, many buy into Pitkin's classic notion that representation means 'acting in the best interest of the public' (Pitkin 1967: 208, 224). In more operational terms this can either mean acting on the wishes of voters when the policy is adopted or acting in a way that the voters would approve once the policy outcomes are known (Manin et al. 1999: 2).

In modern democracies political parties are the main vehicles of structuring the political decision-making process and policy representation (e.g. Dalton et al. 2011). Party government means that political parties present their policy proposals in elections and act upon them once in government (Katz 1986; Budge et al. 2012). At the end of the legislative term, voters can hold the government parties accountable for their deeds and omissions. Policy change thus should follow if the government party or parties have argued in favour of it and were elected upon such policy proposals. There are thus clear normative expectations suggesting this outcome. Political actors' desire for re-election should also be a strong self-interested motive to honour their electoral pledges. Sabatier (1998: 119) has labelled the replacement of one dominant issue coalition by another as the standard model in political science. We can formulate the following hypothesis:

H1. *Nuclear energy policy change will result from a party or a coalition of parties with programmatic commitment to such change, assuming government office, and replacing actors committed to maintaining the policy status quo.*

Yet the literature on political parties' pledge fulfilment suggests that neither single-party governments nor coalition governments in which parties agree on a specific issue always live up fully to their claims (Thomson et al. 2012). One reason might be that the issue is minor, technical, and likely to go unnoticed, far from causing electoral punishment. Nuclear energy clearly is an issue prominent enough that such a mismatch between promise and acting would not remain unnoticed. It is thus important to consider why political parties may change their mind, not acting on their promises. The question, 'when do actors significantly deviate from or reverse a taken policy position?' of course, is one not only relevant to parties coming to government with a commitment to policy change, but to all political parties. In our context it is particularly important when government policy change occurs *without* prior replacement of the government. To develop our expectations regarding the conditions under which such behaviour may occur, we draw on the literature on policy change, policy responsiveness, and party goal conflicts.

2.3.2 Responsive Parties

Political parties compete in elections on the basis of competing policy platforms. Hence, the voters are confronted with *policy packages* and by some means have to choose between them. Yet for any single political party it seems almost impossible to put together a consistent policy package consisting exclusively of those policies that find the approval of all citizens potentially inclined to vote for that party. Consequently, voters are forced into an optimizing decision: choosing the platform that promises the greatest overall benefit (Thurner 2000). While this is a highly complex cognitive challenge, it becomes even more demanding when voters begin discounting party claims (Grofman 1985), try to anticipate government coalitions, and incorporate the outcome of post-election inter-party policy negotiations into their voting decision (Kedar 2005, 2009). Most voters are therefore likely to apply simpler heuristics and focus on party positions on a few issues salient to them (Baumgartner and Jones 2002; Jones and Baumgartner 2005). Transferred to our context, policy change should be more likely when significant changes occur with respect to the salience of the nuclear energy issue.

> H2. *Nuclear energy policy change is likely to result from significant changes in the salience the issue has to voters.*

We should, however, think about high issue salience as a necessary but not sufficient condition. We also need to consider the voters' issue preferences. If they largely agree on the current policy, no change is likely to result from increased attention to it. Conversely, policy change should be more likely when significant salience shifts occur and when many voters are critical about the current policy. Voters may not only attach more or less attention and concern to an issue over time, but also change their mind on it. Later we specify conditions that might cause such opinion change on the nuclear energy issue. Here we conjecture:

> H3. *Nuclear energy policy change is likely to result from massive shifts in public opinion, amounting to majority support for a new policy.*

As we have noted, in taking positions on single issues, individual political parties cannot please all voters. This is simply impossible because of preference diversity among the citizens. Nor do political parties need to do so. Quite simply, a party's position with regard to a system's traditional cleavages and its resulting overall policy package may put off many voters regardless of the party's position on issues that are not structured by these cleavages such as nuclear energy. Hence, even when such a party takes a position on a new issue favoured by these voters, they will not vote for the party. Conversely, traditional alignments of voters with specific parties may override disagreement on individual issues. Thus, parties may reckon that they do not have to adapt their positions on specific issues to maintain their traditional voters. Therefore, actual party strategy change requires careful and shrewd consideration by the actors, taking into account different groups of voters.

We can single out three groups of voters that are the most likely candidates to be considered relevant for party strategies: (1) issue-undecided voters, (2) voters without or with weak party affiliations, and (3) issue-inconsistent voters. All three groups are potentially mobile voter segments. *Issue-undecidedness* relates to voters who do not hold closed and stable attitudes towards an issue. These voters are probably more susceptible to external influences and hence framing efforts of parties (Thurner 2010; Schöning et al. 2015). The larger this group, the more parties should invest in efforts to convince this group or at least not to scare them. Similarly, voters without a party affiliation or with a weak one who share the party's issue position are voters who might be won by the party strengthening its commitment to its existing policy, and, when in government, selling itself as the guarantee for policy stability. Thus, again, no party repositioning or government policy change is likely to occur.

Finally, *issue-inconsistency* relates to voters with issue attitudes that conflict with the relevant positions of 'their' party (Thurner 2010).[2] 'Their party' means some kind of party alignment and can be measured either by stated party loyalty, previous voting behaviour, or by voting intentions. We expect those voters to be more prone to attitudinal or behavioural change due to framing efforts by political parties and other actors. Such internally divisive issues are potentially dangerous for parties and at the same time create key target electorates for their competitors. If the affected party's counter-framing is not successful, policy change might be the only chance to keep issue-inconsistent voters. We hence conjecture:

H4. *Policy change is more likely when government parties have large shares of issue-inconsistent voters.*

As policy change may also alienate voters, such party behaviour of course requires that more voters can thereby be newly attracted or kept than lost. Parties having relevant shares of voters with opposed attitudes on a salient issue face tricky problems of political communication to avoid tensions and vote losses. Most of the time such accommodative communication strategies also involve some kind of policy adaptation. Such electoral considerations as determinants of policy change are more likely the closer parties or coalitions are to critical thresholds such as parliamentary representation, strongest party status, or parliamentary majority.

2.3.3 The Goals of Political Parties and Governments

Notwithstanding the importance of electoral support for political parties, winning votes is just one of their goals (Harmel and Janda 1994; Müller and Strøm 1999; Sjöblom 1968; Strøm 1990; Nohrstedt 2005). Political parties also care about policies. Policy choices can either be of a principled or of a pragmatic nature (Tavits 2007). While principled policy goals cannot be compromised without undermining the very rationale of the party, pragmatic ones can be traded for

---

[2] The concept of issue-inconsistent voters bears similarities with that of cross-pressured voters (Berelson et al. 1954). While cross-pressured voters are divided between conflicting group loyalties (which would suggest different vote choices), issue-inconsistent voters have to cope with a conflict between their party loyalty and their issue preference.

other policies or compromised in order to achieve goals such as winning votes or government office. The issue of nuclear power is of particular interest, as it is of principled nature for some parties and voters, but of pragmatic nature for others. As a matter of fact, being against nuclear energy may result from either or from both rationales. In contrast, we are not aware of relevant political actors who are in favour of nuclear energy for principled reasons. While actors may be strongly in favour of nuclear energy, such commitment always rests in pragmatic thinking about the issue, for instance related to expected economic welfare, energy security concerns, or other priorities. Nuclear energy as such is then merely a means to achieve these other goals that may also be achieved by other means (though these are considered less effective or efficient or sufficiently available). Although typically not included in the list of moral politics, the nuclear energy issue bears some of its characteristics (Engeli et al. 2012; Heichel et al. 2013). Opponents of nuclear energy consider it morally unacceptable to risk the life, health, and wealth of many for the economic gains of a few and to burden future generations with the heritage of nuclear waste without solutions for its disposal. Greens are the archetypical representative of this type of concerns. In terms of political conflict and morality, nuclear energy thus is a 'hybrid issue' (Knill 2013: 311) as no strong moral counter-argument exists. Rather, proponents of nuclear energy use instrumentally rational arguments such as belittling the associated risks and stressing the welfare effects of energy supply, or meanwhile highlighting the negative climate impact of using fossil fuels.

Political parties holding pragmatic views on nuclear energy may adapt their preferences in response to changing economic and energy security conditions and nuclear accidents. In reality, such pragmatic changes in taking policy positions are likely to be invoked to justify policy change even when electoral opportunism is the driving factor. We expect that the presence of parties holding principled (generally negative) positions on nuclear energy in parliament helps to keep the issue on the agenda. Likewise, we expect that (expected) high electoral performance or even government participation of such parties leads to decisions to terminate or phase out nuclear energy.

> H5: *Governments will turn away from nuclear energy (if still committed to it) whenever a Green party participates in government.*

Based on these arguments we can also predict nuclear energy policy stability in countries without nuclear energy and countries that are already in the process of phasing out nuclear energy:

> H6: *No pro-nuclear energy policy change will be made whenever a Green party participates in government.*

As parties with principled positions on nuclear energy cannot participate in government when a pro-nuclear energy course is maintained, the other parties' decision to team up with such opponents of nuclear energy de facto implies their agreement to a policy reversal. Understanding nuclear energy policy reversals that result from the inclusion of parties with principled positions on the issue thus requires understanding why parties holding pragmatic positions choose such partners. In the trivial case, these parties take partly critical positions on nuclear energy for pragmatic reasons (e.g. concerning its economic viability) and hence the government parties agree on a policy direction that, by tendency, is anti-nuclear though for different reasons and with varying intensity. In contrast, parties holding positive positions on nuclear energy have to make policy sacrifices to forge such coalitions. They may do so because it is the only way to get or hold on to government office. The desire for government office is a strong motive for individual politicians and political parties (Riker 1963; Martin and Stevenson 2001; Müller and Strøm 1999) and it may be considered worth making substantial policy concessions to achieve this. Government office is attractive as such but also because of the large influence over public policy it brings. Nuclear energy policy concessions then must be weighed against policy gains in a vast array of public policies. In many situations we cannot disentangle the parties' office and policy motivations, as they are observational equivalents in their striving for government office. We thus conjecture:

> H7: *Government policy will turn away from nuclear energy if required to allow political parties with pragmatic positions on the issue the winning of, or holding on to, government office in coalition cabinets.*

2.3.4 Costs Inflicted by Opponents of Government Policy

According to the revised version of the 'advocacy coalition' approach, situations 'in which all major [issue] coalitions view a continuation of the current situation as unacceptable' (Sabatier 1998: 119) are likely to lead to policy compromise. By definition, compromise is not a full policy reversal but something in-between a U-turn change and the unchanged continuation of the current policy. Such limited reversals may play out as full reversals of some programme part (with continuation of the remaining programme), a downscaling of the entire programme or large parts of it, or some compromise along its time dimension (see previous section). It is impossible to provide an exhaustive list of costs, as ingenious political entrepreneurs will come up with new ideas as to how government policy might be frustrated, delayed, or burdened with considerable financial or image costs. To name just a few such strategies, opponents may use appeals to courts, parliamentary obstruction, testimonials of moral authorities or celebrities, peaceful mass demonstrations, violent activism, or whatever they consider useful and is available to them. We thus need to rely on the qualitative analysis of the cases to specify whether such costs had been inflicted or not. Clearly, this bears the dangers of ex-post rationalization in case of policy change and ignorance of similar costs in other situations. Still, sidelining the measurement problem for now, in line with the 'advocacy coalition' expectations, we conjecture:

> H8: *Partial policy change by an acting government is more likely when policy continuity is heavily challenged by a vital opposition.*

2.3.5 New Evidence from External Developments and Events

The major theoretical approaches to public policy-making—the policy streams model of John Kingdon (1984), the advocacy coalition framework as developed by

Paul Sabatier (1988, 1998) and associates (Weible et al. 2009; True et al. 2007), and the punctuated-equilibrium theory as developed by Bryan D. Jones, Frank R. Baumgartner and associates (Baumgartner et al. 2008, 2011; Baumgartner and Jones 1993, 2002; Baumgartner and Mahoney 2005)—all consider changes external to the decision-making situation important for how the actors perceive the issue and decide upon it. Obvious candidates for such external developments in our context are the factors already mentioned in Chapter 1 as the drivers behind the nuclear energy revival: rising prices of oil and natural gas, import dependencies coupled with increasing concerns about supply security, and increasing concern about the environmental effects (CO_2 emissions) of carbon-based energies. We thus expect that:

H9: Pro-nuclear energy policy change is more likely the more the energy supply of countries depends on the import of carbon-based energy sources (coal, oil, gas) and the less potential they have for developing alternative energies.

Relevant developments external to the decision-making situation thus include gradual changes in structural factors but singular events can also be important. Think, for instance, of the dispute between the Ukraine and Russia over the former's supply with natural gas cutting off a large part of the European gas supply for several days in 2009, the wars in the Middle East that have temporarily prevented, reduced, or threatened oil and gas imports from some of Europe's most important suppliers (the two Gulf Wars in 1990–1 and 2003, respectively, the Libyan revolution in 2011, and the rise of Islamic State since 2014), or the military conflict over Ukrainian territory that unfolded since 2014 which has caused return to a kind of Cold War between the West and Russia, one of Europe's main energy suppliers. The EU boycott on Iranian oil from 2012 to 2016, sanctioning Iran's programme of developing nuclear military capacity, had a similar effect. Such instances are likely to influence how decision-makers in the energy policy community define their challenges and they also figure prominently in attempts at framing nuclear energy as a resolution to energy security concerns. Such events and their interpretations are likely also to affect how citizens think about the choices in energy policy. For instance, the MIT study on the future of nuclear energy (MIT 2003) has suggested that, as soon as energy costs increase, some segments of voters will trade off the perceived costs and risks of nuclear power against the individually experienced incidence of energy costs (commuting, heating). This kind of scenario unfolded in the 2000s before the beginning of the financial and economic crisis in 2008.

Clearly, not all developments and events are instrumental to increasing social acceptability of nuclear energy. Declining or stagnating world market prices for fossil fuels, for instance, should have the opposite effect to that just outlined. This scenario has unfolded since 2008. In particular, we consider accidents in nuclear power stations as events that potentially frighten citizens and make decision-makers aware of the risks associated with nuclear energy production. They also highlight the possibility of unforeseen contingencies and the problems emerging from the interaction of nuclear technology with its natural and human environment. Three such accidents stand out: Harrisburg (Three Mile Island) in 1979, Chernobyl in 1986, and Fukushima in 2011. Each of these accidents constituted a significant challenge to nuclear energy. As already noted in Chapter 1 they signify instances where policies—the nuclear energy programmes—produced 'negative feedback' (i.e. outcomes that make the policy less acceptable) (Hood 1994; Weaver 2010).

Yet each accident has its specifics that make generalization difficult, and limit its influence on public opinion and decision-makers. The Harrisburg accident caused only limited damage, certainly in the short term. The Chernobyl case was fraught with outdated technology and suffered from or accelerated the decline of the Soviet empire. Also, few countries expect earthquakes of a magnitude similar to the one that shocked Japan in 2011. And even fewer countries have nuclear facilities exposed to the destructive forces of tsunamis such as the Fukushima site. Moreover, these accidents did not affect many West European voters directly (with Chernobyl being a partial exception) and as such may have their own 'half-life period', meaning that their impact on the perception and reasoning of voters becomes weaker with the time that has passed since the accident (Csereklyei 2013). We therefore should not wonder when such events do not cause uniform policy reactions throughout the world. Rather, we should expect that differences in the objective conditions listed above and the relevant actors' capacity of framing these accidents (e.g. as due to case-specific, unique conditions or as the outcome to be expected from the use of high-risk technology) and setting the public agenda lead to different policy outcomes. In general terms, we can formulate the following hypothesis:

> H10: *Nuclear energy policy decisions made in temporal proximity to nuclear power accidents are more likely to turn away from nuclear energy to some extent or increase its costs (e.g. abandoning the entire programme or parts of it, reducing its scope, delaying its implementation, or introducing new safety requirements).*

Making decisions on nuclear energy in temporal proximity to nuclear power accidents increases the likelihood of strong public opinion signals to decision-makers, protest events, and the Green parties' electoral strengthening and acceptability to other parties. Therefore, actors in favour of nuclear energy will try to avoid making nuclear energy policy decisions in such contexts or opt for delaying decisions on the substance of the nuclear energy programme by making concessions along the time dimensions (e.g. opting for moratoria, commissioning special checks of power stations or scientific reports). Conversely, actors taking a stance against nuclear energy will try to put the nuclear energy issue on the agenda for decision-making in such contexts.

2.3.6 Path Dependence

Our overview of the history of nuclear energy in Chapter 1 has revealed some broad cross-national trends regarding the use of nuclear energy. Yet for many reasons individual countries have started considering the nuclear energy option at different points in time. Such differences in timing can be consequential. Gerschenkron's (1962: 7) famous insight from the study of industrialization that 'the development of a backward country may, by the very virtue of its backwardness, tend to differ fundamentally from an advanced country' applies here, but it can mean two different things. On the one hand the relative latecomer can avoid the errors of the pioneers (e.g. investing in a specific technology that does not establish itself on the market), copy the forerunners' most rewarding decisions, and thereby speed up the process of building up a sizeable nuclear energy production with lower unit-costs (second mover advantage). On the other hand, barriers to the use of nuclear energy generally have become increasingly relevant over time. Most prominently, citizen concerns about nuclear energy were rarely present initially but have impacted on political decision-making since the 1970s (e.g. Flam 1994; Kitschelt 1980; Jasper 1990; Joppke 1993; Nelkin and Pollak 1981; Rootes 2007). Hence, entering the process of going nuclear early guaranteed an easy ride, while late entrance implied more resistance and uncertain outcomes in many democracies (first mover advantage).

At any point in time, energy policy has to build on the legacy of the energy policy conducted in the past, amounting to the present structure of energy production and consumption (Pierson 2004). Consequently, a country heavily invested in nuclear energy is constrained in two ways: first, there are considerable sunk costs (i.e. what has been invested so far might become a 'stranded investment' in case of radical policy change) and inevitable future costs (e.g. from the nuclear facilities' dismantling and permanent disposal) that in the case of rapid phasing out are not balanced by sufficient returns on investment. Thus, a sudden end to nuclear energy comes with a bundle of financial problems that need to be resolved in that case (boiling down to the 'who pays?' question). Clearly, money spent on a nuclear energy exit cannot be used for other policy goals and these may be more important even to political decision-makers and citizens who might never have opted for nuclear energy when it was originally introduced and expanded. In line with recent analyses (see Fuhrmann 2012; Gourley and Stulberg 2013; Csereklyei 2013) we therefore expect the following outcome:

H11: *Countries heavily invested in nuclear energy are likely to continue on their pro nuclear path.*

A second constraint comes from the problem of substitutability. Taking out nuclear energy production causes a more or less sudden reduction in energy supply, particularly in the electricity sector. The issue then is to find alternative sources of supply, which may come from the accumulation of alternative capacities, importation, or both. Again, this is related to the magnitude of nuclear energy production and the phase-out pace. Small countries with little nuclear energy and alone in its abandonment may find substitution relatively easy. However, when many and major countries decide to depart from nuclear energy, the capacity constraints may constitute a harder challenge. Clearly, politicians and citizens will consider such factors when making decisions on nuclear energy. We thus conjecture:

H12: *If countries heavily invested in nuclear energy reverse their policy, they will adopt a strategy of partial or gradual change (see previous section).*

As already indicated, the longer such processes are stretched over time, the greater the chances that the decisions are subject to further reversal.

Reversing a phase-out decision poses its own set of problems. Depending on the time that has lapsed between the implementation of an exit from nuclear energy, reviving nuclear power may face problems from being disconnected from state-of-the art technological development (impinging on building and maintaining nuclear power facilities and the training of personnel). Moreover, the problem of nuclear energy's social acceptability may have further aggravated. We thus expect that:

> H13: *The more time has passed since nuclear energy has been effectively abandoned, the less likely a return to it becomes.*

The bivariate formulation of our hypotheses is a deliberate simplification of reality. We have already mentioned how issue preferences and issue saliency interact. We will provide a few examples of how the hypotheses may be conditioned by other factors, some of which we will discuss. Yet, given the complexities of nuclear energy policy and political competition in modern democracies, it seems impossible at this stage to provide a full set of such conditionalities.

The lack of endowment with domestic resources may make a country decide at an early point in time (mostly in the 1950s) to establish nuclear energy as a long-term source for economic growth. Such a choice, however, is dependent on the will of the governing elites to actually aim for a path of accelerated growth, which typically requires the presence of factors way beyond the availability of energy. If such factors are lacking, however, slow and low economic growth may lead to a self-enforcing dynamic where countries are not in need of an expansive energy path.

Other factors included in our hypotheses are clearly rooted in more fundamental attitudes and values and their development. For instance, public opinion towards nuclear energy and its susceptibility to change will depend on the general risk attitudes prevalent in a country (e.g. Sjöberg 1999; Kam and Simas 2010). Similarly, the readiness to sacrifice short-term economic gains, the presence and strength of Green parties, and willingness to protest are rooted in the relevance of post-materialist value change in a country (e.g. Abramson and Inglehart 1995; Inglehart and Welzel 2005; Dalton and Welzel 2015).

There is also considerable interdependence between the causal factors we have identified in our hypotheses. For instance, we expect the impact of exogenous shocks and focusing events such as nuclear energy disasters on policy strategies to depend on the institutional structures (e.g. electoral systems), pre-mobilization of social forces, and competitiveness of anti-nuclear parties. Parties in government will react the more acutely to a disaster, the larger and sustained the opposition to nuclear energy already is in a country. Clearly, parties under such conditions are much more vulnerable and should propose quicker, more extensive, and credible policy changes.

The factors expected to exert influence on nuclear energy policy decisions discussed so far mostly relate directly to the policy, office and electoral goals of political parties, or the substance of the nuclear energy issue. Similar to the classic studies of Kitschelt (1986) and Midttun and Rucht (1994), we now turn to political structures. These exercise a rather indirect influence on political decisions by influencing the power various political actors have in the policy-making process and by narrowing their sets of strategic choices. Yet whenever it is easy to predict the direction of a specific factor's influence on nuclear energy policy, it is hard to foresee that its impact on the outcome will be decisive. Conversely, we may expect the impact of other factors to be more significant, but it is less clear in which direction they will move the policy. We therefore indicate the potential effects of political institutions but refrain from formulating expectations in the form of hypotheses.

2.3.7 Institutions: Input Structures

Political institutions structure the articulation of political demands and influence how political preferences are translated into authoritative decisions. Although institutions are also subject to change, they often exhibit a great amount of stability and remain unchanged through individual decision-making processes. In a long-term perspective institutional reform and both its intended and unintended effects can be quite consequential for policy outcomes. As our observation period spans several decades, we are indeed confronted with relevant institutional change and thus within-country variation of factors impacting on actors' strategies. Notwithstanding such developments, most institutional variation is not over time but between the countries covered during our observation period. Our discussion of institutions singles out a number of features that allow differentiating between countries and time periods and generating expectations about the decision-making processes and their outcomes.

Representative and Direct Democracy

We have noted that modern democracies rely primarily on representative political institutions. While many constitutions reserve a few issues—typically particularly consequential ones that are expected to be very rare (such as sovereignty issues or major constitutional changes)—to the referendum device, policy issues (such as nuclear energy) as a rule do not fall in that category (Strøm et al. 2003: 689–90). Yet politicians may nevertheless return decision-making power on such issues to the people by holding a referendum. Resorting to the ultimate principal—the citizens—when it is not constitutionally required must be related to political competition. Direct democratic instruments are strongest when they allow for bottom-up ('uncontrolled') initiated referendums (Smith 1976; Qvortrup 2000). Where such instruments are in place, decisions on issues are potentially tied to public opinion in a much more direct way. Clearly, the specific rules under which people can invalidate laws or write new ones can make a great difference. Also, the rules on observing the outcome of referendums can differ, though given the normative power of direct democratic choices we might expect that the issue preferences of referendum majorities will prevail regardless of these rules. Fully informed and exclusively policy-motivated governments should hold optional referendums only when they reckon that they will win. Yet, both conditions are not always given. The possibility that governments may fail to correctly predict the outcome of a referendum and sometimes other government concerns (e.g. silencing public or intra-party dissent) suggest that a referendum might be held even when its outcome is unpredictable. In any case, we expect that policy reversals are more likely when nuclear policy decisions can be made via referendum.

Electoral Systems

Electoral systems provide crucial incentives for party competition. In our context we can distinguish their impact on the composition of the party system, on issue representation, and on alternation in government.

Low entry thresholds are usually connected to proportional electoral systems. They invite the creation of single-issue parties taking polar positions on issues. The parliamentary representation of Green parties as the issue-owners of anti-nuclear positions is closely related to the existence of proportional electoral systems (Kitschelt 1986). Such parliamentary representation clearly is functional for keeping the nuclear power issue on the political agenda. This, in turn, may impact other parties' position-taking. More specifically, parties competing for the same pool of voters may adapt their issue position. Going beyond such indirect influence, single-issue parties may impact nuclear energy policy once they become necessary as permanent partners in voting alliances or government coalitions (on coalition governments see hypothesis H5). We thus conclude that PR electoral systems are friendlier towards principled adversaries of nuclear energy and increase their chances to have an impact on government policy.

In the classic perspective, majoritarian electoral systems bring about two-party competition and single-party governments endowed with parliamentary majorities, and they enforce a strong and direct connection between public opinion and government policy (Duverger 1954). Note, however, that this strong linkage relates to those issues that are central to both the individual voters and their parties. As long as majority parties remain in tune with their voters with regard to such issues, they are relatively free to decide on other issues. Hence, we should expect a close correspondence between public opinion on the nuclear power issue and government policy when the issue is salient, but expect more government autonomy once this is not the case.

One generally admired property of majority systems is that they allow for 'voting the rascals out'. One practical consequence is that change in government is typically wholesale rather than a partial alternation (Mair 1997: 207–9). On the one hand, policy reversal should be more likely when the government is fully replaced. Such wholesale alternation may result in no party in cabinet office that is closely linked to and defending the policy status quo. On the other hand, the very logic of majority systems is to compete for the median voter. This, in turn, suggests that the policy status quo will largely reflect the preferences of the median voter and that major changes are unlikely. We can see the first argument to take precedence when intra-party dynamics lead to a radicalization of both major parties. Yet even in such situations nuclear energy may not loom prominently in inter-party conflict and even encompassing policy change resulting from government replacement may spare it.

2.3.8 Institutions: Output Structures

Political institutions are also important as part of a system's output structure by influencing the capacity of national governments to implement their policies (Kitschelt 1986; Midttun and Rucht 1994). We single out two factors—the vertical power structure of countries and the political economy of the electricity sector—but clearly other factors also influence state capacity.

Vertical Power Divisions within Countries

Any study that aims at understanding policy outcomes needs to be concerned with the territorial organization of government, in particular if each layer provides an opportunity structure for party competition in its own right. While it may be sufficient to focus on a particular layer of politics in some countries and policy areas, others have a more complex vertical division of powers and hence require a multi-level perspective. Clearly, federal states have their own system of divided and shared jurisdictions and the issue of nuclear energy may place itself in one or more layers. Such vertical divisions of power are potentially important in at least two ways. First, each level of government is a political decision-making arena in its own right and may develop its own distinct approach with regard to any issue at stake. The state electorates may like or dislike nuclear energy, for instance, and different conditions of political competition may provide state politicians with incentives to opt for policy choices very different from those preferred at the federal level. Second, national-level party competition may interfere and guide the behaviour of state politicians. Maintaining party cohesion over different levels of government in policy-making can smooth the relations between states and the federation and help policy coordination. Yet, it can also mean the opposite, making state-level decision-making a roadblock to federal government policy (Feigenbaum et al. 1993; Scharpf 1988; Tsebelis 2002) and providing an additional input structure with access points and channels. Even local government may be important if its consent is required, for instance, in granting construction permissions for nuclear facilities. How the vertical divisions of power interact with political incentives remains essentially an empirical question that we will address in this volume.

Political Economy of the Electricity Sector

Finally, we expect the organization of the electricity industry to impact a country's nuclear energy policy. In line with Kitschelt's notion that 'government control over market participants is a key variable of government effectiveness' (1986: 64), we expect that the more the electricity sector is under the tutelage of politics, the greater the room for political manoeuvre (Parris et al. 1987). National goals such as energy independence, or helping to develop a nuclear engineering industry, should not loom on the agenda of profit-seeking enterprises in the energy-producing sector. And such market-oriented enterprises should be expected to put up resistance against political decisions that are violating their business interests. Generally, we would expect the autonomy of politics to make policy reversals to be greatest when the electricity sector is under public ownership and least given when it is dominated by foreign capital. Additionally, we have to account for the nuclear reactor industry's presence in a given country and its transnationalization.[3] A strong presence of this industry in a country should

---

[3] A quite insightful study by the IAEA (2008) shows that the structure of this industry is permanently in flux, and thus at least partly detracts from individual states' influence. For instance, the German company Siemens bypassed the first German exit decision in 2002 by bringing its nuclear business into French-led AREVA. This cooperation was conceived as 'squeezing', and the company tried to exit and

produce additional lock-in effects. In countries with public ownership there may also be a party-political dimension involved if jobs in the electricity sector are handed out to party trustees. While adherents of the government parties might bow to their wishes, nominees of opposition parties may be more inclined to put up resistance. In many such instances the government may be able to bribe economic interests into acquiescence. Yet purchasing the industry's submission to political authority means acknowledging the budgetary costs of fundamental policy change. Any such change constitutes, in essence, a policy disaster that may involve considerable budgetary consequences. In contrast, a politically directed energy sector may help minimize the costs of public policy U-turns. In short, we expect policy reversals to be politically less costly and hence more likely when the energy sector is under political control.

In line with our study's focus, this discussion has concentrated on the political influence on the electricity industry. Yet, we should not forget that there is also an inverse relationship; political closeness, at the same time, is an inroad to regulatory capture (Stigler 1971). Politicians have learned to understand and act upon their political incentive structure. However, their judgement is less developed when the issues at stake do not directly touch upon it. Here a trusted relation with the electricity industry may well mean that such interests write government policy. In practical terms this means that government policy may follow the industry's design as long the issue is not politicized and taking a prominent place on the public agenda.

2.3.9 EU Integration

For EU member states the process of European integration has gradually changed the context of national energy policy in general, particularly with regard to nuclear energy. Note that the origins of nuclear energy policy in most member states predate European integration. The Euratom Treaty of 1957 entrusted the European Atomic Energy Community with important tasks in nuclear research, servicing the national nuclear programmes, and ensuring nuclear safety by pooling the necessary resources. Yet, energy policy-making remained a national prerogative until the Single European Act of 1986 began to establish a single European energy market. National resistance delayed the creation of the internal market in electricity until 1996 (Directive 96/92/EC). Further EU regulation was required to ensure the opening of domestic markets and establishing a competitive European electricity market (Directive 2003/54/EC, Regulation 1228/2003: 'Cross Border Electricity Trading Regulation'). Although much remains to be

---

to collaborate with the Russian state-owned nuclear energy sector. Legal problems of leaving the AREVA agreement and the second German exit decision in 2011 led the company to abandon the nuclear sector. Optimistic expectations about the future of nuclear energy caused mergers and acquisitions and the formation of firm alliances in the pre-Fukushima period. Accordingly, Toshiba bought a majority share of Westinghouse in 2006 and took on board as co-owner Kazatomprom, the Kazakh State-owned uranium producer. Alliances were formed by AREVA and Mitsubishi Heavy Industries (MHI) (to develop a new 1,000 MW(e) nuclear power plant in 2006) and General Electric (GE) and Hitach (to provide services for operating BWRs and to compete for new reactor projects around the world in 2007).

done to physically integrate the national markets, traditionally structured by natural monopolies and inward-bound transmission capacities, the regulatory framework of a single European market seems largely in place by now, and regional electricity markets are emerging. This allows for regional specialization in energy production and the legally unrestricted flow of energy between member states. While regional specialization typically rests on natural endowments and technological advance with regard to nuclear energy, we also have to think of regional differences in the social acceptability and political viability of different energy production technologies. In other words, the integration of European energy markets provides incentives to specialize in the production of nuclear energy and export of electricity in some countries and it simultaneously allows other countries to satisfy their demands without going through the troubles of establishing domestic production (of course, the 'easy way out' may not be cheap financially and may involve other problems as well).

The EU recognizes the right of member states to decide autonomously which form of energy they want to produce on their territory. Against the background of such a national prerogative, the EU has been assigned with important policy-making tasks that have potential impact for member states' nuclear energy policies. The Lisbon Treaty of 2007 established EU jurisdiction over energy policy with respect to four broad goals: ensuring the functioning of the energy market; ensuring security of energy supply in the Union; promoting energy efficiency and energy saving and the development of new and renewable forms of energy; and promoting the interconnection of energy networks (Article 176 A). As we have already seen, some of the EU initiatives in these areas clearly favour the use of nuclear energy, at least by aiming at resolving associated problems such as safety concerns.

The Single European Act had already established EU jurisdiction over environmental policies. Provided that different forms of energy have their specific environmental problems, related regulation can change the incentives for the use of specific energy forms and consequently impact the energy mix of countries. Perhaps the most prominent decision relevant in this context is the EU commitment to the Kyoto goals that has resulted in the obligation to reduce CO_2 emissions by 8 per cent (from 1990 emissions) until 2012. The EU also participates in the 'Kyoto II' regime that has a time horizon until 2020. We have already seen that the EU promotes the use of nuclear energy as a means to meeting that goal.

The market logic to which the EU largely subscribes does not always work in favour of nuclear energy. Specifically, making nuclear energy a business investment that can mobilize private capital is challenging. Nuclear energy has always required state intervention favourable to it, including public investment into nuclear research, guarantees for long-term investments, and the state limiting and taking over liability risks. All this is actually at odds with the EU's market logic and potentially EU rules. However, in October 2014, the European Commission approved UK plans to subsidize the construction and operation of a new nuclear power plant at Hinkley Point to be in line with EU state aid rules. Whether this signals a special adherence of the Commission to nuclear power has to be seen. In any case, its current Commissioner Miguel Arias Cañete, a former Spanish Minister with affiliation to the People's Party, is convinced that meeting European energy and climate challenges without nuclear energy is not feasible.

Notwithstanding some aspects working in the other direction, in sum increasing European integration has tended to improve the cost–benefit ratio of nuclear energy. At the same time, it has removed obstacles to regional specialization in producing specific forms of energy. Overall, increasing integration thus should benefit the use of nuclear energy in the EU, though not necessarily in each member state.

2.4 CONCLUSION

This chapter has reviewed the political science literature on nuclear energy policy. Building on these approaches, in particular on the studies of Kitschelt (1986) and Midttun and Rucht (1994), we have developed a number of specific expectations regarding which factors might exercise influence on nuclear energy policy decisions and their directionality. We have also formulated some more general expectations about the extent to which institutional factors may impact the fate of nuclear energy more indirectly, by shaping the endowments of individual actors and by influencing the political decision-making process. We will return to these hypotheses in the concluding chapter of the volume in a comparative analysis of Western Europe. Between the two introductory and the concluding chapters, we present some more specific analyses. We first address the role of nuclear energy in the energy mix of European countries in Chapter 3. Here we test a kind of 'technocratic' perspective that assumes the countries' use of nuclear energy can be explained exclusively by their endowments with natural resources and the resulting energy dependencies. In Chapter 4 we turn to political variables. Taking a comparative perspective the chapter shows to what extent nuclear energy has been contested in Western Europe since the 1970s. It addresses the extent to which citizens have been sceptical or hostile towards nuclear energy, the magnitude of citizen protest against nuclear energy, and how important Green political parties have become over the period of investigation. The chapter also highlights some relations between energy dependency and attitudes towards nuclear power and between institutional factors and the strength of the Greens. Chapters 5 to 11 then provide in-depth analyses of the nuclear energy trajectory and the political processes behind the public policy outcomes in seven Western European countries. Naturally, these chapters focus on their cases rather than addressing the overarching hypotheses. They provide analyses in their own right, but they are also building blocks for the comparative analysis in the concluding chapter. However, there we go beyond the set of countries covered with case studies in this volume and we return to the hypotheses and expectations formulated in this chapter.

REFERENCES

Abramson, Paul R., and Ronald Inglehart (1995). *Value Change in Global Perspective*. Ann Arbor: University of Michigan Press.

Andersen, Svein S., and Atle Midttun (1994). 'Environmental Opposition in Norwegian Energy Policy: Structural Determinants and Strategic Mobilization', in Helena Flam (ed.), *States and Anti-Nuclear Movements*. Edinburgh: Edinburgh University Press, 233–63.

Baumgartner, Frank R., and Bryan D. Jones (1993). *Agendas and Instability in American Politics*. Chicago, IL: University of Chicago Press.

Baumgartner, Frank R., and Bryan D. Jones (eds) (2002). *Policy Dynamics*. Chicago: University of Chicago Press.

Baumgartner, Frank R., Bryan D. Jones, and John Wilkerson (2011). 'Comparative Studies of Policy Dynamics.' *Comparative Political Studies*, 44(8): 947–72.

Baumgartner, Frank R., and Christine Mahoney (2005). 'Social Movements, the Rise of New Issues, and the Public Agenda', in Davis S. Meyer, Valerie Jenness, and Helen Ingram (eds), *Routing the Opposition*. Minneapolis, MN: University of Minnesota Press, 65–85.

Baumgartner, Frank R., Suzanna De Beuf, and Amber E. Boydstun (2008). *The Decline of the Death Penalty and the Discovery of Innocence*. Cambridge: Cambridge University Press.

Berelson, Bernard R., Paul F. Lazarsfeld, and William N. McPhee (1954). *Voting: A Study of Opinion Formation in a Presidential Campaign*. Chicago: University of Chicago Press.

Budge, Ian, Hans Keman, Michael D. McDonald, and Paul Pennings (2012). *Organizing Democratic Choice: Party Representation over Time*. Oxford: Oxford University Press.

Campbell, John L. (1988). *Collapse of an Industry: Nuclear Power and the Contradictions of U.S. Policy*. Ithaca, NY: Cornell University Press.

Csereklyei, Zsuzanna (2013). *Measuring the Impact of Nuclear Accidents on Energy Policy*. Working Paper, 151. Vienna: Department of Economics, Vienna University of Economics and Business Administration.

Dahl, Robert A. (2000). *On Democracy*. New Haven: Yale University Press.

Dalton, Russel J., and Christian Welzel (2015). *The Civic Culture Transformed: From Allegiant to Assertive Citizens*. Cambridge: Cambridge University Press.

Dalton, Russel J., David M. Farrell, and Ian McAllister (2011). *Political Parties and Democratic Linkage*. Oxford: Oxford University Press.

Diani, Mario (1994). 'The Conflict over Nuclear Energy in Italy', in Helena Flam (ed.), *States and Anti-Nuclear Movements*. Edinburgh: Edinburgh University Press, 201–31.

Duverger, Maurice (1954). *Political Parties: Their Organization and Activities in the Modern State*. London: Methuen.

Engeli, Isabelle, Christopher Green-Pedersen, and Lars Thorup Larsen (eds) (2012). *Morality Politics in Western Europe: Parties, Agendas and Policy Choices*. Basingstoke: Palgrave Macmillan.

Feigenbaum, Harvey, Richard Samuels, and R. Kent Weaver (1993). 'Innovation, Coordination, and Implementation in Energy Policy', in R. Kent Weaver and Bert A. Rockman (eds), *Do Institutions Matter?* Washington, DC: Brookings Institution, 42–109.

Flam, Helena (ed.) (1994). *States and Anti-Nuclear Movements*. Edinburgh: Edinburgh University Press.

Fuhrmann, Matthew (2012). 'Splitting Atoms: Why Do Countries Build Nuclear Power Plants?' *International Interactions*, 38: 29–57.

Gerschenkron, Alexander (1962). *Economic Backwardness in Historical Perspective*. Cambridge, MA: Belknap Press of Harvard University Press.

Gourley, Bernard, and Adam N. Stulberg (2013). 'Correlates of Nuclear Energy', in Adam N. Stulberg and Matthew Fuhrmann (eds), *The Nuclear Renaissance and International Security*. Stanford, CA: Stanford University Press, 19–49.

Grofman, Bernard (1985). 'The Neglected Role of the Status Quo in Models of Issue Voting.' *Journal of Politics*, 47(1): 230–7.

Hall, Peter (1993). 'Policy Paradigms, Social Learning, and the State.' *Comparative Politics*, 25(3): 275–96.

Harmel, Robert, and Kenneth Janda (1994). 'An Integrated Theory of Party Goals and Party Change.' *Journal of Theoretical Politics*, 6(3): 259–87.

Heichel, Stephan, Christoph Knill, and Sophie Schmitt (2013). 'Public Policy Meets Morality: Conceptual and Theoretical Challenges in the Analysis of Morality Policy Change.' *Journal of European Public Policy*, 20(3): 318–34
Hood, Christopher (1994). *Explaining Economic Policy Reversals*. Buckingham: Open University Press.
IAEA (2008). *Annual Report*. Vienna: IAEA.
Inglehart, Ronald, and Christian Welzel (2005). *Modernization, Cultural Change, and Democracy*. Cambridge: Cambridge University Press.
Jasper, James M. (1990). *Nuclear Politics: Energy and the State in the United States, Sweden, and France*. Princeton: Princeton University Press.
Jones, Bryan D., and Frank R. Baumgartner (2005). *The Politics of Attention: How Government Prioritizes Problems*. Chicago: University of Chicago Press.
Joppke, Christian (1993). *Mobilizing Against Nuclear Energy: A Comparison of Germany and the United States*. Berkeley, CA: University of California Press.
Kam, Cindy, and Elizabeth N. Simas (2010). 'Risk Orientations and Policy Frames.' *Journal of Politics*, 72(2): 281–96.
Katz, Richard S. (1986). 'Party Government: A Rationalistic Conception', in Francis G. Castles and Rudolf Wildenmann (eds), *Visions and Realities of Party Government*. Berlin: Walter de Gruyter, 31–71.
Kedar, Orit (2005). 'When Moderate Voters Prefer Extreme Parties: Policy Balancing in Parliamentary Elections.' *American Political Science Review*, 99(2): 185–99.
Kedar, Orit (2009). *Voting for Policy, Not Parties: How Voters Compensate for Power Sharing*. Cambridge: Cambridge University Press.
Kingdon, John W. (1984). *Agendas, Alternatives, and Public Policies*. New York: Longman.
Kitschelt, Herbert P. (1980). *Kernenergiepolitik: Arena eines gesellschaftlichen Konflikts*. Frankfurt am Main: Campus.
Kitschelt, Herbert P. (1986). 'Political Opportunity Structures and Political Protest: Anti-Nuclear Movements in Four Democracies.' *British Journal of Political Science*, 16: 57–85.
Knill, Christoph (2013). 'The Study of Morality Policy: Analytical Implications from a Public Policy Perspective.' *Journal of European Public Policy*, 20(3): 309–17.
Mair, Peter (1997). *Party System Change: Approaches and Interpretations*. Oxford: Oxford University Press.
Manin, Bernard, Adam Przeworski, and Susan C. Stokes (1999). 'Introduction', in Adam Przeworski, Susan C. Stokes, and Bernard Manin (eds), *Democracy, Accountability, and Representation*. Cambridge: Cambridge University Press, 1–26.
Martin, Lanny W., and Randolph T. Stevenson (2001). 'Government Formation in Parliamentary Democracies.' *American Journal of Political Science*, 45(1): 33–50.
Midttun, Atle, and Dieter Rucht (1994). 'Comparing Policy Outcomes of Conflicts over Nuclear Power: Description and Explanation', in Helena Flam (ed.), *States and Anti-Nuclear Movements*. Edinburgh: Edinburgh University Press, 383–415.
MIT (2003). *The Future of Nuclear Power: An Interdisciplinary Study*. Harvard, MA: MIT.
Müller, Wolfgang C., and Kaare Strøm (eds) (1999). *Policy, Office, or Votes? How Political Parties in Western Europe Make Hard Decisions*. Cambridge: Cambridge University Press.
Nelkin, Dorothy, and Michael Pollak (1981). *The Atom Besieged: Extra-Parliamentary Dissent in France and Germany*. Cambridge, MA: MIT Press.
Nohrstedt, Daniel (2005). 'External Shocks and Policy Change: Three Mile Island and Swedish Nuclear Energy Policy.' *Journal of European Public Policy*, 12(6): 1041–59.
Parris, Henry, Pierre Pestieau, and Peter Saynor (1987). *Public Enterprise in Western Europe*. London: Croom Helm.
Pierson, Paul (2004). *Politics in Time: History, Institutions, and Social Analysis*. Princeton: Princeton University Press.

Pitkin, Hannah Fennichel (1967). *The Concept of Representation*. Berkeley, CA: University of California Press.

Preglau, Max (1994). 'The State and the Anti-Nuclear Power Movement in Austria', in Helena Flam (ed.), *States and Anti-Nuclear Movements*. Edinburgh: Edinburgh University Press, 37–69.

Qvortrup, Mads (2000). 'Are Referendums Controlled and Pro-Hegemonic?' *Political Studies*, 48(4): 821–6.

Riker, William H. (1963). *The Theory of Political Coalitions*. New Haven: Yale University Press.

Rootes, Christopher (ed.) (2007). *Environmental Protest in Western Europe*, 2nd edn. Oxford: Oxford University Press.

Sabatier, Paul A. (1988). 'An Advocacy Coalition Framework of Policy Change and the Role of Policy-Oriented Learning therein.' *Policy Sciences*, 21(2): 129–68.

Sabatier, Paul A. (1998). 'The Advocacy Coalition Framework: Revisions and Relevance for Europe.' *Journal of European Public Policy*, 5(1): 98–130.

Scharpf, Fritz W. (1988). 'The Joint-Decision Trap: Lessons from German Federalism and European Integration.' *Public Administration*, 66: 239–78.

Schöning, Norbert, Paul W. Thurner, and Martin Binder (2015). 'Indifferenz und Inkonsistenz als Moderatoren von Framing-Effekten: Ein Laborexperiment am Beispiel der Kernenergie', in André Bächtiger, Susumu Shikano, and Eric Linhart (eds), *Jahrbuch für Handlungs- und Entscheidungstheorie*, 9: 127–60. Wiesbaden: Springer VS.

Sjöberg, Lennart (1999). 'Risk Perception in Western Europe 10 Years After the Chernobyl Accident', in K. Andersson (ed.), *VALDOR: Values in Decisions on Risk*. Stockholm: European Commission DG XI, 343–51.

Sjöblom, Gunner (1968). *Party Strategies in Multiparty Systems*. Lund: Studentlitteratur.

Smith, Gordon (1976). 'The Functional Properties of the Referendum.' *European Journal of Political Research*, 4(1): 1–23.

Sovacool, Benjamin K., and Scott Victor Valentine (2012). *The National Politics of Nuclear Power: Economics, Security, Governance*. London: Routledge.

Stigler, George (1971). 'The Theory of Economic Regulation.' *Bell Journal of Economics*, 2(1): 3–21.

Strøm, Kaare (1990). 'A Behavioural Theory of Competitive Political Parties.' *American Journal of Political Science*, 34(2): 565–98.

Strøm, Kaare, Wolfgang C. Müller, and Torbjörn Bergman (eds) (2003). *Delegation and Accountability in Parliamentary Democracies*. Oxford: Oxford University Press.

Tavits, Margit (2007). 'Principle vs. Pragmatism: Policy Shifts and Political Competition.' *American Journal of Political Science*, 51(1): 218–29.

Thomson, Robert, Terry Royed, Elin Naurin, Joaquín Artés, Mark Ferguson, Petia Kostadinova, and Catherine Moury (2012). 'The Program-to-Policy Linkage: A Comparative Study of Election Pledges and Government Policies in Ten Countries.' Paper prepared for the 2012 Annual Meeting of the American Political Science Association, New Orleans, 30 Aug.–2 Sept.

Thurner, Paul W. (2000). 'The Empirical Application of the Spatial Theory of Voting in Multiparty Systems with Random Utility Models.' *Electoral Studies*, 19(4): 493–517.

Thurner, Paul W. (2010). '"Issue-Unentschiedene" und "Issue-Inkonsistente" als Targetpopulationen? Das Beispiel Kernenergie (1987–2005)', in Thorsten Faas, Kai Arzheimer, and Sigrid Roßteutscher (eds), *Information-Wahrnehmung-Emotion: Politische Psychologie in der Wahl- und Einstellungsforschung*. Wiesbaden: VS Verlag, 333–53.

True, James L, Bryan D. Jones, and Frank R. Baumgartner (2007). 'Punctuated-Equilibrium Theory: Explaining Stability and Change in Public Policymaking', in Paul Sabatier (ed.), *Theories of the Policy Process*, 2nd edn. Boulder, CO: Westview Press, 155–88.

Tsebelis, George (2002). *Veto Players: How Political Institutions Work.* New York: Russel Sage Foundation; Princeton: Princeton University Press.

Way, Christopher (2013). 'The Politics of the Nuclear Renaissance', in Adam N. Stulberg and Matthew Fuhrmann (eds), *The Nuclear Renaissance and International Security.* Stanford, CA: Stanford University Press, 154–74.

Weaver, R. Kent (2010). 'Paths and Forks or Chutes and Ladders? Negative Feedbacks and Policy Regime Change.' *Journal of Public Policy*, 30(2): 137–62.

Weible, Christopher M., Paul A. Sabatier, and Kelly McQueen (2009). 'Themes and Variations: Taking Stock of the Advocacy Coalition Framework.' *Policy Studies Journal*, 37(1): 121–40.

3

Comparative Policy Indicators on Nuclear Energy

Paul W. Thurner and Wolfgang C. Müller

3.1 INTRODUCTION

This chapter provides an overview of the relevance of nuclear power as an energy source in Europe over the last two decades. It addresses the economic and 'technocratic' rationales for maintaining and expanding nuclear power capacities. These rationales are mainly captured by the concept of energy security (see von Hippel et al. 2011). Accordingly, securing the continuous physical supply of energy at affordable price levels is essential for economic growth and for the international status of nation states. Given the importance of energy security, it is a crucial parameter for the political survival of governments and politicians: voters and the economy alike demand policies to guarantee a steady supply of energy and competitive energy prices. Energy shortages, even if only temporary, would inflict considerable damage on incumbents. And high prices of energy are not only unpopular per se but also increase inflation rates and dampen economic growth. For all these reasons, politicians, parties, and governments are highly sensitized to related risks, and they try to reduce uncertainties by actively promoting innovation, investments, and diversification. As we have seen in Chapter 1, in the 'technocratic' perspective nuclear energy has traditionally been associated with lowering the risk of interrupted supply chains and guaranteeing a stable and low price of electricity. In this chapter we take these assertions at face value—as the dominant way of thinking among political decision-makers (certainly in the 'golden age' period of nuclear energy from the 1950s to the 1970s) and ask to what extent the actual usage of nuclear energy can be explained by the countries' dependencies on imported energy. For that purpose, we employ various indicators on energy production, consumption, and import dependency over time and space. Thus, we are able to directly address the relevance of the rationales that traditionally have been employed in the debate on nuclear energy.

The time horizon for developing, planning, and using nuclear energy counts in decades. This large-scale technology necessitates huge and long-term investments, and it requires setting priorities in the political allocation of assets. The literature has stressed high degrees of industrialization, a high level of technological development, competitiveness in the global economy, and high per capita consumption of energy as necessary (but not sufficient) conditions for the usage of nuclear energy (see Kitschelt 1982; Fuhrmann 2012). A country's energy security is higher the less it depends on external resources. Import dependency may be strictly related to non-endowment with traditional energy resources such as coal, oil, gas, and water suitable for hydroelectric power production. The more a country lacks such resources, the more it is expected to go 'nuclear' in the course of an expansionary economic path. More recently, the European Commission accentuated in its Energy Security Strategy (EC 2014a) that import dependency is even aggravated the more a countries relies on few providers, i.e. the higher supplier concentration in oil, gas, and solid fuels (see also Cohen et al. 2011). Note, however, that the availability of domestic energy may induce a self-enforcing, positive feedback process (see Baumgartner and Jones 2002), leading to an even higher demand for imports, and therefore to high dependency despite natural endowment with such sources. Additionally, the gradual depletion of domestic sources may increase import dependency (e.g. UK) over time, or the coming into commercial use of 'new' energy sources (such as wind) may lead to a decrease in energy dependency (e.g. Denmark, Portugal).

In the remainder of the chapter, we provide an overview of the relevance of nuclear energy worldwide with a focus on the European Union's and especially West European energy production patterns during the post-1990 period. Thus we follow the developments for a period of about two and a half decades.[1] This allows us to answer the following questions. Have countries 'gone nuclear' after the 'golden age' period of this technology? In those countries that employ nuclear energy, how much does this technology contribute to their respective energy mixes over time? Do we observe an expansion or a reduction in the role of nuclear energy? And are there patterns in the countries' energy profiles that help us understand why some choose this technology while others refrain from doing so? As already mentioned, in this chapter we are exclusively interested in the often-cited 'technocratic' rationales. Thus, do governments turn to or expand nuclear energy production in order to avoid energy dependency? Do countries endowed with natural energy resources abstain from building up nuclear energy capacities? What are the energy profiles of EU member states and what role does nuclear energy take in these configurations? We address these questions by looking at selected time series of the outcomes of nuclear energy policies. The next section shows to which degree countries built up nuclear energy production capacities. The outcomes in our observation period (1990 to 2013) of course reflect the endowment of countries with natural resources and their economic development from the 1950s through the mid-1970s, the time of the 'atomic consensus' among elites and citizens' acquiescence.

A second set of questions relates to countries formerly belonging to the Soviet bloc and now members of the European Union. They had to adjust to Western security standards and partly to shut down old Soviet-design nuclear power plants (NPPs). This 'reset' of energy production patterns created new choice situations. On the one hand, the countries could respond to increasing concerns about nuclear

---

[1] As such, we tie to the thread of most of the literature ending by the end of the 1980s after the Chernobyl accident.

energy that had undermined its political viability in several other countries. On the other hand, they were left with nuclear 'endowments' way beyond the closed-down plants (other NPPs that could be 'upgraded' to Western standards, know-how, a population accustomed to nuclear energy production, and nuclear waste that had to be deposed of, reducing the unit costs for storage of more such waste). It is therefore particular interesting which role the Eastern enlargement countries assign to nuclear energy in the post-Soviet era (Marples and Young 1999; Polanecký and Haverkamp 2011) and to compare it to the uninterrupted Western European paths.

3.2 THE EU PUT INTO THE WORLD CONTEXT: FACTS

In October 2007, the European Commission provided a so-called 'Nuclear Illustrative Programme' (COM(2007) 565) where it described the political status quo of nuclear energy in the EU member states and proposed future action. In November 2010, the Energy 2020 strategy of the EU Commission continued to assign nuclear energy a crucial role in the energy mix of the European Union: 'The contribution of nuclear energy, which currently generates around one third of EU electricity and two thirds of its carbon-free electricity, must be assessed openly and objectively' (EC 2010: 5). Nuclear energy continues to be a major contributor of energy production also in the European Energy Security Strategy proposed by the Commission in 2014 (EC 2014a).

A comparison of the contribution of nuclear energy to electricity generation and overall energy consumption highlights the relevance of this technology in the EU (see Figures 3.1 and 3.2). At the end of 2013, the EU continues to be the largest producer and user of nuclear energy and electricity world-wide. In terms of gross inland consumption, the EU generated 226 Mtoe based on nuclear energy (the USA was second, with 188 Mtoe). This accounts for almost 14 per cent of the cumulated energy consumption in this area. Nearly one-third of the world's overall nuclear energy consumption took place within the EU. Concerning electricity production, nuclear energy in 2013 amounts to 833 TWh (the USA is second, with 790 TWh) which equals 26 per cent of the consumption within the EU. At the end of 2013/2014, fourteen EU member states run 136 NPPs for electricity production (see Table 3.1). Viewed from a global perspective, for both absolute numbers and relative shares, it becomes evident that the EU as a whole is heavily relying on nuclear energy. However, there are considerable variances between the single members. France stands out with almost 40 per cent of its total consumption being based on nuclear energy, whereas other countries like Austria, Denmark, Portugal, and Greece do not employ nuclear energy at all. In between, we see countries heavily relying on this energy carrier, like Belgium, many Eastern European EU countries, and Switzerland from Western Europe outside the EU.

As of the beginning of 2015, fourteen of the EU-28 countries were using nuclear energy: Belgium, Bulgaria, the Czech Republic, Finland, France, Germany, Hungary, the Netherlands, Romania, Slovenia, Spain, Sweden, and the United Kingdom. Of the non-EU members in Western Europe, Switzerland employs nuclear energy. Table 3.1 shows the nuclear energy production capacities built

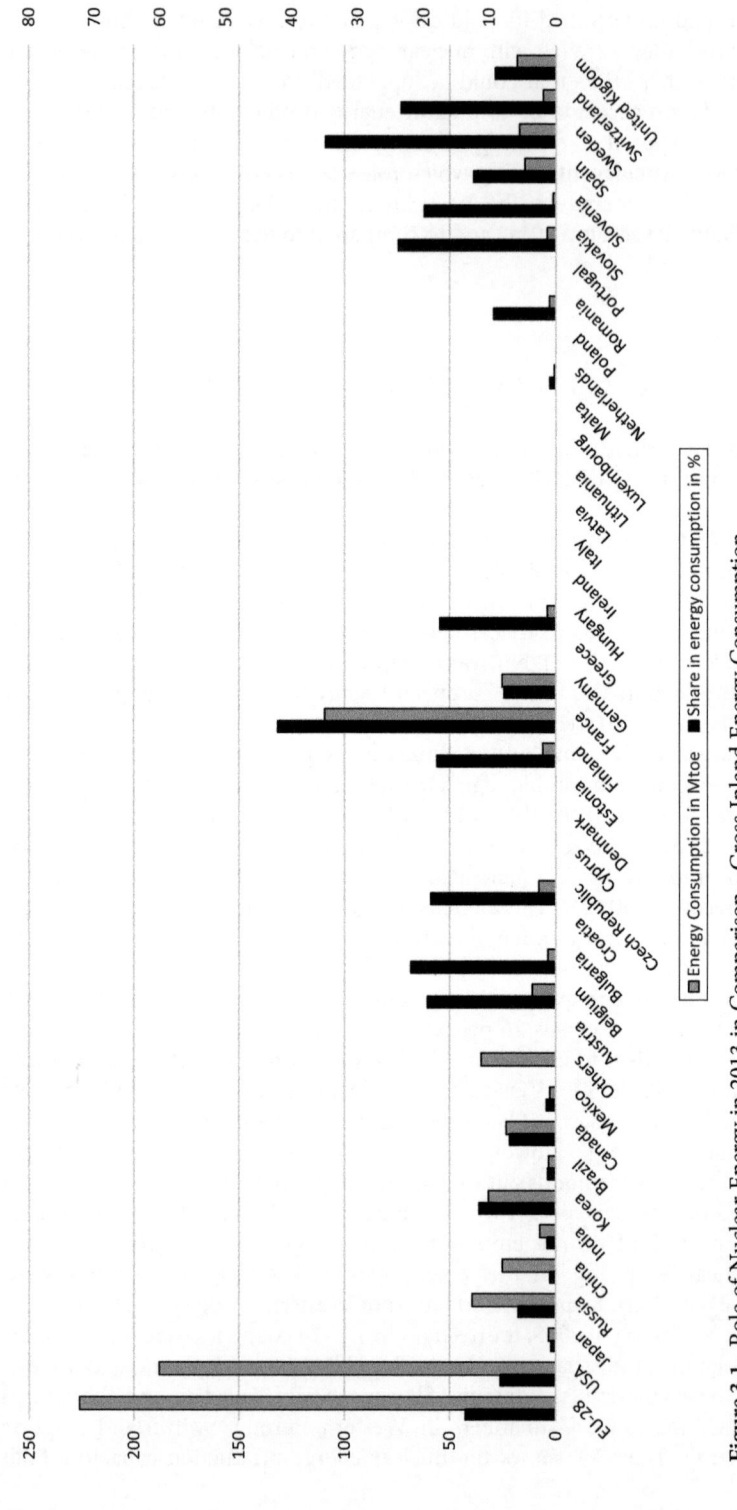

Figure 3.1. Role of Nuclear Energy in 2013 in Comparison—Gross Inland Energy Consumption

Source: Eurostat 2015, <http://ec.europa.eu/eurostat/web/energy/data/database>. For countries outside EU: BP (2014): <http://www.bp.com/en/global/corporate/about-bp/energy-economics/statistical-review-of-world-energy.html>.

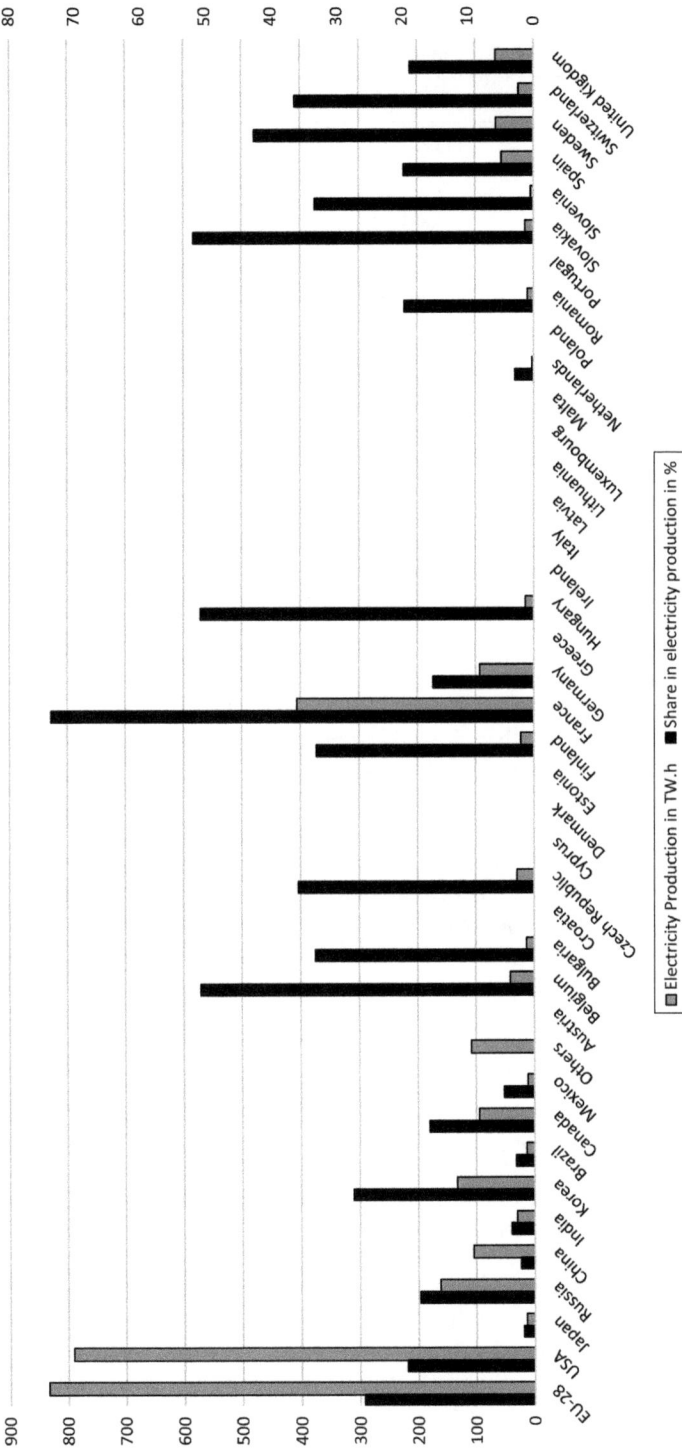

Figure 3.2. Role of Nuclear Energy in 2013 in Comparison—Absolute Electricity Production (TW.h) and Shares in Domestic Electricity Production (%)

Source: IAEA (2015): <http://www.iaea.org/PRIS/CountryStatistics/CountryStatisticsLandingPage.aspx>.

Table 3.1. Nuclear Power Plants in the EU, in Operation and under Construction, 2015

	Nuclear power plants in operation		Nuclear power plants under construction	
	(N)	Net-capacity (MWe)	(N)	Net-capacity (MWe)
EU-28	136	125,383	4	2,218
Belgium	7	5,927	-	-
Bulgaria	2	1,906	-	-
Czech Republic	6	3,884	-	-
Finland	4	2,752	1	1,60
France	58	63,13	1	1,63
Germany	9	12,068	-	-
Hungary	4	1,889	-	-
Netherlands	1	0,482	-	-
Romania	2	1,3	-	-
Slovakia	4	1,815	2	0,880
Slovenia	1	0,688	-	-
Spain	7	7,121	-	-
Sweden	10	9,474	-	-
United Kingdom	16	9,243	-	-
Switzerland	5	3,308	-	-

Note: Countries covered by case study chapters in this volume appear in bold.

Source: IAEA, <http://www.iaea.org/PRIS/CountryStatistics/CountryStatisticsLandingPage.aspx>, Jan. 2015.

up in these countries. From this, it becomes obvious that there is quite some heterogeneity of countries within Europe concerning the use of nuclear energy. The selection of our in-depth case studies reflects this broad variation: we have countries with large NPP fleets like France and Germany, countries with a small (Netherlands) or middle-sized nuclear energy sector (Switzerland, Sweden) and countries that have completely abandoned NE, such as Austria and Italy. We focus especially on Western Europe, because the former COMECON countries did not autonomously control their energy policies. Such external influences on the nuclear strategies of these countries also arose in the process of accession to the EU. Responding to demands of the EU-15 countries some accession candidates shut down old Soviet-type reactors that did not live up to European security standards (see Table 3.2).

If we compare the development of the fleet of NPPs in Europe (see Figures 3.3 and 3.4), over time, we see that the construction of NPPs follow a bell-shaped function, reaching its peak in 1980 with seventy-six NPPs being simultaneously under construction, then ebbing down to a very low level with less than ten NPPs under construction after 1990. The graph showing the number of NPPs simultaneously in commercial operation, contrarily, exhibits the well-known sigmoid logistic shape of technological innovations. This applies also to the capacities of electricity in construction and in commercial operation (see Figures 3.4 and 3.4). However, a different interpretation may apply here: it could be deduced from these figures that European countries decided—explicitly or implicitly—to freeze the construction of new reactors. After the 'storms' of protest and the emergence of new political challengers trying to enter parliaments in the 1970s and 1980s, most governments shied away from continuing earlier plans of

Table 3.2. Nuclear Power Plants Removed from the Grid in Eastern European EU Accession States

Country	Nuclear endowment from Soviet era and post-Soviet change	Status quo
Lithuania	NPP Ignalina (the only NPP in Lithuania; two blocks with a total capacity of about 2700 MW; first block shut down in 2004, second block at the end of 2009).	By 1 Jan. 2010 Lithuania had disconnected its NPP from the grid.
Slovakia	NPP Bohunice (four blocks in total; two blocks of these four blocks were shut down during EU accession process; first block at the end of 2006; second block at the end of 2008; each block with total net capacity of about 440 MW, in total 880 MW).	This shutdown of nuclear capacity made Slovakia a net electricity importer; Slovakia currently plans to compensate this nuclear production with two new blocks in the Slovak NPP Mochovce with total net capacity each of about 440MW.
Bulgaria	NPP Kosloduj (six blocks in total; four blocks were shut down during EU accession; two blocks with a total capacity of 880 MW at the end of 2002, and the two remaining blocks with total capacity of 880 MW at the end of 2006).	Plans of renewing nuclear capacity with a new NPP (Belene) in cooperation with Russia and the German firm RWE were first postponed in 2011 and eventually abandoned in March 2012 for economic reasons. A 2013 referendum initiated by a new government to revise the decision failed (because of low turnout) but signalled considerable support for nuclear energy in the population. In the same year, the parliament decided to suspend the project. After the recent elections, the new Prime Minister Oresharski announced his intention to restart discussion.

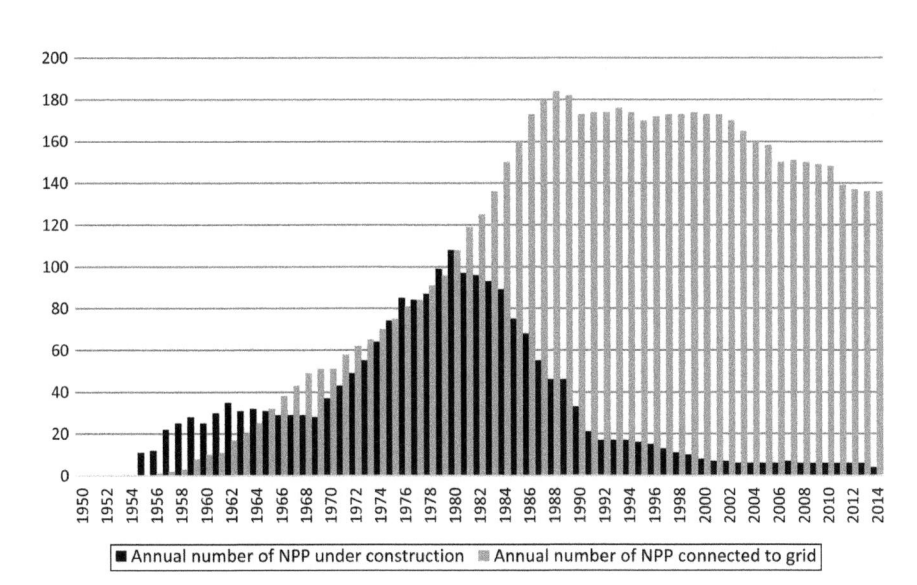

Figure 3.3. Annual Number of NPPs in Construction and in Commercial Operation in the EU-28 Plus Switzerland 1960–2014

Source: OECD/IAEA 2014, own presentation.

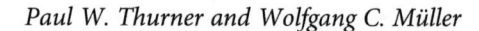

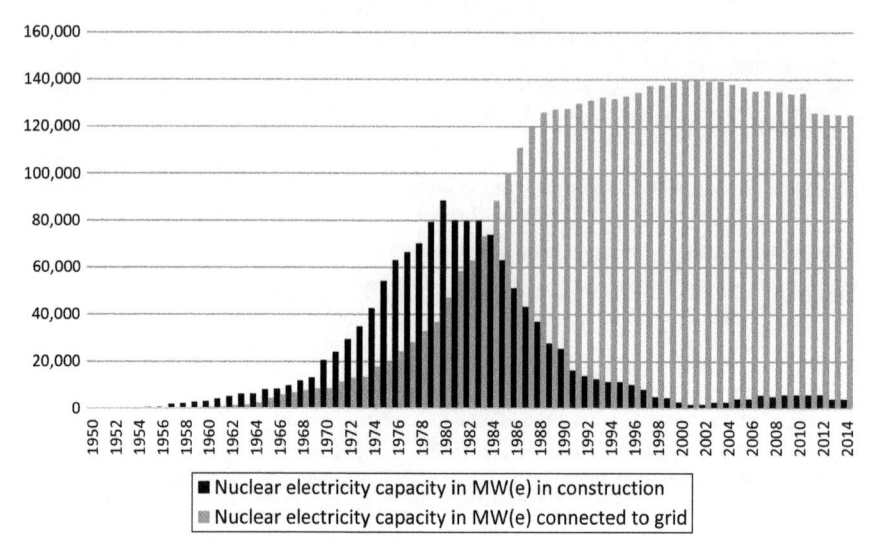

Figure 3.4. Nuclear Electricity Capacity in Construction and in Commercial Operation in the EU-28 Plus Switzerland 1960–2014
Source: OECD/IAEA 2014, own presentation.

extending the fleets. The realized implementation of capacities in many cases allowed a breather—and a wait for the development of a new generation of reactors.

3.3 EXTERNAL ENERGY DEPENDENCY OF EU MEMBER STATES

Do countries set up nuclear energy capacities in order to avoid dependency on external provision of energy? The theoretical perspective proposed by Keohane and Nye (1977, 2000) hints that, due to international and transnational asymmetric interdependencies, countries try to substitute sensitive trade inflows as much as possible with the aim of reducing sensitivity and avoiding vulnerability. In order to assess international restrictions on the energy security of individual countries, we focus, first, on energy dependency over time. According to Eurostat, energy dependency is defined as 'the extent to which an economy relies upon imports in order to meet its energy needs. The indicator is calculated as net-imports divided by the sum of gross inland energy consumption plus bunkers'.[2] The dependency of the EU-27 is more than 50 per cent since 2004. However, this average hides large differences between countries (see tables in the Appendix to this chapter): currently, there is only one net-exporter, namely Denmark (since 1999)—except in 2013. In that year, Denmark for the first time in many years performed as a net importer. Generally, Denmark is one of the leading countries in renewable energies, or, to be more precise, wind power. Interestingly, it has

---

[2] Source: Eurostat.

neither hydroelectric power, nor coal resources, and it does not produce nuclear energy. In 2013, renewables account for about 11 per cent of final energy consumption and 51 per cent of electricity generation. Additionally, Denmark disposes of substantial offshore oil and gas reserves in the North Sea that are expected to secure net exports until at least 2020 (see the IEA's Energy Report for Denmark in 2012: 109 ff.). The UK was a net exporter mainly of fossil fuels between 1994 and 2003. However, this country experienced a depletion of its oil and gas resources, and will be more and more a net importer in the future: its domestic oil and gas production peaked around 2000 and by 2006 it had already extracted about 70 per cent of its total possible oil and 65 per cent of its total possible gas reserves (see the IEA's Energy Report for the UK in 2006: 128 ff.). Poland became a net exporter for one year only (in 1995). The relatively low dependency of Poland rests on its large coal reserves that are heavily used for electricity generation (92 per cent of domestic energy in 2004). Poland exports electricity, mostly to the Czech Republic and Slovakia. Being on the one hand obliged to reduce this carbon-intensive energy production with its high CO_2 emissions, and being highly dependent on Russian oil and gas on the other, Poland now intends to build NPPs.

In Figure 3.5, we partition the degree of overall import dependency into quartiles. Here, we can distinguish a group with a low degree (up to 25), consisting of the Czech Republic, Denmark, Poland, and UK. The second group (26–50) includes at the same time nuclear energy producing countries (Bulgaria, Sweden, Netherlands, Romania) and one 'nuclear free' country (Estonia). Extremely dependent (76–100) are some highly industrialized countries (Italy, Belgium) but mostly smaller economies such as Ireland, Portugal, Malta, and Cyprus. The

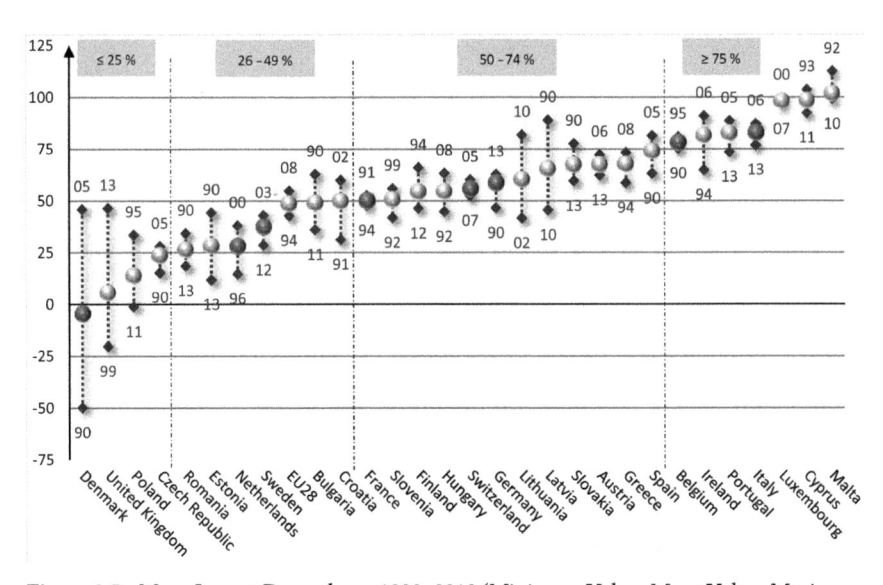

Figure 3.5. Mean Import Dependency 1990–2013 (Minimum Value–Mean Value–Maximum Value)

Note: Countries in dark are covered by case-study chapters in this volume. Values on the max and min whiskers indicate the year of that value. Full time series are available in the Appendix to this chapter.

largest group consists of those countries exhibiting a high dependency (51–75, e.g. Germany, Finland, Switzerland, and Spain). As we have seen, not all of these highly dependent countries have NPPs. At the same time, many countries that have NPPs are nevertheless highly dependent on energy imports.

Given that energy policies are such a long-term endeavour, it is obvious to ask whether countries experience large changes over time—say a ten-point difference in the nineteen-year period under observation. This would indicate significant discontinuities in economic production and political planning as compared to the generally preferred smoothed paths and stability. With the exception of Austria, Belgium, France, Sweden, and Switzerland, all other countries have experienced such remarkable changes, or are constantly extremely dependent anyway—like Luxembourg, Cyprus, Malta, and Portugal. For instance, although still relatively small compared to most other countries, Poland dramatically increased its import-dependency by about thirty percentage points from 1990 to 2009. However, a series of countries also reduced their dependency quite importantly, in particular Bulgaria, Estonia, Finland, Latvia, Lithuania, Slovakia, and Switzerland (see Appendix), i.e. countries relying heavily on nuclear energy. A recent compilation of measures on supplier diversification versus concentration highlights an additional aspect. Countries like Bulgaria, Poland, Lithuania, and Slovakia meet their demand for crude oil nearly exclusively from Russia. Moreover, Russia is nearly the exclusive provider of natural gas for Austria, the Czech Republic, Finland, Estonia, Latvia, and Lithuania (see EC 2014b).

3.4 NUCLEAR ENERGY AS PART OF THE ENERGY MIX OF EU COUNTRIES

Are those countries that have a sizeable nuclear energy production less dependent on energy inflows than countries without or with limited nuclear energy capacities? Finding such a relationship would support the hypothesis that countries try to substitute in order to reduce vulnerability (Keohane and Nye 2000), which seems to be corroborated by the study of Fuhrmann (2012). First, we calculate the share of nuclear energy contributing to a country's overall energy portfolio in order to assess its relevance. We calculate nuclear energy's contribution to gross domestic energy consumption and to the generation of electricity, respectively. Again, we focus on the period since 1990. Main decisions on energy policy have, of course, been made earlier and impact the displayed relationship.

Figure 3.6 provides the contribution of NPPs in the EU-28 plus Switzerland to Gross Inland Consumption (GIC). GIC is defined as the quantity of energy consumed within the borders of a country and calculated by the formula: 'primary production + recovered products + imports + stock changes − exports − bunkers (i.e. quantities supplied to sea-going ships)'.[3]

---

[3] Source: Eurostat, May 2009. Statistical pocketbook 2010: EU Energy and Transport in figures, Link: <http://ec.europa.eu/energy/publications/statistics/statistics_en.htm>.

Comparative Policy Indicators 57

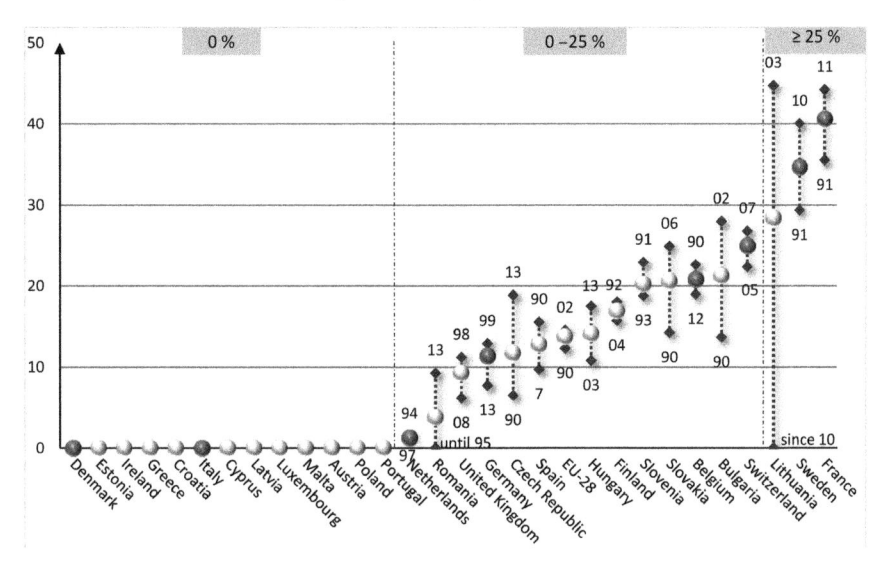

Figure 3.6. Mean Share of Nuclear Energy in Gross Inland Consumption 1990–2013 (Minimum Value–Mean Value–Maximum Value)

Note: Countries in dark are covered by case-study chapters in this volume. Values on min and max whiskers indicate the year of that value. Full time series are contained in the Appendix to this chapter.

If we classify countries according to the mean relative contribution of nuclear energy to gross energy consumption over the period 1990–2013, three groups of countries can be distinguished. First, there are those without NPPs. The second group comprises countries with a 'low' contribution (>0 to 25) of nuclear energy to GIC. It consists of countries such as the Netherlands (with the lowest share) and Switzerland (with the highest share). The third group consists of Lithuania, France, and Sweden, where nuclear energy contributes a quarter to a third of GIC.

Figure 3.7 classifies the countries according to the mean contribution of nuclear energy to gross electricity generation. Gross electricity generation is measured at 'the outlet of the main transformers, i.e. the consumption of electricity in the plant auxiliaries and in transformers is included'.[4] Again, we calculate the percentages.

The focus on electricity generation provides partly a different picture, because electricity may contribute differently to gross inland energy consumption. Not surprisingly, France turns out to have the highest nuclear energy share in electricity contribution. However, Belgium, Lithuania, and Slovakia also rely heavily on nuclear energy. Note that the case studies in this volume include countries representing all four quartiles.

Is there a bivariate relationship between import dependency, supplier concentration on the one hand, and nuclear energy consumption, and electricity generation on the other hand? According to the 'technocratic perspective' on the functions of nuclear energy, higher nuclear energy shares should reduce import dependency. This

---

[4] <http://epp.eurostat.ec.europa.eu/tgm/table.do?tab=table%26init=1%26language=en%26pcode=ten00091%26plugin=1>.

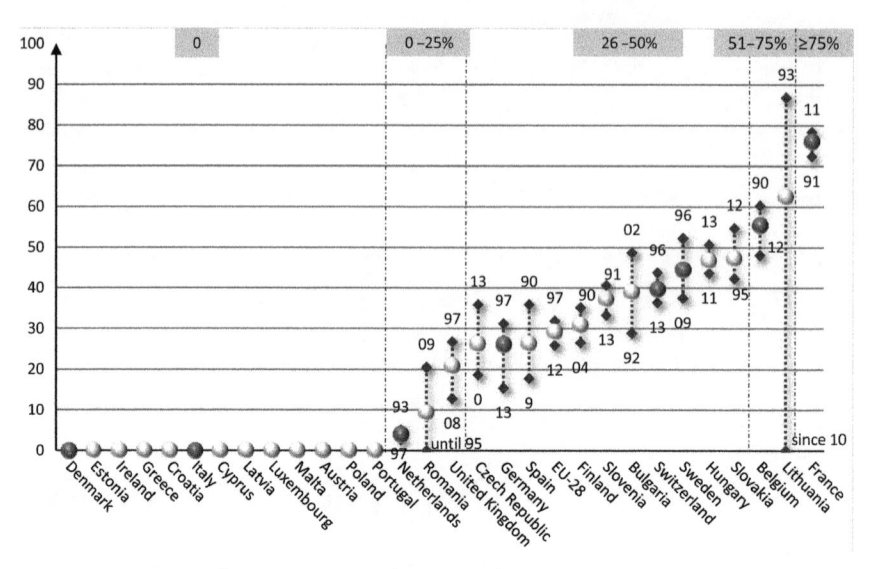

Figure 3.7. Mean Nuclear Energy Contribution to Electricity Generation 1990–2013 (Minimum Value–Mean Value–Maximum Value)

Note: Countries in dark are covered by case studies in this volume. Values on the max and min indicate the year of that value. Full time series are available in the Appendix to this chapter.

is a well-known and obvious argument that is accepted not only by advocates of nuclear energy. The same applies to the argument that those countries using nuclear energy are able to export electricity in the emerging integrated European electricity market. In the following bivariate analyses we use the most recent data of 2013, differentiating for the EU-28 plus Switzerland on the one hand, and the EU without former satellite states of the Soviet Union. We put forward the following hypothesis:

H1: The larger the relative contribution of nuclear energy to electricity generation/gross inland consumption, the smaller the external energy dependency.

Figures 3.8 and 3.9 show the relationship between dependency (y-axis) and share of nuclear energy on electricity (x-axis). The first of these figures leaves out those countries that do not to use nuclear energy. We use the average share of nuclear energy of electricity production and GIC between 1990 and 2013 and the average dependence proportion in that period. The second graph includes these zero-share countries.

Counter-intuitively, this clearly demonstrates that there is a rather strong positive relationship indicating that nuclear energy does not lead to a reduction of energy dependency. It seems to be a reaction to dependence, but less so an effective action against dependence. Interestingly, the curvilinear association implies that there is a point where the usage of nuclear energy actually lowers dependency, but only for countries with very high shares (such as France and Lithuania). The inclusion of countries without nuclear energy hides this relationship.

The same pattern occurs for nuclear energy's contribution to GIC. The inclusion of zero-nuclear countries would blur the relationship. However, the curvilinear relationship is even more pronounced in this case.

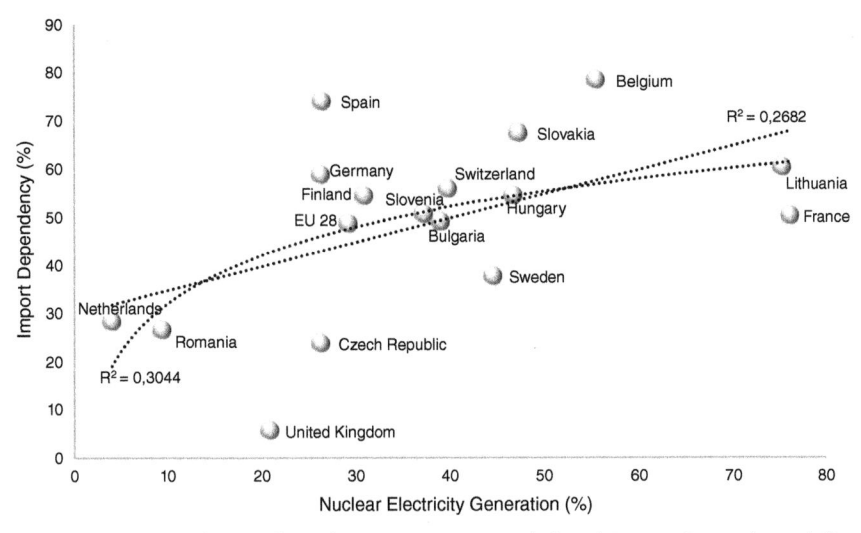

Figure 3.8. Scatterplot: Nuclear Electricity Generation (%) and Import Dependency (%)

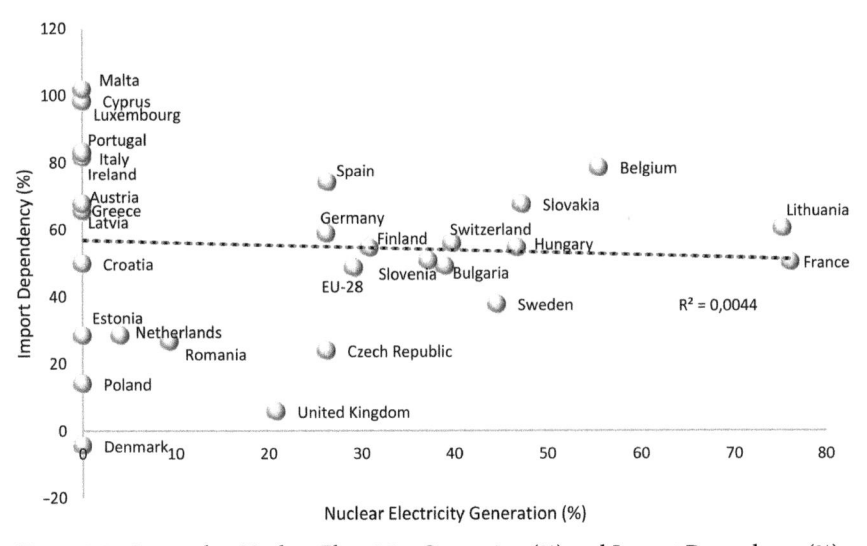

Figure 3.9. Scatterplot: Nuclear Electricity Generation (%) and Import Dependency (%)

As Figure 3.10 shows, *H1* is not corroborated. The weak correlation is especially due to countries having no nuclear energy production at all and at the same time being not import-dependent at all (e.g. Denmark—due to offshore oil and gas resources and wind power) or to a very low degree only (Estonia due to oil shale, Poland due to coal). On the other hand, there are countries with quite high levels of import dependency with at the same time quite high levels of nuclear energy shares in consumption and electricity generation (Belgium, France, Slovakia,

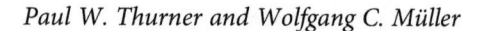

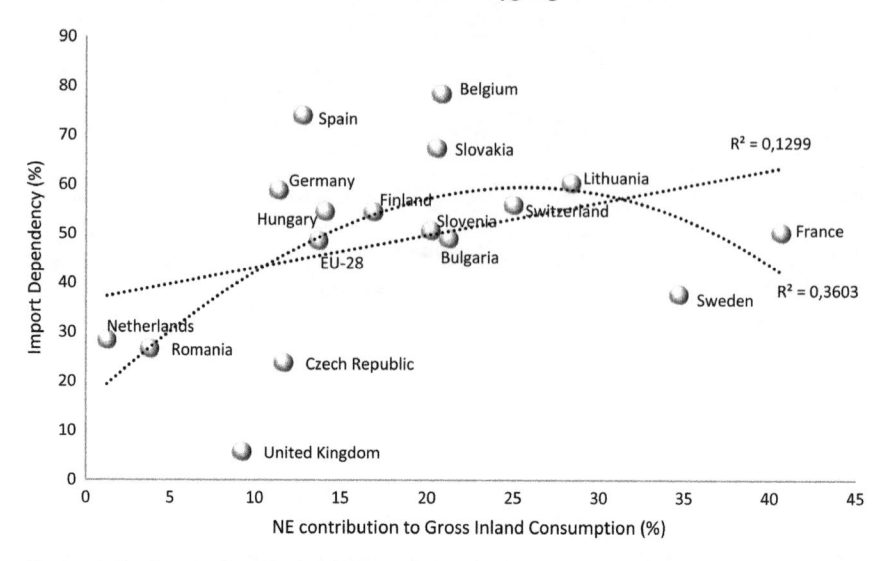

Figure 3.10. Scatterplot: Nuclear Energy Contribution to Gross Inland Consumption (%) and Import Dependency (%)

Lithuania), indicating that these countries' energy efficiency and/or endowments with other energy sources seem to be comparatively lower. However, the relationship might be more complex: The usage of nuclear energy may not lead to a smaller external dependency because it is functioning as a feedback factor stimulating the economy even more. If energy efficiency is not substantially improved, economic growth then may simply require the continued use of the other energy sources and thus perpetuate import dependency.

3.5 CONCLUSION

Nuclear energy has played a different role in the provision of energy in different countries and periods. The chapter has shown that increasing contributions of nuclear energy to electricity production and gross inland energy consumption are only slightly negatively correlated with import dependency on fossil fuels. The simple idea that nuclear energy will quasi-automatically lead to energy security thus turns out to be simplistic.

Having seen huge differences in the energy paths chosen by comparable countries the question remains why this is the case. There seems to be much more politics in these choices than objective conditions. We will address this question empirically in the remainder of this volume.

APPENDIX

Table 3.A1. Share of Nuclear Energy in Gross Inland Consumption (1990–2013)

	1990	1991	1992	1993	1994	1995	1996	1997	1998	1999	2000	2001	2002	2003	2004	2005	2006	2007	2008	2009	2010	2011	2012	2013
EU-28	12.31	12.67	13.04	13.58	13.59	13.60	13.82	14.10	13.94	14.20	14.12	14.31	14.52	14.31	14.32	14.11	13.95	13.38	13.44	13.61	13.44	13.78	13.51	13.58
Belgium	22.63	21.79	21.90	21.68	19.78	19.78	19.67	21.40	20.40	21.62	20.95	20.40	21.69	20.75	20.58	20.81	20.76	21.85	19.83	21.37	20.16	21.51	18.98	19.39
Bulgaria	13.68	15.28	14.43	16.42	18.71	19.65	20.31	22.07	21.60	22.35	25.37	26.21	27.99	23.18	22.97	24.43	24.72	18.95	20.52	22.61	22.26	22.16	22.45	21.90
Czech Republic	6.51	6.94	7.22	7.68	8.15	7.56	7.72	7.46	8.13	8.84	8.53	9.03	11.37	14.99	14.94	14.20	14.56	14.62	15.17	16.58	16.22	17.00	18.32	18.86
Germany	11.07	10.89	11.97	11.65	11.51	11.57	11.70	12.56	11.98	12.88	12.78	12.55	12.34	12.47	12.53	12.30	12.27	10.86	11.34	10.97	10.89	8.79	8.05	7.74
Spain	15.54	15.20	15.00	15.50	14.67	14.01	14.64	13.38	13.57	12.88	12.98	12.95	12.45	11.81	11.62	10.29	10.74	9.72	10.73	10.44	12.31	11.61	12.42	12.33
France	35.57	35.54	36.89	39.52	40.04	40.25	40.14	41.08	39.23	39.88	41.57	40.73	42.22	41.92	41.97	42.10	42.54	41.98	41.72	40.70	41.31	44.23	42.48	42.15
Lithuania	28.01	26.62	35.50	36.26	25.60	36.02	39.37	36.17	38.82	33.38	31.48	36.76	42.62	44.74	42.71	31.14	26.68	27.76	27.99	33.58	0.00	0.00	0.00	0.00
Hungary	12.28	12.84	14.12	13.60	14.16	13.82	13.64	13.69	13.82	14.08	14.52	14.16	13.95	10.81	11.80	12.98	12.70	14.16	14.40	15.86	15.80	16.16	17.35	17.49
Netherlands	1.35	1.22	1.40	1.44	1.44	1.43	1.42	0.84	1.32	1.34	1.34	1.32	1.30	1.29	1.21	1.27	1.13	1.31	1.29	1.35	1.18	1.33	1.23	0.92
Romania	0.00	0.00	0.00	0.00	0.00	0.00	0.75	3.09	3.32	3.66	3.84	3.80	3.70	3.16	3.62	3.65	3.58	4.92	7.19	8.53	8.37	8.29	8.36	9.27
Slovenia	20.87	22.95	19.86	18.85	21.07	20.30	18.96	19.83	20.10	18.80	19.04	20.02	20.76	19.33	19.67	20.72	19.52	20.03	20.87	20.98	20.19	22.02	20.36	19.93
Slovakia	14.26	15.43	15.44	16.27	18.36	16.65	15.91	15.59	16.38	18.81	23.25	23.74	24.79	24.80	24.03	24.31	24.91	22.42	23.80	21.97	21.38	23.15	24.23	23.79
Finland	17.25	17.23	18.02	17.79	16.20	16.93	15.88	16.39	17.03	17.97	17.82	17.64	16.39	15.81	15.72	17.38	15.73	16.18	16.48	17.91	15.84	16.69	17.09	17.95
Sweden	37.08	40.05	33.73	32.92	37.33	35.05	36.35	35.11	36.30	36.50	30.24	36.27	34.18	34.82	38.54	36.61	34.85	34.86	33.42	29.61	29.37	31.38	33.17	34.89
United Kingdom	8.05	8.37	9.12	10.49	10.28	10.33	10.53	11.20	11.21	10.72	9.52	10.03	9.97	9.87	8.88	9.00	8.44	7.31	6.18	8.63	7.55	8.98	8.95	9.06
Switzerland	24.24	23.29	23.61	24.04	24.78	25.61	25.34	25.08	25.14	25.06	25.90	24.86	26.01	26.27	25.73	22.36	25.52	26.80	25.55	25.39	24.78	26.58	24.80	23.39

Note: The values for Austria, Cyprus, Denmark, Estonia, Greece, Ireland, Italy, Latvia, Luxembourg, Malta, Poland, Portugal, and Romania are 0 in these years.

Source: Eurostat 2012, http://ec.europa.eu/eurostat/web/energy/data/database; European Commission 2012, Country Factsheets—EU-27 (27 member states), EU-28 from 2011 EU-28 (Version 1.2); Switzerland: Eurostat; own representation.

Table 3.A2. Electricity Generation by Origin: Nuclear 1990–2013 (%)

	1990	1991	1992	1993	1994	1995	1996	1997	1998	1999	2000	2001	2002	2003	2004	2005	2006	2007	2008	2009	2010	2011	2012	2013
EU-28	29.42	29.88	30.36	31.70	31.23	31.08	31.60	31.89	30.93	31.14	30.40	30.07	30.14	29.52	29.26	28.77	28.22	26.51	26.51	26.58	26.38	26.62	25.91	25.99
Belgium	60.28	59.66	60.24	59.22	56.24	55.50	56.90	60.11	55.25	57.72	56.99	57.74	57.57	55.55	54.94	54.36	54.06	53.88	53.28	51.37	50.01	52.97	48.12	50.67
Bulgaria	35.97	34.95	28.90	34.82	38.50	40.67	42.88	42.76	41.50	42.35	45.52	45.67	48.71	41.70	41.49	43.05	43.58	35.05	36.23	36.71	33.72	33.29	34.67	33.44
Czech Republic	20.24	20.18	20.75	21.54	22.15	20.10	20.11	19.55	20.50	20.84	18.69	20.03	24.98	31.78	31.85	30.52	31.46	30.25	32.45	33.77	33.27	32.96	35.27	35.87
Germany	28.18	27.64	29.93	29.47	28.85	28.90	29.19	31.23	29.33	30.80	29.84	29.61	28.45	27.48	27.39	26.53	26.50	22.19	23.41	22.86	22.35	17.72	15.89	15.44
Spain	35.91	35.81	35.34	35.84	34.22	33.38	32.30	29.10	30.27	28.36	27.91	27.12	26.05	23.79	22.77	19.62	19.95	17.94	18.67	17.78	20.41	19.50	20.53	19.77
France	74.24	72.35	72.57	77.50	74.95	75.99	77.06	78.01	75.53	74.89	76.46	76.24	77.87	77.55	77.81	78.13	78.08	76.82	76.23	76.21	74.85	78.35	74.59	73.63
Lithuania	0.00	0.00	0.00	0.00	0.00	0.00	0.00	0.00	0.00	0.00	0.00	0.00	0.00	0.00	0.00	0.00	0.00	0.00	0.00	0.00	0.00	0.00	0.00	0.00
Hungary	48.29	45.81	44.07	41.91	41.92	41.23	40.41	39.46	37.51	37.26	40.29	38.79	38.59	32.25	35.35	38.69	37.54	36.73	37.02	42.96	42.17	43.59	45.90	50.71
Netherlands	4.75	4.37	4.81	5.04	4.89	4.88	4.79	2.72	4.10	4.33	4.30	4.17	4.00	4.07	3.66	3.92	3.46	3.94	3.80	3.67	3.28	3.59	3.79	2.83
Romania	0.00	0.00	0.00	0.00	0.00	0.00	2.32	9.28	9.81	10.33	10.39	9.98	9.97	8.80	9.74	9.22	8.90	11.19	17.15	20.48	19.12	18.55	19.63	19.71
Slovenia	39.22	40.63	33.89	34.97	37.14	38.55	36.92	38.72	37.31	36.00	35.55	37.05	38.76	38.48	36.43	39.68	37.48	38.65	38.89	35.52	34.94	39.36	35.68	33.35
Slovakia	45.84	47.06	46.52	46.69	48.57	42.32	43.34	43.34	43.46	45.81	52.47	53.37	55.36	57.30	55.70	56.36	57.33	54.65	57.67	53.84	52.35	54.48	54.74	53.37
Finland	35.14	33.41	33.06	32.41	29.48	29.94	28.15	30.31	31.16	33.08	32.07	30.68	29.87	27.16	26.55	32.96	27.98	28.91	29.61	32.66	28.35	31.63	32.60	33.18
Sweden	45.77	51.37	42.64	41.37	50.46	46.44	52.26	46.14	45.67	46.63	38.68	43.91	45.76	49.39	50.52	44.95	46.29	44.29	41.88	37.51	38.29	39.49	37.70	42.53
United Kingdom	18.31	19.57	22.03	25.29	24.73	24.52	25.63	26.74	26.24	24.95	21.71	22.59	21.91	21.55	19.55	19.76	18.28	15.10	12.80	17.43	15.44	17.86	18.51	18.79
Switzerland	42.07	39.42	39.29	37.85	36.74	39.50	43.73	40.27	40.70	37.06	39.17	37.02	40.54	40.76	41.11	39.13	43.43	41.11	40.18	40.44	38.83	42.46	37.42	36.41

Note: The values for Austria, Cyprus, Denmark, Estonia, Greece, Ireland, Italy, Latvia, Luxembourg, Malta, Poland, Portugal, and Romania are 0 in these years.

Source: European Commission 2012, Country Factsheets—EU 27 Member States (Version 1.2); Switzerland: Eurostat; own representation. Eurostat 2015. http://ec.europa.eu/eurostat/web/energy/data/database.

Table 3.A3. Energy Dependency 1990–2013 (%)

	1990	1991	1992	1993	1994	1995	1996	1997	1998	1999	2000	2001	2002	2003	2004	2005	2006	2007	2008	2009	2010	2011	2012	2013
EU28	44.26	44.81	45.69	43.91	42.82	43.03	43.69	44.60	45.92	45.09	46.70	47.37	47.52	48.84	50.16	52.25	53.63	52.92	54.73	53.67	52.78	54.02	53.35	53.19
Belgium	75.17	77.01	78.03	76.67	79.79	80.87	80.46	78.34	80.80	76.92	78.12	80.59	77.51	79.57	79.83	80.12	79.63	76.79	80.73	75.52	77.96	75.78	76.07	77.52
Bulgaria	62.75	61.13	56.16	58.06	54.57	55.89	55.88	51.04	49.97	48.69	45.90	45.84	45.68	46.34	48.14	46.69	45.61	50.68	51.67	45.06	39.60	36.04	36.06	37.82
Czech Republic	15.41	15.90	15.96	16.12	18.17	20.61	24.22	24.13	25.14	25.14	22.90	25.13	26.40	25.07	25.49	28.01	27.80	25.08	25.08	27.18	25.62	27.99	25.32	27.94
Denmark	45.79	39.84	37.28	27.41	27.34	33.40	21.79	15.63	5.64	−16.47	−35.05	−27.95	−41.83	−31.35	−47.00	−49.83	−35.49	−24.11	−20.47	−19.74	−15.69	−5.55	−2.96	12.30
Germany	46.51	51.61	54.54	55.49	56.72	56.79	58.69	59.34	60.97	59.22	59.42	60.87	60.11	60.51	60.88	60.43	60.80	58.36	60.77	60.99	60.08	61.62	61.27	62.65
Estonia	44.22	41.55	32.85	34.28	34.91	32.29	28.74	27.94	36.18	34.87	32.16	32.27	29.61	26.69	28.52	26.09	29.22	24.66	24.72	22.01	13.61	11.95	17.04	11.91
Ireland	68.60	67.07	66.62	67.01	64.83	69.46	71.11	76.59	80.74	84.64	84.85	89.49	88.94	89.45	90.45	89.55	90.94	87.55	90.67	88.82	86.51	89.75	84.84	89.00
Greece	61.96	63.07	69.02	66.54	58.66	66.70	68.03	67.55	70.17	66.10	69.51	68.93	71.51	67.52	72.72	68.60	71.88	71.18	73.34	67.58	69.07	65.05	66.46	62.06
Spain	63.15	63.91	66.68	66.26	68.12	71.67	69.97	71.26	74.25	76.56	76.65	74.70	78.51	76.66	77.63	81.43	81.18	79.63	81.26	79.15	76.75	76.37	73.08	70.48
France	52.44	52.47	52.03	47.91	47.68	48.00	48.52	49.17	51.28	51.54	51.49	50.77	51.06	50.58	50.77	51.60	51.43	50.37	50.76	50.92	48.97	48.61	48.02	47.85
Croatia	42.59	31.31	38.12	36.53	42.25	40.59	44.07	46.91	49.15	54.18	52.92	51.82	59.75	55.98	57.22	58.43	53.96	56.40	59.87	50.97	52.07	54.37	53.64	52.24
Italy	84.66	82.03	84.22	80.76	81.09	81.92	81.87	80.76	81.86	82.93	86.47	83.22	86.00	83.98	84.76	84.46	87.14	85.26	85.69	83.25	84.28	81.82	79.28	76.90
Cyprus	98.29	100.73	99.87	103.56	97.02	100.46	98.17	97.70	96.89	101.99	98.61	95.88	100.08	96.11	95.43	100.69	102.52	95.88	97.53	96.32	100.76	92.41	97.03	96.41
Latvia	88.93	85.55	87.50	71.08	72.26	70.44	73.89	60.27	60.70	55.93	60.98	59.32	58.73	63.22	69.43	63.86	66.70	62.46	58.80	60.39	45.51	59.85	56.37	55.86
Lithuania	71.72	70.55	60.72	56.16	64.57	63.09	52.69	55.19	49.77	53.39	59.36	46.17	41.63	43.77	46.57	56.77	62.00	61.21	57.78	49.89	81.82	81.67	80.33	78.30
Luxembourg	99.50	98.59	99.49	98.33	98.78	97.72	99.38	98.49	99.47	97.09	99.60	97.39	98.59	98.39	97.91	97.30	98.10	96.55	97.41	97.45	97.01	97.20	97.39	96.90
Hungary	48.98	45.77	44.75	47.88	47.47	47.92	51.46	51.58	55.06	53.78	55.17	53.51	56.84	61.96	60.93	63.09	62.67	61.20	63.22	58.52	58.07	51.84	52.35	52.35
Malta	100.02	108.73	112.54	100.00	100.01	104.81	100.01	100.00	100.00	109.53	100.26	99.83	99.80	99.83	99.83	99.98	99.96	99.99	99.95	99.93	99.09	101.37	101.00	104.07
Netherlands	22.15	18.03	17.45	16.84	21.44	17.73	14.72	24.34	25.74	29.21	38.00	33.43	33.38	37.19	30.08	37.73	36.85	37.47	34.32	35.85	30.44	29.72	30.70	26.01
Austria	68.53	66.60	68.42	65.73	65.34	66.39	69.53	67.56	70.27	65.16	65.42	64.87	67.87	70.50	70.74	71.33	72.27	68.74	68.67	65.15	62.35	69.98	63.65	62.28
Poland	0.78	0.85	1.02	2.20	−0.90	−1.17	4.66	6.16	8.11	9.51	9.87	9.85	10.64	13.22	14.46	17.21	19.56	25.50	30.26	31.63	31.27	33.45	30.71	25.77
Portugal	84.14	82.35	84.18	82.79	81.52	85.34	80.37	83.86	84.07	87.42	85.07	85.12	84.14	85.48	83.95	88.57	83.98	81.44	83.44	81.35	75.13	77.67	78.94	73.54
Romania	34.27	27.76	29.70	26.90	25.74	30.31	30.73	32.43	28.48	21.08	21.80	26.06	24.11	25.36	30.20	27.65	29.38	31.73	27.99	20.31	21.85	21.59	22.65	18.58
Slovenia	45.66	42.45	41.84	48.24	49.24	50.87	55.29	54.97	52.50	55.85	52.78	50.42	50.64	53.62	52.36	52.47	52.06	52.46	55.09	48.45	49.43	48.15	51.62	47.02
Slovakia	77.54	73.51	75.28	69.62	68.34	68.50	73.19	73.04	71.10	66.53	65.55	62.19	63.94	64.48	67.65	65.31	63.85	68.24	64.26	66.25	62.86	63.98	59.90	59.58
Finland	61.04	57.00	55.97	56.02	65.95	53.48	55.07	56.29	53.40	50.76	55.24	54.91	52.09	58.94	54.32	54.18	53.53	52.87	54.21	53.76	47.86	52.88	46.30	48.73
Sweden	38.16	36.56	40.65	40.65	41.20	38.91	41.60	39.55	39.12	36.87	40.67	37.68	37.23	42.84	36.30	36.78	36.76	35.42	37.06	36.74	36.60	36.17	28.65	31.59
United Kingdom	2.35	5.16	4.05	0.21	−13.68	−16.39	−14.50	−15.38	−16.35	−20.27	−16.86	−9.30	−12.27	−6.38	4.51	13.39	21.17	20.47	26.23	26.33	28.49	36.26	42.20	46.37
Switzerland	59.85	59.57	58.81	54.45	54.53	54.98	58.73	57.01	57.83	52.72	53.23	54.61	55.49	54.39	55.88	60.08	57.04	52.34	54.91	55.37	54.25	–	–	–

Source: European Commission 2012. Country Factsheets—EU 27 Member States (Version 1.2); Switzerland: Eurostat. Own representation.

REFERENCES

Baumgartner, Frank R., and Bryan D. Jones (2002). 'Positive and Negative Feedback in Politics', in Frank R. Baumgartner and Bryan D. Jones (eds), *Policy Dynamics*. Chicago: University of Chicago Press, 3–28.

Cohen, Gail, Frederick Joutz, and Prakash Loungani (2011). 'Measuring Energy Security: Trends in the Diversification of Oil and Natural Gas Supplies.' *Energy Policy*, 39(9): 4860–9.

EC (2010). *Energy (2020): A Strategy for Competitive, Sustainable and Secure Energy*. Brussels: COM(2010) 639.

EC (2014a). *European Energy Security Strategy*. Brussels: COM(2014) 330.

EC (2014b). *In-Depth Study of European Energy Security*. Brussels: SWD(2014) 330 final/3.

Fuhrmann, Matthew (2012). 'Splitting Atoms: Why Do Countries Build Nuclear Power Plants?' *International Interactions*, 38(1): 1–28.

Keohane, Robert, and Joseph Nye (1977, 2000). *Power and Interdependence*. New York: Longman.

Kitschelt, Herbert P. (1982). 'Structures and Sequences of Nuclear Policy-Making: Suggestions for a Comparative Perspective.' *Political Power and Social Theory*, 13(3): 271–308.

Marples, David R., and Marilyn J. Young (1999). *Nuclear Energy and Security in the Former Soviet Union*. Boulder, CO: Westview Press.

Polanecký, Karel, and Jan Haverkamp (2011). *Energy of the Future? Nuclear Energy in Central and Eastern Europe*. Prague: Heinrich-Böll-Stiftung.

von Hippel, David F., Tatsujiro Suzuki, James H. Williams, Timothy Savage, and Peter Hayes (2011). 'Evaluating the Energy Security Impacts of Energy Policies', in Benjamin Sovacool (ed.), *The Routledge Handbook of Energy Security*. London: Routledge, 74–95.

4

The Conflict over Nuclear Energy

Public Opinion, Protest Movements, and Green Parties in Comparative Perspective

Paul W. Thurner, Sylvain Brouard, Martin Dolezal, Isabelle Guinaudeau, Swen Hutter, and Wolfgang C. Müller

4.1 INTRODUCTION

After the outline of the development of the significance of nuclear energy in European countries (Chapters 1 and 3), the question arises whether the respective energy policy choices led to a politicization of the nuclear energy issue in the various countries. In this chapter we investigate to what extent nuclear power has been contested by public opinion, protest movements, and anti-nuclear issue entrepreneurs in Western Europe since the 1970s (i.e. the time when the building of nuclear power reactors in many countries met the first such resistance). We are particularly interested in the issue entrepreneurs' subsequent institutionalization as Green parties and their taking root in the parliamentary party system. As the presence—or absence—of Green parties in the parliamentary arena is a major factor in the policy debate we record the representation and strength of an anti-nuclear voice at this level. This chapter thus prepares the ground for understanding the different trajectories of nuclear energy by comparatively highlighting the parliamentary strength of its 'natural enemies'. We systematically cover all the countries that are represented with country chapters in the present volume. With regard to public opinion and protest behaviour we contextualize by placing them among a larger set of European democracies.

4.1.1 Public Opinion, Protest Mobilization, and Green Party Institutionalization

Anti-nuclear attitudes in public opinion, protest movements, and the institutionalization of opposition to nuclear energy in the form of Green parties are generally considered to be closely related. Generally, the establishment of new parties is more likely when relevant parts of the public mobilize over an issue that has not divided the existing parties. This largely holds true for nuclear energy, but there are relevant deviations indicating that this relationship is not fully cogent. Indeed, the nuclear energy controversy in the 1970s is commonly considered as the 'catalyst' of the emergence of Green and other left libertarian parties. As Kitschelt has pointed out:

> Antinuclear activists first attempted to work through the established parties, but neither conservative nor socialist parties were willing to represent and support them, particularly in countries with high labor corporatism and left party governments. In these countries, a high level of alienation from the established political institutions encouraged left-libertarians to resort to the mobilization of antinuclear movements in order to advance their agenda. (Kitschelt 1988: 219)

In the late 1980s Kitschelt (1986a, 1988) diagnosed that, despite the non-existence of a left-libertarian party, only the US experienced an intense nuclear power debate in the early 1970s. He argued that, despite extensive nuclear power programmes, there was no such debate in Britain, Canada, Finland, Italy, and Japan. Since about 1975, the nuclear power debate intensified in nearly all countries with left-libertarian parties. Kitschelt highlighted France as an exceptional case because the Socialists, the major opposition party at the time, absorbed the issue.[1] He proposed an interesting rationale for the varying intensity of the anti-nuclear conflict: where Social Democrats were part of government, and thus committed to their previous pro-nuclear course, only the 'exit' option remained for anti-nuclear activists and citizens (i.e. extra-parliamentary contestation and the founding of new parties). Kitschelt identified two exceptions to this rule: 'Belgium and Finland implemented ambitious nuclear power programmes during periods of socialist participation in government, but did not witness strong conflicts over nuclear power' (Kitschelt 1988: 221).

Back in 1988, when Kitschelt's study was published, data availability clearly precluded a comparative assessment of the extent and timing of these conflicts:

> The strength or weakness of the nuclear controversy is difficult to determine because cross-national data on the mobilization of opponents to nuclear power are confined to inventories of case studies. Ideally, opinion polls, the incidence of mass demonstrations against nuclear facilities, and politically motivated delays in the construction and licensing of nuclear facilities would be valuable measures of the strength of antinuclear movements. (Kitschelt 1988: 219–20)

Although nearly three decades have passed since this was published, to the best of our knowledge we are the first to take up this suggestion. In this chapter we combine comprehensive and to large extent original data on the evolution of public opinion on nuclear energy, protest movements, and the emergence and electoral performance of Green parties. In so doing, we intend to reconstruct the interplay between the established parties committed to nuclear power programmes and the societal and political self-organization of the 'natural enemies' of nuclear power. Retracing the interplay between these factors will help us better

---

[1] According to Kitschelt, 'an initially intense antinuclear mobilization in the mid-1970s triggered the participation of ecologists in local and regional elections. After that, government repression, the oppositional Socialist Party's attempts to co-opt anti-nuclear activists, and the movement's complete lack of policy impact quelled the mobilization of collective protest' (Kitschelt 1988: 219).

understand the different paths of nuclear energy policy-making in Europe in the remainder of the volume.

4.1.2 Expectations and Hypotheses

In line with the 'nuclear renaissance' argumentation, we test whether hard economic factors (as explored in Chapter 3) impact public opinion on nuclear energy. Accordingly, we expect:

> Public opinion will be the more positive towards nuclear energy the greater the energy import dependency and the greater the share of domestically produced nuclear energy in energy consumption.

Famously, one of the key factors in Herbert Kitschelt's original comparative assessment of (anti-)nuclear energy policy-making was the *openness* of political systems. The more open the political system, the easier the intrusion of the antinuclear opponents. Conversely, the more closed the political opportunity structure for movements, the harder it is to achieve national prominence, and hence the more likely they are to remain marginal and turn to confrontational strategies. Borrowing from Kitschelt (1986a) in this chapter we test the following hypothesis:

> The greater the openness of the political system, the higher the probability of the institutionalization of anti-nuclear movements and the stronger their institutionalization.

From an incentive-oriented perspective we interpret institutional openness as (a) openness of the electoral system (Cox 1990; Ezrow 2008, 2010; Harmel and Robertson 1985), and (b) openness of the political system deriving from the territorial organization of political authority. Low effective thresholds of the electoral system provide those committed to new issues with the incentive to seek direct parliamentary representation. Even if the first attempt is not successful, the incentive to fight for parliamentary entry is unlikely to disappear under such favourable conditions.

Another institutional feature of interest is state structure. More decentralized systems of government, in particular federal states, should provide a favourable institutional environment for political entrepreneurs. Such systems provide multiple access points for entry at the sub-national level and—once the thresholds of representation and relevance have been passed—chances for exercising influence on public policy (see Chandler and Chandler 1987).

These expectations are in line with the observation by Diani and van der Heijden (1994: 378) that the early phases of the anti-nuclear movement in the mid-1970s were 'largely shaped by the most stable properties of political systems' (first and foremost the political institutions).

Transnational issue awareness and exogenous shocks such as Harrisburg (1979), Chernobyl (1986), and Fukushima (2011) may accentuate differences between systems. Thus we expect the hypothesized positive relationship between the political system's openness and Green parties' electoral performance to become more visible over time, especially in the years after Chernobyl. In these years Green parties won parliamentary representation in nearly all non-majoritarian systems.

The causal relationship between public opinion, the size and timing of protest movements, the electoral performance of Green parties, and policy reversals in the domain of nuclear energy is naturally complex—and will be covered in detail in the country chapters and in the volume's Conclusion. Generally, much of recent research seems to indicate that political party positions follow shifts in public opinion (see Adams and Somer-Topcu 2009; Stimson et al. 1995, 2002; Soroka and Wlezien 2010). Yet the real driver of this development, at least in the early periods, may be protest movements 'on the ground'. Such movements are obviously confronted with severe collective action problems. In the long run, we expect these movements to be especially strong when supported by successful Green parties. This feedback process institutionalizes the nuclear energy issue as part of the policy agenda. Parliamentary parties enjoy democratic legitimacy and can provide valuable organizational resources for the protest movements and keep the issue on the parliamentary and public agenda. We therefore expect anti-nuclear policy change to be more likely as Green party strength increases.

4.1.3 Relevance for Policy Choices

It would be naïve to assume established parties do not react to new challengers (see Hug 2001). According to Meguid (2005, 2008) parties can prevent the new entry by undermining the issue's relevance (dismissive strategy) or by being accommodative vis-à-vis the claim and thereby stealing the issue from the niche party (accommodative strategy). Especially in systems with proportional (and therefore open) electoral systems, we would expect established parties to respond to new demands or even anticipate them in order to decrease the risk of electoral losses. This has two potential implications, one for the party system and one for nuclear energy policy. If the nuclear energy issue is absorbed by at least one of the existing parties, policy entrepreneurs may find it much harder to succeed in party formation. An example is the absorption of the issue by the United Left and the Communist Party in Spain at the end of the 1970s. Therefore, the openness of the electoral system is a necessary but not a sufficient condition for observing the emergence and success of Green parties.[2]

Absorption of the nuclear policy issue by established parties can result in some degree of anti-nuclear policy-making. How much may not only depend on the success of the parties acquiring issue ownership but also on where a country stands on its nuclear power trajectory. The less it has invested so far, the more likely is a more fundamental turning away from nuclear energy as a result of competition between the established parties.

Green parties impact the established parties mainly on the left side of the political spectrum. In the short term, their presence undermines the capacity of

---

[2] This may be one reason why Kitschelt did not find a clear relationship between electoral rules and the emergence of Green parties: 'There is no "hard" test for the significance of electoral laws (e.g. a configuration in which electoral rules are unfavorable to new parties)' (Kitschelt 1988: 224).

established left parties to attract voters and win pluralities of the electorate. Yet the long-term effects of Green entry to the party system are less clear, as in later periods such success may potentially allow for the emergence of new alliances, alternative electoral majorities, and more radical policy changes.

The chapter is structured into three major parts. The first part looks at the way public opinion on nuclear energy has evolved since the late 1970s and whether opposition against nuclear energy is related to domestic nuclear energy production or energy import dependency. The second part describes the strength and development of anti-nuclear protest on the streets from 1975 to 2011. Third, we present more detailed information on the establishment and success of Green parties. There we investigate our hypothesis on the effect of political system openness and the success of Green parties. This chapter thus puts the cases discussed in the country chapters in a larger comparative perspective with regard to the political factors that are likely to cause anti-nuclear dynamics in policy-making.

4.2 PUBLIC OPINION

How did public opinion on nuclear energy evolve over time in the countries we consider? Nuclear energy is not popular anywhere. However, the available data show that there are remarkable differences in levels of rejection as well as of the rapidity of public opinion changes within Europe and across time. Unfortunately, we lack long-term time series on these attitudes in many countries, often due to the simple fact that the issue was not relevant for party competition.[3] Thus we rely on a patchwork of surveys with varying question formats, partly for only a subset of our countries. As a consequence of this unsatisfactory data situation, we draw very prudent conclusions on over-time developments only.

Figure 4.1 shows that the Netherlands, France, and Germany had very high refusal levels already in 1978. The governments in these countries were confronted with a near or above the majority of citizens who opposed their policies. It is especially noteworthy that public opinion in France was highly negative at that time—obviously this background did not translate into the policy-making of this country. The Three Mile Island (Harrisburg) accident of 1979 did not cause a common reaction among European citizens. While the trend of public opinion in France, Germany, the Netherlands, and Belgium shows declining shares of citizens who consider nuclear energy an unacceptable risk, we observe the opposite development in Italy between 1978 and 1982. Overall, Harrisburg had no major impact on the electorates' issue opinion. However, the 1984 survey already indicates an increasing rejection of nuclear energy in all these countries. The rise is most remarkable in Belgium. It was the Chernobyl disaster, then, that induced a real 'seismic' shift against nuclear energy in several countries—varying in magnitude between ten and more than twenty percentage points. The steepest

---

[3] There are, amongst others, several (Special) Eurobarometer surveys dealing with attitudes on nuclear energy but later versions do not include the respondents' voting behaviour or party affiliation. None of the other major comparative surveys (European Social Survey, World Values Survey, etc.) measures stances on nuclear energy.

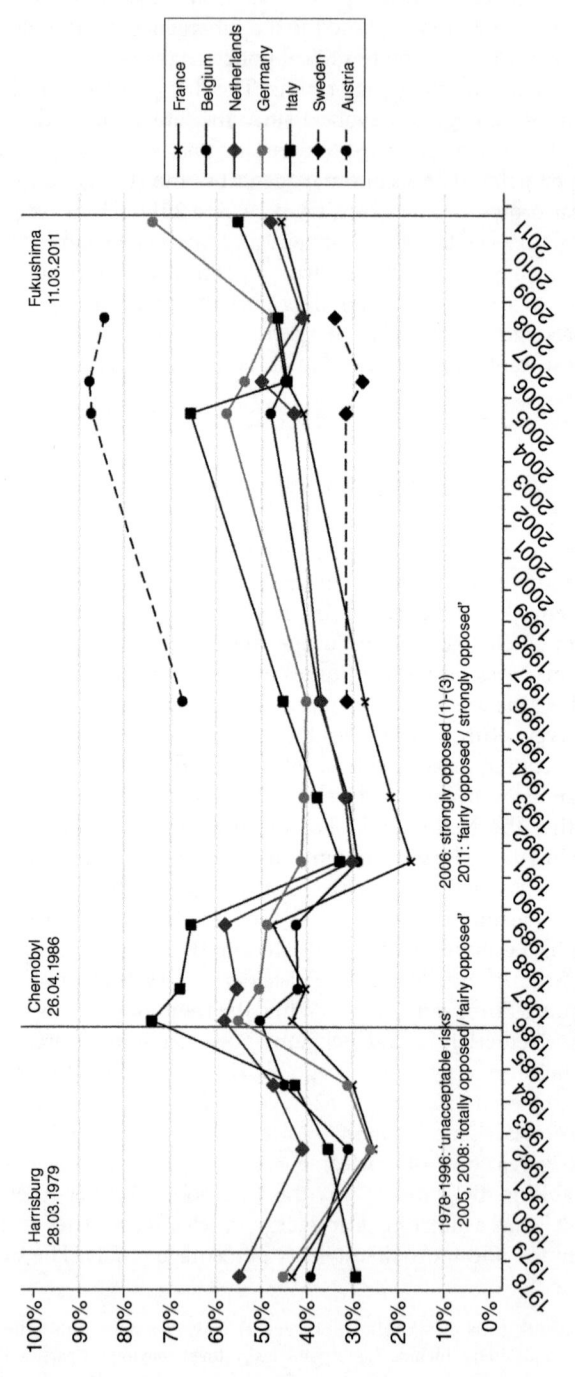

Figure 4.1. Public Opinion Trends in Selected Countries: Opposition to Nuclear Energy (1978–2011)

Notes: Denominator includes 'Don't knows'. EB 75.1 was conducted before Fukushima.

Data sources: Eurobarometer 10A, 17, 22, 26, 28, 31A, 35.0, 39.1, 46.0, 63.2, 65.3, 69.1, 75.1.

increase is observed in Italy, Germany, and the Netherlands. By contrast, Belgian public opinion was barely affected by the Chernobyl disaster.

The Chernobyl effect weakened or even reversed at the beginning of the 1990s. Most surprisingly, the 1993 survey shows a return to pre-Chernobyl rejection levels (e.g. in France, Italy, Belgium, and the Netherlands). Meanwhile, anti-nuclear policy reversals and moratoria on nuclear energy had occurred in Italy and the Netherlands. An explicit legislative or a de facto freezing of nuclear programmes occurred in other countries where no more new reactors were constructed since the mid/end of the 1980s (e.g. Belgium, Germany, the Netherlands (already since 1974), Spain, Sweden (1980–2010), UK (since 1988)). Thus, the planning phase of the fleet of European reactors in most countries dates back to the 1950s to 1970s—with the exceptions of Finland and France which built reactors more recently. In the follow-up surveys (1993, 1996), we observe a steady increase of nuclear power refusal until 2005.

However, the non-acceptance of nuclear energy then decreased markedly in 2006 and 2008 in many countries. It was below 50 per cent in all countries in Figure 4.1 but Austria. This trend in public opinion reflected and/or nurtured the notion of a 'nuclear renaissance' (see Chapter 1). Rapidly rising energy prices (driven by increasing worldwide demand), and the framing of nuclear energy as a solution to problems of energy supply, economic growth, and CO_2 emissions by many decision-makers had affected the perception of voters.

Our time series covering the entire EU ends in 2008. For that year Table 4.1 provides the broadest country coverage of nuclear energy attitudes that we have. Countries are ordered from the most favourable to the most opposed towards nuclear energy (per cent 'in favour' minus per cent 'opposed'). With expanded country coverage (compared to Figure 4.1) country differences increase. While East European countries and a few North European countries that run their own nuclear energy power stations show solid support levels, nuclear energy is almost universally rejected in some of the countries that do without them. If one considers all countries in 2008 (see Table 4.1), an interesting picture emerges. First, there are some countries without nuclear energy (e.g. Austria, Denmark, Greece, Ireland, Italy) which continuously nourish a highly opposed anti-nuclear political culture, with a majority of the electorate rejecting nuclear energy. Second, there are countries using nuclear energy but with moderate opposition (e.g. Finland, Sweden, UK). Finally, there are countries with high dependence on nuclear energy with large shares of citizens who nevertheless oppose it quite fiercely (e.g. Belgium, France, Spain).

A 2011 Special Eurobarometer confined to a smaller set of countries and conducted a few weeks before the Fukushima disaster showed somewhat lower levels of support for nuclear energy but generally replicated the picture of 2008 (Table 4.2).

Although comparative data to map the immediate impact of Fukushima on public opinion are still scarce, some evidence shows that the disaster led to a substantial decline in the acceptance of nuclear energy. Accordingly, a Gallup Global Snap Poll conducted in forty-seven countries in March and April 2011 reported a decline in support for nuclear energy in all but five cases.[4] Yet a cross-country study by Ipsos

---

[4] WIN Gallup, 'Impact of Japan Earthquake on Views about Nuclear Energy', 19 Apr. 2011.

Table 4.1. Approval and Rejection of Nuclear Energy in Twenty-Seven European Countries (2008)

	TOTAL	Totally in favour	Fairly in favour	Fairly opposed	Totally opposed	DK	In favour	Opposed	Net diff.
Bulgaria	1000	28	35	8	5	24	63	13	50
Lithuania	1009	18	46	18	8	10	64	26	38
Czech R.	1070	23	41	24	8	4	64	32	32
Hungary	1000	22	41	21	11	5	63	32	31
Slovakia	1049	15	45	24	7	9	60	31	29
Sweden	1007	30	32	20	15	3	62	35	27
Finland	1001	19	42	27	9	3	61	36	25
UK	1306	13	37	25	11	14	50	36	14
Netherlands	1023	15	40	24	18	3	55	42	13
France	1054	10	42	30	10	8	52	40	12
Slovenia	1026	9	42	35	11	3	51	46	5
Belgium	1012	10	40	37	10	3	50	47	3
EU27	26746	11	33	28	17	11	44	45	1
Germany	1562	12	34	31	16	7	46	47	-1
Italy	1036	12	31	29	17	11	43	46	-3
Romania	1024	4	31	23	15	27	35	38	-3
Poland	1000	12	27	27	19	15	39	46	-7
Estonia	1000	9	32	35	18	6	41	53	-12
Latvia	1004	8	27	36	21	8	35	57	-22
Luxembourg	513	7	27	38	21	7	34	59	-25
Denmark	1032	10	26	26	36	2	36	62	-26
Ireland	1000	5	19	23	31	22	24	54	-30
Portugal	1000	4	19	39	16	22	23	55	-32
Spain	1004	4	20	33	24	19	24	57	-33
Montenegro	500	5	10	22	40	23	15	62	-47
Greece	1000	4	14	27	52	3	18	79	-61
Austria	1008	2	12	33	50	3	14	83	-69
Cyprus	506	3	4	9	71	13	7	80	-79

Source: European Commission, 2008: Special EB 297, Attitudes towards Radioactive Waste, Appendix (fieldwork Feb.–Mar. 2008).

Table 4.2. Approval and Rejection of Nuclear Energy in Twelve European Countries Just Before Fukushima (2011)

%	Strongly in favour	Fairly in favour	Fairly opposed	Strongly opposed	DK	Total 'In favour'	Total 'Opposed'	Net diff.
Belgium	29	33	18	9	11	62	27	35
UK	17	32	24	16	11	49	40	9
Finland	20	32	28	18	2	52	46	6
Czech R.	18	31	30	14	7	49	44	5
Romania	19	22	19	18	22	41	37	4
Poland	17	27	28	16	12	44	44	0
France	12	35	31	16	6	47	47	0
Netherlands	19	29	26	23	3	48	49	-1
All countries	12	24	28	26	10	36	54	-18
Italy	9	19	24	31	17	28	55	-27
Spain	9	15	29	36	11	24	65	-41
Germany	5	16	36	40	3	21	76	-55
Greece	3	5	18	69	5	8	87	-79

Note: Answers to the question: 'To what extent are you in favour of or opposed to the use of the following sources of energy in (OUR COUNTRY)? Nuclear energy'.

Source: EB 75.1.

one year after Fukushima[5] found that the shift of public opinion against nuclear energy was far from being 'seismic'. Indeed, acceptance fell by about eight percentage points on average. In some countries, such as Britain, the status quo ante had already been reached a year after the accident. Hence major variations exist, with Italy and Germany constituting the extreme pole of anti-nuclear attitudes—despite the enormous hunger for energy of these countries.

In the preceding chapters we have recognized objective constraints—at least in the short term—of decision-makers in energy policy. As the hard facts of existing energy supply should be easy to communicate and understand, they might also influence public opinion. To probe such relationships we rely on the last inclusive Special Eurobarometer 2008 on nuclear attitudes (Table 4.1). If we relate the refusal to import dependency and to the contribution of nuclear energy to total gross energy consumption, we indeed see moderate statistical relationships. Yet, counter-intuitively, the higher the import dependency on energy resources, the higher the percentage of opposition towards nuclear energy (Figure 4.2). As expected, the higher the contribution of domesticly produced nuclear energy towards gross inland energy consumption (GIC), the lower the share of refusal in the 2008 survey (Figure 4.3). This latter relationship is of considerable strength, and it demonstrates that the economic reliance on this energy carrier moulds public opinion in a certain way.

---

[5] Ipsos 2012, 'Public Opinion After Fukushima'. This is in line with similar results for the US as published by Bisconti Research, Inc. ('Public Favorability of Nuclear Energy Climbs for Today's Reactors', Future US Development and Global Leadership-Topline-Public-Opinion-Memo, Mar. 2015) and conducted for the Nuclear Energy Institute, a lobbying organization of the US nuclear industry.

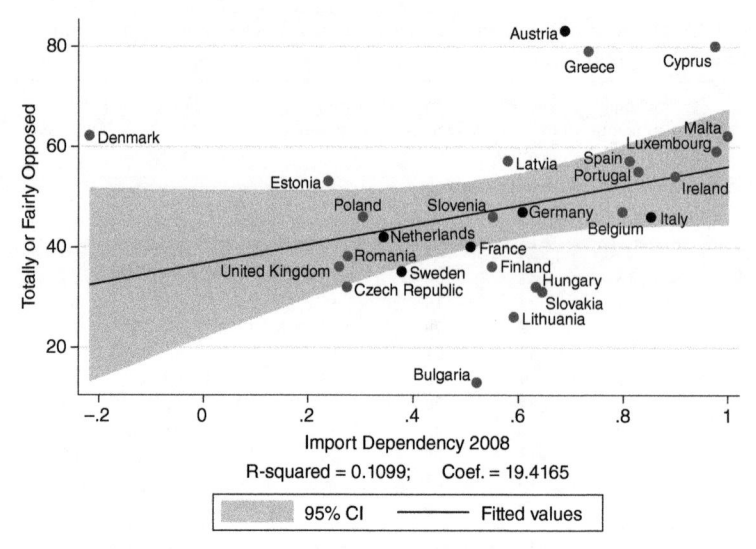

Figure 4.2. Import Dependency and Proportion of Anti-Nuclear Attitudes (2008)
Note: Countries printed in bold are treated in detail in our country chapters.

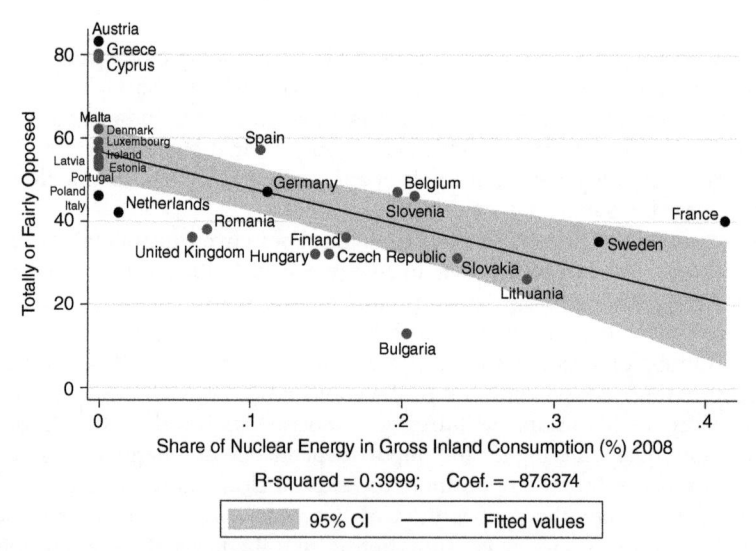

Figure 4.3. Share of Domesticly Produced Nuclear Energy in Gross Inland Consumption and Proportion of Anti-Nuclear Attitudes (2008)
Note: Countries printed in bold are treated in detail in our country chapters.

4.3 PROTEST MOVEMENTS

The anti-nuclear movement and its protest activities played a key role in the debate on nuclear energy policies in the 1970s and 1980s and had its repercussions on public opinion. In the mid-1970s, millions of citizens in more than thirty countries took part in protest activities against the introduction or the extension of nuclear energy production (Rüdig 1990; Giugni 2004). These large-scale protests mobilizing against both the military and civilian use of nuclear power indicated that a once uncontroversial topic had been transformed into a highly politicized and contested issue. At that time, before the emergence and electoral breakthrough of Green parties, studying the policies and politics of nuclear energy in Europe was inextricably related to the study of social movements and protest activities. Since Kitschelt's (1986a) pathbreaking study, social movement scholars have extensively dealt with the question of how the anti-nuclear movement's mobilization level, action repertoire, and impact differed across countries and over time (e.g. Duyvendak and Koopmans 1995; Flam 1994; Giugni 2004; Kolb 2007; Rootes 2003; Rucht 1994b, 1995; Rüdig 1990). However, most of these studies focus on mobilization in the 1970s and 1980s. As the nuclear energy issue has recently re-entered the political stage in many European countries (see Chapter 1), this section traces the development of anti-nuclear protests covering the whole period from 1975 to 2011. Our main aim is descriptive, as we want to answer the question of whether the recent renaissance of the nuclear energy issue has triggered a new wave of anti-nuclear protest mobilization. Our comparative mapping sets the stage for the following in-depth case studies. Specifically, it shows whether (and where) protest politics is an essential part of current nuclear energy politics. We are particularly interested in the way the nuclear accident in Fukushima influenced the activities in the protest arena. These data help highlight the theorized relationships between the openness of the political system, the response of established political actors, and the development of the anti-nuclear protest movement.

4.3.1 The Strength and Development of Anti-Nuclear Protests

To assess the strength and development of anti-nuclear protest mobilization, we rely on protest event analysis, a form of quantitative content analysis of media and some additional sources, to assess changes in protest mobilization (Koopmans 1998; Koopmans and Rucht 2002). This methodological choice follows a long-standing tradition of research on social movements and contentious politics (e.g. Kriesi et al. 1981; Tarrow 1989; Tilly et al. 1975). This mapping of protest events provides a basis for cross-sectional and longitudinal analyses. More specifically, we combine and update existing datasets on anti-nuclear protests in eleven countries (the seven countries covered by the detailed case studies in this book plus Spain, Belgium, Britain, and the United States).[6] Ultimately, we have assembled the largest comparative dataset on nuclear energy protests ever analysed.

---

[6] We mainly combine and update two protest event studies. First, we rely on Kriesi et al.'s (1995) data for France, Germany, the Netherlands and Switzerland (covering 1975 to 1989). This study is

We start with the average mobilization levels for the eight countries that we have information for from 1975 to 2011 (Figures 4.4 and 4.5). Looking at the 1970s and 1980s, our data illustrate the pattern described by Diani and van der Heijden (1994: 358). In most countries the peak of protest against nuclear energy occurred in the late 1970s and 1980s, with the 1990s seeing far less intense struggles. This nicely coincides with the abating of the salience of the nuclear energy issue in the public opinion polls. Only the Chernobyl disaster in 1986 induced a revival of protest mobilization. However, as Rucht (1995: 282) notes, '[w]hatever the specific national situation, by the end of the 1980s the anti-nuclear wave ran out'. On average, anti-nuclear protest did not return until well into the 2000s. In particular, we observe dramatically increased protest activities between 2009 and 2011, following the Fukushima catastrophe.[7]

This 'dominant pattern of development' (Diani and van der Heijden 1994: 358) is visible in most countries in the 1970s and 1980s, whereas the return of anti-nuclear mobilization in the late 2000s is restricted to only a few countries. More specifically, pronounced peaks can be observed recently in Germany, Austria, and Switzerland. These three countries show the highest *average* participation rates over the whole period covered. On average, around 1,500 protesters per million inhabitants were reported as protesting against nuclear energy in Germany, followed by Switzerland (900 participants) and Austria (700 participants). Whereas the Netherlands and France display a medium level of anti-nuclear mobilization (around 450 participants), the other countries lag far behind (below 150 participants).

While no protest event data exist to assess the mobilization levels in Belgium, Spain, and Sweden in the 1970s and 1980s, rough estimates provided by Rucht (1995: 283) indicate a below-average degree of *mass* protest mobilization in these three countries. On a five-point scale, Rucht scores Spain and Sweden as 1 and Belgium as 0. Although Flam and Jamison (1994: 163) refer to the Swedish anti-nuclear movement as 'the largest oppositional movement since the Second World War', its strength in terms of *mass* mobilization in unconventional protest events remained limited (Kitschelt 1986b: 68). This also holds for the Italian and the Spanish cases. In Italy, the main phases of heightened mobilization were around the referendum in 1987 when about 200,000 people marched in Rome for the abolishment of nuclear energy a day before the referendum. Rucht's estimates for

---

based on the coding of all protests covered by the Monday editions of one quality newspaper per country. Based on the same research strategy, Koopmans (1996) added Britain to the sample, Kriesi et al. (2012) added Austria and coded the years 1990 to 2005 as well, while Giugni (2004) collected protests focused on nuclear energy, ecology and peace in Italy and the United States from 1975 to 1999. Second, we draw on the work of Rootes (2003) and collaborators who collected data on environmental protests in eight European countries for the period 1988 to 1997 (Britain, France, Germany, Greece, Italy, Spain, the Basque Country, and Sweden). While both studies adopted a very similar research strategy, Rootes's (2003) data are based on the coding of *all* editions of one quality newspaper and covers more action forms (e.g. litigations and indoor assemblies). For our comparative analyses, we extracted the subsample of Monday protests and dropped these additional action forms. For Belgium, which is missing from these datasets, we rely on the national protest event data collected by Walgrave and Vliegenthart (2012) that covers demonstrations for the 1990s only.

[7] This rise is not reflected in the absolute number of protest events shown in Figure 4.4. It is important to note that this average is even more heavily influenced by only a few countries.

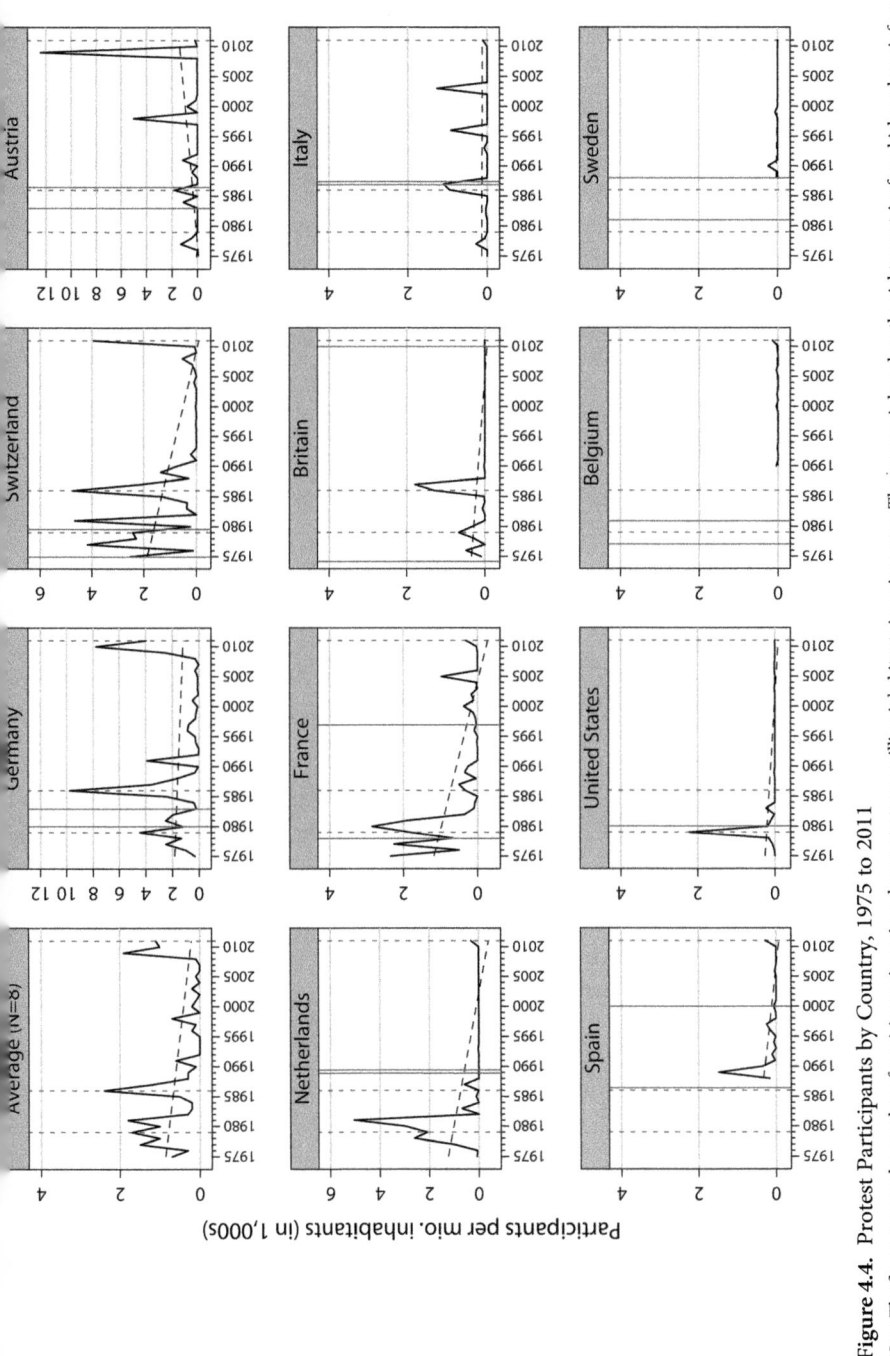

Figure 4.4. Protest Participants by Country, 1975 to 2011

Note: The figure reports the number of participants in anti-nuclear protests per million inhabitants in a given year. The average is based on the eight countries for which we have information on the whole period from 1975 to 2005 (i.e. Austria, Britain, France, Germany, Italy, the Netherlands, Switzerland, and the US). The countries are ranked according to the yearly average over the period covered by our study. The vertical dashed lines highlight the years with major nuclear accidents (Harrisburg in 1979, Chernobyl in 1986, and Fukushima in 2011), the vertical solid line indicates the years when Green parties passed the threshold of authorization and representation, respectively (see Table 4.4). Furthermore, we added a linear trend line.

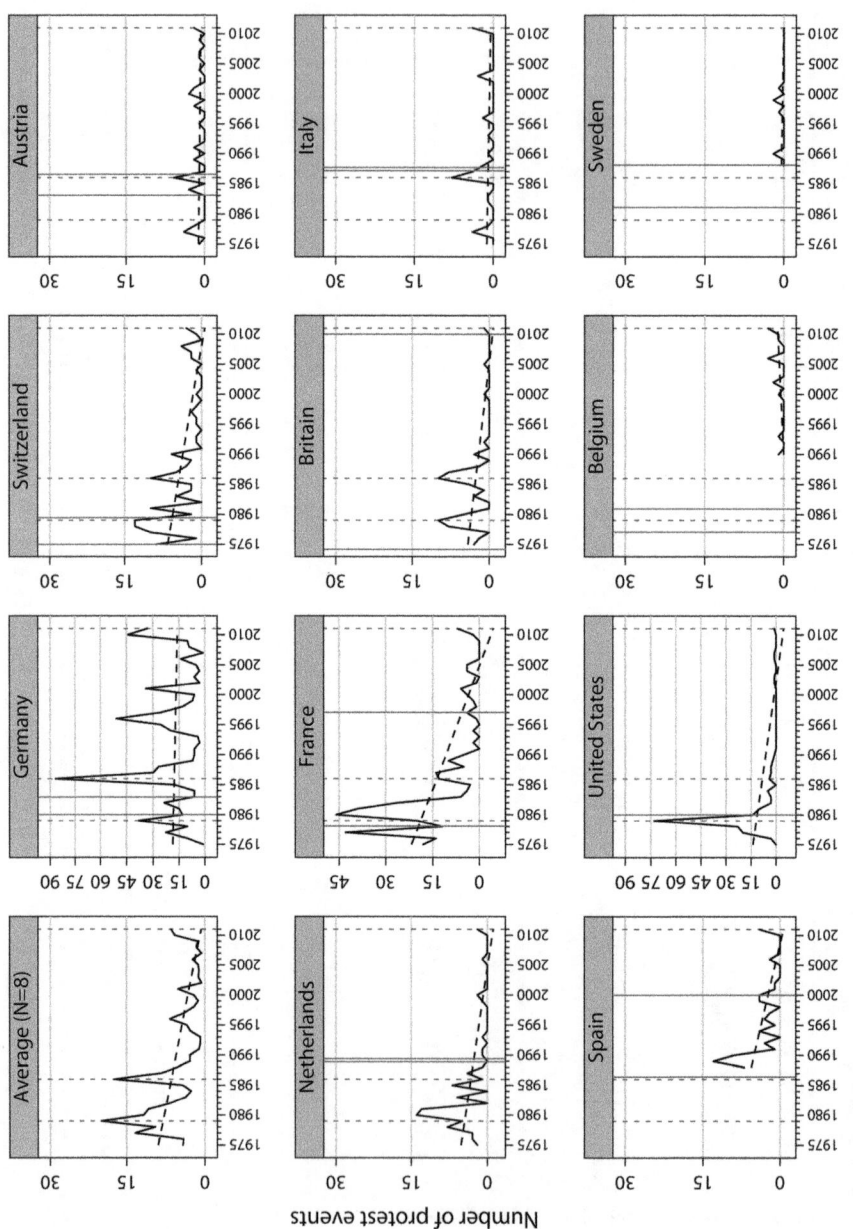

Figure 4.5. Protest Events by Country, 1975 to 2011

Note: The figure reports the absolute number of anti-nuclear protests in a given year. The average is based on the eight countries for which we have information on the whole period from 1975 to 2005 (i.e. Austria, Britain, France, Germany, Italy, the Netherlands, Switzerland, and the US). Note that this overall average is highly influenced by single countries, as the absolute number of protest events depends very much on the size of a country. The countries are ordered as in Figure 4.4. The vertical dashed lines highlight the years with major nuclear accidents (Harrisburg in 1979, Chernobyl in 1986, and Fukushima in 2011), the vertical solid line indicates the years when Green parties passed the threshold of authorization and representation, respectively (see Table 4.4). Furthermore, we added a linear trend line.

Table 4.3. Mobilization Levels by Country and Time Period

	1975–1985	1986/1987	1988–1999	2000–2010	2011
Germany	1.7	6.7	0.7	1.1	4.0
Switzerland	1.7	3.4	0.2	0.1	3.9
Netherlands	1.3	0.3	0.0	0.0	0.3
France	1.2	0.4	0.1	0.2	0.3
Austria	0.4	0.9	0.6	1.2	0.2
United States	0.3	0.0	0.0	0.0	0.0
Britain	0.2	1.1	0.1	0.0	0.0
Italy	0.1	1.0	0.1	0.2	0.1
Spain	-	-	0.2	0.0	0.3
Sweden	-	-	0.0	0.0	0.1
Belgium	-	-	0.0	0.0	0.1
Average (N = 8)	0.9	1.7	0.2	0.4	1.1
Standard deviation	0.6	2.1	0.3	0.5	1.6

Note: Number of participants in anti-nuclear protests per million inhabitants (in 1,000s). The values indicate the *yearly* averages to allow comparison between the different time periods. Values of 1.0 and higher are highlighted in bold.

the other countries are supported by our data presented in Figures 4.4 and 4.5. On the five-point scale, he classifies the mass mobilization against nuclear energy in the 1970s and 1980s in Germany as 5, in Switzerland as 4, in Austria, the Netherlands, and the United States as 3, in France as 2, and in Great Britain and Italy as 1 (see also Kolb 2007: 204–5; Rüdig 1990).

Table 4.3 allows another look at the data by presenting average mobilization levels over five time periods. The numbers underscore that the global renaissance of the nuclear energy issue since the 1990s did not trigger a return of protest mobilization across Europe and the United States. More specifically, the figures underscore that the major nuclear accidents in Chernobyl and Fukushima did not lead to peaks in anti-nuclear protests in all countries. Primarily, the German and Swiss anti-nuclear movements were fuelled by these tragic events. For these two countries, we observe broad-scale protest mobilization in terms of participants per million inhabitants both in 1986–7 and 2011. In both countries, the Greens had already won seats in the national parliament before 1986 (see Figures 4.4 and 4.5). This corroborates our expectation that protest movements have to institutionalize as parties in order to survive.[8] At the same time, Table 4.3 shows that Germany and Switzerland also saw comparatively strong protest movements against nuclear energy in the pre-Chernobyl period. However, the mobilization levels before and after Chernobyl are not consistently related to each other across the eight countries covered by our data.

---

[8] Unfortunately, we lack protest event data for Belgium to confirm the claim that the early success of Green parties is related to higher mobilization levels thereafter. However, anecdotal evidence does not support this hypothesis since Belgium saw no pronounced protest mobilization after the nuclear accident in Chernobyl (Rucht 1995).

4.3.2 The Political Context and the Development of Anti-Nuclear Protests

Although it is beyond the scope of this chapter to systematically explain cross-national differences, we can clearly relate anti-nuclear protest to its wider political context (described in detail in the country chapters). While internal features of the movements (e.g. internal divisions or resources) also matter, the political process approach in social movement research has highlighted that protest activities outside of mainstream political institutions are closely linked to conventional politics in the parliamentary and extra-parliamentary arenas (for overviews, see Hutter 2014: 25–43; Kriesi 2004; Meyer 2004). Diani and van der Heijden (1994: 378) accordingly showed that more closed political opportunity structures make it difficult for a movement to achieve national prominence. Such movements, in turn, are more likely to remain fragmented and to resort to confrontational strategies. While the peaks of the conflict are less closely linked to political context factors, the development in the 1980s was mainly shaped by the more dynamic and flexible way the political elites responded to their challengers.

We highlight these interactions with some illustrative examples for the five countries that witnessed large-scale protest mobilization against nuclear power and that are covered by cases studied in this book. We begin with two countries that witnessed no resurgence of anti-nuclear protests in the 2000s (France and the Netherlands) before moving on to three countries where we observe the opposite (Austria, Germany, and Switzerland).

In France, massive protests against nuclear energy occurred only in the late 1970s and early 1980s. Here, the first large demonstrations against nuclear energy in Europe took place (in the early 1970s) and the movement remained comparatively strong throughout this decade (Figures 4.3 and 4.4). However, despite such mobilization, the French anti-nuclear movement was never really capable of coordinating and acting on the national level (Rucht 1994a). It virtually disappeared in the early 1980s. The movement's decline was mainly caused by the repressive reactions of the state after the violent clashes in Malville (a construction site of a fast-breeder) in 1976, as well as the left-wing parties' decision to continue with the nuclear energy programme after their electoral victory in 1981 (Brouard and Guinaudeau, this volume; Duyvendak 1995; Rucht 1994a) despite anti-nuclear position-taking during the campaign. Many adherents of the anti-nuclear movement felt betrayed by the new President François Mitterrand. At the same time, the Socialists' turn deprived the anti-nuclear movement of its main ally in the arena of established politics. As Rucht (1994a: 148) notes, 'although they saw that Mitterrand's promises were not being kept, the anti-nuclear groups were simply too weak for a rebirth in both quantitative and moral terms'—and given the closedness of the system one might add. This is indicated by the fact that the relevant demonstrations in Alsace or in Paris in 1986 were comprised of just a few hundred participants and hardly received mass media attention.

Similar to the French case, the Netherlands saw no large-scale anti-nuclear protests in 1986 as the anti-nuclear movement in the Netherlands 'was in a rather desperate state at the time of the accident' (Duyvendak and Koopmans 1995: 151). The idea of a public debate as a quasi-official process on energy policy that first emerged in late 1977 led to divisions within the Dutch movement (see Aarts and Arentsen, this volume). In the following years, the radical factions that refused to participate in the debate kept on protesting for the closure of the two existing power plants. After 1981, protest mobilization decreased tremendously when the attempts to shut down the plants failed. While the moderate anti-nuclear groups were quite successful at the beginning of the public debate on energy policy, their efforts did not pay off as the debate had no binding influence on the final decision. Thus, in 1985, the Dutch government declared that it did not accept the debate's conclusion and instead proposed the construction of two new nuclear power plants. As shown by Figures 4.4 and 4.5, this decision did not revitalize protest mobilization in the streets as the radical part of the anti-nuclear movement had fallen apart and the moderate groups had turned to insider tactics and more general energy issues. Furthermore, the Chernobyl accident occurred in the midst of the national election campaign and the government reacted promptly by postponing the decision on the new nuclear plants. Thus, large-scale protest mobilization was unlikely due to the weakness of the anti-nuclear groups and the fact that protesting no longer seemed as urgent. We can observe this in the low participation figures reported for the few anti-nuclear demonstrations that occurred after the accident. As van der Heijden (1994: 123) aptly stated, 'the Chernobyl disaster influenced the stance of the political parties on nuclear energy much more than the activities of the movement (which hardly reacted to the disaster). It brought about unity against nuclear energy, where none had existed earlier'.

Anti-nuclear protests involving the most participants and heated conflicts throughout our observation period took place in Germany (for a detailed summary, see Rucht 2008). Based on participation rates, Germany saw the most pronounced peaks in 1979, 1986, and 2010–11 (Figure 4.4). Although these three peaks were fuelled by tragic nuclear accidents, they were all culminations of protest campaigns against domestic policy decisions. In 1979, the conflict over the geographical concentration of the reprocessing and storage of nuclear waste in the area of Gorleben reached a first peak, whereas the conflicts over the construction of a nuclear reprocessing site in Wackersdorf culminated in 1986. The mass demonstrations from September 2009 onwards were driven by the Christian Democrats and the Liberals' plans to extend the phasing-out period.[9]

The ups and downs of protest mobilization in Germany can only be understood by focusing on the broader political context (e.g. Duyvendak and Koopmans 1995; Rucht 1994b, 2008). First, the policy decisions of the government provided specific objects that an organizationally well prepared movement could focus on in its mobilization. Second, in contrast to the Dutch and French situation, the German political parties were increasingly polarized on the issue (Thurner, this volume). Changing elite alignments and the presence of strong allies are in general regarded as key factors for strong and sustained protest mobilization (McAdam

---

[9] In the wake of the so-called consensus talks (1992/1993) that marked the beginning of the phasing out, the number of people involved in anti-nuclear protests decreased strongly (Figure 4.4). At the same time, the peaks in the number of events shown in Figure 4.5 highlight that protests over nuclear energy have not disappeared in Germany in the 1990s and 2000s (especially the so-called Castor transports led to numerous protests).

1996). In addition to the meanwhile institutionalized 'natural opponent' of nuclear energy, the Green party, the German Social Democrats declared their opposition to the Wackersdorf reprocessing plant in 1984 and, in the autumn of 1986, the national party congress adopted a resolution calling for the phasing out of nuclear energy. Third, the nuclear energy issue led also to controversies between the national government and regional (i.e. Land) governments (mainly those where Social Democrats were in charge). This provided also a more favourable setting for protest mobilization as compared to the more centralized French and Dutch cases.

As indicated by the data, in Switzerland we observe large-scale protests against nuclear energy after the accident in Fukushima. In May 2011, the biggest anti-nuclear demonstration for twenty-five years took place, rallying around 20,000 participants. In contrast to Germany, remobilization occurred after a long period without extensive mobilization on the streets (Giugni and Passy 1999). The last mass demonstrations against nuclear energy dated back to 1986 when Chernobyl revitalized the anti-nuclear forces. As in Germany, the Swiss anti-nuclear movement faced a rather favourable political context characterized by divided elites, strongly established allies (especially the left-wing parties), and a federal political system. The Social Democrats changed to an anti-nuclear position and became crucial political allies of the anti-nuclear movement already in 1978 (Kriesi, this volume). However, the impact of Chernobyl on the Swiss protest landscape was more modest than in Germany and restricted to only a few mass demonstrations. As shown in Figure 4.4, the heydays of anti-nuclear protests in Switzerland were the late 1970s and early 1980s when the conflict over the construction of a nuclear power plant in Kaiseraugst culminated. During this period, the Swiss anti-nuclear movement relied heavily on unconventional activities (especially occupations and mass demonstrations) and became capable of acting at the national level. Since then, the decreasing mobilization levels are linked to yet another crucial aspect of the political context faced by challengers in Switzerland: direct democracy.

Since late 1977, the anti-nuclear forces in Switzerland invested a lot of their efforts in initiating direct-democratic votes on the national and regional (i.e. cantonal) level (for details, see Kriesi, this volume) and forming a Green party. Thus, the anti-nuclear movement is an exemplary case for the institutionalization of the new social movements, which lost their strength in structuring political protest and were integrated into the more formal arrangements offered by the Swiss political system (Giugni and Passy 1999; Hutter and Giugni 2009).

In Austria, protests were also central to the early story of nuclear energy politics in the 1970s, but the number of protesters was lower and the action taken more moderate as compared to the other countries discussed so far (Preglau 1994).[10] After first protests against plans for a Swiss nuclear power plant near the Austrian–Swiss border, anti-nuclear protests started on the local and regional (i.e. Land) level in Vorarlberg in the early 1970s. As shown in Figures 4.4 and 4.5, peaks in protest mobilization occurred later on in the decade when the anti-nuclear movement gained national prominence. The focal point of the conflict

---

[10] This mirrors the Austrian protest landscape more generally and can be linked back to the overall political context faced by challengers at that time (Dolezal and Hutter 2007).

was the Zwentendorf project (e.g. Kok and Schaller 1986). As in other countries, the political elite became more divided on the nuclear energy issue during those years. However, the Austrian Social Democrats, whose support was crucial for the mobilization chances in other countries, were in single-party government and the most pro-nuclear force (Müller, this volume). As Kriesi (1995) shows, this was a very unfavourable situation for new social movements of the left. Nonetheless, the Social Democrats' decisions created opportunities for the anti-nuclear movement. The government's atomic energy information campaign (involving public discussions and symposia) was crucial in this respect. It provided the anti-nuclear groups with a forum for spreading their views and organizing protests. For example, around 8,000 people demonstrated in Zwentendorf on the day of the last (but cancelled) public discussion in June 1977. The government's surprising move to call a referendum in 1978 reopened the formal decision-making process. After its success in the referendum, the anti-nuclear movement demobilized for some years but was revitalized by attempts of the Social Democrats to reverse the referendum's result (Müller, this volume). Protest mobilization peaked around Chernobyl when these attempts came to a sudden end.

In the early 1990s, Preglau (1994: 59) characterized the Austrian anti-nuclear movement as 'a victim of its own success'. However, our data highlight that the days of anti-nuclear protests in Austria were not yet over (Figures 4.4 and 4.5). In contrast to Germany and Switzerland, the strong peaks in the 1990s and 2000s do not reflect protests against domestic policy decisions and are not really fuelled by the events in Fukushima. Rather, large-scale protests were all directed against nuclear power plants in neighbouring countries, especially in the Czech Republic and in Slovakia (Müller, this volume).

The renaissance of the nuclear energy issue from the late 1990s did not trigger a general return of anti-nuclear forces to the streets. In Europe and the United States, anti-nuclear protests were most central in the early phases of the struggle over nuclear energy in the 1970s and early 1980s—the period most studied by social movement scholars. Comparing the countries covered by this book, *mass* mobilization in the protest arena was strongest in Germany at the time, followed by Switzerland, and weakest in Italy and Sweden. Austria, the Netherlands, and France are intermediate cases (Rucht 1995). From the 1990s, protest politics was a very central part of the politics of nuclear energy only in Germany. Although Austria and Switzerland saw peaks in mobilization levels more recently, these peaks are either related to nuclear power plants in neighbouring countries (Austria) or restricted to the latest episode after Fukushima (Switzerland).

Our brief account of anti-nuclear protest development provides strong support for the claim that its explanation requires to pay attention also to the close interactions between protest politics and the activities of political parties in more institutionalized political arenas. As argued in the introduction to this chapter, the institutional openness of the political system in combination with the Social Democrats' responses seem to be key factors explaining the strength of anti-nuclear opposition on the streets. However, only the institutionalization of anti-nuclear protest in the form of successful Green parties leads to a persistence of anti-nuclear protest in later phases. Let us now turn to the institutionalization of this opposition by focusing on the development of Green parties in the same set of countries.

4.4 GREEN PARTIES

Green parties are the institutionalized actors most critical to the use of nuclear energy. Given their roots in the New Social Movements of the 1970s and 1980s all Green parties have linkages to anti-nuclear protests. However, the nature of this relationship varies. In some countries, actors of the anti-nuclear movements were directly involved in the founding of Green parties and this issue was of central, if not unique, importance in the parties' early phases: especially the Green parties in (West) Germany, Austria, Sweden, and France belong to this group (Rootes 1995: 237). Similar to Austria and Sweden, in Italy a referendum on nuclear energy was the crucial event in the early history of the Greens as it led to an unprecedented degree of unity and ultimately enabled the founding of a first national party organization (Rhodes 1995: 171). In Switzerland the Greens' history is not built on a 'defining moment' of anti-nuclear protest (see Seitz 2008), reflecting perhaps the unique decentralized nature of Swiss politics. Finally, in the Netherlands, GroenLinks, a merger of several already existing left parties, was comparatively less focused on nuclear energy and ecological concerns in general. Nevertheless, opposition to nuclear energy is a common denominator of Green party politics throughout Europe, which is also reflected in the Charter of the European Green Party:

> Specifically as regards nuclear energy, Greens stand for a nuclear-free Europe, because of the civil and military threats it poses, because of the burden it puts onto the future generations and because of the security apparatus it needs.
> (European Green Party 2006)

This section provides a short overview of the Green parties' role in the political systems of the seven countries covered by case studies in this book. We compare the Greens' electoral history since the mid-1970s and their stepwise incorporation into institutionalized politics. With respect to the sub-national level of politics we restrict this short exploration to the three federal states dealt with in the subsequent chapters: Austria, Germany, and Switzerland. As argued above, such countries provide a particular favourable political opportunity structure for new parties seeking entry to the party system and aiming for policy impact.

4.4.1 The Greens' Development in Comparative Perspective

Comparing the Greens' development and impact on national (and regional) politics first requires the identification of national parties belonging to this party family. In some of the seven countries this is an easy task, as Green activists very early founded national party organizations which developed in a rather stable way (e.g. Sweden) or where internal disputes such as the famous Fundi–Realo Controversy (Doherty 1992) did not lead to relevant divisions (e.g. Germany). In other countries, however, the Green movements' party history has been shaped by internal struggles and competing Green parties up to the 1990s (e.g. Switzerland, Austria, France).

To identify Green parties, we begin by following the simplest criterion of party family classification (Mair and Mudde 1998): going by *party name*, and adding further information on transnational cooperation and aspects of policy and ideology. Using various sources we provide a short comparative overview of the Greens' development in the seven countries. To structure this exploration, we follow Pedersen (1982) who defined various 'thresholds' a party has to pass during its lifespan. The *threshold of declaration* refers to a party's announcement to participate in elections. As the legal requirements for participating in elections (*threshold of authorization*) are quite low throughout Europe, we put these two initial thresholds together. Next, the *threshold of representation* is the barrier that new parties have to cross to win seats in the legislatures. For this threshold, the country differences are huge. The electoral systems range from majority systems (France, Italy in several elections), and systems of proportional representation with high effective thresholds (partly Switzerland and Germany to a lesser degree) to systems with low entry barriers (Netherlands, Austria). The final *threshold of relevance* is defined as participation in government as proposed by Müller-Rommel (2002).

Table 4.4 displays some important variation in the Greens' development. Already in 1975, Switzerland was the first country to see a Green party running in national elections; it was soon followed by France. The other countries came behind, with Italy (1987) and the Netherlands (1989) coming last. In Italy, this was due to internal discussions on whether to participate in institutionalized politics at all and the local activists' fear of losing their autonomy, which is why only in 1986 a party organization was established on the national level (Diani 1989). In the Netherlands, by contrast, the issues mobilized by the New Social Movements of the 1970s were already incorporated into party competition by various new left parties. Only after their secular decline beginning in the early 1980s was a new Green party founded, as a merger of these predecessors (Lucardie 2006). Its name—GroenLinks (Green Left)—is still reminiscent of the Dutch Greens' particular history. The newly founded De Groenen, by contrast, remained irrelevant.

The *threshold of representation*—winning seats in the national parliament—is the second major step in the Greens' development. This threshold was mostly passed in the 1980s; only the Swiss Greens were successful as early as 1979, whereas the French had to wait until 1997. In France, the majoritarian electoral system is obviously a major challenge for small parties without regional strongholds. But even in 1986, when the Socialists temporarily introduced proportional representation (to weaken the Conservatives), the Greens did not win any seat. Parties that once crossed the threshold of parliamentary representation might be recognized as relevant actors as they receive more publicity and very often also (higher) state subsidies. Continuous parliamentary representation is therefore a major factor for a new party's stabilization. In most cases, the Greens have held on to parliamentary representation after their first success. However, the Swedish Greens lost representation after their first term when the election was overshadowed by an economic crisis, and the Italian Greens are currently without parliamentary representation after joining radical left-wing electoral coalitions in the last two elections. In addition, the West German Greens lost all seats in 1990 but were substituted by their East German counterparts with whom they later merged.

For the last threshold, participation in national government, parties have to become a relevant force in party politics. This was achieved in four of the seven

Table 4.4. Three Major Thresholds in the Development of Green Parties on the National Level

Country	Name of party (as of 2014)	I Declaration and authorisation	II Representation		III Relevance	Current electoral strength
		First candidature[a]	First seats won[a]	Continuous? (years without)	Participation in government	% of votes (year of election)
Austria	Die Grünen	1983	1986	Yes	—	12.4 (2013)
France	Europe Écologie-Les Verts	1978	1997	Yes	1997–2002; 2012–2014	5.5[c] (2012)
Germany	Bündnis 90/Die Grünen	1980	1983	Yes[b]	1998–2005	8.4 (2013)
Italy	Federazione dei Verdi	1987	1987	No (since 2008)	1996–2001; 2006–2008	2.1[d] (2006)
Netherlands	GroenLinks	1989	1989	Yes	—	2.3 (2012)
Sweden	Miljöpartiet de gröna	1981	1988	No (1991–1994)	2014–	6.9 (2014)
Switzerland	Grüne Partei der Schweiz	1975	1979	Yes	—	8.4 (2011)

This table only includes members of the European Green Party (see main text). Candidature, representation, and current electoral strength always refers to the lower chamber of national parliaments.

[a] In several countries predecessor parties fielded the first candidates and won the first seats which is why the literature on Green parties sometimes reports different years.
[b] The West German Greens were not represented from 1990–4 but the East German Bündnis 90 was. In 1993 the two parties merged.
[c] Percentage of votes won in the first round of the parliamentary election.
[d] For 2013, the most recent election, no data are available because the Greens were part of an electoral coalition (Civil Revolution) that received 2.2% of the votes but no seats. The same applies for the election in 2008, where the Greens joined another electoral coalition (Rainbow Left) which received 3.1% of the votes but no seats.

Sources: For the most recent election results see the European Election Database (http://www.nsd.uib.no/european_election_database/). All other data are based on the literature cited in the main text plus numerous additional sources, including the websites of the parties.

countries: for one and parts of a second legislative period in France, and for two in Germany (continuously) and Italy (with an interruption). Since 2014 also the Swedish Greens belong to the group of governing parties. Especially in Germany, but also in Belgium and Finland (two countries not covered by case studies in this book), opposition to nuclear energy played a prominent role in the Greens' experience as governing party. In Germany, the red-green government decided Germany's (first) phasing out of nuclear energy. In Finland, by contrast, the Greens resigned from government during their second term in 2002 in response to a government decision to build a new nuclear power plant (Sundberg and Wilhelmsson 2008) and again in 2014 for similar reasons. In the other cases where Greens participated in national governments, nuclear energy played a much less prominent role. The French Greens managed to include several measures against the further development of nuclear energy in their coalition agreement with the Socialists (Boy 2002: 66) but a phasing out à la Germany was not a realistic option (Evrard 2012). In Belgium, a conflict emerged over the export of nuclear material to Pakistan. However, this debate was framed by the Greens' fear of its potential military use (Buelens and Deschouwer 2002: 124). Finally, in Italy, nuclear energy was a non-issue during the Greens' (first) period in government (Biorcio 2002).

The current electoral strength of the Greens displays huge differences between the seven countries covered by this book. Only one party, the Austrian, recently crossed the 10 per cent mark. The German, Swiss, Swedish, and French Greens constitute a group of parties with a medium level of electoral support. The Dutch and Italian Greens, by contrast, are definitely less successful in the electoral arena.

Note that up to about the early 1990s, additional Green parties participated in party competition on the national level. However, by now in most countries, the Greens' party family is represented by one party only. In the Netherlands, in Switzerland and recently in France, by contrast, the established Greens have to face Green competitors. These are not members of the European Greens but belong to the Green family when referring to other criteria such as policy and ideology (see Mair und Mudde 1998). In the Netherlands, the Partij voor de Dieren (Party for the Animals) competed for the first time in 2003 and has been represented in parliament since 2006. Even though this party focuses almost exclusively on animal rights, its election manifesto also includes opposition to nuclear energy.[11] In Switzerland, the Grünliberale Partei Schweiz (Green-Liberal Party Switzerland) is a split-off from the established Green party and has developed a more liberal profile opposing the left orientation of the Swiss Greens (Seitz 2008: 33–5). Opposition to nuclear energy, however, is also part of the Green-Liberals' programme.[12]

Figure 4.6 shows the Greens' electoral results from 1975 to 2014. To assess the overall strength of the Green parties, the country figures include the parties shown in Table 4.3 (including their predecessors) and the two new forces mentioned above.

---

[11] See <http://www.partyfortheanimals.nl> last accessed May 2015.
[12] See the party's website: <http://www.grunliberale.ch/unsere-positionen.html> last accessed May 2015.

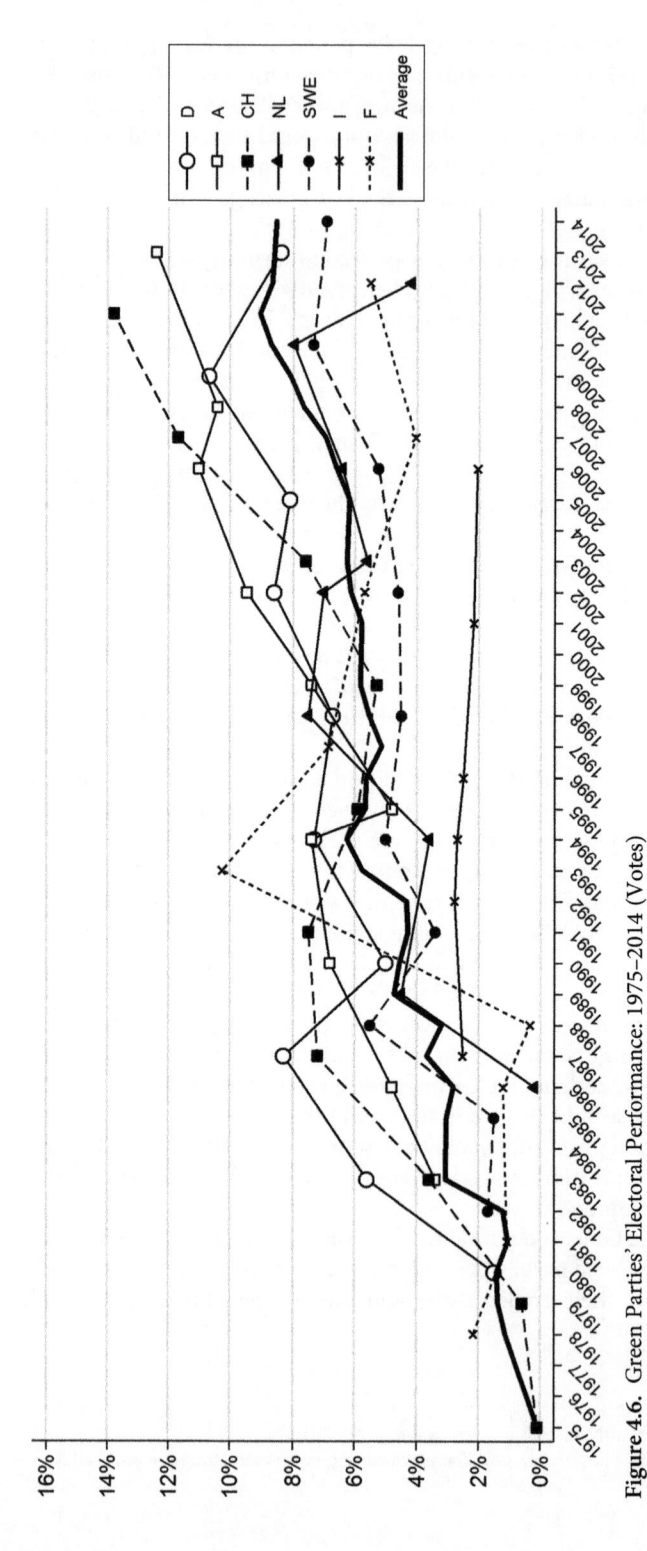

Figure 4.6. Green Parties' Electoral Performance: 1975–2014 (Votes)

Note: Percentages for France refer to the results of the first round (and up to 1993 to various Green parties and candidates which are put together in all sources available), for Germany the Zweitstimmen (second votes, i.e. votes for parties) are included, in Italy the data always refer to the proportional part of the elections.

Sources: See Table 4.4.

4.4.2 Green Parties' Development on the Regional Level

Local and regional levels of government were very important access points, especially in the early phase of the Greens' development. Green parties often achieved their electoral breakthrough at the sub-national level. On the one hand, it is less demanding building up a party organization regionally rather than nationally. On the other hand, the stakes are lower in the game, making voters more willing to vote for new parties, and established political parties more likely to build coalitions with new entrants. Such sub-national coalitions can function as models for subsequent alliances on the national level. Thus federal states provide more favourable political opportunity structures for new challenger parties as the Greens were in the 1970s and 1980s. For this reason we focus on the Greens' sub-national performance in the three classic federal states covered by case studies in this book: Austria, Germany, and Switzerland. The actual degree of federalism heavily varies between these countries, which is why winning seats in regional parliaments and participating in governments has a different importance for the Greens' impact on policy-making. According to the Regional Authority Index (RAI), a formula to assess the strength of federalism with the empirical range among forty-two countries from 0 (most centralized) to 29.3 (most decentralized) (Hooghe et al. 2008), Germany—perhaps surprisingly—is the most decentralized country (29.3), followed by Switzerland (19.5), and Austria (18.0).[13] Similarly, in the index proposed by Lijphart (1999: 189) Germany and Switzerland belong to the top group of 'federal and decentralized' countries, whereas Austria is ranked one category below ('federal and centralized').

In Switzerland and Germany, the Greens won first seats in the legislatures in the late 1970s, in Austria in 1984. At the end of 2014 Greens were represented in all regional parliaments in Austria and Germany. In Switzerland, they had seats in twenty-two out of twenty-five legislatures with partisan elections.

A further step towards institutionalization refers to the Greens' participation in regional governments. The three federal systems not only differ in the political power of their sub-national units but also with respect to the system of government building, which is an important aspect when comparing the success or failure of Green parties in this arena. In Germany, government formation follows a standard parliamentary procedure where parties build majority governments in most cases, either as single-party governments or as coalitions. Hence Green parties typically serve as junior coalition partners—very often together with the moderate Left. In Switzerland, the members of the regional executives are directly elected by the electorate which corresponds to a presidential system of government (Vatter 2002: 41–115). A kind of coalition-building takes place in advance as the parties have to decide whether to field their own candidates or support other parties' aspirants. Finally, Austria has had two types of regional governments in the period observed. Until the 1990s, in seven out of nine Länder party representation in government had to be proportional to their strength in parliament. Within these consociational or power-sharing governments, however, parties

---

[13] The other countries covered by this book are scored as follows: France 16.0, Italy 22.7, Netherlands 14.5, and Sweden 10.0. Hence, Italy has a higher score than Austria.

often built a quasi-coalition, especially to elect the governor (Landeshauptmann) and decide on key issues such as the budget. Two Länder abandoned the proportional system in the 1990s so that now four out of nine have a standard, majority-based system with single-party governments or coalitions. Despite these huge differences the German (1985) and Swiss Greens (1986) nevertheless joined the first regional governments almost in parallel. The Austrians had to wait until 1994 (consociational government) and 2010 (majority government) respectively.

4.4.3 Cross-Sectional Relations between Movements, Parties, and Institutional Openness

The size of protest events clearly coincides with the aggregate level of an adverse public opinion to nuclear energy in Austria, Germany, and Switzerland. These countries also have the best performing Green parties in Europe. When Green parties were running in elections under very unfavourable conditions (for instance, a majoritarian electoral system such as in France) this did not cause the anti-nuclear movement to abandon the protest channel. These strategic choices demonstrate the complex interplay between institutional structures (electoral system, federal system) and actors' strategies over time.

We now explore our hypotheses with bivariate scatterplots. We follow Lieberman (2005) in determining the role of our selected cases on-the-line and off-the-line (i.e. cases that are on or near the fitted relation, and cases where the relationship is clearly under- or overestimated given the value combination of the country). Our major variable of interest is the performance of Green parties.[14]

Figure 4.7 accounts for the disproportionality of the electoral system at the respective elections[15] and for whether the country is a federal system. We present three temporal snapshots: the last election before Chernobyl, the first election after Chernobyl, and the most recent election. The openness of the electoral system is operationalized by the Gallagher (dis)proportionality index (Gallagher and Mitchell 2005). We consider Austria, Belgium, Germany, and Switzerland as federal systems and all other countries in our sample as unitary.

We can corroborate the expected negative relationship between the disproportionality of the system and the Green parties' vote share in Western Europe. Yet in the period before Chernobyl the electoral system explains only about 10 per cent of the variance, whereas the relationship is quite pronounced after Chernobyl and Fukushima. The Netherlands and Italy clearly stand out as special cases: although they had nuclear power programmes, Green parties were much less successful than one would expect given the operating PR electoral systems. In contrast, Great Britain fully meets the theoretical expectation: the most disproportional system

---

[14] Note that (a) in the case of Portugal the Green party 'Os verdes' always runs in an electoral alliance with the Communist party; (b) the Green parties in Greece and Spain are extremely fragmented into splinter groups; (c) the Danish Greens are irrelevant (they took part in elections only in 1987, 1988, and 1990). The red-green alliance is not considered as a Green party.

[15] Note that this is the first representation of the success of Green niche parties along varying electoral systems. Neither Meguid (2005) nor Ezrow (2010) present detailed results for Green parties.

The Conflict over Nuclear Energy 91

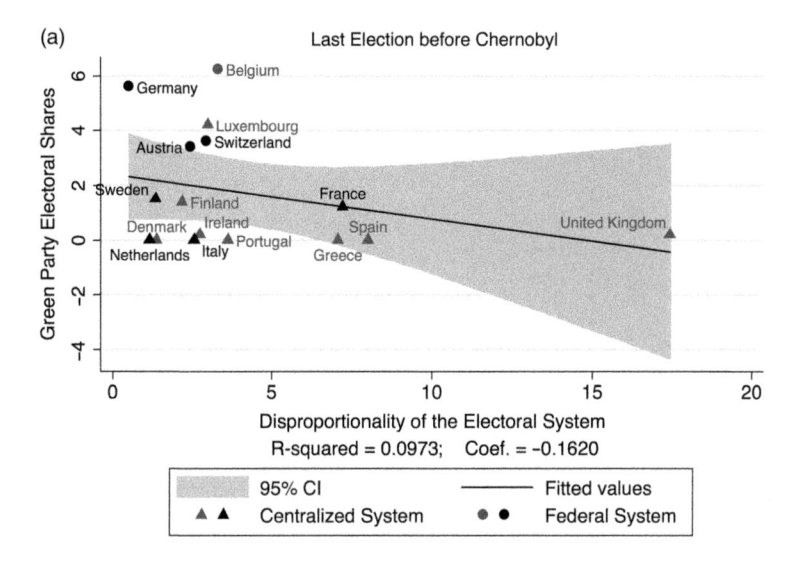

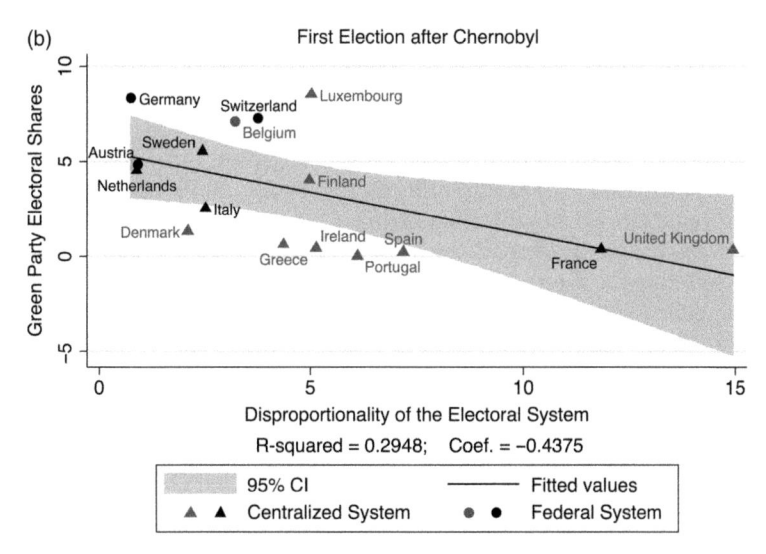

Figure 4.7. (a–c). Disproportionality and Green Party Shares in Three Different Elections
Note: Most recent election results as per 2012. Countries printed in bold are treated in detail in our country chapters.

prevented the parliamentary entry of the Greens until 2010 and discouraged potential Green voters to cast their vote for Green candidates.

Our second indicator of openness—federalism—clearly interacts with the electoral system variable: the four federal countries display higher Green party electoral shares as we would expect by simply accounting for the electoral system. Countries such as Germany, Switzerland, Luxembourg, Belgium, and Austria are

(c) Most Recent Election

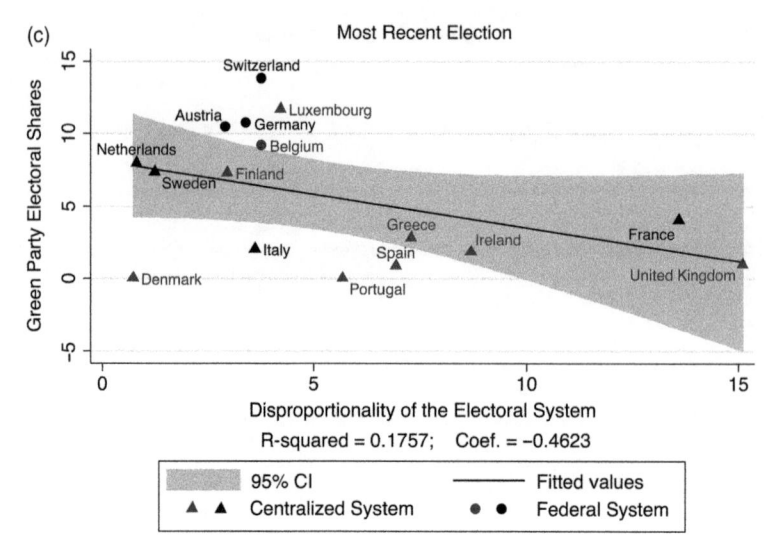

[Scatter plot showing Green Party Electoral Shares vs Disproportionality of the Electoral System, with countries labeled: Switzerland, Austria, Luxembourg, Germany, Belgium, Netherlands, Sweden, Finland, Greece, Italy, Spain, Ireland, France, Denmark, Portugal, United Kingdom. R-squared = 0.1757; Coef. = −0.4623. Legend: 95% CI, Fitted values, Centralized System, Federal System.]

Figure 4.7. Continued

off the line. Note that this effect is maintained throughout the whole observation period. Even more impressive is the negative relationship in the elections just after Chernobyl: the disproportionality variable 'explains' nearly 30 per cent of the variance, thus indicating a clear relevant impact. Yet, this influence weakens the more time passes after the event: in the most recent elections, the R^2 is down to 17.5 per cent. Finally, not all cases conform to the openness/electoral system expectations. Despite having a highly open electoral system, Denmark is very much below-the-line: Green parties show a quite bad performance. This is easy to understand. In addition to other parties owning important Green issues, the country's oil and gas and, more recently, wind resources, have led to early abandoning of the nuclear energy option.

4.5 CONCLUSION

This chapter has looked at the 'natural enemies' of nuclear power: concerned citizens, protest movements, and Green parties. The basic idea is that the presence and strength of these factors is potentially crucial for the development of nuclear power policies in European democracies. We have seen that energy import dependency does not lead to a public opinion favourable to nuclear energy. Although the relevance of nuclear energy in a country's energy mix has a positive effect on its acceptance by citizens, it does not determine public opinion. Hence, there is ample room for political argument and the moulding of public opinion by political actors.

Our exploration of comparative and national public opinion surveys since the late 1970s has identified some general trends and important attitudinal differences towards nuclear energy. The trends move against nuclear energy after Chernobyl, and return to pre-accident levels soon thereafter, followed by a steady increase in discomfort with nuclear energy until the early years of the twenty-first century. Then the concerns slightly relaxed, but even before Fukushima opposition towards nuclear energy increased again. In terms of attitudinal differences we see an enormous range—from countries where those in favour of nuclear energy clearly outnumber those who oppose it, to countries where the majority of citizens reject nuclear energy and only a small minority are in favour. The countries employing nuclear energy are generally friendlier towards it, with supporters outnumbering opponents. Yet in Germany, Switzerland, Spain, and above all Austria solid majorities of citizens opposed nuclear energy even before Fukushima.

Our comparative assessment of protest movements against nuclear energy has again revealed large country differences. Germany stands out as the country that upheld the highest levels of protest activity since the mid-1970s. While several countries had individual periods of more intense street protest, Switzerland clearly comes second over the entire period, in particular with new waves of anti-nuclear protest mobilization in the context of the relevant referendums. Given the case that France also saw widespread protest at an early stage, it seems that especially those countries with many reactors under construction and in use actually induced such heavy campaigns. However, institutional factors together with the strategies of incumbent parties led to no party permanently representing these attitudes in parliament in France.

Neither citizens who adopt a negative attitude towards nuclear energy nor sizeable protests on the streets alone are sufficient to cause anti-nuclear policy change. Rather, such mass attitudes and activist behaviours are factors that are both nourished and used by political parties in their interactions. While established political parties occasionally ride the anti-nuclear wave to foster their electoral and office goals, Green parties are most committed to anti-nuclear policy-making. Our comparative assessment of Green party development singles out the German one as performing best, winning sizeable vote shares and serving in government at both the national and Land levels. Green parties are also relatively strong in Switzerland, Austria, and Sweden. In these countries the 'natural enemies' of nuclear energy are thus most entrenched in the party system. It is here where, a priori, we would consider policy reversals and a turn away from nuclear energy most likely. Again, such outcomes cannot be taken for granted, as much depends on how the established parties play the game. The country chapters that follow study these processes.[16]

---

[16] This chapter is the result of a collaborative effort of data collection. Measurement of public opinion in the selected countries and in the EU generally relies on Eurobarometer data assembled by S. Brouard, I. Guinaudeau, and P. W. Thurner. S. Hutter investigated the occurrence, size and timing of anti-nuclear protest movements, while the occurence, evolution and involvement of Green parties in Europe has been investigated by M. Dolezal. We would like to thank Christopher Rootes and Stefaan Walgrave for kindly providing us with their protest data. Furthermore, we thank Silke Breimaier, Lorenz Hüttenhofer, Ann-Kristin Kölln, Isabelle Plessis, Tobias Schwarzbözl and Mirjam Selzer for their research assistance.

REFERENCES

Adams, James, and Zeynep Somer-Topcu (2009). 'Do Parties Adjust their Policies in Response to Rival Parties' Policy Shifts? Spatial Theory and the Dynamics of Party Competition in Twenty-Five Postwar Democracies.' *British Journal of Political Science*, 39(4): 825–46.

Biorcio, Roberto (2002). 'Italy', in Ferdinand Müller-Rommel and Thomas Poguntke (eds), *Green Parties in National Governments*. London: Frank Cass, 39–62.

Boy, Daniel (2002). 'France', in Ferdinand Müller-Rommel and Thomas Poguntke (eds), *Green Parties in National Governments*. London: Frank Cass, 63–77.

Buelens, Joe, and Chris Deschouwer (2002). 'The Belgian Greens in Government', in Ferdinand Müller-Rommel and Thomas Poguntke (eds), *Environmental Politics*, 11(1): 112–32.

Chandler, William M., and Marsha A. Chandler (1987). 'Federalism and Political Parties.' *European Journal of Political Economy*, 3(1–2): 87–109.

Cox, Gary (1990). 'Centripetal and Centrifugal Incentives in Electoral Systems.' *American Journal of Political Science*, 34(4): 903–35.

Diani, Mario (1989). 'Italy: The "Liste Verdi"', in Ferdinand Müller-Rommel (ed.), *New Politics in Western Europe: The Rise and Success of Green Parties and Alternative Lists*. Boulder, CO: Westview Press, 113–22.

Diani, Mario and Hein-Anton van der Heijden (1994). 'Anti-Nuclear Movements Across States: Explaining Patterns of Development', in Helena Flam (ed.), *States and Anti-Nuclear Movements*. Edinburgh: Edinburgh University Press, 355–82.

Doherty, Brian (1992). 'The Fundi-Realo Controversy: An Analysis of Four European Green Parties.' *Environmental Politics*, 1(1): 95–120.

Dolezal, Martin, and Swen Hutter (2007). 'Konsensdemokratie unter Druck? Politischer Protest in Österreich, 1975–2005.' *Österreichische Zeitschrift für Politikwissenschaft*, 36(3): 338–52.

Duyvendak, Jan Willem (1995). *The Power of Politics: New Social Movements in France*. Boulder, CO: Westview Press.

Duyvendak, Jan Willem, and Ruud Koopmans (1995). 'The Political Construction of the Nuclear Energy Issue', in Hanspeter Kriesi, Ruud Koopmans, Jan Willem Duyvendak, and Marco Giugni (eds), *New Social Movements in Western Europe: A Comparative Analysis*. Minneapolis: University of Minnesota Press, 145–64.

European Green Party (2006). *The Charter of the European Greens*. Adopted at 2nd EGP Congress, Geneva, 13–14 Oct.

Evrard, Aurélien (2012). 'Political Parties and Policy Change: Explaining the Impact of French and German Greens on Energy Policy.' *Journal of Comparative Policy Analysis*, 14(4): 275–91.

Ezrow, Lawrence (2008). 'Parties' Policy Programmes and the Dog that Didn't Bark: No Evidence that Proportional Systems Promote Extreme Party Positioning.' *British Journal of Political Science*, 38(3): 479–97.

Ezrow, Lawrence (2010). *Linking Citizens and Parties: How Electoral Systems Matter for Political Representation*. Oxford: Oxford University Press.

Flam, Helena (1994). *States and Anti-Nuclear Movements*. Edinburgh: Edinburgh University Press.

Flam, Helena, and Andrew Jamison (1994). 'The Swedish Confrontation over Nuclear Energy: A Case of a Timid Anti-Nuclear Opposition', in Helena Flam (ed.), *States and Anti-Nuclear Movements*. Edinburgh: Edinburgh University Press, 163–200.

Gallagher, Michael, and Paul Mitchell (eds) (2005). *The Politics of Electoral Systems*. Oxford: Oxford University Press.

Giugni, Marco (2004). *Social Protest and Policy Change. Ecology, Antinuclear, and Peace Movements in Comparative Perspective*. Lanham, MD: Rowman & Littlefield.

Giugni, Marco, and Florence Passy (1999). *Zwischen Konflikt und Kooperation: die Integration der sozialen Bewegungen in der Schweiz*. Chur: Rüegger.

Harmel, Robert, and John D. Robertson (1985). 'Formation and Success of New Parties: A Cross-National Analysis.' *International Political Science Review*, 6(4): 501–23.

Hooghe, Liesbet, Arjan H. Schakel, and Gary Marks (2008). 'Appendix B: Country and Regional Scores.' *Regional and Federal Studies*, 18(2–3): 259–74.

Hug, Simon (2001). *Altering Party Systems*. Ann Arbor: University of Michigan Press.

Hutter, Swen (2014). *Protesting Culture and Economics in Western Europe: New Cleavages in Left and Right Politics*. Minneapolis: University of Minnesota Press.

Hutter, Swen, and Marco Giugni (2009). 'Protest Politics in a Changing Political Context: Switzerland, 1975–2005.' *Swiss Political Science Review*, 15(3): 427–61.

Kitschelt, Herbert P. (1986a). 'Political Opportunity Structures and Political Protest: Anti-Nuclear Movements in Four Democracies.' *British Journal of Political Science*, 16(1): 57–85.

Kitschelt, Herbert P. (1986b). 'Four Theories of Public Policy-Making and Fast Breeder Reactor Development in France, the United States, and West Germany.' *International Organization*, 40(1): 65–104.

Kitschelt, Herbert P. (1988). 'Left-Libertarian Parties: Explaining Innovation in Competitive Party Systems.' *World Politics*, 40(2): 194–234.

Kok, Franz, and Christian Schaller (1986). 'Restrukturierung der Energiepolitik durch neue soziale Bewegungen? Die Beispiele Zwentendorf und Hainburg.' *Österreichische Zeitschrift für Politikwissenschaft*, 15(1): 61–73.

Kolb, Felix (2007). *Protest and Opportunities: The Political Outcomes of Social Movements*. Frankfurt and New York: Campus.

Koopmans, Ruud (1996). 'New Social Movements and Changes in Political Participation in Western Europe.' *West European Politics*, 19(1): 28–50.

Koopmans, Ruud (1998). 'The Use of Protest Event Data in Comparative Research: Cross-National Comparability, Sampling Methods and Robustness', in Dieter Rucht, Ruud Koopmans, and Friedhelm Neidhardt (eds), *Acts of Dissent: New Developments in the Study of Protest*. Berlin: Edition Sigma, 90–110.

Koopmans, Ruud, and Dieter Rucht (2002). 'Protest Event Analysis', in Bert Klandermans and Suzanne Staggenborg (eds), *Methods of Social Movement Research*. Minneapolis: University of Minnesota Press, 231–59.

Kriesi, Hanspeter (1995). 'Alliance Structures', in Hanspeter Kriesi, Ruud Koopmans, Jan Willem Duyvendak, and Marco Giugni (eds), *New Social Movements in Western Europe: A Comparative Analysis*. Minneapolis: University of Minnesota Press, 53–81.

Kriesi, Hanspeter (2004). 'Political Context and Opportunity', in David A. Snow, Sarah A. Soule, and Hanspeter Kriesi (eds), *The Blackwell Companion to Social Movements*. Oxford: Blackwell Publishing, 67–90.

Kriesi, Hanspeter, Edgar Grande, Martin Dolezal, Marc Helbling, Dominic Hoeglinger, Swen Hutter, and Bruno Wüest (2012). *Political Conflict in Western Europe*. Cambridge: Cambridge University Press.

Kriesi, Hanspeter, Ruud Koopmans, Jan Willem Duyvendak, and Marco Giugni (1995). *New Social Movements in Western Europe: A Comparative Analysis*. Minneapolis: University of Minnesota Press.

Kriesi, Hanspeter, René Levy, Gilbert Ganguillet, and Heinz Zwicky (1981). *Politische Aktivierung in der Schweiz. 1945–1978*. Diessenhofen: Rüegger.

Lijphart, Arend (1999). *Patterns of Democracy: Government Forms and Performance in Thirty-Six Countries*. New Haven: Yale University Press.

Lucardie, Paul (2006). 'Das Parteiensystem der Niederlande', in Oskar Niedermayer, Richard Stöss, and Melanie Haas (eds), *Die Parteiensysteme Westeuropas*. Wiesbaden: VS Verlag für Sozialwissenschaften, 331–50.

Lieberman, Evan S. (2005). 'Nested Analysis as a Mixed-Method Strategy for Comparative Research.' *American Political Science Review*, 99(3): 435–52.

McAdam, Doug (1996). 'Conceptual Origins, Current Problems, Future Directions', in Doug McAdam, John D. McCarthy, and Mayer N. Zald (eds), *Comparative Perspectives on Social Movements: Political Opportunities, Mobilizing Structures, and Cultural Framings*. Cambridge: Cambridge University Press, 23–40.

Mair, Peter, and Cas Mudde (1998). 'The Party Family and its Study.' *Annual Review of Political Science*, 1(1): 211–29.

Meguid, Bonnie M. (2005). 'Competition between Unequals: The Role of Mainstream Party Strategies in Niche Party Success.' *American Political Science Review*, 99(3): 347–59.

Meguid, Bonnie M. (2008). *Party Competition between Unequals: Strategies and Electoral Fortunes in Western Europe*. Cambridge: Cambridge University Press.

Meyer, David S. (2004). 'Protest and Political Opportunities.' *Annual Review of Sociology*, 30: 125–45.

Müller-Rommel, Ferdinand (2002). 'The Lifespan and the Political Performance of Green Parties in Western Europe', in Ferdinand Müller-Rommel and Thomas Poguntke (eds), *Green Parties in National Governments*. London: Frank Cass, 1–16.

Pedersen, Mogens N. (1982). 'Towards a New Typology of Party Lifespans and Minor Parties.' *Scandinavian Political Studies*, 5(1): 1–16.

Preglau, Max (1994). 'The State and the Anti-Nuclear Power Movement in Austria', in Helena Flam (ed.), *States and Anti-Nuclear Movements*. Edinburgh: Edinburgh University Press, 37–69.

Rhodes, Martin (1995). 'Italy: Greens in an Overcrowded Political System', in Dick Richardson and Christopher Rootes (eds), *The Green Challenge: The Development of Green Parties in Europe*. London: Routledge, 168–92.

Rootes, Christopher (1995). 'Environmental Consciousness, Institutional Structures and Political Competition in the Formation and Development of Green Parties', in Dick Richardson and Christopher Rootes (eds), *The Green Challenge: The Development of Green Parties in Europe*. London: Routledge, 232–52.

Rootes, Christopher (2003). *Environmental Protest in Western Europe*. Oxford: Oxford University Press.

Rucht, Dieter (1994a). 'The Anti-Nuclear Power Movement and the State in France', in Helena Flam (ed.), *States and Anti-Nuclear Movements*. Edinburgh: Edinburgh University Press, 129–62.

Rucht, Dieter (1994b). *Modernisierung und neue soziale Bewegungen. Deutschland, Frankreich und USA im Vergleich*. Frankfurt: Campus Verlag.

Rucht, Dieter (1995). 'The Impact of the Anti-Nuclear Power Movements in International Comparison', in Martin Bauer (ed.), *Resistance to New Technology: Nuclear Power, Information Technology and Biotechnology*. Cambridge: Cambridge University Press, 279–91.

Rucht, Dieter (2008). 'Anti-Atomkraftbewegung', in Roland Roth and Dieter Rucht (eds), *Die sozialen Bewegungen in Deutschland seit 1945: Ein Handbuch*. Frankfurt andNew York: Campus, 245–66.

Rüdig, Wolfgang (1990). *A World Survey of Opposition to Nuclear Energy*. Harlow: Longman.

Seitz, Werner (2008). '"Melonengrüne" und "Gurkengrüne": Die Geschichte der Grünen in der Schweiz', in Matthias Baer and Werner Seitz (eds), *Die Grünen in der Schweiz: Ihre Politik. Ihre Geschichte. Ihre Basis*. Zürich: Rüegger Verlag, 15–37.

Soroka, Stuart N., and Christopher Wlezien (2010). *Degrees of Democracy: Politics, Public Opinion, and Policy*. Cambridge: Cambridge University Press.

Stimson, James A., Michael B. Mackuen, and Robert S. Erikson (1995). 'Dynamic Representation.' *American Political Science Review*, 89(3), 543–65.

Stimson, James A., Michael B. Mackuen and Robert S. Erikson (2002). *The Macro Polity*. Cambridge: Cambridge University Press.

Sundberg, Jan, and Niklas Wilhelmsson (2008). 'Moving from Movement to Government: The Transformation of the Finnish Greens', in Kris Deschouwer (ed.), *New Parties in Government: In Power for the First Time*. London: Routledge, 121–36.

Tarrow, Sidney (1989). *Democracy and Disorder: Protest and Politics in Italy 1965-1974*. Oxford: Oxford University Press.

Tilly, Charles, Louise Tilly, and Richard Tilly (1975). *The Rebellious Century, 1830-1930*. Cambridge, MA: Harvard University Press.

van der Heijden, Hein-Anton (1994). 'The Dutch Nuclear Energy Conflict 1973–1989', in Helena Flam (ed.), *States and Anti-Nuclear Movements*. Edinburgh: Edinburgh University Press, 101–28.

Vatter, Adrian (2002). *Kantonale Demokratien im Vergleich. Entstehungsgründe, Interaktionen und Wirkungen politischer Institutionen in den Schweizer Kantonen. Mit einem Vorwort von Arend Lijphart*. Opladen: Leske + Budrich.

Walgrave, Stefaan, and Rens Vliegenthart (2012). 'The Complex Agenda-Setting Power of Protest. Demonstrations, Media, Parliament, Government, and Legislation in Belgium, 1993-2000.' *Mobilization*, 17(2): 129–56.

5

Austria

Rejecting Nuclear Energy—From Party Competition Accident to State Doctrine

Wolfgang C. Müller

5.1 INTRODUCTION: THE RELEVANCE OF THE NUCLEAR POWER ISSUE IN NATIONAL POLITICS

Austria was the first country to ban nuclear energy (in 1978) and it has never reversed this decision. Yet for this book's research question, the Austrian case is a fascinating one; the 1978 decision did not remove the nuclear issue from the agenda, but was followed by a decade of attempts at policy reversal. Had the accident of Chernobyl not intervened in 1986 Austria might have gone nuclear in the late 1980s. The construction of the nuclear power station in Zwentendorf, that despite being completed was never turned on, is a major event in the narrative of post-war Austrian history precisely because it remained on the agenda for about a decade and hence alternative outcomes would have been feasible. The result of banning nuclear energy can be interpreted as 'accident' caused by party competition. From this perspective, abandoning nuclear energy resulted from a collective decision where the outcome did not represent the parliamentary majority's policy preferences. In policy terms, it might have also failed to represent the electorate. The latter statement may seem paradoxical, as the decision was actually made by referendum; yet it is possible that some voters cast their vote to bring down a government they disliked rather than to decide on the specific issue. This is one possible interpretation of the available evidence that was popular among political decision-makers before Chernobyl. Yet by now Austrians seem to have firmly made up their minds on nuclear energy. Indeed, the country remained unaffected by the revival that nuclear energy experienced in the Western world in the early years of the new millennium. Nevertheless, nuclear energy has kept returning as a prominent item of the domestic political agenda. While the earlier periods have received some attention from social scientists (Pelinka 1983; Preglau 1994) little has been published about the more recent developments.

The Austrian case demonstrates how electoral and office concerns of political parties determine their policy position taking. Parties' electoral concerns tie public policy to public opinion and hence serve one representational ideal. Yet the varying abilities of political parties to exercise influence on public opinion and multi-party politics make the translation of public opinion into public policy a complex process with alternative outcomes being feasible. Finally, we see that key public policy decisions gain a life of their own. They help consolidate public opinion, produce spill-over effects into other policy areas, and impact coalition politics.

The chapter proceeds as follows. First, it provides a brief history of nuclear power policy in Austria. Next it introduces the major actors in this policy area, describes the formal jurisdictions, and briefly accounts for the actors' political influence on nuclear energy policy. The rest of the chapter then analyses how political parties and the electorate interacted around the issue and how party competition impacted policy-making. The conclusion addresses explicitly how the trade-offs political parties faced explain the policy outcome.

5.2 POLICY DEVELOPMENT

Austria's early history of nuclear energy policy was not distinguishable from that of other Western countries. In line with the policy of industrial modernization, the first plans for engaging in nuclear power production were developed already in the 1950s. The first research reactor was decided on in 1956 and began to operate in 1960. A research platform for nuclear energy was founded in 1956. In the 1960s, the electricity industry established several firms with specific tasks in the planning and construction of nuclear power stations. In 1969 the decision was made to build the first nuclear power station at Zwentendorf, about 40 km north-west of Vienna. Interestingly, at that point the Länder considered the nuclear power station attractive and consequently even competed over its location (Kreisky 1996: 152; Kriechbaumer 2004: 210; Schaller 1987: 123). Construction works at Zwentendorf began in 1972. The planning for a second nuclear power station in Stein/St. Pantaleon, close to the industrial centre of Upper Austria, began in 1974.

Thus, the electricity industry could rely on political support for going nuclear. Indeed, temporarily, the government was more enthusiastic about nuclear energy than parts of the electricity industry that then prioritized different investments. The 1969 government's 'Energy Concept for Austria', a single-party cabinet of the People's Party (ÖVP), included one nuclear power station. 'Going nuclear' was unanimously supported in a parliamentary resolution in 1969 (i.e. by the ÖVP, the Social Democrats (SPÖ), and by the Freedom Party (FPÖ)). When the SPÖ took over the government in 1970, it seemed that promoting nuclear energy would be a lesser priority. Yet the government soon found its way back to the post-war consensus on the issue. The SPÖ government's Energy Plan of 1975 projected that nuclear power production would begin in 1976. Its contribution to electricity production was expected to be 5 per cent and to rise to 33 per cent by 1985, from a total of four nuclear power stations. At that time, planners estimated annual growth rates in electricity demand of up to 6.5 per cent. In the light of economic stagnation following the first oil crisis, the 1976 Energy Plan reduced these figures, now planning for three nuclear power stations until 1990, providing 20 per cent of the country's electricity supply (Schaller 1987: 173–6). In any case, the 1976 Energy Plan still envisaged a 'prominent role' for nuclear energy.

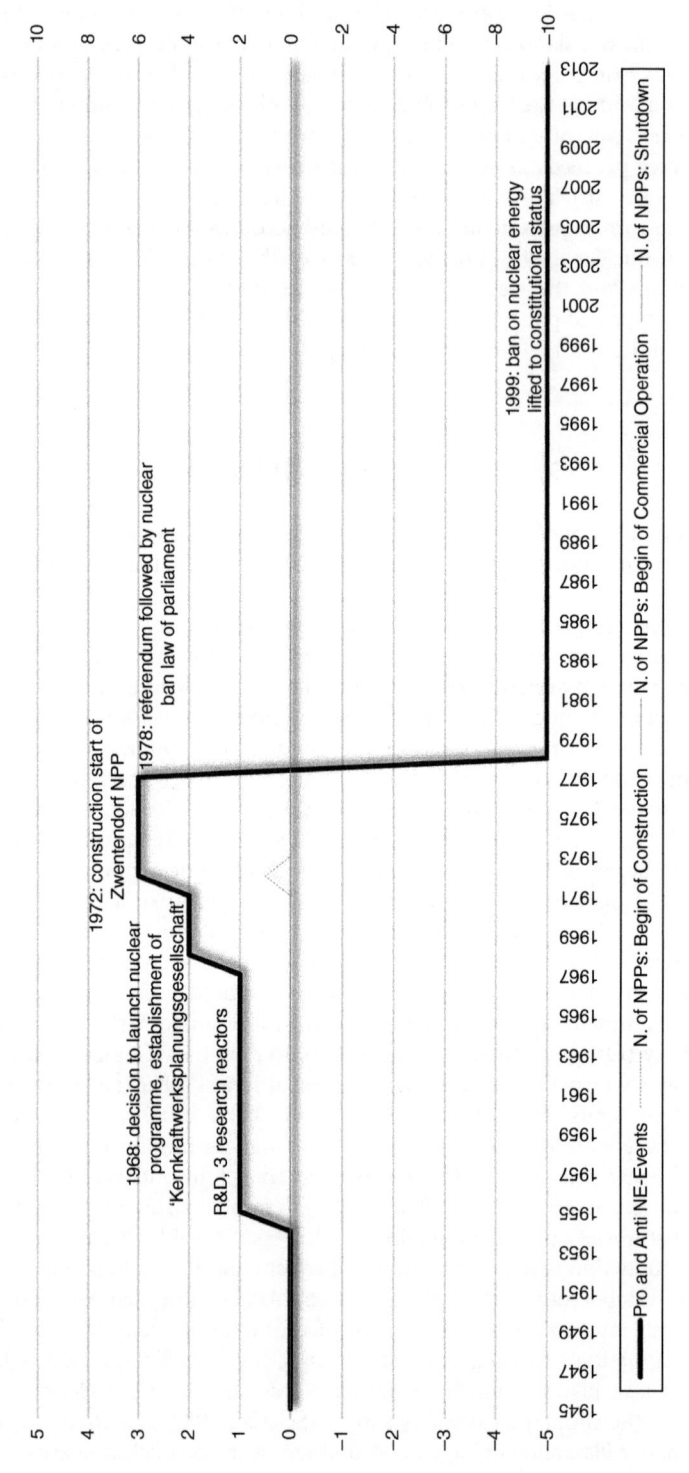

Figure 5.1. Nuclear Energy Policy Development in Austria, 1945–2013

— Pro and Anti NE-Events ········ N. of NPPs: Begin of Construction ——— N. of NPPs: Begin of Commercial Operation ——— N. of NPPs: Shutdown

1968: decision to launch nuclear programme, establishment of 'Kernkraftwerksplanungsgesellschaft'

R&D, 3 research reactors

1972: construction start of Zwentendorf NPP

1978: referendum followed by nuclear ban law of parliament

1999: ban on nuclear energy lifted to constitutional status

Of significant importance for the political debate and the framing of the nuclear power issue by the major parties was that the ÖVP single-party government (1966–70) had only given the general permit to go ahead with the Zwentendorf plant while the subsequent SPÖ single-party government had issued the more specific permits.

The Zwentendorf power station was completed and ready to start operation in 1978. Very late in the game, the government majority in parliament called a referendum. On 5 November 1978 a majority of 50.5 per cent of the voters said 'no' to the 'peaceful use of nuclear power' (49.5 per cent 'yes', turnout 64.1 per cent). On 8 November, the SPÖ introduced a bill to parliament that ruled out the use of nuclear power on Austrian soil. It was unanimously enacted on 15 December (Bundesgesetzblatt 493/1978). All parliamentary parties committed politically to not overturning the law without holding another referendum and without assembling a two-thirds majority in parliament for calling such a referendum (although a bare majority would satisfy the constitutional requirement). In terms of actual legislation only one change took place: in 1999 parliament passed a constitutional law banning the use of nuclear power plants (based on nuclear fission) and the transportation of nuclear fuel through Austria (Bundesgesetzblatt I, 149/1999). In a way this constitutional law formalized the parties' early promises, as revisions require a two-thirds majority in parliament.

Austria has thus incorporated its rejection of nuclear power in its body of constitutional law. In terms of domestic public policy the Austrian nuclear energy story stops here. Figure 5.1 summarizes it in this volume's standard form. As we will see, the politics behind these decisions are not as straightforward as this narrative may suggest. Nor have the politics of nuclear power been confined to the domestic arena.

5.3 ACTORS AND JURISDICTIONS

The issue of electricity production is highly politicized in Austria in the sense that the relevant firms were all under public ownership at the outset of the story. Following the 1947 nationalization of the electricity industry, a mix of central and Land government control emerged, resulting in a complex web of firms under public ownership. The most important are the Verbundgesellschaft, which initially had been given the task to build and run major power stations, and nine Land companies which initially were designated to guarantee local supply. The major political parties, the SPÖ and ÖVP, were closely involved in making appointments to management positions in these firms. For them, the electricity industry was a resource to be employed for several purposes: supporting economic growth, regional development, and providing 'jobs for the boys'. In turn, the major parties and interest organizations were willing to relinquish the payment of dividends from the electricity industry, allow relatively high consumer prices, and be generally supportive to its activities (Lauber et al. 1988; Kok 1991; Sickinger 2004). In this context, nuclear energy became a controversial issue; genuine political considerations—the parties' electoral and office ambitions—were eventually more important than the electricity industry's concerns. A privately organized industry probably would have put up more resistance and thus imposed more direct costs on politics.[1]

Since the banning of nuclear power production, the electricity industry has gone through major changes in ownership. Empty government coffers and ideological zeal for privatization have led to substantial private shares in many Austrian electricity companies. The new owners include foreign firms that are heavily invested in nuclear energy. Yet these changes have not caused the industry to join in the international attempts at reviving nuclear energy, as observed elsewhere in the early twenty-first century. On one hand, such an endeavour would have been an uphill battle with little chance for success. However, the single European energy market renders such moves dispensable as nuclear energy can be produced where resistance is low, while electricity can be transmitted with low cost to places of demand.

Outside the electricity industry, the nuclear power issue mainly affected the business interests of energy-intensive sectors and those enterprises that had hoped to benefit from subcontracting with foreign nuclear engineering firms. As the industry had hoped for the construction of up to fourteen nuclear power stations in Austria by 1980 (Schaller 1987: 167) the stakes were substantial. It was mainly the Federation of Industry that represented these interests. Most of the business community at large, mainly small firms represented by the Business Chamber, however, lacked such direct incentives. It was supportive to nuclear energy because of the general economic arguments that fuelled the debate (from providing cheap and secure energy to the avoidance of stranded investment and costs for the taxpayer).

Before nuclear energy was banned, it was not subject to special legislation. The Ministry of Trade and Commerce was in charge of the electricity sector but its formal competencies with regard to nuclear power stations were far from comprehensive. The building and taking-up operation of such power stations required the consent of local and Land authorities and that of several ministries. Yet most of the steps in the complex process of authorizing the production of nuclear energy had been completed before the issue was politicized. According to the relevant law (the Dampfkesselemissionsgesetz, i.e. the law regulating all emissions from steam generation), the final decision rested with the Minister of Trade and Commerce. It was thus up to the central government whether Austria would go nuclear or not. Yet when it was time for a decision, the issue was already so politicized that party leaders took over and passed new legislation.

As the next section shows in greater detail, the post-war consensus of nuclear energy optimism of the political elite coincided with the grand coalition government of the ÖVP and SPÖ (1947–66) and was maintained throughout the subsequent single-party government of the ÖVP (1966–70). The issue was gradually politicized in the 1970s and remained controversial through most of the SPÖ's single-party government term (1970–83) and the subsequent SPÖ-FPÖ coalition (1983–86). In short, while the SPÖ continued to bank on nuclear energy,

---

[1] In fact, the Verbundgesellschaft was not completely docile. It appealed to the courts for compensation from the ban of nuclear energy but failed. It was eventually rescued from bankruptcy (resulting from the stranded Zwentendorf investment) with the taxpayers' money.

the FPÖ first (beginning in 1972) and later (and to a lesser extent) the ÖVP turned away from it. The Chernobyl accident paved the way for a new period of interparty consensus on nuclear energy, which is now generally rejected. Nuclear energy has become a valence issue, and party competition is based on the competence in fighting its use in neighbouring countries and thus sheltering Austria from the consequences of nuclear accidents. The parties that have entered the party system only after Chernobyl either have anti-nuclear credentials (the Greens) or have joined that competition as it is potentially rewarding electorally.

Over the entire period, political parties were unitary actors in parliamentary voting on nuclear energy issues. Yet, they experienced their internal discussions and conflicts over the issue. The major interest groups closely connected to the main political parties were a part of the post-war consensus. Today none of them assumes a pro-nuclear position with regard to domestic energy production. The trade unions and the business organizations and their intra-party bastions remained longer and more deeply committed to the pro-nuclear consensus than the political parties at large. Thus party leaders are the key actors in decision-making regarding nuclear energy, and for that reason constitute the main focus of this chapter. However, they were not the key actors in putting the nuclear energy issue on the agenda. This was the distinct contribution of grassroots movements.[2]

5.4 VOTER ATTITUDES AND PARTY COMPETITION

This section distinguishes three periods. In the first two, the issue of nuclear energy was at stake in the domestic arena. In the first one the story is largely in line with the developments elsewhere in Western Europe. It contains the breaking up of the post-war consensus on nuclear energy and ends with the decision not to switch on the first, just completed nuclear power station but rather to outlaw nuclear energy production. Thus nuclear energy was 'aborted' rather than 'phased out', as it never had been really 'in' (in the sense of being more than planned capacity and real investment). The second period is that of attempts at reversing that decision. Again, this process was ended abruptly by the Chernobyl accident. In its aftermath the decision was made to maintain the nuclear power 'virgin' status of Austria. Yet, the story does not end here. The same forces that drove domestic nuclear energy policy now play out in nuclear energy foreign policy that takes central stage in the most recent period.

5.4.1 Phase 1: Who is to be Blamed for Going Nuclear?

Before examining the development of the relevant voter attitudes it is worth highlighting the institutional and party system background of party competition.

---

[2] Several studies highlight the role of grassroots protest much more than is possible in the present chapter. See Kitzmüller (1979) and Brandstätter et al. (1984) for the activists' perspective, Schaller (1987) and Preglau (1994); for a comparative perspective see Nelkin and Pollak (1977).

Nuclear energy became an issue in the time of single-party governments and indeed single-party popular majorities. Note that the electoral system of the 1970–92 period pushed proportional representation close to the extreme of forgoing any 'reductive effect'. Combining the Hare method with very large constituencies made it easy for new parties to enter parliament. Likewise, small shifts in electoral support between government and established opposition parties had potential consequences in terms of office. Initially, nuclear energy was not a political issue. When this changed the nuclear power issue fuelled competition between the traditional parties and at times dominated the public agenda. There was no serious outside contender before 1983 (when two Green parties first ran in national elections but failed to win parliamentary representation).

To highlight the parties' positioning, this chapter scrutinizes electoral manifestos, other programmatic statements of the parties, and key policy decisions. Until 1970, the party manifestos (which were generally short and centred on the parties' core issues) contained only few and scattered references to energy policy. If this policy area was mentioned at all, it was with the claim of making the most out of domestic resources, in particular producing hydroelectric energy from the country's rich water resources. In 1966, both major parties mentioned energy planning. The ÖVP referred to developing an 'energy plan for Austria' and the SPÖ called for an energy plan in order to best combine domestic and imported energy sources and to increase domestic electricity production by 30 per cent by 1970. Austria was about to go nuclear, but nuclear energy at that time was uncontroversial and did not require mention in party documents. In their 1970 manifestos, both major parties clearly committed themselves to pushing nuclear power for economic reasons. The ÖVP seemed more interested in speeding up the process, demanding the building 'of a large and high-output nuclear power station as soon as possible'. The SPÖ, in its book-long electoral manifesto (a reissue of its 1968 economic programme), was more concerned about the capacity (600 MW) of the power station than the time schedule. Building such a big one would require the coordination of the electricity industry and thus construction could not begin before 1975. In the early elections of 1971, following a stint of SPÖ minority government, the parties were concerned with other issues. The first oil crisis of 1973 forced energy policy into a more prominent place on the agendas of political parties and decision-makers. The FPÖ had begun to gradually depart from the all-party nuclear energy consensus shortly before that happened. In 1972 it voted against public credit liabilities for the Zwentendorf project. In its energy concept of 1973, the FPÖ listed some of the problems of nuclear energy and proposed delaying further investment until the maturation of the nuclear power technology. Note, however, that the FPÖ did not demand an emergency brake on the nuclear energy programme that was already under way. Rather, it proceeded from the first two nuclear power stations being completed before the moratorium on further investment would set in (Reiter 1982: 161). In contrast, the ÖVP energy concept of 1974 proposed to invest in both hydroelectric and nuclear power, two types of energy that would complement each other and make Austria less dependent on the oil market.

The nuclear energy issue slowly reached the national agenda through the activities of grassroots movements. The first citizen protest against nuclear energy occurred in 1967. Responding to the government's energy concept of 1969, the

League for Public Health (Bund für Volksgesundheit) collected about 100,000 protest signatures against nuclear energy between 1969 and 1974. While these activities did not have much impact, the grassroots protest in Vorarlberg (the most western Land) did. It was directed against the projected Swiss reactor in Rüthi (near the Austrian border and much closer to Vorarlberg than any of the projected Austrian reactors). Beginning in 1972, the protest movement won the support of the regionally dominant newspaper, the *Vorarlberger Nachrichten*, and soon all Land party organizations and the Land political institutions joined in (Schaller 1987: 162–7; Rösch-Wehinger 2009: 81–4). Vorarlberg politicians lobbied the national government to pressure Switzerland to abandon the project. Notwithstanding the fact that Austria was planning to 'go nuclear' itself in the near future, the national government indeed engaged in relevant diplomatic efforts. Whatever effect this had on the Swiss decision-makers, the plan to build a nuclear power station at Rüthi was eventually shelved in 1976. In retrospect, this episode is important as the Austrian nuclear power referendum returned results that varied greatly between the Länder, with Vorarlberg being most negative (84 per cent 'no' votes). Note that the overall referendum result would have been a 'yes' if Vorarlberg had returned a 'no' vote share similar to that of the other Länder rejecting nuclear energy. The episode also foreshadows the concern for foreign nuclear power stations close to the Austrian border that constitute the central focus of the most recent phase of nuclear power politics.

However, on a national scale, grassroots protest was building up only slowly. In 1974, 75,000 citizens signed a petition against the second planned nuclear power station in Upper Austria. In contrast, protest against Zwentendorf and nuclear energy as such continued to remain scattered and rather insignificant.

Surveys conducted in 1975 showed that Austrians were rather sceptical about this type of energy, considering it more risky and potentially harmful than other forms of energy and other risky technologies.[3] To fight such scepticism Chancellor Bruno Kreisky prescribed an information campaign conducted between October 1976 and March 1977 in which both supporters and opponents of nuclear energy were given room (Bundespressedienst 1977; Nowotny 1979). As it turned out, it provided the opponents the opportunity to reach a national audience which they had largely lacked. The overall result of the campaign was that uneasiness about nuclear energy increased. This holds true in comparison with the specific risks of other forms of energy (breaking dams and exploding refineries) and other risk technologies. When framed as a forced choice between dependence on energy imports from the Eastern bloc and Arabian states in 1977, more survey respondents were willing to accept the import dependence risk (41 per cent) rather than the nuclear one (35 per cent).[4] Yet Austrians seemed overwhelmingly willing to bend to the argument that nuclear power was an economic necessity, particularly when faced with the 'fait accompli' of a nearly completed nuclear power station (Schaller 1987: 252–3; Ulram 1990: 131).

In response to the government's nation-wide information campaign, the various protest organizations pooled their resources in a national organization, the

---

[3] 'Atomkraftwerke—gefährlich.' *Journal für Sozialforschung*, 17(2) (1977): 24–6.
[4] 'Unklarheit über Atomkraftwerk.' *Journal für Sozialforschung*, 17(3) (1977): 32–3.

IÖAG (Initiative Österreichs Atomkraft Gegner), in 1976 (Brandstätter et al. 1984: 162–3). Between 1976 and 1978, the grassroots protest accelerated. Although it still constituted a relatively small minority of the electorate, it won considerable public attention and was beginning to pressure the political parties. The first to be affected were the politicians in the municipalities where the nuclear power stations were to be located. Although they did not attempt to bail out of the deal—after all, locating a nuclear power station promised considerable economic benefits for their communities—they responded to citizen concerns by rejecting the permanent disposal of nuclear waste on their soil. This, in turn, highlighted the issue of nuclear waste disposal.

Indeed, it was impossible to find a site for a nuclear waste deposit in Austria. The electricity industry and the government therefore turned to foreign options, exploring Egypt, Iran, India, and France (as the fuel was coming from the French firm COGEMA), yet none of these solutions eventually turned out to work. As no plan for a final disposal site could be presented, the decision-makers resorted to the 'interim' solution of a short-term depot at the site of the Zwentendorf power station. While the promoters of nuclear energy argued this would provide a sufficient time buffer to resolve the final disposal problem, its opponents rejected that claim and insisted on having a solution before turning the key at Zwentendorf.

A second prominent issue was the safety of the Zwentendorf plant. Specifically, it was questioned whether its location was suitable given concerns from geological and hydrological expert assessments that initially had been concealed from the public and were revealed only by accident. If credible, such concerns could reach out to those who were not principled opponents of nuclear energy.

What were the cues the voters received from the parties? The SPÖ was clearly in favour of continuing the country's nuclear energy path and connecting Zwentendorf to the grid. All polls demonstrated that the voters did not miss this message. Yet, SPÖ leader and Chancellor Kreisky was alarmed by the Swedish Social Democrats losing office over the nuclear energy issue in 1976. Repeatedly he warned the SPÖ leadership in their internal deliberations that the issue 'may cost us exactly the one or two percent of the vote that we may then be missing for the majority' (Fischer 1993: 159).[5] Recall that the SPÖ had won a 50.5 per cent majority of the popular vote in the 1975 general election. A 2 per cent vote loss almost certainly would have deprived the SPÖ of its parliamentary majority and thus brought to an end its period of single-party government. Kreisky was therefore keen to maintain the elite consensus underlying Austria's going nuclear.

As mentioned above, the FPÖ had been rethinking its position on nuclear energy since 1972. As the party had traditionally catered to the technical and business intelligence that was keen on scientific progress and economic growth, this move was surprising. Yet, the FPÖ's parliamentary party also included politicians who were amongst the early sceptics of nuclear energy. Individual motivations ranged from (far right) fear for the impact of nuclear radiance on the human genetic heritage to more post-materialist concerns of the liberal wing. Such concerns met with the prospect of developing an electorally rewarding

---

[5] In his memoirs Kreisky (1996: 153) even talks of an expected vote loss of 3–4 per cent points from the nuclear energy issue.

'unique selling proposition' given the underlying scepticism about nuclear energy in the electorate. Consequently, the FPÖ conducted a nuclear energy policy U-turn between 1972 and 1977. In June 1977, it began to take issue with the close-to-completion Zwentendorf power station. A party executive resolution demanded that all safety issues, including the final disposal of radioactive waste, would have to be resolved before Zwentendorf could be switched on. Consequently, the FPÖ rejected legitimizing the ÖVP and SPÖ's 'megalomania', demanding the use of alternative energy forms for an interim period of about thirty years (as then a new form of nuclear energy without radiation would be ready for commercial use) (Reiter 1982: 180).

This left Kreisky with the ÖVP as a potential partner, the party that had proudly welcomed the nuclear power age in Austria in 1969. Yet, various statements of individual ÖVP politicians signalled that this party's support was not guaranteed (Schaller 1987: 263; Stifter 2006: 185). Beginning in the autumn of 1977, intense inter-party negotiations aimed at getting the ÖVP consent in a parliamentary resolution legitimizing Zwentendorf going online. Yet, the ÖVP insisted on the government guaranteeing the safety of the power station (after all, all permits relating to Zwentendorf specifically had been issued by SPÖ ministers) and to show how the nuclear waste problem would be resolved. The negotiations did not show much progress and were eventually terminated by Kreisky. Internal pressure from the nuclear power enthusiasts in the SPÖ and the feeling that the ÖVP was delaying the negotiations only to move 'going nuclear' closer to the next scheduled elections in the autumn of 1979 may account for this decision.[6]

While the trade unionists in the SPÖ were willing to go ahead with connecting Zwentendorf to the grid even without oppositional assent, Kreisky surprisingly suggested an alternative option: a referendum on nuclear power. Expecting a clear majority in favour of using nuclear energy, no policy costs would have resulted but the 'hot potato' would have been placed in the hands of the voters. The SPÖ made attempts to win the ÖVP's support for a referendum. They failed over the question wording, with the SPÖ wanting a vote on Zwentendorf and the ÖVP one on nuclear energy. Yet, an affirmative answer to the latter question would not have resolved the SPÖ's problems, as the government would have remained accountable for all the issues specifically tied to Zwentendorf (such as the choice of the construction site despite the alleged history of devastating earthquakes in the region in earlier centuries or details of construction). Finally, on 28 June 1978, the SPÖ parliamentary majority paved the way for a referendum on 5 November. The text mentioned both the peaceful use of nuclear energy and the switching on of Zwentendorf.[7]

---

[6] Of course, real actors are often not fully informed. According to Fischer (1993: 156), the then leader of the ÖVP parliamentary party group, Alois Mock, revealed many years later that his party would have been ready to make substantial concessions already in 1978 and had not understood why the SPÖ terminated the negotiations about a joint parliamentary legitimization of nuclear energy at that stage.

[7] As the constitution confines the referendum to making decisions on existing legislation, the process was not straightforward. First, the SPÖ passed a law that (a) required one law each for the switching on of any nuclear power station and at the same time (b) contained the permit for Zwentendorf. Next, all parties voted to hold a referendum on that law.

While the party positions of the FPÖ ('no') and the SPÖ ('yes') were clear, the ÖVP needed many words to say 'no'. While upholding its commitment to nuclear energy as such, it continued to focus on the specific problems with Zwentendorf. While the ÖVP did not explicitly recommend its voters to cast a 'no' vote in the referendum, party leader Josef Taus made clear that he would vote 'no' and party functionaries were committed to such behaviour (Stifter 2006: 187–94).

In a desperate attempt to rally SPÖ voters behind the pro-side (on 22 October), Kreisky indicated that he might resign if the referendum did not produce the desired result (Schaller 1987: 333). Table 5.1 suggests that, if anything, it had the opposite effect as ÖVP adherents now had a strong non-policy reason to vote 'no' in the referendum (see also Angermann and Plasser 1979: 23).

Table 5.1 shows how public opinion developed in 1978. The referendum was held on 5 November. Early in the year, opinion polls showed a clear majority in favour of nuclear energy and the switching on of Zwentendorf. Yet, this majority shrank in the course of the year. While a plurality of respondents registered their support for nuclear energy, in some surveys those objecting and those undecided outnumbered the former. Clearly, this trend continued until the referendum and was fuelled by Kreisky's threat of resignation.

It is particularly interesting to look at the party preferences of the respondents and the share of issue-inconsistent voters among the party electorates. SPÖ sympathizers always registered clear majorities in favour of nuclear energy. Yet, the share of firm opponents of nuclear energy among SPÖ voters was sizeable enough to concern the party. Moreover, the longer the debate on nuclear power continued, the more SPÖ sympathizers became issue-undecided.

In a way the ÖVP was in an even more difficult situation than the SPÖ (Ulram 1990: 132). Table 5.1 shows that its electorate was more evenly split over the nuclear issue both before and after being strongly cued by the party. While

Table 5.1. Party Sympathy and Policy Preferences over the Nuclear Power Station at Zwentendorf in Referendum Run-Up and Referendum Voting, January to November 1978

Policy preferences		SPÖ	ÖVP	FPÖ	No party	Total
1978, 1–2	Pro	76	52	79	55	62
	Against	18	43	21	30	30
	No opinion	6	5	0	15	8
1978, 6	Pro	73	50	41	51	58
	Against	26	46	59	39	37
	No opinion	2	4	0	10	5
1978, 7	Pro	67	32	?	?	46
	Against	14	30	?	?	22
	No opinion	19	38	?	?	32
1978, 9	Pro	70	42	46	48	55
	Against	12	31	26	20	19
	No opinion	18	27	28	32	26
1978, 10	Pro	58	25	46	27	39
	Against	13	42	34	24	26
	Undecided/No opinion	29	33	19	50	35

Sources: Brettschneider 1980: 5–6; surveys of the Dr Fessel + GfK institute.

Table 5.2. Referendum Voting Behaviour of Party Sympathizers

Party preference	Yes (In favour of nuclear power)	No (Against nuclear power)	Did not participate
SPÖ	60	15	25
ÖVP	10	63	26
FPÖ	11	52	37
No party affiliation	25	38	38

Source: Survey of the IFES, conducted in the week after the referendum ($N = 1,727$) as reported by Bichlbauer (1979: 32) but recalculated to exclude survey respondents who were not entitled to vote or did not answer the question. Due to rounding errors rows do not always add up to 100.

initially the supporters of nuclear energy just outnumbered the opponents plus those that were undecided, the distribution of opinions shifted dramatically towards the 'no' side in the run-up to the referendum. Here the increasing party polarization, with the ÖVP de facto saying 'no' and SPÖ leader Kreisky's resignation threat weighed in. Thus, massive elite-cuing is behind this shift in public opinion.

In electoral terms, the FPÖ faced a similar electoral trade-off as the ÖVP. Given the insignificant size of the FPÖ at the time, only few voters declared themselves as party supporters; not too much should be read into the figures. In any case, the survey respondents are more likely to represent the party's core constituency from the technical and business sectors than the floatng voters the party wanted to attract with its rejection of nuclear energy.

Non-party-affiliated survey respondents show the same trend as ÖVP sympathizers, though their turning away from nuclear energy is less clear.

Table 5.2 shows the actual voting behaviour of party adherents, as it was recalled in the week immediately after the referendum. The share of voters who were not willing to follow their party's cue is similar in all parties. Although the differences are small, the SPÖ electorate was most willing to vote *against* their party's cuing whereas the FPÖ adherents (who abstained in large numbers) were least willing to follow their party's instructions.

According to another poll taken in the week following the referendum, 19 per cent of those who had voted 'no' in the referendum recorded the recommendation of the party leaders Kreisky ('yes') and Taus ('no') as their main reasons for so doing. Of those who had voted 'yes' 10 per cent identified Kreisky's recommendation as their main reason. They did so in accordance with their general party-political outlook. The party factor also impacted on the non-voting behaviour as a substantial share of abstainers consisted of issue-inconsistent citizens: 18 per cent of those who abstained claimed that they did so because they were torn between party loyalty and issue opinion (Kienzl 1979: 23–5). Both major parties were affected roughly equally: 15 per cent of the abstainers experienced a conflict between their ÖVP loyalty and their pro-nuclear issue opinion while 14 per cent abstained because their SPÖ affiliation conflicted with their rejection of nuclear energy (Kienzl 1979: 27).

Table 5.3 looks prospectively at electoral consequences of the nuclear energy issue. It reveals that it was important to nuclear energy opponents, as many seemed ready to sanction their party for taking a pro-nuclear stand. Accordingly,

Table 5.3. Eligibility of Pro-Nuclear Party (June–September 1978)

Party eligible	SPÖ sympathy		ÖVP sympathy		FPÖ sympathy		No party	
	June	Sept	June	Sept	June	Sept	June	Sept
Yes	91	86	64	58	45	57	68	65
No	6	5	29	22	49	20	22	12
Don't know	3	9	7	20	6	22	10	24

Source: June: Survey of the Fessel + GfK institute; Sept.: Sozialwissenschaftliche Studiengesellschaft SW 7806.

Table 5.4. Voters' Motives in the 1979 General Election

The wrong behaviour of this party with regard to nuclear issue was...	SPÖ voters	ÖVP voters	FPÖ voters	Abstained, other party	All
...the most important motive **not** to vote for a specific party	5	5	9	2	4
...a second motive of relevance	12	5	9	7	9

Source: Fessel + GfK 79/6793.

the ÖVP was particularly vulnerable. This clearly helps understanding this party's behaviour.

The referendum was held less than a year prior to the general election of 1979. Despite the upheaval about Zwentendorf and nuclear energy, the election resulted in the third consecutive majority of the Social Democrats under Kreisky (who had not resigned after the defeat but conversely had received additional authorization by the party executive). The SPÖ again won the majority of both the popular vote and parliamentary seats. To be precise, it was its best result ever. Quite simply, the SPÖ's post-referendum behaviour by taking the lead in outlawing nuclear energy had removed the issue from the agenda. A legal ban on nuclear energy and the promise not to lift it without assembling a two-thirds majority in parliament and holding another referendum was probably more than opponents of nuclear energy inclined to vote for the SPÖ had hoped for. The SPÖ even used testimonials of celebrities praising Kreisky as being the guarantor for upholding the ban on nuclear energy in the 1979 election campaign. Table 5.4 shows that altogether 13 per cent of the voters were in some way influenced by the parties' nuclear policy position taking, though it is hard to establish net winners and net losers on the basis of this indirect evidence.

This section has shown how political parties positioned themselves with regard to the nuclear power issue and how that interacted with voter preferences. In taking positions, party leaders were not unconstrained, given the parties' track records and the interests of intra-party groups to continue with the post-war strategy of economic growth and technological progress. Yet, all parties had internal disputes about nuclear energy. In the SPÖ the trade union wing was most outspoken in favour of nuclear energy.

In the ÖVP the powerful business wing was most committed to nuclear energy (Stifter 2006: 188–90). Only a few individual politicians with national standing and the Vorarlberg Land party organization were equally committed against nuclear energy. The ÖVP's leading role in the development of the Austrian nuclear energy programme, the 50 per cent share of the mostly ÖVP-dominated Land electricity companies in the Zwentendorf plant, and the party's general commitment to the post-war economic growth consensus suggested that anything but low-key support was unlikely. At the same time, the ÖVP was vulnerable itself as voters inclined to support the parties of the centre-right were most likely to harbour 'post-materialist' concerns. Hence, for the party leadership, framing the nuclear issue in a way that would allow reconciling such conflicting concerns and at the same time inflict damage on the SPÖ was the strategic goal.

It is fair to conclude that, according to their sincere policy preferences, both major parties would have preferred Austria going nuclear in 1978. This option represented the post-war economic growth consensus. A considerable amount of money had been invested—about 9 billion schilling for the construction of Zwentendorf alone. More generally, a ban on nuclear energy raised the issue of the country's future energy supply. Such considerations were most prominent amongst the ÖVP business wing and the SPÖ trade unionists. These also occupied the commanding heights in Austria's powerful interest organizations: the Business Chamber, the Federation of Industrialists, the Trade Union Congress, and the Chamber of Labour, respectively. Yet, both parties faced important trade-offs. While small electoral losses could have been very consequential for the SPÖ— ending its majority and single-party government—the ÖVP was threatened by more substantial voter defections but at the same time could benefit greatly from SPÖ losses. Risking nuclear power—and eventually losing it—the major parties followed the vote-seeking imperative. As the remainder of this chapter will show, this also had considerable office implications.

5.4.2 Phase 2: A Second Chance for Nuclear Energy?

In his book on the Kreisky years, the then parliamentary leader of the SPÖ, Heinz Fischer (1993: 161), reveals that some of the SPÖ leaders were somewhat relieved over the referendum's result: it had cleared the agenda and eased the SPÖ's burden. The Three Mile Island (Harrisburg) nuclear accident of March 1979 and the October 1979 election silenced those in the party who felt differently.

Yet, the very close result of the referendum (50.5:49.5) and the low turnout (a mere 64.1 per cent at a time when electoral participation was still very high[8]) invited interpretation. One was that of an 'accidental majority'—resulting from the mixing of anti-nuclear power with anti-Kreisky motives and 'artificially' low turnout. All that provided fuel for those who did not like the referendum's outcome. Soon after the 1979 general elections the most outspoken promoters of nuclear energy began to work towards a revision of the 1978 decision (Müller 1985: 210; Schaller 1987; Kriechbaumer 2004: 220). The Trade Union Federation,

---

[8] The general election immediately preceding the referendum had a turnout of 95.4%, the one following it had a turnout of 94.1%. As the referendum on nuclear power was the first referendum in Austrian history, no domestic yardstick specifically tied to that instrument was available. Abstention was also substantially higher than could be expected from the pre-referendum surveys.

the Chamber of Labour, the Chamber of Business, the Federation of Industrialists, and the Austrian electricity industry founded an energy policy lobbying organization (Gesellschaft für Energiewesen). It was to work against further debacles in the energy sector through proactive strategies and towards a revision of the referendum.

In 1980 a people's initiative sponsored by the Trade Union Federation (and supported by the other economic interest organizations) was organized.[9] To remove the final disposal problem of nuclear waste from the agenda, the interest group leaders commissioned a report from their organizations' experts that stated that the disposal would not be required before the twenty-first century and any early solution would only produce unnecessary costs (Kriechbaumer 2004: 222). The specific demand of the people's initiative was to abolish the legal ban on nuclear power. At that time, a people's initiative required the support of 200,000 citizens (who have to sign before the electoral authorities within a week). The idea was that symbolically the people themselves would require the revision of the referendum and thereby give the political parties a legitimate cause to agree to another referendum. Given that the Trade Union Federation had 1.6 million members and the logistical help of the other interest groups at that time, the support of 420,000 citizens was generally considered disappointing. Similarly disappointing was the result of the counter-mobilization, a people's initiative sponsored by Catholic groups. Their ideas of converting Zwentendorf into a conventional power station and elevating the law banning nuclear power to constitutional rank failed to pass the 200,000 signatures threshold. Issue-inconsistent citizens resolved their problem from being cross-pressured by not signing either of the initiatives and so the party polarization of the referendum was maintained if not strengthened (Gehmacher 1981). The mobilization for the threshold-crossing pro-nuclear initiative was not sufficient for the ÖVP or FPÖ to lend their support to calling a second referendum on the nuclear power issue.

Meanwhile, the owners of Zwentendorf maintained its ready-to-start status, hoping for better times. There was indeed reason to remain optimistic for proponents of nuclear energy. In its 1981 economic programme, the SPÖ maintained 'the peaceful use of nuclear energy in Austria will be necessary to reach the energy policy goal of reducing the share of oil (in energy supply)'. Nor were the interest groups yet ready to give up the fight. Yet, intensified inter-party conflict over economic policy and political scandals made it even more difficult for the major parties to compromise over nuclear power. Moreover, the ÖVP was concerned about the damage such behaviour would cause to its chances in the 1983 elections. Consequently, no deal was made in what would be the SPÖ single-party government's last term.

The SPÖ's electoral manifesto of 1983 did not mention the issue of nuclear energy. However, Kreisky, already ageing and in bad health, was reported to have said that Zwentendorf would be turned on and more nuclear power stations built provided the SPÖ maintained its majority. The ÖVP manifesto maintained that the referendum result must be respected and the FPÖ manifesto continued to

---

[9] A people's initiative is a plebiscitary way of introducing a legislative bill to parliament (Müller 1998).

'forcefully reject the use of nuclear energy at its present state of technological development'. The 1983 national election was the first to be contested by Green parties.[10] The more conservative United Greens of Austria (VGÖ) was under the co-leadership of one of the leading anti-Zwentendorf activists, the geologist Alexander Tollmann, and most of the activists of the leftist Alternative List had credentials from the anti-nuclear movement. Although the number of votes cast for the two Green parties combined (about 3.5 per cent) would have been sufficient to enter parliament, neither of them actually made it. The election result was also bad news for the SPÖ as it lost its majority by a small margin.

Although the nuclear power issue may have motivated Green voters, it was not as prominent as the economic issues that dominated the agenda. As a consequence of the SPÖ losing its majority, Kreisky resigned as Chancellor but still paved the way to a coalition government of the SPÖ and FPÖ. Clearly, the SPÖ's ambition to lift the ban on nuclear energy and to get Zwentendorf online came second to the party's office ambitions and other policy goals. All these seemed more likely to achieve as the dominant partner in a close-to-minimum-winning coalition with the tiny FPÖ than in a grand coalition with the ÖVP. Although an increasing number of ÖVP leaders and voters now were sceptical about nuclear energy, at that point its consent to go nuclear seemed feasible. In contrast, the SPÖ-FPÖ coalition was the combination of the most pro- and the most antinuclear energy party. All the FPÖ was willing to concede was tolerating SPÖ attempts at getting a parliamentary majority for a second referendum outside the coalition (i.e. with the ÖVP). The SPÖ made several moves in that direction that all failed (Müller 1985: 210). These attempts were orchestrated by the decision of the electricity industry in 1985 to dismantle Zwentendorf. This was most likely a desperate attempt to put pressure on the politicians to get their act together.

As Table 5.5 shows, the electorate remained split over the issue. With the exception of two surveys conducted shortly after the Harrisburg accident in 1979, all surveys until 1986 show pluralities in favour of switching on Zwentendorf. Yet, only in two surveys was a majority in favour of so doing. While the share of voters who would vote against nuclear energy in a second referendum remained relatively stable (range 32–9 per cent) those who would vote in its favour fluctuated considerably (range 40–58 per cent). Provided that the undecided voters were leaning more towards nuclear energy perhaps only a few parameters would need to change to make them turn out in a second referendum and support the pro-nuclear energy side. One of the unresolved issues was the final disposal of nuclear waste. In 1983, the Verbundgesellschaft successfully concluded negotiations with both China and Russia to take care of Austria's nuclear waste.[11] With the final disposal problem resolved (by nuclear waste exports) and a 58 per cent majority in the 1985 survey perhaps only a new grand coalition was required to revive the nuclear energy option?

---

[10] At that time the 'Greens' had only begun to emerge from different local citizen initiatives. The most important one held a sizeable delegation in the Salzburg city council. However, it was all but an archetypal Green list.
[11] *Wiener Zeitung*, 5 Nov. 2008. Interview with Walter Fremuth, then CEO of the Verbundgesellschaft, the 50% owner of Zwentendorf.

Table 5.5. Post-Referendum Attitudes on Nuclear Power (Vote Intention in Referendum Today)

Year	Pro nuclear energy	Against nuclear energy	Would not participate*, Undecided/No answer, DK	N
1978, 11 (IFES)	37	31	20*/12	1727
1979, 1 (IFES)	46	33	18*	2000
1979, 2 (IFES)	48	35	16*	2000
1979, 3 (IFES)	49	33	15*	2000
1979, 4 (IFES)	33	49	16*	2000
1979, 5 (IFES)	32	51	16*	2000
1979, 6 (IFES)	42	41	16*	2000
1979, 9 (IFES)	45	37	16*	2000
1979, 10 (IFES)	45	38	15*	2000
1979, 11 (IFES)	41	39	18*	2000
1980, 1 (IFES)	48	36	14*	2000
1980, 2 (IFES)	49	36	13*	2000
1980, 4-5 (F+GfK)	58	32	0/10	900
1980, 8-9 (F+GfK)	44	39	15/2	983
1980, 11 (F+GfK)	36	36	25/3	970
1981, 2 (IFES)	46	29	21/4	1500
1981, 8 (F+GfK)	40	39	20/2	1500
1985, 4-5 (F+GfK)	58	32	0/10	982
1986, 5-6 (F+GfK)	10	87	0/3	900

Sources: Surveys of the IFES according to Bichlbauer (1979: 32), Blaha (1980: 25), IFES (if8102) and surveys of the Dr Fessel + GfK institute.

All attempts at policy reversal came to an abrupt end with the Chernobyl accident of 24 April 1986. Due to the unusual wind conditions at the time, Austria was among the most affected countries. The issue of radioactive pollution caused great public concern and Chancellor Fred Sinowatz was quick to realize: 'Zwentendorf is dead'. Even the most ardent promoter of nuclear power in the top echelons of Austrian politics, Trade Union Federation president Anton Benya, agreed. Consequently, the Zwentendorf reactor was dismantled.

5.4.3 Phase 3: Mission the World and Reap Electoral Gains

With no nuclear reactor left, nuclear energy being legally banned, and even the once most ardent supporters of the nuclear cause having given up on it, did the issue fall into oblivion? In a way this is true, as no survey evidence is available for the twenty years between Chernobyl (Table 5.6) and the recent years characterized by international attempts at reviving nuclear energy. Obviously, those in the position to commission public opinion surveys were no longer interested to monitor closely what the Austrians think about nuclear energy. Rather, the citizens' rejection of nuclear energy was taken for granted. A glance through the press reporting on nuclear energy in this period is sufficient to recognize that media cuing reinforced this attitude.

This rejection of nuclear energy is confirmed by twenty-first-century surveys. These have probed into different aspects and dimensions of nuclear energy.

Table 5.6. Post-Chernobyl Attitudes towards Nuclear Energy in Austria

Year/Month	Question	Pro-nuclear	Anti-nuclear	N
2006/5–6	Strongly–somewhat (7-5) in favour vs strongly–somewhat opposed (3-1)	6	86	1111
2006/10–11	Risks vs advantages of nuclear energy	20	66	1013
2009/9–10		13	75	1001
2006/10–11	Possible to operate a nuclear power plant in a safe manner	28	60	–
2009/9–10		33	63	
2006/10–11	Nuclear energy helps fighting global warming	37	41	–
2009/9–10		29	69	
2006/10–11	Nuclear energy helps to make us less dependent on fuel imports	54	34	–
2009/9–10		47	48	
2006/10–11	Nuclear energy ensures lower energy prices	42	41	–
2009/9–10	... stable energy prices	36	56	
2006/10–11	Use of nuclear energy should be increased vs decreased	6	59	–
2009/9–10		4	66	
2009/9–10	... increased vs decreased provided nuclear energy's advantages in reducing greenhouse gases and import dependence	6	54	–
2007/6	Advantages vs disadvantages of nuclear energy	15	64	1042
2009/9–10	Advantages vs risks of nuclear energy	24	65	
2007/6	Nuclear energy to avoid climate change catastrophe	16	38	
2007/6	Today's technology makes another Chernobyl extremely unlikely	13	70	–
2009/5	Nuclear energy is unassailable, in favour of constructing nuclear power stations	8	?	1043
2009/5–7	Lifting the ban on nuclear power production in Austria	16	78	1200
2009/9–10	Possible to dispose nuclear waste in a safe manner	26	69	–

Sources: 2006/5–6. Special Eurobarometer 262. Energy Technologies: Knowledge, Perception, Measures.
2006/11: Special Eurobarometer 271. Europeans and Nuclear Safety.
2007/5: IILP, IMAS.
2009/5: IMAS Imas international Report 13, May 2009.
2009/5–7: AUTNES. Post-Post Election Survey.
2009/9–10: Special Eurobarometer 324. Europeans and Nuclear Safety.

Table 5.6 summarizes them under the grossly simplifying 'pro' and 'con' labels. Given the many (often fundamentally) different items, Table 5.6 cannot be read as a time series in its entirety (though some issues show up several times). Nevertheless, the emerging picture is clear: whichever item was explored and whatever frame was used, all surveys returned vast majorities against nuclear energy.

After banning the production of nuclear energy, Austria has become an importer of electricity mainly from nuclear power. While the Greens occasionally hinted at the double standard involved in this behaviour, this was not of public concern. It was only in the aftermath of the Fukushima disaster that other parties turned to this issue. The SPÖ-ÖVP coalition under Werner Faymann was quick to promise an end to such imports in 2011. Yet, eventually it turned out that a ban on electricity imports from nuclear production would have violated EU law and hence the idea was dismissed in 2012.

As this episode shows, even when citizens largely agree on a matter and their opinions are strong and stable, and even in the absence of niche parties that cater to the less populated end of the opinion spectrum, this does not render the issue irrelevant. Rather, nuclear power has turned from a position issue in the pre-Chernobyl period into a valence issue (Stokes 1963). In other words, there is general agreement about the desired direction of policy (to dispense with nuclear power altogether) and controversy and competition is about which party or politician is most competent in achieving that goal. But where is the desired policy when no nuclear power station is left to fight and nuclear energy is already legally banned? Austrian politicians have turned to nuclear power elsewhere and chosen to compete over their commitment to preventing harm from abroad. This chapter has highlighted the early fight against a nuclear power station in neighbouring Switzerland. Of course, Austria is surrounded by nuclear power stations and—leaving aside the possible consequences of their closing down on the international energy markets and CO_2 emissions—for nuclear energy opponents it would be attractive to close down all of them immediately. Yet, given the real-world constraints, this does not seem feasible in the short term. Therefore, Austrian politicians have targeted particular dangerous species among nuclear facilities. The first one was the planned German reprocessing plant at Wackersdorf in Bavaria. It had motivated considerable grassroots protest in the bordering Austrian Länder and politicians picked up the case quickly. Between 1985 and 1989, when the construction plans were cancelled due to domestic citizen protest in Germany (see Chapter 7), Austrian politicians took a very active part in the fight against Wackersdorf by tolerating unconventional protest by Austrian citizens (e.g. the blocking of cross-border traffic). It may be fair to conclude that this was first and foremost a play for the domestic Austrian audience, with the question being: who is the best representative of the country's vital interests?

Austrian EU membership (from 1995) triggered concerns that the freedoms of the single market might be used by foreign firms to build nuclear waste disposal sites on Austrian soil, to transport nuclear materials through the country, or even try to invalidate the ban on nuclear energy by appeal to the European Court of Justice. At the same time discussion about a possible future NATO membership of Austria invited thinking about the issue of nuclear weapons on Austrian soil. The Greens voiced these concerns in a people's initiative in 1998. 248,787 citizens (4.3 per cent of those entitled to participate) signed the initiative. Although the ideas may seem a little far-fetched, given the consensus on the issue, a constitutional law was passed that responded to these demands and outlawed such behaviour.

The nuclear power stations in the East European neighbouring countries constituted even more suitable targets than Wackersdorf or abstract nuclear invasion scenarios, particularly after the lifting of the iron curtain. On the one hand, they were generally conceived as less safe than Western plants. On the other hand, these countries' ambitions of joining the EU provided a lever that could be used to exercise real influence. As Austria has been a EU member since 1995 and the accession of new members requires unanimous consent of member states, Austrian politicians could credibly claim in the domestic arena that it was possible to impose Western standards on the accession countries or, if these could not be reached, to enforce the closing down of nuclear power stations.

In terms of national-level party manifestos, the FPÖ was first to add a foreign policy dimension to the nuclear power issue. In its 1986 manifesto it stated 'Now it is time to work for a retreat from nuclear energy internationally, as radioactivity does not know national borders', but the party remained silent on the issue in the subsequent manifestos until 2002. The ÖVP followed in 1990, stating the double goal of 'fighting dangerous nuclear power stations' and 'helping eastern neighbours' in coping with the problem. The 1990 SPÖ-ÖVP coalition agreement committed the government to promoting the phasing out of nuclear energy in neighbouring countries with the goal of building a nuclear-power-free zone in central Europe. In their 1994 coalition agreement (signed after the approval of Austria's EU accession by referendum) these parties committed to maintaining Austria's active role against nuclear energy as EU member state. That claim was repeated in the 1996 coalition agreement. The first SPÖ manifesto containing nuclear power foreign policy dates from 1995. It committed to continuing Austria's anti-nuclear energy policy in the EU. In 1999, both the SPÖ and ÖVP manifestos referred to the chance to impose Western nuclear safety standards on EU accession countries. The ÖVP was more explicit and also mentioned the Czech Temelìn reactor that was still under construction and thus seemed a more suitable target than nuclear power stations already in operation. The manifesto of the Greens talked about 'helping our neighbours to get out of nuclear energy'. The ÖVP-FPÖ coalition taking government office after that election related that claim explicitly to EU enlargement. In 2002, with the Eastern EU enlargement negotiations beginning in October, the manifestos were most detailed and explicit on the nuclear energy topic. The SPÖ, now in opposition, defined more general and long-term goals for Europe such as the exit from nuclear energy, abolishing subsidies for nuclear energy, and the promotion of renewable energy. The ÖVP was more specific, addressing both the EURATOM Treaty and Temelìn. The FPÖ subscribed to the same ideas but used stronger words. The 2003 coalition agreement of the ÖVP and FPÖ was even more explicit, making the pledge that the government would fight the Czech nuclear power station at Temelìn, work towards a revision of the EURATOM treaty, and more. In 2005, the ÖVP-FPÖ coalition agreement stated that promoting anti-nuclear policy would be a core topic of the upcoming Austrian EU presidency. The subsequent agreements of the SPÖ-ÖVP coalitions from 2007 and 2008 again committed the partners to oppose nuclear energy and support efforts to improve nuclear safety in EU context.

How did these commitments translate into political action? One strategy of Austrian politicians was trying to influence relevant decisions at the international level. A series of (largely unsuccessful) attempts were directed at US and European institutions and aimed at preventing the provision of credits devoted to nuclear expansion in the accession countries or engineering grants that should ease phasing out.[12] In 2006, Austria led a coalition against research on nuclear energy in the seventh EU Framework Programme. Most important, however, were EU membership negotiations with the Eastern enlargement countries. Of course,

---

[12] Austria unsuccessfully lobbied the Export-Import Bank of the United States to prevent the granting of a credit for the completion of Temelìn in 1994. In 1995 Austrian MEPs—taking advantage of vast floor absence in the European Parliament—engineered the delay of a credit for the Slovak nuclear power plant Mochovce.

the problems were that nuclear energy is not generally rejected in the EU nor does nuclear safety fall under EU jurisdiction. Yet, based on the argument that states have a role in protecting their citizens, Austria 'was the driving force making nuclear energy an issue within the context of EU enlargement' (Axelrod 2004: 158). The negotiations eventually led to making EU accession conditional on the closing down of seven first-generation reactors (one in Slovakia, two in Lithuania, and four in Bulgaria) and the upgrading of several second-generation reactors in the Czech Republic, Slovakia, Hungary, and Bulgaria (see Chapter 1).

Given that nuclear safety is not included in the EU jurisdiction and the divided opinions on nuclear energy among EU member states, the Council decision on the 'principles, priorities, intermediate objectives and conditions contained in the Accession Partnership with the Czech Republic' from 6 December 1999 (1999/858/EC) only demanded from the Czech Republic to 'continue to ensure high levels of nuclear safety at the Dukovany and Temelìn (upon completion) nuclear power plants'. As this seemed a rather weak obligation, Austrian government officials tried to follow up in bilateral contacts. As Temelìn was not yet completed, Austrian politicians hoped for a second 'Zwentendorf' (i.e. a stop on the project) or, at least, Western safety standards. Yet, Austria had no legal right to demand Czech cooperation or even information. To ensure that, Austria threatened to block the closing of the energy chapter in the EU accession negotiations. At the same time politicians were willing to tolerate the blocking of inter-state motorways between Austria and the Czech Republic by anti-nuclear activists. Overcoming these inconveniences was an incentive for the Czech side to engage in bilateral negotiations with Austria.

Austrian parties competed over what should be demanded from the Czech Republic and how that should be achieved. The case is particularly interesting as the main dividing line in the ÖVP-FPÖ government, with the FPÖ raising maximalist demands: insisting on the stop for Temelìn or otherwise blocking the Czech Republic's accession to the EU.

Concerned about coalition survival, its own electoral prospects, looming international embarrassment, and making some real progress in resolving the problem, the ÖVP behind the back of its coalition partner managed to engineer negotiations with the Czech side also involving EU enlargement commissioner Günther Verheugen. The 'fait accompli' was a bilateral agreement with the Czech Republic (signed in December 2000) that obliged the Czech side to conduct an environmental impact assessment on Temelìn, establish an early warning system, and provide high-quality information on accidents in nuclear power stations, while the Austrian side committed to guaranteeing the free flow of traffic and refraining from upholding accession negotiations.

The FPÖ claimed to be unimpressed. To put pressure on its coalition partner, it organized a people's initiative titled 'Veto against Temelìn'. It was surprisingly proposed in October 2001 and could be signed in January 2002. The initiative demanded the enactment of a constitutional law requiring that Austria's government officials could only allow Czech EU accession under the conditions of the prior closing down of Temelìn and providing a legal guarantee to maintain that status as EU member state. With 914,937 supporting signatures (15.25 per cent of the potential voters) the initiative was well supported. With the initiative, the FPÖ had 'tied itself to the mast' (cf. Elster 1984) and thus established a considerable problem for the coalition.¹³ Perhaps this was even more a threat for the FPÖ's government team. Indeed, in retrospect the people's initiative can be seen already as part of the FPÖ internal power struggle between radicals and the party's team in public office at the federal level that eventually brought down the ÖVP-FPÖ coalition in September 2002.

Federal Chancellor Schüssel managed to counter the initiative move of the FPÖ by conducting further negotiations with the Czech Prime Minister Miloš Zeman (again involving Commissioner Verheugen) that improved on the previous agreement. Foreign Minister Benita Ferrero-Waldner (ÖVP) then was quick to vote for the closing of the energy chapter in the accession negotiations. Subsequent events prevented Temelín coming back as an all-or-nothing issue on the political agenda.¹⁴ Yet, the relief that had followed the bilateral agreements did not last long. Apparently, the interpretations of the Czech concessions had been overly optimistic. Today, frustration about nuclear energy policy in the Czech Republic is the predominant feeling in Austria. The same applies to Slovakia, where Austrian politicians have engaged in unsuccessful activities to prevent the building new nuclear reactors. Needless to say that Austrian parties publicized their ideas and actions in fighting nuclear energy abroad to their best abilities in the domestic arena.

This final episode of nuclear power's trajectory in Austrian politics has shown that, although political parties basically agree on the substantive issue, it would be beneficial to close down particularly risk-prone nuclear power stations in the neighbouring countries. Yet this issue was not without trade-offs. Specifically, Austria was engaged in nested games (Tsebelis 1990) with the accession countries and the other member states. Despite some discomfort about nuclear energy and the labour market implications of Eastern enlargement Austria was overwhelmingly favourable about it. And playing hardball games with regard to the nuclear power issue might have compromised Austria's business interests (as the largest per capita investor in these countries). Finally, exploiting the veto power over accession might have diminished the willingness of other member states to respect legitimate Austrian interests in day-to-day qualified majority decision-making in the EU and made Austria (again, after the recent 'Haider affair') an odd member in the EU. Clearly, government parties, when behaving responsibly, are more constrained than opposition parties. Yet, unconditional vote maximizing may jeopardize government office for both parties already in the government, like the FPÖ, and opposition parties.

---

¹³ The initiative was doomed to fail without the opposition's parliamentary support (i.e. without SPÖ votes) as the two-thirds constitutional majority could not be reached without it. Yet, the SPÖ's 'no' could have been anticipated before the initiative's start and was loud and clear thereafter. Of course, carrying out the initiative's threat—blocking Czech EU access—was first and foremost in the hands of the government and hence the ÖVP. The ÖVP's worst-case scenario therefore was a showdown in the coalition followed by early elections over that issue.
¹⁴ These events include the breakdown of the ÖVP-FPÖ coalition, earthquake elections with the ÖVP triumphing and the FPÖ being reduced to a third of their previous parliamentary strength, the humiliating return of the FPÖ as a docile coalition partner in a renewed coalition with the ÖVP, and eventually the breaking away of the government-oriented wing of the FPÖ, establishing the BZÖ in 2005.

5.5 CONCLUSION

This chapter has followed the trajectory of nuclear energy policy in Austria. It has identified political parties as the main actors and decision-making strongly influenced by party competition. Political parties have three main goals: exercising policy influence, winning votes, and holding government office. Under favourable circumstances these goals do not conflict and can be achieved simultaneously. Often, however, political parties face trade-offs between these goals and can achieve one only at the price of abandoning or neglecting another (Strøm 1990; Müller and Strøm 1999). As this chapter has shown, this was indeed the case in Austrian nuclear energy policy. The policy outcome—first banning nuclear energy, then upholding this decision against all attempts at policy reversal, and finally adding a foreign policy dimension and fighting nuclear energy abroad—resulted from these goal conflicts and the game unfolding between political parties.

In the first period, the main trade-off for two major parties, the SPÖ and ÖVP, was that between policy on the one hand and votes and office on the other. Votes and office were linked as the SPÖ single-party majority government had only three seats' lead over the opposition. The nuclear energy issue had the potential to terminate the SPÖ's popular majority. The stakes were even higher if we consider the likely office consequences of such shifts in electoral support: the 1978 leadership change in the FPÖ[15] had considerably increased the chances that the ÖVP and FPÖ would form a coalition together rather than join a coalition lead by the SPÖ. Hence, even small electoral losses had the potential to have enormous impact in terms of office. Thus, the SPÖ and ÖVP privileged electoral and office goals over policy goals. At the same time, when turning to the referendum device, the SPÖ could hope to get away with only risking but not losing nuclear energy, as the outcome of the referendum initially seemed a safe bet for the pro-nuclear side. The initial goal of the ÖVP was avoiding electoral costs from helping the SPÖ out by legitimizing the Zwentendorf power station. If the SPÖ had followed through that course and let Zwentendorf go online, as suggested by its trade union wing, in an optimistic scenario the ÖVP might have won on all counts. Electoral punishment of the SPÖ would have strengthened the ÖVP (at least in relative terms). A change in government seemed possible. And the new government would inherit nuclear power, so no policy costs would have resulted. Once the SPÖ had chosen the referendum option, the SPÖ forfeiting power over a lost referendum would have been the best result from the ÖVP perspective and probably worth losing nuclear power. Finally, it was initially risky for the FPÖ to switch to the anti-nuclear side despite its core electorate's favourable attitude towards nuclear power. Yet, the overall party politicization of the nuclear energy issue quickly made this a lesser concern. Party politicization strengthened the 'no' side and probably was decisive for the rejection of nuclear power in the referendum.

---

[15] That change was agreed in February 1978, when the party executive nominated Alexander Götz, and completed with the leadership election at the party congress in September 1978, when 398 (of 416) delegates voted for Götz.

In the second phase, the initial situation had changed or soon was to change: nuclear energy was banned and the single-party government of the SPÖ gave way to the SPÖ-FPÖ coalition in 1983 (after another change in the leadership and course of the FPÖ in 1979). The FPÖ stuck to its policy position of rejecting nuclear energy but nevertheless made it into government. While unwilling to vote for nuclear energy, the FPÖ made the concession of tolerating SPÖ attempts at finding a parliamentary majority outside the coalition (i.e. with the ÖVP). As these attempts failed, the attached risk for the FPÖ never materialized. If anything, scepticism in the ÖVP over nuclear energy had increased over time (though in terms of sincere preferences the majority of party leaders was on the pro-nuclear side). Its tactical situation was basically unchanged (until 1983) or even more challenging (1983–6). The ÖVP thus did not want to 'bail out' the SPÖ by supporting nuclear policy reversal and bear electoral costs for such a move without being compensated by government office. As the SPÖ managed to maintain its single-party government (1979–83) and then had chosen to govern with the FPÖ, the ÖVP's priority was breaking the SPÖ majority and from 1983 unseating the SPÖ-FPÖ coalition rather than reviving nuclear energy.

In the third phase, after Chernobyl, nuclear energy was no longer a contested issue in Austria: the parties quickly converged to celebrate the wisdom of the 1978 decision to ban nuclear energy. Yet, the issue did not disappear from the agenda. Now foreign nuclear power stations were the universal targets and the parties competed over their competence in fighting them. Admittedly, it is much more difficult to exercise influence abroad, particularly for a small country that takes extreme positions on the relevant policy dimension among EU member states. The Eastern enlargement process certainly provided a lever but the question was to what extent political parties would allow nuclear power policy goals to compromise other policy goals. The party that took the extreme position, the FPÖ, was least interested in the major policy goal that guided the behaviour of the other parties: EU enlargement. And it was most resentful of the Czech side for its unwillingness to invalidate the Benes decrees expelling ethnic Germans in 1945–6. Hence, the FPÖ hoped to benefit electorally from its position taking but did not face much trade-off in terms of conflicting policy goals. Rather, the trade-off was between votes and policy on the one side and office on the other. ÖVP brinkmanship in international negotiations was meant to shift the balance between these goals by weakening the FPÖ's policy cause. Politically, it was successful, as the coalition did not fall over nuclear energy foreign policy.

Overall, it is difficult to assess the Austrian impact on the modernization of nuclear energy in Eastern Europe and thereby achieving safety gains. The more ambitious goals of redirecting the entire energy policy of the accession countries all failed, as modernized second-generation reactors are still in operation and the closed-down first-generation reactors have been replaced by more recent reactors. At least in retrospect, these goals were more suitable for party propaganda than policy-making. What is clear, however, is that competition over the nuclear energy issue in its foreign policy dimension brought the ÖVP-FPÖ coalition close to collapse and was a milestone to its termination in conflict in 2002.

This chapter has placed party competition at the centre of understanding nuclear energy policy outcome in Austria. Yet, political parties' cost–benefit calculations are influenced by the policy status quo. Several factors have provided a favourable background for the developments outlined in this chapter and have allowed the primacy of party politics in the Austrian case.

- *Timing*. The Austrian decision to ban nuclear energy was taken before the first nuclear power plant began its operation. Although money had been spent on developing the nuclear programme and building the plant, by saying 'no' Austria could maintain its nuclear 'virgin' status. It thus could avoid problems such as having to cope with (sizeable) nuclear waste.
- *Size*. As a small country, substituting domestic nuclear energy production by energy imports seemed costly but feasible.
- *Alternatives*. Being endowed with some natural energy resources (water not yet used for generating hydroelectric power, a modest amount of oil and gas, wood) and potential for large-scale energy savings, the claim that nuclear energy could be substituted for was plausible.
- *Political control*. At the time of making the crucial decisions the energy sector was under public ownership.
- *Path dependence*. Once the decision to abandon nuclear energy had been made and the Chernobyl accident had occurred it was easy to converge on a new anti-nuclear policy consensus. There were no nuclear power stations to remind decision-makers of their previous opinions and no major interests that would keep fighting in an uphill battle. The resulting one-sided cuing of the citizenry by politicians and media alike have brought about overwhelming rejection of nuclear energy in Austria. While many countries experienced a popular rejection of nuclear energy immediately after the Chernobyl accident but bounced back to a more split public opinion over the issue, the immediate post-Chernobyl attitudes were frozen in Austria.

Today no political party or major interest group promotes nuclear energy and hence a policy reversal. No relevant mass media argue against this consensus. Despite privatization and liberalization, the electricity sector has remained under political control and is not actively lobbying for nuclear energy. Nuclear power thus is categorically and—for all practical purposes—unanimously rejected. This is the 'state doctrine' referred to above. If nuclear power is mentioned in the context of domestic energy production it is to legitimize other forms of energy production that are unpopular for other reasons (such as destroying nature or transforming landscape). Thus, notwithstanding the pre-Fukushima international revival of nuclear energy with lifetime extensions, nuclear energy investment decisions, and efforts at reversing earlier phasing-out decisions in many Western countries, the nuclear energy cause seems solidly dead in Austria. This chapter has shown how this outcome relates to party competition, circumstantial factors, and path dependence. It is easy to imagine how different conditions at critical junctures could have paved the way for different outcomes.[16]

---

[16] Thanks to Hannes Auer, Michael Danzer, Nikolaus Eder, and Manès Weisskirchner for excellent research assistance and to Peter A. Ulram for granting access to Dr Fessel + GfK surveys. This research has greatly benefited from work in the Austrian National Election Study (AUTNES). Funding by the Austrian Research Fund (FWF) (S10903-G11) is gratefully acknowledged.

REFERENCES

Angermann, Erhard, and Plasser, Fritz (1979). 'Wahlen und Wähler in Österreich 1977–1978', in *Österreichisches Jahrbuch für Politik 1978*. Vienna: Verlag für Geschichte und Politik, 1–23.

Axelrod, Regina (2004). 'Nuclear Power and EU Enlargement: The Case of Temelìn.' *Environmental Politics*, 13(1): 153–72.

Bichlbauer, Dieter (1979). *Studie zur Volksabstimmung über die friedliche Nutzung der Kernenergie in Österreich aus demokratietheoretischer und soziologischer Sicht. Endbericht.* Vienna: Österreichische Gesellschaft zur Förderung der Forschung.

Blaha, Peter (1980). 'Zwentendorf nach Zwentendorf.' *Journal für Sozialforschung*, 19(2): 21–9.

Brandstätter, Lidia, Grosser, Michael, and Werthner, Hannes (1984). 'Die Anti-AKW-Bewegung in Österreich', in *Umdenken. Analysen grüner Politik in Österreich*. Vienna: Junius, 157–77.

Brettschneider, Rudolf (1980). 'Wahlen und Wähler in Österreich 1978/79', in *Österreichisches Jahrbuch für Politik 1979*. Vienna: Verlag für Geschichte und Politik, 1–15.

Bundespressedienst (ed.) (1977). *Kernenergie*. 4 vols. Vienna: Bundespressedienst.

Elster, Jon (1984). *Ulysses and the Sirenes*. Cambridge: Cambridge University Press.

Fischer, Heinz (1993). *Die Kreisky-Jahre 1967–1983*. Vienna: Löcker.

Gehmacher, Ernst (1981). 'Meinungsbildung zum Pro-Zwentendorf-Volksbegehren.' *Journal für Sozialforschung*, 21(1): 69–75.

Kienzl, Heinz (1979). 'Der atomare Rückschlag.' *Journal für Sozialforschung*, 19(1): 19–27.

Kitzmüller, Erich (1979). 'Österreich—verspäteter Atomzwerg oder nicht atomarer Anfänger?', in Lutz Metz (ed.), *Der Atomkonflikt*. Berlin: Olle und Wolter, 226–48.

Kok, Franz (1991). *Politik der Elektrizitätswirtschaft in Österreich*. Baden-Baden: Nomos.

Kreisky, Bruno (1996). *Der Mensch im Mittelpunkt: Der Memoiren dritter Teil*. Vienna: Kremayr & Scheriau.

Kriechbaumer, Robert (2004). *Die Ära Kreisky. Österreich 1970–1983*. Vienna: Böhlau.

Lauber, Volkmar, with Hellriegl, Manfred, and Kok, Franz (1988). 'Paradigmenewechsel in der Elektrizitätswirtschaft.' *Österreichische Zeitschrift für Politikwissenschaft*, 17(3): 231–48.

Müller, Wolfgang C. (1985). 'Die Rolle der Parteien bei Entstehung und Entwicklung der Sozialpartnerschaft', in Peter Gerlich, Edgar Grande, and Wolfgang C. Müller (eds), *Sozialpartnerschaft in der Krise*. Vienna: Böhlau, 135–224.

Müller, Wolfgang C. (1998). 'Plebiscitary Politics and Party Competition in Austria.' *Electoral Studies*, 17(1): 21–43.

Müller, Wolfgang C., and Strøm, Kaare (eds) (1999). *Policy, Office, or Votes? How Political Parties in Western Europe Make Hard Decisions*. Cambridge: Cambridge University Press.

Nelkin, Dorothy, and Pollak, Michael (1977). 'The Politics of Participation and the Nuclear Debate in Sweden, the Netherlands, and Austria.' *Public Policy*, 25(3): 333–57.

Nowotny, Helga (1979). *Kernenergie: Gefahr oder Notwendigkeit?* Frankfurt am Main: Suhrkamp.

Pelinka, Anton (1983). 'The Nuclear Power Referendum in Austria.' *Electoral Studies*, 2(3): 253–61.

Preglau, Max (1994). 'The State and the Anti-Nuclear Power Movement in Austria', in Helena Flam (ed.), *States and Anti-Nuclear Movements*. Edinburgh: Edinburgh University Press, 37–69.

Reiter, Erich (1982). *Programm und Programmentwicklung der FPÖ*. Vienna: Braumüller.

Rösch-Wehinger, Anna (2009). *Die Grünen in Vorarlberg: Von den sozialen Bewegungen zur Partei*. Innsbruck: Studienverlag.

Schaller, Christian (1987). *Die österreichische Kernenergiekontroverse: Meinungsbildungs- und Entscheidungsprozesse mit besonderer Berücksichtigung der Auseinandersetzungen im das Kernkraftwerk Zwentendorf bis 1991. Dokumentation—Analyse—Interpretation.* Doctoral Dissertation: University of Salzburg.

Sickinger, Hubert (2004). 'Politische Rahmenbedingungen und deren Auswirkungen am Beispiel der Elektrizitätswirtschaft', in Ewald Nowotny, Christoph Parek, and Ronald F. Scheucher (eds), *Handbuch der österreichischen Energiewirtschaft.* Vienna: Manz, 159-78.

Stifter, Gerald (2006). *Die ÖVP in der Ära Kreisky 1970-1983.* Innsbruck: Studien Verlag.

Stokes, Donald E. (1963). 'Spatial Models of Party Competition.' *American Political Science Review*, 57(2): 368-77.

Strøm, Kaare (1990). 'A Behavioral Theory of Competitive Political Parties.' *American Journal of Political Science*, 34(3): 565-98.

Tsebelis, George (1990). *Nested Games.* Berkeley, CA: University of California Press.

Ulram, Peter A. (1990). *Hegemonie der Erosion: Politische Kultur und politischer Wandel in Österreich.* Vienna: Verlag Böhlau.

6

Nuclear Politics in France

High-Profile Policy and Low-Salience Politics

Sylvain Brouard and Isabelle Guinaudeau

6.1 INTRODUCTION

On 8 January 2015, Ségolène Royal, French Minister of Ecology, Sustainable Development, and Energy, announced her intention to 'plan the building of a new generation of reactors that will replace the older plants when they can no longer be refurbished'.[1] This clearly signals the enduring commitment of France to nuclear energy even after the events at Fukushima in March 2011. Contrary to the situation in many other European countries, French nuclear policy has never experienced a major policy reversal, nor was it ever seriously challenged—even if, for the first time ever, a law capping nuclear electricity production was adopted in 2015 (Table 6.A1, in Appendix 2). Therefore, in the present book, France offers a control case and enables us to identify, in a comparative perspective, factors explaining why this country did not phase out.

The continuity of the French pro-nuclear policy has given rise to the second largest set of nuclear plants in the world (59 reactors), behind the United States (104). Since the creation of the Atomic Energy Commission in 1945, €188 billion have been invested in nuclear research and development as well as in nuclear facilities.[2] The results of this policy in the long run are striking. Since the 1970s, energy production in France has tripled due to the massive development of nuclear energy. At the same time, the use of domestic natural resources (coal, gas, oil) has declined steadily. As shown in Figure 6.1, around 75 per cent of French electricity now comes from nuclear plants. France is therefore worldwide the country that relies most on nuclear energy. This policy enabled France to reduce the level of oil importation from the end of the 1970s to the mid-1980s and to stabilize it during the following years (see also Chapter 3). The fast growth in energy consumption—from 150 million tons of oil equivalent (Mtoe) to 250 Mtoe

---

[1] <http://www.usinenouvelle.com/article/segolene-royal-il-faut-batir-de-nouvelles-centrales-nucleaires.N307067>.
[2] Report of the Cour des Comptes (2012): cf. <http://www.ccomptes.fr/Publications/Publications/Les-couts-de-la-filiere-electro-nucleaire>.

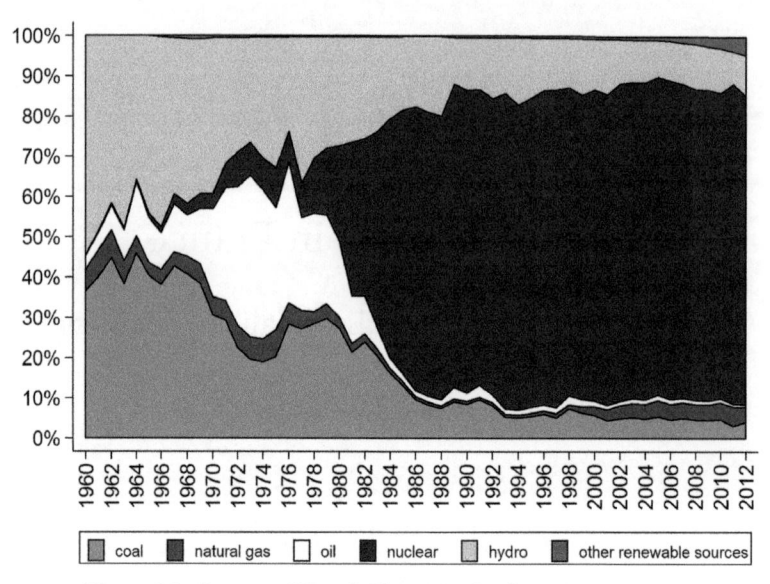

Figure 6.1. Sources of French Electricity Production 1960–2012

in thirty-five years—was secured by nuclear energy. So, despite the lack of domestic natural resources, the level of foreign energy dependence has regularly decreased to reach around 50 per cent. For many years, electricity supply in France had been higher than the demand, so that France was even able to export electricity (Guillaumat-Taillet 1987; Hadjilambrinos 2000).

The new French nuclear projects also stem from an industrial policy aiming to support the state-owned nuclear industry. A sustained programme of nuclear buildings made it possible to keep the country's nuclear industry alive. With the French giant company AREVA producing 'third-generation' nuclear plants, France wanted its nuclear industry to gain new markets abroad. The former President Nicolas Sarkozy explicitly affirmed his will to prove that France relies on its own nuclear technology by building new nuclear plants.

Since the end of the Second World War, the nuclear energy priority has never been deeply challenged in France. The French pro-nuclear policy has been intensively scrutinized by political scientists and various explanations have been put forward. First, French nuclear policy has been described as a mechanical answer to the specific national situation characterized by the lack of natural resources. However, many other countries in the same situation did not develop any nuclear programme, whereas countries with natural energy resources did do so. Frank Baumgartner explains the differences in nuclear policy in France and in the US by the specificity of the French scientific community, which is smaller and more homogeneous than the American one (Baumgartner 1990). Nonetheless, there are also anti-nuclear scientists in France who publish public appeals against nuclear energy. Many have also suggested that the encapsulated bureaucratic decision-making process (Hecht 1998; Jasper 1988; Kitschelt 1986; Rucht 1994) keeps 'nuclear power off the political agenda' (Baumgartner 1990) and explains the enduring pro-nuclear policy. Notwithstanding such claims nuclear energy issues have been a main topic of the legislative and parliamentary agendas since the beginning of the 1950s. From the same perspective, the economic weight of the nuclear complex composed by the electricity company and the nuclear industry was also seen as a reason for the continuity in French energy policy. However, to be fully relevant from a comparative perspective, these factors should have prevented any policy reversal in Germany as well. Other scholars suggested that the continuity of French nuclear policy resulted from a pro-nuclear public opinion. However, the evidence does not support this explanation either. Support for nuclear energy from the French public opinion has been far from massive. French public opinion is more or less equally divided with fluctuations driven by the media coverage of the nuclear issue. Nevertheless, there has been a pro-nuclear consensus among the French governing parties (Nelkin and Pollak 1980)—only recently challenged under the electoral pressure of the Greens—associated with a low saliency of the nuclear energy issue in the political competition. Social movements against nuclear energy failed to structurally influence the French nuclear policy as well as the party system until the end of the 1990s.

The present chapter argues that a policy reversal would have needed a partisan agent to implement an anti-nuclear policy. From a comparative perspective, the continuity of the French pro-nuclear policy appears to be the result of an avoidance of politicization by the main French political parties, reinforced by the increasing inertia of the French nuclear policy inheritance. The avoidance of politicization resulted partly from the features of the electoral system; coalition-making constraints were also relevant. Recent changes in the nuclear policy stances and policies can be understood against the background of the electoral rise of the Green Party. They may also be interpreted as counterfactual proof of electoral system effects and coalition-making constraints.

6.2 POLICY DEVELOPMENT

In 1945, the creation of a specialized nuclear research centre—the Commission for Atomic Energy (CEA)—marked the beginning of the French nuclear programme. Three different motivations shaped this decision. First, there was the fundamental scientific aim to intensify the involvement of the French research community in nuclear research. Second, in the context of post-war reconstruction, policy-makers were interested in exploring the possibility of a civilian use of nuclear energy for the production of electricity. Finally, developing the technology required to create nuclear weapons was the third objective followed by the first post-World War II government in starting the French nuclear programme (Hecht 1998). De Gaulle and the French army wanted to avoid another defeat and to gain independence vis-à-vis the United States and the Soviet Union.

In 1951, the junior minister Félix Gaillard proposed the first five-year development plan for nuclear energy that was adopted a year later by Parliament. There was a consensus on going nuclear even though the Communist Party wanted to avoid any military use of atomic energy, and rightist parties prevented the participation of communist sympathizers in the programme. This plan gave birth to the first nuclear plant in 1956 (G1 in Marcoule) and to the research and development of a second plant, built in 1959. Framed by the idea of independence and industrialization, the programme did not rely on the existing American technology but chose a new French technology (graphite-moderated, gas-cooled) elaborated by the CEA to produce nuclear energy. EDF (Electricité de France), the electricity company nationalized in 1945, succeeded in setting up collaboration with the CEA on the first nuclear plant. Since then, the EDF-CEA association has structured the field of nuclear policy. Nuclear electricity has been commercialized by EDF since 1966.

The 1960s were crucial in shaping the French nuclear policy. Following De Gaulle's return to power, the army and the CEA were focused on French nuclear independence and on the production of plutonium for the nuclear weapon programme. Conversely, in order to 'modernize France' EDF wanted to intensify nuclear energy production, relying on the more efficient and robust American technology based on pressurized water reactors instead of graphite-moderated reactors. In 1969, the government decided to split military and civilian logics, allowing EDF to use its preferred technology. The building of a new wave of nuclear plants directly stems from this decision. This new industrial perspective occurred before the oil crisis of 1973–4, even if the crisis reinforced it. Under the 'Messmer plan', announced in 1974, the objective was to build thirteen new plants before 1980, fifty before the middle of the 1980s, and 200 before 2000. This overly ambitious programme was only partially realized, given the over-estimation of the growth of electric consumption in France (Bataille and Galley 1999; see also Guillaumat-Taillet 1987).

Nuclear policy was not contested in Parliament until 1997 and anti-nuclear stances were kept outside the political institutions (Nelkin and Pollak 1981; Kitschelt 1986; Rucht 1994). However, the 1970s marked an upsurge in the opposition to nuclear plants. Protest around several construction sites arose from local actions to massive demonstrations and violent confrontations with the police. The mobilization reached its peak in Creys-Malville against the Superphénix fast-breeder reactor in 1976 and 1977. The anti-nuclear protests kept on at the beginning of the 1980s with only limited policy results. The building of nuclear plants was suspended during a brief period after Mitterrand's election in order to allow an assessment of the energy policy and a debate on it in Parliament. This debate did not challenge nuclear energy policy. Only the construction of one planned nuclear plant was cancelled in 1981 (in Plogoff). The 1998 decision to stop the Superphénix plant, to which we will return with further detail, was part of the government coalition agreement between the Socialist, Communist, and Green parties. This was highly symbolic for opponents of nuclear energy, given the numerous demonstrations this experimental plant had provoked for two decades.

Nevertheless, the level of nuclear energy production remained unaffected and indeed kept on growing. In 2005, the building of nuclear plants was relaunched with the first building of a European pressurized reactor (EPR) reactor in France. On 31 January 2009, the French president announced the building of a second third-generation nuclear plant by EDF in Flamanville, as well as the prolongation of the lifetime of the existing plants to forty years. After a fifteen-year pause (1990–2005) these episodes clearly signalled the industrial and political will to start a new development phase of nuclear energy in France. This orientation has not been seriously called into question after the accident of Fukushima in March 2011. New security investigations resulted in demands for new investments in the existing plants, but no plant was closed. On the contrary, a life-term extension of the nuclear plant from the original forty years to fifty or sixty years was discussed. EDF announced €55 billion investment for the required refurbishments.

The 2012 political alternation halted this new development phase. The closure of the oldest plant, located in Fessenheim, has been announced, even if not effective yet, and the second EPR project is stalled (while the building of the first one is maintained). In addition, a law about energy transition was adopted in 2015, which limits for the first time the allowed level of nuclear energy production to the current level of power of French nuclear plants: 63.2 GW. The main practical consequence is that eighteen months before the new EPR reactor will be connected to the grid (expected in 2018), EDF will have to close older nuclear plants—Fessenheim and another one—representing the same amount of power, to comply with the law. The decrease of the proportion of nuclear energy in electricity to 50 per cent is to be compensated by an increase in renewable energy production (technically, production of nuclear energy is limited to the current level, while electricity consumption is expected to grow). This scenario was EDF's preferred alternative, while the government did not support the progressive and partial phasing out of nuclear energy advocated by the Greens, in order to decrease its contribution to the energy mix. If France is still not experiencing a policy reversal (as there is no phasing out and the building of new nuclear plants is expected), the recent decisions represent a turning point: they are the first explicit policy stopping the development of nuclear energy in France.

6.3 ACTORS AND JURISDICTIONS

When dealing with this French exception, some scholars point to the specificity of the French scientific community, which is considered to be smaller and more homogeneous than in other countries, with a quasi monopoly of the Corps des Mines graduates in key positions and a concentration of R&D resources towards research carried out within the state-controlled institutions, EDF and the CEA (Baumgartner 1990; Delmas and Heinman 2001: 449; Schneider 2009). This literature has revealed strong links between nuclear research, nuclear industry, and nuclear policy. Boudia describes how policy-makers, scientists, and industrialists in charge of nuclear programmes have responded to growing public distrust with the creation of information and public relation devices (Boudia 2003) and how they have used scientific expertise in order to promote the social acceptability of nuclear energy and to resist social protest (Boudia 2008).

Nonetheless, since the mid-1970s, French scientists, in particular nuclear physicists, have mobilized and signed public appeals against nuclear energy (Topçu 2006), so that some scientific expertise might back attempts to modify the direction of French energy policy. Famous examples are the founding mobilization of thousands of scholars, in 1975, and the establishment of the Commission for Independent Research and Information on Radioactivity (CRIIRAD in

French), an organization created after Chernobyl with the objective of providing independent measures of radioactivity.

In a related vein, most authors explain that French citizens' distrust towards nuclear energy was not channelled into policy-making as the decision-making process was described as 'encapsulated', 'technocratic', and 'bureaucratic' (Kitschelt 1986; Jasper 1988; Rucht 1994; Delmas and Heinman 2001; Schneider 2009) and is supposed to have kept 'nuclear power off the political agenda' (Baumgartner 1990). In this view, policy-making is dominated by the executive, in interaction with experts, technocrats, managers, and administrators of the nuclear sector. Crucial decisions are taken behind closed doors, with little room left for a democratic or political debate over energy policy choices. The institutional setting thus leaves no chance for the polarization of French public opinion finding any expression in the politicization of nuclear energy policy in either party or parliamentary debates.

The central state, the executive, and the central administration indeed play a crucial role in nuclear policy-making, both as to expertise and decision-making (Lucas 1979; Rucht 1994; Delmas and Heinman 2001). The CEA and EDF developed plans that were submitted for the government's approval (often to the ministries of industry, research, defence and environment) and, in the Fifth Republic, to the President. EDF and the CEA were transformed and partially privatized in the 2000s. Yet the influence of the executive remains critical, notably through the appointment of chairmen and administrators in both institutions. The executive also continues to exert a decisive influence over energy policy and planning as well as the regulation of the energy market via the approbation of infrastructure projects, the regulation of electricity prices, the public shares in groups such as EDF, AREVA, or ENGIE (formerly known as GDF-Suez) and the activities of the energy regulation commission, which are closely controlled by the government. A main justification for this persistent state control is the French concept of *mission de service public*, which implies the guaranteeing of an equal and universal access to electricity.[3]

Until now, the construction of nuclear plants has been supervised either by the CEA or by EDF, which signed contracts with industrial groups for the different components of the reactors. To satisfy the energetic demand at lower costs, concentration in the energy sector has been favoured. Four huge groups had dominated the sector for a long time: Cogema (a CEA department dealing with R&D and nuclear safety), EDF (the sole company engineering nuclear plants), the Empain-Schneider group (building the main components of the plants through its subsidiaries Framatome and Creusot-Loire), and the Alstom-Atlantique branch of the CGE group. Since 2001, the main group is AREVA (which resulted from the merging of the CEA Industry department with Framatome and Cogema).

This 'policy of champions' had fostered the emergence of what had been until recently high-performing and competitive groups that were deemed to follow a strategy of internationalization (Delion and Durupty 2010). AREVA became the leading group worldwide in the nuclear energy sector. Backed by the state, it captured markets resulting from a rebirth of nuclear energy in the late 2000s, such as in

---

[3] These objectives are defined in the 2000 law on electricity (Wise 2005: 54–5).

China, India, or the United States. However, facing many financial, operational and commercial challenges after the break-up of its joint-venture with Siemens, it sold most of the non-nuclear related assets as well as some of its nuclear related ones to EDF. EDF has also acquired 100 per cent of British Energy in early 2009. This makes it the first electricity producer and provider worldwide, thereby strengthening its competitiveness in the market for building new plants. From this perspective, not only has the privatization of energy groups remained partial, but their new status has also allowed public groups to gain influence through an offensive policy of mergers and acquisitions. Being a main shareholder in these groups allows the central state to influence energy prices as well as industrial strategies, as shown by the two following examples. On one hand, in January 2010, the French state prevented GDF-Suez from running up considerable debts in order to buy the British group International Power. On the other hand, the French state decided in 2010 to give EDF the leading role in the French nuclear industry, in order to improve the competitiveness of the French nuclear industry abroad and to appease the increasing tensions between AREVA and EDF. After numerous failures, the only new nuclear plant to be built abroad by AREVA-EDF is the Hinkley Point C plant in the United Kingdom.

Since the late 1990s, French nuclear policy conflicts with EU competition policy, which implies opening the market to international competitors. In European comparison, the liberalization of the energy market was slow and limited in France (OECD 2005, 2009). EDF remains highly dominant for the construction of nuclear plants, electricity production, and transport for several reasons: its former investments make electricity possible at relatively low cost and the persistence of regulated electricity prices parallel to—substantially higher—market prices given the conception of electricity as a public service is an obstacle to free competition. The French state, the public bodies, and labour unions from the energy sector have been resisting the Europeanization of energy policy by delaying the transposition of liberalization directives, by protesting against them, and bypassing competition rules using the creation of subsidiary companies and groups in which the state is a minority but significant shareholder (Van den Hoven and Froschauer 2004; Humphreys and Padgett 2006; Bauby and Varone 2007). In 2009, after entrusting the EDF with the construction of the new EPR, a decision that had been criticized by the European Commission, the French President indicated that the order for a forthcoming third EPR plant (that has not materialized yet) would go to one of EDF's competitors, probably GDF-Suez—a group in which the French state had a stake of over one-third. So, despite initiatives taken by the European Commission in order to weaken the dominant position of EDF—such as control of acquisitions and calls to cede parts of the group's production to competing companies as long as competition cannot be considered free (Wise 2005: 55–6)—Europeanization has overall been limited, and France has maintained its tradition of industrial policy.

Activities related to nuclear energy are controlled by the Institute of Radio-protection and Nuclear Safety, which was originally part of the CEA, the Nuclear Safety Agency, an independent administrative agency directed by five commissars appointed directly by the President of the Republic, the President of the National Assembly, and the President of Senate. In a nutshell, the respective influence of the different players in the nuclear policy field—the President of the Republic,

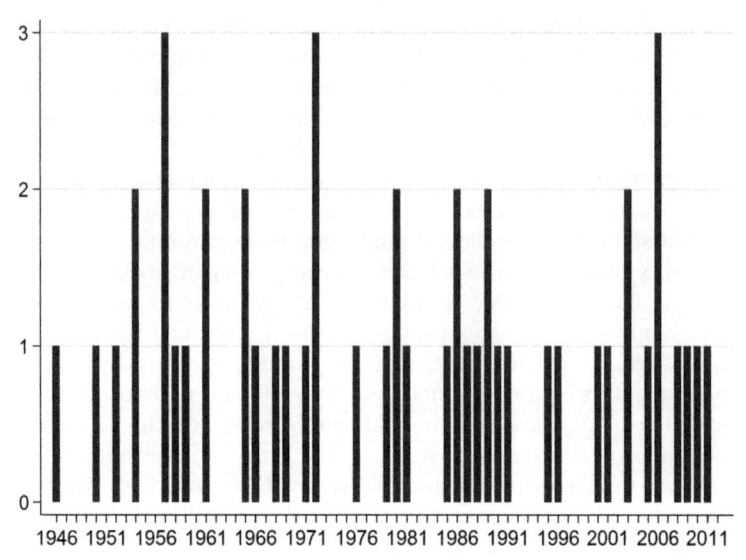

Figure 6.2. Number of Statutes Regarding Nuclear Energy Issue

the government, Parliament, the CEA, and EDF—has evolved towards a reinforcement of the role of the executive and in particular of the President over the course of the Fifth Republic, as indicated by the creation in 2008 of the Nuclear Policy Council chaired by the French President. The deregulation of the electricity market has affected nuclear energy policy-making towards the margins.

If the existence of a restricted, integrated, and homogeneous policy network can thus not be denied, asserting that nuclear energy issues are mostly or entirely kept off the political agenda and out of democratic arenas, such as the Parliament (Colson 1977; Hatch 1986: 150-4), or that there is no division of power in this field (Delmas and Heinman 2001) would be an exaggeration. Contrary to widespread belief, initiatives and the elaboration of decisions emanate from the executive, but their adoption is regularly submitted to a parliamentary vote, so that problems of nuclear energy have been a substantial part of the legislative agenda since the early 1950s. Even without counting the annual budget laws, which often contain dispositions regarding expenses or taxes related to nuclear facilities, forty-nine laws dealing with nuclear energy have been voted and adopted in the French parliament since 1946 (Figure 6.2).

Concrete and major decisions involving the allocation of state credits have been scrutinized and voted on by French MPs, such as the five-year plans for the development of atomic energy adopted in 1952 and 1957, the law on the experimentation of nuclear energy and on basic industries contributing to the general equipment of the country (1959), the electrical equipment programme of 1961 and the creation of the EURODIF society, specializing in uranium enrichment and established in France. More recently, in 2005, parliament adopted a law defining the direction of energy policy, which firmly confirms the crucial place of nuclear electricity in the French energy mix.

This is not to say that all choices in nuclear policy have been submitted to a parliamentary vote. Specific decisions regarding the timing, geographical implantation, and the conditions of the construction of nuclear plants mostly take the form of decrees (i.e. acts possibly taken by the executive only). However, the government has been entitled to make decrees on nuclear energy by law, most importantly the 1946 law on the nationalization of electricity and gas and the 1961 law against atmospheric pollution and odours (articles 2, 4, and 8), on the basis of which the 11 December 1963 decree set the conditions of authorization, creation, and exploitation of nuclear facilities.[4] When faced with growing popular contestation, this legislative setting might have been amended to change the decision-making process regarding new nuclear plants. This is, indeed, what occurred in 2006, when the law on nuclear transparency and security was adopted as the first (French) legislative frame specifically designed for nuclear activity. Since then, an independent organization, the Nuclear Safety Authority, plays an important role in the authorization of new plants and in ensuring transparency towards the public and parliament.

The adoption of the 2006 law and the subsequent revision of the institutions ruling nuclear activities have opened a window of opportunity for politicizing nuclear energy. In previous decades, already, such opportunities had been provided through the regular agenda-setting of questions of nuclear cooperation (AIEA, EURATOM,...) and of nuclear safety. Between 1965 and 2006, we were able to identify no less than twenty-two laws dedicated to matters of safety of nuclear power plants, treatment sites, and radioactive waste disposal sites. Given this focus on risks and uncertainty, these deliberations could have given rise to a democratic debate on the direction of French energy policy and to an effective parliamentary scrutiny. The substantial place reserved for issues linked to nuclear energy may also be illustrated by the considerable attention devoted to it by the parliamentary committee specializing in technological and scientific issues: Office Parlementaire d'Evaluation des Choix Scientifiques et Techniques. Since its creation in 1983, thirty-six reports (out of 198) deal with the nuclear energy issue, with reflections on the consequences of Chernobyl, nuclear safety and security in France and beyond, the management of highly radioactive waste, the costs of the production of nuclear electricity, the lifespan of power plants, the future of the French nuclear sector, and so on.

In short, the institutional setting of French nuclear energy policy alone cannot be blamed for the absence of democratic debate. There is no institutional factor definitively preventing parliamentary representatives from making energy policy a salient issue, or from channelling citizens' negative feedback regarding French nuclear energy policy. Several nuclear development programmes have been submitted to a parliamentary vote, as were the laws that have shaped the decision-making rules of nuclear energy policy. Although the decision to construct new plants has not been put on the parliamentary agenda for decades, MPs have deliberated on reports covering all facets of nuclear energy, as well as on a series

---

[4] The 1972 law authorizing the creation of enterprises exercising, on French soil, electrical activity of European interest, and the 1976 law on installations classified for environmental protection, are also quoted as a reference in many nuclear energy decrees.

of laws on issues of nuclear research, cooperation, responsibility, and safety. Yet, the related parliamentary debates never gave rise to any major cleavage before the first election of Green MPs in 1997. All parliamentary parties supported the successive plans of nuclear development and expansion in the 1950s, 1960s, and 1970s. In debates over French energy policy, MPs seem to share common objectives that are very favourable to the nuclear sector: to secure nuclear activities, to legitimate them, to develop them, and to convince European partners of their necessity. The absence of visible and influential controversy thus seems to result from nuclear energy being treated by MPs as a valence issue. In the remainder of the chapter, we argue that this depoliticization cannot be understood without taking party politics and coalition-related strategies into account.

6.4 POLITICAL COMPETITION OVER NUCLEAR ENERGY

A pro-nuclear consensus amongst major political parties and the depoliticization of the issue have been among the conditions of the enduring commitment to nuclear energy in France, as we show in a first part of this section. This might be explained by a similar consensus amongst the French citizens. The lacking of polarization on this issue would simply reflect the absence of electoral incentives to politicize the nuclear issue. In the second part of this section, we will show that attitudes towards nuclear energy have changed across time but have been negatively oriented most of the time. In the third part of the section, we present evidence that nuclear energy was also a very salient issue in the French mass media during specific periods. In the fourth part of the section, we will analyse the level of congruence between partisan leanings and attitudes towards nuclear energy, as well as its evolution across time. As electoral incentives to politicize the nuclear issue were present, the final section studies how electoral and coalitional politics affects nuclear issue attention and preference and provides a new explanation of the patterns of the French nuclear policy.

6.4.1 Political Parties' Positioning with Regard to the Nuclear Power Issue

Given the rise of anti-nuclear protest in the 1970s[5] and the growing importance of nuclear energy, a politicization of nuclear policy could have been expected. In fact, before the creation of the Green Party in 1984, the only party opposed to nuclear energy was the small Unified Socialist Party that partly merged with the Socialist Party in 1974 and disappeared in 1989. In fact, French political parties mostly avoided this issue.

---

[5] Stemming mainly from ecology movements and from local collectives like 'Stop Golfech', 'Tchernoblaye', or the initiatives federated within the network 'Sortir du nucléaire', this contestation took numerous forms, from petitioning and mobilizing to mass demonstrations or spectacular actions.

Political parties had many opportunities to oppose each other over nuclear energy issues in the parliamentary arena but no parliamentary party challenged nuclear energy before the Greens had MPs. The continuity of French nuclear energy policy is largely grounded in this lack of politicization. This low salience in party competition is illustrated by the minor attention devoted by parties to nuclear energy in their electoral manifestos (Figure 6.3). To estimate the level of attention to the nuclear energy issue in the party manifestos in a comparative manner, it is additionally important to provide the level of attention to further relevant political issues. The salience of farmer and culture-related issues as measured by the Comparative Manifesto Project comparatively illustrates the modest level of attention to nuclear energy within the four main parliamentary parties. Nuclear energy has been by far less salient than other issues of similar or even smaller scope, such as 'farmer' and 'culture' issues. It has played a marginal role in manifestos of the main left-wing parties. Even the Gaullist Party, that pushed the expansion of nuclear energy during their time in government, did not prioritize that topic in its party manifestos. Only the Greens devote considerable attention to nuclear energy in their manifestos. Since 1958, only in 2007 and 2012 did electoral platforms of all main parties deal with nuclear energy. Therefore, even if the level of attention to nuclear energy is still comparatively weak, the nuclear energy issue has started to be included in French electoral campaigns.

For a long time, this issue had not been politicized—in other words, it was not an issue on which the major political parties had visible divergences (Barthe 2006). Despite the vocal and widespread protests among civil society towards the end of the 1970s, the major parties remained steadfast in their pro-nuclear stance. We systematically coded the positions enshrined in each party's electoral platform from 1958 onwards, placing each policy position on the policy scale from 5 (expansion of nuclear energy) to –5 (forbid nuclear power). The positions occupied on this scale by the main French parties, shown in Figure 6.4, reveal the broad consensus that has long reigned on the issue of nuclear energy. Between 1958 and 1988, all political parties, except the PS in 1981, maintained a clearly pro-nuclear stance. This consensus and the fact that nuclear energy policy was largely absent from party programmes are indicators of the depoliticization of the issue. This can be explained with respect to both the parties' key preferences that disposed them to support more or less the production of nuclear energy, and to strategic considerations.

For historical reasons, the parties flying the Gaullist flag and the Communist Party (PCF) were the political forces most in favour of nuclear power. It is also worth noting that both parties often made use of the same types of argument to champion the cause, pointing to the advantages of this technology in terms of economic well-being, employment, independence, and competitiveness (Hecht 1998). Gaullist parties were historically involved in initiating and developing nuclear energy: they defended a consistent position over time, and remained committed to 'consolidating the production of nuclear energy'. The 2007 platform emphasized the comparative benefits of the French nuclear programme, its advantages in terms of reducing greenhouse gases, whist at the same time recognizing 'citizens' right to access all useful documents regarding the risks of nuclear energy and the methods used in France to prevent these risks'. Shorter in length, the 2012 platform maintained this position, citing support of the nuclear industry

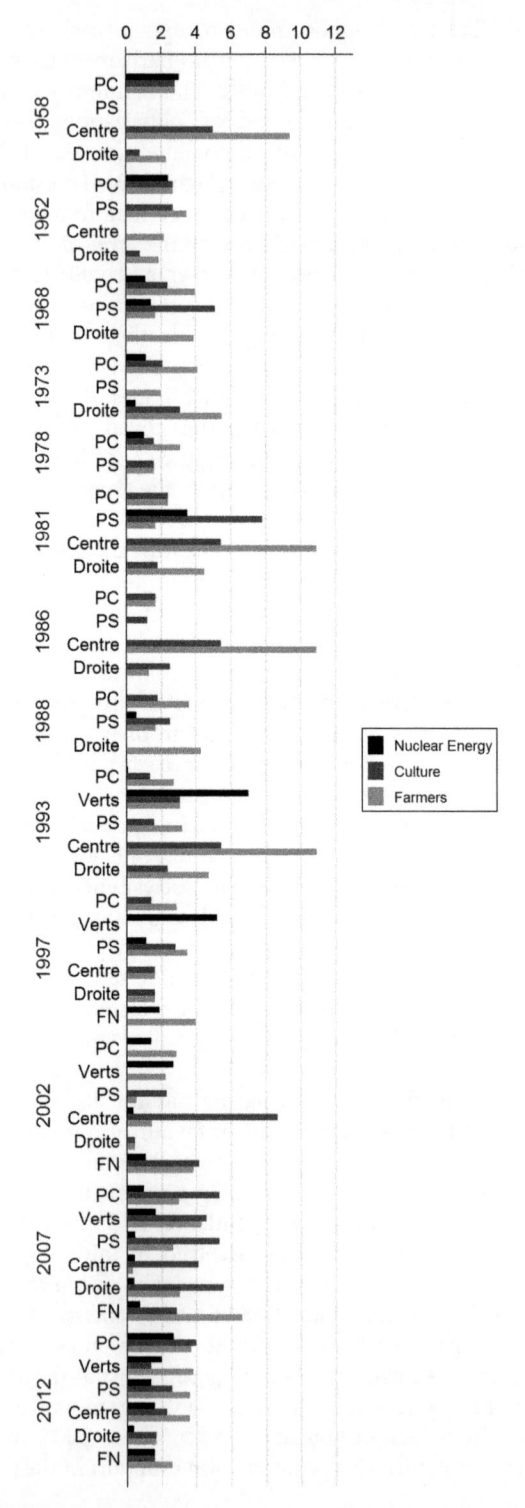

Figure 6.3. Attention to Nuclear Energy, Farmers and Culture in French Party Manifestos (% of words)

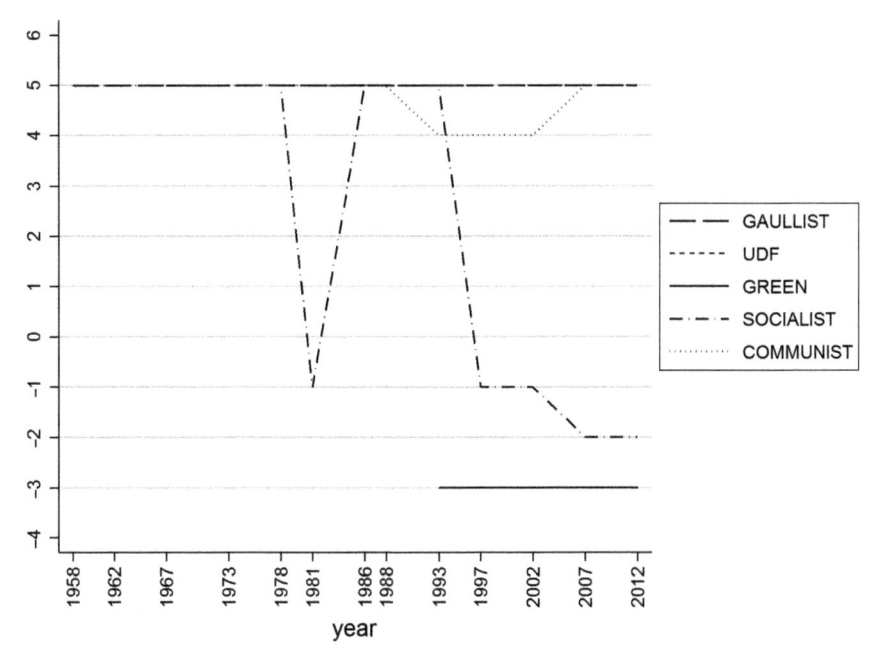

Figure 6.4. French Party Stances on a Pro-Nuclear–Anti-Nuclear Energy Scale

as a component of sustainable development policy and the advantages of 'safe, cheaper energy'.

As far as the PCF is concerned, there are three main reasons for its enduring pro-nuclear stance. Important to this party's ideology is a belief in the power of science and technology to transform the world as well as in its positive impact on the standard of living. The fact that the USSR had been committed in massively developing nuclear energy had also strengthened the pro-nuclear stance of the Communist Party. Finally, the high number of Communist scientists involved in French nuclear research as well as the strength of the communist trade union CGT in EDF reinforced the attachment of the PCF to the French nuclear policy. For example the first director of the CEA, Frédéric Joliot-Curie, was a researcher publicly known as a member of the Communist Party.

The parties at the centre of the political spectrum, the majority of which were absorbed by the UDF from 1978 onwards, also actively supported the development of nuclear energy, in particular under the presidency of Valéry Giscard d'Estaing, between 1974 and 1981. In more general terms, the parties in power avoided challenging the validity of a programme that was crucial for the country's electricity supply and in which large sums had been invested.

The PS was not historically or ideologically predisposed to promote nuclear energy in the same way as the Communists, the Gaullists, or the Centrists. On the contrary, its links with the largely anti-nuclear trade union CFDT (Garraud 1979) compelled this party to challenge the energy policy decisions made in the 1960s and 1970s. In fact, prior to the foundation of the Green Party, the stance most critical of nuclear power was that of the Socialists in 1981. Whilst he did not explicitly call pro-nuclear energy policy into question, François Mitterrand did table a number of proposals in order to respond to the anti-nuclear movement: reinforcing the security checks at nuclear power stations, limiting the nuclear programme to the power plants under construction until the country had delivered its verdict on the programme via referendum, and a framework law which guaranteed that citizens would be able to hold their leaders accountable, particularly on security issues related to nuclear energy.

This situation continued until 1993: no political party opposed to nuclear power obtained more than 3 per cent of the vote in legislative elections and the PCF remained the favoured coalition partner of the PS. However, the first electoral victories of the pro-environment parties and the continued decline of the PCF radically altered the state of play: the PS was now forced to accommodate the Greens in its proposals. As far as this development is concerned, Figure 6.4 clearly represents the programmatic U-turn on the part of the PS in 1997 when, for the first time in its history, it signed a government agreement with the Greens. Socialist policy proposals started to move towards those of the Greens on the nuclear issue. The tone associated with nuclear energy is negative in the 1997 platform: 'We will change the course of the French energy policy by adopting a moratorium on the building of nuclear plants, by increasing the incentives to energy savings and to the development of alternative energy. We are going to close the fast breeder reactor Superphénix'. In 2007, the Greens committed to phasing out nuclear power by 2030, whilst the PS promised to 'reduce the share of nuclear energy in France's final energy consumption by increasing the share of renewables in this consumption to 20 per cent by 2020 and to 50 per cent in the longer term'. Similar discrepancies between the two parties' programmes were evident in 2012, with the Greens promising to orchestrate the 'total phase out of nuclear energy within 20 years' and the Socialists' position remained similar to that adopted in 2007. In 2012, the PS proposed increasing 'the share of renewable energies in order to reduce dependence on nuclear energy, to the extent that the share of nuclear energy in the production of electricity would fall from 75 per cent to 50 per cent by 2025', in the words of the party's candidate François Hollande. The PS also promised a debate on energy policy, as well as 'a moratorium on the growth of nuclear energy' by 'the conclusion of [that] debate'. According to the PS candidate, in concrete terms, that equated to 'the completion of the Flamanville site' and the shelving of the Penly project,[6] 'at least during the next five year term'.[7] The PS also committed to closing the Fessenheim plant.

Against this backdrop, as suggested by the widespread attention to the nuclear energy issue in 2012, an unprecedented politicization of nuclear power happened in 2011–12 even if the issue was already hotly discussed during the TV debates involving the opposing candidates, which took place between the two rounds of the presidential election 2007. The new politicization does not appear to have stemmed so much from a change in the parties' positions on the issue as from a higher emphasis on the issue during the campaign. Until 1988, nuclear policy was

---

[6] Read on 3 Mar. 2012 on the site <http://francoishollande.fr/actualites/contre-le-projet-epr-de-penly>.
[7] Read on 3 Mar. 2012 on the site <http://www.media-part.fr/journal/france/150212/nucleaire-recul-de-francois-hollande-sur-l-epr-de-penly>.

an issue on which all parties broadly agreed. Subsequently a point of increasing controversy, it was avoided for strategic reasons. In 2012, the right-wing Gaullist party (UMP) decided to underscore the differences between its own views on nuclear power and those held by the PS and the Greens.[8] First and foremost, this strategy allowed the party to draw attention to the differences of opinion both within the PS-Green coalition and within the PS itself. Such disagreements led to a public debate between the two parties, before and after the coalition agreement was signed, namely on the issue of MOX fuel. To use a metaphor coined by Hillygus and Shields (2009), all that remained for the UMP to do was drive deeper the wedge that already divided the Green-PS coalition. With this strategy, the UMP also sought to defend the decisions made by Jacques Chirac and Nicolas Sarkozy to build new reactors in Flamanville (in 2005) and Penly (in 2009). The strategy saw them defend these decisions by successfully reframing the issue of nuclear power in terms of competitiveness, jobs, purchasing power, and the reduction of greenhouse gases in order to counterbalance the risk-focused arguments put forward by the opposition (Brouard et al. 2013).

To sum up, nuclear energy, after being consensual and depoliticized for a long time, has become increasingly visible, disputed, and politicized.

6.4.2 Weak Public Support for Nuclear Energy

Data constraints make studying long-term trends in public opinion a tricky enterprise. From that point of view, nuclear policy is not an outlier (Jasper 1988). Some questions were asked only once or twice. Several questions have been asked for a long time, but not every year. Conversely, other questions were asked twice or more in some specific year and for some years, we also have multiple indicators. Moreover different questions may lead to different answers. Furthermore, response categories of the questions changed in some cases. Unfortunately, in the data we gathered there are no items having been asked identically every year during a forty-year period. So, we have a heterogeneous dataset in terms of frequency, timing, and response categories. In order to remedy this problem and to assess French public opinion about nuclear policy, we use the measure of 'public mood' developed by James Stimson in his study of liberalism versus conservatism in the United States (Stimson 1991). Based on the 'Dyadic Ratio Algorithm', the measure of public mood has been used increasingly to create a single public opinion indicator from heterogeneous datasets (Baumgartner et al. 2008). Public mood captures the shared variation over time of different series of questions tapping the same dimension. The public mood is an aggregated measure based on survey marginals. Another advantage of the public mood approach is to go beyond question-wording-induced bias by changing it.

---

[8] This was also the case for Jean-Luc Mélenchon's Left Party, which advocated a wholesale re-evaluation of French energy policy choices following an 'immediate public national debate' examining all available alternatives, 'including the phasing out of nuclear power and maintaining a secure, state-owned nuclear industry'. Once this debate had been held, Mélenchon's programme promised that a referendum would be organized to decide between these possibilities.

Following Stimson's guidelines, we included in our indicator of public mood about nuclear energy all questions asked at least three times, which allow a clear distinction between positive and negative feelings about nuclear energy. As advocated by Stimson, the ratio of positive feelings from the sum of positive and negative feelings for each question is used to compute the public mood about nuclear energy: the resulting 'nuclear support index' estimates the relative level of nuclear support in France. People that choose neither a positive answer nor a negative answer were not included in the calculus of the ratio. By construction, the nuclear index is sensitive to the change in mind from positive to negative feelings or vice versa, but also from indifferent and ambivalent feelings to positive and negative feelings.

The nuclear support index is computed using the software WCalc designed by James Stimson[9] and is based on 312 results from twenty-four different question wordings, collected from thirteen sources (surveys and barometers). The data were collected from nine different sources, covering thirty-nine years from 1975 to 2013. There is one year—1985—without any data. Conversely, in 1986, many data are available but one question was asked at the very beginning of the year and the remaining questions after the Chernobyl accident. It might be reasonably argued that distinguishing before and after Chernobyl is key to understanding the dynamics of public opinion towards nuclear energy. Furthermore, the best proxy to public opinion in 1985 is probably public opinion at the very beginning of 1986. This is why we filled the year 1985 by attributing the early 1986 polling result to that year. Consequently, the year 1986 is estimated only with polling results after the Chernobyl accident.

The first striking observation is, regarding most of the period considered, the absence of majority support for nuclear energy among French citizens (Figure 6.5).

Figure 6.5. Level of Support to Nuclear Energy in France 1975–2013

[9] The software is available at <http://www.unc.edu/~jstimson/resource.html>.

Despite the bias of our support index towards more support (since this indicator measures the proportion of supportive respondents among those who positioned themselves, this proportion would be substantially lower when calculated in relation to the whole sample), our index exceeds 50 per cent only over the 1975–86 period, with values situated between 48.8 per cent and 58.4 per cent and an average of 55.4 per cent. This timing is surprising, as it is set against the background of the strongest anti-nuclear mobilizations in French history.

The Three Mile Island accident in 1979 does not seem to have had any short-term impact at this aggregate level (as the highest support of the period is measured in 1982), but this support declined over the 1980s, especially after the Chernobyl accident in 1986. This trauma caused a rapid collapse, with a drop by 18.7 points in the public mood within five years. Interestingly, perhaps due to the fading memory of Chernobyl, or due to the increasing visibility of alternative framings, this trend was reversed in the 1990s, marked by a progressive and incremental increase until 2000—paradoxically, by the mid-term of the Jospin government, which involved the Green Party for the first time.

However, even when the mood indicator reached a peak in 2000, it remained under 48 per cent, and a new low in the public mood towards nuclear energy was reached in 2011, with 40 per cent. Nevertheless, unlike the Chernobyl accident, the Fukushima accident did not induce a decrease in nuclear support but ended a steady four years decline (–7 points). In fact, at the end of 2011, nuclear support among French public opinion started to sharply rise again (Brouard et al. 2013; Brouard and Guinaudeau 2015). It is still too soon to assess the long-term effects of the Fukushima-related debates but we should notice that in 2012–13, our indicator of support for nuclear energy comes close to 50 per cent for the first time since the early 1980s. The increase in support observed in 2012 and 2013 may be surprising at first sight, in the aftermath of the Fukushima accident and in the context of the diminishing support of public opinion for nuclear power plants in most countries (Ramana 2011; Bonneval and Lacroix-Lasnoë 2011), the phasing out decided by four of France's direct neighbours and the reflections on the safety of the French plants. As shown elsewhere, this development can be understood as a campaign effect with a higher politicization, the reframing of nuclear energy issue, a stronger presence in the media, and the first hint of a party-issue alignment in the electorate (Brouard et al. 2013).

From this aggregate analysis of public opinion, it is difficult to argue that there has been a consensus about nuclear energy amongst the French citizens. Even if French public opinion displays, in comparative perspective, fairly exceptional traits (Franchino 2014), a clear majority in favour of the nuclear issue has rarely existed. There were incentives to politicize the nuclear issue in order to break the existing political alignment and to win more votes. Particularly during the second half of the 1980s, the level of nuclear support was historically weak in France.

6.4.3 The Varying Public Salience of the Nuclear Issue

Political parties' incentives to politicize an issue depend on the state of public opinion but also on the public salience of the issue. Politicizing an issue is a way to increase its salience. But events and mobilizations sometimes give salience to issues without purposive politicization by politicians and parties. Despite methodological problems (Wlezien 2005), the 'Most Important Problem' indicator is usually used (Smith 1980). Unfortunately, no comparable indicator exists in France. Like numerous previous studies, we studied the media content in order to estimate the salience of the nuclear issues in the public sphere. In fact, studies show that media set the agenda for public opinion (McCombs and Shaw 1972) and party competition—even if media agendas are also partially shaped by other agendas (Soroka 2002). We analysed the articles dealing with the nuclear issue in *Le Monde*, which is usually acknowledged as the leading newspaper in France over the entire post-war period. We used the content of *Le Monde* as a proxy of the French media agenda given that the level of inter-media consistency is generally high according to the media studies, even in heterogeneous countries such as Belgium or Canada.[10] Moreover, the crucial role played by this newspaper in placing the nuclear energy issue on the media agenda has already been clearly shown (Blanchard 2010): other media outlets were quick to adopt the *Le Monde's* priorities—these included dailies (*Libération*), weeklies (*Le Point* and *L'Express*), and television news broadcasts (France 2). Blanchard concluded that 'the issue of nuclear power gained prominence in the public sphere largely to . . . a short-term domino effect among France's various media outlets' and *Le Monde* played a pivotal role in this process.

Estimating the importance of the media coverage of an issue enables us to estimate the salience of an issue. Figure 6.6—which presents the number of articles per year—shows the ebbs and flows of the nuclear issue on the media agenda. Broadly speaking, nuclear energy received only limited attention from the late 1970s onwards, although it did occasionally come under the media spotlight. At the end of the 1970s, attention to the nuclear issue was at a high. The years 1977–81 were marked by vehement anti-nuclear protests in France—protests at least equivalent in scope to those seen in West Germany during the same period—mobilization that explains the increased prominence of nuclear issues in the media. The Three Mile Island accident in 1979 provided fuel for the media. In 1977, more than two articles per day were dedicated to the nuclear energy issue, often on the front page. It then declined steadily until 1981. Whilst the early 1980s saw the anti-nuclear movement lose impetus and the issue depoliticized, the years that followed saw media interest in the issue spike on four separate occasions.

The first was in 1986, in the aftermath of the Chernobyl disaster. This accident in 1986 directed public attention once more to the nuclear issue. Nevertheless, the media attention quickly faded away again. The period between 1988 and 1996 was one of low tide for the nuclear issue. Most of the articles were short news rather than front-page material. The second peak in 1997, sparked by the controversy

---

[10] In order to measure the media coverage of nuclear energy in *Le Monde*, we used three different sources. Between 1977 and 2001, the articles related to nuclear energy were identified using *Le Monde's* annual index. Publication of this index ceased in 2001. As a result, we used a second source, the search engine <http://www.lemonde.fr> (the data were collected in Feb. 2013). As the graph indicates, the number of relevant articles varied according to the source used (electronic or printed). However, the broad trends depicted are similar, making it possible to reliably conclude that media coverage of the issue between 1977 and 2012 did in fact evolve as shown, even if comparing levels of media attention in the issue at the beginning and end of the period studied is an activity which must be undertaken with caution.

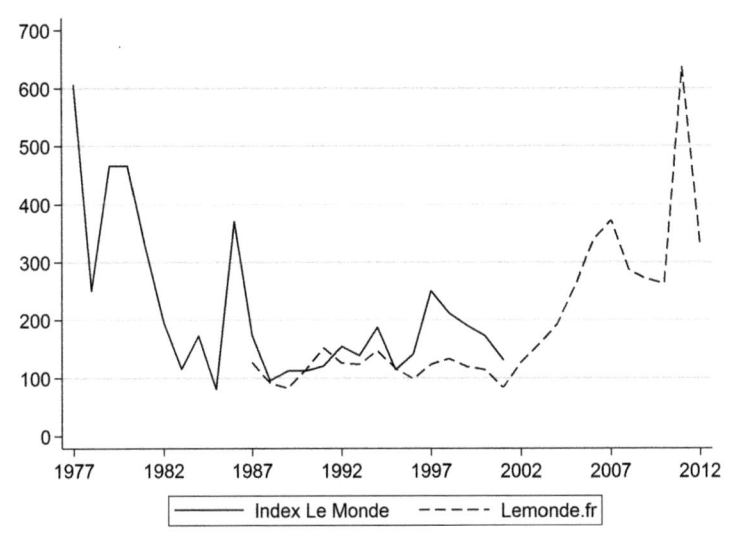

Figure 6.6. Media Attention to Nuclear Energy in France 1977–2012

surrounding the nuclear waste reprocessing plant in The Hague (Baisnée 2001), the arrival in government of ministers from environmental parties, and debates on the decommissioning of French nuclear power plant Superphénix. Numerous articles were also published about the nuclear debate in Germany. Nevertheless, the nuclear issue did not keep a high level of salience for a long time. Ten years later, the nuclear issue experienced a new peak of attention, triggered not only by the 'nuclear renaissance' and the decision to recommence the development of EPR reactors in France following a lengthy break in construction, but also by the debates on nuclear proliferation (often related to the Iranian nuclear programme), cost and availability of energy, and the potential role of nuclear power in the fight against climate change.

Interest in the issue peaked for a fourth and final time in 2011, in the wake of the Fukushima disaster. However, the fact that media exposure of nuclear issues was at an all-time high in 2011–12 cannot be explained solely by the Fukushima disaster: the extensive media coverage was also the result of the unprecedented politicization of the issue of nuclear power during the presidential election campaign. A detailed analysis of the various phases of media coverage of nuclear power confirms the crucial role played by these two factors (Brouard et al. 2013). The media coverage of the issue of nuclear power did increase sharply in March 2011 before remaining relatively extensive until June 2011. After this lengthy period of intensity, media interest in the issue of nuclear power dropped to the average levels recorded during previous summers before increasing once more in September and October 2011—a result of the debates on the nuclear power staged during the primary elections of the French Socialist Party (PS). These debates saw Martine Aubry, an advocate of phasing out nuclear power, go head-to-head with François Hollande, in favour of abandoning the 'all-nuclear solution'.

Media interest in the issue peaked again in November 2011, with an average of more than three articles per day. The period coincided with the turbulent conclusion of the programmatic and electoral negotiations between the Greens and the PS. The tensions between them in fact opened a window of opportunity for the unprecedented politicization of the nuclear issue. Whilst this debate raged, the President of the Republic and members of the presidential majority, along with several pro-nuclear interest groups, also broached the issue, in order to distinguish their own views from those expressed by the PS and the Greens. Media interest in the issue finally began to wane in December 2011, but remained relatively intense until spring 2012.

Thus attention on nuclear energy has gone 'up and down' (Downs 1972). Most of the time, nuclear energy has not been in the forefront of the media agenda. Nevertheless, the nuclear issue was a salient dimension of the media agenda at four different moments: at the end of the 1970s, 1986, at the end of the 1990s and during recent years. So, beyond the state of public opinion, the public salience the nuclear issue in the media has opened some windows of opportunity to politicize the nuclear issue during the three last decades.

6.4.4 The Discrepancy between Partisan Proximity and Nuclear Preferences

The level of nuclear support among party leaners is presented in Figure 6.7.[11] It differs notably among the supporters of leftist and rightist parties: while the majority of the electorate of parties of the right and far-right supports nuclear energy, this proportion is much smaller among Communists and Socialists and especially among ecologists (around 20 per cent). However, after the level of nuclear support among the supporters of all four traditional governing parties had eroded since the early 1980s, the level of support reached again its maximum in 2012.

The rise and peak in nuclear support affects all party electorates, even if not to the same extent. For both rightist parties, the level of nuclear support decreased from three-quarters in 1980 to a slight majority in 2005: the progressive decline of nuclear support among centrist party leaners has been totally reversed in 2012; and while this support experienced a drastic decrease among Gaullist supporters following the Chernobyl accident, their 2012 upsurge in nuclear support (90 per cent) is striking and typical of a politicization effect. Following a similar pattern, PS sympathizers became much less supportive after 1986, to fall from a 50-50 balance to under 40 per cent until 2012, when it came back to its initial level. This also applies to the Communist Party. Nevertheless the 2005 and 2012 increases should be interpreted with caution. In fact, the survey question differs from the others. Moreover, the number of people being close to the Communist Party has been very limited for fifteen years as, for a decade, far left-wing parties as well as the new Left Party have become significant electoral players in France. By contrast with the Communist Party, their sympathizers are more anti-nuclear (even if the 2012 reframing had a great effect on far-left-wing leaners). In fact the Left Party leaners were the only ones adversely affected by the reframing of the issue

---

[11] We used the same question asked in three waves of the survey 'The French and Science' fielded in 1982, 1989, and 1994, as well as in a 1980 SOFRES poll. We also used two complementary surveys: a 2005 IFOP survey and the last wave of the TriÉlec survey 2012 (May 2012). The level of nuclear support represents the percentage of respondents taking a position in favour of nuclear energy.

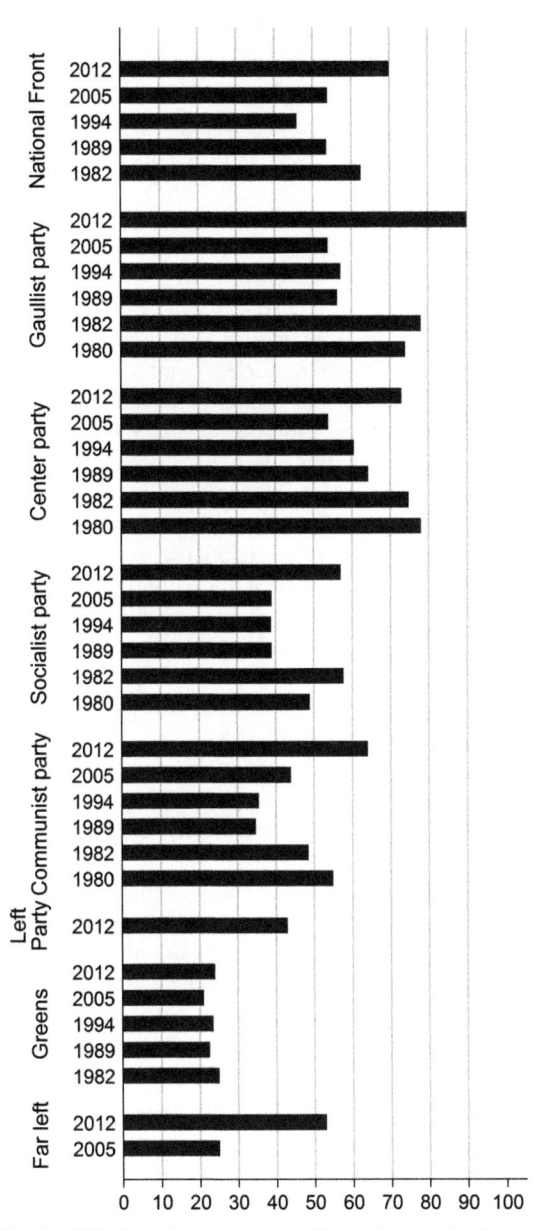

Figure 6.7. Level of Nuclear Support among Party-Leaners in France, 1980–2005

following the Fukushima catastrophe: nuclear support decreased among them during the presidential campaign 2012. With the Greens, the Left Party was the only one with a majority of anti-nuclear sympathizers. Ecologist-leaners were the only ones unaffected by the Chernobyl explosion, the Fukushima accident, and the 2012 politicization of the issue. Their level of nuclear opposition has always been high and stable.

As there has been a clear pattern of decline in nuclear support among party sympathizers of each party since 1980 and all French parties but the Greens and emerging far-left parties have remained favourable to the use of nuclear energy, the congruence between issue preference and partisan proximity has been low in a specific part of the electorate. Those opposed to nuclear energy have been badly represented by the enduring electoral supply. In our data, from around 70 per cent in 1982 (Figure 6.8), the anti-nuclear part of the electorate, close to a pro-nuclear party, reached its peak in 1989 after the Chernobyl accident, when nearly 90 per cent of the anti-nuclear citizens were at the same time supporters of pro-nuclear parties. In 1994, the corresponding figure was at the 1982 level. In 2002, the answers to a different survey question—with three possibilities: building new nuclear plants, no new nuclear plants, stopping existing nuclear plants—show a similar level of discrepancy between anti-nuclear preferences and partisan proximity. Given the evolution of party positions and the increasing politicization of the issue, significant changes occurred in 2012: the proportion of anti-nuclear citizens close to a pro-nuclear party is at its minimum (30 per cent). Conversely, the proportion of pro-nuclear citizens, close to an anti-nuclear party is at the highest level (35 per cent), partly because of the successful reframing of the issue. Even if the congruence between voters' and their preferred party's position has never been so high for nuclear energy, the realignment process is still going on. Nonetheless, the long-run discrepancy between nuclear policy preference and partisan proximity is striking: why didn't the divergence between issue preference and partisan proximity produce a major political realignment before 2012?

6.4.5 Parties' Electoral and Coalitional Strategies

From a comparative perspective, the continuity of the French pro-nuclear policy is, first of all, rooted in the interaction between the avoidance of politicization by the main French political parties and the increasing inertia of the French nuclear policy inheritance. Political, economic, and policy factors all explain the absence of a phase-out followed later by a new phase-in observed in other countries.

To achieve a policy reversal, anti-nuclear social protest would have needed partisan allies as in other countries that experienced a phase-out. The incentives for politicizing the nuclear energy issue were high for some parties at some moments in time. As the pro-nuclear policy was implemented by the rightist coalition, either the leftist parties or a new ecologist party might have played this role. The leftist parties neither politicized nor opposed (or only weakly and lately opposed) nuclear energy before the Green party rose at the end of the 1980s. And it was only after it became a significant player in government that French nuclear policy has been altered if not reversed. To understand why, two critical junctures of both the nuclear policy and the political history of France will be analysed: first the period of nuclear expansion despite alternation (1973–85) and second the period of halting nuclear development under pressure from Greens (1989–2002, 2012–14).

Two phenomena coincided during the second part of the 1970s and the first half of the 1980s: the acceleration of the nuclear programme and the slow path towards alternation in government. It was one of the key moments of the nuclear

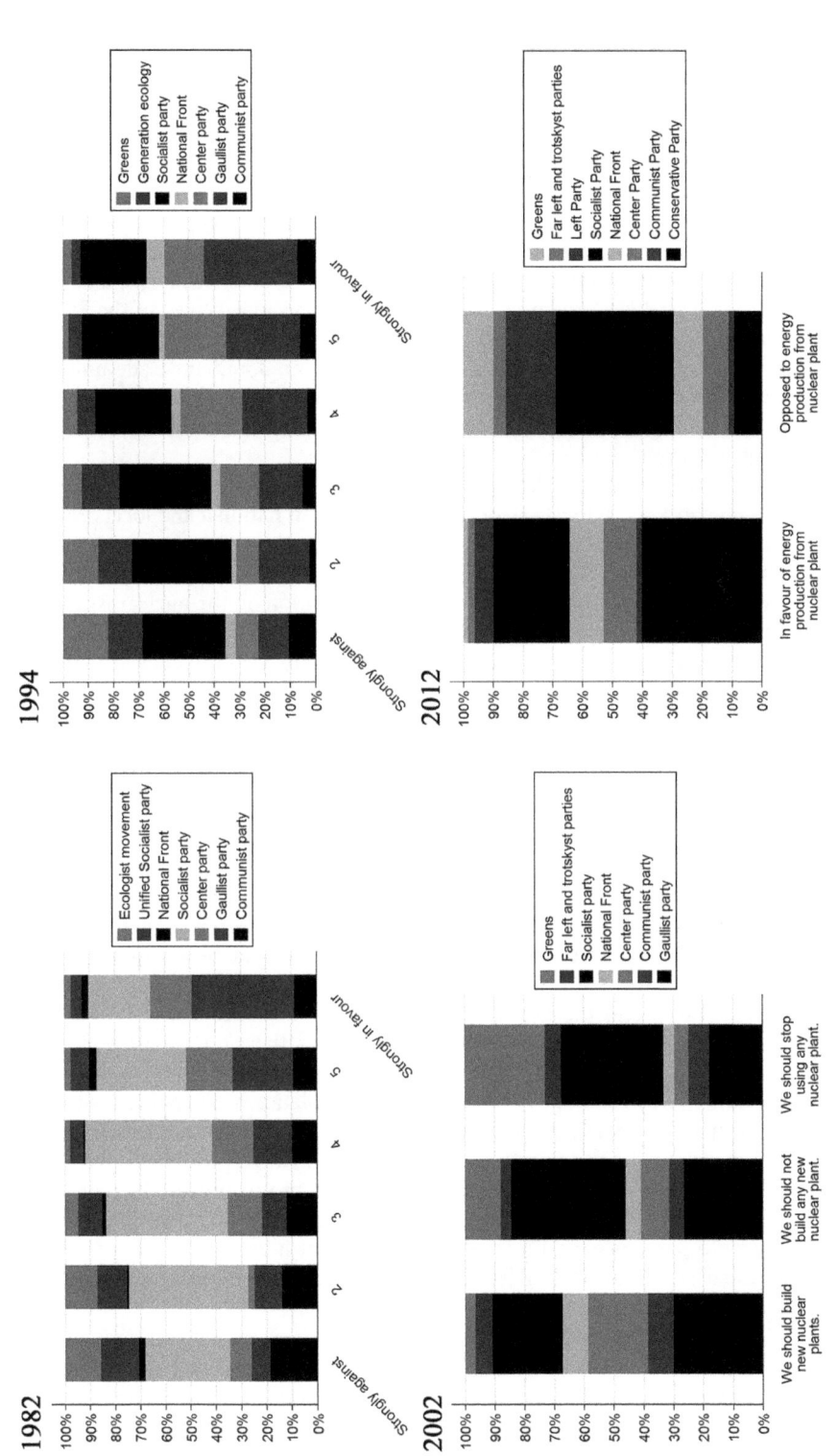

Figure 6.8. Level of Inconsistency between Policy Attitudes and Partisan Leaning of French Voters, 1982, 1994, 2002, and 2012

policy with the building of numerous new nuclear plants and the rise of nuclear electricity production. An anti-nuclear stance from the opposition—soon to become the governing coalition—or a phase-out at that stage of the French nuclear programme might have had more consequences on the scope of the French nuclear programme than at any other following stage.

The Communist Party had supported the civil nuclear policy from the beginning of the French nuclear programme. At the end of the 1970s, the anti-nuclear protest was mainly driven by a coalition of environmentalist activists, anarchist groups, and Trotskyist organizations. The potential responsiveness of the PCF to the anti-nuclear protest was decreased by the historic rivalry between the PCF and these groups. Moreover the Communist CGT was the dominant trade union in EDF and the nuclear sector. Hence the pro-nuclear stance of the PCF was not challenged during the late 1970s protests. The PCF may be described as a policy-seeker at that time.

The Socialist Party was closer to the anti-nuclear side than the Communist Party. Some Socialist activists were heavily involved in national and local protests against the nuclear policy. The only officially anti-nuclear mainstream organization, the trade union CFDT, was traditionally a close ally of the Socialist Party. So there were real incentives to realign the partisan position on the nuclear issue and politicize it in order to win votes. Nevertheless the Socialist Party neither switched from a pro-nuclear to an anti-nuclear stance nor politicized the nuclear issue.

The Socialist Party and its leader François Mitterrand were obviously office-oriented at this period, because alternation and winning office was the explicit top priority objective. Due to differences with the PCF, the PS fell short of this objective in the 1978 legislative election: it was fifteen seats short of reaching a majority. In 1981, however, the aligned left managed to win the presidential election—even the PS alone won a majority of seats. It is not doubtful that achieving some policy gains in the social and economic area was a central concern of the Socialist Party leadership. Whether these policies were a substantive goal or an instrumental one is difficult to determine, but this does not matter from our perspective. In both cases, nuclear policy stances had to be compatible with accessing power and reforming the French social and economic policy. At the end of the 1970s and the beginning of the 1980s, the only available coalition partner in order to secure a winning coalition was the Communist Party. As the Communist Party had a strong commitment to its own policy stances, the Socialist Party was constrained to adopt a policy platform compatible with the Communist Party. State intervention in the economy by nationalization and an active industrial policy was a common ground that made it possible to overcome the failure to agree on a common policy manifesto and to provide the core of a coalition agreement between both parties. A firm and politicized anti-nuclear stance would perhaps have attracted more votes, but it would undoubtedly have undermined a coalition of the left and thereby rendered impossible the alternation in government aimed for in 1981.

Policy-related arguments went against a phase-out of the nuclear programme as well. During the 1970s, François Mitterrand had steadily emphasized the importance of remaining independent as to the energy supply and even promoted the idea of turning back to the French graphite technology. Furthermore, the interventionist socio-economic policy would have been undermined by a phase-out of the nuclear programme in two ways. First, the current nuclear policy perfectly fitted with the economic policy to be conducted by the Socialists as the planning and building of numerous nuclear facilities was led by a state-owned company. Moreover, the programme would ensure cheap energy for future industry development and give jobs to thousands of employees. From the Socialist economic policy perspective, stopping such a programme would have been inconsistent. Secondly, the most important part of the nuclear plants was already under construction or nearly finished. Thus, a drastic phase-out would have been very costly. The most expensive part of the nuclear programme had already been realized and hence would have been stranded investment of great magnitude. Finding alternative energy supply on the market and paying for it would have constituted another hurdle. The necessary funds to finance the policy would not have been available for the nationalization policy strongly desired by the coalition of the left.

In October 1981, after the PS came to power, the National Assembly adopted an energy programme based on the so-called Hugon report, elaborated by a working group after the elections. It significantly deviated from the propositions formulated by the PS six months earlier, while still in opposition (PS 1981[12]). The importance of nuclear energy for the energy supply had largely increased, while reduced means were allocated to economizing the use of energy and developing renewable energies (Martin 1982). This gave rise to reproaches against the government for reneging on its electoral promises. The government responded that it could not afford to take the risk of an underestimation of the electricity consumption and highlighted the need for a minimal continuity in industrial policy.[13] Policy inheritance and the costs of a policy reversal also clearly deterred the Socialist Party from switching policies and politicizing the nuclear issue.

Finally, as long as the entry costs in the French political system were high enough to forbid any party with anti-nuclear stances from being pivotal, the Socialist Party had incentives to stick to its traditional pro-nuclear stance. Only symbolic pay-offs for anti-nuclear activists were delivered as, for example, the criticisms directed against the undemocratic implementation of nuclear policy by the rightist government (e.g. the location of the nuclear plants) before 1981 or the cancellation of the Plogoff nuclear plant after the leftist coalition won the presidency and a legislative majority in 1981. These symbolic pay-offs challenged neither the use of the nuclear energy itself nor the buildings of new nuclear plants after 1981. The relevance of this explanation is underscored by the contrast between the two periods analysed.

Although if the ecology movement has run in the French national elections since the presidential contest of 1974 (gaining 1 per cent), it has become important in the electoral competition only since the end of the 1980s. Thus, Mitterrand could afford to reject ecologist demands and insist on the indispensability of nuclear energy at the national Congress of the Socialist Party in Nantes in 1977.

---

[12] These proposals for government energy policy until 1990 stress the decoupling of economic growth and energy consumption, workers' security, and ecology.

[13] According to Roger Fajardie at the PS national Congress of Valence in Oct. 1981: 'when the Party was in opposition, certain choices could be postponed or be blurred. It is not possible anymore to act so as soon as one is in charge of public affairs' (see also the speeches of Pierre Mauroy and Bernard Morin).

During the March 1989 municipal elections, ecologist lists attracted many votes[14] and 1,300 of them became municipal councillors. Soon after this major breakthrough, the European parliamentary election was a second success for the Green Party (10.6 per cent) in June 1989. In 1992, for the first time in their history, ecologists were represented in a decision-making institution. Indeed, they were the true winners of the 1992 regional elections (Habert et al. 1992). With 14.3 per cent of votes, more than 200 ecologists entered the French regional councils. Beyond these results, the distribution of seats and political parties located the two ecologist parties as pivotal players in many regions (Brouard 1999). Indeed, ecologists participated in regional coalitions with either rightist or leftist parties. They also provided external support for formal minority governments. The 'decentralization' policy initiated in the 1980s that gave more power to local elected institutions and created a new layer of regional government has given new opportunities for the ecologists to become a relevant political player. Nevertheless, ecologist gains have not been limited to second-order elections. The 1993 legislative elections confirmed the new electoral strength of the ecologists with nearly 8 per cent of the vote. And in the 1995 presidential election, the Green candidate gathered more votes than ever. So since the end of the 1980s, despite the structural instability of the ecologist organizations and leaderships,[15] their increasing electoral and strategic importance appears as an obvious trend.

At the same time, electoral support for the Socialist and Communist parties had significantly dropped. So ecologists, and amongst them the Green Party, put them under pressure at three levels: electorally, by taking votes from their traditional leftist constituencies; politically, by raising new issues for the electoral agenda; and strategically, by appearing as the pivotal player in a forthcoming winning coalition. In reaction to this, the Socialist Party began introducing new policy stances in order to cope with the triple challenge of limiting electoral losses, dealing with new issues, and being able to build a new broad coalition. In fact, beyond the traditional coalition of the left, the Socialist Party understood progressively that a winning coalition needed to include the Green Party. Given the high likelihood of a landslide victory of the rightist coalition in 1993, the 1997 legislative election was the first time when the coalition-making—that gave birth to the 'plural left' coalition—included the Green Party. Hence the impact of the ecologist challenge on the Socialist and Communist Party could be studied at that time.

The Greens have been strongly committed to an anti-nuclear stance. At least on this issue, the Greens have been policy-oriented. Thus the nuclear energy issue gained a new relevance for the Socialist Party that needed to take a stance compatible with the likelihood of forming a coalition with the Green Party and the Communist Party. So new policy proposals from the Socialist Party were needed in order to allow a common ground on the nuclear policy issue to signal the Socialists' willingness to form a coalition with the Green Party and concede what might be presented as policy achievements of the Green Party. Already, at the national congress of Rennes in March 1990, the attention to environmental issues and the question of the reaction to Greens' electoral success was a sensitive issue: the

---

[14] Ecologist lists attracted 8% of the votes in 132 towns of 9,000 inhabitants or more where such a list was presented.

[15] For an exhaustive story of the political ecology in France, see Benhamias and Roche 1992; Sainteny 1992; Prendiville 1993; Delwit and De Waele 1999.

Socialist MPs Julien Dray and Yvette Roudy both used the example of nuclear policy in their speeches to illustrate the growing preoccupation of the electorate with environmental issues, while Marie-Noëlle Lienemann, another MP who made a speech at the Rennes Congress, presented this issue as the embodiment of productivism: 'We are the only Socialists in Europe to stick to this soothing discourse on nuclear energy. Don't believe you will be able to avoid questioning this policy'.

As mentioned earlier, the change regarding the nuclear policy stance of the Socialist Party in its campaign to the 1997 legislative election is striking. The 1997 Socialist platform clearly anticipated a coalition with the Greens and therefore leaned unambiguously towards the anti-nuclear side: a moratorium was promised. It might be argued that other factors than the anticipation of the next coalition-making game can explain the change in the Socialist proposals related to nuclear policy. The impact of the Chernobyl accident in 1986 is probably one of these factors. This dramatic event negatively altered the policy image of nuclear energy and caused some substantial policy realignments all across Europe. However, if the Chernobyl accident was the driving force behind the change of the nuclear policy stance of the Socialist Party, we should have been able to see it as soon as 1988. Yet the 1988 Socialist platform was their most pro-nuclear party manifesto ever.[16]

Beyond the Socialist party manifesto nuclear policy was for the first time affected by an effective Green pressure in 1997–8, when Greens entered the plural left coalition (1997–2002) with the PS and PC. The government decided on the closure of the experimental plant running the fast-breeder reactor Superphénix. Yet, this reversal was mainly symbolic and did not hinder the connection of new nuclear plants to the electricity grid and a peak in nuclear electricity production. The promised moratorium on nuclear plant construction was never voted on, even if it was de facto implemented. This is not necessarily linked to the Greens being in government, as the nuclear development plan was already fully realized and as no nuclear plant reached its projected end of life during this period. Nevertheless as soon as the right-wing coalition came back to power in 2002, the nuclear programme was immediately relaunched with the decision to build a new plant in Flamanville, followed by a second one in 2009, planned in Penly. If the Greens did not achieve a reduction of the weight of nuclear energy, they probably precluded a further extension of the French nuclear programme as long as they were in office. Given the highly constraining legacy of past policy choices, downsizing the nuclear programme would have been more costly in 1997 than in 1981: the discrepancy between political time and policy time gave the Greens little opportunity to further challenge French nuclear policy.

The logic induced by the changing coalition-related incentives has persistent effects in party manifestos and government policy. The second Socialist-Green governing coalition (2012–14) has also halted the development of nuclear energy in France. The 2012 political alternation was associated to three decisions: the

---

[16] For instance, the programme asked: 'Which country is the only one that succeeded in developing the nuclear energy in order to overcome the scarcity of our natural resources? It is ours, because it succeeded in organizing a twenty-year plan, which no private company would have been able to do'. In 1988, despite the Chernobyl accident, the nuclear policy was still presented positively within the state interventionism frame. In a manner reminiscent of some Communist manifestos, the Socialists even use the example of nuclear energy as a main illustration of the merits of planning and nationalization, the two pillars of their economic programme.

announcement that the oldest nuclear plant (Fessenheim) will be shut down at least at the end of 2016; the nuclear plant under construction (Flamanville) will be finished and connected to the grid; the newest project (Penly) is cancelled. In addition, as already mentioned, nuclear power is on the verge of being capped to the current power of its existing reactors by the final approval in 2015 of the law regarding the energy transition.

There has not been any major policy reversal in the French nuclear energy policy. Nevertheless, when an anti-nuclear party, the Greens, became a pivotal coalition partner, the Socialist Party started to amend its policy platform. Furthermore, the growth of the French nuclear programme stopped when the anti-nuclear party was part of the governing coalition. The lack of coalition-related incentives to adopt an anti-nuclear stance in the key growth period of the French nuclear programme explains the exceptional reliance on nuclear energy in France. Conversely, when coalition-related incentives did exist, the trajectory of the French nuclear policy has been significantly altered by the new coalition, within the limits of the policy legacy. Such an outcome proves counter-factually that beyond policy inheritance and economic and financial constraints, politicization and coalition-building are the key factor to understand the continuity of the French nuclear energy policy.

6.5 CONCLUSION

The long de-politicization of nuclear policy resulted not in the least from the pattern of party competition in France. We have underscored that many incentives have existed, for French parties, to change their position and to politicize the nuclear issue. This issue has been on the political agenda for more than fifty years and has been highly salient on the agenda of social movements and during some periods of the media. Public opinion has most of the time been more anti-nuclear than pro-nuclear. However, nuclear energy has not been on the electoral (or political) agenda (i.e. the set of policies contested between political parties) until an anti-nuclear party became electorally relevant and induced new coalition-related incentives. The features of the electoral system and the constraints of coalition-making fostered a pro-nuclear consensus among French parliamentary parties. New policy proposals and policy changes were introduced only by the late 1990s, when the Greens became a relevant player in the electoral as well as coalitional games.

Policy inheritance, as well as budgetary and economic constraints has, however, drastically limited the range of the possible policy reversals but also of a renewal of the nuclear reactors. Given that cutting the public deficit and decreasing the debt are likely to remain the main aims of any future French government, a massive plan for building new nuclear plants is difficult to implement in the short or middle run despite the recent announcement of the Energy Minister. As extensions of the life-duration of the existing plant will not go on forever and as the construction of new plants requires more and more time, policy inheritance as well as budgetary and economic constraints might in the next decades have the reverse effect and induce a progressive decrease of nuclear energy production in France. Nevertheless the rising politicization of the issue, with a strong and public commitment to nuclear energy by right-wing parties and sympathizers, has the potential to inhibit this trend in case of a 2017 alternation.

APPENDIX 1: POLICY DEVELOPMENT GRAPH

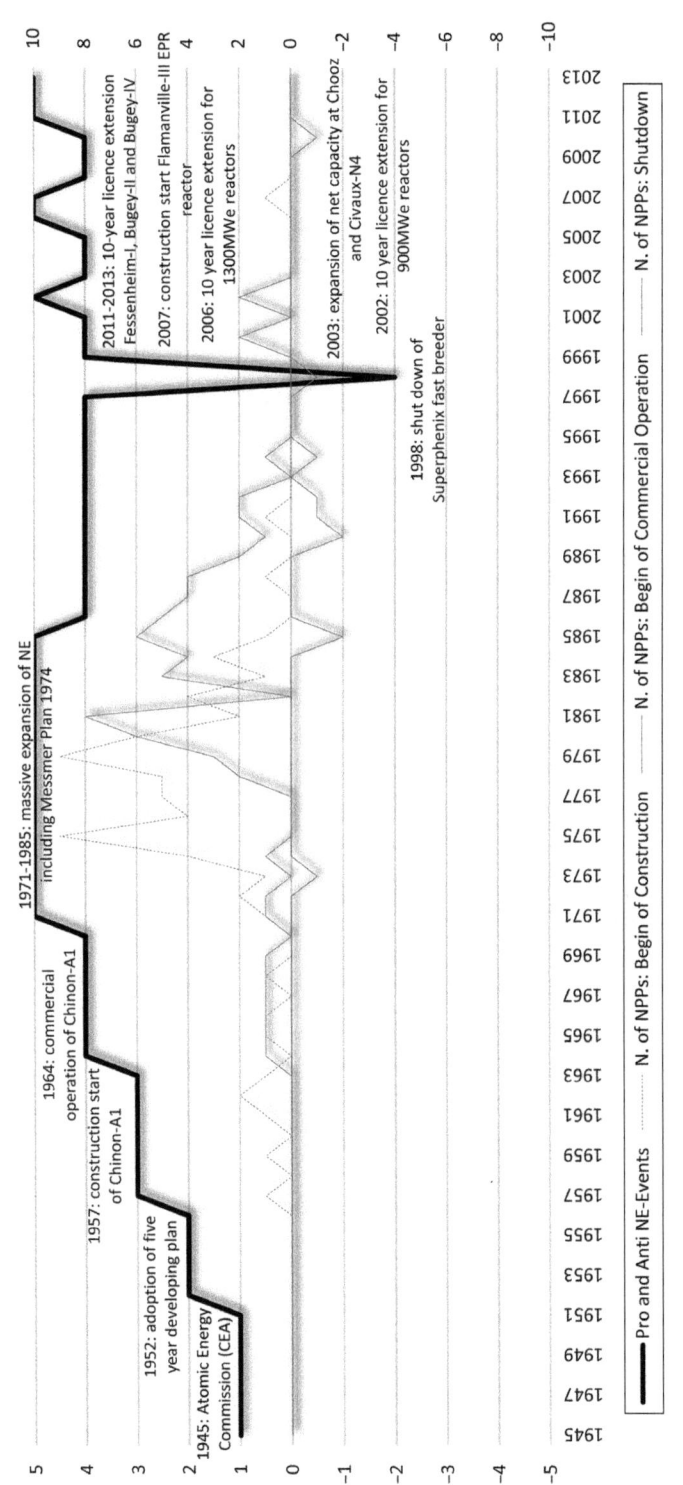

Figure 6.A1. Nuclear Energy Policy Development in France, 1945–2013

APPENDIX 2: MAIN EVENTS OF THE NUCLEAR FRENCH POLICY

Table 6.A1. Main Events of the Nuclear French Policy

Year	Policy decision
1945	Nuclear research: Creation of the Commissariat à l'Energie Atomique (CEA)
1951	Proposal of a nuclear energy programme
1952	Decision to go nuclear approved by the Parliament
1958	Criticality date of the first commercial nuclear plant Marcoule G2
1959	Grid date of Marcoule G2 nuclear plant
1970	The 6th plan (1971–5) decided the building of 8000 MW of nuclear power
1974	Messmer plan: 13 new nuclear plants (13 Mwe) every two years
1981	Moratorium & cancelation of the Plogoff nuclear plant
1982	Re-starting of the building of nuclear plants
1991	Closure of the nuclear programme launched in 1974 with the order of a last reactor (Civaux)
1998	Dismantling of fast-breeder experimental nuclear plant Superphénix
2005	Decision to build a new EPR nuclear plant (Flamanville 3—start in 2012)
2009	Decision to build a new EPR nuclear plant (Penly—start in 2017) & increase of the life time of the existing nuclear plant to 40 years (+10 years)
2012	Cancelation of the Penly plant and announcement of the closing of Fessenheim before 2017
2015	Adoption of a law that caps nuclear power

REFERENCES

Baisnée, Olivier (2001). 'Publiciser le risque nucléaire: La polémique autour de la conduite de rejets en mer de l'usine de la Hague.' *Politix*, 14(54): 157–81.

Barthe, Yannick (2006). *Le pouvoir d'indécision: La mise en politique des déchets nucléaires*. Paris: Economica.

Bataille, Christian, and Robert Galley (1999). *Rapport sur l'aval du cycle nucléaire*, ii, *Les coûts de production de l'électricité*. Paris: Rapport de l'Office parlementaire d'évaluation des choix scientifiques et technologiques, 1359, available at: http://www.assemblee-nationale.fr/11/rap-off/r1359-02.asp#P23_776.

Bauby, Pierre, and Frédéric Varone (2007). 'Europeanization of the French Electricity Policy: Four Paradoxes.' *Journal of European Public Policy*, 14(7): 1048–60.

Baumgartner, Frank R. (1990). 'Keeping Nuclear Power Off the Political Agenda.' Paper presented at the Workshop on the Comparative Political Economy of Science: Scientists and the State, Los Angeles, 12–14 Jan.

Baumgartner, Frank R., Suzanna L. De Boef, and Amber E. Boydstun (2008). *The Decline of the Death Penalty and the Discovery of Innocence*. Cambridge: Cambridge University Press.

Benhamias, Jean-Luc, and Agnès Roche (1992). *Des Verts de toutes les couleurs: Histoire et sociologie du mouvement écolo*. Paris: Albin Michel.

Blanchard, Philippe (2010). *Les médias et l'agenda de l'électronucléaire en France: 1970–2000*. Doctoral thesis in political science. Paris: Université Paris-Dauphine.

Boudia, Soroya (2003). 'Exposition, institution scientifique et médiatisation des controverses techno- scientifiques: Le cas du nucléaire (1945–2000).' *Mediamorphoses*, 9: 47–52.

Boudia, Soroya (2008). 'Sur les dynamiques de constitution des systèmes d'expertise scientifique: Le cas des rayonnements ionisants.' *Genèses*, 70(1): 26–44.

Bonneval, Laurent, and Cécile Lacroix-Lasnoë (2011). *L'opinion publique et européenne et le nucléaire après Fukushima*. Paris: Fondation Jean Jaurès.
Brouard, Sylvain (1999). *Partis politiques et politiques publiques dans les gouvernements locaux: L'exemple des groupes et élus écologistes dans les régions métropolitaines*, PhD dissertation, Institut d'Etudes Politiques de Bordeaux.
Brouard, Sylvain, and Isabelle Guinaudeau (2015). 'Policy Beyond Politics? Public Opinion, Party Politics and the French Pro-Nuclear Energy Policy.' *Journal of Public Policy*, 35(1): 137–70.
Brouard, Sylvain, Florent Gougou, Isabelle Guinaudeau, and Simon Persico (2013). 'Un effet de campagne.' *Revue française de science politique*, 63(6): 1051–79.
Colson, Jean-Philippe (1977). *Le nucléaire sans les Français*. Paris: Maspero.
Cour des Comptes (2012). *Les coûts de la filière électronucléaire*. Paris: Rapport Public Thématique.
Delion, André G., and Michel Durupty (2010). 'Chronique du secteur public économique.' *Revue française d'administration publique*, 133(3): 169–77.
Delmas, Magali, and Bruce Heiman (2001). 'Government Credible Commitment to the French and American Nuclear Power Industries.' *Journal of Policy Analysis and Management*, 20(3): 433–56.
Delwit, Pascal, and Jean-Michel De Waele (eds) (1999). *Les partis Verts en Europe*. Brussels: Complexe.
Downs, Anthony (1972). 'Up and Down with Ecology: The Issue Attention Cycle.' *Public Interest*, 28(1): 38–50.
OECD (2005). 'Concurrence sur les marchés de produits et performance économique.' *Etudes économiques de l'OCDE*, 10/2005: 7–91.
OECD (2009). 'Renforcer la concurrence pour accroître l'efficacité et l'emploi.' *Etudes économiques de l'OCDE*, 5/2009: 113–46.
Franchino, Fabio (2014). 'The Social Bases of Nuclear Energy Policies in Europe: Ideology, Proximity, Belief Updating and Attitudes to Risk.' *European Journal of Political Research*, 53(2): 213–33.
Garraud, Philippe (1979). 'Politique électro-nucléaire et mobilisation: La tentative de constitution d'un enjeu.' *Revue française de science politique*, 29(3): 448–74.
Guillaumat-Taillet, François (1987). 'La France et l'énergie nucléaire: Réflexions sur des choix.' *Revue de l'OFCE*, 19(1): 1989–227.
Habert, Philippe, Pascal Perrineau, and Colette Ysmal (1992). *Le vote éclaté*. Paris: Département d'études politiques du Figaro & FNSP.
Hadjilambrinos, Constantine (2000). 'Understanding Technology Choice in Electricity Industries: A Comparative Study of France and Denmark.' *Energy Policy*, 28(15): 1111–26.
Hatch, Michael T. (1986). *Politics and Nuclear Power: Energy Policy in Western Europe*. Lexington, KY: University Press of Kentucky.
Hecht, Gabrielle (1998). *The Radiance of France: Nuclear Power and National Identity After World War II*. Cambridge, MA: MIT Press.
Hillygus, D. Sunshine, and Todd G. Shields (2009). *The Persuadable Voter: Wedge Issues in Presidential Campaigns*. Princeton: Princeton University Press.
Humphreys, Peter, and Stephen Padgett (2006). 'Globalization, the European Union, and Domestic Governance in Telecoms and Electricity.' *Governance*, 19(3): 383–406.
Kitschelt, Herbert B. (1986). 'Political Opportunity Structures and Political Protest: Anti-Nuclear Movements in Four Democracies.' *British Journal of Political Science*, 16(1): 57–85.
Jasper, James M. (1988). 'The Political Life Cycle of Technological Controversies.' *Social Forces*, 67(2): 357–77.
Lucas, Nigel D. (1979). *Energy in France: Planning, Politics and Policy*. London: Europa Publications.

Martin, Jean-Marie (1982). 'Chronique sur l'énergie: Tendance de la consommation (1979-1981) et nouvelles orientations de la politique énergétique française (1981-1990).' *Revue d'économie industrielle*, 20(1): 101-13.

McCombs, Maxwell E., and Donald L. Shaw (1972). 'The Agenda-Setting Function of Mass Media.' *Public Opinion Quarterly*, 36(2): 176-87.

Nelkin, Dorothy, and Michael Pollak (1980). 'The Political Parties and the Nuclear Energy Debate in France and Germany.' *Comparative Politics*, 12: 127-41.

Nelkin, Dorothy, and Michael Pollak (1981). *The Atom Besieged: Extraparliamentary Dissent in France and Germany.* Cambridge, MA: MIT Press.

Prendiville, Brendan (1993). *L'écologie, la politique autrement? Culture, sociologie et histoire des écologistes.* Paris: L'Harmattan.

PS (1981). *Energie: L'autre politique.* Paris: Club socialiste du Livre.

Ramana, M. V. (2011). 'Nuclear Power and the Public.' *Bulletin of the Atomic Scientists*, 67(4): 43-61.

Rucht, Dieter (1994). 'The Anti-Nuclear Power Movement and the State in France', in Helena Flam (ed.), *States and Anti-Nuclear Movements.* Edinburgh: Edinburgh University Press, 129-62.

Sainteny, Guillaume (1992). *Les Verts.* Paris: PUF.

Schneider, Mycle (2009). 'Nuclear Power in France: Trouble Lurking behind the Glitter', in Lutz Mez, Mycle Schneider, and Steve D. Thomas (eds), *International Perspectives on Energy Policy and the Role of Nuclear Power.* Brentwood: Multi-Science Publishing, 55-83.

Smith, Tom W. (1980). 'America's Most Important Problem: A Trend Analysis, 1946-1976.' *Public Opinion Quarterly*, 44(2): 164-80.

Soroka, Stuart N. (2002). *Agenda-Setting Dynamics in Canada.* Vancouver: UBC Press.

Stimson, James A. (1991). *Public Opinion in America: Moods, Cycles, and Swings.* Boulder, CO: Westview Press.

Topçu, Sezin (2006). 'Nucléaire: De l'engagement "savant" aux contre-expertises associatives.' *Nature, Science Société*, 14: 249-66.

Van den Hoven, Adrian, and Karl Froschauer (2004). 'Limiting Regional Electricity Sector Integration and Market Reform: The Cases of France in the EU and Canada in the NAFTA Region.' *Comparative Political Studies*, 37(9): 1079-1103.

Wlezien, Christopher (2005). 'On the Salience of Political Issues: The Problem with "Most Important Problem".' *Electoral Studies*, 24(4): 555-79.

Wise, Michael (2005). 'Droit et politique de la concurrence en France.' *Revue sur le droit et la politique de la concurrence*, 7(1): 7-91.

7

Germany

Party System Change and Policy Reversals

Paul W. Thurner

7.1 INTRODUCTION

As in many other political systems, the nuclear energy issue proved to be highly conflictive and polarizing from the mid-1970s until the German parliamentary election in 2009. After the post-Fukushima phase-out decision by an originally pro-nuclear Christian-Democratic-Liberal government coalition in 2011, the issue disappeared from the campaign agenda. Nuclear energy is clearly one of the key issues for understanding the structure and development of the more recent German party system. This issue contributed at least partially to the parliamentary entry of the Green Party, and to the replacement of government coalitions in 1983, 1998, and in 2009. In 2000/1, the Social Democratic-Green government decided on a first gradual phase-out of nuclear energy. This first phase-out decision is especially interesting because the political decision implied that nineteen nuclear power plants (NPPs), which had produced up to nearly 30 per cent of Germany's electricity in the 1990s, would have to be shut down successively. More importantly, it implied that the application of this technology would have been definitely terminated by about 2022–3. This decision was partly annulled by a new government coalition of CDU/CSU and FDP in December 2010, and re-established after the Fukushima catastrophe in 2011. Regarding the sequence and speed of the implementation of antipodal decisions and in view of the respective implied sunk costs, these are undoubtedly the most far-reaching policy reversals in a democratic system with regard to a large-scale high-technology ever. Thus the German case constitutes a crucial case in studying the conditions of policy reversals.

The pre-1985 history of German nuclear energy policy-making and politics has been described and explained in great detail, and put into its comparative context by Herbert Kitschelt (1980, 1983, 1986a, 1986b). In contrast, the post-Chernobyl phase has seen rather few policy studies.[1] In this chapter I provide new data and interpretation that capture the entire post-war period. Special attention will be given to major policy reversals, without at the same time neglecting periods of

---

[1] See especially the important contributions by Rüdig (2000, 2003).

continuity despite pressures to reverse. I argue that German nuclear energy policy has seen three major reversals since the late 1990s. Even before these major policy reversals, two important changes of the German nuclear energy policy occurred. The first such change became visible in declining governmental financial support as expressed in the yearly R&D budgets from the mid-1950s to 2014. A steady increase in government support culminated in an exceptional peak in 1982 but then was followed by successive reductions. Behind these numbers were at least three important policy discontinuities that became clear by the end of the 1980s: first, the non-connection of a fast-breeder reactor (FBR) to the grid by the end of the 1980s; second, the withdrawal in 1989 from building a large-scale reprocessing plant in Bavaria (Wackersdorf); third, the actual freezing of new constructions (post-1982) and of new commercial operations (post-1989) (see Figure 7.1). This reflects a wait-and-see strategy as well as far-reaching adjustment of the conservative-liberal governments at that time struggling with extra-parliamentary pressures and the political fall-out of disasters. The explicit phase-out decision was electorally promised and implemented by the first SPD-Green government in 2000–2. The second explicit re-reversal came under the conservative-liberal coalition, taking office in 2009. This government intended to follow the international trend and to gradually retake the nuclear path. As a first step, it extended the lifetime of the operating nuclear power stations. However, in the aftermath of the Fukushima disaster, it re-established the previous phase-out decision and introduced what is now known as the German *Energy Transition* (*Energiewende*).

Despite important increases in shares of renewable energies—the contribution of solar energy to electricity generation increased from 1.97 per cent in 2010 to 4.7 per cent in 2013, that of wind power 6 per cent in 2010 to 8.4 per cent in 2013—nuclear energy continues to constitute a relevant part of the German energy mix, namely 22.4 per cent in 2010 and 15 per cent in 2015, with peaks of 35 per cent in the 1990s. This share actually amounted to about 46 per cent in 2010 (Federal Ministry of Economics and Technology) if we consider the so-called base provision (*Grundlaststromversorgung*): the permanently required electricity in the grid which, due to the lack of storing capacities, cannot be replaced by solar or wind power. According to the Federal Ministry for the Environment and Nature Conservation and Nuclear Safety there have been about 30,000 employees in this sector in 2010. Nuclear energy contributes to the avoidance of 100 to 150 million tons of carbon dioxide (CO_2).

Germany is tenth in Europe in per capita energy consumption – after Belgium, the Netherlands, Luxemburg, and France. With the exception of large coal deposits, Germany possesses only minor stocks of fossil fuels—and is therefore heavily dependent on imports of oil and gas. Note, however, that due to the deindustrialization in Eastern Germany, due to technological progress, and to increased energy efficiency, the country has experienced a stagnation of energy consumption since the 1990s.

In 2014 there were still nine nuclear plants at eight sites under operation (Brokdorf, Grohnde, Emsland, Grafenrheinfeld, Philippsburg, Neckarwestheim, Isar-2, Grundremmingen A and B). Eight plants had to be closed after the Fukushima disaster. There is a clear asymmetry in the geographical spread of the location of sites that are concentrated in five Länder (Bavaria, Baden-Württemberg, Hesse, Lower-Saxony, Schleswig-Holstein). One reason for this asymmetry is that these

Länder (unlike North Rhine Westfalia (NRW) and Saarland) had no important coal resources. Another reason for the concentration of nuclear power stations is that for a long time these Länder have been governed by conservative parties. Finally, all nuclear reactors (of the VVER-440 MWe type) in East Germany were shut down immediately after reunification due to security problems. In West Germany, at the time of the Fukushima disaster six units have been boiling water reactors (BWRs) and twelve have been pressurized water reactors (PWRs).

The main question to be answered is: which causal factors initiated the series of policy changes? And counterfactually: why do we observe stability despite political pressure for change? My central argument will partly relativize the early conclusions of Kitschelt (1980, 1983, 1986a, 1986b) with regard to the period of expanding nuclear energy: in my view, it was exactly the openness of the German political system—namely the features of its electoral system in combination with its decentralized federal system—which made it possible for a Green Party not only to cross the threshold of parliamentary representation, but also to become *the 'issue owner'* of nuclear energy for a long time. Only the successive *institutionalization* of a protest movement as a political party and its participation in regional and federal coalition governments guaranteed the continuation of high issue attention[2] and made these policy reversals possible. Only the accumulation of political resources—voters, money, social and human capital—allowed the Green Party continuously to organize the protests and to become a competitive and credible seller of alternative viable policy options. Afraid of losing voters, all established parties had to readjust their issue positions and policies. I combine the analysis of voter attitudes towards nuclear energy with content analysis of party manifestos in order to corroborate this new interpretation of the issue of the evolution of nuclear energy in Germany.

7.2 POLICY DEVELOPMENT

In the following section I describe a series of events, major reversals against nuclear energy, that have to be explained later by introducing the relevant causal factors and their interplay.

Until the mid-1970s, a permissive consensus prevailed between the four major parties (CDU/CSU, SPD, FDP), the trade unions, the Federation of the German Industry, and science—rather than a deliberate closure of and by the political-administrative system. These actors collaborated in developing nuclear energy technology; the nuclear energy issue was not politicized—neither in society (see Kitschelt 1980; Radkau 1983; Czada 1993) nor in the political-administrative system. Nuclear energy policy consisted of a combination of science and technology policies and Land and local infrastructure policies—especially private–public water supply and electricity companies played an important role. There was neither important opposition nor pressure groups considering nuclear energy dangerous and pleading for alternative energy sources.

---

[2] This can be seen from the high number of protest events (see Chapter 4).

As can be seen from the event scale (see Figure 7.1), the expansive period starts in the early 1960s. Its starting point was laid down by the Ministry of Atomic Affairs, created in 1955 and taken by Franz J. Strauss. He proposed a first nuclear programme aiming to bring together scientists, to buy research reactors from the US and the UK, and finally develop a fleet of German reactors. This policy was perpetuated by his successors in three follow-up programmes. The visualization shows that the construction beginning of the whole German fleet of reactors falls into the period between 1961 and 1981. Until 1989 reactors already under construction were finalized and commissioned. Even if the contribution to electricity production expanded in the following years, these indicators clearly show that the expansive path was politically suspended then. What are the main decisions reflecting this political halt?

7.2.1 Early Adjustments I: Reducing Nuclear Energy Research Subsidies

One of the most important indicators in assessing the dynamics of policy agendas is budget change (see Jones and Baumgartner 2005). Applied to our policy field, this means: to which extent did government budgets support nuclear energy from the late 1952 to the present? Support not only implies direct subsidies, but also includes preferential treatment (e.g. with regard to taxing, disregarding external costs and the costs of removal of plants, etc.), contributions to international organizations (e.g. to IAEA) and to transgovernmental institutions (EURATOM). There is a fierce and, until now, unresolved debate about the real amount of financial flows from the state to the nuclear industry. This debate extends to whether these flows should be considered subsidies or initial funding needed by any large-scale innovative projects, and in the case of nuclear energy, as fully profitable.[3] Without taking either perspective, the following section focuses exclusively on the expenditures for R&D allocated to nuclear energy as presented by DIW (2007) and as reflected in the follow-up budgets (Figure 7.2). I report both real price-adjusted values and percentage changes. The expenditures grew continuously until the early 1980s, with an exceptional high increase in 1982. In Jones and Baumgartner's terminology (2005) such budget changes of exceptional magnitude are 'punctuations'. After 1982, the public expenditures for nuclear energy research declined remarkably and continuously. Note that this also applies to expenditures for coal and other fossil energy sources, whereas R&D expenditures for renewable energy have now steadily increased. Expenditures for nuclear fusion technology have not changed remarkably since the mid-1980s. In 2006 real prices, the German government spent €24.1 billion over the 1974–2007 period—according to the calculations of DIW (2007).

---

[3] For recent arguments and empirical evidence see the expert opinion of the German Institute for Economic Research (DIW) (2007) initiated by then Green-led Ministry of Environment, or the update of data from the perspective of atomic energy lobbyists, see Weis et al. (2011). Note that the temporal patterns of these money flows for R&D is similar in both perspectives despite differences in absolute values. A main problem in calculating the money flows is, for instance, whether to include or exclude disposal research, risk co-insurance, and fusion technologies.

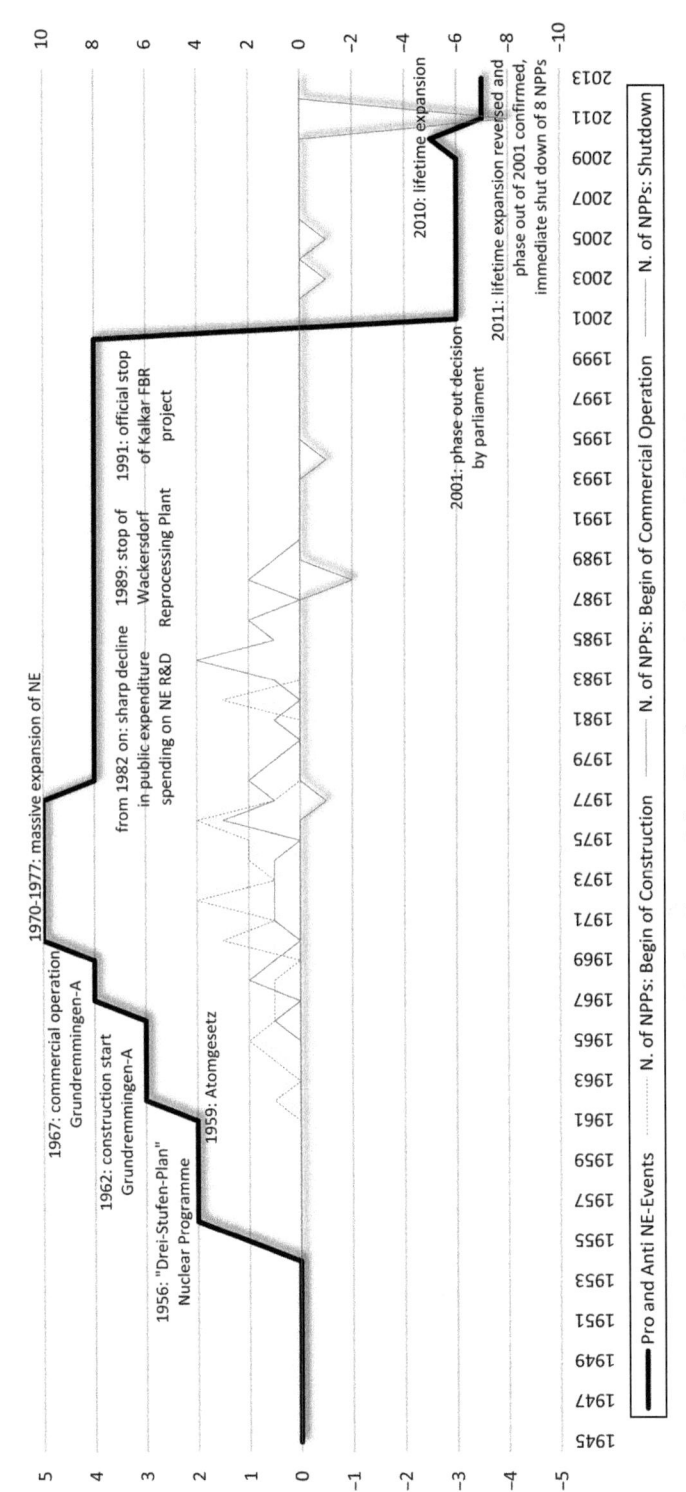

Figure 7.1. Nuclear Energy Policy Development in Germany, 1945–2013

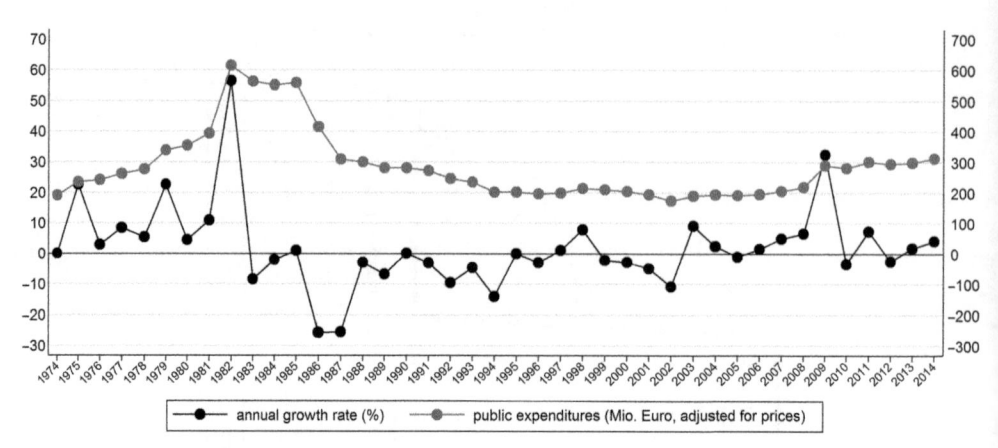

Figure 7.2. Public Expenditures for R&D in Nuclear Energy: Percentages of Budget Changes (Adjusted for Prices) 1974–2014
Source: DIW 2007: 16, BMBF 2008/2010/2012/2014, own calculation.

Over the entire period from the 1950s through 2007, the DIW estimated €40 billion R&D of public expenditures allocated to nuclear energy in 2006 prices. Note that in the beginning, the regional governments also participated extensively in nuclear energy R&D expenditures amounting to about €5 billion (in 2006 prices) (DIW 2007). The reduction in R&D expenditures after 1982 reflects on the one hand the maturation and the commercialization of the technology—which contributed increasingly to the provision of electricity. However, this reduction seems also indicative of the following two political reorientations: halting both the fast-breeder reactor technology and the Wackersdorf reprocessing plant. The renewed peak in 2008 indicates increases in research but especially in the quadrupling of the 2008 amount for the removal of shutdown reactors.

7.2.2 Early Adjustments II: Stopping the Fast-Breeder Reactor (FBR)

One of the important early reversals in German nuclear energy policy was the halt in the construction of a commercial FBR in Germany in response to the anti-nuclear movement's demands. This decision provided clear evidence to observers and activists alike that protests could be effective. The case is essential for the understanding of the history of the anti-nuclear movement (see Rucht 2008) and its transformation into the Green Party.

The Kalkar FBR was a joint project of Germany, Belgium, and the Netherlands that had been started in 1972. The objective was to use nuclear fuel more efficiently and to reduce dependency on uranium imports. After the beginning of construction in 1973, the Kalkar site experienced large-scale demonstrations. The plant was completed in 1986, but never went into operation. Numerous lawsuits had led to interruptions of the construction. A special inquiry committee of the Federal Parliament imposed an interruption of the construction for four years in order to achieve stricter safety requirements. Successive cost increases led to a total investment of €3.5 billion. It was the SPD-FDP government in North Rhine-Westphalia that was mainly responsible for the delaying measures. It had already adopted an anti-nuclear position in 1978. This was relevant beyond the Kalkar project, as it undermined the credibility of the federal government—also an SPD-FDP coalition. The necessity of a FBR and of nuclear energy was increasingly questioned. Whereas Chancellor Helmut Schmidt (SPD) intransigently promoted nuclear energy both nationally and internationally, the size of an anti-nuclear faction—led by Erhard Eppler—within the SPD increased in the late 1970s.[4] The issue was considered so important that Chancellor Schmidt threatened internally several times to resign. In a highly polarizing election campaign in 1980 between the challenger Strauss—the former and first Minister for Atomic Affairs—and incumbent Schmidt, the latter was nevertheless able to gather the anti-atomic movement behind the SPD. Being confronted with two undesirable alternatives, the new leftist movement still rallied behind the SPD—and caused the new alternative, the Green Party, to win only 1.5 per cent of the votes in the 1980 parliamentary elections. With regard to the FBR, the NRW Ministry of Economics tactically denied granting a partial construction licence. Despite these successive waiting games (later to be imitated, not invented, by the first Green minister in Hesse, Joschka Fischer), the FBR was ready for operation in 1985. Yet the NRW ministry responsible for its commissioning again denied its permit for years—against the will of the central government (now consisting of a coalition government of CDU/CSU-FDP). The NRW government asserted incalculable risks and argued that former partial licences had been accepted only with reservations. Consequently, it did not allow nuclear fuel elements to be inserted in the reactor. Protracted examinations of the reactor aimed at delaying the process until the FBR could be prevented. In the context of decreases in energy consumption, electricity-producing companies did not push vigorously enough to achieve commissioning. The Chernobyl disaster of 1986 further increased the reservations against the operation of a FBR. Finally, the conservative-liberal coalition in federal government declared the official halt on the FBR project in 1991. Due to the eminent sunk costs, the NPP Kalkar was now generally considered an investment black hole.

7.2.3 Early Adjustments III: Stopping the Wackersdorf Reprocessing Plant

The first plans were to build a reprocessing plant in Gorleben, Lower Saxony. Due to demands to share the waste management burden, Bavaria, under its Minister President Strauss, took over the task of building a large reprocessing plant in 1980 in a former coal-mining region that suffered from massive unemployment at that time. Partly violent demonstrations and occupations of the site followed. To the surprise of the Bavarian government, the mostly rural local population supported

---

[4] For an overview of the strategic challenges of the SPD confronted with these new-leftist currents since the mid-1970s see Scarrow 2004.

the protesters and citizens flooded the licensing authorities with objections. In 1989, the operating companies lost interest in this project and decided to reprocess nuclear fuels in cooperation with the French and British reprocessing plants in The Hague and Sellafield, respectively. The abandonment of Wackersdorf in May 1989 was generally seen as another defeat of the pro-nuclear coalition and an important partial victory in the fight against nuclear energy. Actually it meant the end of the intention to build up and guarantee the whole processing cycle of nuclear fuel in Germany. The decision induced future attention cycles, because utilities had now to carry nuclear fuels over long distances to The Hague and Sellafield. These transports fuelled future campaigns of the Green Party because it gave visible testimony to their main argument: the 'unresolved' question of the final disposal of nuclear waste (see Rüdig 2000). In order to understand this policy change as a genuinely political decision, it must be remembered that, by the end of the 1980s, the CDU/CSU-FDP government that had replaced the SPD-FDP coalition in 1982 was under continuous pressure due to extra-parliamentary mobilization of the anti-nuclear and peace movements. The Chernobyl disaster was followed by the establishment of the Ministry for the Environment, Protection of Nature, and Reactor Safety in June 1986. Note, however, that the violently contested reactor in Brokdorf simultaneously started operating in September 1986. In 1988 and 1989 three further new plants were activated. Political pundits and public opinion researchers expected a clear defeat of the government under Chancellor Kohl in the next election scheduled for January 1991. However, German unification in 1989 turned the policy mood and forcefully introduced a change of the issue agenda with the need to integrate and rebuild Eastern Germany at the top. Whereas former SPD Chancellor Brandt expected a leftist majority already in the mid-1980s, an acceleration of anti-nuclear policy-making was stopped due to other priorities—the integration and reconstruction of Eastern Germany—and the rallying behind incumbent Chancellor Kohl. Nuclear energy was only a minor topic in the reunification election in 1990, as candidates unanimously consented to switching off five Soviet-type reactors in East Germany (Greifswald) and abandoning three further reactors at that site—two under construction and one already completed and ready for commercial operation. However, in the mid-1990s the attention to nuclear energy revived due to the already indicated Castor transports of nuclear fuel to/from The Hague and Sellafield. Therefore, in the 1998 parliamentary election, the Greens mobilized successfully against nuclear energy—and paved the way for the first phase-out decision.

Abandoning the fast-breeder reactor and the reprocessing plant, the freezing of R&D budgets and of new reactor constructions were adjustments taken by the governing Christian-Democratic and liberal parties. These parties were clearly for nuclear energy, but given the fierce extra-parliamentary pressure, these parties were satisfied with the achieved status quo. The next section describe the sequence of major policy reversals.

7.2.4 Reversal I: Phasing Out Nuclear Energy

In 1998, the first coalition government in German history of the SPD and Greens was formed, i.e. a government of two decidedly anti-nuclear parties. In their coalition agreement, the parties consented to change the Atomic Energy Law and on a definite nuclear energy phase-out. This intention had already been made explicit earlier in the coalition contract of the SPD-Green government in Lower Saxony of 1990. Note that this coalition was led by the later Federal Chancellor Schröder. However, after the 1998 success it took nearly four years until the so-called Act on the Structured Phase-Out of Nuclear Power for the Commercial Production of Electricity[5] was officially promulgated. This indicates that working out this legal act was extremely complicated and required hard bargains— negotiated both between the coalition parties and between the government and the German nuclear energy industry. In order to assess the assertiveness of the pro- and anti-nuclear coalitions respectively, one should consider the initial demands. The Green Party had demanded an immediate phase-out in its 1998 electoral manifesto. However, terminating a previously unrestricted operating licence would have violated constitutional law, as it would have implied an expropriation of the utilities. Such behaviour, in turn, would have led to enormous financial compensation claims. Therefore, the pragmatic wing of the Green Party realized that it had to agree on a compromise that would fall short of immediate shutdowns. The approach taken was to allow utilities to continue operation of NPPs for a specified number of years to allow for a sufficient return on investments. Contested issues included the number of years before the shutdown and whether it should occur at a specified point in time, or vary between plants according to the number of years the relevant plant had been in operation. Even within the Green party no single option enjoyed unanimous support, with a range from immediate shutdown (as demanded by the radical faction) to granting a grace period of five years after the promulgation, and a one-by-one NPP shutdown twenty-five years after the beginning of their operation.

The new Chancellor Gerhard Schröder decelerated the original momentum. He had already been involved in so-called 'consensus talks' with the nuclear energy industry since 1992/3 that aimed at an 'orderly' termination of nuclear energy. The SPD had committed to a phase-out in its party programmes and electoral manifestos since 1987, any other policy would have undermined its credibility. However, Chancellor Schröder and the Minister of Economic Affairs Werner Müller, a former manager of energy company VEBA, wanted to avoid the payment of compensation to and opening conflict with a powerful industry that the SPD had previously heavily supported. Consequently, Chancellor Schröder continued a consensual approach. He allowed for an extended negotiation process and publicly criticized and even excluded the Green Minister of the Environment Jürgen Trittin from top-level meetings with the CEOs of the nuclear energy industry. Utilities were in a rather comfortable bargaining position: having mostly written off the high start-up costs, utilities generated considerable profits from their NPPs and therefore had strong economic interest 'to ensure as long a working life for their reactors as possible'. The 'stakes' involved in terms of phasing out existing nuclear reactors were thus quite high, much higher than in the case of other countries such as Austria or Italy that had earlier opted for a non-nuclear future (Rüdig 2000: 49–50).

---

[5] Gesetz zur geordneten Beendigung der Kernenergienutzung zur gewerblichen Erzeugung von Elektrizität.

In the end, the final result was a gradual phase-out until 2021–3. This gradual phase-out decision occurred after the mean total operation time of NPPs was fixed at thirty-two years. However, the reference point was decided to be the total amount of electricity produced by a NPP, allowing for the transfer of quotas from one plant to another. Thus, some NPPs were expected to operate for a longer time period. The agreement also fixed the end of the transport of nuclear waste and its reprocessing in 2005. Investigations for final nuclear waste disposal were to be renewed and the examination of the suitability of Gorleben temporarily suspended. As a consequence, utilities were required to dispose nuclear waste at the sites of NPPs.

The CDU/CSU and the FDP heavily criticized the phase-out decision, arguing that German NPPs had the highest safety standards worldwide and that nuclear energy would contribute to preventing climate change. In contrast, environmental associations criticized the phase-out decision as a complete fake, because the remaining operation time would be no different from what the utilities had planned for anyway. Comparing the initial bargaining demands with the outcome, there is indeed some truth in this criticism.

What is much more important, however, is the fundamental change in the declared objectives of the 1959 Atomic Energy Act in its 2001 version. In the 1959 version, the aim was to promote the use of nuclear energy. Section 1 of the 2002 Atomic Energy Act now reads as follows: 'The purpose of this act is: 1. to phase out the use of nuclear energy for the commercial generation of electricity in a structured manner, and to ensure ongoing operation up until the date of discontinuation'. This fundamental change of goals had far-reaching repercussions on research and investments in Germany, and caused a relocation of the companies' nuclear business to other countries. Thus in 2001, Siemens, the long-time technologically leading company in the nuclear energy industry, brought its nuclear energy corporation into a joint venture with the French company Areva—on rather bad terms. While the abandoning of the reprocessing plant in Wackersdorf and of the FDB project constituted only a leaving of the expansion course (see Figure 7.1), the phase-out decision was clearly a major policy reversal, turning nuclear energy policy-making into the negative area of our scale—at least with regard to national policy-making. At the international level, the SPD-Green coalition continued to fulfil its obligations, to contribute to IAEA and to EURATOM. However, it did not join the Global Nuclear Energy Partnership.

7.2.5 Reversals II and III: Re-phasing-in and Re-phasing-out

During the 2005–9 legislative term, the SPD and CDU/CSU coalition accepted a tacit stalemate in nuclear energy policy-making. Due to the SPD's veto position, there was no room for fundamental changes. Nevertheless, this period was characterized by intense quarrels between the CSU-led Ministry of Economics (Minister Michael Glos) and the SPD-led Ministry for the Environment (Minister Sigmar Gabriel). Glos initiated a Project Group on Energy Policy Programme in 2008. In its first report this group demanded a prolongation of the operation time of NPPs from the legal status quo of thirty-two years to a minimum of forty years. In contrast, Gabriel used his office for a continuous public agitation against nuclear energy and especially against the waste deposit site Gorleben. This should also be understood against the background of the first permission by the highest courts and in accordance with Atomic Law of a final waste deposit site in 2007—the so-called Schacht Konrad. This site is qualified for low and medium high degrees of radioactive waste—i.e. for about 90 per cent of the waste produced in Germany. Thus, a crucial argument in the anti-nuclear debate—the unresolved final deposit question—seemed to be at least partially challenged.

In December 2010, in accordance with their 2009 campaign positions, the new CDU/CSU-FDP government cancelled the phase-out decision of 2002 and granted an extension of twelve lifetime years on average per NPP. Note, however, that this same government did not modify §1.1 of the Atomic Law: 'The objective of this law is to abandon nuclear energy in an orderly way'—again in accordance with their programmatic commitment to consider nuclear energy as a 'bridge technology'. Thus, this legal act cannot be seen as a return to nuclear energy. However, many observers interpreted this partial reversal only as a first step to be followed by a smooth return to nuclear energy once more advanced technologies such as Generation IV reactors were ready and nuclear energy acceptance increased, against the background of raised costs of other forms of energy. In this sense, in 2009 Siemens began to reorient its nuclear energy business towards a Russian cooperation. This clearly indicated its renewed willingness to invest in this technology and reclaim its earlier autonomy lost in the cooperation with French Areva. Thus, our scale in Figure 7.1 returns to 'commercial operation' as before.

However, the Fukushima event led to a sudden, definite, and consensual end of nuclear energy in Germany—despite some marginal disagreement in the FDP and lobby groups. Even many Christian Democratic politicians admitted that they had changed their opinion due to a completely new assessment of risks. Only three months after the re-phasing-in decision, i.e. on 15 March 2011, the same government declared a moratorium with a three-month shutdown of all reactors and ordered systematic security checks. All seven plants built before 1980 had to stop production immediately. After a dramatic loss of the elections in the Baden-Württemberg Land elections of 27 March, the federal cabinet decided on 6 June 2011, that eight plants should be shut down immediately. The nine remaining plants were to be shut down successively until 2022—thus re-establishing the phasing-out decision of the SPD-Green precursor government. Regarding the sequence and speed of implementing these antipodal decisions and considering the implied sunk costs, these are undoubtedly the most far-reaching policy reversals ever in a democratic system in the use of a large-scale high-technology. As a consequence, in September 2011 Siemens announced a complete withdrawal from the nuclear energy business, and abandoning long-term cooperation plans with the Russian company Rosatom. The main operating companies are E.ON, RWE, EnBW, and Vattenfall Europe—the products of fusions in the electricity industry over the years. These companies reported billions of losses over the next years—after years of high profits—and announced the loss of ten thousand jobs. Vattenfall, E.ON, and RWE have filed lawsuits against the forced shutdowns, which are still pending. In December 2016, the Federal Constitutional Courts ruled that the nuclear exit decision was legitimate. Despite stipulating an agreement until 2018 on compensations for investments based on the re-phasing-in decision, the Court thereby confirms in principle the legality of the phase-out II.

Assessing the sequence and timing of the policy development, it is quite obvious that, despite enormous extra-parliamentarian pressures against nuclear power, a necessary condition for clear reversals in the pre-Fukushima period was a government consisting of parties with clear anti-nuclear positions. During the Kohl era 1983–98, only adjustments were carried out, especially in the face of two disasters. The Social-Democratic Party had to take a new identity in the energy policy area in order to find a new, leftist majority from 1998 to 2005.

7.3 ACTORS AND JURISDICTIONS

This section gives special attention to the inherent conflict between a policy-deciding federal government and policy-implementing governments at the Land level—even if they share the same party affiliation. There are no specific stipulations with regard to the preferred energy provision in the German Constitution (Grundgesetz, GG). However, the German Constitutional Court has ruled that energy should be part of public services. Its regulation is therefore deemed necessary, because of the Länder responsibility to guarantee energy and the respective infrastructure in accordance with the postulate of social welfare of Art. 20, 1 GG. The main legislation is constituted by the Atomic Energy Act (Atomgesetz, AtG, 1959/1960—see Ziegler 2011).[6] Its declared objective was to 'promote nuclear research and the development and use of nuclear energy for peaceful objectives'. In a previous version of the German constitution, according to Art. 74, 1, Nr. 11a GG, regulation with regard to energy provision was in the 'concurrent competence' of the Länder.[7] The postulate of the 'equality of standards of living' clause in Art. 72, 2 GG allowed the federal state to exploit these shared competences while the Länder were administratively required to implement the decisions under the Atomic Law (1959) (Bundesauftragsverwaltung). Since the 'Reform of Federalism I', an important reform of the German constitution in 2006, the federal level has now exclusive jurisdiction over nuclear energy (Art. 73, 14 GG; see Pielow et al. 2007). Furthermore, Art. 87 GG enables the federal state to use autonomous agencies like the Federal Office for Radiation Protection, established in 1986,[8] or the Federal Office for the Regulation of Nuclear Waste Management in 2014.

Notwithstanding the prevailing political consensus until the mid-1970s, it makes sense to identify the actors that engineered the *positive discrimination* of

---

[6] The historical background and policy process is described e.g. by Radkau 1983; Radkau 2008; Kitschelt 1980.

[7] In areas of competing legislation, the Länder are allowed to decide on public policies as long as the federal state does not make use of these competencies.

[8] See Gesetz über die Errichtung eines Bundesamtes für Strahlenschutz. This agency assigned to the BMU was established in 1986 and was endowed with responsibilities for the approval of intermediate storage of nuclear fuels, their transportation, as well as for the construction and operation of disposal facilities for radioactive materials.

nuclear energy and the early regulatory regime, leading to the enormous path dependencies. The short answer is clearly a pro-growth and pro-nuclear advocacy coalition (see e.g. Rüdig 2000). In order to understand the emergence of this coalition it is useful to focus on its sectorial institutionalization, especially within the ministries deciding on nuclear energy policies. The policies of the conservative-led governments under Chancellor Adenauer in the 1950s laid the basis for the emphasis on nuclear energy as *the* energy option in order to become independent of coal and fuel imports. This emphasis was not put into question by the following governments led by the Social Democratic Party (SPD), but rather accelerated under its Chancellors Brandt and Schmidt.

The main ministries involved in the development of nuclear energy have been the Ministry of Economics, and the—over the years differently labelled— ministries for technology, science, environment, and interior, respectively. Tracing the institutional evolution of these ministries with regard to their responsibilities is telling: different labelling and the shifting and reshifting of parts of the jurisdictional responsibilities between them are indicative of the underlying jurisdictional and bureaucratic dynamics of the political agenda. The importance attributed to nuclear energy was already visible in the creation of the Federal Ministry for Atomic Affairs (Bundesministerium für Atomfragen) in 1955. It had the explicit task of developing the peaceful usage of nuclear energy and to achieve independence from foreign energy resources. This ministry headed by Franz Josef Strauss initiated the so-called Atomic Commission in 1956 and established, in close synergy with scientists, private companies, and regional administrations, a series of nuclear research centres (e.g. Jülich, Karlsruhe, Munich, Hanover, etc.). The first research reactor in Munich came under construction in 1957—only about one decade after the Second World War. This was possible due to the Paris treaty and the German renouncement of nuclear weapons, and because the German government joined the International Atomic Energy Agency in the same year. In 1958, a commission for reactor safety was set up. In the same year, the first nuclear research programme was launched; it was followed by three successive programmes in 1963 (DM 2.5 billion), 1968 (DM 5 billion), and 1973 (DM 6.1 billion). As other research-based technologies were also successively subsidized, another more general labelling occurred in 1962 in which the now responsible Federal Ministry of Scientific Research was established. After the Chernobyl disaster, the Federal Ministry for Environment, Nature Conservation, and Nuclear Safety was formed in June 1986. The nuclear division of the Research Ministry was shifted to this new ministry, implying that a clearly pro-nuclear line was incorporated into a ministry in charge of environment policy. This originally pro-nuclear stance changed definitely with the taking of ministerial office by a minister of the Green Party in 1998. The anti-nuclear tendency was maintained under a Social Democratic minister in 2005, and even under a Conservative minister since 2009. In contrast, the responsibility for technology policy and especially for the security of energy supply remained in the Ministry of Economic Affairs. Accordingly, the latter department was continuously in conflict with the Ministry for the Environment— even in coalition governments of the SPD and Greens.

Centralized oversight over NPPs was planned as part of the establishment of the new Ministry for the Environment in 1986. The ministry was intended to preside over the committee of the responsible ministries of the Länder (Länderausschuss für Atomenergie, established in 1958). According to the original version of the Atomic Law (§7) the Länder had the competence to approve and to monitor the construction, operation, and decommissioning of NPPs. However, the involvement of Green parties in Länder such as Hesse, Lower Saxony, Hamburg, and Schleswig-Holstein politicized the originally apolitical issue (see Czada 1993). Due to the fragmentation, overlapping of competencies, and the necessary interplay between the Länder and the federal government, nuclear energy policy-making increasingly became a nested game that required a negotiation mode (see Czada 1993). In this set-up it became increasingly possible to veto pro-nuclear policy-making of individual Länder and the federal government, and also to infuse policy alternatives from the periphery to the centre. This is one of the reasons why the Federalism Reform I recentralized this policy area and transferred exclusive legislative competencies to the Federation.

According to the Repository Site Selection Act in 2013, the Federal Office for Radiation Protection is now responsible for the site selection of wastes, which constitute the policy left-overs.

7.4 VOTER ATTITUDES AND PARTY COMPETITION

Why these reversals and, especially, why the phase-out decision(s)? Why at these points in time, and why not earlier? And why the respective magnitude of the reversals? From the 1950s to the end of the 1970s, the German political elites were not inclined to envisage alternative energies (see Kitschelt 1980, 1983). Undoubtedly, the mobilization of movements, and partly the radicalization of protest, played an important role for the policy reversals (see Rucht 2008). In order to understand the complete chain of these reversals, however, one has to trace the process that led to successive windows of opportunity. The major phase-out decision in 2002 has to be understood in the context of a whole series of earlier policy modifications and adjustments. Already, at the beginning of the 1990s, attempts to build new NPPs in Germany had come to an end. A de facto halt on constructing new plants is already reflected in the 'consensus talks' beginning as early as 1992, where the nuclear energy industry signalled its readiness to back down. At the same time, the fusion option and that of a new generation of safer reactors remained open. I argue that the institutionalization of the Green Party[9] as an institutionalized movement entrepreneur (i.e. as part of parliaments *and* governments) is a necessary precondition for the continuation of the extra-parliamentary protest, and of the repositioning of other parties, of the energy companies, and of the nuclear energy technology firms. The chapter therefore traces the evolution of the Green Party that is intricately interwoven with the anti-nuclear protest movement. Furthermore, the ups and downs of the definition of nuclear energy as a macro-issue (see Baumgartner and Jones 1993; Kingdon 1995), and the continuation of the attention cycle (i.e. the presence of an issue on the political macro-agenda) is reflected in the development of individual-level

---

[9] See Panebianco (1988) for the concept of the organizational institutionalization of parties.

issue saliency (see Wood and Vedlitz 2007) in successive steps. To serve this purpose, the chapter provides time series on public opinion, clearly showing that the electorates of all the established parties were split over the nuclear energy issue. The early surveys already indicate the potential for electoral shifts that then actually occurred with the entry of the Greens. The other parties had enormous difficulties in taking credible positions on this issue over time. Due to the internal attitudinal splits of their electorates, these parties were forced to readjust their policy positions and to accept and even initiate the reversals described. The section shows that the reactive reflection and position-taking of the established parties is mirrored in their party programmes and electoral manifestos.

7.4.1 The Institutionalization of the German Green Party

In their analyses of the German anti-nuclear movement, Kitschelt (1980) and Rucht (2008) stressed the importance of mobilization from below. However, there is no such thing as a permanent grassroots or self-mobilization of protest (see Olson 1965; Marwell and Oliver 1993), as successful politicization requires organization and resources. Upon that premise, this chapter argues that German nuclear policy energy reversals have been caused by the very institutionalization of the Green party and its successive electoral successes. The concept of institutionalization of a party means that it had accessed parliaments and governments and was involved in policy-making at different levels of the German multi-level system. Becoming a viable option for a government coalition, and actually participating in governments increased the visibility and power of the Green Party. The strategic use of these opportunities by its leaders indicates that only a match between opportunity structures and apt entrepreneurs leads to electoral success and effective realization of policy positions. It is this party that gave the protest movement a voice, provided financial support and encouragement, co-organized protest events of unseen magnitude, and thus put pressure on the established parties to readjust and to reframe their pro-nuclear positions successively.

The Green Party emerged from local Green lists presented at regional elections since spring 1977. In November 1977, a new environmental party was founded in Lower Saxony. In the 1978 state elections in Hesse and Bavaria, Green party lists won 2 per cent and 1.8 per cent, respectively. In 1979, the Greens for the first time entered a Land parliament in Bremen. In 1980, the Green federal party was founded, and the Land election successes continued, winning 5.3 per cent in Baden-Württemberg. These events were paralleled by the protests against the Gorleben final waste deposit reaching completely new dimensions. However, the results of the 1980 federal election (1.5 per cent) showed on the one hand that the Green party was still a local and regional phenomenon. On the other, the clash campaign between incumbent Chancellor Schmidt and the former Atomic Minister F. J. Strauss as challenger absorbed this cleavage at the national level: the nuclear energy issue was now on the national campaign agenda. Land governments already played waiting games with the federal government with regard to licensing NPPs and the investigation of possible sites for final waste disposal. Nevertheless, electoral successes of the Greens spiralled into a permanent mobilization against the SPD-FDP government in 1981.[10] The Green Party was the key centre in organizing these protests. Political participation is crucially driven by expectation formation. Due to the intermediate electoral successes and the accessibility of the party system, the movement gained momentum. On 6 June 1982 the Green Party increased its share to 7.7 per cent in the Hamburg regional election. Also in June, more than 500,000 demonstrated in Bonn against US President Ronald Reagan. In September 1982, the Greens achieved 8 per cent in the elections in Hesse. This prompted SPD leader Willy Brandt, whose party had won 42.8 per cent there, to foresee a new, leftist coalition option emerging for national politics. However, in October 1982, SPD Chancellor Schmidt, a fervent proponent of nuclear energy, did not survive a vote of confidence—and a strictly pro-nuclear coalition of the CDU/CSU and FDP took over federal government. The SPD had by that time been completely split over nuclear energy for years. For instance, recall the abandonment of the FBR by important intra-party actors. Nevertheless, time series of public expenditure on R&D still display an enormous final increase in 1982.

In the federal election in 1983, the Green Party won 5.6 per cent and entered Federal Parliament for the first time. In the context of a relatively low representational threshold, voters with a clear anti-nuclear attitude now shifted their choices. The Green Party had entered the 'system' and now worked from within Parliament to change policies. One of the party's key figures in this period was Joschka Fischer, one of its founders and part of the pragmatic faction. Initially responsible for the organization of the federal parliamentary group, the basic democratic rotation principle which the Greens then obeyed forced him out of Federal Parliament in 1985. Continuing his career in Hesse, he became the first ever Green minister in a coalition with the SPD, taking up the Ministry for Environment and Energy in the Land government. As Rüdig (2000) convincingly argues, this period was extremely important for anti-nuclear policy-making, because the Green Party now disposed of resources to develop legal tactics to impede nuclear energy—and to keep it on the agenda. Fischer had quite spectacularly used the nuclear energy issue to put forward an ultimatum causing the break-up of the coalition government in Hesse in 1987. He refused to license a nuclear company. Despite the loss of government participation, Fischer used the institutional role of parliamentary opposition quite ingeniously. He re-entered the Hesse government in 1991 as Minister of Environment, Energy and Federal Affairs until 1995. His spectacular fights with the Federal Minister of Environment made him the de facto leader of the Greens. In 1994 Fischer left for the Federal Parliament and prepared the party for government participation in 1998. The electoral manifestos and the Green campaign were fundamentally oriented against nuclear energy.

Rüdig (2000) wonders why the German Green Party focused so much on the nuclear energy question once they were in a government coalition—unlike the Greens in government in other countries (e.g. in Finland or Belgium). The most likely answer is that the German Greens understood quite clearly that they had become the owners of the nuclear energy issue. As a consequence, any

---

[10] To provide a few examples, on 18 Feb. 1981 more than 100,000 people demonstrated against the NPP Brokdorf. On 10 October 1981 more than 300,000 protested for peace and disarmament in Bonn.

ineffectiveness in dealing with this question in a government would have destroyed their very reputation and thus prevented their further development towards larger market shares. Note, however, that becoming the owner of this issue in the German setting was not self-evident, as the SPD had made a U-turn in their nuclear energy policy already in the mid-1980s, and were now also rejecting nuclear energy. Yet, for a long time, the Green Party was perceived as the only new-leftist actor credibly rejecting nuclear energy. Without the successful institutionalization of the protest movements into a party, achieving such a major policy reversal would be hard to imagine. Although the Christian Democratic and Liberal parties introduced the first modifications to the policy of expanding nuclear power, they did so under increasing pressure from the Green Party that had just entered parliament. This would have been impossible without the quite open German electoral system and it allowed for the gradual integration of grassroots protest into the federal policy-making system. With hindsight, the German political system was not as closed for reform efforts as the rather pessimistic assessments in Kitschelt's (1980, 1983) early analyses suggest.

The second institutional feature of Germany that contributed to the outcome is federalism. It allowed the Greens to 'march through the institutions' step-by-step (rather than hope for the 'big bang' electoral breakthrough at the national level), taking advantage of mid-term fatigue with the national government. Moreover, the Green Party participation in Land governments allowed not only the blocking of nuclear energy implementation, but also devoting public resources to elaborating new policy options—such as the policies on renewable energies.

7.4.2 Changes in Public Opinion

From its very beginning, the protest movement has been investigated extensively by public opinion surveys (see Renn 1977; Battelle Institute 1977). Figure 7.3 is the first attempt to put together a complete time series of nuclear energy attitudes from 1977 through 2011, drawing on the Politbarometer time series of the Forschungsgruppe Wahlen (FGW). All percentages relate to the full sample (i.e. they include all parties, abstention, no answers, missings, and don't knows, and combining the last three categories into one single one as their separation over time proved impossible).

The Harrisburg accident had already noticeably changed German public opinion on nuclear energy. The share of 'don't knows' decreases permanently from nearly 20 per cent to a very small fraction. However, the 'shutdown immediately' segment increased only marginally. Interestingly, it seems to amount already to about 40 per cent at that time. The explicit 'pro-nuclear energy' segment remained rather unimpressed, remaining also at about 40 per cent. The 'shutdown immediately' question format, however, biased the answers. After introducing another category, asking whether the existing NPPs should be kept, but no more new plants to be built, the new category absorbed a steady increasing share of respondents—up to more than 75 per cent in the mid-1990s. Again, differentiating this category between those which prefer to 'use only existing plants as long as possible' and 'use only existing plants but shut them down as soon as possible', it turns out that these two segments were of nearly the same size (c.45 per cent). In the 1990s, the

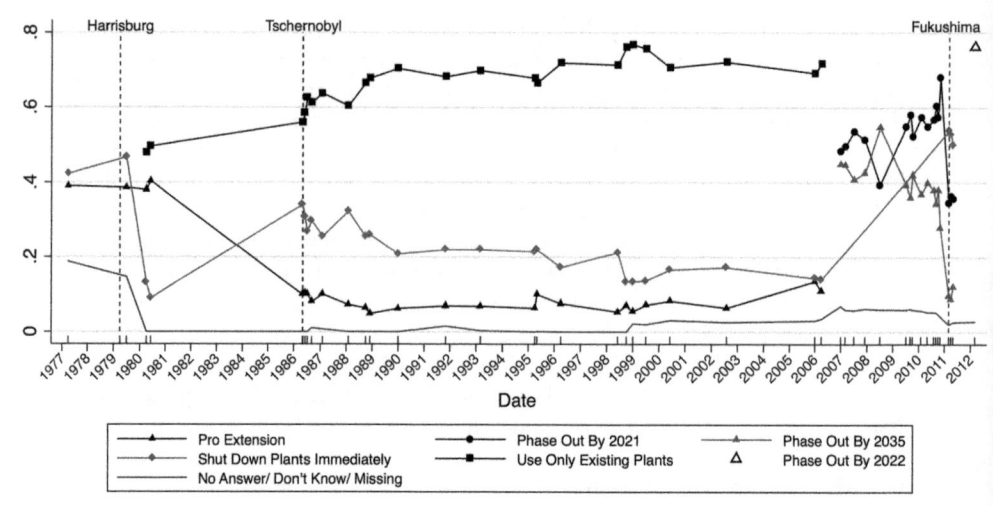

Figure 7.3. Development of Attitudes towards Nuclear Energy

Note: Eastern Germany included since 1991.

category 'use them as long as possible' increased. It is this background which the long-lasting Kohl governments accepted, and did nothing to provoke a destabilization of this very large majority of the electorate consenting with the status quo.

In the long-term development of German public opinion, the Chernobyl disaster constituted nevertheless a watershed that is visible in the dramatic reduction of the pro-extension segment thereafter. At the same time, the 'shutdown immediately' segment steadily decreases from 1998 to 2006. The share of survey respondents in favour of the NPPs' operation time extension considerably increased during this period. Note that in 2006, that is after the first phase-out, the question format has been adapted, providing respondents with two phasing-out dates, 2022 and 2035, respectively. While these segments supporting one or the other oscillate between c.40 and 50 per cent in the 2006–9 period, with a small advance of the 2022 date, in one survey in 2008 the segment preferring the 2035 date prevailed. However, the politicization of the issue on the occasion of the annulment of the phasing-out decision in 2009–10 led again to a dramatic increase in those demanding the '2022 phase out', while the segment preferring the 2035 date decreased. In November 2010, 69 per cent wanted to maintain the phasing-out decision instead of extending the lifetime of NPPs. In March 2011, after the Fukushima disaster, 55 per cent preferred an immediate shutdown, 34 per cent a return to the original phasing-out decision before the prolongation in December 2010. A majority of voters continue to be against nuclear energy also in 2013 according to the national election survey.

Whereas the development of aggregated issue attitudes provides a general background for the understanding of political decisions, attitude dynamics below this global pattern may be more important. Here the concept of 'issue inconsistency' (Thurner 2010; Schöning et al. 2015) helps identify potentially volatile voter segments. Accordingly, we can expect especially those voters with issue attitudes that are in conflict with the official positions of 'their' party, to be

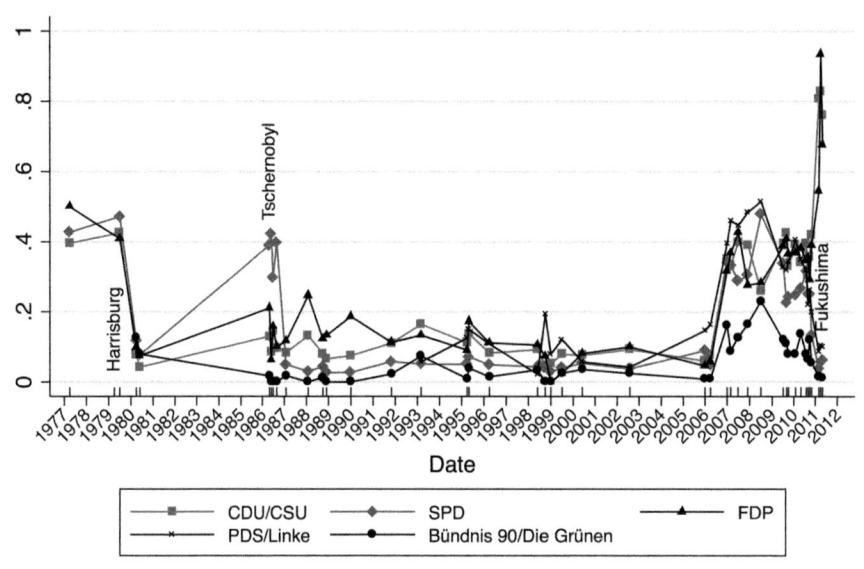

Figure 7.4. Share of 'Inconsistent Voters' 1977–2011
Sources: Politbarometer 1977–2011, Election Study 1987.

more prone to attitudinal or behavioural changes.[11] We expect that inconsistency between voters' individual policy attitudes and their intention to vote for a party taking a policy position that is in conflict with these attitudes may have perceptual and behavioural consequences for these 'issue-inconsistent' voters. To provide one example, voters are 'issue-inconsistent' when they favour phasing-out nuclear power, but at the same time have a global preference for the Christian Democratic parties, or, to provide another example, when they are pro-nuclear energy but voters of the SPD after its repositioning in the mid-1980s. As soon as parties have large portions of voters with such conflicting issue attitudes, problems also arise with regard to taking coherent positions and with integrating attitudinal heterogeneity. This is of special importance for issues that are highly polarizing and that have a high potential for conflict.

The CDU/CSU (40 per cent), the FDP (50 per cent) as well as the SPD (43 per cent) exhibited very high shares of inconsistent voters by the end of the 1970s (Figure 7.4). Note, however, that this fact must have been especially alarming for the incumbent government parties, the SPD and the FDP. The SPD experienced considerable struggles between its factions. The drop in shares in 1980 is due to the new question format. In 1977–9, respondents had three options: (a) build new reactor, (b) production of energy not using nuclear energy, (c) don't know. Since 1980 the question included the option: shut down immediately. Interestingly, the proportion of inconsistent vote intentions for the SPD increased dramatically in 1986 up to 40 per cent. This prepared the way for the historical U-turn of this party in position-taking. In contrast, the voters of the CDU/CSU

---

[11] E.g. due to framing efforts by political parties and other actors.

incorporated only about 10 per cent of such respondents at this period. This proportion increased to about one-third in the 1990s to 2005, however with a low salience for these voters (see Mauerer et al. 2015). After the Fukushima disaster, more than 70–80 per cent of those indicating a vote intention for the CDU/CSU and the FDP also were against the usage of nuclear energy. This was an alert for the CDU/CSU to change position in order not to lose government.

The conclusion, therefore, is that parties had to adjust at least partially to the described heterogeneity of their voters. Partially means that it is quite possible to attract and incorporate voters with conflicting attitudes—as long as these attitudes are not salient and not the top-priority decision criteria for the relevant voters. However, as soon as these change, due to exogenous shocks and/or effective and competitive campaigning, parties have to decide how to position and/or how put weight on such an issue. The next section shows how this adjustment proceeded in the position-taking in party programmes and electoral manifestos.

7.4.3 Party Position-Taking in Electoral Manifestos

Until 1975 the nuclear energy issue can be characterized by a 'permissive consensus'. According to the influential work of Kitschelt (1980), despite increasing demonstrations and non-legal occupations of building sites in Whyl and Brokdorf in the 1974–6 period, there was no real competitive politicization before 1980. A closer and systematic look at the electoral manifestos—see also Figures 7.5 and 7.6—shows that this interpretation applies only to the two main political parties, the SPD and CDU/CSU: they decided to form a 'cartel of silence' with regard to nuclear energy in 1976. In contrast, the FDP reserved two sub-chapters of its 1976 manifesto 'Freedom—Progress—Achievement' for nuclear energy by highlighting citizens' rights and their protection, granting priority to these goals over economic considerations. Clearly, this is not in line with the later FDP positions that

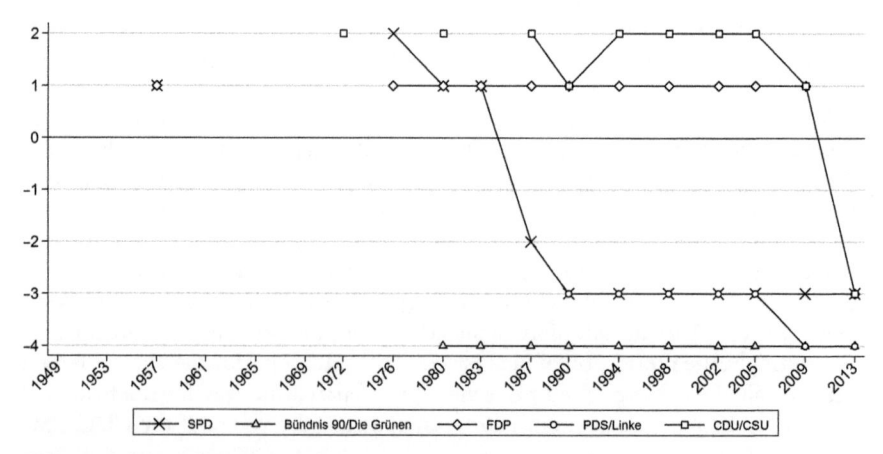

Figure 7.5. Parties' Position-Taking in German Electoral Manifestos

Note: 2 'Unconditional support', 1 'Weak, conditional support', 0 'No commitment', −1 'Freezing', −2 'Downsizing', −3 'Gradual or immediate shutdown, exit', −4 'Forbidding'.

transformed into *the* party of economic freedom with a clear pro-nuclear course. In terms of the spatial theory of voting, the FDP opened rather opportunistically a new dimension of competition in the 1976 election in the sub-dimension of nuclear energy. Its strategic repositioning as a government party resulted from the increasing grassroots mobilization against the construction of NPPs and the incentive to take a position not represented until then by the established parties. However, in its 1980 election manifesto, the Christian Democratic parties reacted to the public mood and to the strategic move of the competing parties. They now extensively took a position for nuclear energy (devoting 597 words to that issue—indicating a high saliency). In their electoral campaign, the CDU/CSU criticized the SPD-FDP coalition for blocking the further development of nuclear energy that was seen as indispensable for achieving energy security and securing jobs. Contrarily, the SPD meanwhile began to withdraw from its original position. Nuclear energy in the 1980 manifesto was considered only an option that could be either included or excluded from the future German energy mix.[12] Challenger Strauss accused Chancellor Schmidt of being both for and against nuclear energy. The 1980 FDP electoral manifesto continued to list all problems of nuclear energy in an extensive section (1,630 words).

The 1983 electoral manifesto of the Christian Democrats refrained from explicitly mentioning nuclear energy. The party recognized that its electorate and parts of its rank and file showed heightened ecological affinities. Thus, former CDU Member of Parliament Herbert Gruhl, having left the party in 1978, founded the Ecological Democratic Party in 1982 with the intention to appeal to conservative voters. The SPD took another step towards an anti-nuclear energy position in its manifesto by committing to provide no more money for FBRs and making further usage of nuclear energy dependent on its safety and the resolution of the waste disposal problem. However, the saliency of the nuclear energy issue remained low (see Figure 7.6). The FDP now moved towards being silent on the issue, spending no more than fourteen words on it in the 1983 electoral manifesto: nuclear energy is only legitimate as long as waste disposal is secured.

In the 1983 election, the German party system experienced a dramatic change: the entry of a new type of party—the Green Party. Why this success? Surely, this party also covered citizens' rights issues, peace and disarmament, and third world questions etc. Nevertheless, the core issue of this party was its anti-atomic stance. This becomes even more plausible against the immediate historical background. In 1982, two new NPPs (Emsland, Isar-2, and Neckarwestheim-2) as well as the uranium enrichment facility Gronau visibly went under construction. Even more symbolically, the highly contested Gorleben final nuclear waste disposal received partial approval in 1983. Although the FDP and SPD had begun to reposition themselves with regard to the nuclear energy issue, their participation in a government making everyday pro-nuclear decisions and their greater concern for their economic reputation undermined their credibility as anti-nuclear parties. The SPD lost 4.7 percentage points, the Green Party gained 4.1. Thus, despite being aware of the problem of ecological fallacy, it

---

[12] 'The nuclear energy option should be maintained, the option to renounce nuclear energy in the future should be opened.' (SPD manifesto 1980: 18).

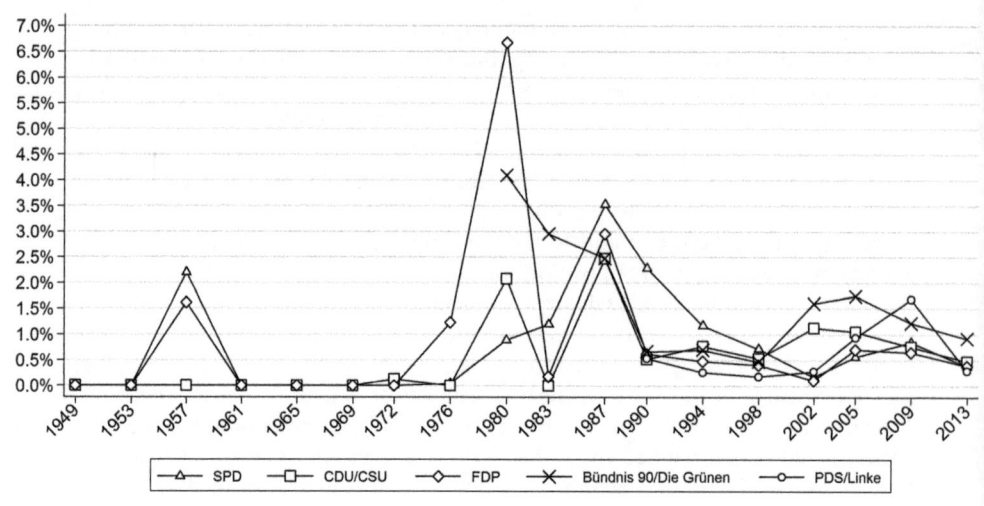

Figure 7.6. Share (%) Nuclear Energy in Electoral Manifestos
Own calculation.

seems legitimate to say that we observe a shift of party preferences due to the issue of nuclear energy.

In the 1987 election, one year after Chernobyl, the repositioning of the former pro-nuclear energy SPD, in opposition, was already completed. It legitimized this re-orientation by an extensive argument in its manifesto (685 words). For the first time, the SPD replaced the term 'Nuclear Energy' by 'Atomic Energy' which has a more negative connotation. Now the CDU/CSU was also under pressure to legitimize extensively its position (579 words). Despite granting much room to safety concerns and arguing that nuclear energy should be considered a transitory technology, the message was unequivocal: nuclear energy should be kept as a part of the energy mix, especially in order to avoid air pollution. The FDP continued to accentuate the priority of safety considerations, and it now joined the SPD in explicitly refusing the Kalkar FBR. However, we observe a smooth repositioning by the accentuation of the necessity of nuclear energy for economic and environmental reasons.

In the 1990 reunification election all parties except the Greens allocated only low or medium saliencies to the nuclear energy issue. The Christian Democrats accentuated the 'CO_2-reduction' frame, the FDP played again the 'transitory technology' card, and the SPD now emphasized the Chernobyl disaster and demanded a phase-out. In 1994, we observe again rather low saliencies. The Christian Democrats continued to link nuclear energy to environmental benefits and Germany's high security standards. In 1998, the FDP pleaded to keep the nuclear option open. The SPD promised to phase out as soon as possible—thus paving the way for a coalition government with the Green Party. Even the CDU/CSU chose a positive environmental framing—reducing CO_2 emissions and expanding renewables. Nuclear energy was mentioned in only one sentence as being an indispensable part of the energy mix. For several years, the Left party was undecided on whether to demand an immediate shutdown or rather a gradual phase-out. In the 2005 election, it finally tried to overbid the Red-Green phasing-out decision.

Note that the Green Party continued to put high saliency on nuclear energy in all its manifestos and programmes. The Greens expressed their unconditional commitment to an immediate shutdown of all NPPs and 'to use all available administrative, economic and legislative means to implement such a policy' (Rüdig 2000: 54). In 2002, the FDP, now in opposition, joined the Christian Democrats in emphasizing the CO_2 reduction implications of nuclear energy. The Christian Democrats blamed the government's 'wrong decision' to phase out. In 2002, both parties claimed that nuclear energy should be part of the German energy mix. In 2005, the Christian Democrats especially advanced the perspective that Germany would lose its leading international position in nuclear technology. In extensive energy chapters in its 2005 and 2009 manifestos, the FDP explicitly declared the phase-out decision to be economically and ecologically wrong. The party now clearly prioritized economic reasoning—contrary to the extensive safety considerations in previous campaigns. In the 2009 manifesto, the Christian Democrats promised explicitly a lifetime extension for NPPs. In 2013, nuclear energy was still a topic, despite all parties now accepting the phase-out decision. The Green Party proposed to increase the security requirements for all operating NPPs. CDU/CSU, Greens, and SPD proposed to take efforts to internationalize higher security standards, or even to abandon the technology internationally.

Systematically comparing manifestos this way gives an additional impression about the trajectory of adjustments of parties, but is also telling about sequencing, imitation and predating, polarization and playing-down strategies in political communication and competition. Over time, the most remarkable changes in position-taking can be observed in the manifestos of the SPD and FDP. The U-turn of the SPD was induced by the challenge of the new left (see Scarrow 2004). After having lost parts of this voter segment to the new party, the Greens, the Social Democrats tried to secure viable government majorities by adjusting in this issue, at the same time risking the loss of parts of their traditional segments like the unions. Note that phase-out has always been non-negotiable for the German Greens. The FDP changes can be explained by the location of this party in the two-dimensional policy space. The party rather opportunistically played the citizens' rights dimension in the late 1970s and before its change of coalition partner in 1983. Successively, it up-sized its economic profile and tried to attract economy-affine voter segments. The most obvious change in terms of saliency can be seen in the manifestos of the Christian Democrats. The party increasingly emphasized the energy problem. This is understandable in the context of the inconsistent voter share among its potential voters. Sticking to the aspiration to be a mass party attracting more than 40 per cent requires enormous communicative efforts in order to balance these different attitudes.

7.5 CONCLUSION

As this chapter has documented, there were several adjustments during the Christian-Democratic-Liberal coalition government period 1983–8, followed by three major reversals in the course of German nuclear energy policy. Until the 1980s, Germany followed a course of nuclear energy expansion typical for advanced industrial democracies opting for this energy carrier. This course was even intensified by a final exceptional increase in R&D expenditures for nuclear energy purposes by the SPD-FDP government coalition in 1982. Given the mobilization of anti-nuclear grassroots protest since the mid-1970s and voters' attitudes, this constituted a remarkable policy decision against large parts of the SPD rank and file. At that time the SPD continued to put more emphasis on its traditional coalition with the pro-growth trade unions and neglected that large parts of its core clientele had different and, more importantly, highly politicized attitudes. Actually, with regard to attitudes this also partly applies to the other established parties. However, the Christian Democrats were not in government, and the FDP quite opportunistically took an oppositional stance within the government—by playing the card of protecting the citizens' rights of anti-nuclear protesters.

The Green Party's parliamentary entry in 1983 was the result of a partial de-alignment of new leftists from the SPD dissatisfied with its pro-nuclear course. Together with the reorientation of the FDP towards coalition government with the Christian Democrats, it led to the Social Democrats' loss of governmental power for fifteen years. One may argue that the SPD repositioned itself too late and too indecisively in 1980 and 1983 to prevent the breakthrough of the Greens. However, given the party's internal heterogeneity of highly politicized attitudes and its pro-nuclear energy policy record, it is difficult to imagine how it could have avoided these hardships, even with hindsight.

The first steps of limiting Germany's expansionist nuclear energy course were made by the subsequent CDU/CSU-FDP government: the halt of the FBR and of the reprocessing plant in Wackersdorf, and the actual freezing of the construction of new reactors. These decisions were due to the fact that large numbers of the voters of these parties took a negative attitude towards nuclear power. The pressure of the anti-nuclear forces was not strong enough during this time to induce a major change of policy. The major reversals of nuclear energy policy begin with the dramatic phasing out in 2002 of the SPD-Green government, due to the new commitment of the SPD against nuclear energy from 1983. In a different government constellation it might have remained a symbolic stance, but not in a coalition with the Greens. This party was tied inextricably to the commitment to abandon nuclear energy and compromising it probably would have led to splitting the party. Thus, coalition politics—but also balancing between party factions—was crucial for party position-taking and government policy. Notwithstanding such constraints of parties, the actual phase-out decision only made explicit what was already implicit in the energy policy since the 1990s, namely to stop building new plants while continuing to run the existing ones. This is reflected in the fact that the remaining operation time of NPPs granted the energy companies approximated their claims. This part of the phasing-out decision in 2002 was rather symbolic.

The second major reversal of Germany's nuclear energy policy was the extension of the remaining operation time of existing NPPs by the CDU/CSU-FDP that took government office in 2009. By itself, this was not yet a return to nuclear energy as a permanent part of the German energy mix but given the more pro-nuclear attitudes of the government parties the energy companies believed that they would manage to build the new line of the European Pressurized (Generation IV) Reactor on the established nuclear sites. Yet, this seems to be definitely excluded after the third major reversal: the post-Fukushima phasing-out decision of the same government. This decision seems to constitute the final blow to nuclear power in Germany.

REFERENCES

Battelle Institute (1977). *Einstellung und Verhalten der Bevölkerung gegenüber verschiedenen Energiegewinnungsarten*. Bonn: Bundesministerium für Forschung und Technologie.
Baumgartner, Frank R., and Bryan D. Jones (1993). *Agendas and Instability in American Politics*. Chicago: University of Chicago Press.
Czada, Roland (1993). 'Konfliktbewältigung und politische Reform in vernetzten Entscheidungsstrukturen: Das Beispiel der kerntechnischen Sicherheitsregulierung', in Roland Czada and Manfred G. Schmidt (eds), *Verhandlungsdemokratie, Interessenvermittlung, Regierbarkeit*, Opladen: Westdeutscher Verlag, 73–100.
DIW (2007). *Abschlussbericht zum Vorhaben Fachgespräch zur Bestandsaufnahme und methodischen Bewertung vorliegender Ansätze zur Quantifizierung der Förderung erneuerbarer Energien im Vergleich zur Förderung der Atomenergie in Deutschland. Im Auftrag des BMU*. Berlin: Deutsches Institut für Wirtschaftsforschung.
Jones, Bryan D., and Frank R. Baumgartner (2005). *The Politics of Attention: How Government Prioritizes Problems*. Chicago: University of Chicago Press.
Kingdon, John W. (1995). *Agendas, Alternatives, and Public Policies*. New York: Harper Collins.
Kitschelt, Herbert P. (1980). *Kernenergiepolitik: Arena eines gesellschaftlichen Konflikts*. Frankfurt am Main: Campus.
Kitschelt, Herbert P. (1983). *Politik und Energie: Eine vergleichende Untersuchung zur Energie-Technologiepolitik in den U.S.A., der Bundesrepublik, Frankreich und Schweden*. Frankfurt am Main: Campus.
Kitschelt, Herbert P. (1986a). 'Political Opportunity Structures and Political Protest: Anti-Nuclear Movements in Four Democracies.' *British Journal of Political Science*, 16(1): 57–85.
Kitschelt, Herbert P. (1986b). 'Four Theories of Public Policy-Making and Fast Breeder Reactor Development in France, the United States, and West Germany.' *International Organization*, 40(1): 65–104.
Marwell, Gerald, and Pamela Oliver (1993). *The Critical Mass in Collective Action: A Micro-Social Theory*. Cambridge: Cambridge University Press.
Mauerer, Ingrid, Paul W. Thurner, and Marc Debus (2015). 'Under Which Conditions do Parties Attract Voters' Issue Reactions? Party Varying Issue Voting in German Election 1987–2013.' *West European Politics*, 38(6): 1251–73.
Olson, Mancur (1965). *The Logic of Collective Action: Public Goods and the Theory of Groups*. Cambridge, MA: Harvard University Press.
Panebianco, Angelo (1988). *Political Parties: Organization and Power*. Cambridge: Cambridge University Press.
Pielow, Johann-Christian, Hans-Martin Koopman, and Eckhart Ehlers (2007). 'Energy Law in Germany', in Martha M. Roggenkamp, Catherine Redgwell, Iñigo Del Guayo, and Anita Rønne (eds), *Energy Law in Europe: National, EU, and International Regulation*. Oxford: Oxford University Press, 623–716.
Radkau, Joachim (1983). *Aufstieg und Krise der deutschen Atomwirtschaft 1945–1975. Verdrängte Alternativen in der Kerntechnik und der Ursprung der nuklearen Kontroverse*. Reinbek: Rowohlt.
Radkau, Joachim (2008). 'Von der Kohlennot zur solaren Vision: Wege und Irrwege bundesdeutscher Energiepolitik', in Hans-Peter Schwarz (ed.), *Die Bundesrepublik Deutschland: Eine Bilanz nach 60 Jahren*. Cologne: Böhlau, 461–86.

Renn, Ortwin (1977). *Kernenergie aus der Sicht der Bevölkerung: Analyse von Einstellungen und Motiven*. Forschungszentrum Jülich: Bericht des Forschungszentrums Jülich (KFA-AKI-IB-1/77).

Rucht, Dieter (2008). 'Anti-Atomkraftbewegung', in Roland Roth and Dieter Rucht (eds), *Die Sozialen Bewegungen in Deutschland seit 1945: Ein Handbuch*. Frankfurt am Main: Campus, 245–66.

Rüdig, Wolfgang (2000). 'Phasing Out Nuclear Energy in Germany.' *German Politics*, 9(3): 43–80.

Rüdig, Wolfgang (2003). 'The Environment and Nuclear Power', in Stephen Padgett, William E. Paterson, and Gordon Smith (eds), *Developments in German Politics 3*. Basingstoke: Palgrave Macmillan, 248–68.

Scarrow, Susan E. (2004). 'Embracing Dealignment, Combating Realignment: German Parties Respond', in Peter Mair, Wolfgang C. Müller, and Fritz Plasser (eds), *Political Parties and Electoral Change*. London: Sage, 86–110.

Schöning, Norbert, Paul W. Thurner, and Martin Binder (2015). 'Indifferenz und Inkonsistenz als Moderatoren von Framing-Effekten: Ein Laborexperiment am Beispiel der Kernenergie', in André Bächtiger, Susumu Shikano, and Eric Linhart (eds), *Jahrbuch für Handlungs- und Entscheidungstheorie. Band 9*. Wiesbaden: Springer VS, 127–60.

Thurner, Paul W. (2010). '"Issue-Unentschiedenheit" und "Issue-Inkonsistenz" bei den Einstellungen der Deutschen zur Kernenergie, 1987–2005', in Thorsten Faas, Kai Arzheimer, and Sigrid Roßteutscher (eds), *Information-Wahrnehmung-Emotion: Politische Psychologie in der Wahl- und Einstellungsforschung*. Wiesbaden: VS Verlag für Sozialwissenschaften, 333–53.

Weis, Michael, Katrin van Bevern, and Thomas Linnemann (2011). 'Forschungsförderung Kernenergie 1956 bis 2010: Anschubfinanzierung oder Subvention?' *atw*, 56(8/9): 466–8.

Wood, Dan, and Arnold Vedlitz (2007). 'Issue Definition, Information Processing, and the Politics of Global Warming.' *American Journal of Political Science*, 51(3): 552–68.

Ziegler, Eberhard (2011). *Atomgesetz mit Verordnungen*. Baden-Baden: Nomos.

8

Why Italian Nuclear Energy Policy Failed Twice

Fabio Franchino

8.1 INTRODUCTION: THE TRAJECTORY OF NUCLEAR ENERGY POLICY

The history of nuclear energy policy in Italy is characterized by major shifts. A period of great innovation was followed by major delays in capacity expansion, ultimately culminating in a full reversal. Figure 8.1 illustrates the gross production and capacity of nuclear energy, also as shares of national electricity production and capacity (see also Table 8A.1).

By 1964, three nuclear power plants (NPPs) were operating, comprising a gross capacity that exceeded 550 MWe. In the 1960s, the country was a world leader in nuclear energy production. Throughout the 1970s, these plants supplied more than 3,000 GWh a year to the electricity grid from 3,176 GWh in 1970 up to 4,428 GWh in 1978. After a long period of stagnation and rising tensions, the fourth and final plant was completed in 1978, adding 650 MWe of capacity, which eventually increased to more than 800 MWe in 1981. But by that time nuclear energy amounted to less than 3 per cent of the total capacity of electricity plants across Italy.

Production peaked between 1982 and 1986, when more than 6,700 GWh of electricity a year were produced (about 4 per cent of gross national energy production). However, the 1980s saw also the end of nuclear energy policy. The accident at Chernobyl heightened the conflict within the government coalition. On the one side, the Christian Democratic Party (DC) and other small parties advocated a moratorium of the planned expansion. On the other side, the Socialist Party (PSI) argued for an exit from nuclear energy production. The government decided to discontinue temporarily the supply of electricity to the grid. After an inconclusive early election, the success of an anti-nuclear referendum, and a government crisis, the plants were permanently shut down and the policy remained off the political agenda for the next twenty years.

The issue re-emerged in the late 2000s with the nuclear energy renaissance. This recent attempt to restart the programme suffered a similar fate after the accident at Fukushima. In a second referendum, the policy relaunch was overwhelmingly

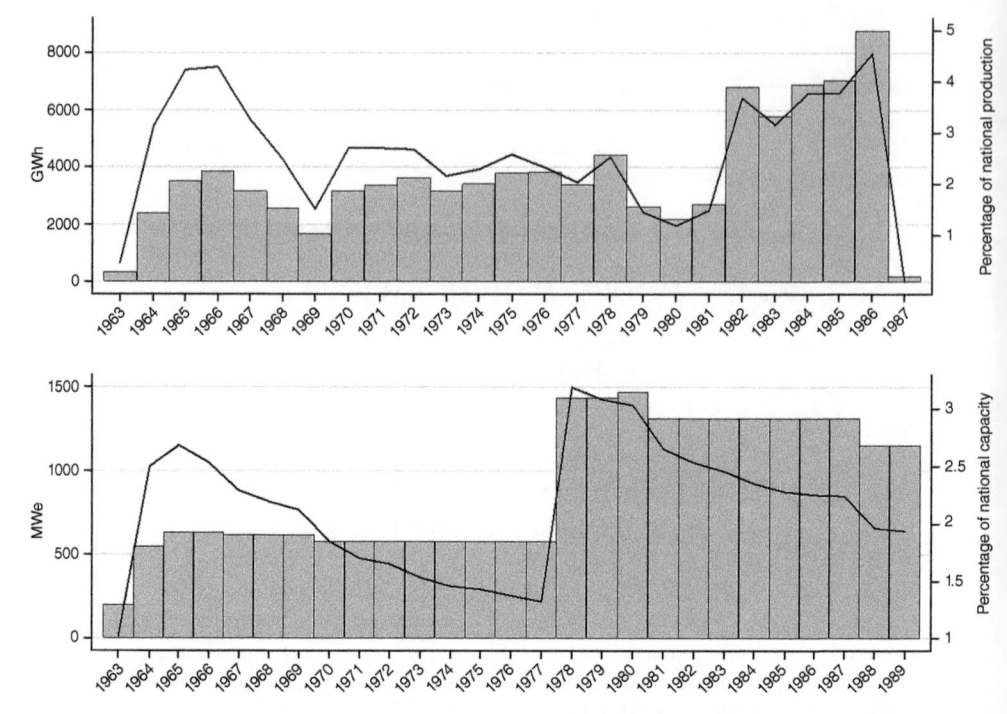

Figure 8.1. Gross Electricity Production and Capacity from Nuclear Energy, 1963–1989
Note: Bars plot electricity production (Gwh) and capacity (MWe), lines plot percentages. Data from Terna.

rejected and plans have been abandoned. The current government of February 2014 includes some nuclear energy supportive politicians, such as the Environment Minister Gian Luca Galletti (Union of Centre, UdC), but, despite the high external energy dependency, the issue is unlikely to resurface in the foreseeable future.

In this chapter, I assess the key factors that have influenced this policy trajectory. Italy is a particularly interesting case because several elements discussed in Chapter 2 play an important role. I will show that the catalyst for the initial bout of innovation was the intense competition among energy producers in the 1960s. In the crucial 1970s, however, the nationalization of electricity production and the emerging power of the regions severely delayed plans to increase capacity. In the aftermath of the Chernobyl accident, coalition politics and electoral pressures, in the context of a referendum challenge and the limited capacity that was accumulated over time, are crucial to explain the policy reversal of the 1980s.

A more favourable public opinion and a fair presence of issue-inconsistent voters combined with the lack of intra-coalitional conflict over this issue explain the resurgence of the policy in the late 2000s. A second referendum serendipitously coincided with another major accident (Fukushima), hence leading to another popular rejection.

8.2 POLICY DEVELOPMENT

I first review the major developments in nuclear energy policy, emphasizing the main legislative and executive measures. These events are summarized in the nuclear energy policy scale in Figure 8.A1 in the Appendix. I will also suggest some causal factors, but the systematic analysis of these policy choices is carried out in section 8.4.

8.2.1 Public and Private Ventures of the 1960s

Research on nuclear energy began with CISE (Centro informazioni studi e esperienze), privately funded by Edison, Cogne, and FIAT in 1946 (Zaninelli and Borroni 1996). In 1952, the National Research Council established the National Committee for Nuclear Research (CNRN), an academic research institution. This public–private divide would soon spill over onto the production and commercialization of electricity from nuclear energy.

In December 1955, Edison and the state-owned Finelettrica, the largest electricity-producing companies, set up SELNI (Società Elettronucleare Italiana). This company did not operate for the first year and a half because of internal divergences about the location and type of plants to build. In March 1957, Finelettrica left and set up SENN (Società Elettronucleare Nazionale). In the same month, ENI (Ente Nazionale Idrocarburi, the state-owned hydrocarbons corporation) established SIMEA (Società Italiana Meridionale per l'Energia Atomica).

The race was on. SIMEA built the first NPP in Latina (Lazio). It supplied the first kilowatt to the grid in January 1964. At the time, it was the largest in Europe. SENN built the first European large boiling water reactor in Garigliano (Sessa Aurunca, Campania) with the support of CNRN. The plant was connected to the grid in January 1964. SELNI built a plant in Trino Vercellese (Piedmont) which was connected in October 1964. Trino NPP was an initiative of Edison, which was concerned about plans to nationalize electricity production.

By the mid-1960s, the electricity capacity of Italian NPPs could reach 590 MWe, the third largest in the world after the United States and Great Britain (Figure 8.1; Corbellini and Velonà 2008: 19–31; Curli 2000: 54–8; Fornaciari 1997: 11–32).

All these NPP projects were independently conceived. This reflected competition between private and public producers and among state-owned companies. There was no comprehensive policy at the national level. For instance, no ministerial authorization for the construction of the Trino NPP was issued, simply because the terms of such authorization were not clear. Even the competences of the nuclear safety authority were poorly defined (Fornaciari 1997: 64). By the time the relevant measures were adopted in 1962, the construction of the three plants was well under way.

8.2.2 Regulatory Framework and Consequences of Nationalization

The first serious attempt to regulate the production of nuclear energy dates back to a bill that merged an April 1959 proposal by sixteen senators from the Communist

Party (PCI), which promoted the nationalization of electricity production, and a December 1959 government proposal of Industry Minister Emilio Colombo (DC), which instead was based on private production. It took until the end of 1962 for Parliament to adopt the measure. The delay was predominantly due to the reform of CNRN, which became the National Committee for Nuclear Research (CNEN) with Law 933/1960, and to ongoing discussions about nationalization.

Soon after these issues were dealt with, the Parliament approved, under extreme urgency, Law 1860/1962 on the peaceful use of nuclear energy. The almost completed plants in Latina and Garigliano would not have been allowed to operate in the absence of this law. It set out the administrative procedures for granting authorizations and the obligations of NPP operators concerning technical and economic capabilities, radioactive waste disposal, and financial liability in case of accident. The government then adopted Presidential Decree 185/1964 on nuclear safety when the Latina plant began operating.

Nationalization was agreed with Law 1643/1962 and ownership of SELNI, SENN, and SIMEA was transferred to the state-owned electric energy corporation ENEL (Ente Nazionale per l'Energia Elettrica) in February 1965. However, nationalization delayed the construction of NPPs in the second half of the 1960s, despite a 7 per cent annual increase in electricity consumption. The majority of electricity (61.6 per cent) was produced by private companies and up to 1,200 of these had to be transferred into state ownership (Commissioni Speciali della Camera e del Senato 1962: 64–5; Curli 2000: 29). Merging and integrating this variegated set of small, large, private, and public companies took several years (Castronovo 1988; Corbellini and Velonà 2008: 32).

There were also obstacles specific to nuclear energy. Other state-owned enterprises, such as ENI, might not have wanted ENEL to replace fossil fuels with nuclear power in the energy mix.[1] Furthermore, the conviction for embezzlement in 1964 of Felice Ippolito, CNEN general secretary and member of ENEL governing board, may have caused further delays (Ippolito and Simen 1974).

More importantly, the existing plants were still prototypes that produced electricity at a higher cost than conventional plants did. They could not guarantee uninterrupted supply as well. The Trino plant was suspended from 1967 to 1969 for modifications to the reactor. The capacity of the Latina plant was reduced by 20 per cent in 1969 because of corrosion problems. In those periods of strong energy demand, Arnaldo Maria Angelini, ENEL chief executive, voiced doubts about the competitiveness and reliability of nuclear energy. Policy-makers opted for more traditional and reliable sources (Corbellini and Velonà 2008: 28; De Paoli 2011: 25) and the share of NPP capacity over national capacity declined (see Figure 8.1).

8.2.3 Plans, Delays, and Failures

Nationalization led to centralization of decision-making under the Interministerial Committee on Economic Planning (CIPE, see section 8.3.2). In July

---

[1] In Feb. 1974, the Christian Democratic, Socialist, Social Democratic, and Republican parties were prosecuted for receiving illegal funds allegedly in exchange of favouring oil over nuclear power.

1966, the committee approved the construction of a NPP, under the initiative of Industry Minister Giulio Andreotti (DC). In 1969, ENEL opted for Caorso in Emilia-Romagna. The construction started in January 1970, but connection to the grid took place in May 1978 and commercial operations began only in December 1981. Delays were due to minor malfunctions and regulatory interventions of the DISP (Directorate for Nuclear Safety and Health Protection of CNEN). After the Three Mile Island accident of March 1979, works were suspended. They restarted only after an expert commission on nuclear safety recommended upgrades, causing further delays (Corbellini and Velonà 2008: 44–5; Fornaciari 1997: 71). These events increased public attention to nuclear safety and led to the organization of the first anti-nuclear groups.

In March 1973, Industry Minister Enrico Ferri (Social Democratic Party, PSDI) declared his support for expanding nuclear energy power. Soon after the increase in oil price following the Yom Kippur war, CIPE approved in December 1973 an ENEL plan to build four NPPs and located the first two near the Lazio–Tuscany border and the Abruzzo–Molise border.

Problems soon started to emerge. The first impediment was institutional. Following a constitutional requirement, the Parliament established in 1970 fifteen ordinary-statute regions with competences in urban planning, regional development, and public works. Regions were also entitled to coordinate with the central government on energy policy. Regional assemblies, which appointed regional governments, were directly elected for the first time in June 1970.

In view of these constitutional obligations, Law 48/1967 set up a Consultative Interregional Committee, chaired by the Minister of Budget and Economic Planning. The committee was created to examine planning issues with a regional dimension, including the selection of NPP sites. This reform did not spell immediate trouble. In June 1974, the Consultative Interregional Committee located the first reactor in Montalto di Castro (Lazio). Regional involvement meant delays however. The Lazio region only gave its approval in September 1976 and the government its go-ahead in February 1979 (Corbellini and Velonà 2008: 47–8; Fornaciari 1997: 86). The whole process from CIPE approval to the beginning of construction took more than a year and a half longer than in the case of the Caorso plant. Locating the site, clearing authorizations, and opposition from local and environmental movements compounded the delay. The construction was also suspended by the city mayor because of a presumed increased seismic risk. Works restarted at the end of 1980 after the green light of an expert commission (Fornaciari 1997: 87).

On the other hand, regional involvement meant doom for the second reactor. The project was abandoned after several years of strong local opposition and unwillingness by Abruzzo and Molise to provide a site.

Nevertheless, the first National Energy Plan (NEP), drafted in 1975 by Industry Minister Donat Cattin (DC), established an ambitious objective of constructing twenty NPPs. The programme was based on the (grossly optimistic) estimate that the historic growth rate of electricity demand of 6.6 per cent a year would continue. Its objective was to meet 64 per cent of national demand with NPPs by 1990 (Fornaciari 1997: 112–25). In December 1975, CIPE approved the plan, recommending the immediate start of the public procurement procedures for eight 1,000 MWe NPPs. A plan to increase capacity by further 8,000 MWe was to be approved by 1977. Technical features were standardized under the Unified Nuclear Project, while regulatory and safety control was conferred upon CNEN-DISP. The government also invested heavily in CIRENE, a domesticly developed reactor project.

The establishment of the regions meant that Law 1860/1962 required complementary measures, so the Parliament approved Law 393/1975 on site selection of NPPs. This measure established that CIPE was responsible for approving ENEL multi-year plans for new NPPs, in agreement with the Consultative Interregional Committee. After approval, the regions had to indicate within five months at least two plant locations. In case of inaction, the government would step in and select the sites. After a safety review, the regions had to approve the final location within two months. If a region failed to comply, CIPE would step in again.

Plans to expand capacity proceeded. In October 1975, the Consultative Interregional Committee approved the building of four NPPs; two in Piedmont and two in Lombardy. As required by the 1975 NEP, the Parliament adopted a resolution demanding the construction of four further NPPs in October 1977 and CIPE approved this measure two months later.

8.2.4 Reversal

At the beginning of the 1980s, only four NPPs were operating (Latina, Trino Vercellese, Garigliano,[2] and Caorso). The 1981 NEP, drafted by Industry Minister Giovanni Marcora (DC), envisaged only three NPPs (about 6,000 MWe overall) to be built in Lombardy, Piedmont, and Apulia by 1998. Because of the overestimated electricity demand and construction delays, plans were halved and replaced by the import of electricity and natural gas.

The policy momentum was still in favour of nuclear energy, however.[3] The regions failed to identify locations within the deadline of Law 393/1975, despite a new law on the compensation of localities (Law 8/1983) that was almost unanimously adopted in November 1982. Therefore, CIPE chose two sites for each region in February 1983. In January 1985, the Piedmont region approved the construction of Trino II, close to the existing site of Trino Vercellese. The next month, a ministerial decree authorized ENEL to start the works. Trino II was the first to be built according to the guidelines of the Unified Nuclear Project.

Meanwhile, the Industry Minister Renato Altissimo (Liberal Party, PLI) revised the 1981 NEP by moving forward the construction of NPPs for an aggregate capacity of 4,000 MWe. After parliamentary approval, CIPE located them in Veneto, Sicily, Campania, and Basilicata in March 1986.

One month later, the Chernobyl accident eventually meant the termination of nuclear energy policy. This reversal will be analysed in greater detail below. Suffice to say here that, in October, the government of Bettino Craxi (PSI) discontinued the supply of electricity to the national grid from the Caorso plant. This was portrayed as a *temporary* decision taken during a fuel reload, in view of a likely referendum on the issue. The Latina plant followed the same

---

[2] This plant closed due to a malfunction in Aug. 1978. It no longer produced electricity and was expected to shut down in the early 1980s.

[3] Even the lukewarm government of the Socialist Bettino Craxi decided to finance research on nuclear fusion in Oct. 1983.

fate in November, while the Trino plant was *temporarily* disconnected from the grid in March 1987.

After the rejection of the nuclear programme in the referendum of November 1987, the five-party government coalition adopted a resolution demanding the government of Giovanni Goria (DC) to (a) prepare a new national energy plan with a five-year moratorium on the construction of NPPs, (b) terminate the Trino II works, (c) shut down the Latina plant, and (d) establish a commission to evaluate the technical and economic feasibility of converting the Montalto di Castro plant. Meanwhile, the government had proceeded on suspending the works at this site until the end of January 1988. Note that, according to this resolution, the plants of Caorso and Trino were supposed to remain operational.

In December 1987, CIPE adopted the relevant decisions with regard to Trino II and Latina NPPs. However, the feasibility commission, chaired by the economist Luigi Spaventa, advised against the conversion of the Montalto di Castro plant. For reasons I will explain, this option turned out to be politically unfeasible. Works were suspended and the plant was converted to fossil fuel combustion.

The 1988 NEP, adopted in August and drafted by the Industry Minister Adolfo Battaglia (Republican Party, PRI), referred only to research on nuclear power. The Unified Nuclear Project and participation at NERSA, the French-led Superphenix consortium, were terminated. The CIRENE project was essentially abandoned. In May 1990, the Parliament adopted a resolution demanding the permanent shutdown of the plants in Caorso and Trino Vercellese. In July, CIPE, under the Andreotti government, duly obliged.

8.2.5 Attempted Relaunch and New Regulatory Framework

The policy disappeared from the political agenda until it resurfaced following the nuclear power renaissance of the 2000s. The first timid step was in November 2007 when the government of Romano Prodi (Olive Tree) joined the Global Nuclear Energy Partnership, a US-initiated international partnership to promote the use of nuclear power, and signed a US–Italy bilateral agreement on cooperation in energy research and development.

More ambitiously, the government of Silvio Berlusconi (People of Freedom, PdL) adopted a decree law in June 2008 where it set out a new national energy strategy. Some of the most important measures concerned (a) a national conference on energy and the environment, (b) the building of NPPs, and (c) the signing of international agreements for the development of the nuclear energy sector.

The Parliament converted the decree to Law 133/2008 soon after, while the Economic Development Minister Claudio Scajola (PdL) began working on a plan to build four third-generation NPPs by 2020. ENEL and the French EDF signed a memorandum of understanding in February 2009 and, in August, they set up the joint venture Nuclear Development Italy (Sviluppo Nucleare Italia). In September 2009, the government signed a similar agreement with the US administration, which would have presumably involved Westinghouse, General Electric, and Ansaldo Nucleare.

On the regulatory side, Law 99/2009, a government-sponsored bill adopted in July 2009, demanded the government to adopt regulations on the siting of NPPs, nuclear waste storage, and compensations for local communities.[4] The law also established a Nuclear Safety Agency and outlined the procedure for the selection of NPPs.

As I will analyse in greater detail in this chapter, these plans unfolded between March and June 2011. After the Fukushima accident, the government hastily adopted Decree Law 34/2011 that halted the nuclear programme and called for the adoption of a new national energy strategy within twelve months. The decree was converted into Law 75/2011 in May. This moratorium however did not succeed in avoiding a referendum which was planned for June. This public consultation led to the repeal of the provisions in Law 133/2008 concerning the construction of NPPs. Apart from research, the 2013 national energy strategy does not foresee new initiatives.

8.3 ACTORS AND JURISDICTIONS

Before moving on to the explanation of this policy dynamics, I discuss in this section the policy process and introduce the main societal and constitutional actors having a stake in and impacting on nuclear energy policy-making.

8.3.1 Market Operators

The three nuclear energy companies (SELNI, SENN, and SIMEA) of the 1950s resulted from two cleavages underpinning the energy market: a north–south and a private–public divide. The shareholders of the SELNI initially comprised both private[5] and state-owned companies from the IRI-Finelettrica group. The latter left SELNI and established SENN with the objective of developing a state-owned nuclear energy sector in southern Italy. SIMEA was the initiative of ENI, another public-owned company.

Following nationalization, ENEL became solely responsible for electricity production and transmission, and partially responsible for distribution. It managed the planning, construction, and operation of NPPs. ENI was in charge of nuclear fuel and Ansaldo was the components supplier. After the termination of the policy, ENEL nuclear energy division moved into nuclear waste management and plant decommissioning.

In 1992, ENEL was incorporated into a joint-stock company, with the Treasury Ministry as the main shareholder, in anticipation of the liberalization of the electricity sector in 1999. That year ENEL nuclear power activities were transferred to the state-owned SOGIN (Società Gestione Impianti Nucleari), which is in charge of waste management and decommissioning. The private company Ansaldo Nucleare is active abroad in NPP construction and decommissioning.

---

[4] For this purpose, the government adopted Legislative Decree 31/2010.

[5] Edison of Milan, SADE of Venice, SELT-Valdarno of Florence, SRE of Rome, and SGES of Palermo.

8.3.2 Policy Process: Government, Regions, and Referendum

The Ministry of Economic Development, formerly the Ministry of Industry, is in charge of policy formulation and implementation, including the licensing procedure of NPPs and related facilities. Between 1975 and 1988, it drafted the three multi-annual NEPs, in consultation with ENEL. The NEP was the key document setting out the plans, procedures, and deadlines for the production, transmission and distribution of energy across the country. In 2008, Decree Law 112 replaced the NEP with the national energy strategy. The latest one has been adopted in 2013, after extensive consultation with private and public operators.

The key executive institution in charge of adopting and implementing these plans is the Inter-ministerial Committee on Economic Planning (CIPE), established by Law 48/1967. CIPE is chaired by the Prime Minister and composed of several ministers with competences over economic planning and development. The deputy chair is the minister in charge of budgeting, economic planning, or development. CIPE takes decisions about building new plants, selecting sites, terminating works, and shutting down operating plants. However, since government survival depends on the support of a parliamentary coalition, CIPE has been nothing more than a rubber stamp for the Parliament in some circumstances.

Regional consultation is constitutionally mandated and regulated by Law 393/1975 and Legislative Decree 31/2010 (see section 8.2). In order to strengthen regional involvement in policy formation, the Consultative Interregional Committee was replaced in 1983 by a permanent State–Regions Conference. Regional competences have been expanding and several national policies now require regional consultation. A constitutional reform in 1999 introduced the direct election of regional executives and one in 2001 repealed the central government's power to suspend regional legislation. Disputes between regions and the central government are referred to the Constitutional Court. Local authorities are also consulted and a permanent State–Cities and Local Authorities Conference has operated since 1996.

The Ministry of the Environment is responsible for the environmental compatibility of nuclear projects. Safety regulation and supervision is currently performed by the Department of Nuclear, Technological, and Industrial Risk that is being moved under the National Inspectorate on Nuclear Safety and Radioprotection, established in March 2014. The inspectorate reports to the Ministries of Environment and Economic Development. Originally, this department (called DISP) was part of CNEN, the research committee promoting nuclear technology. In 1982, it was separated from research with the establishment of the National Commission for the Research and Development of Nuclear Energy and Alternative Energy (ENEA). It has undergone three more reforms since.

The abrogative referendum also plays a central role in policy-making. According to the Constitution, the repeal of a law or parts thereof can be subject to public consultation if demanded by five regional assemblies or at least half a million citizens. The result of a referendum carries through only if a majority of the electorate participates. The law implementing these provisions was adopted in 1970. The Constitutional Court establishes whether a referendum proposal complies with these provisions.

8.3.3 Parties and Electoral Systems

In the post-war period, the Italian party system can be roughly divided in two phases. The first period comprised governments that were centred on the DC with variously sized coalition partners, most notably PSI. PCI, the main opponent, has never been formally in government. As we shall see, PSI turned out to be the party that developed the most sceptical views about nuclear energy, with serious consequences for policy-making. The open-list proportional representation electoral law in force in this period had the usual consequences of inhibiting strategic voting in the electorate and facilitating the entry of new electoral and legislative parties into the political arena.

The second period begins in 1994 and comprises alternating right- and left-of-centre coalition governments, with pro-nuclear energy policy opinions that are more clearly identifiable with right-of-centre parties. The two electoral systems operating in this period display more majoritarian features: a mixed dependent system[6] from 1993 to 2005 and a closed-list bonus-adjusted proportional representation system thereafter.

8.4 POLITICAL COMPETITION OVER NUCLEAR ENERGY

8.4.1 Party Positioning and Coalition Politics in the 1960s: Nationalization of Electricity Production

Nuclear energy was not contentious in the 1960s. Policy-makers simply reacted to the activism of market operators. This is not to say that these operators lacked political sponsors. ENI President Enrico Mattei had close links to the left wing of the DC. IRI President Aldo Fascetti was a DC Member of Parliament until 1958. Only SELNI did not have obvious links to the political establishment, but were powerful shareholders in FIAT and Edison. Giorgio Valerio and Vittorio De Biasi, Edison President and General Manager respectively, did not hide their opposition to the most salient issue of the day: the nationalization of electricity production and transmission (Fornaciari 1997: 14).

Nationalization was put on the political agenda in 1956 by a joint PCI-PSI bill, but it was strongly opposed by PLI that supported the DC minority government of the time. The initiative gained support only after the Prime Minister Amintore Fanfani (DC) replaced this external support with a centre-left coalition with PSDI and PRI in February 1962. At the end of that year, the government majority in Parliament adopted the nationalization law with the support of PSI and PCI. PLI, a right-wing party (MSI), and other smaller parties voted against. In the lower chamber, the bill received extensive support—404 ayes out of 478 votes (Mori 1992; Silari 1989).

---

[6] Three-quarters of the seats were allocated by a single-member district plurality system and the remaining seats by proportional representation. For the Senate, the application of the proportional formula was dependent on the distribution of votes produced by the majoritarian formula.

Nationalization paved the way for Law 1860/1962 on the peaceful use of nuclear energy. After solving some outstanding issues, especially with regard to accident liability, this law was supported by PCI, PSI, and even MSI. CIPE became the key executive committee in charge of nuclear energy policy-making. Its first main decision was the approval of the construction of a NPP (later located at Caorso) in July 1966, during a centre-left coalition government.[7]

In sum, a policy in its infancy was matched with a lack of overt opposition in society and within the DC dominated governments. The NPPs at Latina, Garigliano, and Trino Vercellese faced no opposition from local authorities or groups. Nationalization was the most salient energy-related issue in the 1963 and 1968 general elections—supported by left-wing parties and the centre-left coalition government, carried out by the latter, and opposed by PLI and other smaller conservative parties.

8.4.2 Regionalization, Party Positioning, and Coalition Politics in the 1970s

Aside from the delays implementing nationalization (see section 8.2.2), centralization did not expedite policy-making for two reasons.[8] First, the regulatory framework on nuclear safety was now fully operational. As you may recall, DISP's demands to tighten safety standards—even more stringent after the Three Mile Island accident—delayed the construction of the Caorso plant.

Second, Law 48/1967 now required the government to involve the Consultative Interregional Committee in the selection of NPP sites. This involvement was inconsequential in the case of the Caorso NPP because the regional committee representatives were unelected officials without democratic legitimacy. This soon changed with the first direct regional elections in 1970. Recall that CIPE approved in December 1973 a proposal of the Industry Minister Ferri (PSDI) to build four NPPs to be located near the Lazio–Tuscany and the Abruzzo–Molise borders. The fate of these two sites is revealing.

The Lazio regional council that approved the Montalto di Castro site in September 1976 was run by a PCI-PSI coalition, presided over by Maurizio Ferrara (PCI). The PCI was also the most voted for party in the electoral constituency of Montalto di Castro in both the 1970 and 1975 regional elections. This party therefore played a key role, in spite of the incipient opposition from local and environmental movements. On the other hand, the regional assemblies of Abruzzi and Molise, which failed to locate the second site, were DC dominated. Throughout the 1970s this party held the absolute majority of seats in Molise and almost the absolute majority in Abruzzi. In other words, intra-party conflict torpedoed the second project.

Despite these setbacks, politics in the first half of the 1970s was still favourable to nuclear energy. Government coalitions were dominated by DC, which coalesced, among others, with the openly pro-nuclear PRI and PSDI. Ministers of

---

[7] It included DC, PRI, PSDI, and PSI.

[8] Government changed frequently in this period but politicians remained the same, so it is unclear whether this high turnover caused delays as well.

Industry were mostly Christian Democrats. Electoral manifestos made no mention of energy policy in the 1972 general elections. The policy temporarily dropped off the political agenda after the heated debates about nationalization of the previous decade.

It came to the forefront only after the first oil crisis. Coalition politics however explain a great deal of the content of the 1975 NEP—the most ambitious nuclear energy programme ever drafted. In November 1974, Aldo Moro (DC) replaced his co-partisan Mariano Rumor as Prime Minister in a DC-PRI minority coalition government, which interrupted the alliance with PSI and PSDI for the next four years—they provided only external support. This turned out to be the longest period since 1962 that these parties would stay out of government.[9] The Deputy Prime Minister, Ugo La Malfa, was from the PRI, one of the most outspokenly pro-nuclear parties. Moreover, parties were keen to dispel allegations that they received illegal funds in exchange for favouring oil over nuclear power, as argued in an ongoing judicial investigation (see n. 1).

CIPE began in earnest to implement the 1975 NEP and to update the regulatory framework. In March 1975, the DC-PRI coalition government proposed a new bill on the site selection of NPPs. The intent was to expedite decision-making, especially in view of the ongoing reticence of Abruzzo and Molise to provide a site. The proposal was approved by the relevant parliamentary committees of the Chamber and the Senate in their legislative capacity, which meant almost unanimous approval by the Parliament.[10] It became Law 393/1975 (see section 8.2.3).

The first oil crisis brought nuclear energy policy to the forefront of the political debate in the 1976 general elections, but heightened salience did not mean divisions (see Figures 8.A2 and 8.A3 in the Appendix displaying party positions on and salience of nuclear energy). The electoral manifestos of both DC and PCI emphasized the urgency of implementing the NEP with its planned expansion of capacity. Other parties, especially PSDI and PSI, were more concerned about the impact of inflation on real wages and advocated price stability. If a difference had to be found, left-wing parties put more stress upon a fair distribution of costs and benefits and proper regional involvement. After PCI came very close to overtaking DC, the DC minority governments from July 1976 to March 1979 received external support from PCI. This so-called 'historic compromise' presided over the kidnapping and killing of Moro by the terrorists of the Red Brigades in early 1978.

Clouds were gathering on the horizon of nuclear energy policy as well. Overt public opposition to nuclear plants began in the mid-1970s. Environmental organizations were already active (e.g. Italia nostra, WWF Italia, and Club di Roma) and rapidly establishing (e.g. Amici della terra and Lega ambiente). A small left-libertarian and anti-nuclear power party (Radical Party, PR) succeeded in gaining four seats in the lower chamber. The first anti-nuclear power demonstration took place in December 1976 at Montalto di Castro and PR considered collecting signatures for a referendum. Several other demonstrations

---

[9] Four single-party (DC) governments between Feb. 1962 and Nov. 1974 did not last more than six months on average. They paved the ground for subsequent centre-left coalitions.

[10] When the bill arrived for final approval at the Industry and Trade Committee of the Chamber of Deputies in July 1975, fifteen out of sixteen committee members voted in favour.

followed, but they tapered out at the end of 1977 when the municipality of Montalto di Castro approved the project.

Nevertheless, nuclear energy began shaping party positions more incisively. As set out in the NEP, in October 1977, DC, PCI, PSDI, and PRI adopted a parliamentary resolution demanding the construction of further four plants, on top of the eight already planned. The resolution was opposed by PR, MSI, and a small extreme left party (Democrazia Proletaria, DP). Notably, PSI abstained.[11]

The second oil crisis and the Three Mile Island accident shaped the political debate during the 1979 general elections. The benign neglect of the public towards this policy began to erode (see section 8.4.3). Parties discussed safety issues for the first time during an electoral campaign. PCI called for the establishment of a national committee on health and safety and for moving DISP from CNEN to the Ministry of Health Service. CNEN was considered too pro-nuclear to monitor safety in an independent fashion. It also advocated delegating to the regions more competences for assessing NPP environmental impact. For several parties, including PSDI (a government party during the elections), regional and local authorities had to approve NPP sites, de facto legitimizing delays and weakening the effects of Law 393/1975.

Overall, the main political parties—both in government and in opposition— remained cautiously pro-nuclear, although PSI was increasingly sceptical. DC held on to its position, while PCI lost support for the first time since 1953. The parties that intermittently coalesced with DC gained votes. The small anti-nuclear PR more than tripled its seats in Parliament. As we shall see, this election would have major implications. First, however, we discuss the developments of public attitudes towards nuclear energy.

8.4.3 Public Opinion about Nuclear Energy (1978–89)

The analysis of public attitudes must be done with caution because questions vary and may be misleading, especially if surveys are conducted for private companies. Surveys also tend to concentrate during periods in which the issue is salient. Figure 8.2 illustrates the distribution of attitudes in favour and against nuclear energy from surveys carried out by Eurobarometer since 1978. The questions between 1978 and 1996 are the most comparable. The questions of the last two surveys employ different scales.[12]

Most apparent is the impact of nuclear accidents. In 1978, 59 per cent of Italians (excluding non-respondents) considered the employment of nuclear energy worthwhile, while only 32 per cent thought that the technology involved

---

[11] The pro-nuclear PLI voted in favour of expansion but abstained in another section of the resolution because it advocated more regional and local involvement. Protests in Molise and Montalto di Castro were in progress.

[12] The question in the first set of surveys is: 'Here are three opinions about the development of nuclear power stations, which use atomic energy for the production of electricity. Which of these three statements comes closest to your own opinion on the development of nuclear power?' The answer categories were: Worthwhile (for), no particular advantage/neither develop nor abandon (balanced), unacceptable risks (against). The 2006 survey employs a seven-point opposition-support scale, while the 2008 survey uses a four-point scale.

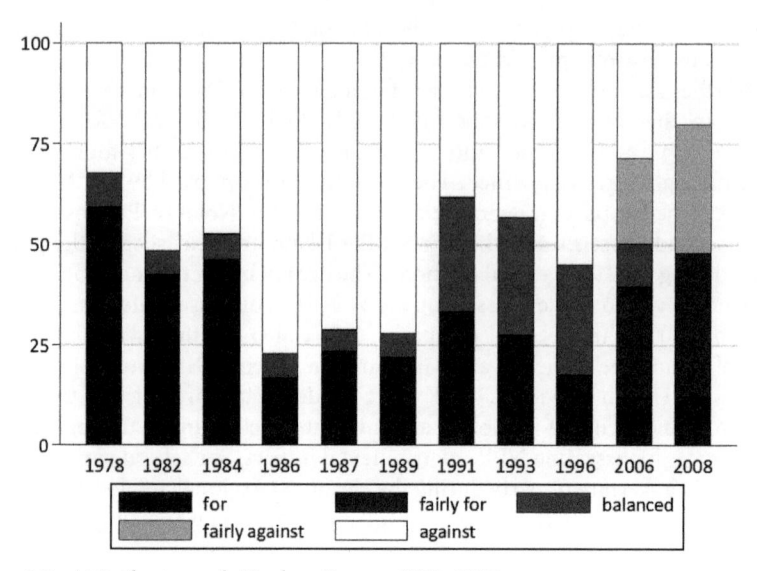

Figure 8.2. Attitudes towards Nuclear Energy, 1978–2008

Sources: Eurobarometer studies ZA0995, ZA1208, ZA1321, ZA1544, ZA1713, ZA1751, ZA2031, ZA2347, ZA2898, ZA4507, and ZA4743.

unacceptable risks. After the Three Mile Island and Chernobyl accidents, this latter figure steeply increased to 77 per cent in 1986. The Italian public remained strongly critical throughout the 1980s.

Figure 8.3 illustrates the ideological distribution of respondents opposing nuclear energy (the white and light-grey sections of the bars in Figure 8.2).[13] Throughout the 1980s, a plurality of opponents to nuclear energy reported left-of-centre political orientations (and a plurality of all respondents was left-wing). Franchino (2014) finds that this ideological divide tended to intensify in the spatial proximity of NPPs. Moreover, pro-nuclear views were weakly rooted even in right-wing individuals because they displayed high volatility in the aftermath of accidents.

This public opinion dynamic was not unique to Italy however (Franchino 2014). We have to move to party positioning and coalition politics to explain the policy reversal.

8.4.4 Referendum, Party Positioning, and Coalition Politics in the 1980s: Reversal

At the beginning of the 1980s, political support was shifting away from DC. In 1981, Giovanni Spadolini (PRI) was the first non-DC Prime Minister of the

---

[13] Opponents are subjects that score between 1 (strongly opposed) and 3 in the 2006 survey and those that are at least fairly opposed in the 2008 survey. In a self-reported 1 (left) to 10 (right) ideological scale, left-wing respondents score lower than five while right-wing respondents score higher than six.

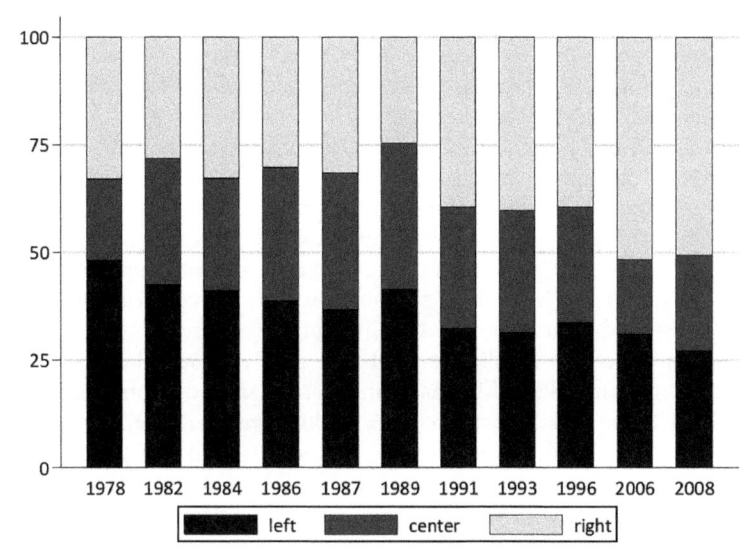

Figure 8.3. Ideological Distribution of Opponents of Nuclear Energy, 1978–2008
Sources: See Figure 8.2.

post-war period. He led a five-party coalition (DC-PSI-PSDI-PRI-PLI) that was going to rule for the next decade. This novelty had initially no implications for the plans to expand nuclear energy capacity. Indeed, PRI was probably the most open supporter of nuclear power (Ascheri 1988). Its 1979 manifesto criticized parties that were concerned about the diversification of energy supply but acquiesced to popular pressures for halting the expansion.

In the 1983 electoral campaign, the positions over nuclear energy of the parties that were likely to form the government were still fairly homogeneous. DC emphasized the need to speed up the construction of new plants. PRI and PLI remained supportive, though underscoring the safety dimension. Only PSI appeared to adopt a more lukewarm position. It emphasized research on nuclear fusion, but it still supported the implementation of the 1981 NEP. The opposition was more divided. While PCI was in favour, PR and DP were strongly against. Nonetheless, the issue was not particularly salient. DC lost fifty-five seats for the benefit of its coalition partners, especially PRI and PSI. The latter party drained votes also from PR, who lost eight seats. In the opposition, PCI lost votes, while DP managed to have seven representatives.

The best performance of PSI in fifteen years, combined with poorest performance of DC since 1948, paved the way for Bettino Craxi, the PSI leader, to become the Prime Minister of the five-party coalition in August 1983. The incentives facing PSI are central to understanding the events that followed. Both DC and PCI were losing support in favour of various medium to small-sized parties. PSI, the largest among them, had been competing with PCI along the traditional economic left–right dimension with mixed results. But in the early 1980s, it began to capitalize on the emerging left-libertarian, environmental, and post-modern issues (Inglehart 1977; Inglehart and Flanagan 1987; see section 8.4.3). Competition was tough along this new dimension as well because, as you may recall (see section 8.3.3), the barriers to entering the political arena were low, given the electoral system operating at the time. The Greens presented candidates for the first time in the 1985 regional elections (they successfully entered Parliament in 1987). This party and the anti-nuclear PR were frustrating PSI's aspirations to become a significant player in Italian politics. Indeed, the first measure of the Craxi government was to finance the more environmentally friendly nuclear fusion, as pledged during the electoral campaign.

On the other hand, the policy momentum was still in favour of nuclear energy. At the end of 1985, the government parliamentary majority approved with the support of PCI the Altissimo plan to move forward the construction of NPPs. Things then started to unravel after the Chernobyl disaster.

The circumstances for a policy reversal were highly favourable. At the time of the incident, only the NPPs of Latina, Trino Vercellese, and Caorso were supplying electricity to the grid. In October 1986, Paolo Fornaciari (1997: 92), the ENEL engineer in charge of the Unified Nuclear Project, asserted that the Montalto di Castro NPP was only 60 per cent complete. The works at Trino II had only just started. The contribution of nuclear energy to total electricity consumption had inexorably decreased from 4 per cent in 1965 to slightly more than 1 per cent in the early 1980s (Figure 8.1; Fornaciari 1997: 290). Since 1964, the Caorso NPP constituted the only significant capacity expansion. Imports of electricity and natural gas were meeting the increased demand, as foreseen by the 1981 NEP. Finally, the oil price dropped in 1986 to pre-crisis levels.

The cost of a policy reversal in nuclear energy increases with capacity. As the number of plants increases, policy choices become more path-dependent (Levi 1997; Pierson 2000). Given a capacity that barely exceeded 2 per cent of electricity production capacity nation-wide, path dependency could have hardly kicked in. The costs of a full reversal were not perceived as exorbitant at least for some parties, especially if weighed against electoral gains.

Soon after the Chernobyl accident, several motions and questions were put before the Parliament requiring the government to conduct a safety review, adopt a moratorium, and hold a national conference on energy. PSI became decisively anti-nuclear. Returning from the general conference of the German Social Democratic Party in August 1986, Claudio Martelli, PSI deputy head, declared his opposition to nuclear power. According to Martelli, it was nonsense to continue with the programme because Italy had fallen behind in the expansion of capacity. In September, Labour Minister Gianni De Michelis (PSI) suggested replacing nuclear energy with natural gas imported from Algeria and the Soviet Union. As we have discussed, a referendum was to be expected, so the Craxi government discontinued the operation of the three NPPs between October 1986 and March 1987.

The government was severely split. In November 1986, DC national executive committee unanimously approved a document stating that the construction of NPPs had to proceed. In February 1987, Industry Minister Valerio Zanone (PLI) convened a national conference on energy as requested by Parliament. The conference was supposed to be an opportunity to exchange views between experts in the energy policy community and politicians. The large majority of experts supported nuclear energy, but politicians deserted the meeting by and large. The conference was boycotted by the Greens, but it was also criticized by

Achille Occhetto, PCI general secretary, and by the trade unions (Fornaciari 1997: 250).

In April 1987, DC withdrew its support for the government. Craxi apparently breached an informal agreement with Ciriaco De Mita, the DC leader, to leave the premiership to a Christian Democrat after a year. More substantive issues were on the table however, given the suspension of NPP electricity production. Meanwhile, PR collected signatures for three referendums, which were supposed to be held in June. PSI signalled its support, but DC opposed them. The crisis resulted in an early election and the referendums were moved back to November.

The nuclear issue was now at the forefront of the campaign debate. All parties supported a national and international safety review, greater international coordination, and tighter controls, but they differed on the terms of the moratorium. For DC, works at Montalto di Castro and Trino Vercellese had to continue. The plants should have started operating once safety reviews were carried out and tighter control procedures were in place. DC also supported investments in NPPs abroad, with a view of increasing imports. PSI disagreed emphatically: the construction of NPPs should be halted and investment should be directed toward safer energy sources, energy savings, and research. The Greens were pushing for a full reversal. PCI supported the moratorium with a view to substituting nuclear energy with alternative sources in the long term, but their track record of supporting the policy was a liability.

The result of the June 1987 elections was a stalemate. Both DC and PSI won seats (fourteen and nineteen respectively) at the expense of their smaller coalition partners. PCI faced the strongest setback by losing twenty-seven seats, while the two small anti-nuclear parties, PR and DP, gained six seats overall. The Greens, for the first time competing in national elections, obtained almost a million votes for the lower chamber, bringing fourteen representatives to Parliament.

Although PSI had the best performance in twenty years, the electoral outcome did not alter the balance of power vis-à-vis DC, which consolidated its position as the largest party. After four years, it was now time for a Christian Democrat (Giovanni Goria) to be the Prime Minister of the five-party coalition. There were no alternatives to such a composition. A DC-PCI coalition might have been more in favour of nuclear energy, but it was highly improbable. After the traumatic experience of the historic compromise, DC was determined to avoid any deal with PCI. A PCI-PSI coalition with smaller anti-nuclear parties was politically unlikely because it excluded the largest party (DC) and, numerically, it was barely feasible in the Senate.

The composition of the Goria government was revealing of the conflicts in the coalition. The Ministry of Industry was held by the pro-nuclear Adolfo Battaglia (PRI), but the increasingly important Ministry of Environment was under Giorgio Ruffolo (PSI), a renowned scholar of sustainable development.

Because of the elections, the referendums were moved to 8–9 November 1987. They proposed the repeal of (1) the provisions in Law 393/1975 according to which CIPE could step in if the regions failed to locate and approve new NPPs sites, (2) the financial aid to local authorities hosting nuclear or coal power stations, and (3) the provisions allowing ENEL to participate in the construction and management of NPPs abroad.

DC was in a difficult predicament because these were clearly *its* policies. But the party had already had bad experiences with the referendums on divorce and abortion, which it promoted but resolutely lost. Sensing the widespread public concern about nuclear safety (see section 8.4.3), it might not have wanted to be perceived as losing touch with the public and, especially, it wanted to avoid the risk of being on the losing side with PCI, in a campaign against PSI, left-libertarian, and green parties. It would have weakened its position in government. DC therefore indicated its support for the first two questions. Similarly, the (initially critical) PCI did not want to coalesce with DC, so the party followed PSI in supporting the repeal of all three issues. PRI and PLI remained resolutely against.[14]

Only 65.1 per cent of the electorate voted (the lowest turnout until then), but the results were decisive: 80.6 per cent voted in favour of repeal in the first issue, 79.7 per cent in the second, and 71.9 per cent in the third.

The outcome was a setback for DC and it was almost fatal for the strained government coalition. Divisions persisted. The occasion for another confrontation was the budget proposal which received lukewarm support. Goria offered his resignation on 14 November but it was rejected by the President of the Republic. He decided to remain in office and presented a new programme on 20 November. The nuclear energy issue was then incorporated in a resolution, signed by the five government party whips, which provided for the Caorso and Trino NPPs to remain operational (see section 8.2.4). The executive attached a motion of confidence to this resolution—a clear sign of how divisive the issue was. The motion passed on 18 December solely with the support of the five government parties.

Conflict lingered on. PSI did not accept the recommendation against the conversion of the Montalto di Castro plant and it withdrew its support for the government in March 1988. The new cabinet—composed of the same parties but with De Mita (DC) as Prime Minister—had to comply with PSI's demands. Works were suspended and the plant was converted to fossil-fuel combustion. The government programme referred to the need to maintain a 'nuclear presidium' in Trino and Caorso, but no reference was made to a reconnection to the grid.

In sum, there was no credible alternative to the five-party coalition in the second half of the 1980s and PSI made its participation in government conditional upon a full pullout from nuclear energy. The policy remained off the political agenda for the following twenty years.

8.4.5 Public Opinion about Nuclear Energy (1991–2011)

Before analysing the attempt to relaunch the policy, it is worth going back to public attitudes. Throughout the 1990s, opponents exceeded supporters of nuclear energy by nineteen percentage points; 28 per cent of respondents had a more balanced opinion. In the last two Eurobarometer surveys in the 2000s, 51 per cent of respondents remained critical, but 44 per cent were supportive (see Figure 8.2). Figure 8.4 displays the attitudes reported by a miscellaneous set of recent surveys. Different methodologies and (some strongly leading) questions explain the considerable variance. Public support however appeared to be on the increase. Where

---

[14] For an analysis of the debate in the media see Cantone et al. (2007).

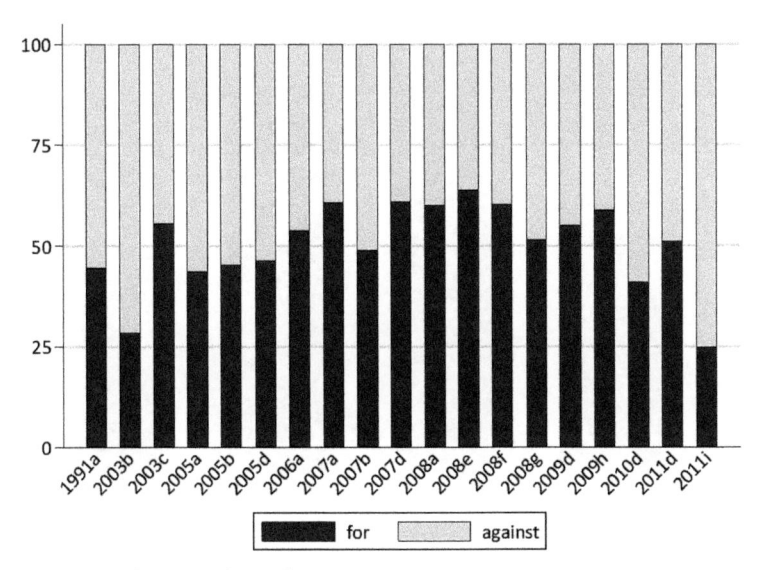

Figure 8.4. Attitudes towards Nuclear Energy, 2000s

Sources: (a) SWG 1991, 2005, 2006, 2007, 2008; (b) Observa, 2003, 2005, 2007; (c) Datamedia 2003; (d) Ferrari Nasi and Grisantelli 2005, 2007, 2009, 2010, 2011; (e) GfK Eurisko 2008; (f) Ekma 2008; (g) Demos and pi 2008; (h) Ipsos Public Affairs 2009; (i) Gnresearch 2011.

the same instrument and methodology has been employed (e.g. the six SWG surveys suffixed by the letter a), a relative majority favoured a relaunch, while around 10–14 per cent were undecided. This moderate pro-nuclear change in public opinion preceded and maybe fomented government plans.

Figures 8.5 and 8.6 display the distribution of opinions about nuclear energy by ideology and partisan allegiance respectively. Recall that in this period pro-nuclear energy opinions can be more clearly associated with centre and right-wing parties. In the pre-Fukushima period, the proportion of issue-inconsistent voters (i.e. those in disagreement with their party's position, Thurner 2010) is not trivial. Between 10 and 28 per cent of supporters of centre-right parties, such as PdL and Northern League (LN), opposed nuclear energy. Issue inconsistency was more diffused as we move left. According to Figure 8.5, 27 per cent of centrist voters opposed nuclear energy, in disagreement with the policy of parties such as UdC. Actually, a large majority of UdC voters disagreed with their party according to Figure 8.6. This is a large disparity. These figures thus invite caution but they may be indicative of weakly entrenched pro-nuclear views (Franchino 2014). More to the left, between 27 and 42 per cent of supporters of centre-left parties, such as Italy of Values (IdV) and the Democratic Party (PD), were instead in favour of nuclear energy. In other words, issue-inconsistent voters were twice as likely to be found among left- than right-wing voters.[15] This may have been of comfort for plans to restart the programme, to which we now turn.

---

[15] Similar results are reported in a survey conducted by PD in Sept. 2007: 46% of centre-left respondents were in favour of nuclear energy (46% were against), while only 23% of the centre-right respondents were against (68% were in favour).

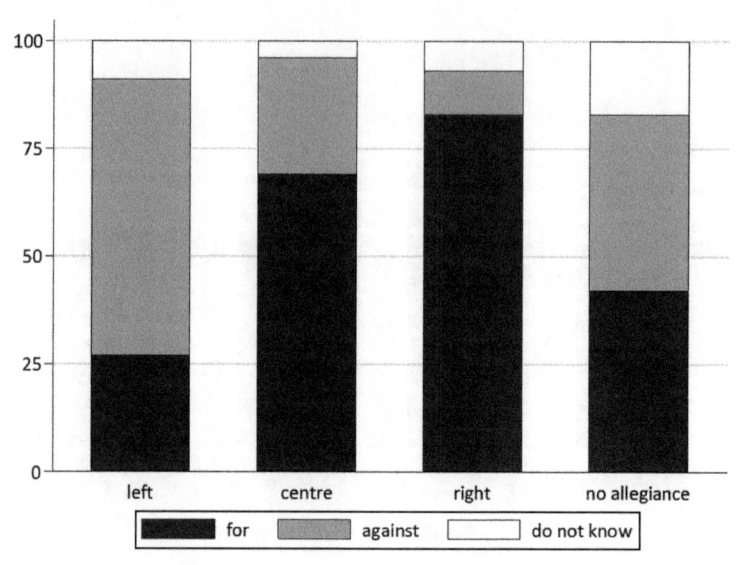

Figure 8.5. Attitudes toward Nuclear Energy and Ideology

Source: SWG Survey, July 2008. Question: The debate about nuclear power as an alternative energy source is back. Today, given the energy crisis and pollution problems, would you be in favour or against investing in nuclear energy?

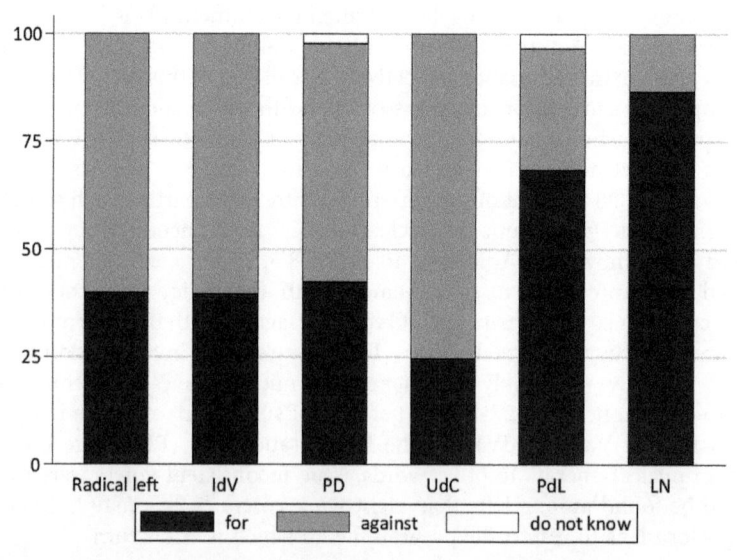

Figure 8.6. Attitudes towards Nuclear Energy and Partisanship, 2009

Source: Ferrari Nasi and Grisantelli, Jan. 2009. Question: Can you tell us if you agree or disagree with this statement? Italy should return to employing nuclear energy for civilian use.

8.4.6 Referendum, Party Positioning, and Coalition Politics in the Last Decade: Attempted Relaunch

Nuclear energy slowly crept back on the policy agenda during the 'nuclear renaissance' period (see Chapter 1). In the 2006 elections, the manifestos of both the centre-right and the centre-left alliances[16] advocated participation in international research projects on third-generation NPPs. These initiatives seemed to have sparked renewed interest in this policy. However, the centre-left manifesto added a vein of scepticism: 'A resumption of the nuclear program in Italy today is not feasible'.

The barely winning centre-left coalition government turned out to be short-lived and took no significant steps.[17] Italians had to go back to the polls in 2008. During this electoral campaign, centre-right parties, especially PdL, UdC, and other smaller parties, reiterated the need to participate in research programmes. PD was not explicit in its manifesto, perhaps in order to gloss over internal dissent. Even references to nuclear energy research were dropped. IdV, an electoral ally of PD, was also silent (two years later, it would promote a referendum). The Greens and the small Left Rainbow Party were clearly opposed.

In June 2008, the government of the victorious PdL-NL centre-right coalition adopted the decree law on the national energy strategy that put nuclear energy back on the agenda. According to the government, a return to nuclear energy would lower greenhouse gas emissions, external dependency, and electricity costs. Once the decree was converted into Law 133/2008, the programme started to be implemented under the leadership of Economic Development Minister Scajola (PdL). In August 2008, the executive sponsored an important bill which became Law 99/2009, once adopted by the government parties (see section 8.2.5). The small pro-nuclear centre party UdC was in opposition and abstained.

These measures were subject to a few constitutional reviews promoted by eleven regions—ten of which were run by centre-left parties. The only marginal success of these initiatives was that the Constitutional Court established that regional consultation was compulsory prior to the authorization to build a NPP, but regional opinions remained not binding.

On the other hand, a referendum on the provision of Law 133/2008 regulating the construction of NPPs turned out to be fatal. The promoter was IdV, an opposition party which began collecting signatures in 2010. At a first sight, the threat looked minor. Since 1995, no referendum reached the threshold of voter participation required to validate the outcome. Serendipitously, two factors raised public awareness. First, the Fukushima accident of March 2011 revived public concerns about nuclear safety. We have seen in section 8.4.5 that there were many issue-inconsistent voters among the public. These voters are more prone to attitudinal or behavioural change due to framing efforts (Chong and Druckman 2007a, 2007b), so the accident offered much needed help to the anti-nuclear cause.

---

[16] The centre-right House of Freedoms, headed by Silvio Berlusconi, was a four-party coalition (Go Italy, National Alliance, Northern League, and the Union of the Christian Democrats). The centre-left Union, headed by Romano Prodi, was essentially a two-party coalition (Olive Tree and a small communist party).

[17] Apart from signing the Global Nuclear Energy Partnership.

As a matter of fact, the last column in Figure 8.4 reports the outcome of a survey conducted in March 2011 by Gnresearch for the centre-left daily *La Repubblica* (Gualerzi 2011). The proportion of supporters dropped by a full twenty percentage points and the share of opponents almost doubled. Second, public disaffection with the government was mounting, as emerged with the resounding and surprising success of centre-left candidates at important mayoral elections in May 2011.

The referendum offered another opportunity for an anti-government statement.[18] Sensing defeat, in March 2011, the government hastily adopted Decree Law 34/2011 that halted the nuclear programme and called for the adoption of a new national energy strategy within twelve months. Its clear intent was to avoid the referendum. The decree was converted into Law 75/2011 in May. However, the Court of Cassation ruled, by majority, that these measures were not enough to avoid the referendum because they constituted only a temporary postponement, rather than a permanent repeal. Following constitutional jurisprudence, the Court argued that the legislative intent behind the new law was still pro-nuclear as it (implicitly) included and did not explicitly exclude the use of nuclear energy even in the short term. The referendum should therefore be allowed and applied to the provisions of Law 75/2011 instead. The Constitutional Court upheld this ruling unanimously.

A dry read of these provisions does not indicate a certain return to nuclear power, nor is their temporary nature explicit. Even so, one can easily find temporary measures which last several years and successful referendums with almost no consequences.[19] On the other hand, Berlusconi's public declaration to restart the programme within one or two years did not help. Given an electorate that sharply turned sceptical, government's manoeuvring did not go down well and was portrayed by anti-nuclear groups as a ploy to subvert public opinion. According to the mentioned Gnresearch survey, 91 per cent of the respondents declared their intention to vote. Among these, 71 per cent supported the repeal. With public opinion largely on its side, the Court was in an ideal situation to exert influence. It was a highly publicized issue, with costless public monitoring of executive non-compliance (Vanberg 2001, 2004).

Pro-nuclear parties in both government (PdL and LN) and opposition (UdC and FLI, a small break-away party) did not issue voting instructions. Berlusconi and several centre-right leaders publicly stated that they would not vote, hoping that the participation threshold would be missed. On the other camp, aside from the referendum promoters (i.e. IdV and PR), anti-nuclear views began to congeal within PD, the largest opposition party. Preference aggregation was not completely smooth. When PD leader Pierluigi Bersani signed the Global Nuclear Energy Partnership a few years earlier, he appeared warmer towards nuclear energy (Maurizi 2011). Moreover, in October 2010 the renowned oncologist Umberto Veronesi was appointed president of the newly established Nuclear Safety Agency. Veronesi was a high-profile PD senator who held pro-nuclear energy views. In

---

[18] Subject to referendum was also a provision which allowed ministers to procrastinate turning up in court. It offered another vehicle for signalling resentment directly against Berlusconi.

[19] Recall the *temporary* suspension of the nuclear plants in 1986–7. In 1993, a referendum repealed the Ministry of Agriculture, which was swiftly transformed into the Ministry of Agricultural Policies and Forestry.

February 2011, PD's national assembly nevertheless declared its opposition to the government's programme and supported the referendum.

On 12–13 June 2011, after sixteen years of failed attempts, 54.8 per cent of the electorate participated in the consultation and a considerable 94.1 per cent voted for the repeal. The government abandoned the project. Nuclear energy disappeared from the 2013 elections and it is likely to remain off the political agenda for the foreseeable future.

8.5 CONCLUSION: EXPLAINING POLICY CHOICES

Several factors discussed in Chapter 2 help us understand these policy developments. We leave aside here economic and environmental pressures, which have been common across Western Europe, and consider three sets of variables.

First, consider the institutions, such as the electoral system and the provisions for holding referendums and regulating regional involvement. They do not explain directly policy choices but structure the context within which voters decide, parties develop positions, and policy-makers plan and implement measures.

Second, public opinion dynamics provided the social support for policy change, as it evidently did throughout the whole period when the public shifted first against, then in favour, and then back against nuclear energy. This dynamic does not differ from that of other European countries with nuclear power (Franchino 2014), but social support could become a necessary condition for the permanence of a policy when abrogative referendums are available. A successful referendum is no guarantee of a full repeal but it weights the odds against continuity.

Moreover, issue-inconsistent voters offer opportunities for party repositioning and, possibly, policy change. See the left-wing voters that were at odds with PCI pro-nuclear policy in the 1970s and 1980s or with the sceptical positions of their parties in the 2000s. The former inconsistency eventually led to a repositioning of PCI; the latter encouraged a relaunch of nuclear energy policy.

The third sets of factors to consider are party positioning and coalition politics. These dynamics heavily depend on the electoral systems, which shape voting behaviour and political competition, and on referendums, which may raise issue salience and likelihood of policy change. PSI began repositioning in the late 1970s in order to take advantage of an increasingly critical public opinion and a fledgling environmental movement that appealed to left-wing post-materialist voters. Repositioning occurred under the threat of anti-nuclear parties entering politics and it had the advantage of eroding electoral support for PCI, its pro-nuclear competitor on the left. Similarly, in the 2000s right-of-centre parties were particularly keen to take advantage of an electorate—much of which was of centre-left orientation—that was warming up to the idea of nuclear energy.

Coalition politics is the most proximate cause of policy change. Changes in government composition indeed explain nationalization, the ambitious 1975 NEP, and the relaunch of the policy. Nationalization became feasible when PLI was excluded from government. The NEP was produced under a pro-nuclear DC-PRI coalition that left out less enthusiastic parties (e.g. PSI) from policy formulation. The relaunch in the 2000s gained momentum only after a centre-right coalition won office.

Major plans and decisions correlate with intensified debates about energy in general and nuclear energy in particular. Nationalization was an important campaign issue in the 1963 and 1968 elections, as was nuclear energy in the 1976 and 1979 elections. But increased salience does not necessarily imply increased intra-coalitional conflict. There was almost unanimous agreement about expanding capacity and improving safety in the second half of the 1970s. On the other hand, after a massive shift in attitudes, nuclear energy was *the* most salient and divisive issue in the 1987 electoral campaign, as emerges from the party manifestos (see Figures 8.A2 and 8.A3). Coalition politics is the key to understanding the reversal.

Several factors converged in the run-up to this decision. For a host of reasons, including regionalization, expansion plans suffered severe delays and investment in nuclear energy was limited. The energy sector was under full political control and the government did not need to face resistance from private operators. Finally, the return of cheap oil made alternative sources attractive. These factors weakened path dependency and reduced the costs of a reversal. The Chernobyl accident then sharply heightened popular concerns about safety, which were strongly conveyed at the referendum.

None of these factors are sufficient to explain reversal in my view however. Italy was once a major innovator in the field and investments were not trivial. Participation at the referendum was not overwhelming and, in other circumstances (see n. 19), politicians have only complied with the letter but not with the spirit of these consultations. The reference to a 'nuclear presidium' was clearly designed to avert a full pullout. Instead, a sufficient condition was that PSI made its unavoidable participation in government conditional upon a full pullout. There was no need in this case for a green party to be in government—a credible threat to enter the political arena was enough. On the other hand, office-seeking[20] considerations prevailed in DC, a party that was unwilling to sacrifice premiership and government to nuclear energy.

In case of the attempted relaunch, its timing can be explained by a government with a strong electoral mandate and no intra-coalitional differences over the issue. The coincidence of another accident with an upcoming referendum was just serendipitous. Persevering with the policy after this consultation would have been a political liability, and it may have been reversed anyway, were a centre-left coalition to win the next elections. Also, there were no sunk costs, only legislative and executive measures.

Italy is still investing in nuclear energy research, so one cannot rule out other attempts to relaunch the programme. Economic and environmental pressures are not receding, but the common energy market of the European Union is somewhat alleviating their impact. For the policy to re-emerge, one has to wait for a committed government, benign public opinion, and no further accidents. Even so, other hurdles, from regional involvement to referendum, will not disappear.

---

[20] On votes-, office-, and policy-seeking incentives of parties see Harmel and Janda (1994), Müller and Strøm (1999) and Tavits (2007).

APPENDIX 1: RAW DATA FOR A NUCLEAR ENERGY POLICY SCALE

Table 8.A1. Raw Data for a Nuclear Energy Policy Scale

Year (yyyy-mm)	Event description	Pronuclear (+), Antinuclear (-)	Comments
1946	Private companies set up the research centre Cise (*Centro informazioni studi e esperienze*)	=	research related/ private sector
1952-06	National Research Council establishes the *Comitato Nazionale per le Ricerche Nucleari* (National Committee for Nuclear Research, CNRN).	=	research related
1955-12	Main Italian electricity producing companies set up the *Società Elettronucleare Italiana* (Italian Electronuclear Company, Selni)	+	public-private venture
1957-03	Finelettrica establishes the *Società Elettronucleare Nazionale* (National Electronuclear Company, Senn)	+	
1957-03	Eni (*Ente Nazionale Idrocarburi*—the state-owned hydrocarbons corporation) establishes the *Società Italiana Meridionale per l'Energia Nucleare* (Southern Italian Company for Nuclear Energy—Simea)	+	
1958-11	Latina plant: Construction started	+	
1959-11	Garigliano plant: Construction started	+	
1960-08	Parliament replaces the CNRN with the *Comitato Nazionale per l'Energia Nucleare* (National Committee for Nuclear Energy, CNEN), detached from the National Research Council—Law 933 of 11 September 1960	=	research related
1961-07	Trino plant: Construction started	+	
1962-12	Law 1643 of 6 December 1962 on the nationalization of production, import, export, transport, transformation, distribution and sale of electric energy under Enel *Ente nazionale per l'energia elettrica* (National Agency for Electric Energy)	=	
1962-12	Law 1860 of 31 December 1962 on the peaceful use of nuclear energy	+	
1963-05	Latina plant: Connected to electricity grid	=	technical
1964-01	Latina plant: Commercial operation	+	
1964-01	Garigliano plant: Connected to electricity grid	=	technical
1964-06	Garigliano plant: Commercial operation	+	
1964-10	Trino plant: Connected to electricity grid	=	technical
1965-01	Trino plant: Commercial operation	+	
1965-02	Selni, Senn, and Simea (nuclear energy companies) transferred to Enel, following Law 1643 of 6 December 1962	=	
1966-07	CIPE[†] approves the construction of a new nuclear power plant	+	
1967	Electricity production of the Trino plant suspended for modifications to the internal structure of the reactor	=	technical

(*continued*)

Table 8.A1. Continued

Year (yyyy-mm)	Event description	Pronuclear (+), Antinuclear (-)	Comments
1969	Electricity production of the Trino plant restarted	=	technical
1969	Enel locates the new plant in Caorso	+	
1970-01	Caorso plant: Construction started	+	
1971-06	CIPE approves the five-year research plan (1971–5) of the CNEN	=	research related
1971-12	Parliament adopts Law 1240 of 15 December 1971 restructuring the CNEN and separating the National Institute of Nuclear Physics from the CNEN.	=	research related
1973-12	CIPE approves a plan to build four new plants and locates the first two near the Lazio-Tuscany border and the Abruzzo–Molise border	+	
1974-06	Consultative interregional committee supports locating the first reactor in Montalto di Castro (Lazio).	=	consultation only
1974-10	CIPE approves the five-year research plan (1974–8) of the CNEN (National Committee for Nuclear Energy)	=	research related
1975	First National Energy Plan (NEP): objective of constructing twenty new plants.	+	action plan
1975-08	Law 393 of 2 August 1975 on site selection of nuclear power stations	+	
1975-10	CIPE decides that four new plants will be built in Piedmont and Lombardy	+	
1975-10	Consultative interregional committee supports locating two new plants in Piedmont and two in Lombardy.	=	consultation only
1975-12	CIPE approves chapter III of the first NEP on nuclear energy expansion and specifies that the public procurement procedures for building eight new plants should begin immediately	=	
1976-09	Lazio region approves the location of the site at Montalto di Castro	=	not binding
1977-10	Parliament approves a resolution supporting the nuclear power expansion plan (building of four plants, starting public procurement procedure for four other plants, option for four more plants)	+	resolution supporting earlier CIPE plans
1977-12	CIPE (re)approves a) building of four new plants (that have been already contracted out) and b) starting of public procurement procedure for four more units, with the options of additional four units	=	earlier CIPE decisions reaffirmed
1977-12	Municipality of Montalto di Castro approves the project for a new nuclear power plant	=	not binding
1978-05	Caorso plant: Connected to electricity grid	=	technical
1979-02	Montalto di Castro plant: Construction started	+	
1979	Montalto di Castro city mayor suspends plant construction after the Three Mile island accident	=	

Italy: Two Policy Failures

1980-04	CIPE approves the five-year research plan (1980–4) of the CNEN (National Committee for Nuclear Energy)	=	research related
1980	Montalto di Castro plant construction restarts	=	
1981	Second NEP: objective of constructing only three new plants (planned expansion of nuclear energy capacity halved)	-	action plan—back down from previous plan
1981-04	CIPE approves five-year CNEN PEC reactor project	=	research related
1981-12	Caorso plant: Commercial operation	+	
1981-12	CIPE approves the second NEP	+	
1982	The Parliament replaces the CNEN with the *Comitato Nazionale per la Ricerca e lo Sviluppo dell'Energia Nucleare e delle Energie Alternative* (National Committee for the Research and Development of Nuclear Energy and Alternative Energy Sources, ENEA)	=	research related
1982-01	CIPE approves the National Plan on Energy Research (*Piano Nazionale di Ricerca per l'Energia*)	=	research related
1982-03	Garigliano plant: Shutdown	=	technical shutdown
1983-02	CIPE identifies two plant sites for each region (Lombardy, Piedmont and Apulia) for the three new plants.	+	
1983-10	CIPE approves funding of research on nuclear fusion	=	research related
1985-03	CIPE approves the five year Funding Programme of ENEA (1985-9)	=	research related
1985-01	Piedmont region approves the construction of Trino II	=	not binding
1985-02	Trino II plant: Construction started	+	
1985-12	Parliament approves a resolution supporting an amendment (proposed by the industry minister) of the second NEP increasing the planned capacity expansion by 4000 MW	+	
1986-03	CIPE decides to locate the new plants in Veneto, Sicily, Campania or Basilicata and approves the update to the second NEP	+	
1986-10	Caorso plant: Energy supply to grid discontinued	-	
1986-11	Latina plant: Energy supply to grid discontinued	-	
1987-03	Trino plant: Energy supply to grid discontinued	-	
1987-11	Outcome of nuclear power referendums in favour of repeal	-	referendum
1987-11	Montalto di Castro plant: Works suspended (CIPE decision)	-	
1987-12	Parliament approves resolution (attached to a motion of confidence) demanding (a) a new national energy plan with a five-year moratorium on the construction of new plants, (b) the termination of the works for Trino II, (c) the shutdown of the Latina plant	-	

(continued)

Table 8.A1. Continued

Year (yyyy-mm)	Event description	Pronuclear (+), Antinuclear (−)	Comments
	and (d) the establishment of a commission to evaluate the technical and economic feasibility of converting the nearly finished plant of Montalto di Castro to other uses		
1987-12	Latina plant: Shutdown (CIPE decision)	−	
1987-12	Trino II plant: Works suspended (CIPE decision)	−	
1988-08	Government approves the Third NEP that terminates the Unified Nuclear Project, participation at NERSA, the French-based Superphenix consortium, and the CIRENE	−	halt to nuclear energy production/also research related
1989	Montalto di Castro plant converted to fossil fuel combustion	−	
1990-05	Parliament approves resolution demanding the permanent shutdown of the plants in Caorso and Trino Vercellese	−	
1990-07	Trino plant: Shutdown (CIPE decision)	−	
1990-07	Caorso plant: Shutdown (CIPE decision)	−	
1991-08	Following the abandonment of research on nuclear energy, ENEA is renamed *Ente per le Nuove Tecnologie, l'Energia e l'Ambiente* (Agency for the New Technologies, Energy and Environment), Law 282 of 25 August 1991	=	research related
2007-11	Signing of the Global Nuclear Energy Partnership, a US-initiated international partnership to promote the use of nuclear power	=	statement of principles only
2008-06	Decree Law 112 of 25 June 2008 on a national energy strategy (national conference on energy and the environment, building new nuclear energy plants, signing of international agreements for the development of the nuclear energy sector). Converted into Law 133/2008.	+	
2009-07	Parliament adopts Law 99 of 23 July 2009 (request for government regulation on site location, establishment of Agency for Nuclear Safety (*Agenzia per la sicurezza nucleare*), establishment of procedures for choosing the types of plants). ENEA is renamed *Agenzia nazionale per le nuove tecnologie, l'energia e lo sviluppo economico sostenibile* (National Agency for the New Technologies, Energy and Sustainable Economic Development), investment in nuclear energy re-activated.	+	
2009-08	Enel and Edf establish the joint venture Nuclear Development Italy (*Sviluppo Nucleare Italia*).	+	
2009-09	Government signs memorandum of understanding with the US administration for	+	

	development of nuclear plants (Westinghouse, General Electric and Ansaldo Nucleare)		
2010-02	Legislative decree 31 of February 15, 2010, government regulation on site location	+	
2011-03	Decree Law 34 of 31 March 2011—a twelve month moratorium—converted into Law 75/2011	-	
2011-06	Outcome of nuclear power referendum in favour of repeal	-	referendum

† CIPE: Inter-ministerial committee on economic planning (*Comitato interministeriale per la programmazione economica*) chaired by the prime minister and composed by several ministers with competences over economic planning and development.

Data on plant construction, connection, commercial operation and shutdown available from <http://www.iaea.org/programmes/a2> (with the exception of the Montalto di Castro and Trino II plants).

APPENDIX 2: GRAPHS

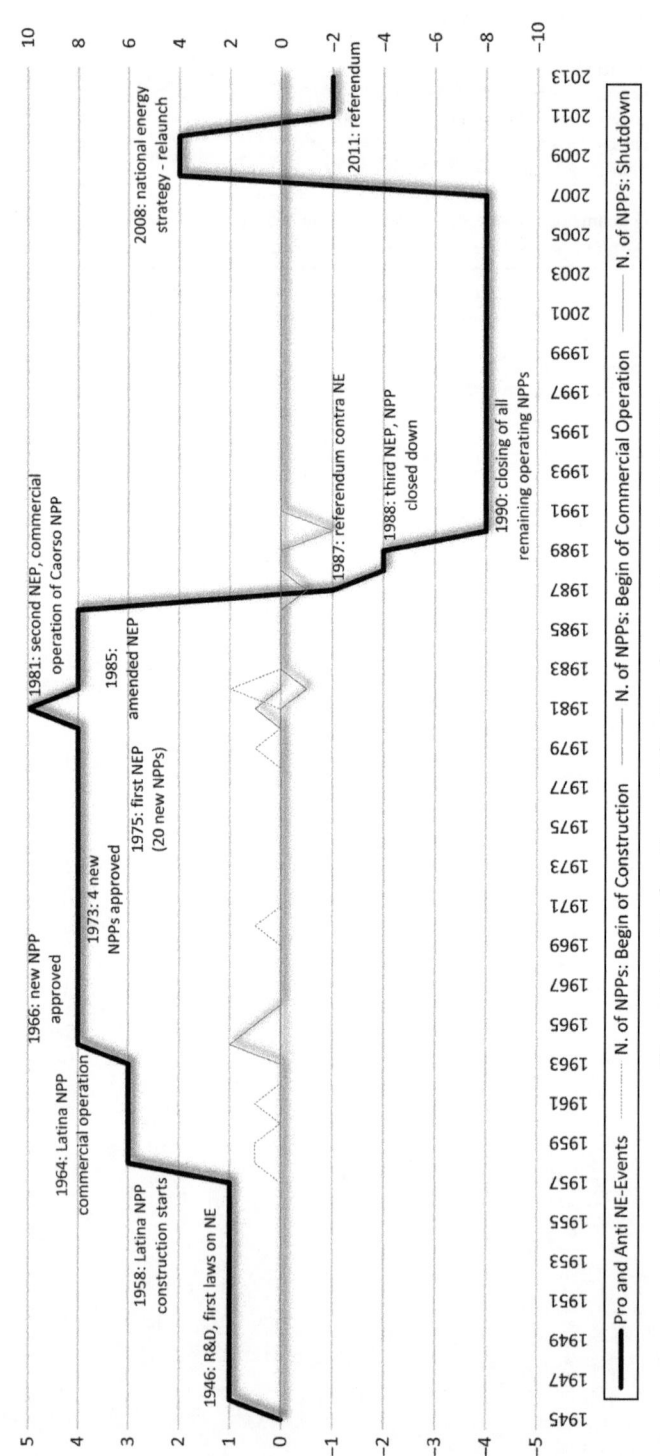

Figure 8.A1. Nuclear Energy Policy Development in Italy, 1945–2013

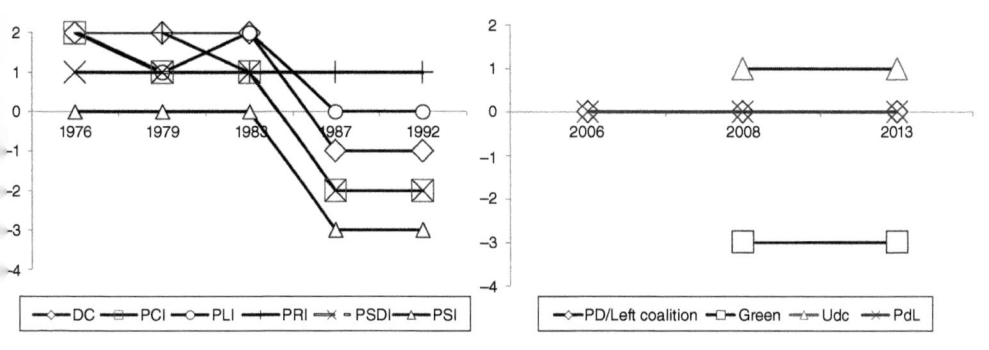

Figure 8.A2. Parties' Position-Taking in Italian Electoral Manifestos

Note: 2 'Unconditional support', 1 'Weak, conditional support', 0 'No commitment', −1 'Freezing', −2 'Downsizing', −3 'Gradual or immediate shutdown, exit', −4 'Forbidding'. In the left panel, we have omitted three small parties (first PR and DP, then the Greens) that advocated exit.

Source: Electoral manifestos and interviews. In 1992 and 2013, there were no references to nuclear energy. We assume that parties held the same positions.

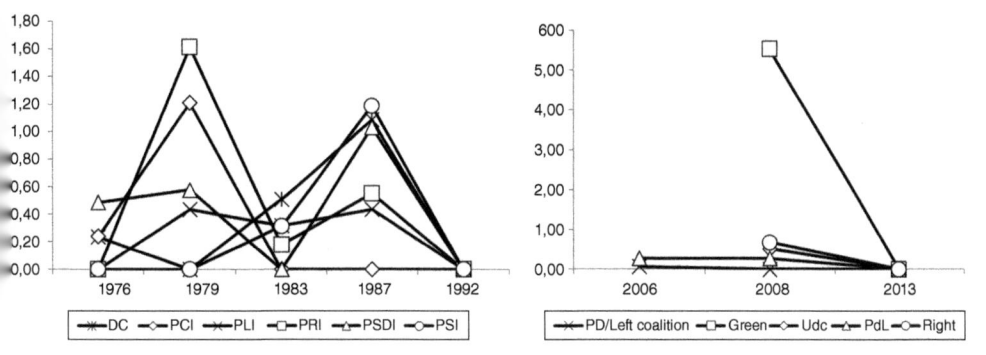

Figure 8.A3. Nuclear Energy Salience in Party Electoral Manifestos (%)

Note: Share of words in quasi-sentences on nuclear energy policy out of the total number of words.

Source: Electoral manifestos.

REFERENCES

Ascheri, Giacomo (1988). *Giovanni Spadolini: Prima Presidenza Laica.* Rome: Editalia.

Cantone, Marie Claire, Giancarlo Sturloni, and Giancarlo Brunelli (2007). 'The Role Played by Stakeholders in the Public Debate that Brought Italy out of the Club of Nuclear Energy Producers.' *Health Physics,* 93(4): 261–6.

Castronovo, V. (1988). 'Le Nazionalizzazioni nelle Politiche Economiche del Secondo Dopoguerra in Europa.' Conference proceedings on La Nazionalizzazione dell'Energia Elettrica: L'Esperienza Italiana e di Altri Paesi Europei, 9–10 Nov., Bari: Laterza.

Chong, Dennis, and James N. Druckman (2007a). 'Framing Theory.' *Annual Review of Political Science,* 10: 103–26.

Chong, Dennis, and James N. Druckman (2007b). 'Framing Public Opinion in Competitive Democracies.' *American Political Science Review,* 101(4): 637–55.

Commissioni Speciali della Camera e del Senato (1962). *La Nazionalizzazione dell'Energia Elettrica in Italia*. Rome: Studium.

Corbellini, Francesco, and Franco Velonà (2008). *Maledetta Chernobyl: La Vera Storia del Nucleare in Italia*. Milan: Francesco Brioschi.

Curli, Barbara (2000). *Il Progetto Nucleare Italiano (1952-1964): Conversazioni con Felice Ippolito*. Soveria Mannelli: Rubettino.

De Paoli, Luigi (2011). *L'energia nucleare: Costi e benefici di una tecnologia controversa*. Bologna: Il Mulino.

Franchino, Fabio (2014). 'The Social Bases of Nuclear Energy Policies in Europe: Ideology, Proximity, Belief Updating and Attitudes to Risk.' *European Journal of Political Research*, 53(2): 213-33.

Fornaciari, Paolo (1997). *Il petrolio, l'atomo e il metano: Italia nucleare 1946-1997*. Milan: 21mo Secolo.

Gualerzi, Valerio (2011). 'Nucleare, tre italiani su quattro dicono "no" alle nuove centrali.' *La Repubblica*, 22 Mar.

Harmel, Robert, and Kenneth Janda (1994). 'An Integrated Theory of Party Goals and Party Change.' *Journal of Theoretical Politics*, 6(3): 259-87.

Inglehart, Ronald (1977). *The Silent Revolution: Changing Values and Political Styles among Western Publics*. Princeton: Princeton University Press.

Inglehart, Ronald, and Scott C. Flanagan (1987). 'Value Change in Industrial Societies.' *American Political Science Review*, 81(4): 1289-1319.

Ippolito, Felice, and Folco Simen (1974). *La questione energetica: Dieci anni perduti, 1963-1973*. Milan: Feltrinelli.

Levi, Margaret (1997). 'A Model, a Method, and a Map: Rational Choice in Comparative and Historical Analysis', in Mark I. Lichbach and Alan S. Zuckerman (eds), *Comparative Politics: Rationality, Culture, and Structure*. Cambridge: Cambridge University Press, 19-41.

Maurizi, Stefania (2011). 'Intrigo nucleare.' *L'Espresso*, 12 (24 Mar.): 57-62.

Mori, G. (1992). 'La nazionalizzazione in Italia: Il dibattito politico economico', in Giovanni Zanetti (ed.), *Storia dell'industria elettrica in Italia*, v. *Gli sviluppi dell'Enel, 1963-1990*. Bari: Laterza, 147-73.

Müller, Wolfgang C., and Kaare Strøm (eds) (1999). *Policy, Office, or Votes? How Political Parties in Western Europe Make Hard Decisions*. Cambridge: Cambridge University Press.

Pierson, Paul (2000). 'Path Dependence, Increasing Returns, and the Study of Politics.' *American Political Science Review*, 94(2): 251-67.

Silari, Fabio (1989). 'La nazionalizzazione elettrica in Italia: Conflitti di interessi e progetti legislativi 1945-1962.' *Italia Contemporanea*, 177: 49-68.

Tavits, Margit (2007). 'Principle vs. Pragmatism: Policy Shifts and Political Competition.' *American Journal of Political Science*, 51(1): 151-65.

Thurner, Paul W. (2010). '"Issue-Unentschiedenheit" und "Issue-Inkonsistenz" bei den Einstellungen der Deutschen zur Kernenergie, 1987-2005', in Thorsten Faas, Kai Arzheimer, and Sigrid Roßteutscher (eds), *Information—Wahrnehmung—Emotion: Die Bedeutung kognitiver und affektiver Prozesse für die Wahl- und Einstellungsforschung*. Wiesbaden: VS Verlag, 333-53.

Vanberg, Georg (2001). 'Legislative-Judicial Relations: A Game-Theoretic Approach to Constitutional Review.' *American Journal of Political Science*, 45(2): 346-61.

Vanberg, Georg (2004). *The Politics of Constitutional Review in Germany*. Cambridge: Cambridge University Press.

Zaninelli, Sergio, and Mariarosa Borroni (1996). *Ricerca, innovazione, impresa: Storia del CISE: 1946-1996*. Bari: Laterza.

9

Nuclear Power and Politics in the Netherlands

Kees Aarts and Maarten Arentsen

9.1 INTRODUCTION

In the Netherlands, the share of nuclear power in electricity generation is small by all standards (5 per cent in 1990 and 2.9 per cent in 2013). The country hosts only one operational nuclear power plant (450 MW in Borssele), and one dormant reactor (50 MW in Dodewaard) preparing for dismantling. These small numbers, however, do not reflect the magnitude and intensity of the nuclear debate in the Netherlands since the early 1950s. The country started its nuclear path following the international trend of developing the nuclear option as part of the energy portfolio. In this way the nuclear option became part of intense societal and political debate and conflict, with peaks in the 1970s and 1980s. In those years the country intensively discussed and disputed nuclear power, but plans were faded out as a consequence of the Chernobyl accident. After 1986 an extension of nuclear power production was discussed, but concrete plans were never developed. The debate has continued until 2015, but with less passionate ideological positions than before. To date (March 2015) nuclear power production is, as ever before, not preferred by the majority of the Dutch population.

In the subsequent sections of this chapter, we describe and analyse the policy development of nuclear power production in the Netherlands (9.2), followed by an overview of the actors and jurisdictions in this policy area (9.3) and a systematic overview of political competition over nuclear energy (9.4).

9.2 POLICY DEVELOPMENT

The focus on nuclear power in the Netherlands followed the 'Atoms for Peace' programme initiated by the United States in the early 1950s.[1] The Dutch wanted to engage in nuclear technology, considered as a promising future technology at

---

[1] This section draws on Arentsen (2009). For detailed descriptions of the early episodes in Dutch nuclear history see Verbong and Lagaaij (2000), Andriesse (2000), and De Jong (1987).

the time. The promise of nuclear technology was politically translated into the ambition of the Dutch government to have nuclear-based power generation by 1962 and a gradual change from fossil to nuclear electricity production in the following years. To effectuate the ambition of a nuclear future, a national nuclear industry uniting the relevant expertise of the country was initiated. The idea was not only to have nuclear-based electricity generation, but to develop a Dutch nuclear industrial cluster able to design, produce, and export Dutch nuclear technology. The building of a first experimental boiling water reactor of 50 MW started in 1965 in Dodewaard, and this reactor was connected to the grid in 1969.

The national ambition was however frustrated in two ways. First, in 1959 a large natural gas field had been discovered in the province Groningen (followed later by new discoveries of natural gas). In the 1960s, natural gas quickly became an important fuel in electricity production in the country next to coal and fossil oil. The second such development was a move of one of the (then) regional electricity companies in 1969. This public utility, PZEM (later EPZ) in the province Zealand, purchased a complete nuclear power plant in the United States without involving either the Dutch national government or the other Dutch electricity companies. PZEM wanted to produce cheap electricity mainly for industrial purposes (in nearby Vlissingen a French company had recently built an energy-intensive aluminium plant). The news about the purchase of the nuclear reactor shocked both the government and the other electricity companies. From that time on the Dutch government took a stronger leading position in the country's nuclear debate. The EPZ nuclear power plant, built in Borssele, was connected to the grid in 1973.

Responding to the first oil crisis, the Dutch government in 1974 published a White Paper on energy policy. This White Paper announced the construction of three new nuclear power plants of 1,000 MW each—two in the country itself, and one in collaboration with Germany, on German soil (Kalkar, across the border near Nijmegen). Investing in nuclear energy was part of the fuel diversification strategy of the government to reduce resource dependency. The plan to build two new nuclear plants and especially the Dutch participation in the Kalkar project dominated the political and the nuclear power agenda during the 1980s. In the early 1970s, the Dutch government proposed a new tax of 3 per cent on household energy bills in order to finance the Kalkar project. In 1973 this proposal won a majority in parliament, even though all left-wing parties opposed it. The 'Kalkar tax' as it was widely known, was enacted by July 1973, but it remained so controversial that it was discontinued by January 1977. Kalkar, the fast-breeder reactor, thus became the symbol of the anti-nuclear movement in the Netherlands (and in Germany as well). In the end 'the battle of Kalkar' was won by the anti-nuclear movement and the reactor was never put into operation. The project was cancelled in its final stage on account of tremendous costs (particularly in Germany).[2]

By the end of the 1970s the controversy over nuclear electricity production became so strong that the Dutch government tried to mitigate societal pressure by organizing a nation-wide energy debate. This unprecedented event started in June 1981 and lasted two years. A steering committee appointed by the government

---

[2] The Kalkar site was later transformed into a leisure park—Wunderland Kalkar—by a Dutch entrepreneur.

organized numerous debates and lectures all over the country, and also commissioned several research projects. Despite the good intentions, the debate was not a success. The atmosphere required for an open dialogue on energy was simply absent at the time, since a shared definition and understanding of the underlying problems was also missing. The debate was meant for the exchange of information, consultation, national hearing, research, and documentation on the future energy supply of the country. In reality, a single question—being either in support of or against nuclear power—dominated the debate. One of the conclusions of the debate was that extension of the country's nuclear power capacity was not obvious, given the preference of the majority of the population (Stuurgroep MDE 1984: 352).

However, the then incumbent government coalition of Christian-democrats and conservative liberals (CDA-VVD) ignored the apparent preference of a majority of the population, and continued to focus on extending the country's nuclear energy capacity in power generation. The government reconfirmed its earlier intention to increase the nuclear share in power generation by some 2,000 to 4,000 MW.[3] Parliament approved the governmental intentions and the electricity industry was put in charge of the effectuation of the Dutch ambitions. Then the Chernobyl accident radically changed the Dutch nuclear power horizon. The continuation of the nuclear route was interrupted and later completely stopped by the accident.

The CDA-VVD government coalition in charge at the time of Chernobyl initiated a wide and intensive review of the nuclear energy option (De Jong 1987: 278–9). All aspects of nuclear power were intensively analysed and assessed—safety aspects in particular. The assessment took several years but could not change the prospects for a nuclear route in Dutch electricity generation. According to the Minister for Economic Affairs at the time, the country would have to decide about new nuclear options within a time frame of ten to fifteen years, given the increasing global energy demand, the corresponding shortage, and the climate change problem. Environmental groups were very critical about the governmental assessment of the nuclear energy plans. They published a reaction under the title 'The Dutch nuclear file can be closed as well as the nuclear power plants'.[4] They pleaded for energy efficiency improvements, energy saving, and renewable forms of energy. Dutch electricity producers united in the SEP[5] hoped for a new future for nuclear energy, but by 1993 the government had decided to cancel the country's ambitions in that area. A year later, the government decided to close down the Dodewaard plant by 1997, to be followed by the closure of Borssele in 2003. In 1997 the Dodewaard nuclear power plant did close down, leaving Borssele as the only operational nuclear power plant.

After the 1993 decision to cancel the plans for the building of more nuclear power plants, the Dutch nuclear energy front became quiet. Energy transition for a carbon-neutral energy supply became the overall guiding concept. The idea of transition expressed the need for a complete system change in a time frame of twenty-five to fifty years (see Rotmans et al. 2000). In this context nuclear energy

---

[3] *Nota Elektriciteitsvoorziening in de jaren 1990*, Dutch Parliament, No. 18830.
[4] <www.energie.nl>, Dossier kernenergie, Energierapport 1993.
[5] Samenwerkende Electriciteitsproducenten, Cooperating Electricity Producers.

re-entered the political debate. In the 2005 Energy Report, nuclear energy was introduced as a strategy to mitigate the climate change problem. The report did not announce any investments in nuclear power but stressed the necessity of the option for future energy provision, by arguing that nuclear R&D should continue to receive public funding, and by encouraging domestic research groups to intensify international collaboration. The 2005 Energy Report presented nuclear power as a sustainable energy option and a potential answer to the climate change challenge for the first time in the twenty years after Chernobyl (Ministerie van Economische Zaken 2005).

Meanwhile, in 2000 the earlier government decision to close the Borssele nuclear plant by 2003 had successfully been challenged in a court of justice by the plant's personnel. In the absence of legal grounds to close the plant, the government first decided to extend the operation of the Borssele nuclear power plant by ten, and then by twenty years, until 2033. The decision to extend the operation resulted from the expected costs of a forced early closure, but climate change and security of supply were also used to legitimate the decision politically. It was required that the safety requirements must be excellent and must be assessed every five years.

In 2004 the Rathenau Institute for technology assessment explored the nuclear landscape in the Netherlands (Rathenau Instituut 2004). The report confirmed the unchanged societal aversion to nuclear power. Public opinion had hardly changed and was about the same as in the 1970s according to the report (see also section 9.4). In early 2006, about a month after the governmental decision to extend the lifetime of the Borssele plant, the Junior Minister[6] for the Environment suggested nuclear energy as one of the Netherlands' options to mitigate the climate change challenge, in reference to the Kyoto target. Then EPZ, one of the current owners of the Borssele nuclear power plant, applied for a new nuclear power plant at the current location in Borssele. However, the 2007–10 Dutch government coalition of CDA, PvdA, and Christen Unie postponed the decision-making regarding a new nuclear power plant.

The 2008 Energy Report (Ministerie van Economische Zaken 2008) introduced several nuclear scenarios. The first one assumes that the current situation is continued, with only one nuclear power plant operating until 2033 in combination with nuclear-produced electricity imports. In the second scenario, the Netherlands only invests in generation IV (inherently safe) nuclear power plants. Since this technology is expected to be commercially available around 2020, such a power plant could only be operational in the Netherlands after 2030. A third scenario assumes a replacement investment when the Borssele plant closes down in 2033. In the fourth and final scenario, the Borssele plant will be replaced and one or two new nuclear power plants will be built. The Energy Report concludes that, whatever future decision will be taken, somewhere around 2020 the ongoing Dutch debate in one way or another should draw conclusions to continue nuclear after 2033, when the current plant is closed.

---

[6] Since 2002, environmental policy has been part of the portfolio of a Junior Minister rather than the Minister at the Ministry for the Environment and Physical Planning.

Dutch public opinion on nuclear power continues to be mixed, diverse, and on balance critical. This is clearly reflected by a report of the national Social and Economic Council on nuclear energy (SER 2008). The Council shows disagreement on the future role of nuclear energy in the Dutch fuel mix. The positions range from pro-nuclear power at one end of the spectrum to anti-nuclear power at the other end. All parties listed their detailed perspective in the appendix of the report. The council as a whole recommended continuing nuclear research.

In particular the right-wing coalition of VVD and CDA that came into office in 2010, supported by Geert Wilders's PVV, gave a boost to the nuclear option in the Netherlands. Its positive signals about nuclear energy were echoed by the owners of the Borssele nuclear power plant who announced their willingness to invest in new nuclear capacity in the Netherlands. Two licence applications were filed. By July 2011, several months after the Fukushima nuclear disaster, the licence applications were being processed but in January 2012 the applications were withdrawn (because of the bad economic climate at the time). The right-wing government coalition continued its plan for facilitating a second nuclear reactor in the Netherlands but the Japanese disaster made the coalition announce that safety will be the dominant criterion for decision-making on the second nuclear reactor. According to the coalition, nuclear energy must continue as an option in the Netherlands to meet the increasing electricity demand until 2050.

Initiatives to develop a second nuclear reactor stopped in the course of 2012 because of the high investment risks in combination with the changing production conditions of electricity due to the increase and preferred load of electricity from renewable resources. The Fukushima disaster was hardly discussed in the context of expanding nuclear energy in the Netherlands. Fukushima initiated a debate on nuclear safety and safety standards in the EU resulting in so-called stress tests and international monitoring and control of safety. The Netherlands is committed to these international agreements. Fukushima did not reactivate the Dutch debate on nuclear energy of the 1970s and 1980s. The policy agreement of the new 2012 government coalition of VVD and PvdA did not mention nuclear energy at all.

In summary, Figure 9.1 depicts the major policy reversals of the Netherlands over the past seventy years. Until 1974, policies were directed at a stepwise extension of nuclear energy. The public and political debate that followed the 1974 Government White Paper and the ensuing plans for the Kalkar project bought this extension to a halt. In 1994, phasing out became the official policy, but it was never completely enacted as ten years later the licence of the Borssele plant was extended for several decades.

9.3 ACTORS AND JURISDICTIONS

The actor scenery in the Dutch nuclear landscape is diverse and ranges from nuclear proponents to nuclear opponents and from nuclear professionals to nuclear non-professionals. The proponent/opponent groups are inhabited by all kinds of actors. Both have their political representation in national political parties, with some clearly in favour and some clearly against nuclear energy. In between are political parties taking a more pragmatic position (see also next section).

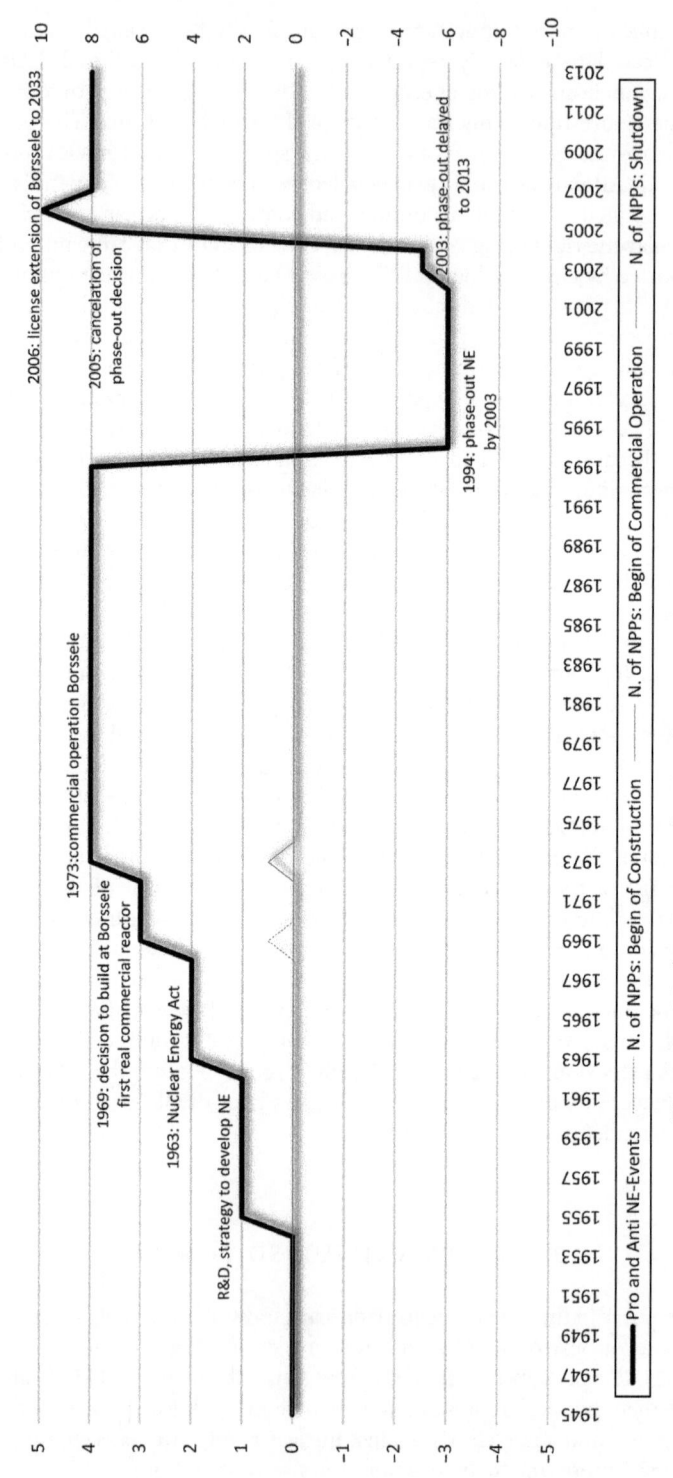

Figure 9.1. Nuclear Energy Policy Development in the Netherlands 1945–2013

Environmental groups and organizations are strong opponents of nuclear energy in the Netherlands. They always have been. The larger, longer existing, organizations all have a tradition in the anti-nuclear movement of the 1970s and 1980s. They inform the public about the hazards and risks of nuclear energy and participate in the societal energy debate of the country. When appropriate, they take and communicate strong positions against nuclear energy. The anti-nuclear movement in the Netherlands is still active, among others by running two websites with well-documented information about the history of nuclear energy and resistance in the Netherlands.[7] The protest is now concentrated and focuses in particular on the siting of the Dutch national nuclear waste organization COVRA, located near the nuclear power station in Borssele.

Industry in general and the electricity industry in particular has been part of the proponent side of nuclear energy.[8] Big industry always considered nuclear energy as a must for the sake of security of the electricity supply. In the 1970s the electricity industry, well organized and coordinated at that time, tried to develop its own nuclear capacity, but the attempt failed for several reasons (Andriesse 2000; Arentsen 2009). Decisions about new power plants are no longer taken domestically because the former public utilities have been taken over by foreign companies after the liberalization of the Dutch energy market in 2004 (Arentsen and Künneke 2003). In recent years, the investments made in the Netherlands were in coal- and gas-based power stations (ECN 2012).

Apart from the proponent/opponent distinction another line separates the actors in the nuclear landscape: professionalism.[9] The application of nuclear energy is highly professionalized in all its aspects and well institutionalized, internationally (UN, EU) and nationally. The internationally agreed technical rules and standards are implemented in Dutch law. Nuclear activities are legally based on the Nuclear Energy Law of 1963, which covers all peaceful applications of nuclear and radioactive materials and waste in the Netherlands, as well as safety and protection against ionizing radiation.

Licensing of nuclear activities as well as monitoring and control of nuclear activities is a responsibility of the national government. All nuclear and safety expertise and knowledge is concentrated in the Dutch Nuclear Inspectorate established in 2014. Previously the expertise and responsibility of the Inspectorate were shared among five different government ministries: Economic Affairs, Social Affairs and Employment, Environment Affairs, International Affairs, and Transport. Now the responsibilities are concentrated in the Ministry of Economic Affairs and the Ministry of Infrastructure and the Environment. Both ministries share the Nuclear Inspectorate as the expert organization on all aspects of nuclear including safety. Regional and local jurisdictions have no responsibility or task in nuclear energy.

Nuclear science and technology at Dutch universities and technological institutes are part of the professional arena. So is the Dutch nuclear waste organization COVRA. This company is responsible for the transport and storage of nuclear waste of all

---

[7] <http://www.laka.org> and <http://www.kernenergieinnederland.nl>.

[8] There is one uranium enrichment company located in the Netherlands, Urenco. This company uses centrifuge technology to enrich uranium.

[9] See Arentsen (1998).

categories and for research on geological storage. A final part of the professional arena of Dutch nuclear energy is the radiological safety profession, which is responsible for radiological safety on Dutch premises and the radiological workers.

9.4 POLITICAL COMPETITION OVER NUCLEAR ENERGY

In the previous sections, nuclear energy policy in the Netherlands has been summarized with hardly any reference to the role of specific political parties. The major policy reversals—in the 1970s, after Chernobyl, and in more recent years before and after Fukushima—are however direct consequences of the positions taken by political parties. In this section we therefore focus first on policy reversals of the major political parties (9.4.1). Since Dutch governments are always based on coalitions of various parties, the next section (9.4.2) discusses how the party positions have led to government policies. In section 9.4.3 the positions of voters on the issue of nuclear energy are presented, as well as voters' perceptions of party positions.

9.4.1 Party Positions on Nuclear Energy

The party system of the Netherlands is traditionally fragmented. The combination of social segmentation according to class and religious lines with an electoral system of pure proportional representation (a single, nation-wide district and an electoral threshold of only 0.67 per cent) has been conducive to the rise of fringe parties. In 2012, the 150 seats in the Second Chamber of parliament were won by eleven parliamentary parties, the largest of which (VVD) got just over one-quarter of the votes. Four years later, in 2016, another six parliamentary groups had been formed after disagreement within some of the parties. The Christian Democratic CDA (a merger of former Roman Catholic, Dutch Reformed, and Calvinist parties), the Social Democratic PvdA, and the conservative-liberal VVD have in different combinations formed the core of the government coalitions.

Until the early 1970s and the first oil crisis, these major political parties were all in favour of further developing nuclear energy in the country. The first reversals occurred in the mid-1970s in the CDA and PvdA.[10] In 1977, the CDA programme for the parliamentary election emphasized that restraint was needed in the use of nuclear energy, given the risks and uncertainties associated with the technology. Before 1977, the constituent parties of the CDA (KVP, ARP, and CHU) did not mention nuclear energy at all in their election programmes. In the 1981 and 1982 election programmes, the CDA not only wanted restraint in the use of nuclear energy in the Netherlands, but also opposed building new nuclear power plants, at least until the outcome of the nation-wide energy debate of the early 1980s was clear.

---

[10] The policy reversals discussed in this section are largely based on an analysis of the election programmes of Dutch political parties, which can be accessed at the Documentatiecentrum Nederlandse Politieke Partijen of the University of Groningen at <www.dnpp.nl>.

The CDA's increased restraint with regard to nuclear energy was however slowly given up after the conclusion of the nation-wide energy debate, and in defiance of the Chernobyl accident. The 1986 and 1989 election programmes stated that expansion of nuclear energy production 'could not be excluded'. The 1994 and 1998 programmes recommended that the expansion of nuclear energy should be investigated. The CDA election programmes of 2002, 2006, and 2010 stated that new nuclear power plants should be built in the Netherlands. Nuclear energy is regarded as a means for reducing CO_2 emissions in electricity production during the transition to using renewables, provided that the production and the storage of waste are as safe as possible. In 2012, however, nuclear energy would 'no longer be necessary in the long run'. In short, the CDA, after some hesitation about the nuclear option in the late 1970s and early 1980s, gradually evolved into a political party with a pro-nuclear programme but has taken a less outspoken stance in the most recent elections.

The social-democratic PvdA also did not mention nuclear energy in its election programmes before 1977. For the 1977 election, the PvdA programme announced bluntly that no new nuclear power plants should be built, and that the Kalkar project 'should not get a sequel'. Recall that the PvdA and other left-wing parties had opposed the Kalkar tax proposal in 1973 (see section 9.2). In the following years, the position of the PvdA became more and more anti-nuclear. From 1981 until 1989, its election programme stated that the existing nuclear plants should be closed down as soon as possible. From 1994 onwards, until the 2006 programme, 'as soon as possible' was changed into 'immediately', and no new nuclear power plants should be built. The PvdA thus shows a gradually growing aversion to nuclear energy over the 1977–2010 period. The 2006 programme stated: 'when we invest sufficiently in energy saving, renewables... and clean fossil fuels, nuclear energy is... not needed'. The 2010 and 2012 programmes underlined that nuclear energy was no long-term solution to energy shortages and that the party opposed the building of a new nuclear power plant.

Of the three traditional large parties, the conservative-liberal VVD has always been the most outspoken proponent of nuclear energy. The 1971 election programme of the VVD simply stated under the header of 'technological development' that 'nuclear energy promises to become a rich, cheap and clean source of energy'. The programme also mentions the desirability of international cooperation in the field of nuclear energy. The nuclear option as a means for making European energy less dependent on other parts of the world returns in the 1977 programme. Four years later, the VVD programme also contains nuclear energy as a potentially attractive option, although the associated problems of safety and waste need careful attention. The VVD advocates correct and balanced government communication on nuclear energy, 'so that unnecessary anxiety is taken away'. In the next years, nuclear energy was consistently regarded as a part of a diversification policy in electricity production. Until 1998, the VVD also emphasized that the existing nuclear power plants should be kept operational. From 2002 onwards, the party opted for an increase in the number of nuclear power plants. The 2010 programme states that a second nuclear plant near Borssele should be built as a replacement of coal-fired plants. In 2012 the tone has slightly changed: a new plant *may* be built, based on the latest technology.

Among the smaller and/or newer political parties in the Netherlands, the Green Left and Socialist Parties are consistently anti-nuclear. At the other end of the political spectrum, Pim Fortuyn's LPF was pro-nuclear energy in 2002, and Wilders's PVV in 2006 and 2010 simply stated that new nuclear reactors should be built. In 2012 the tone of the PVV programme has slightly changed, too: 'nuclear energy is to stay, on the condition that it is safe and responsible'.

D66, which has carried government responsibility several times since its foundation in 1966, was anti-nuclear energy especially in the 1981–2002 period. The party mentions various problems associated with nuclear power production (safety, waste), and explicitly prefers oil and natural gas to nuclear energy. Since 2006, D66 has shown a cautious policy reversal towards a more pro-nuclear position. The 2006 programme states that, with the present state of technology, new nuclear power plants do not have priority and cannot receive government subsidy, but the existing plants can play a role in the transition towards renewables. This position was echoed in the 2010 and 2012 programmes.

This brief overview of party policies on nuclear power shows that, before 1977, nuclear energy was hardly or not politicized at all. Nuclear energy was seen as a technological development that could benefit Dutch energy production in the future, rather than as the result of a policy-making process and a political decision. Only from 1977 onwards do the main political parties take explicit and different positions on nuclear energy. The CDA shows a clear, continuous movement from reluctance concerning nuclear energy towards a pro-expansion position. During the same period, the PvdA moved from the same position of reluctance towards an anti-nuclear position. Of the three major traditional parties, the VVD has always been, and still is, the most outspoken proponent of nuclear energy. Finally, D66 has evolved from an anti-nuclear position towards one that does not preclude the use of nuclear energy anymore. The Fukushima disaster has resulted in slightly more negative positions on nuclear energy than before. Party positions on nuclear power have thus always tended to follow the dominant left–right conflict dimension in Dutch politics. On its own, the issue of nuclear power plants has not been a highly salient one. Except in 1981, voters have never ranked energy-related issues among the most important problems facing the country. In contrast, environmental pollution dominated these rankings in both 1972 and 1989, and is also mentioned quite often in other years.

9.4.2 Government Coalitions and Nuclear Energy

When nuclear energy became politicized in the late 1970s, the centre-right government coalition consisted of CDA and VVD (1978–89, with a short-lived exception in 1981–2). In this period the government first organized the broad social debate on energy in 1981–3 (see section 9.2). As noted above, the government did not follow the majority in terms of public opinion at the time, and decided in favour of keeping the existing nuclear plants operational while planning for additional nuclear capacity.

In response to the 1986 Chernobyl accident, the CDA-VVD coalition initiated further research, but despite widespread distrust of nuclear power plants the government emphasized that nuclear energy was still needed for medium- or long-term energy production.

In 1989, CDA and PvdA formed a new centre-left coalition. This coalition decided that the Netherlands would give up its nuclear ambitions, and drafted a plan for the closure of the two existing nuclear plants in Dodewaard and Borssele. Then from 1994 until 2002, PvdA, VVD, and D66 constituted a coalition government. This government involved left- and right-wing parties but not the centrist Christian-democrats. In the first part of this period, the Dodewaard plant was actually closed, but the Court of Justice prevented the planned closure of Borssele.

In 2002, the CDA retook its position in the heart of the government—first in a coalition with the LPF and VVD, and after the 2003 election with the VVD and D66. The coalition agreement of the latter government mentioned that the Borssele plant would be closed by 2013—an important issue for the minor coalition partner D66. But the closing date depends also on the plans of the owner of the plant. Although official government policy maintained that 2013 would be the year of closure, informal negotiations between the owners and the ministry of Economic Affairs continue. Only in early 2006, did D66 finally agree to an extension of the Borssele plant to 2033.

The CDA-PvdA-CU (Christen Unie, an orthodox-Calvinist small political party) government that took office in 2006 agreed not to build new nuclear plants during its term of office; the Borssele plant would remain operational. The 2010 election, called after this coalition split up, brought VVD and CDA together in a new coalition, which also received parliamentary support from the anti-Islam PVV. The new coalition's policy plans aimed for less dependency on foreign countries for energy consumption, and expansion of nuclear energy production. The Fukushima disaster did not lead to a change in the official position of the Dutch government on nuclear energy.

After early elections in 2012, a VVD-PvdA coalition was formed. As mentioned earlier, its coalition agreement was silent on nuclear energy.

Thus, the main reversals in government policies neatly reflected the party composition of the government. As noted before, party positions on nuclear energy generally followed the dominant left–right conflict dimension of Dutch politics. When this conflict dimension was less prominent (as in the 1994–2002 period with PvdA-VVD cooperation), nuclear energy was an even less salient issue than it was at other times.

9.4.3 Citizens' Positions and Perceived Party Positions

Citizens' attitudes towards nuclear energy are available through surveys from 1977 onwards.[11] The main survey question on nuclear energy was introduced as follows:

---

[11] The data analysed in this section come from the Dutch Parliamentary Election Studies, 1977–2012. The data can be obtained from major data archives and from <www.dans.knaw.nl>. For more information, refer to <www.dpes.nl>.

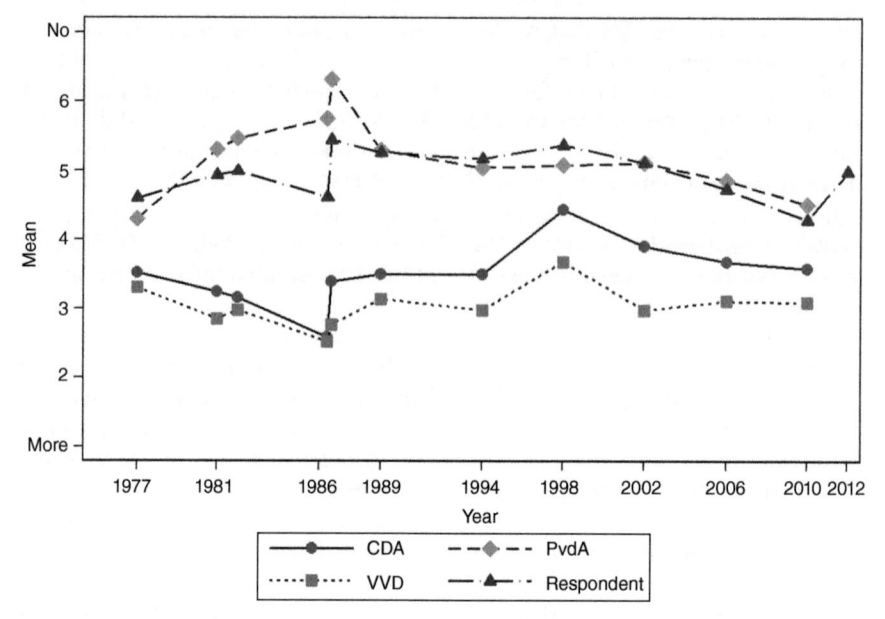

Figure 9.2. Mean Respondent Position on Nuclear Power Plants and Perceived Party Positions

Source: Dutch Parliamentary Election Studies, unweighted data.

As you may know some people fear that within the foreseeable future a shortage of energy in the world will occur. One means of fulfilling this need is to build nuclear power plants. Some people therefore believe that the Netherlands should quickly increase the number of such plants. On the other hand, others consider the dangers too great and think that no nuclear power plants should be built at all.

A show-card is then presented with a seven-point scale running from 1 'more nuclear plants' to 7 'No nuclear plants'. The respondent is asked first to place the most important political parties on this scale, and finally him/herself. The question has been asked in this format at the time of each parliamentary election from 1977 until 2010; in 2012 only self-placement on the scale was assessed.[12]

Figure 9.2 presents the mean respondent position as well as the mean perceived positions (by all respondents) of the three major political parties during the entire period: CDA, PvdA, and VVD. In 1986, the survey question was asked twice: both before and after the parliamentary election of 21 May. The Chernobyl accident first reached the news in the Netherlands on 30 April. The pre-election survey of the Dutch parliamentary election study had just been finished. Thus, Chernobyl also provided a natural experiment of the impact of a nuclear disaster on attitudes towards nuclear energy (for analyses see Visser 1994; Van der Brug 2001).

Figure 9.2 shows that the mean respondent position is not somewhere in the middle of the perceived positions of the major parties, as one might have expected. Instead, the mean respondent position is consistently skewed towards the 'no

---

[12] In 2006 and later, the introduction was shortened but the question remained essentially the same.

nuclear plants' position. The mean respondent position was for several years (1977, 1989–2002) even more anti-nuclear than the perceived position of the PvdA, the most outspoken anti-nuclear one of the major parties. The figure also shows that the respondents perceive clear differences between the three major parties. CDA and especially VVD are seen as relatively clearly more pro-nuclear than PvdA. It is noteworthy that the trends through time do not simply follow the main policy reversal discussed above. We argued that the position of the PvdA became more anti-nuclear from 1977 until 1994, and remained fiercely anti-nuclear from 1994 until 2006. In the perception of the Dutch voters, however, the PvdA moved again towards a less extreme position from 1986 onwards. In a similar contrast with the analysis of their election programmes, in the eyes of the voters CDA and VVD first moved towards more extreme pro-nuclear positions in 1977–86, only to bend towards less extreme positions from 1986 until 1998.

There is an obvious explanation for these counter-intuitive findings. How respondents position political parties on issues that do not dominate the campaign depends not only on the issues involved but also on the general perceptions of how parties compete for votes. When the major political parties are perceived to be clearly different on important policy issues, these differences are often projected onto whatever issue is presented. Reversely, when differences between parties on the major issues are relatively small, respondents tend to observe smaller differences between parties on every issue. Figure 9.2 echoes the polarization of the Dutch party system in the 1972–86 period, and the depolarization in the 1989–98 period (Aarts et al. 1999).

Finally, Figure 9.2 shows the large shift in (perceived) positions of both the major parties and the respondent immediately after the Chernobyl accident in 1986, as well as the shift in respondent positions after Fukushima in 2011 (perceived party positions are not available in 2012). Both Chernobyl and Fukushima were turning points for Dutch nuclear ambitions. The survey data show that both events also deeply affected public opinion. Even twenty years after Chernobyl the mean respondent position was still more anti-nuclear than just before the accident.

This point can be illustrated in more detail with another survey question. In 1986, respondents were asked both before and after the accident whether the (then) two operational nuclear power plants in the Netherlands should continue to be used, or should be shut down. Table 9.1 contains the result:17 per cent of the respondents changed their opinion from pro- to anti-nuclear, whereas only 4 per cent changed in the other direction.

Table 9.1. Chernobyl and Public Opinion on Operational Nuclear Power Plants. Responses to Question Item: 'Close Existing Nuclear Plants?'

		Before accident	
		No	Yes
After accident	No	47%	4%
	Yes	17%	33%
			100% (1,147)

Source: Dutch Parliamentary Election Study 1986; unweighted data.

We now turn to the positions of the voters for various parties. As already discussed, some parties—most notably the PvdA, Green Left, and its predecessors, and until 2003 also the D66—have consistently opposed the use of nuclear energy at least since 1977. The largest of these, PvdA, has gradually become a more outspoken opponent. In contrast, CDA has since 1977, until 2010, gradually become more pro-nuclear. The VVD has consistently been in favour of using and possibly expanding nuclear energy. The new populist-right parties, LPF followed by the PVV of Geert Wilders, have been outspoken proponents of expanding the nuclear option. In short, on one pole of the nuclear energy policy dimension we expect strong support for the Green Left, PvdA, and D66. On the other pole we expect strong support for VVD, and from 2002 onwards also LPF and PVV, and a growing support for CDA.

For four sample years (1977, 1989, 1998, 2012), the relevant data are presented in Figures 9.3a–d, which show how voters at various positions of the nuclear policy dimension actually voted in the parliamentary election. For the 1977 election (see Figure 9.3a), the voter's position on nuclear energy is not very strongly correlated with vote choice, but some directions are visible. Opponents of nuclear energy tend to vote more often for PvdA and D66, and also for some of the smaller parties that include the forerunners of the Green Left. VVD and CDA are more popular among the proponents of nuclear energy. However, the relationship between nuclear preference and voting behaviour is at best moderately strong.

In 1989 (Figure 9.3b) this relationship is more pronounced. Green Left, PvdA, and D66 are relatively much more popular among the opponents of nuclear energy, whereas VVD and CDA show the opposite pattern. It is noteworthy that in 1989, just as in 1977, PvdA is also quite popular among the relatively small group of staunchest supporters of nuclear energy. In 1998 (Figure 9.3c) and in 2012 (Figure 9.3d), basically the same conclusions hold. There is a moderately strong

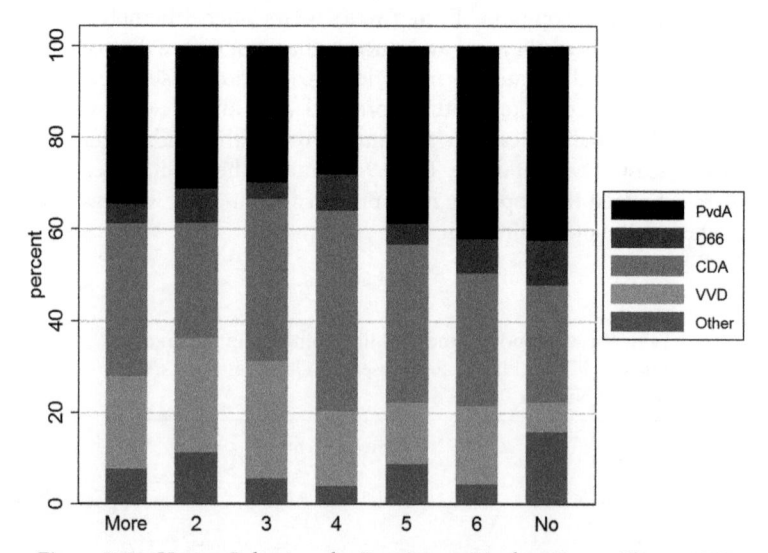

Figure 9.3a. Voting Behaviour by Position on Nuclear Power Plants, 1977

Source: Dutch Parliamentary Election Study 1977, unweighted data.

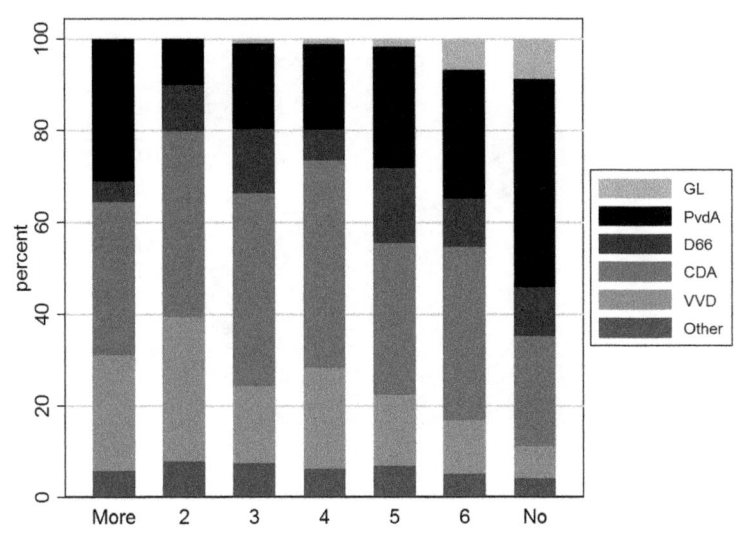

Figure 9.3b. Voting Behaviour by Position on Nuclear Power Plants, 1989
Source: Dutch Parliamentary Election Study 1989, unweighted data.

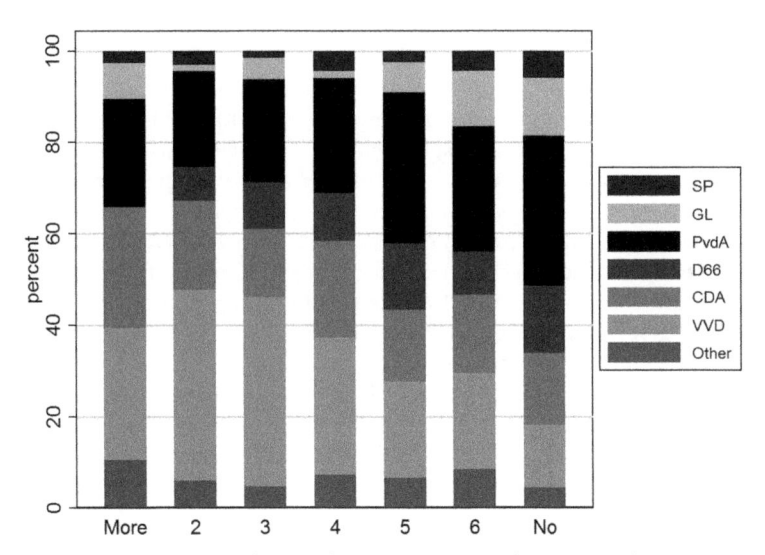

Figure 9.3c. Voting Behaviour by Position on Nuclear Power Plants, 1998
Source: Dutch Parliamentary Election Study 1998, unweighted data.

relationship between the voter's position on nuclear energy and his/her voting behaviour. But the position on nuclear energy in itself contributes only very modestly to the explanation of voting behaviour. Other political issues, especially those related to the socio-economic dimension of politics (e.g. the desired level of income differences) are much more important (Aarts et al. 1999; Van Wijnen 2001).

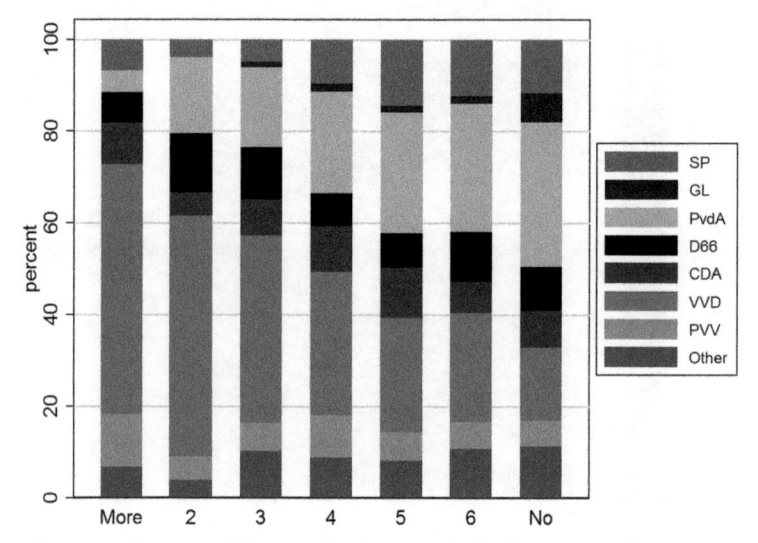

Figure 9.3d. Voting Behaviour by Position on Nuclear Power Plants, 2012
Source: Dutch Parliamentary Election Study 2012, unweighted data

Figure 9.4 provides an overview of the mean position of the voters of various parties through time. Voters of some of the parties have been considered as a single group for clarity of presentation. Green Left was founded only in 1989, but its constituent parties have retrospectively been merged. Also, the orthodox-Reformed parties have merged, and LPF and PVV (two distinct parties in 2002, respectively 2006) together form a single line in the graph.

Figure 9.4 reconfirms the pattern discussed with Figure 9.3 (where the percentages have been computed reversely). Supporters of SP, Green Left, PvdA, and D66 are the strongest opponents of nuclear energy. Supporters of the CDA, VVD, the orthodox-religious, and the populist-right parties have different positions. But does this mean that the latter voters are pro-nuclear?

Perhaps the most striking feature of Figure 9.4 is that the mean positions of voters of all parties—including the parties that clearly supported nuclear energy—are almost all of the time in the upper half of the issue dimension. This means that the voters of practically all parties are, on average, opposed to nuclear energy. The exceptions are VVD and CDA voters before Chernobyl, and VVD voters more recently. Earlier (see Figure 9.2) we have shown that the mean perceived party positions of CDA and VVD were almost all of the time in the lower half of the nuclear energy dimension (tending towards more nuclear plants), whereas the mean respondent position was in the upper half (tending towards less nuclear plants). Figure 9.4 thus reinforces the suggestion that voters of right-wing parties did not follow their party on the issue of nuclear energy, but instead remained by and large opposed to nuclear energy.

This conclusion is reinforced by a final view on survey data. Figure 9.5 shows for the main four parties CDA, PvdA, VVD, and D66 during the 1977–2010 period, the positions of the voters for those parties, and their perception of

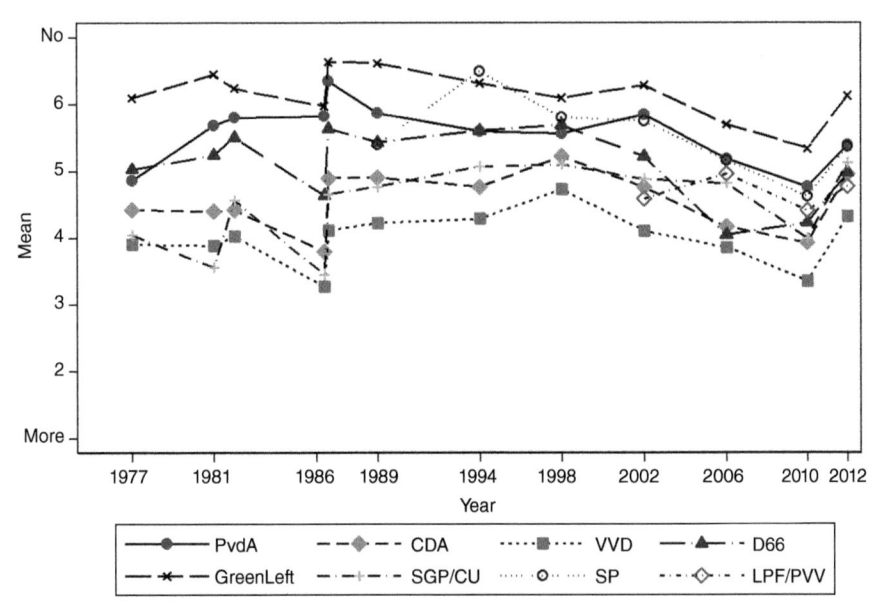

Figure 9.4. Mean Position on Nuclear Power Plants of Voters of Various Parties

Source: Dutch Parliamentary Election Studies, unweighted data

GreenLeft: or its predecessors; SGP/CU: or their predecessors

where their party stands. For all four parties, the mean voter position is more antinuclear than the perceived position of the party they voted for. For CDA and VVD this difference is relatively large, often exceeding one point on a seven-point scale. Over the years the CDA and VVD voters have approached each other somewhat on nuclear energy, but the positions of the voters and their parties do anything but coincide. Proper data after 2010 are not available; it therefore remains unclear how the differences between voter and party positions have further developed in the wake of Fukushima.

9.5 SUMMARY AND CONCLUSION

Our analysis has shown how nuclear energy was initially welcomed in Dutch politics as a new promise: as an appealing technology liberating the country from energy shortages. In the early 2000s nuclear energy assumed once more the status of a new promise: this time as means for securing energy supply in the face of climate change, and for energy independence. The Fukushima disaster has put an end to such ambitions, at least for the time being. If anything can be learned from the Dutch experience with nuclear energy, it is the political resilience of the issue.

In the years since the early 1950s, nuclear energy was barely developed as a serious option in Dutch electricity production. With only a single reactor in the

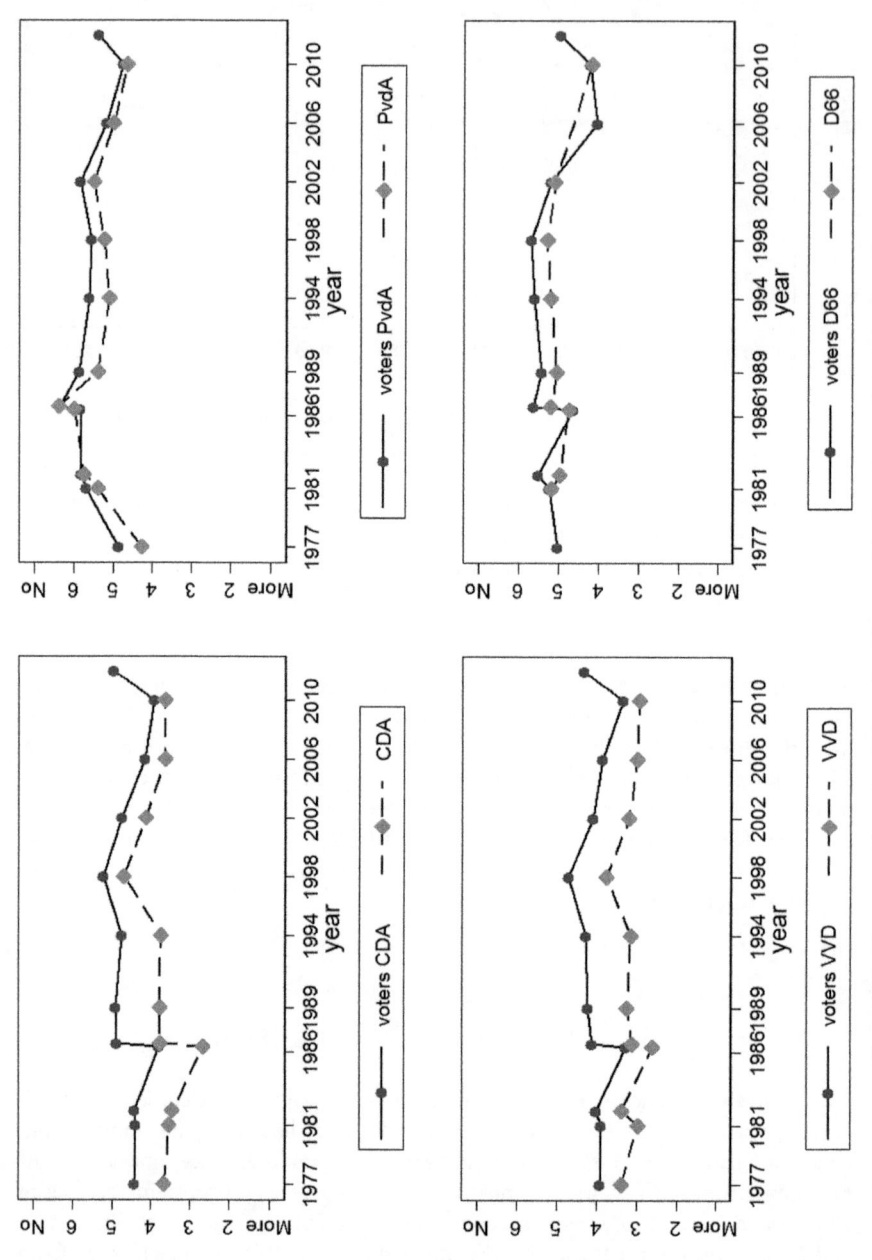

Figure 9.5. Voters and Perceived Party Positions on Nuclear Power Plants for Four Parties

country, the economic role of the technology is still marginal. Chernobyl gave the nuclear option a final blow, or so it seemed. After the accident in 1986, popular support for nuclear energy faded almost completely away and for many years blocked any nuclear ambition.

Before Chernobyl, both the government and the electricity industry were strongly decided in their nuclear ambition despite widespread aversion on the side of the population. Even the conclusions of the national energy debate could not stop the government's intention to build two new nuclear reactors in the country. Without Chernobyl (and all other circumstances equal) at least two more nuclear reactors would have been operating in the Netherlands. Chernobyl stopped these intentions but some twenty years after the accident the nuclear alternative has made a resurgence. But it was not a second start in nuclear-based power production in the Netherlands. Popular aversion has remained strong; voters for pro-nuclear parties are distinctly more anti-nuclear than their preferred party; and companies do not have any nuclear ambitions. On top of all this, the 2011 Fukushima disaster resulted in taking new positions and actual policy reversals: Political parties and voters shifted towards the anti-nuclear position, and even the filed applications for building new plants at the Borssele site were eventually withdrawn.

In the case of the Netherlands, the most important policy reversals around nuclear energy occurred in 1993, seven years after Chernobyl. It is no coincidence that the government coalition by that time was different from the one in power during the Chernobyl disaster: the anti-nuclear PvdA had replaced the pro-nuclear VVD (cf. Hypothesis 1 in Chapter 2). It is however not the case that this reversal followed a massive shift in salience or support among the general public. In the Netherlands, most people have been opposed to nuclear energy for the whole period under consideration, and despite resulting in fierce social protest nuclear energy has never been among the most important national problems in the eyes of voters (Hypotheses 2 and 3 are thus not confirmed).

The case of the Netherlands also underlines the importance of path dependency in adopting nuclear technologies. Had the country not discovered huge supplies of natural gas in the early 1960s, the urgency to invest in alternative energy sources—including nuclear energy—would have been much higher. This implies that without discovering natural gas fields, the Netherlands would probably have had a larger fleet of nuclear power plants when policy reversal was on the agenda and more inertia at work.

Finally, as this chapter demonstrates, government policies in consensus democracies with many political parties and coalition governments are relatively unresponsive to changes in the electoral fortune of these parties. In the end, there is always at least one party that continues to hold office from one coalition to the next, which provides at least some continuity in government policies. It is hard, or even impossible to imagine a new Dutch government implementing a nuclear energy policy that is radically opposed to that of the previous government—something not uncommon in many other countries.

History does not simply repeat itself: a renewed social opposition against nuclear energy identical to that in the late 1970s and early 1980s is unlikely to occur. But at the same time the nuclear issue remains controversial and politically extremely sensitive.

REFERENCES

Aarts, Kees, Stuart E. Macdonald, and George Rabinowitz (1999). 'Issues and Party Competition in the Netherlands.' *Comparative Political Studies*, 32(1): 63-99.
Andriesse, Cees D. (2000). *De Republiek der Kerngeleerden*. Bergen: Uitgeverij Beta Text.
Arentsen, Maarten J. (1998). 'The Invisible Problem and How to Deal with it: National Policy Styles in Radiation Protection Policy in the Netherlands, England and Belgium', in Marie-Louise Bemelmans-Videc, Ray C. Rist, and Evert Vedung (eds), *Carrots, Sticks and Sermons: Policy Instruments and their Evaluation*. New Brunswick, NJ: Transaction Publishers, 211-31.
Arentsen, Maarten J. (2009). 'Contested Technology: Nuclear Power in the Netherlands', in Lutz Mez, Mycle Schneider, and Steve Thomas (eds), *International Perspectives on Energy Policy and the Role of Nuclear Power*. Brentwood: Multi-science Publishing, 321-33.
Arentsen, Maarten J., and Rolf W. Künneke. (2003). 'Dilemmas of Duality: Gas Market Reform in the Netherlands', in Maarten J. Arentsen and Rolf W. Künneke (eds), *National Reforms in European Gas*. London: Elsevier, 103-33.
Brug, Wouter van der (2001). 'Perceptions, Opinions, and Party Preferences in the Face of a Real World Event: Chernobyl as a Natural Experiment in Political Psychology.' *Journal of Theoretical Politics*, 13(1): 53-80.
ECN, Energie-Nederland en Netbeheer Nederland. (2012). *Energy Trends 2012*. Amsterdam: ECN.
Jong, J. J. de (1987). 'Kernenergie', in H. G. de Maar (ed.), *Energierecht*. Alphen aan den Rijn: Samson H.D. Tjeenk Willink, 275-301.
Ministerie van Economische Zaken (2005). *Energie Report 2005*. The Hague: Ministerie van Economische Zaken.
Ministerie van Economische Zaken (2008). *Energie Report 2008*. The Hague: Ministerie van Economische Zaken.
Nota Elektriciteitsvoorziening in de jaren 1990. Dutch Parliament, No. 18830.
Rathenau Instituut (2004). *Het nucleaire landschap: Verkenning van feiten en meningen over kernenergie*. Werkdocument 94. The Hague: Rathenau Instituut.
Rotmans, Jan, René Kemp, Marjolein van Asselt, Frank Geels, Geert Verbong, and Kirsten Molendijk (2000). *Transities & transitiemanagement de casus van een emissiearme energievoorziening*. Maastricht: ICIS BV.
SER, Social and Economic Council (2008). *Kernenergie en een duurzame energievoorziening*. The Hague: Social and Economic Council.
Stuurgroep MDE (1984). *Maatschappelijke Discussie Energiebeleid: Het Eindrapport*. The Hague: Stuurgroep MDE.
Verbong, Geert, and Alexander Lagaaij (2000). 'De belofte van kernenergie', in Johan W. Schot, Harry Lintsen, and Arie Rip (eds), *Techniek in Nederland in de twintigste eeuw, deel II Delfstoffen, energie, chemie*. Zutphen: Walburg pers, 239-57.
Visser, Max (1994). 'Policy Voting, Projection and Persuasion: An Application of Balance Theory to Electoral Behavior.' *Political Psychology*, 15(4): 699-711.
Wijnen, Pieter, van (2001). *Policy Voting in Advanced Industrial Democracies: The Case of the Netherlands 1971-1998*. Enschede: University of Twente.

10

The Will of the People? Swedish Nuclear Power Policy

Sören Holmberg and Per Hedberg

10.1 INTRODUCTION

Sweden is an interesting case in the history of nuclear energy as it was politicized already in the early 1970s, and since then official nuclear policies have changed many times and rather dramatically—from a strongly pro-nuclear position, to fading out nuclear energy with a fixed end-date, to renewing the Swedish nuclear energy industry, to fading out nuclear energy. The main drivers of these policy changes were the parties' changing policy positions, Green party institutionalization, and changing government compositions.

Sweden began its nuclear energy history early, with great optimism and great ambitions (Anshelm 2010). The country not only built the largest per capita nuclear energy production capacity in the world, it also aimed to control the full cycle of nuclear energy (from uranium production to reprocessing), building up an internationally competitive industry of nuclear energy technology, and, for some time, also had the goal of producing nuclear weapons for the purpose of self-defence. Step-by-step these goals have been abandoned. As already indicated, with regard to nuclear energy this was a confrontational process with three major policy reversals. Politicization of the nuclear energy issue began in the 1970s and it continues until today, although periods of confrontation and decision-making have alternated with periods when none of the major actors actively worked for policy change.

Today, Sweden has ten operating nuclear power reactors providing more than 40 per cent of the country's electricity demand. Of all nations in the international 'nuclear energy club' only four have relied more on nuclear energy than Sweden in 2013. In absolute terms, Sweden was the fourth-largest producer of nuclear energy in Europe in 2013 and none had a larger per capita production (OECD 2014). The current minority government of Social Democrats and Greens favours the phasing out of nuclear power and its replacement by alternative energies but faces internal tensions over this issue and can rely only on weak parliamentary support. Perhaps for these reasons and the tension between long-term investments and short-term government change the current Prime Minister Stefan Löfven has referred to 'the need of a broad agreement that can last' (Reuters, 1 October 2014) and the outlook of freezing the status quo until 2018.

10.2 POLICY DEVELOPMENT

Initially, Swedish nuclear power policy[1] did not evolve very differently from the general pattern discernible in many other Western democracies. Nuclear hopes were very elevated in the 1950s and 1960s. In 1955, Sweden opted for an ambitious and supposedly 'independent' programme ('Swedish Path') that initially aimed to cover the full nuclear cycle (Kaijser 1992: 443). The goal was national independence from energy imports that had been seriously restricted in two world wars and international crises. A state-owned development company, AB Atomenergi, was started already in 1947. In 1954 the first research reactor (R1) was activated in downtown Stockholm. Four years later it was thoughtfully moved outside Stockholm. In the mid-1960s, a Swedish uranium mine was operational, but was quickly shut down in 1969 for lack of profitability. The first commercial reactor, Oskarshamn 1, was commissioned in 1966 and went operational in 1972. During these early gung-ho years for nuclear projects, Sweden also seriously discussed the possibility of building an atomic bomb of its own. Those bomb ideas were not definitely shelved until 1968, a decision that also buried the ambition to cover the full nuclear cycle including a reprocessing plant.

Before the 1970s official projections were of twenty-four reactors by 1990. Note, however, that market actors had a strategic interest in producing inflated estimates (Kåberger 2007: 228–9). Bringing nuclear expansion plans in line with reduced increases in electricity demand (and thereby helping the electricity industry to avoid energy prices decline due to overcapacity) in 1970 all five parties unanimously decided to limit the Swedish build-up of reactors to eleven. All these policy adaptations were driven by economic factors.

The politicization of the nuclear energy issue began around 1973. Responding to the first oil crisis, in 1975 parliament decided to further expand nuclear energy but to cap the maximum number of reactors to be built at thirteen. In 1977, a new law introduced tougher requirements for starting up new reactors and in 1979 parliament decided to limit the number of Swedish nuclear reactors to twelve. In 1980 a (consultative) referendum on the use of nuclear energy was held on the initiative of the Social Democrats. It was followed by a Riksdag decision to phase out nuclear power in Sweden. Yet, the phase-out was not to be immediate. It was to take place over a thirty-year period, allowing the already operational six nuclear power plants and those six under construction to be used for the full projected twenty-five-year lifetime (Kaijser 1992).

After the 1986 Chernobyl accident Sweden put extra restrictions on nuclear research and eventually decided to start the phase-out by the late 1990s (Kaijser 1992: 457). In 1997, a parliamentary majority consisting of Social Democrats, Centre Party, and Left Party enacted a law to close the oldest reactors in Barsebäck (the only nuclear site close to major cities—Lund and Copenhagen) before the set time limit. As a consequence, Barsebäck I and II were closed down (in 1999

---

[1] Most of the policy data has been collected and put together by Rebecka Åsbrink as research assistant in the project Energy Opinion in Sweden.

and 2005, respectively) with the owners being financially compensated by the state (Kåberger 2007: 231).

Already at the beginning of the 1990s public policies started to become a bit less negative towards the use of nuclear power. In 1991 the Social Democrats, the Liberals, and the Centre Party agreed to stick to the old commitment to phase out all reactors by 2010. This agreement did not mention anything about when to start the close down. Instead it was emphasized that welfare and jobs must be considered and that the phase-out process would not be commenced until renewable production of electricity has been achieved at reasonable prices. The phase-out had become less imminent.

In 2006 the Non-Socialist Alliance won the elections and formed a new government replacing the Social Democrats who had run Sweden since 1994. In that year, the Centre Party, the first party turning 'anti-nuclear' in the 1970s, had again changed its position towards nuclear energy, declaring a short-term phase-out unrealistic. The change of government meant that no reactors were to be shut down in the foreseeable future and that the restrictions on nuclear research were lifted. Furthermore, in 2009, the government decided to make it possible to build new nuclear reactors in Sweden when the old ones are worn out. It also decided that nuclear waste would be finally deposed on the sites of a nuclear power station and narrowed down the choice to two of them (Roßegger 2014). Swedish nuclear power policy had changed rather profoundly.

In 2010, ahead of the elections, the parliament—with the Red-Green opposition voting 'no'—formally determined to phase out the phase-out plan and to make it possible to construct new nuclear plants in Sweden, although not more than ten. In the fall of 2010 the new more positive nuclear power policy was solidified since the Alliance won the election and was re-elected as the governing coalition.

Another turn occurred in 2014 when the non-socialist government lost the election and was replaced by a minority cabinet of the Social Democrats and Greens. The Greens promised to close down two nuclear power stations before their scheduled decommissioning date in the 2014–18 legislative period. Yet this is to be done not by special purpose legislation (which would trigger compensation payments to nuclear energy producers) but by changing the tax structure in a way that would make nuclear energy less profitable (Swedish Reuters, 29 October 2014). In 2015, Vattenfall as well as E.ON announced that they would close down four reactors earlier than previously planned.[2]

Figure 10.1 summarizes the described policy developments in the categories used throughout the volume and also provides information about the size of Swedish nuclear energy production over time.

---

[2] In 2016, five political parties (Social Democrats and the Greens as government parties together with three non-socialist opposition parties (Centre, Christian Democrats, Conservatives)) agreed on the goals of the future Swedish energy policy. The Left Party as well as Sweden Democrats and the Liberals were not part of the deal. In the agreement, it was stated that in 2040, 100 percent of electricity production should be renewable; with the added clarification that: 'This is a goal, not a stop date forbidding nuclear power, neither a phasing out of nuclear power with a political decision'.

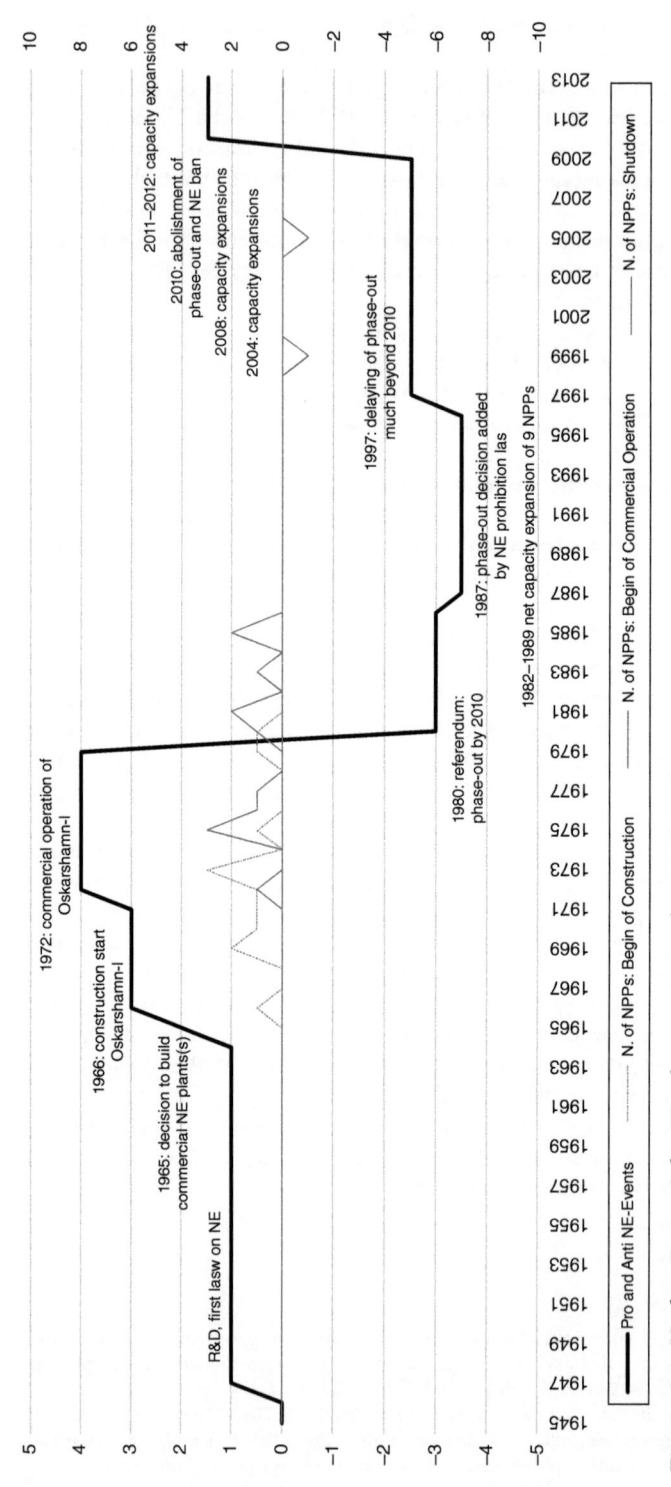

Figure 10.1. Nuclear Energy Policy Development in Sweden, 1945–2013

Note: The left-hand scale axis refers to nuclear energy events; the right-hand scale axis refers to the numbers (n) of reactors (beginnings of reactor constructions, of industrial operation, and reactor shutdowns). This depiction ends with the year 2013. After completion of this chapter there is in 2014 another policy reversal. The social democratic and green coalition government declared they would work out binding plans for phasing out nuclear energy (−2) in the foreseeable future. In the same year there was also a massive increase in the tax burden on nuclear energy, making it as energy source more expensive.

10.3 ACTORS AND JURISDICTIONS

Nuclear energy falls in the ministerial jurisdiction of the Ministry of Enterprise, Energy and Communications (previously called Ministry of Industry) since 1969 (previously it belonged to the Ministry of Finance). Yet the 'main instrument of state intervention' (Kaijser 1992: 441) in the early period of nuclear energy development in Sweden was the State Power Board (Vattenfall) that started as one of the administrative agencies through which most of the Swedish administration is run. It was the single most important actor in this emerging sector (Sahr 1985: 27-31). Effective from 1992 Vattenfall was no longer a state board but a state-owned company that later was partly privatized. Safety and environmental concerns fall under the jurisdiction of the Ministry for the Environment. Meanwhile, a network of government agencies handles nuclear energy matters, including the Swedish Energy Agency, the Energy Markets Inspectorate, and Svenska Kraftnät, responsible for the transmission system, and the Swedish Radiation Safety Authority and the Swedish Environmental Protection Agency.

Today, Swedish nuclear plants are owned by a mixture of public and private companies (Lönnroth 2009). State-owned Vattenfall has a majority owner share in the plants at Ringhals and Forsmark. The Oskarshamn plant has a group of private companies, including E.ON, as majority owners. Before it was shut down, Barsebäck had Sydkraft, a private company, as majority owner. When the phase-out of Barsebäck was decided, Vattenfall stepped in as a majority owner.

Sweden was one of the few countries that built up a domestic nuclear technology industry. The key actor in this area was ASEA. Already in the 1950s it had the ambition to become one of the world leaders in heavy electric equipment, defining nuclear energy as one of its areas of importance (Kaijser 1992: 442, 450-2). The majority of Swedish and two Finnish reactors are ASEA designed. Once the demand for nuclear equipment vanished, ASEA reoriented itself and in 2000 it sold its nuclear energy sector to Westinghouse. Today, not much is left from the Swedish nuclear energy technology industry (Lönnroth 2009).

Local municipalities always had a strong role in the process of planning and licensing nuclear power plants. Although the government has the prerogative of declaring an area to be of 'national interest' for the purpose of building nuclear energy facilities against a municipality's will it is unlikely to make use of it (Michanek and Söderholm 2009: 4093-4). As Jaspar (1990: 134) has correctly observed, the relevant decisions on the building sites had been made in the 1960s before nuclear energy became problematized.

Major policy decisions in nuclear energy policy have taken the form of laws. This prescribes a major role for government, parliament, and political parties. Since the politicization of the nuclear energy issue in the early 1970s the political parties have been the major actors. The Swedish party system is characterized by a strong left-right divide (with the Social Democrats, Left Party, and Greens on the one side and the Conservatives, Liberals, Christian Democrats, and for most part, the Centre Party on the other side). These parties have surrounded the extreme right-wing Sweden Democrats (in parliament since 2010) by a *cordon sanitaire* and excluded them from parliamentary cooperation.

Parliament is the major site for nuclear policy-making since the issue's politicization (Jasper 1990: 134). The centrality of parliament is partly due to the fact that Sweden has a strong tradition of minority cabinets (Bergman 2000). In the period that roughly comprises the time when nuclear energy became politicized, from 1970 until 2015, fifteen of the eighteen cabinets had minority status (Cabinets Palme II to Löfven). The three exceptions were the non-socialist coalitions of 1976 and 1979, headed by Prime Minister Thorbjörn Fälldin and the 2006 Alliance government headed by Fredrik Reinfeldt. This means that in order to introduce policy change, the government must find parliamentary support either within its own ideological bloc or by reaching out across the dominant left–right divide.

As already mentioned, a referendum was important in the history of Swedish nuclear energy. Invoking the referendum mechanism, however, is the prerogative of parliament and hence party-political considerations.

As everywhere, societal interests try to exercise influence on parties and lawmakers. Industrial confederations and trade unions, in particular in the energy and energy-intensive sectors, have traditionally been powerful allies of the nuclear industry (Kåberger 2007: 229).

Environmental groups were already players early in the game. In the 1950s and 1960s, they had a pro-nuclear impact on energy policy-making as their main concern was to keep the last remaining wild rivers in the north of the country free from hydroelectric power stations (Kaijser 1992: 452; Sahr 1985: 31–3). Things changed in the late 1960s. The Swedish anti-nuclear movement was an important agenda setter and societal force prior to the 1980 referendum but largely fell dormant thereafter (see Chapter 4).

10.4 POLITICAL COMPETITION OVER NUCLEAR ENERGY

10.4.1 Party Position-Taking on Nuclear Energy

As everywhere, nuclear energy was not a controversial issue in Swedish politics for a long time. The plan to build eleven nuclear reactors in Sweden had been supported by all parties in 1973. No debate, no conflict, everything calm. At the time energy policies were the topic for experts and a very limited number of politicians. Mass media were silent and the general public ignorant (Holmberg and Asp 1984; Holmberg et al. 1977; Holmberg 1978). In this atmosphere, the first Swedish reactor started operations in 1972.

The tranquillity was, however, about to change drastically. In 1973 the Centre Party (formerly the Agrarian Party) suddenly ended the unity between the parties and came out against a build-up of nuclear power in Sweden. This move had been preceded by anti-nuclear movement protest and critical reporting in the important newspaper *Dagens Nyheter* since 1971. The Centre Party's policy change had been attributed to the influence of the new party leader Thorbjörn Fälldin taking a moral stand on nuclear energy while other leaders of this party may have seen that a critical position on nuclear energy would increase the party's electoral chances with the urban electorate. The Centre Party was soon accompanied by the Left Party (previously the Communists). A politicization process started, fuelled by the international oil crises. Nuclear power became front-page news and an opinion-forming period commenced which in terms of scope and intensity is unmatched in modern Swedish history (Holmberg 1991b; Holmberg et al. 1977; Jasper 1990; Sahr 1985; Vedung 1979, 2002).

This happened while nuclear power began to generate electricity and quickly reached 20 per cent of total electricity production already in the 1970s. It reached a level of at about 45–50 per cent in the mid-1980s.

The conflict pattern that emerged between the parties was very unusual for Swedish politics. Traditionally, most political issues in Sweden are structured by the dominant left–right dimension. That did not happen for the nuclear conflict, however. The non-socialist Centre Party was joined by a socialist party, the Left Party, and by the Christian Democrats (not represented in parliament at the time) in opposing nuclear power expansion. Favouring nuclear power were the Social Democrats, the Liberals, and the Conservatives.

The initial reaction of the governing Social Democrats was to try to get the issue under control by calling for a two-year moratorium on the start of new nuclear power projects and to put in a cap of thirteen nuclear power plants (Jasper 1990: 140). Given the state of nuclear power development in Sweden this was symbolic politics as it would not have slowed down the programme as planned. At the same time a national information campaign was initiated, as the Social Democratic leaders believed that their rationalistic approach to energy policy would convince the vast majority of Swedes (Sahr 1985).

The 1976 elections ended the long period of Social Democratic government (since 1944), bringing to power a non-socialist coalition government of the Centre Party, Liberal Party, and Conservative Party under Prime Minister Fälldin, the Centre Party's chairman. While the nuclear energy issue had figured prominently in the campaign of the Centre Party, its two coalition partners had played down the issue so as not to undermine the chance to unseat the Social Democrats. Still, the issue had been prominent and the Social Democrats associated their defeat with it (Lönnroth 2009; Nohrstedt 2005).

The differences over the nuclear energy issue between the non-socialist parties became visible soon after government formation. Inexperience and the perspective that any government without its participation would be more friendly towards nuclear energy led the Centre Party to compromise and basically accept ten nuclear power plants already existing or in construction. In 1978 the coalition broke over the eleventh to be newly constructed (Flam with Jamison 1994: 185; Sahr 1985: 97–8). According to some sources, the Liberals had taken an uncompromising position in government as they recognized their chance to continue as single-party government with the tacit support of the Social Democrats (Flam with Jamison 1994: 185). A Liberal party minority cabinet was formed that worked hard to settle the nuclear energy issue by introducing a cap of twelve nuclear power plants as a final target of expansion (a compromise with the now less expansionist Social Democrats). Yet the Three Mile Island accident in the USA that was widely publicised in Sweden prevented the bill from being passed (Jasper 1990; Nohrstedt 2005; Sahr 1985).

Against the background of the accident, and in order to overcome their internal split over the nuclear power issue and to clear the agenda for the 1979 elections, the Social Democrats agreed to an old request from anti-nuclear groups to arrange a referendum on the future of nuclear power in Sweden. The Liberals and

Conservatives immediately accepted this idea. The referendum was to be held after the 1979 elections. This election brought another non-socialist majority. With the nuclear energy issue removed from the agenda by the referendum ahead, a non-socialist majority government of the Centre Party, Liberal Party, and Conservative Party could be formed again under Prime Minister Fälldin (Jasper 1990; Sahr 1985).

The referendum was held in early 1980. The choice was between three alternatives. Alternatives I and II, arguing for an expansion of nuclear power before an eventual phase-out, won by a combined share of 58 per cent of the vote. The anti-nuclear alternative (III) got 39 per cent, with 3 per cent handing in a blank vote. Alternative III specified no nuclear build-up and a fast phase-out of existing reactors within ten years.

The victory for the pro-nuclear side had a serious catch, though. On the ballot paper of Alternative I (*phase-out at end of plants' lifetime*; supported by the Conservatives) as well as on the ballot of Alternative II (*phase-out at end of plants' lifetime; important future power plants should be publicly owned*; backed by Social Democrats and Liberals) it was stated that nuclear power would be phased out in Sweden sometime in the future. Alternative III suggested *stopping construction and phase-out* the existing six operating reactors by 1990.

This made the referendum tricky to interpret. At the time Alternative I and II, most clearly Alternative I, were perceived as pro-nuclear. Yet, on the ballots there was talk of a phase-out. Sweden had a referendum where you could not vote but for phasing out nuclear power. There was no alternative arguing in favour of the Nuclear Society.[3]

As a follow-up to the referendum, the Riksdag decided that all Swedish nuclear reactors should be shut down in the year 2010 by the latest. Sweden had opted for a nuclear phase-out policy. All parties except the Conservatives accepted 2010 as the terminal year for nuclear power in Sweden.

The official phase-out policy did not, however, preclude that Sweden kept on phasing in new reactors. In the years immediately following the referendum, in 1981–5, five reactors were activated in Sweden. Then the Chernobyl accident occurred (in 1986). Due to the prevailing wind conditions, fall-out was particularly high in Sweden. Earlier that year the Social Democrats (who had returned to government in 1982) had proposed decommissioning the first reactors before the end of the 1990s. More radical proposals vanished with increasing time distance from the accident and eventually, in 1991, a parliamentary voting coalition of Social Democrats, the Centre Party, and Liberals determined that the phase-out should start by the late 1990s and be finished in 2010. The Social Democrats had hoped that a broad party consensus would permanently remove the nuclear energy issue from the agenda (Nohrstedt 2008). Yet the Left Party did not agree, neither did the Greens (a post-referendum party that had entered parliament in

---

[3] The reason behind the three alternatives was a tactical decision by the Social Democrats and the Conservatives. They did not want to be behind a joint alternative and thought it advantageous to have two 'pro-nuclear' alternatives against only one 'anti-nuclear' alternative. Two anti-nuclear parties—the Left party and the Centre Party—voted against the three alternative solutions in parliament but were outvoted by a majority composed of Social Democrats, Liberals, and Conservatives (Jasper 1990: 228).

1988). They wanted a faster phase-out, while the Conservatives considered the phase-out too quick and were against the terminal year 2010.

The three-party anti-nuclear alliance was not to last long. Already in 1997 the Liberals left. They had become sceptical of the phase-out policy and eventually joined the Conservatives and started to argue for building new reactors. Instead, the Left Party joined the anti-nuclear alliance and it was decided that the phase-out should start by shutting down Barsebäck I and II. Located just outside Malmö and close to Copenhagen, these reactors were the only ones close to major cities. Less noticed at the time was that the parliamentary decision also stated that the terminal year 2010 should be dropped. The end year for the phase-out process now was left unspecified.

In 1999 Barsebäck I was definitely closed. Sweden had concretely started to phase out nuclear power. In 2005 the process continued when Barsebäck II was also decommissioned. At the same time, a research reactor at Studsvik was shut down as well. It seemed like Sweden was really going to phase out nuclear power.

But then came the 2006 election. The four non-socialist parties, the Conservatives, Liberals, Christian Democrats, and the Centre Party, formed an Alliance and made a nuclear compromise not to shut down any nuclear plants in the upcoming four years if they won the election. It meant that the Centre Party left the nuclear phase-out issue coalition with the Social Democrats. This move occurred against the background of facing the Greens as a permanent addition to the party system and acquiring ownership over the anti-nuclear issue. Under the leadership of Maud Olofsson since 2001 the Centre Party had been moving to the centre-right, trying to combine economic soundness, showing a special concern for small and medium-sized enterprises, with concern for environmental issues. Still, neither the Centre Party nor the Christian Democrats were strong supporters of nuclear energy. Both parties continued to have large shares of issue-inconsistent voters (see Chapter 2 for this concept), meaning that the party electorates were almost evenly split between those who had a preference for abolishing nuclear energy and using it at the time of alliance formation and taking government office (Holmberg and Weibull 2008). The Centre Party now promoted nuclear energy as a kind of 'bridge technology' that would be used until sustainable solutions based on new technologies could replace it. The political communication strategy thus was not to accept nuclear energy in principle but to use it for somewhat longer without specifying the exact date of phase-out. The context of EU energy policies and the commitment to fight climate change by following a decarbonization strategy are also relevant here (Nohrstedt 2014).

The Alliance won the election and formed a new government replacing the Social Democrats. As a consequence, the phase-out policy was placed on hold and all former restrictions on nuclear research were abolished. Suddenly, only one year after the shutdown of reactor II in Barsebäck, the phase-out process did not seem as inevitable any more.

In 2009 it became evident that Swedish nuclear power policy was about to change very profoundly. After some inter-party wrangling, the governing Alliance agreed to abolish the phase-out plan. It was also agreed that it would be possible to build new reactors in Sweden when the old ones are worn out. Ironically, in the previously agreed-upon terminal phase-out year of 2010, parliament decided in agreement with the Alliance policies to abolish the phase-out plan and make it possible to construct new nuclear power plants in Sweden, however, not more than a maximum of ten (Nohrstedt 2014). The Red-Green opposition composed of the Left Party, Social Democrats, and the Greens voted against. They still supported the phase-out option.

In the election of 2010 the non-Socialist Alliance once more proved victorious, reaffirming their resolve not to phase out nuclear power in Sweden. The Red-Green pre-electoral coalition with a phase-out policy on their platform lost. The loss was especially hard for the Social Democrats who had their worst election since Sweden became a democracy in 1921 (Oscarsson and Holmberg 2013).

If in 2005 it seemed like Sweden was about to phase out nuclear power, in the aftermath of the 2010 election it seemed like Sweden would start to build new reactors if that was economically viable. At least it was a real possibility. Phasing out was out, phasing in was in. As the fixed licensing periods for nuclear power plants had been replaced by a periodic safety review (the first round in 2014–18) the door was open to make such decisions at a convenient point in time.

But then came the accident in Fukushima. Although Swedish public opinion was shaken when it happened, no policy changes were decided as a consequence of the Japanese accident. In terms of public opinion, the immediate reaction was an increase in favour of phasing-out nuclear power by some twenty percentage points (Holmberg 2011b).

The nuclear energy issue was not particular prominent in the 2014 campaign, however (Karlsson and Oscarsson 2015). The non-socialist government lost seats and eventually was replaced by a minority cabinet of the Social Democrats and Greens. Only the Greens had promised a closing down of 'several old reactors' in their manifesto while the Social Democrats had stressed seeking cross-party agreement on energy production. At the time of writing, the new government has not announced that it will try to go for another direct reversal of the Swedish nuclear energy policy. Yet the Greens aim to use the market mechanism to make nuclear energy production less attractive by removing hidden government subsidies and thereby invite nuclear energy producers to retire unprofitable nuclear power plants and make investment in a new generation of such plants too costly and risky. This strategy may work, as can be seen from Vattenfall's and E.ON's announcement in 2015 to close down four reactors ahead of previous closing plans because of 'declining profitability and increased costs' (AFP). If so, government replacement has meant another policy reversal, though this time thorough the back door.

10.4.2 Handling Nuclear Power in a Representative Democracy

But what about the people? Have they actively taken part in the nuclear ride or have they merely been amazed onlookers or maybe only passive followers? The simple normative claim that ultimately the will of the people shall rule in a democracy is obviously of great interest when we study the development of nuclear power. So the question is: have people's views affected how the nuclear energy trajectory has evolved? Yet in representative democracies the people are not supposed to be the sole sovereign. Elected politicians are intended to play an independent role as the representatives of the people.

The representative system is set up to work through an active interplay between voters/principals and representatives/agents/policies. Voter opinions should influence elected politicians and how policies are enacted, at the same time as the views of the people are affected by what representatives say and do. A dynamic interplay between voters and representatives/policies is the driving engine in the representative system.

A new research area that has emerged during the last couple of decades is focused on this interplay between different actors/levels in a democracy (Page and Shapiro 1983). The field is usually called opinion–policy research. But it might as well be called research into dynamic representation (Holmberg 2011a). The focal point is the across time relationship between the will of the people and the policies formulated by elected officials. The decisive question is who leads whom? We talk about a top-down representational system if elected representatives and policies dominate opinion formation on the mass level. People do as they are told and/or are influenced by what they see. If, on the other hand, elected politicians and enacted policies are affected by public opinion we talk about a bottom-up system. Then the will of the people rules (Holmberg and Esaiasson 1988; Brothén and Holmberg 2010).

Black and white either–or models are seductive, their simplicity makes them easy to digest and apply. Elite pull or mass push, representation from above or from below, elite- or mass-driven opinion change, are all good examples of such simplified dichotomous models. In empirical tests they all come out grey, not black or white. Representative democracy is never 100 per cent run from above or 100 per cent run from below. Elite pulls coexist with mass pushes (Stimson 2007; Holmberg 2011a; Holmberg and Hedberg 2013). Consequently, the interesting question is one of degrees. Are policy changes more often elite or mass driven? To what extent is democratic decision-making best characterized as representation from above or from below?

10.4.3 Public Opinion on Nuclear Power

The first Swedish opinion polls on the issue of nuclear power were taken at the beginning of the politicization period in the years 1973/74. They revealed large proportions of 'don't know' answers and a majority favouring expanding nuclear power in Sweden. However, already in late 1974 and early 1975 public opinion shifted drastically under the influence of an intensive debate and a majority came to support a 'no' to a nuclear build-up (Holmberg and Hedberg 2009). The antinuclear majority among voters was to prevail until after the elections of 1976, and would help unseat the Social Democratic government.

Going into the election of 1979 and the 1980 referendum public opinion turned more positive towards nuclear power, interrupted only by a short negative spike immediately after the Three Mile Island accident in the USA in the spring of 1979. In the referendum the two alternatives that at the time were perceived as pronuclear won by 58 per cent to 39 per cent for the anti-nuclear alternative. But since all alternatives talked about eventually phasing out nuclear power, the Swedish parliament decided on a long-term phase-out policy in 1980.

After the referendum, nuclear power quickly lost its number one position on the public agenda. In the lead-up to the elections of 1976 and 1979 nuclear power was singled out as the most important issue by 21 and 26 per cent of the voters. Since then, however, the comparable proportions of voters mentioning nuclear or energy issues as important has been substantially smaller—between 1 and 5 per cent in the elections in the 1982–2010 period. Nuclear power was not depoliticized on the mass level, but it became less politicized.

After the referendum and the return-to-normalcy process that followed, public opinion did not change much for a number of years. If there was a trend in those years it was a weak one favouring nuclear power. The stillness was to change dramatically with the Chernobyl accident in 1986. As in many other European countries, support for nuclear power plummeted. In the short term attitudes to nuclear power became ten to twenty percentage points more negative depending on what measure we entertain. Yet the effect was only temporary. In some measurements the upturn in anti-nuclear sentiments was still present two years after the accident. But in most surveys, the impact was gone within a year of the catastrophe.

The last years of the 1980s and especially the elections of 1991 that brought a non-socialist government to power meant a strong upsurge in pro-nuclear views in Sweden. The decidedly anti-nuclear years of the late 1970s were definitely gone.

In the following we will leave the narrative and look more closely at what results from a couple of surveys reveal about how Swedish public opinion has evolved across the forty years between the mid-1970s and the first decades of the 2000s. The data come from the Swedish National Election Studies and from the SOM Institute, both located at the University of Gothenburg.

The curves in Figures 10.2 and 10.3 show how mass attitudes to nuclear power have developed since the issue was politicized in the mid-1970s. In Figure 10.2, nuclear opinion is measured using a subjective self-classification question with three explicit response alternatives: in favour, against, or no opinion. The advantage as well as drawback of a simple self-classifying question is that it lacks any specific policy content. The advantage is that the question can be used across time even though the debate over nuclear issues might shift in focus. The drawback is equally evident. Since the question lacks specific policy content, the meaning of 'in favour' or 'against' answers could change across time.

In contrast, our other measurement series depicted in Figure 10.3 is based on a question specifying a number of concrete policy options related to the long-term use of nuclear power in Sweden. The question wording has been identical across time, although the exact formulation and number of response alternatives have changed somewhat over time. In the most recent surveys the response alternatives have been five: 'Abolish nuclear power very soon'; 'Abolish nuclear power, but not until our present reactors are worn out'; 'Use nuclear power and renew/modernize the reactors, but do not build any more reactors'; 'Use nuclear power and build additional reactors in the future'; 'No definite opinion'.

The longest time series portrayed in Figure 10.2 and based on self-classifications reveal that opposition to nuclear power was most pronounced in 1976. It also shows that anti-nuclear identifications were more common than pro-nuclear identifications up until the election of 1988. After that, beginning in 1991, Swedes have more often classified themselves as in favour of nuclear power than as against—most decidedly so in the election of 2006. The long-term trend has

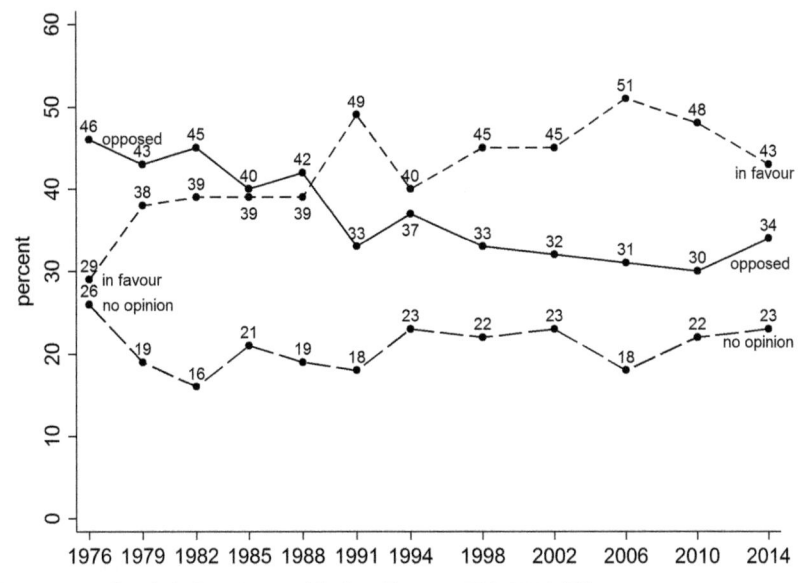

Figure 10.2. Swedish Opinion on Nuclear Power 1976–2014 (%)

Note: The figures for 1976 come from Holmberg et al. (1977). The figures in 1979–2014 come from the Swedish National Election Studies (SNES). Percentages are computed among all respondents. Question: There are different opinions on nuclear power as an energy source. What is your view? Are you mainly in favour or mainly opposed to nuclear power or don't you have any decided opinion?

been in favour of the use of nuclear power. In 1976, only 29 per cent identified themselves as 'in favour' of nuclear power. The comparable figure had risen to 51 per cent in 2006 and to 48 per cent in 2010. However, after the Fukushima accident support for nuclear power has weakened somewhat, down to 43 per cent in 2014.

Our other time series starting in 1986 and based on a more policy-specified survey question shows the same trend (Figure 10.3). Support for the long-term use of nuclear power in Sweden has gone up from 30 per cent at the time of the referendum in 1980—and from a low of 12 per cent a couple of months after the Chernobyl accident—to 51 per cent in 2009. During the same period, support for a phase-out of nuclear power diminished from 66 per cent in 1980 and a high of 75 per cent in 1986, after the Chernobyl disaster, down to 31 per cent in 2009.[4] Pre-Fukushima the relative majority of Swedes changed from being in favour of a phase-out of nuclear power up until 2001 to supporting a continued use of nuclear power from the year 2003 and up until the Fukushima meltdown. The Japanese accident once again shifted the opinion balance. Starting in the spring of 2011, Swedish opinion returned to being more in favour of phasing out nuclear power than to keeping using it.

---

[4] The fading out of the opinion effect of the Chernobyl accident is clearly visible in Figure 10.3. Support for phasing out nuclear power goes down from 75% in 1986 to 66% in 1988 and to 57% in 1990 (see Holmberg 1991a, 1991b).

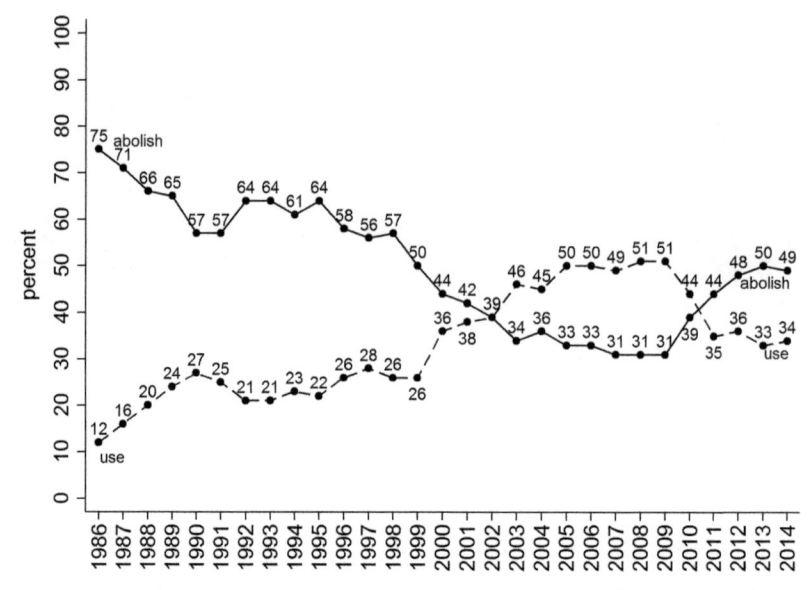

Figure 10.3. Swedes on the Use of Nuclear Power as an Energy Source (%)

Note: The SOM Institute, University of Gothenburg; annual nationwide surveys in Sweden; sample size 3,000 persons 16–85 years old; mail questionnaires with an average response rate of 60%. The survey question asks about Swedes' opinion on the use/long-term use of nuclear power as an energy source in Sweden. Response alternatives, including a 'no opinion' alternative, are phrased as fairly concrete policy proposals and have varied somewhat over the years. The number of substantial response alternatives was five up until 1996/97, but thereafter reduced to four. The words 'use nuclear power' and 'phase-out nuclear power' have all the time been used in the response phrasings, making it possible to distinguish between people in favour of using nuclear power versus people in favour of phasing-out nuclear power. Changes in question wording have occurred over the years. See Holmberg and Hedberg (2015) for further details. In 1980, support for the use-alternative was 30% and for the abolish-alternative 66% (Holmberg and Asp 1984).

Ironically, most of the pre-Fukushima opinion shift happened when Sweden finally started to phase out nuclear power in the years 1999–2005, when the two reactors at Barsebäck outside Malmö were shut down. In 1998, before the closing of reactor I at Barsebäck, 57 per cent supported the phase-out plan. Six years later in 2005, after Barsebäck II was closed down, only 33 per cent still supported the phase-out process. Neither of the shutdowns had majority support among Swedes (Holmberg and Hedberg 2009). On the contrary, at the time a majority opposed the closing of the reactors, including most followers of the Social Democratic Party—the governing party together with the Centre Party and the Left Party made the decision to shut down the reactors.

In terms of self-identification a relative majority of Swedes declared themselves in favour of nuclear power already in the early 1990s. In more concrete policy terms, however, the same relative majority did not materialize until ten years later in the early 2000s—after the phase-out process had started and people began to have second thoughts. Today, after the Fukushima accident a clear relative majority of Swedes once again identify themselves as in favour of phasing out nuclear power and want Sweden to stop using nuclear power in the long term.

How these changes came about on the level of the different party supporters is highlighted in Figures 10.4 and 10.5. Sympathizers with most parties have become

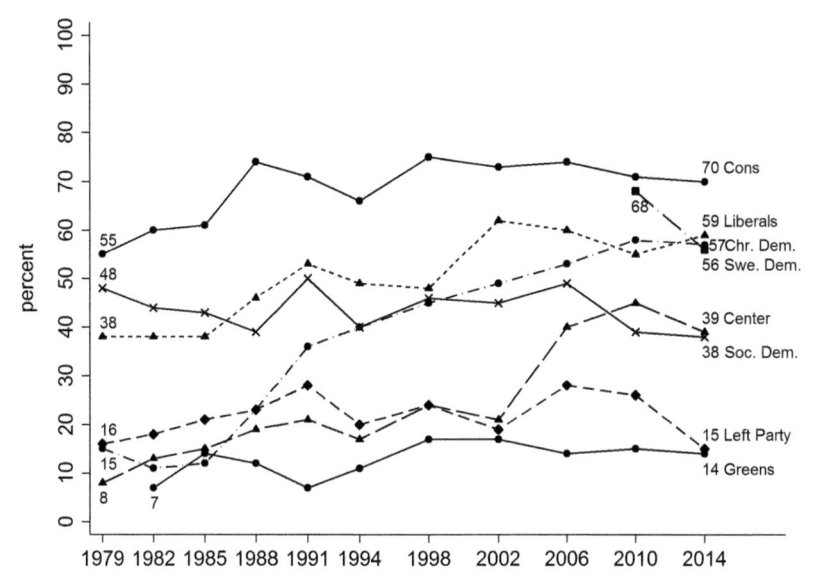

Figure 10.4. Percentage in Favour of Nuclear Power among Voters for Different Swedish Parties 1979–2014

Note: See Figure 10.3 for the question wording. The data come from SNES. The result for New Democrats in 1991 is 66% in favour. For Feminist Initiative (FI) the % in favour is 15 in 2014.

more supportive of nuclear power over the years, but clearly more so for some parties than for others.

Looking at Figure 10.4, the line-up of the parties at the time of the referendum is very evident among their voters. Supporters of the anti-nuclear parties ('Alternative 3' parties in 1980)—the Centre Party, Communists, Christian Democrats, and the Greens—are decidedly more negative to nuclear power than supporters of the more nuclear-positive parties, especially compared to followers of the Conservatives (an 'Alternative I' party in the referendum), but also in comparison to supporters of the Social Democrats and Liberals ('Alternative II' parties in 1980).

With two exceptions, the increase in support for nuclear power has occurred across all parties but at a very different pace. If we compare the situation at the elections in 1979 and 1982 with opinions in 2014, support for the nuclear option has increased most clearly among voters for the Christian Democrats (+42 percentage points) and the Centre Party (+31 points). The comparable upturn is smaller among voters for the Liberals (+21 points) and the Conservatives (+15 points). The change is considerably less visible among voters for the Red-Green parties, +7 point among Green voters, while among Left Party and Social Democratic voters support for nuclear power has decreased by –1 and –9 points, respectively.

Looking at relative majorities across time for different party voters it is interesting to note that most party groups have not shifted their majority position. More supporters of the Conservatives and the Social Democratic Party have always identified themselves as in favour of nuclear power rather than against; more so among Conservatives, however, than among Social Democrats. In a similar fashion, most followers of the Greens and the Left Party have always

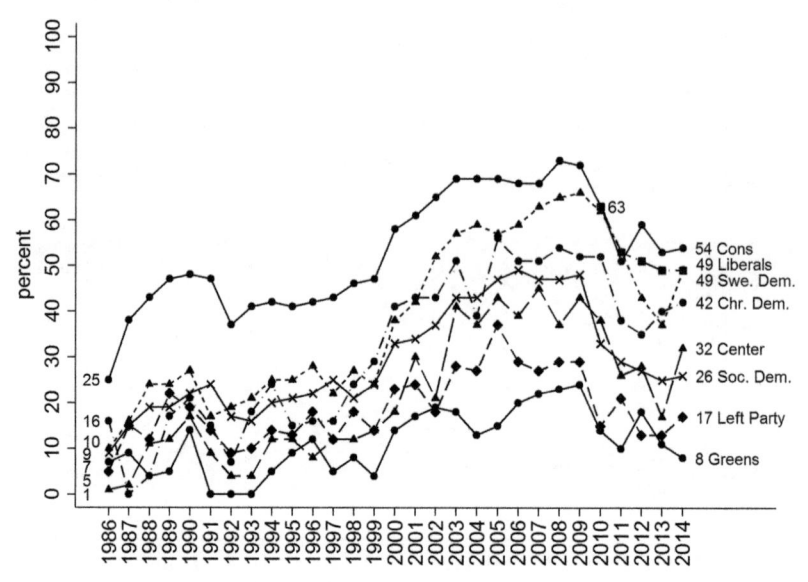

Figure 10.5. Percentage in Favour of Using Nuclear Power among Swedes with Different Party Sympathies

Note: See Figure 10.3 for the question wording. For Feminist Initiative (FI) the result in 2014 is 9% in favour of nuclear power. Among all, those in favour were 34% in 2014.

classified themselves as against nuclear power. Centre Party voters were close to switching side to be predominantly in favour of nuclear power in the election of 2006, but not quite. But in 2010 they did. And in 2014 they again switched back to be more against than in favour.

Two party groups have changed side more clearly. In 1988 most Liberal supporters began to identify themselves as being in favour of nuclear power. Previously most Liberals saw themselves as anti-nuclear. Christian Democratic voters made the same journey a few years later. Since the election of 1994 most Christian Democrats have identified their nuclear position as in favour. Before that a relative majority of Christian Democrats were describing themselves as anti-nuclear.

Now, focusing on how the more policy-based nuclear attitudes have changed among different party groups, it is apparent that most developments basically are the same as for the measurement based on the self-classification question. As is shown in Figure 10.5, support for using and not phasing out nuclear power has increased among sympathizers of all parties compared to the situation in 1986; most noticeable among Liberal (+39 points) and Centre Party supporters (+31 points).[5] The shift among Social Democrats, Christian Democrats and Conservatives sympathizers has been more modest and close to the average for the whole population

---

[5] Most of the opinion changes in favour of nuclear power among Liberal Party and Centre Party supporters have occurred in the 2000s when the policies of the two parties have become markedly more pro-nuclear. A potential top-down opinion formation process from party to followers is one possible explanation for what has happened, more clearly so for the Liberal than for the Centre Party supporters (Holmberg and Hedberg 2009).

(+22 points). Least attitude change in the direction of using nuclear power is found among supporters of the Left Party (+12) and the Greens (+1 points).

The result for the Social Democrats is worth noting especially. The change in direction of a more positive attitude to nuclear power among Social Democrats is most apparent when we talk about the phase-out policy and not at all when we look at how Social Democrats identify themselves as 'pro' or 'con' nuclear power. In terms of self-identification, Social Democrats of today are actually less pro-nuclear than in the late 1970s. However, the relative majority of Social Democratic sympathizers have all along been identifying as pro-nuclear and that has not changed. But when it comes to concrete policies present-day Social Democratic sympathizers are less in favour of a nuclear phase-out than was the case in the 1980s.

What we see is remnants of the old 'Alternative II' policy from the referendum. It proposed to first build up and use nuclear power and then slowly phase out all reactors as they got worn out. Two messages were deliberately sent. Social Democrats and 'Alternative II' were in favour of nuclear power in the short and intermediate term, but against in the long run. And that is still today the mindset of many Social Democrats—postpone the phase-out as long as possible, but eventually nuclear power has to be abolished.

Supporters of the other party behind 'Alternative II' in the referendum, the Liberals, have taken a different and more decisive route. They have abandoned not only the phase-out plan. They have also stopped identifying themselves as against nuclear power. Most of them are now wholeheartedly in favour of a nuclear future.

However, examining the results from the latest survey in 2014, it is noticeable that the phase-out plan is now—post-Fukushima—supported by relative majorities among followers of all parties, except three: the Conservatives, the Liberals, and the Sweden Democrats. Most Swedes in 2014 and most sympathizers with a majority of the parties, including the two governing ones, are in favour of phasing out nuclear power, not keeping using it.

10.4.4 Public Opinion Effects on Official Nuclear Policy

The ultimate question of whether across time there has been any relationship between Swedish nuclear power policy and what people want can be given a straightforward answer. Yes, there has been a very evident relationship. In the early 1970s, when Sweden started the nuclear build-up, most Swedes with an opinion were or became positive. Then in the late 1970s and the 1980s, in a parallel fashion, official policy as well as public opinion became more negative and in favour of phasing-out nuclear power. Later, in the 1990s, official policy was stable and still in support of a phase-out and so was public opinion. When around the millennium mass opinions on nuclear power started to decidedly turn more positive, official policy followed suit a couple of years later. In 2010, the Riksdag in concord with a majority of the people determined to abolish the phase-out plan. Sweden was to use nuclear power, not phasing it out. Then came the Fukushima catastrophe and Swedes once again turned more negative about nuclear solutions and in 2014 elected a new government bent on phasing out nuclear power.

This bird's eye view of how official nuclear policy and public opinion have travelled together gives a selective but on the whole accurate picture of the developments. Naturally, it needs to be refined and fleshed out in more detail—not least to be able to address the question whether policies have affected opinions more often than opinions have affected policies.

With the data at hand, one possibility is to systematically study the extent to which public opinion and official policy has changed in the same direction across the eleven mandate periods covered by our investigation, starting with the period 1976–9 and ending with 2010–14. When opinion and policy shift in tandem and turn more negative to nuclear power like in the years 1979–82, we classify the change as being in the same direction. If opinion or policy stays the same while the other moves, we classify the case as indecisive. Mandate periods where nuclear policy and public opinion have changed in opposite directions, one becoming more positive at the same time as the other has become more negative, are classified as changes in different directions. It happened, for example, in the years 1976–9.

Across our eleven mandate periods slightly more than half witnessed parallel changes in the same direction for official nuclear policy and public opinion (55 per cent). Policy and opinion became more positive or more negative in tandem. Only two cases (18 per cent) reveal a change pattern with a shift in different directions. In the period 1976–9 as well in 1994–8, citizens became more positive to nuclear power while official policy turned somewhat more negative. The remaining three periods show indecisive change patterns, with in all cases policy being stable while opinion moved (27 per cent). Thus, official Swedish nuclear power policy has most often changed together and in a parallel fashion with Swedish nuclear opinion across the roughly forty years between 1976 and 2014. Rarely has policy moved one way and the will of the people the other way. That is positive news for representative democracy in Sweden. The system works as intended.

If we in a similar manner inspect the change patterns between party policies and the opinions of party supporters across the eleven mandate periods we can base the conclusions on many more cases (seven parties across eleven mandate periods). And reassuringly enough, the mean outcome for seven parties over the thirty-eight-year period is much the same as when we studied the relationship between the general public and official policy. Parallel changes are more common than changes in different directions even for the relationship between party policy and the opinions of party sympathizers. Party policies and the views of party voters tend to go together much more often than the other way around, when they move in different directions. Apparently, for the nuclear power issue, Swedish representative democracy in most cases also works as intended on the party level.

So far, what the analysis has shown is that change patterns between Swedish nuclear policies and opinions more often tend to move together across time than in opposite directions. What we, however, have not said anything about is who follows whom? Or to express the question somewhat sharper: do policy changes tend to be driven by opinion and/or opinion changes? Or is it more often the other way around, that changes in public opinion tend to be driven by policy and/or policy changes?

One way to empirically address these questions is to apply time-lagged time series analysis. We study the relationship between policy or opinion change in a previous period with policy or opinion change in a later period. And we do that separately with first opinion and then policy time-lagged as 'causal' factors. It is important to emphasize that the analysis cannot in any sense prove causal relationships. What the results can indicate are degrees of *potential* effects of opinion on policy or *potential* effects of policy on opinion.

Unfortunately, the outcomes of the time-lagged analyses are not very conclusive. Most changes are of the indecisive kind, meaning, in most cases, that opinion changed while policy stayed stable. Furthermore, in the minority of cases where we could see dual time-lagged changes, it is about as common to find potential effects of opinion on policy as it is to find potential effects of policy on opinion.

Consequently, the conclusion must be that given our data we cannot determine who—opinion or policy—follows whom most frequently on the nuclear issue. We more firmly can conclude is that nuclear opinion and policy to a large extent move together in Sweden. But on the question of who leads whom, the jury is still out.

An interesting bit of evidence that can strengthen the case for potential opinion effects can be picked up from a series of Swedish studies of political representation (see Figure 10.6). Beginning in 1985, Swedish members of parliament have been asked some of the same survey questions on nuclear power as the voters. Across the last twenty-five years we can systematically follow the development of nuclear attitudes in the Riksdag as well as among the electorate.

In a dynamic fashion we can study whether the opinions of members have tended to lead the way and voters followed suit, or if the process has been the

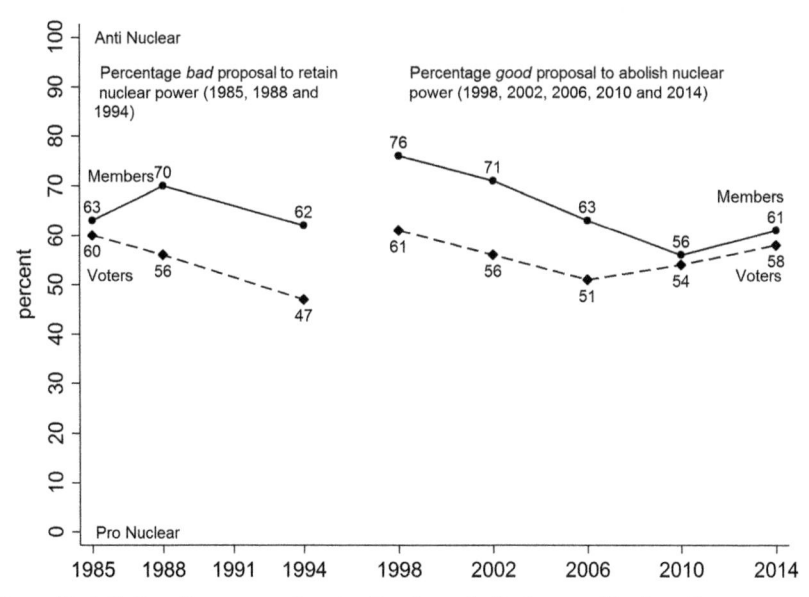

Figure 10.6. Policy Representation in Sweden—Attitudes on Nuclear Power among Members of Parliament and Eligible Voters in 1985–2014 (%)

Note: The results come from the Swedish National Election Studies 1985–1994 (Oscarsson and Holmberg 2013), SOM Sureys (Holmberg 2015), and the Swedish Riksdag Studies (Brothén and Holmberg 2010; Karlsson and Oscarsson 2015). Members stand for members of the Swedish Parliament and voters for eligible voters. Percentages have been calculated among respondents with explicit opinions, excluding don't know and middle of the road-answers ('neither good nor bad') (see Holmberg 2011).

opposite with politicians' opinions following voter opinion over time. In the first case we talk of representation from above, in the second case we have representation from below. In Sweden, most issues tend to be of the representation from above kind (Holmberg 2011a). Issue opinions are more elite-driven than mass-driven.

The nuclear issue, however, is an exception. Opinion formation on the nuclear issue has not been potentially elite-driven. Ever since our first study in 1985, members of the Swedish Riksdag have on average been more negative about the use of nuclear power than the general public. But like voters, politicians have across time become more positive to nuclear power, yet never becoming more positive—or as positive—as the electorate.[6]

The nuclear views of the politicians have followed public opinion in slowly accepting the long-term use of nuclear power and not phasing it out. Thus, since the mid-1980s we have a clear case of representation from below on the nuclear issue. Potentially, members' nuclear attitudes have been influenced by what the voters think. Mass opinions have affected elite opinions.

10.5 CONCLUSION

Sweden represents an interesting case in the history of nuclear energy because of the size of its programme and three policy reversals. The country started out early with an planned full-cycle programme and even today nuclear energy production is the world's largest per capita. The planning and early build-up were generally welcomed as modernization, promising energy security and economic growth. Sweden was able to build in a fast sequence six commercial reactors in the 1970s. These high investments and the heavy contribution of these reactors to electricity production were objective hard facts for all subsequent governments, just like the high dependence on oil imports (H9).

Up to the 1960s even environmentalists were positive about nuclear energy as a means to protect the last wild-flowing rivers from hydroelectric exploitation. Anti-nuclear protests began in the early 1970s. The Centre Party's going 'anti-nuclear' in 1973 made the issue one of party competition and it has remained one such issue until today. For a long time this issue did not follow the left–right conflict dominating Swedish party competition and has seen cross-bloc party alliances. The nuclear power issue was prominent in the 1976 elections that brought to an end the period of Social Democratic rule.

Several attempts were made to remove the nuclear energy issue from the agenda of the party system. The most consequential was the 1980 referendum. The referendum outcome granted the nuclear energy programme time to complete its build-up and use of its production capacity but required politicians to fix an end date for its eventual termination. Granting each nuclear power plant the then

---

[6] Note that after the Fukushima accident attitudes towards nuclear power have become more negative among Swedish citizens, as well as among MPs. But still, on average, MPs are more negative about nuclear power than the general public.

projected full lifetime of twenty-five years, 2010 was set as the end date for the use of nuclear energy. This was the first major policy reversal that would make Sweden a country without nuclear energy by that year.

When that date was approaching, another major policy reversal appeared on the agenda. In 2010, the parliament in a narrow vote supported the non-socialist government's proposal to lift the ban on nuclear energy and to allow building a new generation of nuclear power plants on the sites already used for that purpose.

The third major policy reversal so far is only declaration. The new government of Social Democrats and Greens that took office in 2014 agrees on the phasing out of nuclear energy, but the precise when and how are still unclear.[7] Currently it seems that making nuclear energy carry its costs and making it less profitable, and employing the market mechanisms for its termination, is the preferred strategy.

These policy reversals have been brought about by a number of mechanisms and contexts. When discussing these we refer to the hypotheses put forward in Chapter 2. The first mechanism in the causal chain is party position change. While all parties supported the nuclear industry until the early 1970s, the Centre Party turned anti-nuclear in 1973, the Left Party and later the Social Democrats followed, and eventually the Centre Party switched back to become a reluctant supporter of using nuclear energy longer than initially planned. It is remarkable that the Swedish Centre Party—contrary to the Finnish Centre Party that was the driving pro-nuclear force in the 1960s—turned to environmental issues already at the end of the 1960s. It is obvious from hindsight that it was the structure of party competition which led to the clear anti-nuclear position-taking of the Centre Party: given the upcoming anti-nuclear movements and the increasingly anti-nuclear tendencies in the public opinion, this position-taking was highly strategically informed, i.e. the will to gain governmental power (H7). Thus, the promise of Thorbjörn Fälldin to shut down the existing reactors until 1985 contributed to the victory of the Centre Party in 1976.

The Social Democrats' electoral loss was a real warning signal to other parties of this political family in Europe. It indicated that the nuclear energy issue could be a decisive one. Still, the Centre Party's efforts in 1978 not to complete the planned nuclear build-up led to a government crisis because the Liberal and the Conservative parties did not follow the Centre Party in calling for a referendum then. The discussion of a referendum was refuelled by the Harrisburg disaster.

Due to the early absorption of the environmental and nuclear energy issue in Swedish politics, the Green Party entered the parliament only in 1988. Yet for further developments the institutionalization of the Greens in the Swedish parliamentary party system is an important factor. In line with H1 and H5, the second relevant mechanism is government replacement. Both the 2010 policy reversal and the announced post-2014 reversal are directly related to change in government and the parliamentary power distribution. The third mechanism, of course, was the referendum.

At the level of individual parties we see that the two most important ones that changed their position on nuclear energy, the Centre Party and the Social

---

[7] According to the five-party agreement from 2016, all Swedish electricity production should be renewable by the year 2040.

Democrats, have the largest shares of issue-inconsistent sympathizers. This is in line with H4. Similarly, the issue positions of these parties on nuclear energy are more qualified than those of their government allies. While all parties have genuine policy preferences concerning nuclear energy, their motivations are complex, weighing in concern for other policy goals such as economic growth, energy security, and climate change. Nevertheless, we have seen that important moves on the nuclear energy issue such as the Centre Party's going 'anti-nuclear' in 1973 and its reluctant acceptance of pro-nuclear policy change in the 2000s served the party's electoral goals and prepared the re-establishment of a non-socialist bloc government in 2006. Similarly, the Social Democrats' moves and position-taking have reflected the party's concern for closing its ranks and helping its electoral goals.

In sum, in the Swedish case, the increasing issue salience is related to the turning away from nuclear energy in the 1970s and decreased issue salience was a favourable condition for the decision to extend the lifetime of nuclear power plants and to allow their renewal (H2). The Swedish trajectory also supports the relevance of nuclear power accidents—Three Mile Island, Chernobyl, and Fukushima—for policy changes in the expected direction (H10). Finally, the Sweden case also provides some support for the relevance of path dependency in terms of being invested in nuclear energy. This is evident from the long grace period given to nuclear energy in the 1970s, followed by the re-reversal under the non-socialist Alliance government, and perhaps also from the cautious moves of the current Red-Green government (H11, H12).

Swedish official nuclear power policy, party policies, and public opinion have to a remarkable extent followed each other over the last forty years since the nuclear issue was politicized in the mid-1970s. Yet, we cannot conclusively determine who led whom. What we can conclude, however, is that most changes have been parallel. Official policy shifts have in a majority of cases been done in tandem with changes in relevant party policies—mostly in concord with changes among parties in government—and also most often in the same direction as swings in the public opinion.

In the early 1970s, all parties and the majority of the Swedish people agreed with official policy. Sweden was to go nuclear. Then in the late 1970s and in the 1980s, all parties' policies as well as public opinion became decidedly more anti-nuclear, as did official policy. After a referendum, Sweden was now to phase out nuclear power (after a period of first finishing the build-up). Somewhat later, in the 1990s, official policy was still to phase out all nuclear reactors and the policy had a strong backing in public opinion as well as in the policy of the governing Social Democratic Party. When public opinion began to turn more pro-nuclear in the years around 2000 (Holmberg 1999, 2000)—ironically at the same time as Sweden started the phase-out process by closing down two reactors—with some delay, official policy as well changed and became more positive about the use of nuclear power. Most parties' nuclear policies followed suit and adjusted to a more pro-nuclear stance; noticeably not the Social Democrats, however. In 2010, a non-socialist government elected in 2006 and re-elected in 2010 decided—with support of a majority of the electorate—to phase out the phase-out plan and to open up the possibility to build new reactors in Sweden. Once more, official policy was to go nuclear. And once more, the decision was taken in accordance with the will of the people. But then Fukushima happened and Swedish opinion changed. The phase-out option bounced back to majority position and in the 2014 election a new anti-nuclear government was elected.

Together and hand in hand Swedish politicians and people walked into the Nuclear Society in the early 1970s. A nuclear build-up was decided and became the official policy of the land. Then second thoughts appeared, resulting in a referendum and a phase-out policy supported among parties and people as well as manifested in official policy. The phase-out era was to last about thirty years. In the early 2000s, however, afterthoughts followed the second thoughts. Sweden once more changed its nuclear course. Together and hand in hand the majority of the people and—this time not all politicians—but the governing non-socialist politicians determined to go back to the policies of the early 1970s and once more walk Sweden into the Nuclear Society. However, the Fukushima accident blocked that path. Sweden is now back to walking away from the Nuclear Society. The trajectory of the Swedish case is thus compatible with but does not directly support H3.

When it comes to the functioning of representative democracy, our normative conclusion must be positive. On the whole, Swedish representative democracy and nuclear power policy have worked well together. Hand in hand most of the time, parties, politicians, and the public have formed and changed policies. It may look like a fairy tale, but apparently representative democracy sometimes works as intended.

REFERENCES

Anshelm, Jonas (2010). 'Among Demons and Wizards: The Nuclear Discourse in Sweden and the Re-Enchantment of the World.' *Bulletin of Science, Technology and Society*, 30(1): 43–53.

Bergman, Torbjörn (2000). 'Sweden: When Minority Cabinets are the Rule and Majority Cabinets the Exception', in Wolfgang C. Müller and Kaare Strøm (eds), *Coalition Governments in Western Europe*. Oxford: Oxford University Press, 192–230.

Brothén, Martin, and Sören Holmberg (eds) (2010). *Folkets representanter*. Göteborg: Statsvetenskapliga institutionen.

Flam, Helena, with Andrew Jamison (1994). 'The Swedish Confrontation over Nuclear Energy: A Case of a Timid Anti-Nuclear Opposition', in Helena Flam (ed.), *States and Anti-Nuclear Movements*. Edinburgh: Edinburgh University Press, 163–200.

Holmberg, Sören (1978). 'Pressen och kärnkraften. En studie av nyhetsförmedling och debatt i 20 tidningar under 1976 års valrörelse.' *Statsvetenskaplig tidskrift*, 81(4): 211–38.

Holmberg, Sören (1991a). *Svenska folkets åsikter om kärnkraft och slutförvaring efter Tjernobyl*. Stockholm: SKN.

Holmberg, Sören (1991b). *The Impact of Party on Nuclear Power Attitudes in Sweden*. Stockholm: SKN.

Holmberg, Sören (1999). 'Kärnkraftsopinionen på tröskeln till 2000-talet', in Sören Holmberg and Lennart Weibull (eds), *Ljusnande framtid*. Gothenburg: SOM Institute, 323–36.

Holmberg, Sören (2000). 'Kärnkraften – en stridsfråga även under 2000-talet?', in Sören Holmberg and Lennart Weibull (eds), *Det nya samhället*. Gothenburg: SOM Institute, 321–8.

Holmberg, Sören (2011a). 'Dynamic Representation from Above', in Martin Rosema, Bas Denters, and Kees Aarts (eds), *How Democracy Works: Participation and Representation in Modern Societies*. Amsterdam: Amsterdam University Press.

Holmberg, Sören (2011b). 'Kärnkraftsopinionen pre-Fukushima', in Sören Holmberg and Lennart Weibull (eds), *Lycksalighetens ö*. Gothenburg: SOM Institute, 215–22.
Holmberg, Sören, and Kent Asp (1984). *Kampen om kärnkraften*. Stockholm: Publica.
Holmberg, Sören and Peter Esaiasson (1988). *De folkvalda*. Stockholm: Bonniers.
Holmberg, Sören, and Per Hedberg (2009). 'Party Influence on Nuclear Power Opinion in Sweden.' Department of Political Science, University of Gothenburg. Paper presented at a Conference on Nuclear Power Attitudes in Western Europe. Mannheim, 24–5 Apr.
Holmberg, Sören, and Per Hedberg (2013). *Public Opinion on Energy across Time and Space*. Gothenburg: Department of Political Science, University of Gothenburg.
Holmberg, Sören, and Lennart Weibull (eds) (2008). *Skilda världar*. Gothenburg: SOM Institute.
Holmberg, Sören, Jörgen Westerståhl, and Karl Branzén (1977). *Väljarna och kärnkraften*. Stockholm: Publica.
Jasper, James M. (1990). *Nuclear Politics: Energy and the State in the United States, Sweden, and France*. Princeton: Princeton University Press.
Kåberger, Tomas (2007). 'History of Nuclear Power in Sweden.' *Estudos Avançados*, 21(59): 225–42.
Kaijser, Arne (1992). 'Redirecting Power: Swedish Nuclear Power Policies in Historical Perspective.' *Annual Review of Energy and the Environment*, 17: 437–62.
Karlsson, David, and Henrik Oscarsson (2015). *The Swedish Riksdag Study 2014*. Gothenburg: Department of Political Science, University of Gothenburg.
Lönnroth, Måns (2009). 'Chernobyl Plus 22 – the Swedish Case', in Lutz Mez, Mycle Schneider, and Steve Thomas (eds), *International Perspectives on Energy Policy and the Role of Nuclear Power*. Hockley: Multi Science Publishing, 371–85.
Michanek, Gabriel, and Patrick Söderholm (2009). 'Licensing of Nuclear Power Plants: The Case of Sweden in an International Comparison.' *Energy Policy*, 37(10): 4086–97.
Nohrstedt, Daniel (2005). 'External Shocks and Policy Change: Three Mile Island and Swedish Nuclear Energy Policy.' *Journal of European Public Policy*, 12(6): 1041–59.
Nohrstedt, Daniel (2008). 'The Politics of Crisis Policymaking: Chernobyl and Swedish Nuclear Energy Policy.' *Policy Studies Journal*, 36(2): 257–78.
Nohrstedt, Daniel (2014). 'Understanding the Context of Nuclear Energy Policy Change in Sweden', in Michael Hill (ed.), *Studying Public Policy*. Bristol: Polity Press, 55–67.
OECD (2014). *Nuclear Energy Data* (NEA No. 7197). Paris: OECD.
Oscarsson, Henrik, and Sören Holmberg (2013). *Nya svenska väljare*. Stockholm: Norstedts Juridik.
Page, Benjamin I., and Robert Y. Shapiro (1983). 'Effects of Public Opinion on Policy.' *American Political Science Review*, 77(1): 175–90.
Roßegger, Ulf (2014). 'Programme Elements of Swedish Nuclear Waste Management: Implementing with What Results?' *Energetika*, 60(1): 54–68.
Sahr, Robert C. (1985). *The Politics of Energy Policy Change in Sweden*. Ann Arbor: University of Michigan Press.
Stimson, James (2007). 'Perspective on Representation: Asking the Right Questions and Getting the Right Answers', in Russel J. Dalton and Hans-Dieter Klingemann (eds), *Oxford Handbook of Political Behavior*. Oxford: Oxford University Press, 850–62.
Vedung, Evert (1979). *Kärnkraften och regeringen Fälldins fall*. Stockholm: Rabén & Sjögren.
Vedung, Evert (2002). *The Politics of Swedish Energy Policies*. Uppsala: Department of Government.

11

Switzerland

Hanspeter Kriesi

11.1 INTRODUCTION

Switzerland has five nuclear power plants (NPPs) today, producing 37.4 per cent of its electricity (2009). The first NPP (Beznau I) was put into service in 1969, Beznau II and Mühleberg followed in 1972, Gösgen in 1978, and Leibstadt in 1984. The first three NPPs were constructed without any resistance; an anti-nuclear opposition did not yet exist. In fact, in the 1960s, environmentally conscious experts and all parties explicitly supported the peaceful use of nuclear energy, since it seemed to be more respectful towards the environment than the use of fossil fuels or of hydroelectric power. With these NPPs, Switzerland belongs to the countries with the highest per capita production of nuclear energy in Western Europe. In Switzerland, resistance against nuclear power only took shape in the early 1970s, as a reaction to the licence authorizing the construction of a sixth nuclear power plant (NPP) in Kaiseraugst (close to the city of Basel) in 1969. In the early 1970s, two additional NPPs were planned in Verbois (Canton of Geneva) and Graben (in the Canton of Berne). None of these three NPPs was ever built. It was only in 2007 that the Swiss federal government announced a replacement of existing units. In 2008, the electricity industry submitted requests for the authorization of three new NPPs to the federal authorities. For the details of the development of the amount of MW planned, under construction, and produced in Switzerland, we refer the reader to Chapter 3.

Once the implementation of the Swiss nuclear power policy had gotten under way, its further development has been punctuated by four critical junctures, each of which was preceded by a set of focusing (or contingent, precipitating) events. The occupation of the construction site of the planned NPP in Kaiseraugst by the anti-nuclear movement in 1975 constitutes the first critical moment. This event marked the starting point of the escalation of confrontation between the pro- and anti-nuclear forces. The opposition to Kaiseraugst had been building since the project received the general authorization licence, but the focusing event that created the signal for the occupation came when excavation works for the foundation of the project started. Subsequently, the escalating confrontation between the two camps in the nuclear policy domain led to the increasing importance of the direct-democratic arena for the decision-making in this domain. The challengers of the nuclear power programme made effective use of the direct-democratic instruments at the federal and at the cantonal level, which are readily available for challengers in Swiss politics, and eventually succeeded in blocking this programme at least temporarily by means of their popular initiatives (Giugni and Passy 1997; Giugni 2004). Their eventual breakthrough came in 1989/1990, when the Kaiseraugst project was abandoned and a set of energy policy decisions were taken, which introduced, among other things, a ten-year moratorium on the construction of new NPPs.

This partial success of the movement constitutes the second critical moment, which took advantage largely from another focusing event, the Chernobyl disaster in 1986. This catastrophe not only served to revitalize the Swiss anti-nuclear movement, but also strengthened its allies in the parliamentary arena and weakened the pro-nuclear forces. But since the freeze on nuclear expansion settlement was only temporary, nuclear power came back on the agenda of federal politics in the early 2000s. Prompted by the end of the ten-year moratorium, the issue of nuclear power was reopened and the third determining moment came in 2003, when two new initiatives of the anti-nuclear coalition were defeated in a popular vote, and a new Federal Nuclear Energy act was adopted by Parliament, which opened the door for the replacement of the five ageing NPPs by another generation of NPPs. Figure 11.1 presents the general outline of the Swiss nuclear energy policy scale, which is clearly punctuated by the two federal votes on the freeze on nuclear expansion/pulling out of nuclear energy. The final critical juncture, the catastrophe at Fukushima in Japan, again had far-reaching consequences for Swiss nuclear energy policy. It led to the adoption of a plan to phase out nuclear energy in Switzerland by Parliament.

The importance of the direct-democratic arena for the Swiss energy policy in general is documented by the fact that, from the late 1970s through early 2015, the Swiss have been called upon to vote on energy policy at the federal level no less than thirteen times, with at least eight votes on nuclear power. This corresponds to roughly 4 per cent of the votes at the federal level during this period. A similar number of votes took place on agricultural, tax or labour market, pension, or transportation issues. Only on health (24), immigration (21) and institutional (19) issues were there clearly more votes. To these federal votes, one should add many cantonal and municipal votes dealing with energy policy in general, and nuclear power in particular (consultative votes on the construction of NPPs, the construction of waste disposal sites, and the question of political support for nuclear power more generally). Compared to other policy domains, energy policy is highly contested and gives rise to very intense direct-democratic campaigns. On average, energy policy campaigns have been more than twice as intense as the average campaign and only foreign policy in general and Swiss relations to the EU in particular are even more intense.[1]

To understand the Swiss case, it is also very important to take into account the federal structure of the state and the close relationship between the electricity industry and the cantons—the regional member states of the Swiss Confederation,

---

[1] This can be shown by comparing the campaign intensity of all the votes that have been taking place at the federal level between 1981 and 2008 (own calculations based on own data, available from the author).

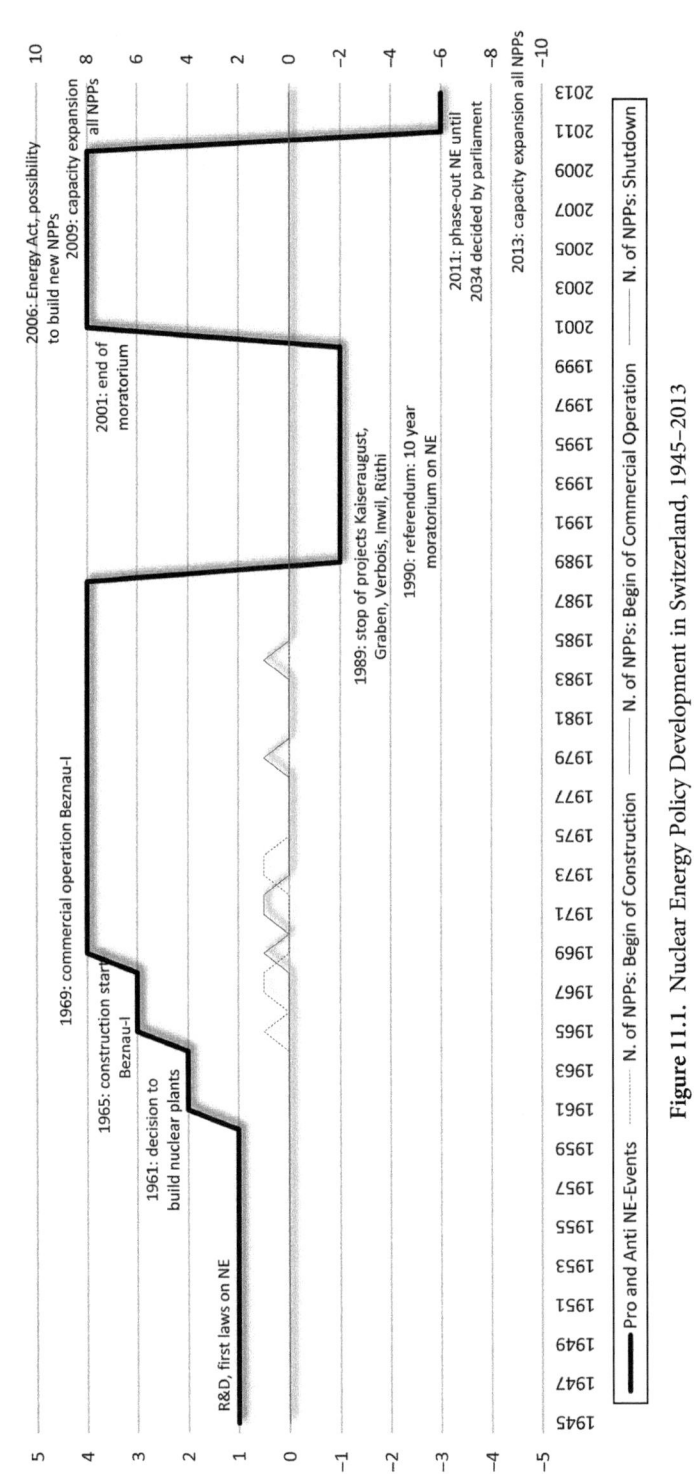

Figure 11.1. Nuclear Energy Policy Development in Switzerland, 1945–2013

which play a key role in energy policy. With the exception of nuclear energy policy, which falls under the regulatory competence of the federal government, energy policy falls under the jurisdiction of the cantons that are also heavily engaged in the electricity industry, because they partially own most of the electrical power plants in the country. The Federal Office for Energy was responsible for the regulation of nuclear energy in Switzerland until 2009, when a new, independent regulatory agency, the Federal Nuclear Safety Inspectorate (ENSI), was created. This new institution is charged with the supervision of the Swiss nuclear power plants, of the temporary stocks of nuclear wastes in the country, and of the Swiss nuclear research institutes. There is no nuclear industry proper in Switzerland. As is pointed out by Yamasaki (2007: 136), Switzerland did not benefit from the catalysing effect of a research and development programme on NPPs, as was the case in France or in the UK. Rather, in line with the hypothesis of Midttun and Rucht (1994: 393), the close relationship between the electricity industry and the cantonal states originally facilitated the implementation of an ambitious nuclear power programme. In addition, this programme benefited from strong support by the centre-right parties who occupy a dominant position at every level of the Swiss polity. It was only when a forceful anti-nuclear movement made its unexpected entry onto the regional, and then onto the national political scene that this ambitious programme was called into question, and temporarily stopped.

In this chapter, I shall first present the development of the Swiss nuclear energy policy in some more detail. Next, I shall introduce the key actors and coalitions who have shaped this policy, before I turn to a discussion of the political competition over nuclear energy, where I shall put a heavy accent on public opinion and the attitude of the voters to nuclear energy policy. As we shall see, up to the catastrophe in Japan in spring 2011, the future of nuclear energy in Switzerland looked more promising than it did before, but these promises were probably based on some illusions linked to the outcome of the decisive popular votes in 2003. In the context of this chapter, it will, of course, not be possible to do justice to the exceptionally rich details of the issues involved. Rather, the chapter will outline in very broad strokes the various aspects of this very important policy domain, which has heavily occupied Swiss politics ever since the late 1960s.

11.2 POLICY DEVELOPMENT

The regulatory framework of Swiss nuclear energy policy goes back to 1946, when the Federal Parliament adopted the first federal act for the promotion of nuclear energy. In 1957, the constitutional basis for the federal legislation in nuclear energy policy—Article 24 of the Federal Constitution—was adopted in a popular vote, which attributed the competence for nuclear energy to the federal state (see Table 11.1). Based on this article, the law on nuclear power was rapidly elaborated and adopted by Parliament two years later, in 1959. The law was shaped by the interests of the nuclear energy lobby. Thus, the development of nuclear power was left to (semi-)private corporations. For the construction of NPPs, these corporations had to obtain a federal licence, but the federal authorities were expected to

Table 11.1. Energy Policy Milestones in Switzerland

Major proposals/popular votes	Year of initiation/ adoption by Parliament	Popular votes	Date of vote	Share of yes votes	Cantons with yes majority
Constitutional article on nuclear energy	-	comp ref	24 Nov. 1957	77.3%	22
Law on nuclear energy	1959	-	-	-	-
Authorization licence for Kaiseraugst	1969	-	-	-	-
First initiative of anti-nuclear movement	1975	initiative	18 Feb. 1979	48.8%	10
Nuclear energy act ('counter-proposal')	1978	option ref	20 May 1979	68.9%	-
Constitutional article on energy	1981	comp ref	27 Feb. 1983	50.9%	11
'Atomic' initiative	1980	initiative	23 Sept. 1984	45.0%	6
'Energy' initiative	1980	initiative	23 Sept. 1984	45.8%	6
Agreement on NPP Kaiseraugst	1989	-	-	-	-
Constitutional article on energy	1987	comp ref	23 Sept. 1990	71.1%	23
Decree on the utilization of energy	1990	-	-	-	-
'Stop' initiative	1987	initiative	23 Sept. 1990	47.1%	7
'Moratorium' initiative	1986	initiative	23 Sept. 1990	54.6%	19.5
'Solar' initiative	1995	initiative	24 Sept. 2000	31.9%	0
Counter-project 1: promotional tax	1995	comp ref	24 Sept. 2000	46.6%	4.5
Counter project 2: ecological tax	1995	comp ref	24 Sept. 2000	44.6%	2.5
Law on energy	1998	-	-	-	-
Law on liberalization of electricity market	1999	option ref	22 Sept. 2002	47.4%	-
'Stop' initiative II	1998	initiative	18 May 2003	33.7%	0.5
'MoratoriumPlus' initiative	1998	initiative	18 May 2003	41.6%	1
Law on nuclear energy	2003	-	-	-	-
Law on nuclear power liability	2008	international ratification	2011?	-	-
Request for three new NPPs by electricity industry	2008	-	-	-	-
Phase-out of nuclear energy until 2034 decided by Parliament	2011	-	-	-	-
'Phasing out' initiative submitted by Green party	2012	initiative	Popular vote pending	-	-
Government presents proposal for new energy policy 'Energy strategy 2050'	2012	-	-	-	-
'Energy tax instead of VAT' initiative by Green liberal party	2012	initiative	8 Mar. 2015	24.6%	0
Parliament adopts first set of measures of new energy strategy (including phasing out of NPPs)	2016	-	referendum vote pending	-	-

accord such a licence without further ado, once the relevant criteria were fulfilled. Moreover, the liability for future NPPs was limited to 40 Mio SFr., for greater damages, the law envisaged coverage by federal funds. At the time, the left criticized these aspects of the law, which, from its point of view, tended to privatize future benefits, and to socialize future losses (Kriesi 1982: 13–16).

However, the left was not yet fundamentally opposed to the development of nuclear power.

Based on this regulatory framework, an ambitious nuclear power programme took shape, which only ran into difficulties at the end of the 1960s. The resistance started in the regions of Basel and Geneva, where NPPs were planned at Kaiseraugst (AG) and Verbois (GE). In both cases, the proximity of NPPs to be built or under construction in the neighbouring countries (Wyhl and Schwörstadt in Germany, Fessenheim in France in the case of Kaiseraugst, Creys-Malville in France in the case of Verbois) contributed to the sensibility of the regional populations to the dangers of NPPs and to the rise of powerful anti-nuclear mobilizations. Opposition also emerged in the regions of Gösgen and Leibstadt, where NPPs were already under construction, as well as in the region of Graben, where yet another NPP was to be built. The mobilization proved to be most forceful in the region around Basel, however, where it took on the character of a broad popular movement, which, as already pointed out, culminated in the occupation of the construction site of the future NPP in Kaiseraugst on 1 April 1975, the day when excavation works for the foundations of the future plant began. The occupation lasted eleven weeks. When it finally ended thanks to successful negotiations between the occupants and the Swiss federal government, the context for the Swiss nuclear energy policy had fundamentally changed.

With the occupation of Kaiseraugst, the anti-nuclear movement lost its regional character and constituted itself as a national actor. At the same time, however, the movement split into a moderate and a radical wing (Schroeren 1977: 126–34), which both proceeded to launch their own anti-nuclear challenges at the national level. The moderates were the first to make use of the direct-democratic instruments and launched their first popular initiative a few days before the end of the occupation. It envisaged a democratization of the licensing procedures, to be newly designed in such a way that no future NPP could have been constructed in Switzerland, although the text of the initiative did not explicitly oppose the construction of NPPs. Before the vote on this federal initiative took place in early 1979, the anti-nuclear movement achieved a first success due to the acceptance of its first cantonal initiative by a two-thirds majority in the Canton of Basel City in 1977. This was also the year of the first peak of the movement's mobilization in Switzerland (see Figure 11.2). After a very intense campaign, the initiative of the movement at the federal level was eventually rejected by a very close margin of 51 to 49 per cent in February 1979, although large majorities of voters supported the initiative in the regions with future NPP sites (Kriesi 1982: 33–44).

A federal act, of limited duration and adopted in 1978 as an informal counterproposal to the first federal initiative of the anti-nuclear movement, amended the existing law with the introduction of a detailed procedure for authorizing the construction of future NPPs. In the future, this procedure was to consist of two main components: the 'general authorization license' (*Rahmenbewilligung*) and the 'supply of evidence for the demand' (*Bedarfsnachweis*). Most importantly, the amended law proposed a democratization of the licensing procedure by subjecting the issuance of a licence for the construction of a new NPP to the optional referendum. This meant that the voters would, without any doubt, be called upon to vote on any new NPP by the opponents of nuclear power. This

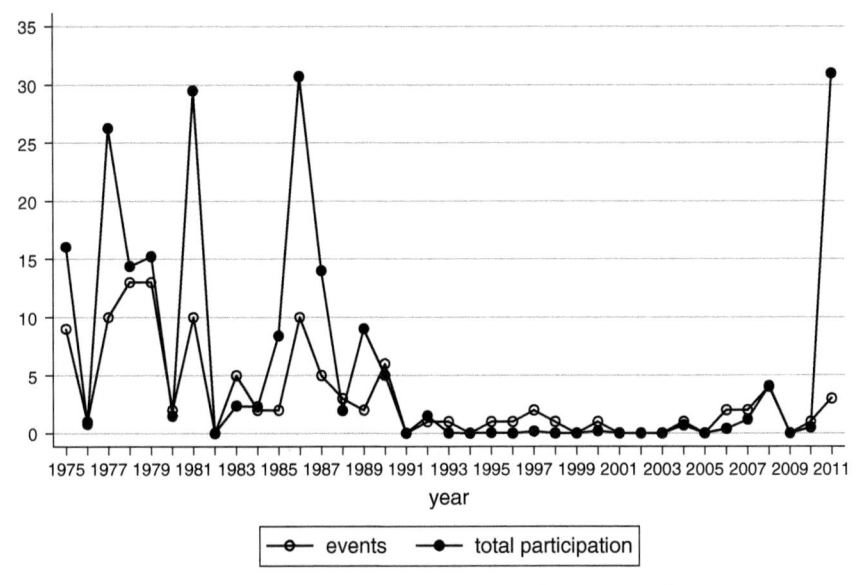

Figure 11.2. Development of the Mobilization by the Anti-Nuclear Movement in Switzerland

Events: number of protest events organized by the anti-nuclear movement per year; total participation: total number of participants (in thousands) in these events per year.

Source: PEA-dataset, see Hutter and Giugni (2009) and Chapter 4.

federal act was itself submitted to a popular vote, because the radical wing of the anti-nuclear movement, for which the act did not go far enough and which wanted to submit the NPP projects to the compulsory referendum, had successfully launched a referendum against it. Only a few days before the Three Mile Island (TMI) accident, the act was accepted by a two-thirds majority of the voters in May 1979.

In spite of this result, and although the movement's initiative had not passed, the close outcome of the vote on the initiative in February 1979 caused a rupture in the pre-existing equilibrium in Swiss energy policy, which did not allow for rapid re-equilibration. As a result of the proven clout of the anti-nuclear movement, Swiss energy policy has been at an impasse for an extended period of time, given the intransigence of the opposing coalitions (Rieder 1998: 220). Until the early 2000s, both the pro-nuclear coalition and the anti-nuclear coalition held veto positions. Their vetoes were based on their documented, mutual strength in direct-democratic votes, which allowed both of them to have recourse to a popular vote, if they were not able to impose themselves in the parliamentary or administrative arenas. In 1980, the moderate wing of the anti-nuclear movement made a second attempt to initiate the stepwise reduction of nuclear energy, by launching another two initiatives (see Table 11.1): their 'atom initiative' proposed 'a future without new nuclear power plants', whereas their 'energy initiative' proposed 'a safe, economically sound and environmentally friendly energy supply', i.e. the replacement of nuclear energy by power-saving measures and the promotion of renewable energy. The movement's radical wing had also launched its own initiative 'for the interruption of the exploitation programme of nuclear energy', which called for the stopping of the construction of the fifth NPP in Leibstadt, and for the progressive shutdown of all existing NPPs. The radicals failed to attain the required quorum of 100,000 signatures for their initiative. The two initiatives of the moderates, in turn, were rejected in a popular vote in 1984, although both were supported by a sizeable minority of roughly 45 per cent of the voters.

In the early 1980s, not only did the anti-nuclear movement fail to achieve its goal of shutting down the nuclear power plants, but the government's energy policy also proved to be at an impasse. Parallel to the emerging confrontation on nuclear energy, the broader Swiss energy policy debate had intensified as a reaction to the oil crisis of the early 1970s. A federal commission (GEK) had been instituted in 1974, whose task it was to elaborate a comprehensive plan for the Swiss energy policy. The final report of this commission was published in 1978, defining goals for Swiss energy policy and some scenarios to attain it. Based on this report, a constitutional amendment was elaborated that should have attributed a more important regulatory role to the federal government, whose manoeuvring room in energy policy in general had been restricted to information providing, and the initiation of cooperative arrangements with and between cantons, and with private actors from the business community (Jegen 2003: 70). Just like the two initiatives of the anti-nuclear movement, this constitutional amendment failed in a popular vote in February 1983—because of the resistance of the cantons. Although it obtained a (very narrow) popular majority, it did not obtain a majority of the cantons.

In the 1980s, the nuclear policy debate focused mainly on the project of Kaiseraugst. In 1981, the federal government provided the project with a new 'general authorization licence'—a step which provoked the mobilization of 20,000 opponents of nuclear power in a demonstration (see Figure 11.2). The two chambers of parliament confirmed the measure in 1983 and 1985 respectively. But the project still lacked a renewed authorization for construction. At this point, the catastrophe in Chernobyl intervened, which, together with economic and technological considerations, sounded the death knell for this most famous NPP project in Switzerland; since the mid-1970s, when it was stopped by the occupation, the project had not only become technologically outdated, but it was also no longer economically viable. Given the increasing costs of the project, the electricity industry realized that it could import electrical power at a much cheaper rate from France. Two parliamentary motions, submitted by members of Parliament close to the electricity industry in 1988, led to the final withdrawal from the project in 1989 (Jegen 2003: 76-9). After Kaiseraugst had been shelved, Graben, which had met with strong, unexpected resistance as well, was denied its general authorization licence in 1979, and Verbois was never granted a licence for construction either.

The Chernobyl catastrophe not only proved to be the catalyst for the reappraisal of the nuclear power programme on the part of the electricity industry, it also remobilized the anti-nuclear movement (see Figure 11.2), and incited it once again to launch two popular initiatives—one proposing to put an end to nuclear energy in Switzerland (the 'stop' initiative), the other proposing a freeze of ten years for the construction of any additional NPPs (the 'moratorium' initiative). Both initiatives were submitted to the popular vote in 1990, and, to the surprise of many, the 'moratorium' initiative passed, obtaining a majority of 54.6 per cent of the vote and also a majority of the cantons. This partial victory of the movement constituted a second landmark event for the anti-nuclear movement (Rieder 1998: 231–2). In the same vote, a second, watered-down version of the constitutional amendment on energy policy was accepted by an overwhelming popular majority and by all the cantons. This amendment clarified the powers of the different levels of government and provided for a more active role of the federal government in matters of energy policy. After the occupation of the site in Kaiseraugst, this triple vote in 1990 constitutes the second major turning point in Swiss nuclear energy policy.

The moratorium on nuclear energy opened a 'window of opportunity'—a temporary 'energy peace' as the Energy Minister declared at the time, which was to be used for intensified legislative action at the federal level. On the one hand, the anti-nuclear movement completely demobilized after its success at the polls (see Figure 11.2), and subsequently it only manifested itself in the direct-democratic arena where it was also supported by its allies among the political parties. Thus, the Green Party, represented in the federal parliament since 1983, used the moratorium to propose two popular initiatives that promoted renewable energies—the 'solar initiative' and the 'environmental initiative'. The first proposed the introduction of an additional tax on energy for the promotion of solar energy; the second asked for the introduction of a fiscally neutral tax on non-renewable fuel. Both initiatives were submitted to the authorities in 1995. Parliament responded by presenting two counter-projects, one for each initiative, which incited the Greens to withdraw their environmental, but not their solar initiative. Subsequently, the two counter-projects and the solar initiative were all three rejected by the voters in September 2000. In addition, the problem of nuclear waste disposal remained on the agenda throughout the 1990s. Local resistance against the chosen sites for waste disposal plants also used direct-democratic instruments at the regional and local level. Thus, in 1995 and 2002, the voters of the Canton of Nidwald twice pronounced a veto against the Wellenberg site, the location chosen by Nagra,[2] the national agency charged with the development of a workable waste disposal policy since 1978, for the disposal of weakly radioactive waste. On both occasions, the voters refused to provide Nagra with a cantonal licence for test drilling. In February 2011, in a national consultation procedure, a large majority of 80 per cent of the voters in this small canton once again opposed Nagra by demanding Wellenberg be eliminated from the list of possible sites for radioactive waste deposits. New locations were proposed in January 2015.

On the other hand, the electrical industry tried to 'patch up' (see Visser and Hemerijck 1997: 57) its cosy relations with the cantonal states, and the federal government tried to incite private actors to cooperate 'in the shadow of the state' (Scharpf 1997). It launched programmes promoting the reduction of energy consumption ('Energy 2000'), and of CO_2 emissions. Legislative progress, however, was slow in coming. The federal law on energy, implementing the constitutional

---

[2] National association for the storage of radioactive waste (Nationale Genossenschaft für die Lagerung radioaktiver Abfälle).

amendment from 1990, was eventually adopted in 1998, but only because major issues such as the introduction of a tax on energy were deferred to future legislation. In cooperation with the parliamentary committees in charge of energy policy, the ministry resorted to non-decision-making and decoupling of issues to get some of the pending legislation passed. This means that major issues such as the liberalization of the electricity market, the introduction of a tax on energy, and the support of alternative energy sources (such as solar energy) were not settled. The liberalization of the electricity market was tackled by a separate legislative process. The corresponding new law was again attacked by a referendum launched by the labour unions, and voted down in September 2002, after similar measures had already failed at the cantonal level in Zurich and Nidwald in 2001.

As a result of these failures, once again energy policy found itself at a considerable impasse, which the anti-nuclear movement tried to resolve in its favour with yet another set of two popular initiatives, one demanding the progressive abandonment of nuclear energy, the other, more moderate one, asking for an extension of the freeze (the 'MoratoriumPlus' initiative). Both of these initiatives were launched before the end of the moratorium, but came up for the vote only in spring 2003, together with a set of seven other proposals. In this unusual accumulation of proposals submitted to the vote, the two initiatives dealing with nuclear energy drew less attention during the campaign than had been the case in the past, and both were voted down by considerable margins—the more moderate initiative obtained only 41.6 per cent of the vote, while the more radical one obtained even less (33.7 per cent).

The failure of these last two initiatives of the movement constituted the third turning point in Swiss nuclear energy policy. Together with the renewal of the law on nuclear energy in 2003, which the federal government proposed to parliament in 1999 as an indirect counter-proposal to the two initiatives, their rejection clarified the situation.[3] The new law contained several concessions to the anti-nuclear coalition, such as new dispositions concerning the regulation of nuclear waste (a ten-year moratorium, from 2006 until 2016, was established for fuel reprocessing), as well as dispositions concerning the procedures of NPP licensing (to obtain a general authorization license for an NPP construction, a concrete plan for nuclear waste management is to be proposed by nuclear operators, and the issuing of future general authorization licences is to be submitted to the optional referendum). The ordinance based on this law was implemented in February 2005. In 2008, the revision of another key law in this policy domain—the new law on nuclear power liability—was adopted by the Federal Parliament.

In 2007, the federal government decided on a new general orientation of energy policy, which was to be based on four pillars: the improvement efficiency of energy, the increase of the share of renewable energies, the construction of new large power plants, and an active foreign policy in the energy domain. As a transition measure, the government believed that the construction of new nuclear power plants was necessary, given the gap in the electricity supply predicted for

---

[3] As stipulated by Article 107 of the new nuclear energy law (Kernenergiegesetz, KEG) of 21 Mar. 2003, this new law was to be published only after the withdrawal of the two initiatives or after their rejection in the popular vote.

the years after 2020. In other words, the federal government was still betting on nuclear energy. A study of Avenir Suisse, the think tank of the Swiss business community, came to a similar conclusion: for the period after 2022, it predicted a shortage in the electricity supply in Switzerland (Meister 2008). In June and December 2008, the Swiss electricity industry requested the authorization of the construction of three new nuclear power plants—one each in Gösgen, Beznau, and Mühleberg.

By spring 2011, when the Japanese catastrophe occurred in Fukushima, the general licensing procedures for the three new projects had progressed considerably. In 2009, the energy committee of the Council of States—the second chamber of the Swiss parliament—had suggested that the two competing giants from the electricity industry, which were planning the three new plants, should find a compromise for the construction of only two projects (instead of the three requested), given its expectations that only two would be needed. In November 2010, the nuclear energy inspectorate ENSI, which had examined the projects from a strictly technical point of view, gave positive advice for granting them the general authorization licence. Subsequently, the licensing requests for the new projects were submitted for consultation to the cantons and other interested parties. As part of this procedure, a consultative referendum was held in the Canton of Berne, where the people could express themselves on the desirability of the construction of a new plant in Mühleberg. The vote took place in February 2011, shortly before the catastrophe in Fukushima. Interestingly, the red-green majority of the cantonal government opposed the construction of a new plant, while the centre-right majority of the cantonal parliament supported it.[4] The vote was purely consultative and limited to the Canton of Berne, but it was of symbolic importance for Swiss energy policy as a whole. In a very close decision, 51 per cent of the voters decided to accept the construction of a new nuclear power plant in Mühleberg. Given the outcome of this vote, the federal government was expected to formulate its message for the Federal Parliament about the construction of the new plants by 2012, which, in turn, was expected to take its decision in favour of their construction in 2013. This decision would certainly be attacked by a referendum, the outcome of which was not guaranteed, even before the Japanese catastrophe had occurred. If the people accepted the new projects, procedures for granting the construction licence could be set in motion, which could still be opposed by legal complaints. Even under the most optimistic scenario for the nuclear industry, a new nuclear power plant would not have been in operation before the mid-2020s.

The catastrophe of Fukushima fundamentally changed the course of the procedures set out for the new nuclear power plants. Immediately after the catastrophe, the new federal energy minister, a Christian democrat, stopped the licensing procedure for the three projects. The ENSI was asked to analyse the reasons for the accident in Japan, and to draw possible conclusions for Switzerland. Moreover, the safety of the existing Swiss nuclear power plants was to be subject to close examination. These

---

[4] Since cantonal parliaments and governments are elected separately, based on different electoral systems (majoritarian for the governments, proportional for the parliaments), it is possible that the majorities in the two bodies do not coincide.

decisions rendered obsolete the recent popular vote in the Canton of Berne (which would have to revote once the procedures were to be taken up again). Moreover, they not only reopened the debate on the new projects, but also on the continued operation of the older plants (Beznau I and II, and Mühleberg). Mühleberg, the licence of which had only been extended to an unlimited period in late 2009, came under particular scrutiny because its reactor was of the same type as the reactors operating in Fukushima. As in many other countries, the future of nuclear energy became highly compromised in Switzerland.

The catastrophe of Fukushima incited the Greens to launch yet another popular initiative to get out of nuclear energy. This initiative asked for the phasing out of the Swiss NPPs by 2029, when the youngest NPP would have terminated forty-five years in operation. The initiative obtained the required number of signatures and was submitted to the government in November 2012.[5] In reaction to the catastrophe of Fukushima, to everybody's surprise, the Swiss government adopted a similar stance. In late May 2011, it decided to progressively phase out nuclear energy. The National Council, the first chamber, confirmed this decision in early June. In late September 2011, just before the Federal elections, a large majority of the Council of States, followed suit after a heated, emotional debate, effectively taking energy policy out of the election campaign.

The government moved with unusual speed to implement this decision. Already in spring 2012 it presented its proposals for the new energy policy—'Energy Strategy 2050'—and submitted it to the traditional consultation procedure. In 2013, the final proposal of a first set of measures, which were intended to serve as an 'indirect counter-proposal' to the Greens' phasing-out initiative, was submitted to the National Council to discuss it. The National Council ended up adopting a somewhat modified version in December 2014. Two elements above all were contested in this set of measures: the size of the subsidies for renewable energies, and the phasing out of NPPs. As far as the latter is concerned, the government shared the goal of the Greens to phase out NPPs. It rejected the construction of any new NPPs. However, with respect to the existing NPPs, it played for time by proposing not to limit the lifespan of the three most recent out of the five existing NPPs. The industry had previously announced that it calculated a duration of operation of at least sixty years, which would take the last of the existing NPPs well beyond the deadline fixed by the Greens' initiative in 2029. The National Council eventually adopted a compromise solution that did not limit the duration of operation of existing NPPs, but required the submission of a long-term operation concept for NPPs after the completion of forty years of operation. It also introduced the possibility for financial compensation, in case the existing NPPs were to lose their licence for security reasons before their lifespan anticipated by the industry had come to an end. The second chamber accepted this proposal in 2016, but the final decision is still pending, because the SVP (Swiss People's Party) launched a referendum against it. The popular vote on the phasing out initiative took place after the final parliamentary decisions on the

---

[5] In the aftermath of Fukushima, the Green Liberals also mobilized for another initiative related to energy policy and which asked for the replacement of VAT by an energy tax. This initiative, which has only a tenuous relationship with nuclear energy policy, was voted down by an overwhelming popular majority in early 2015.

'Energy Strategy 2050' in November 2016. A majority of 54.2 percent of the voters rejected the initiative, which means that the phasing out will proceed at a slower pace than desired by the initiative.

11.3 ACTORS AND COALITIONS

Traditionally, energy policy in Switzerland and elsewhere has been dominated by what Broadbent (1998) calls the 'pro-growth coalition'. With the rise of the anti-nuclear movement, a second, 'pro-ecology coalition' has established itself, too. The pro-nuclear and the anti-nuclear coalitions are, in turn, subsets of these two broader coalitions (see Jegen 2003; Kriesi and Jegen 2001).

The *pro-growth coalition* has three basic components in Switzerland, which correspond to the 'ruling triad' in Broadbent's (1998) study of environmental politics in Japan: cantonal governments, the three major parties of the centre- (FDP, CVP) and populist right (SVP), and the business community. First of all, the *cantons* (and, one should add, major cities) have traditionally been key actors in the use of the important hydraulic resources of the country, and, consequently, in the control of the electrical power industry, including NPPs. The big utilities and systems' operators in Switzerland are all, at least partially, owned by the cantons. The cantons, especially the ones in the Alpine region, receive a large part of the revenue linked to hydroelectric power plants and the members of the cantonal governments have been heavily involved in the management of this industry. In the context of the federal Swiss state, the cantons, however, do not just play the role of energy producers. Until the adoption of the constitutional amendment in 1990, the federal government had a very limited jurisdiction in energy policy only. Rather, energy policy, with the only exceptions of nuclear power and taxes on gasoline, fell under the jurisdiction of the cantons.

The cantonal governments do not, however, homogeneously favour the 'pro-growth' coalition. Depending on the regionally variable pressure exerted by the ecology and anti-nuclear movements, some cantons have adopted a rather more 'pro-ecology' stance. Thus, as mentioned above, in 1977 already, the voters in the canton of Basel city had accepted an initiative requiring their cantonal government to oppose NPPs. Similarly, to mention another example, Geneva voters accepted an amendment to the cantonal constitution in 1986, imposing on the cantonal authorities an anti-nuclear power policy. According to this amendment, the Geneva cantonal authorities are held to oppose, by all legal and political means at their disposition, the installation of NPPs, of radioactive waste disposal, and of reprocessing facilities of radioactive waste on their territory or on immediately surrounding territories (an addendum especially directed against the, now abandoned, retreatment plant at Creys-Malville in neighbouring France). Moreover, given the void in energy policy at the centre, while most cantons have been content with non-decision-making and delaying decisive action, some cantons—pressured by their urban population and regional anti-nuclear movements—have adopted a very active and innovative policy in the domain of energy efficiency (Delley and Mader 1986). In the more active cantons, parts of the cantonal administrations, especially the technical experts of energy efficiency, have become key players in the 'pro-ecology' coalition.

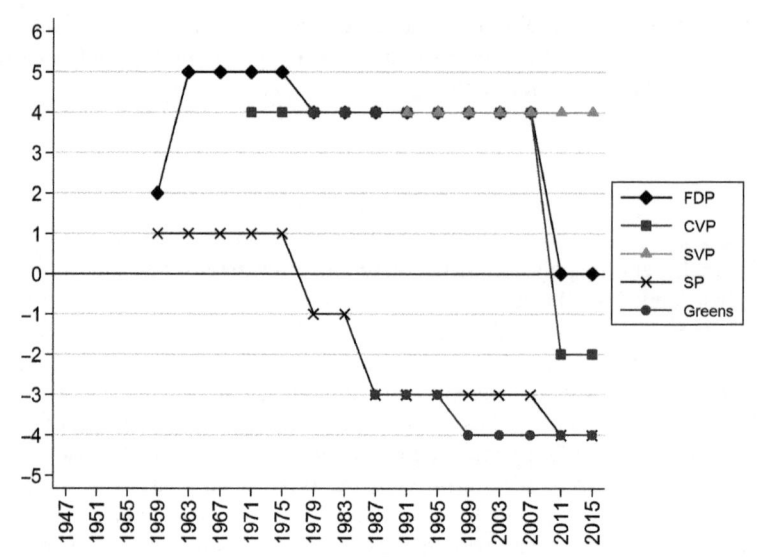

Figure 11.3. Party Scales

Source: Swiss party manifestos, voting recommendations for federal initiatives of the anti-nuclear movement (if voting recommendations deviate from manifesto declarations, voting recommendations are used), and (for the most recent positions) voting behaviour in Parliament. Note that the most recent positions of the FDP and the CVP are difficult to determine, because they are divided on the issue of nuclear energy and avoid addressing it in their programme.

The *three major political parties of the centre and populist right*, who have dominated the federal government and, in varying compositions, most of the cantonal governments, up to the present, have always been closely linked to the business community in general and, through their members of the cantonal governments and the so-called 'energy forum', to the electricity industry in particular. The 'energy forum' is a common platform for the energy industry and the parliamentarians close to the business community. On the business side, the forum regroups the representatives of the different types of energy sources and of the energy-consuming branches (machine industry, banks, insurance, and small and medium-sized business). On the parliamentarian side, it can count on no less than 130 among the 246 members of the two chambers of Swiss parliament. Figure 11.3 presents the party scales for Switzerland. As this figure shows quite clearly, the three major parties of the centre and populist right have always supported nuclear energy until the most recent past. The position of the CVP has not always been as clear-cut as that of the other two parties, however, even if it has consistently opposed the anti-nuclear initiatives. Thus, some of its cantonal sections deviated from the party's national pro-nuclear recommendation in the 1990 votes, and, right after the accident of Chernobyl, in its 1987 electoral programme, the party even proposed to avoid the construction of new nuclear power plants in the future.[6] In the more recent past, the CVP party base has

---

[6] The coding in Figure 12.3 for the CVP in 1987 and 1991 is based on its opposition to the anti-nuclear initiatives, and not on its party programme.

become much more divided with respect to nuclear energy. This incited the party to dilute its support of nuclear energy in its programme for the 2011 elections, which it adopted early in the year before the Japanese catastrophe. After the Fukushima catastrophe, the CVP minister of energy became one of the driving forces of the new phasing out strategy.

In the energy policy domain, the *business community* is mainly represented by the electricity industry. Additional key actors of the business community include the interest associations of the other types of energy sources, and the peak association of Swiss industry, Economiesuisse. The growth orientation comes in two variants: a technological production orientation, and an economic market orientation. Both 'technological enthusiasts' and economic 'cost-benefiters', in Jasper's (1990: 25) terms, belong to the 'pro-growth coalition'. The 'technological enthusiasts' are mainly represented in the electricity industry, which has long been a domain of engineers. Based on forecasts suggesting a continuously growing demand, this industry has above all been preoccupied with guaranteeing the supply of a sufficient amount of energy for the worst-case scenario. Thus, when its expansive nuclear power programme met with popular resistance, the industry proceeded to secure for itself expensive importation rights for nuclear power in France, to be able to keep up with its demand forecasts. When, to its great surprise, the demand for electricity declined for the first time in 1993, it responded with a price increase to maintain its income, faithful to its monopolist tradition, but quite out of touch with a changing market context.[7] The 'cost-benefiters' are typically represented in the other parts of the business community, which tends to be more preoccupied with the costs of the energy (especially in energy-intensive branches of industry). Moreover, within the business community, the interests of the providers of different fuel types—oil, gas, coal, nuclear power, hydroelectric, wind, and solar power—do not necessarily coincide.

In the course of the 1990s, the dominant 'pro-growth' coalition has been subjected to *additional internal tensions,* given the decision by the European Union *to liberalize its electrical energy market.* Whereas the international sector of the Swiss business community received the ideas for liberalizing the electricity market with open arms, the liberalization issue added to the plight of the electricity industry. Part of the economy producing for the national market, the latter has long been one of the most protected and most cartelized sectors of the economy. It has not been used to a competitive environment and has benefited from its cosy relations with the state. The difficulties proved to be most important for its nuclear power branch, because some of the NPPs (e.g. Leibstadt) produce the most expensive electricity. The liberalization issue has exerted strong pressures for the restructuring of the entire electrical industry, which until very recently has been highly fragmented and decentralized: a wave of mergers and restructuration has drastically reduced the more than 1,000 electricity producers and no less than seven system operators which made up the Swiss electrical industry in the past. By 2009, two new giants have emerged that will dominate the industry in the future together with BKW, another electricity producer: the

---

[7] Swiss electricity prices have traditionally been relatively low for households, but rather high for industry.

Axpo holding (a joint venture of Axpo (formerly NOK), CKW, and EGL-Laufenburg) and the Alpiq holding (under whose umbrella EOS and Atel (formerly Motor-Columbus, the corporation responsible for the Kaiseraugst project) have merged and which also includes a participation of EDF). Together, these two conglomerates provide electricity for roughly three-quarters of the Swiss population. Along with the BKW, the two giants were the driving forces for the construction of new NPPs. Alpiq has submitted a project for the replacement of Gösgen, and Axpo has created a joint venture with BKW (Resun AG—Replacement Suisse Nucléaire) for the replacement of the nuclear power plants in Mühleberg and Beznau.

The *pro-ecology coalition* is the privileged domain of the 'moralists' in Jaspers's terms, that is, organizations that are sceptical about the possibilities of continued growth and that plead for the preservation of non-renewable resources, for energy-saving, and for the reduction of destructive external effects on the environment that are caused by energy production. But on this side, too, we find a fair share of 'technological enthusiasts' and 'cost-benefiters'. The pro-ecology coalition has its roots in the *anti-nuclear movement*. The campaigns of the anti-nuclear movement have greatly strengthened the position of the 'pro-ecology' coalition in the Swiss energy policy domain. The movement has found allies within the political system—above all among the parties of the left. The traditional Social Democrats (SPS) and, since the early 1980s, the Green Party (GPS) embraced the cause of the anti-nuclear struggle and became ardent defenders of an anti-nuclear position in the parliamentary arena (see Figure 11.3). In the course of the 1980s, the alliance broadened with the institutionalization of an increasing number of organizations of the ecology movement (Kriesi 1996) and the shift in the focus of the energy policy debate from the nuclear energy to the broader issues of energy efficiency and sustainable development. The alliance could now also count on allies in the federal and cantonal administrations—among others former movement members who had made their entry into the public administrations.[8]

The position of the Swiss Social Democrats is of particular importance in this context, because it deviates from the respective party positions in some other European countries. Originally, the Social Democrats were part of the pro-nuclear coalition as well. Since 1959, they had been part of the ('magic formula') grand coalition governing the country at the federal level, and it was a Social Democrat—Willy Ritschard—who was the member of the federal government responsible for energy policy at the critical moment of the mobilization at Kaiseraugst. The popular Ritschard very clearly defended a pro-nuclear point of view and forcefully mobilized the voters in the name of the government's pro-nuclear position against the first initiative of the anti-nuclear movement in 1979 (Degen 1993: 110). At this point, his party had, however, already turned against nuclear energy. The transformation process started surreptitiously with the key event of Kaiseraugst. Until Kaiseraugst, nuclear energy had not been a salient issue for the party, and the regional movement against Kaiseraugst had, at first, been a centre-right movement. By chance, the Social Democrats' national president at the time, Helmut

---

[8] A case that illustrates this point is the former director of the Swiss WWF, who became the head of the federal office of environmental protection.

Hubacher, was a member of the National Council representing the City of Basel, and as such he became highly sensitive to the anti-nuclear position when faced with the Kaiseraugst occupation. Together with other national politicians from the left, he acted as an (eventually successful) intermediary between the movement (whose radical wing did not want to negotiate with the government) and the federal government (some of whose centre-right members favoured an intervention by the army to clear the site). After Kaiseraugst, the anti-nuclear perspective progressed in the party and, at its congress in 1978, i.e. at a time when the Green Party had not even been founded in Switzerland, it officially adopted an anti-nuclear position. Not all sections of the party agreed to this change of position at the time[9] (i.e. Ritschard was not the only one with a pro-nuclear position in the party). However, a clear majority voted in favour of the new position, which the party has unwaveringly defended ever since.

Faced with plans to construct new NPPs in the early 2000s, the pro-ecology coalition was reorganizing as well, and a new coalition took shape that promised to mobilize against the construction of any new plants. The alliance against new NPPs included thirty-two organizations, among which the Social Democrats, the Greens, and the small Christian Socialist party, as well as environmental organizations such as Greenpeace and the WWF. The alliance promised to launch a referendum against any new general authorization licence. In addition to the two broad coalitions, we can distinguish a third group of actors—the *intermediaries* who take an ambiguous position in this policy area. They include the federal government and administration as well as regional actors.

The reactions of the 'pro-ecology' coalition to the catastrophe in Fukushima were predictable: its members insisted on the phasing out of nuclear energy, and, as we have already seen, the Greens launched a popular initiative to that purpose. On the 'pro-growth' side, however, the reactions were more complex and to some extent unexpected. While the national-conservative SVP remained a staunch supporter of nuclear energy, the Liberals (FDP) surprised everybody by their declaration that pursuing the construction of new nuclear power plants was no longer feasible. They had not become opposed to nuclear power (they were still in favour of maintaining the existing nuclear power plants in operation, provided they fulfilled the required safety standards), but they no longer believed that new nuclear power plants had any chance of being accepted by the population. For purely pragmatic reasons and to play for time, they thus proposed to search for alternatives to the current technology of nuclear energy (including a new generation of nuclear power plants). They abstained in the parliamentary vote on phasing out nuclear power plants in June 2011, as a result of their profound internal divisions on this issue.[10] By contrast, the CVP, which had already started to move away from nuclear power before Fukushima, now definitely joined the anti-nuclear camp, led by its member of the federal government, Doris Leuthard, who had taken over as energy minister shortly before the catastrophe. The party

---

[9] The section of the canton of Aargau, where two nuclear power plants (Beznau I and II) were already operating, or the section of the canton of Berne, resisted the change of position.

[10] They participated in a subsidiary vote, on a motion of the Green Party, which revealed that ten members of the liberal group voted with the anti-nuclear camp, nineteen with the pro-nuclear camp, and five abstained in this vote as well (*NZZ* 133 (9 June 2011), p. 11).

leadership imposed this new line on hesitating members of parliament, partly arguing pragmatically like the Liberals (no popular majorities for nuclear energy could be expected for many years to come), partly economically (necessity to provide investors with clear signals for future investments), and partly invoking the risks involved in this technology. Electoral reasons may have played a role as well, given the coming federal elections in fall 2011. However, the question of the coherence with its smaller allies in the political centre—the Green-Liberals, a split off from the Green Party in 2007, the Evangelical Party (EVP) and the BDP, a split off from the SVP, all of whom had joined the anti-nuclear camp already before (GLP, EVP) or right after Fukushima (BDP)—does not seem to have influenced the CVP's decision. In the debate on the 'Energy Strategy 2050' in the National Chamber, the so-called 'Fukushima Alliance' composed of CVP, BDP, and the Red-Green camp held firm. In contrast to the Red-Green camp, both CVP and BDP, however, opposed the Greens' initiative, which essentially means that they wanted to give the phasing out of NPPs more time. By contrast, the Liberals and the SVP opposed the new energy strategy, and in particular the phasing out of nuclear energy.

11.4 POLITICAL COMPETITION OVER NUCLEAR ENERGY

In order to show the impact of the third turning point on the Swiss nuclear policy debate in particular, we have analysed this debate in the most important newspapers of the four largest Swiss cities—Zürich, Basel, Berne, and Geneva—for the ten-year period 1999–2008 (see Utz 2009).[11] As our analysis shows, the focus and the tone of the debate changed profoundly after the third turning point. During the five-year period from 1999 up to and including 2003—the year of the adoption of the new nuclear energy law—procedural issues at the federal and cantonal levels, the phasing out of nuclear energy, waste disposal, and the moratorium dominated the debate. All of these issues became considerably less prominent after 2003. With the rejection of the two pending initiatives, the moratorium completely disappeared from the agenda, the phasing out and waste disposal became less relevant, and procedural issues were considered settled and no longer preoccupied the public to the extent they did in the earlier period. On the other hand, the construction of new NPPs, which was rather a non-issue before, became the dominant issue of the debate after 2003. In addition, the debate now increasingly turned to questions of efficiency and supply (the 'supply gap' question), and

---

[11] The newspapers chosen were: Zurich: *Neue Zürcher Zeitung* (NZZ), Basel: *Basler Zeitung* (BaZ), Berne: *Der Bund*, Geneva: *Le Temps*. The databank Factiva served as the source for the digital versions of the newspaper articles. the selection was made based on a list of keywords (in German): kernkraft* OR kernenergie* OR kernreaktor* OR reaktor* OR nucleaire* OR AKW* OR KKW* OR 'atomarer abfall' OR 'atomare abfälle' OR atomenergie* OR atomkraft* OR atommüll* OR atomreaktor* OR atomstrom* OR atomwärme* OR atomwirtschaft* OR atomaire* OR atomique* OR endlager* OR radioaktiv* OR radioacti*. This procedure provided 3,093 articles. Based on a thorough reading of these articles, we made a selection of 301 articles, which contained at least one actor positioning himself with respect to a sub-issue of nuclear energy. The results of the analysis reported here are based on these 301 articles (Utz 2009).

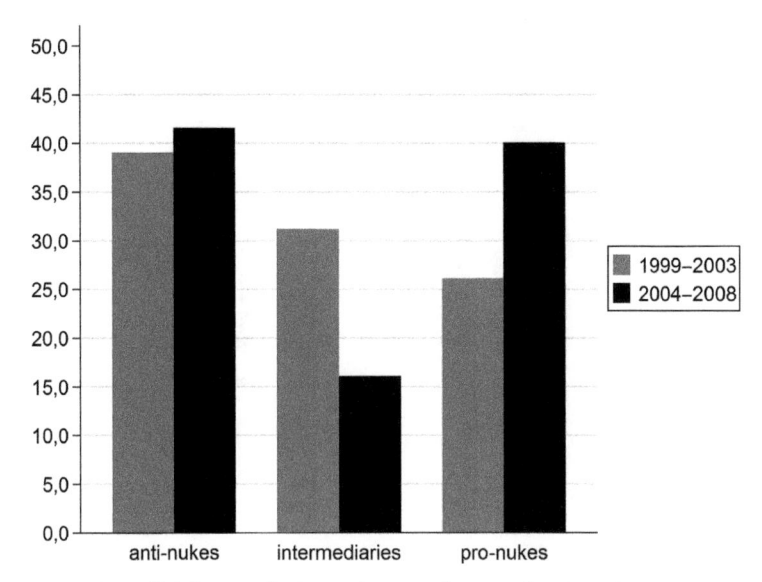

Figure 11.4. Overall Salience of Major Groups of Actors by Period: Percentages of All Mentions in the Press

Source: Analysis of data provided by Utz (2009).

to alternative sources of energy (gas and renewable energy). Moreover, the tone of the debate (i.e. the average positioning of the contributions to the debate) became more negative with regard to all the issues that had been more important during the earlier period, while, with one exception (efficiency and supply), it became more positive with regard to the issues that predominated during the more recent period. The more favourable tone was especially notable for gas power plants and for the construction of new NPPs.

Based on this analysis of the nuclear energy debate in the major Swiss print media from 1999 to 2008, we can now also analyse the effect of the third turning point on the relative salience of the two coalitions and of the intermediary group of actors in the media. Figure 11.4 shows the changing salience of the different types of actors from the first to the second period. Most conspicuously, the salience of the pro-nuclear side increased to the detriment of the intermediaries. While the anti-nuclear coalition had received more media attention before the turning point in 2003, the two camps obtained virtually the same media coverage after the adoption of the new nuclear energy law. In particular, the electricity industry and the two governing parties that have always been most clearly in favour of nuclear energy—FDP and SVP—became much more prominent than they were before. By contrast, the federal government and administration, that were, in fact, the most prominent actors during the first period, lost much of their prominence with the settlement of the key legislative issues.

We have also coded the framing of the debate by the different types of actors. Frames correspond to the arguments given by the actors for the justification of their position on a given sub-issue. Figure 11.5 shows the overall distribution of frames over the three major groups of actors. The alternative frames in this figure

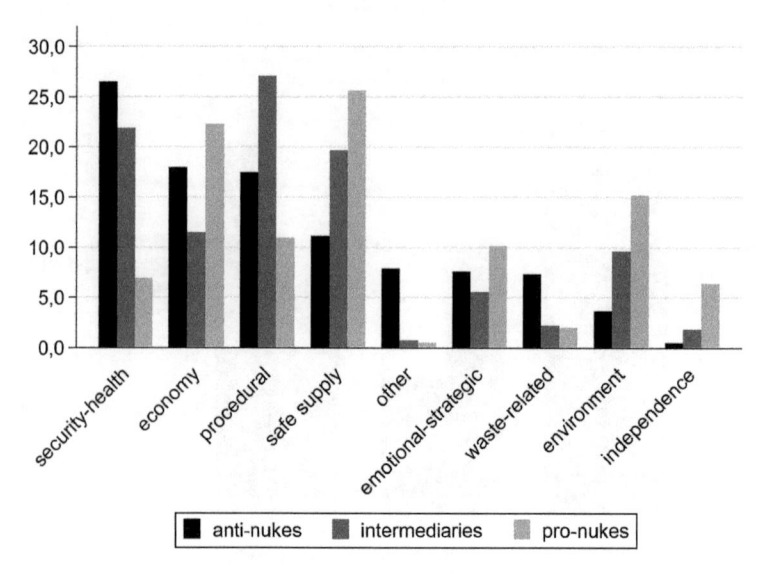

Figure 11.5. Overall Use of Frames by the Three Major Groups of Actors: Percentages
Source: Analysis of data provided by Utz (2009).

are ordered from left to right according to the frequency with which they have been used by the anti-nuclear movement. As is immediately apparent from this figure, while each camp uses a wide variety of arguments, the camps nevertheless differ with regard to their privileged frames. Thus, to justify their positions, the anti-nuclear activists mainly use security and health arguments, while the pro-nuclear actors heavily argue for securing supply and, surprisingly, for the reduction of CO_2 and SO_2 emissions (environment). The actors with intermediary positions privilege procedural arguments. Economic arguments are almost equally invoked by anti- and pro-nuclear actors. Note also that emotional arguments are not very prominent on either side. More detailed analyses show that arguments concerning the safe/reliable/secure supply of energy gained in importance for all three groups of actors after the 2003 turning point.

There are no systematic time series for documenting the development of Swiss public opinion on nuclear energy in the long run. Patching together data from several different sources, it is, however, possible to get a general idea of its development (see Figure 11.6). The change in public opinion in the course of the 1970s is documented by several surveys (Kriesi 1982: 3): while only about one-fifth of the population was critical of nuclear power before Kaiseraugst, this percentage rose to about 50 per cent in the late 1970s. After the Chernobyl accident, opposition to nuclear power rose again to a high of 58 per cent in 1989—the time of the adoption of the moratorium. During the 1990s, opposition to nuclear power rose even further, to reach an unprecedented peak of 76 per cent in 2001. By the time of the vote on the two last initiatives of the anti-nuclear movement, the share of people opposed to nuclear power was still very high. Against this background, it appears, at first, puzzling that the two initiatives were rejected in 2003—a puzzle to which I shall return shortly. It is only under the

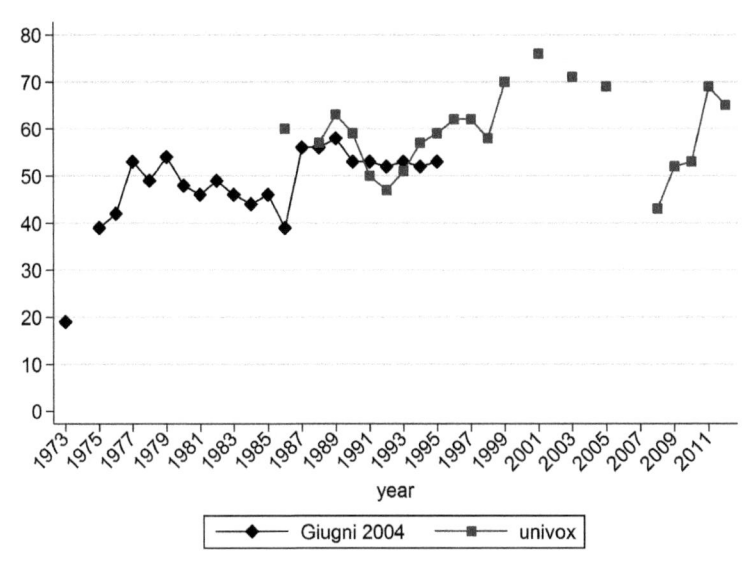

Figure 11.6. Development of Public Opinion on Nuclear Energy: Percentage of People Against

Source: 1973 (Kriesi 1982: 3); 1975–95 (Giugni 2004: 203, 244) % of people who say that nuclear energy is rather negative or very negative; 1986–2012 (gfs-Zürich: univox) % of people who agree that the risks of nuclear energy are not acceptable.

impact of the financial and economic crisis in 2008 that opposition to nuclear power seems to have decreased temporarily to the levels prevailing in the mid-1980s.[12] After Fukushima, however, the opposition to nuclear energy regained the levels of the early 2000s, with more than two-thirds of the Swiss public agreeing with the statement that 'the risks of nuclear energy are not acceptable'.

To get a better idea of Swiss public opinion on nuclear power, we can look at the three surveys that were held after the popular votes on the initiatives in 1984, 1990, and 2003.[13] Before we turn to the analysis of the voting choices, I would like to point out an important procedural aspect of the votes on nuclear energy, which is easy to overlook, but which most likely has had a decisive impact on the outcome of the vote in 2003: the composition of the proposals submitted to the voters on a given date. In 1984, the double initiatives were submitted to the popular vote as a package without any other proposals. In 1990, they were submitted together with the revised constitutional amendment on energy policy, and with a minor modification of the law on traffic. In 2003, by contrast, the two initiatives were part of an exceptional number of nine proposals that were submitted to the voters on a single occasion. Such a large number of proposals had never before (and never

---

[12] The 2008 survey of gfs, on which these figures are based, was held in November of that year, i.e. after the collapse of Lehman Brothers.
[13] These surveys are part of the VOX surveys, which take place regularly after the federal popular votes in Switzerland. They refer to VOX nos. 23, 40, and 82. These surveys are available from the Voxit databank at FORS, the Swiss social science data archive at the University of Lausanne, under the numbers 23, 40, and 82.

since) been submitted on a single date. Seven of these proposals were initiatives. In addition to the two initiatives related to nuclear energy, these initiatives dealt with various, unconnected issues—vocational training, the handicapped, housing, public health, and Sundays without traffic. The last two proposals had been put on the agenda by optional referendums launched by some citizens' action committees against modifications of the laws on the armed forces. Given the dire consequences of this unprecedented accumulation of proposals submitted to the voters together with the two initiatives of the anti-nuclear coalition, it is important to note that this exceptional accumulation was not the result of some Machiavellian strategy on the part of the government, but rather the unanticipated outcome of the manoeuvring by initiative committees: independently of one another, several of these committees had sought to put their initiative on the agenda of the last voting date before the federal elections in fall 2003, in order to be able to have an influence on the outcome of these elections.

The number of projects submitted on a given date is crucial in our context, because of a straightforward relationship which exists between the number of projects submitted to the vote on a given date and the degree of the voters' awareness of the proposals submitted to the vote: the share of unaware voters increases steeply with the number of proposals.[14] Compared to an overall average of 27 per cent, it reached an absolute maximum (an average of 43 per cent unaware voters per proposal) in the vote of 18 May 2003, the unprecedented vote on nine proposals. This effect is highly significant and holds up even if we control for the complexity of the proposals. Accordingly, the level of awareness was also much lower than it had been previously for the two initiatives on nuclear energy submitted on that date. As Figure 11.7 shows, the share of voters with a high level of policy-specific awareness—i.e. of voters who are capable of citing the title of the proposal and its overall contents in response to open questions—reached 81 and 87 per cent respectively in 1984 and 1990, but only 29 per cent in 2003.[15]

This result is not surprising, given the complexity of the menu offered to the voters in May 2003. However, the outcome was aggravated by the fact that the opponents of the initiatives—led by economiesuisse, the peak association of the Swiss business community—purposely exploited this situation by launching a massive campaign proposing the voters to vote '7 times no, and 2 times yes' (i.e. 'no' against all seven initiatives, and 'yes' for the two modifications of the law about the armed forces). This came down to a refusal to enter into a discussion on the substance of the propositions of the seven very different initiatives. This strategy paid off, since all the seven initiatives were rejected, including the two initiatives of the anti-nuclear coalition.

As already discussed, both in 1990 and 2003, the voters had to make a choice about two initiatives, a radical proposal asking for an end to nuclear energy and a more moderate proposal in favour of a moratorium. There were many more voters who chose a 'double no' in 2003 than in 1990, in spite of the fact that the

---

[14] This result is based on an analysis of all the projects submitted to a popular vote at the federal level between 1981 and 2008.

[15] This and the subsequent results in this section are based on active voters only, i.e. the citizens who did not participate in the votes are not taken into account.

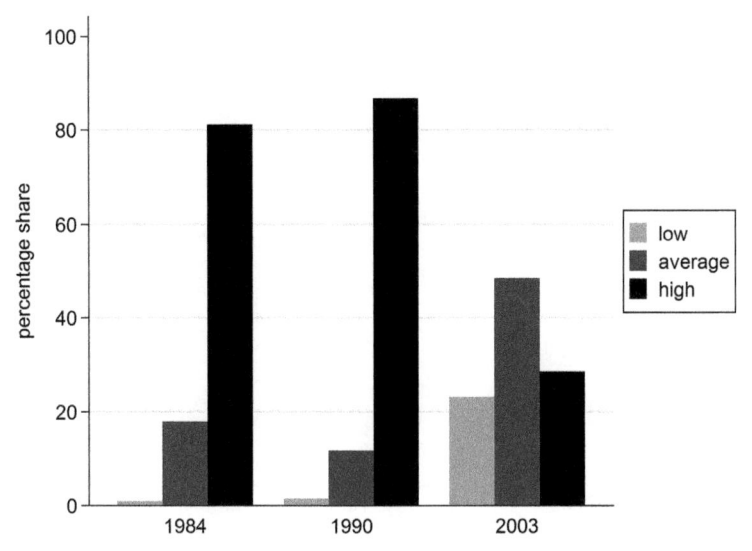

Figure 11.7. Level of Policy-Specific Awareness in the Three Votes on Nuclear Energy (%)
Source: Vox surveys 23, 40, 82.

general attitude on nuclear energy had become less favourable by 2003. This result should be interpreted as an indication of the voters' disorientation in 2003. As it turns out, in 2003, but not in 1990, the vote choice heavily depended on the voters' level of awareness. In 1990, almost all the voters were highly aware (87 per cent), and the few unaware voters opted just as frequently in favour of the initiatives as the highly aware among them. In 2003, by contrast, not only was the overall level of awareness much lower, but unaware voters also opted more frequently for the pro-nuclear camp (Gamma = 0.28***). The 'double no' was generally more frequent in 2003 than in 1990, but the difference was especially large among the unaware (see Figure 11.8). Conversely, the share of 'double yes' was particularly low among the unaware in 2003. This is to suggest that much of the defeat of the two initiatives in 2003 is due to the fact that there were not only many more unaware voters in 2003, but many more unaware voters who massively voted a 'double no', most likely because of the strategy of the opponents of the seven initiatives. Assuming for the 2003 vote a level of awareness comparable to that of 1990, and assuming that voters with a given level of awareness would all have voted the way the voters with that level of awareness actually did in 2003, the 'MoratoriumPlus' initiative, but not the stop initiative, would have been accepted by the voters in 2003.

In 2009, a majority of survey respondents (54.6 per cent) were 'rather'/'fully' in favour of a replacement of the existing nuclear power plants. Asked more specifically how they would vote if there were a vote on the construction of new nuclear power plants 'next Sunday', 47.5 per cent said they would vote in favour of the construction, but an equal percentage indicated that they would reject such plans. In August 2010, public opinion was still deeply divided on this issue, but the share of supporters of new nuclear power plants had dropped to 43 per cent, while the share of opponents had risen to 49 per cent. After the Fukushima catastrophe,

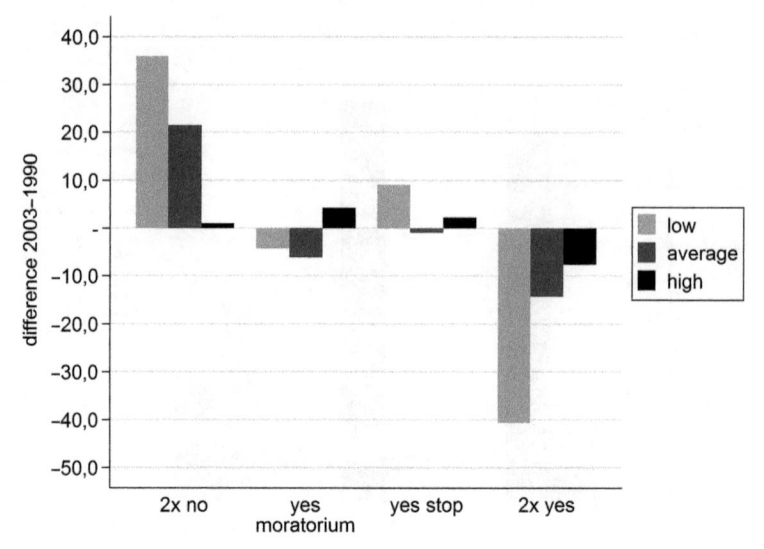

Figure 11.8. Difference in Vote Shares 2003–1990, by Level of Awareness (%)
Source: Vox surveys 23, 40, 82.

public opinion changed dramatically against nuclear energy: 69 per cent of the respondents now indicated that they would vote against the construction of new nuclear power plants.[16]

11.5 CONCLUSION

As I have tried to document in this chapter, the Swiss nuclear power policy underwent two partial policy reversals and is about to perform a full policy reversal since 2011. First, the ambitious nuclear programme of the Swiss electricity industry met with increasing resistance and was eventually stopped by the combined effects of the decision to shelve the projects of Kaiseraugst, Graben, and Verbois, and of the ten-year moratorium for the construction of new NPPs. This first partial policy reversal has, at least in part, been brought about by the strong mobilization by the anti-nuclear movement, which effectively used all the levers available in the open Swiss political system. Technological and economic considerations may have played a role in the decision to abandon Kaiseraugst, too. But had the movement not mobilized very broad resistance against the project of Kaiseraugst, this plant would have been built, and had the moratorium not called for a time of reflection, the nuclear power programme might have been resumed already at an earlier date. The first reversal was partial, because the moratorium was limited in time, and because the more radical proposal to stop the programme altogether had not been accepted by the Swiss voters.

[16] Univox (see Figure 11.6).

The second partial policy reversal brought about a revival of the nuclear power programme. After the defeat of the last two initiatives of the anti-nuclear coalition and the adoption of the new nuclear energy law, the tone of the nuclear power debate in Switzerland decisively changed in favour of nuclear energy, the government envisaged the construction of new NPPs, as a transitory solution to close the predicted shortfall in electricity supply, and the electricity industry was, indeed, planning the construction of at least two new NPPs to replace some of the ageing NPPs of the first generation. This second policy reversal should be considered as only partial, nevertheless, because the change of tone of the elite's debate was entirely premised on a bogus success at the polls and because of the concessions made by Parliament to the 'anti-nuclears' in the new 2003 law. As I have shown here based on a comparison of the voting behaviour of the voters in 1990 and 2003, their decision on the two initiatives of the anti-nuclear movement in 2003 was a sham, and could by no means be taken as an indication of the actual position of the majority of the voters on nuclear energy in a future vote. Moreover, as a result of the concessions made by the Parliament in the new nuclear energy law of 2003, the general authorization licence for any new NPP had to be submitted to a popular vote, the outcome of which was anything but certain, even before the catastrophe at Fukushima in spring 2011.

After Fukushima, the Swiss nuclear power policy is engaged in what appears to be a full policy reversion. The construction of new NPPs is now out of question, and the debate is focusing mostly on the duration of the phasing out of the existing NPPs. The illusion of majoritarian support for new NPPs created by the result of the vote in 2003 has become irrelevant. The impact of this catastrophe on public opinion and party positions has been profound, with major consequences for the plans to construct new nuclear power plants in Switzerland. In the aftermath of this catastrophe, a third, and this time complete reversal in Swiss nuclear energy policy is shaping up: the phasing out of Swiss nuclear power plants once and for all.

The Swiss case confirms the general thrust of this volume's approach. Swiss nuclear power policy was decisively shaped by party coalitions (H1), which reacted to shifts in salience of this issue among the voters (H2) and to shifts in public opinion (H3), as indicated by the outcome of the popular votes on the initiatives of the anti-nuclear movement. The latter shifts have been heavily influenced by nuclear disasters (H10) and by policy opposition (H8). The Swiss case is set apart from the other countries by two specificities of the Swiss polity.

First, Swiss nuclear energy policy has been decisively shaped by the institutional opportunity of direct-democratic instruments, which allowed the policy opposition to mobilize in conventional channels in order to force binding popular votes. The opposition has successfully launched its initiatives at moments when the issue of nuclear energy was particularly salient in the public's mind—after the Kaiseraugst occupation, after the Chernobyl disaster, and after Fukushima—and it benefited from the massive shifts in public opinion in the popular votes.

Second, the rather limited role of the Greens in the Swiss case distinguishes it from the German one. In Switzerland, the policy reversals took place without the Greens ever having been part of the federal government (accordingly, H5 and H6 have not been relevant for the Swiss case). The relative unimportance of the Swiss Greens for nuclear power policy may be explained by the fact that the

Swiss Social Democrats, who have always been part of the government during the period under study, adopted an anti-nuclear stance very early on. In a way, the Social Democrats have pre-empted the field for the Greens in this particular policy domain. Yet this is not to say that the Greens have been unimportant for Swiss nuclear energy policy. This is illustrated by the fact that they successfully launched an initiative that put pressure on the government in the wake of Fukushima and more generally the Greens have been an important part of the pro-ecology coalition. However, they have never been the only, nor have they been the most important party of principled opposition against nuclear energy in Switzerland. Finally, the Swiss Christian-Democrats provide the most obvious illustration for a pragmatic anti-nuclear position in this policy domain (H5). The party's turn, which intervened after the Fukushima disaster and shortly before the federal elections in 2011, and which was engineered by its popular energy minister, is likely to have been motivated by the desire to defend its only seat in government and possibly gain an additional seat with the support of a popular cause.

REFERENCES

Broadbent, Jeffrey (1998). *Environmental Politics in Japan: Networks of Power and Protest*. Cambridge: Cambridge University Press.

Degen, Bernard (1993). *Sozialdemokratie: Gegenmacht? Opposition? Bundesratspartei?* Zürich: Orell-Füssli.

Delley, Jean-Daniel, and Luzius Mader (1986). *L'Etat face au défi énergétique*. Lausanne: Payot.

Giugni, Marco (2004). *Social Protest and Policy Change: Ecology, Antinuclear, and Peace Movements in Comparative Perspective*. Lanham, MD: Rowman & Littlefield.

Giugni, Marco, and Florence Passy (1997). *Histoires de mobilisation politique en Suisse: De la contestation à l'intégration*. Paris: l'Harmattan.

Jasper, James M. (1990). *Nuclear Politics: Energy and the State in the United States, Sweden, and France*. Princeton: Princeton University Press.

Jegen, Maya (2003). *Energiepolitische Vernetzung in der Schweiz: Analyse der Kooperationsnetzwerke und Ideensysteme der energiepolitischen Entscheidungsträger*. Basel: Helbing & Lichtenhahn.

Kriesi, Hanspeter (1982). *AKW-Gegner in der Schweiz*. Chur: Rüegger.

Kriesi, Hanspeter (1996). 'The Organizational Structure of New Social Movements in a Political Context', in Doug McAdam, John D. McCarthy, and Mayer N. Zald (eds), *Comparative Perspectives on Social Movements: Political Opportunities, Mobilizing Structures and Cultural Framings*. Cambridge: Cambridge University Press, 152–84.

Kriesi, Hanspeter, and Jegen, Maya (2001). 'The Swiss Energy Policy Elite.' *European Journal of Political Science*, 39: 251–87.

Meister, Urs (2008). *Strategien für die Schweizer Elektrizitätsversorgung im europäischen Kontext*. Zürich: Avenir Suisse.

Midttun, Atle, and Dieter Rucht (1994). 'Comparing Policy Outcomes of Conflicts over Nuclear Power: Description and Explanation', in Helena Flam (ed.), *States and Anti-Nuclear Movements*. Edinburgh: Edinburgh University Press, 383–415.

Rieder, Stefan (1998). *Regieren und Reagieren in der Energiepolitik: Die Strategien Dänemarks, Schleswig-Holsteins und der Schweiz im Vergleich*. Berne: Haupt.

Scharpf, Fritz W. (1997). *Games Real Actors Play: Actor-Centered Institutionalism in Policy Research*. Boulder, CO: Westview Press.

Schroeren, Michael (1977). *z.B. Kaiseraugst: Der gewaltfreie Widerstand gegen das Atomkraftwerk: Vom legalen Protest zum zivilen Ungehorsam*. Zürich: Verlag Schweizerischer Friedensrat.

Utz, Kathrin (2009). *Die Renaissance der Kernenergie in der Schweiz*. Lizentiatsarbeit, Institut für Politikwissenschaft, Universität Zürich.

Visser, Jelle, and Anton Hemerijck (1997). *'A Dutch Miracle': Job Growth, Welfare Reform and Corporatism in the Netherlands*. Amsterdam: Amsterdam University Press.

Yamasaki, Sakura (2007). 'Policy Change in Nuclear Energy: A Comparative Analysis of West European Countries.' PhD thesis. Université catholique de Louvain, Département des Sciences Politiques et Sociales.

12

Conclusion

Explaining Nuclear Policy Reversals

Wolfgang C. Müller, Paul W. Thurner, and Christian Schulze

12.1 INTRODUCTION

In this final chapter we aim to generalize from Western Europe's experience with nuclear energy policy-making, trying to understand the factors that have driven national decisions and that account for different energy policy trajectories of the countries. In so doing, we follow a three-track strategy. In the next section we confine ourselves to the seven countries intensively analysed in this book's case studies. These include the most complex cases that have gone through one or more nuclear energy policy reversals. Here we have the most in-depth evidence that allows us to evaluate the hypotheses formulated in Chapter 2.

Next we extend the scope of our analysis to all of Western Europe. For this purpose, we have written short analytical narratives of the trajectory of nuclear energy in the remaining countries that are presented in the Appendix to this chapter. They contain the information on which we build in the third section. In these country profiles, we systematically discuss for each case which factors were crucial in determining nuclear energy policy reversals. Our approach in writing these studies is a complement to the highly useful country profiles provided by the IEA, the IAEA, and other institutions as we are focusing on political parties' communication and decision behaviour. While facts and figures that dominate the existing reports are important, in the end it is politics that transforms them into strategies and decisions—the focus of our perspective. In the third section of this chapter we look at West Europe more synoptically, distinguishing four groups of countries in terms of nuclear energy policy reversals and discussing the communalities and differences between the countries in each group.

In the fourth section we turn to statistical analysis, trying to detect quantitative regularities and relationships. This perspective supplements the causal reasoning based on the in-depth analysis of cases. Note that our dependent variable is different in the qualitative comparative and in the statistical analyses. In the qualitative comparative analysis we focus on the most fundamental decisions: going 'nuclear' or not, expanding or freezing an existing nuclear energy programme, and maintaining nuclear energy or phasing it out. In the statistical analysis we focus on policy decisions directed *against* the use of nuclear energy.

Finally, we study slightly different time periods in these sections. Overall our various analyses thus complement rather than duplicate each other.

While the pioneering studies in this research field had a strong focus on antinuclear movements that challenge the existing system of well-aligned established parties and economic interests (Kitschelt 1986; Midttun and Rucht 1994), our approach considers the nuclear energy issue more as a 'normal' issue—though one with special qualities—in the political game.

In the final section of this chapter we briefly summarize its results and use the insights of the present volume to discuss the future of nuclear energy in Western Europe.

12.2 THE HYPOTHESES EVALUATED

In Chapter 2 we formulated thirteen simple bivariate hypotheses on how a number of factors will influence the fate of nuclear energy. These hypotheses are overlapping (or nested) in terms of having different generality. While not conditionally independent they interact in complex ways in the different contexts. Drawing on this book's seven country case studies we here discuss how these hypotheses have fared. In so doing, we mostly look at the major changes in nuclear energy policy that have occurred but also at the countries more generally to put these cases of actual decisions in greater context.

Our first hypothesis is related to political parties and their role in the system of government and hence the basic paradigm of party democracy, where parties compete by taking issue positions and act on these promises when in government (Dalton et al. 2011; Thurner 1998, 2000). The basic normative idea is to ensure that the important policy choices of a nation are tied to the electoral process. As a consequence, individual parties would remain committed to the issue positions of their electoral manifestos until they have gone through another election with different issue positions. Public policy change then results from parties that are committed to such change taking office. Hypothesis 1 captures this logic:

> H1. *Nuclear energy policy change will result from a party or a coalition of parties with programmatic commitment to such change, assuming government office, and replacing actors committed to maintaining the policy status quo.*

Turning to empirical observations, our seven in-depth country studies present a more nuanced bag of evidence. The archetypical programme-election-policy mechanism has been behind policy adaptations or reversals in four countries—France, and partly in Germany, Spain, and Sweden.[1] In Austria, Italy, and

---

[1] Reference is made to the French Socialist-Greens alliance in 1981 and 1997 (abandoning particularly controversial nuclear energy projects), the return to a strictly pro-nuclear course under the Conservative President Nicolas Szarkozy in 2007, and the capping of the nuclear energy programme under the Socialist-Green governments after 2012 in France, the Red-Green phase-out decision in Germany and its revision by the succeeding CDU/CSU-FDP government in Germany, the freezing of the nuclear energy programme in the 1980s by the PSOE government and expanding reactor capacity under the PP government from 2004, and the reviving of nuclear energy under the non-Socialist government taking office in 1997 and the Red-Green post-2014 attempts to phase out in Sweden.

Switzerland the major public policy reversals were the result of referendums or of governments that switched their position in the anticipation of direct-democratic decision-making. Although the parties may have promised more than they eventually delivered (e.g. in France) these full or partial reversals of nuclear energy policy in the seven case study countries have largely been tied to the process of electoral or referendum democracy. This is not true of the other policy reversals in the case study countries that have resulted from post-election bargaining between parties or spontaneous policy responsiveness of the government, disregarding their earlier programmatic announcements.

Our second hypothesis relates to the electoral salience of the nuclear energy issue. We highlighted the theoretical distinction between the attribution of salience at the level of voters and parties, respectively.

H2. Nuclear energy policy change is likely to result from significant changes in the salience the issue has to voters.

Admittedly, our compiled evidence on voters' issue salience with regard to nuclear energy is limited. To our own surprise, in many countries there have been only few if any systematic national surveys on the issue. To the extent that specific survey items are available, nuclear energy is rarely in the top ranks of the 'most important problems' (MIP) in open-ended questions indicating the directly elicited salience. Given the fact that opinion pollsters, drawing on focus groups and pilot studies, are typically very aware of issues' potential salience in electorates, the (lack of) availability of survey questions is telling in itself. In early periods, and in some countries using nuclear energy to a greater extent, the issue was not really a 'hot' one. Exceptions are periods with major nuclear energy disasters. There is more evidence on issue salience from the supply side of politics that, of course, does not translate directly into voters' issue salience. By and large it suggests that mainstream parties did not devote much attention to the nuclear energy issue in their manifestos. Even the peaks of attention to this issue in the manifestos are small if compared to that devoted to other issues. Nuclear energy has not been a core issue of any of the European mainstream parties because most of the time there was little to gain by emphasizing it. There are exceptions to this rule. The chapters on Sweden and Italy have highlighted the issue entrepreneurship of the Centre Party and the PSI, respectively. In the German case, the Social Democratic Party (SPD) developed after its U-turn in the mid-1980s into a fierce opponent of nuclear energy in order to contest the issue leadership of the Green Party. Of course, the situation is fundamentally different for Green parties. For them and anti-nuclear movements it is critical to influence the electoral issue agenda. Without their efforts to enter the electoral market, and the nuclear energy accidents of Chernobyl and Fukushima, the fate of nuclear energy in Western Europe would have been a different one.

A major precondition for Green breakthrough and anti-nuclear policy reversal is the change of public opinion:

H3. Nuclear energy policy change is likely to result from massive shifts in public opinion, amounting to majority support for a new policy.

Explaining Nuclear Policy Reversals 289

The underlying normative idea here is issue responsiveness. It is based on the understanding that democratic governance requires a constant exchange between the government and the governed (Dahl 2000) and adaptation of policies to new situations and new demands. The principle of short-term responsiveness may thus conflict with the tying of policy to the electoral process ex ante (before taking office) (Manin et al. 1999). This hypothesis, therefore, is substantively different from H1.

Empirically, the thermostatic model of politics expects, and provides evidence for, mutual adaptation of public policy and public opinion (Soroka and Wlezien 2010). With regard to the nuclear energy issue, the evidence assembled in our case studies is mixed. On the one hand, there are countries where such adaptation is nearly absent and considerably delayed at best. The chapter on France demonstrates that there is no direct linkage between public opinion and public policy. This country continued its massive nuclear energy expansion programme despite the electorate having adopted a negative attitude. In the case of France we also see that public opinion was strongly moulded by the established parties protected by the majoritarian system. Similarly, for the Netherlands Kees Aarts and Maarten Arentsen in Chapter 9 clearly state that H3 has to be rejected. This result is astonishing given the country's pure PR system. Similar to France, most voters were against nuclear energy as long as public opinion time series on this issue exist and real policy change was not connected to massive shifts in issue opinion among voters.

On the other hand, the link between public opinion and public policy is stronger in the remaining countries, although public policy change cannot always be related to massive short-term shifts in public opinion. In Germany, for the major policy decisions, the link to short-term public opinion shifts is not very strong. The Red-Green phase-out decision of 2001-2 was not linked to any particular public opinion shift. Although the Conservative-Liberal government's partial reversal of this decision by extending reactor lifetime in 2010 was preceded by a rather affirmative public opinion shift in the context of the 2008 campaign, a public opinion change in the opposite direction had already occurred when the issue was decided in 2010. In contrast, the post-Fukushima return to the previous phase-out date in 2011 mirrors a massive short-term shift in public opinion against nuclear energy. The earlier smaller policy changes in German nuclear energy policy brought public policy gradually in line with evolving public opinion but they are not short-term responses to massive opinion transformations.

In Italy, we find the closing-down decision of 1987-90 related to more long-term public opinion change described in Chapter 8 as the gradual 'greening' of Italian society and to a massive short-term push from Chernobyl. The attempts at a revival of nuclear energy in the 2000s were also rooted in more long-term public opinion change in the context of climate change and increasing energy prices and considered to be stable by the decision-makers. It was a massive short-term public opinion shift in the other direction caused by the Fukushima accident that led to referendum defeat and ended the revival plans in 2011.

In Austria, nuclear energy policy change was related to massive shifts in public opinion. As Chapter 5 shows, the 1978 referendum decision against nuclear energy reflected a dramatic short-term shift in public opinion that occurred in the referendum campaign. Opinions were strongly moulded by the parties in the run-up to the referendum. Chernobyl caused another massive and lasting shift against nuclear energy that has been reflected in symbolic politics since then.

For Sweden, Sören Holmberg and Per Hedberg in Chapter 10 document a strong relationship between the development of public opinion and public policy. Sweden turned away from nuclear energy in the short period where nuclear energy was rejected by referendum. The country abolished the phasing-out policy when public opinion had swung back to majority support for nuclear energy, and returned to a phasing-out policy when public opinion shifted again after the Fukushima disaster.

In no other country should the public opinion mechanism work as strongly as in Switzerland, given the direct-democratic instruments that have subjected each major policy decision to referendum since 1978. In his chapter Hanspeter Kriesi shows that public policy by and large mirrored public opinion. He also argues that the only exception—the rejection of two anti-nuclear initiatives in 2003—is most likely due to the electorate's lack of information in what was a complex decision-making situation.

Overall, thus, nuclear energy policy has been effectively isolated from public opinion in some countries. In contrast, in the majority of our cases public policy largely developed in tune with public opinion but often with considerable time gaps. Policy reversals thus mostly reflected evolutions in public opinion but not necessarily short-term ones.

Given the mostly weak link between public opinion shifts and public policy change, it is important to take a closer look at political actors and their rationales:

H4. *Policy change is more likely when government parties have large shares of issue-inconsistent voters.*

This hypothesis emerges from the idea that political parties are adapting their issue positions and public policy in a strategic manner. More specifically, they care most about their own (potential) voters. The two types of voters the government parties are most likely to lose are those without or with only a weak party affiliation and voters who disagree with their preferred party's policies on important issues. While a general party preference pulls issue-inconsistent voters towards their party, their nuclear energy issue preference pushes them away and towards another party (Thurner 2010). Policy change should be the more likely the more such issue-inconsistent voters the government parties have. In the respective party's best-case scenario, policy change can remove such inconsistencies without creating new ones of relevance (for instance, because the other voters are ambivalent on the issue or have only low-intensity preferences).

The hypothesis is generally supported by the evidence provided by the case studies—as long as the very restricted availability of appropriate surveys allowed us to test it. Yet how the issue-inconsistency mechanism has precisely worked differs widely over the cases. It therefore merits taking a closer look at the individual cases.

In France all parties had many issue-inconsistent voters since such policy preference measures are available. As Sylvain Brouard and Isabelle Guinaudeau show in Chapter 6, the case supports the hypothesis insofar as of the leading government parties the Socialists, the established party that eventually adjusted its policy and turned marginally against nuclear energy, had by far the highest share of issue-inconsistent voters.

As Chapter 7 demonstrates, all German parties switched their positions on nuclear energy in the course of time. The more they suffered from issue-inconsistency among their voters, the earlier they switched their positions. The SPD, faced with many voters deserting to the Greens, moved first. The FDP remained always highly ambivalent on the nuclear energy issue. Both pro-business parties, the FDP and the Christian Democrats, officially turned away from nuclear energy after Fukushima and their electoral disaster in Baden-Württemberg two weeks later.

In Switzerland, as Chapter 11 shows, the first government party that turned away from nuclear energy, the Social Democrats, had internal rifts over the nuclear energy issue early on while the other parties of the permanent ('magic formula') coalition government were still largely united on pursuing a pro-nuclear course. While this change of the Social Democrats' position had no direct impact on government policy, the post-Fukushima one of the CVP did. As Kriesi notes, the CVP's party base had become much more divided with respect to nuclear energy in recent years, distinguishing it from the other hitherto pro-nuclear energy government parties. This party's repositioning was the trigger for the 2011 government decision to phase out nuclear energy.

In the Netherlands voters of practically all political parties are, on average, opposed to nuclear energy but nuclear scepticism is stronger in the electorates of the left parties. The majority of party voters of the centre-right thus were not following their parties' cues on the nuclear energy issue. Chapter 9 shows that the CDA—the party that switched from the pro- to the anti-nuclear side in coalition with the PvdA that made the (eventually inconsequential) decision to fix a date for terminating nuclear energy—had indeed more nuclear-sceptical voters then the Liberals who continued to hold on to nuclear energy.

In Italy issue-inconsistency was also important. The 'greening' of the PSI, beginning in 1987, was mainly an offensive move to exploit the issue-inconsistency of its main competitor, the oppositional PCI. Yet at the same time the PSI was under threat from the Radical Party and the emerging Greens. While the policy change of the government was enforced by referendum, the PSI as a government party was important to ensure that the anti-nuclear referendum outcome was actually honoured—in contrast to other referendum outcomes that had been perverted before by actual government policy. Although it eventually failed, the move of Berlusconi's Pole of Liberty (PdL) to rejuvenate nuclear energy in the 2000s followed a similar logic as the PSI's issue entrepreneurship in the 1980s. Relying on a relatively homogeneous support base, the PdL tried to exploit the issue-inconsistency of the left's electorate by invoking the referendum mode.

In Austria issue-inconsistency of the governing Social Democrats was modest compared to that of the opposition parties, the People's Party and Freedom Party. This problem caused the People's Party to avoid clear positioning on the nuclear energy issue for a long time and eventually to oppose the specific reactor and the government's work rather than nuclear energy per se. Notwithstanding these troubles of its greatest competitor, the governing Social Democrats had a thin advance only over them. Even a small share of voters drifting away due to the nuclear energy issue could have put an end to their reign. Although the party remained firm in its position on the issue, its choice of the referendum mode was largely due to issue-inconsistency among party voters. The Social Democrats' calculation was that the referendum would allow both, keeping these voters loyal to the party in elections and, by exploiting greater issue-inconsistency among non-Socialist voters, winning the referendum. While the first bet was successful, the second was not.

> H5: *Governments will turn away from nuclear energy (if still committed to it) whenever a Green party participates in government.*

With regard to this hypothesis we have to consider only a few countries and office periods. There has been no Green government participation thus far in Austria, the Netherlands, and Switzerland, or in Italy when the country was employing nuclear energy. In the remaining countries and periods our case studies support the hypothesis. Germany's first phasing-out decision and Sweden's most recent attempts to use the market mechanism to enforce an exit from nuclear energy provide strong support. Even pro-nuclear France accepted anti-nuclear energy changes, although rather muted ones, when the Greens participated in government.

> H6: *No pro-nuclear energy policy change will be made whenever a Green party participates in government.*

Again the number of episodes with Green government participation is very limited in our sample of seven countries but all evidence from the four that have a relevant experience—France, Germany, Italy, and Sweden—supports the hypothesis.

> H7: *Government policy will turn away from nuclear energy if required to allow political parties with pragmatic positions on the issue the winning of, or holding on to, government office in coalition cabinets.*

This hypothesis derives from the desire for government office, one of the strongest motivations among political leaders (Riker 1962). Government office can be a goal in itself or instrumental. Taking a pragmatic attitude on nuclear energy considers the status quo and weighs different policy and political goals against each other. The parties we focus on here were positively associated with nuclear energy at some point and probably would have maintained that course if this had been the most likely way to win or hold on to government office.

The first party in government confronted with a critical challenge over nuclear energy was the Swedish Social Democrats. Perhaps underestimating the issue's potential power, they upheld their commitment to nuclear energy. Nuclear energy policy was one of the issues that contributed to their electoral defeat in 1976 and loss of government power. This not only caused the Swedish Social Democrats to rethink their issue position but warned political leaders in all democracies that the nuclear energy issue might have the power to make and break majorities and bring to office or down a government. Our case studies do not suggest that incumbent governments held on to nuclear energy when they considered this an issue that could lose them the election. Of course pro-nuclear energy governments were occasionally replaced by alternative governments, but not *because* of their commitment to nuclear energy. Our case study evidence suggests that the nuclear energy issue has not sufficiently shaped the voters' preferences to be labelled a 'decisive' issue in any further election. Knowing about its potential, government parties have been careful to engage in the 'management' of this issue and to show policy responsiveness if this was considered necessary to achieving their office goals.

We first look at episodes where issue position change has helped win government office. Several policy reversals are related to such preceding changes of parties' policy positions. While we do not question that much of such repositioning may involve soul-searching and re-evaluating issue positions given real-world changes and events, we are interested in whether these party changes were required for or functional to winning office. The Swedish Centre Party is a particular interesting case. It was the first mainstream party to reject nuclear energy and later returned to accepting it. The first change in the 1970s (turning anti-nuclear) improved its electoral competitiveness dramatically, the second one in the 2000s helped to forge the Non-Socialist Alliance. Both issue position changes were followed by periods of government office with nuclear energy policy reversals. In a similar vein, the German Red-Green alliance would not have been possible without the SPD adopting a critical position on nuclear energy. While we will never know how insistent the SPD under its leader Gerhard Schröder would have been on this policy goal in an alternative government coalition, the Red-Green one that actually formed after the 2008 elections decided the first German nuclear energy phase-out. Another case of 'functional' party position change preceding the winning of government office is the French PS. In need of the Greens as allies, the Socialists in opposition opted for a turn in nuclear energy policy both in the 1990s and in 2012, and followed up with terminating parts of the nuclear energy programme in both government periods (cancelling the Superphénix and individual reactor projects and de facto freezing the nuclear energy programme under Prime Minister Lionel Jospin and capping the programme under President Hollande).

Other nuclear energy policy changes were made by government parties still committed to nuclear energy when they took office. The most dramatic one occurred in Germany where the CDU/CSU-FDP cabinet under Chancellor Angela Merkel made a full U-turn, returning to the Red-Green phase-out policy the same government had begun to dismantle only a few months earlier. The Fukushima accident and its political fallout, especially the removal of a conservative-liberal government in Baden-Württemberg in the elections two weeks later, strongly suggested that holding on to power after the next election might indeed require policy responsiveness. The behaviour of Italy's strongest government party, the Democrazia Cristiana, was not quite so obviously party-strategic, when it decided to respect the referendum outcome. Yet, as Fabio Franchino (in Chapter 8), points out, such honouring of a referendum outcome was not a strong normative imperative in Italy but rather the result of the DC's accepting the blackmailing of its indispensable coalition partner, the PSI, and thus primarily due to the party's office goals. Similarly, in the Netherlands, the CDA was willing to adapt its nuclear energy position to its changing coalition partners, just before the major changes in Dutch nuclear energy policy were enacted. Two governments also shelved massive expansion plans for nuclear energy in response to the Chernobyl and Fukushima accidents and called for a time-winning nationwide energy debate after the Three Mile Island accident. In the latter case, however, the government reacted more immediately to protest behaviour that had been fuelled by the accident. These decisions were first and foremost issue management without paying the price of a more fundamental policy reversal.

The hypothesis is perhaps most difficult to evaluate for the Austrian case. The Social Democrats' strategy of holding a referendum in 1978 was an attempt to serve the party's office ambitions without forsaking its policy goal, as it banked on winning the referendum. The party taking the lead in outlawing nuclear energy thereafter and presenting itself in the 1979 election as the guarantor of the referendum outcome, however, clearly was functional for its office goals. Yet trying to revitalize the nuclear energy issue after the referendum was not (and, as a consequence, facing Green competitors in the 1983 election for the first time).

Given the 'magic formula' permanent coalition, government participation was hardly at stake for any of the major parties in Switzerland. Notwithstanding electoral considerations of individual parties, the post-Fukushima acceptance of nuclear energy phase-out by two previously pro-nuclear parties to a large extent was a willingness to adapt to the realities of how the issue would fare in future Swiss direct-democracy decision-making.

H8: *Partial policy change by an acting government is more likely when policy continuity is heavily challenged by a vital opposition.*

This hypothesis draws on expectations from the revised version of the 'advocacy coalition' approach (Sabatier 1998). Policy change then does not require replacing the government. Nor is it driven by substantive preference change of governments, caused, for instance, by changed objective conditions (such as discovery of natural resources). Rather it is the government's making concessions with the goal to make the policy's opponents relent and to win public approval for its responsiveness and reasoned approach. Such government concessions can be both substantive (affecting nuclear energy policy decisions) and procedural (the way how these policy decisions are made). The alternative would be to remain strictly on course and use parliamentary majorities and, if required, the state's coercive means to impose government policy (a kind of 'toughening-out' strategy such as Margaret Thatcher's handling of the British miners' strike) (Richardson 1982).

When we look at the narratives of the policy process in our case study countries there is evidence for both strategies. The Swedish Social Democrats' government was the first one to be challenged. Remaining firm on the subject matter, its information campaign was an attempt to win the argument by means of information and persuasion. The 1976 election defeat, by the Social Democrats' own understanding, was the price for remaining firm on the economic and nuclear energy policy issues at stake. The subsequent non-Socialist government formed without substantive agreement on the nuclear energy issue and eventually fell over it. For the time being, the issue was settled by referendum. Other Swedish governments came to office with a clear position on the nuclear energy issue and remained on course. No concessions were made in France where the government implemented its programme of nuclear expansion notwithstanding considerable extra-parliamentary protest early on. Given the leftist background of most protest and the majoritarian electoral system, the conservative governments in office at the time of strong mass protest were not particularly concerned about electoral punishment. Concessions were forthcoming only under the governments of the left of President Mitterrand (symbolically giving up one strongly challenged reactor project), Prime Minister Jospin, and President Hollande. They all agreed to make these concessions while still in opposition to improve their chances of winning power. If anything, once in power, real concessions fell short of what had been indicated before.

In the other countries typically governments have no such clear records of remaining firmly on their initially chosen nuclear power course. Typically, governments remained steadfast for a while but offered concessions when it turned out that the opponents of their policy could inflict considerable electoral or political costs on them. Procedural concessions cover the spectrum from moratoria, freezing the status quo for years (Netherlands after Chernobyl, Switzerland, following up upon the Kaiseraugst conflict, Germany after 1982), to invoking the referendum mode (only in Austria and Italy (in 2011) was the referendum government-initiated while referendums in Italy (in 1987), Sweden, and Switzerland were enforced by other actors). Substantive government concessions to the opponents of nuclear energy range from abandoning particular controversial parts of the nuclear energy programme such as reprocessing and building fast-breeder reactors (France, Germany, Netherlands) and giving up on individual reactor projects with particularly strong local protest (France, Italy) to fully blown reversal (Germany in 2011, in a rather proactive move of the government). Partial concessions may be also reached more easily in strong bicameral systems such as Germany, where there are incentives for governmental parties to relax their policy positions. At the same time, opposition parties may exploit a sub-national arena to polarize the debate and to attract deviant voters.

> H9: *Pro-nuclear energy policy change is more likely the more the energy supply of countries depends on the import of carbon-based energy sources (coal, oil, gas) and the less potential they have for developing alternative energies.*

This hypothesis would better be evaluated quantitatively and with a larger sample. To simplify things, we only look at the extreme cases: countries currently not using nuclear energy. Of the case study countries these are Italy and Austria. These are also the most energy import-dependent ones in our sample of seven (see Chapter 3, Figure 3.5). Yet Italy is much more import-dependent than Austria. At the same time the per capita production of alternative energy is much higher in Austria.[2] We thus should expect Italy to be more likely to make attempts at returning to nuclear energy than Austria. If we disregard the time from shortly after the referendum until Chernobyl in Austria, this expectation is met by the evidence, given the failed attempt under Berlusconi.

> H10: *Nuclear energy policy decisions made in temporal proximity to nuclear power accidents are more likely to turn away from nuclear energy to some extent or increase its costs (e.g. abandoning the entire programme or parts of it, reducing its scope, delaying its implementation, or introducing new safety requirements).*

---

[2] Eurostat, 'Primary Production of Renewable Energy, 2003 and 2013'. Document YB15-de.png.

The 1979 Three Mile Island accident may have prevented a settlement of the nuclear energy issue in Sweden and clearly helped the anti-nuclear side in the 1980 referendum. Otherwise it did not directly impact on major nuclear energy policy decisions in the seven countries considered here. In contrast, Chernobyl and Fukushima were not only much more severe accidents but also much more consequential in terms of decision-making.

France is the single case study country where nuclear energy policy was not affected by Chernobyl. In Sweden Chernobyl enforced legislation on the phasing-out decision already made in 1980. In Austria, Chernobyl was the death stroke to the already struggling attempts at reversing the decision to abandon nuclear energy. Given that it already had been outlawed no public policy resulted, but the event forced the electricity providers into a final set of firm-level withdrawal measures. In Germany, no immediate policy measures were taken but the context was set for important policy adaptations—terminating the fast-breeder reactor and reprocessing projects—in the next few years. Similarly, in Switzerland the Chernobyl disaster was functional for a negotiated ending of the Kaiseraugst conflict and agreeing on a moratorium for nuclear expansion. In Italy the Soviet reactor accident exercised considerable influence on the 1987 referendum terminating nuclear energy. In the Netherlands, nuclear expansion plans were shelved and a review process was set in motion. Notwithstanding a revival of nuclear expansion plans years later, the process of real expansion could never be set in motion again. The world of Western European nuclear energy politics would never be the same as before Chernobyl.

The Fukushima accident was even more consequential for the fate of nuclear energy in Western Europe. While it did not impact the nuclear energy policy of the incumbent Conservatives in France, it influenced the position-taking of the oppositional Socialists. In 2012, they committed to a policy of capping the nuclear energy programme and abandoning reactor projects. All this turned into government policy when the PS took office in the same year. In Sweden, Fukushima caused a massive swing in public opinion, turning nuclear energy supporters into a minority, and paving the way to an important yet not full policy reversal by the Red-Green government taking office in 2014. In Italy Fukushima brought down the attempt of the Berlusconi government to revive nuclear energy with the help of the referendum instrument, resulting in a major defeat of the government. In the Netherlands, Fukushima ended another attempt at revitalizing nuclear energy, although no formal decision was taken. Policy-relevance was most immediate in Germany and Switzerland. In both cases governments exercised a full reversal of nuclear energy policy. The CDU/CSU-FDP cabinet under Angela Merkel did so only a few months after it had begun to dismantle the Red-Green exit policy by extending the lifetime of existing reactors. Even the nuclear-free Austria reacted to Fukushima, engaging in more symbolic politics and international-level activity to fight nuclear energy.

> H11: *Countries heavily invested in nuclear energy are likely to continue on their pro-nuclear path.*

Clearly, investment (in particular if not yet fiscally depreciated) and energy dependency are important arguments in the debate about nuclear energy and constitute incentives to defend or aim to revitalize it. Our seven case studies comprise some of the world's leading nuclear energy countries. Nevertheless, all but one of these countries had decided at some point to abandon nuclear energy or to freeze its development. The country most invested and most dependent on nuclear energy, France, indeed continues on the nuclear path while all other of our case study countries have at some point abandoned nuclear energy. Yet there is no linear relationship between investment (measured by the share of nuclear energy in electricity consumption) and the timing of exit decisions (assuming that it would take the most invested ones longer to make this decisions). Nor does the current outcome, with the low-invested Netherlands remaining in the pool of nuclear energy countries and highly invested Germany and Switzerland on the exit route, reflect the basic reasoning behind the hypothesis.

> H12: *If countries heavily invested in nuclear energy reverse their policy, they will adopt a strategy of partial or gradual change.*

This hypothesis is universally confirmed by the trajectory of the case study countries that decided to abandon nuclear energy despite being heavily invested. Heavily invested Germany, Switzerland, and Sweden decided for long-term phase-outs. Looking at the other end of the continuum, in nuclear energy exit countries running only few old reactors (Italy) or having only one not yet activated (Austria) full withdrawal was implemented very quickly.

> H13: *The more time has passed since nuclear energy has been effectively abandoned, the less likely a return to it becomes.*

In three of our case study countries—Sweden, the Netherlands, and Germany—incoming governments had inherited both a relatively recent nuclear energy phase-out policy and a fleet of nuclear power plants still active. As we have seen, these governments found it easy to abandon the phase-out policy. Hypothesis 13 therefore probes the cases where nuclear energy has been effectively abandoned in that no reactor is working and other measures have been taken to dismantle the nuclear energy programme. Although our case studies include all the countries that have exited nuclear energy after at least building one reactor for industrial energy production, only Austria and Italy have reached this stage. For all the other countries currently on an exit route (another) policy reversal should be less challenging as the relevant structures and conditions for running a nuclear energy programme are obviously given.

In Austria, exiting nuclear energy in 1978, these structures were quite costly maintained for several years after the outlawing of nuclear energy as the energy providers, the major interest groups, and the government aimed at a policy reversal. Although the dismantling set in already before Chernobyl, after several attempts at reversal had failed, the developments since then have decisively closed the nuclear energy case. While technically a nuclear energy revival might still be feasible, it is not politically. A country once almost evenly split in terms of public opinion, with the economic and political elites largely in favour of nuclear energy, has turned into a solidly anti-nuclear country where rejection is nearly universal in the population and politicians compete on their anti-nuclear energy credentials.

In contrast, Italy started a process of reviving nuclear energy about twenty years after its exit in 1987/1990 and a projected restart of new nuclear power plants thirty-five years later. The Fukushima accident intervened and the attempt failed but given the decision-making rules it might otherwise have been successful. Substantial time passed since the exit from nuclear energy thus is not a sufficient condition to preclude attempts at revival of nuclear energy.

12.3 COMPARATIVE CASE STUDY ANALYSIS

We now turn to a comparative analysis of nuclear energy policy in all of Western Europe. The goal of our discussion is to identify the factors explaining why individual countries reversed their nuclear energy policy. In order to fully understand nuclear energy decision-making we need to look beyond actual policy reversals. Rather than focusing exclusively on actual policy reversals, we need to focus on the *decision situations* more broadly, considering what was on the agenda of actors who had the formal power to make nuclear energy policy decisions.

For the required information we draw on the detailed reconstructions of the political decision-making processes on nuclear energy in Western Europe. As mentioned, we draw on two types of studies. One is the seven country chapters in this volume. These analyses provide in-depth information on the trajectories of nuclear energy and the factors that exercised crucial influence on this process and its outcomes. In these case study chapters, the authors have used all available information to reconstruct the causal story. Similar to what our country experts have done in their case study chapters, in synoptic analyses of the remaining ten countries we have tried to draw on a variety of sources[3] to uncover the main causal lines of their nuclear energy policy. These case-by-case studies appear at the back of this chapter (Appendix). In the present section we bring the information from all the country analyses together.

Collectively, these country studies show that nuclear energy was indeed universally accepted in the 1950s. Any Western European country that could seriously think of mastering the challenge of 'going nuclear' planned to do so at some point in time. Yet the subsequent trajectories of nuclear energy were very different in the various countries. Some withdrew early from their nuclear energy plans, others established nuclear energy programmes but then made policy reversals, and still others continued on the nuclear energy track. Accordingly, we structure our discussion in four panels of countries:

(1) those that never planned to go into nuclear energy production,
(2) those with planning for a nuclear energy programme but early withdrawal from these plans,
(3) those that built and mostly used nuclear power plants but at one point decided to withdrew from nuclear fission,
(4) those that built up a nuclear energy programme and never decided to abandon it.

The countries in groups 1 and 4 never made an explicit reversal of their nuclear energy policy, though the outcome is obviously very different. The countries in groups 2 and 3 have made reversals in their nuclear energy policy. The difference

---

[3] Unfortunately, the literature on some of smaller countries with early withdrawal from nuclear energy is rather thin. Most of these primarily historically oriented contributions also appeared too late to be used for the important comparative studies of Kitschelt (1986) and Midttun and Rucht (1994). Our country profiles also differ from those provided by the International Atomic Energy Agency and the World Nuclear Association. Despite providing valuable information these reports do not focus on the decision situations and the strategic considerations of the respective governments.

is that the reversals of group 2 countries were low-cost while those of group 3 were high-cost due to large sunk costs for investment in nuclear energy programmes and greater political risk for the decision-makers. The two groups also distinguish themselves by the finality of the current state of nuclear energy policy. While we can safely assume that group 2 countries will maintain their policy status quo, this is less the case with group 3 countries. Finally, group 3 is not homogeneous with regard to the extent of the current use of nuclear energy and what lastly had been decided on the future of nuclear energy.

12.3.1 Group 1: Nuclear Energy Abstainers

The first group is confined to four of the smallest and/or least populated countries in Western Europe—Andorra, Cyprus, Iceland, and Malta—that are also geographically quite peripheral and for long have been economically weak. These states thus clearly lacked practically the necessary preconditions for 'going nuclear' and therefore did not seriously consider this option at one point. In order not to inflate our sample with irrelevant cases we exclude these countries from further consideration. That all other countries did plan for the use of nuclear energy at some point in time is testament to the fact that nuclear energy in the 1950s and 1960s was almost universally accepted as the up-and-coming energy technology of the twentieth century (see Chapter 1).

12.3.2 Group 2: Early Complete Withdrawal from Nuclear Energy

This group comprises Denmark, Greece, Ireland, Luxembourg, Norway, and Portugal.[4] All these countries had nuclear energy ambitions at some point, but then withdrew. Why did they not take the final steps to nuclear energy? According to our detailed country profiles, the central actors responded to the following interacting factors: anti-nuclear movements and citizen attitudes, competitive party strategies, lateness in the process of developing nuclear energy, the prospect of soon tapping alternative energy resources, and/or economic resource constraints.

Our country profiles indicate that anti-nuclear movements indeed managed to mobilize considerable resistance against going nuclear. The snapshot of nuclear energy attitudes from the first Eurobarometer surveys with relevant items available for these countries (Figure 12.1) shows the fruits of these efforts: in none of these countries did a majority of respondents consider nuclear energy 'worthwhile'. Although nuclear energy supporters were the plurality in Denmark, Luxembourg, and Ireland, Figure 12.1 shows that the shares of citizens rejecting or accepting nuclear energy were similar-sized in Denmark and Luxembourg, while nuclear energy rejection prevailed in Greece and Portugal. Moreover, large shares of respondents did not record a firm opinion. This early snapshot, of course, is taken at different times in the national policy processes but it shows that the public opinion environment was not favourable to nuclear energy in any

---

[4] For short analyses of these countries see this chapter's Appendix.

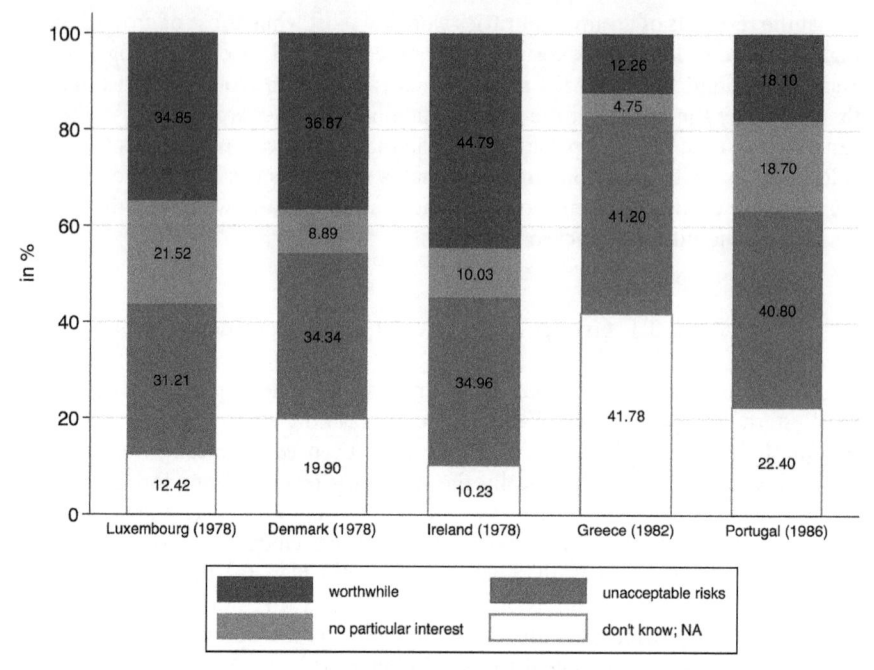

Figure 12.1. Attitudes towards Nuclear Energy in the first Eurobarometer Available

Note: Question format: all new developments in the industrial field imply effort, time and money, They may also involve risk. Here are three opinions about the development of nuclear power stations, which use atomic energy for the production of electricity. Which of these three statements comes closest to your own opinion on the development of nuclear power?

Sources: EB 10A, 17, 26, 46.0.

of these countries around the time when critical decisions about nuclear energy were made.

Figure 12.2 shows how public opinion developed in the countries of group 2. While anti-nuclear attitudes peaked after Chernobyl, even when memory of the accident faded away in most countries a majority of respondents continued to oppose nuclear energy.

Against the background of anti-nuclear mobilization and a large share of citizens rejecting nuclear energy in all countries the issue had party-political relevance. In all these cases, Green parties were electorally weak. Yet in Denmark and Norway 'left-to-the-traditional-left' parties politicized environmental issues and nuclear energy very early on. As a consequence, the Social Democrats adjusted their positions. As major parties used to form single-party minority cabinets in these countries they did not want to give too much room to their leftist competitors, nor did they want to radically break with the post-war policy of economic growth. A natural strategy of adjusting party policy positions in government is to delaying decisions. In Greece and Portugal, the nuclear energy issue was absorbed in the traditional left–right conflict, with left parties being more negative about nuclear energy. Electoral concerns and delaying decisions were not confined to the parties of the left, however. Provided they were in government

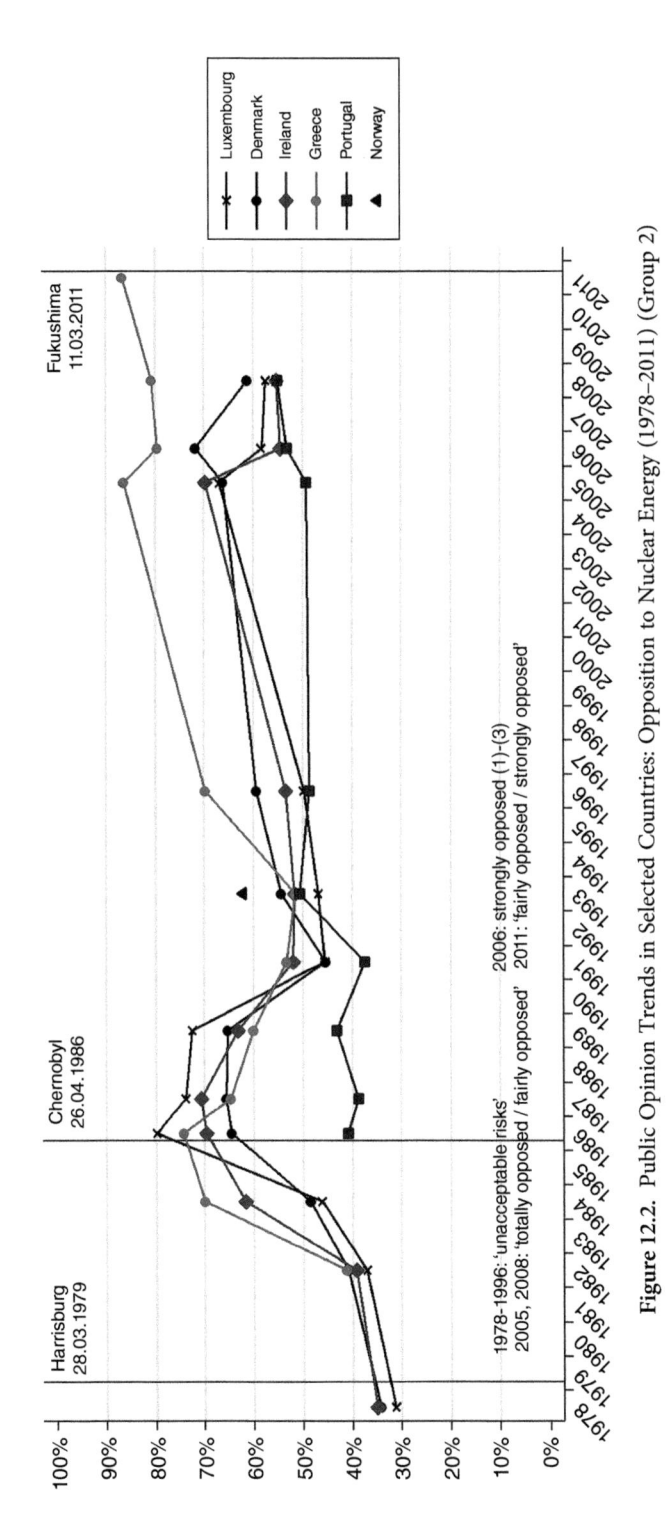

Figure 12.2. Public Opinion Trends in Selected Countries: Opposition to Nuclear Energy (1978–2011) (Group 2)

Note: EB 75.1 was conducted before Fukushima.

Sources: Eurobarometer 10A, 17, 22, 26, 28, 31A, 35.0, 39.1, 46.0, 63.2, 65.3, 69.1, 75.1.

(as in Ireland or Luxembourg) the centre-right parties also followed this track. In both cases conservative governments on a pro-nuclear course had lost elections and, although other issues may have been more important, these parties were more concerned about the electoral risks associated with a pro-nuclear energy course when they returned to government.

Of course, anti-nuclear movements and critical citizens were not unique to these countries in the 1970s or 1980s, whenever they retreated from their nuclear energy ambitions. However, these countries were laggards in developing nuclear energy industrially. None of them had built reactors for energy production by the 1970s, the time when anti-nuclear movements begun to flourish and to exercise cross-border impact. In this political environment the costs of initiating specific reactor projects were politically too high because the Social Democratic parties and even centre and liberal parties had abandoned the earlier pro-nuclear policy consensus. Quite simply, the nuclear energy issue now was credible as a threat to existing party loyalties. In the cases of Ireland and Greece this process was fuelled by the Three Mile Island and Chernobyl accidents, respectively, that were proximate to the making of important decisions on nuclear energy.

We also need to consider more structural contextual conditions. With regard to Denmark, Ireland, and Norway and partly even Greece we refer to the endowment of these countries with plenty of energy resources (oil, gas, lignite), or at least the perception thereof in the case of Ireland (which proved to be fallacious).[5] In the first three cases the relevant discoveries were recent and with such prospects it was considered not necessary to continue on the nuclear path. While this was not the case with Luxembourg, its small size gave room for a different economic strategy: de-industrialization and a turn to service industry. Under such conditions responsiveness was cheap, as it did not require sacrificing policy goals close to the heart of the parties such as economic growth or welfare state expansion. In the cases of Greece and Portugal, we have also to account for the difficult transition phase to democracy and in the latter case also the government's empty coffers due to the hugely costly decolonization wars. These were simply not the conditions to engage in a long-term programme with high start-up costs and only long-term investment amortization.

12.3.3 Group 3: Countries with Nuclear Energy Policy Reversals

The countries in this group are Austria, Belgium, Italy, Germany, the Netherlands, Spain, Sweden, and Switzerland.[6] They went down the nuclear energy track much further than the group 2 countries. All of them built nuclear power plants and all but one also produced nuclear energy. Yet all these countries at some point decided to abandon the nuclear energy track. However, they are not in the same pool when we consider the final outcome of nuclear energy policy (as of 2015). First, all countries but Austria and Italy have active reactors connected to the grid.

---

[5] In the Irish case gas stocks were rapidly ebbing. Today, Ireland is heavily dependent on oil imports and inflows of electricity from Britain, and the nuclear energy issue is being debated again.

[6] All countries but Belgium and Spain are covered in country chapters; for these two see the detailed country profiles in the Appendix.

Secondly, of the countries with active nuclear energy programmes all but the Netherlands produce major shares of their electricity in nuclear power reactors. Thirdly, while the reversal countries share the property of once deciding against the further use of nuclear energy, not all have upheld this decision.

While Germany decided to phase out under the Red-Green government in 2002 it extended reactor lifetime in 2011, presumably as a first step to nuclear energy revival, but returned to about the original Red-Green phasing-out strategy after Fukushima in the same year. Sweden has gone from phasing out after the 1980 referendum with a long time-frame, to a policy of speeding up this process by the early closing down of some reactors and an earlier end-date for nuclear energy in 1991, to lifetime extension and a policy of renewal on the existing sites after 2006, to a government policy—not yet specific regulation—of using the market mechanism to terminate nuclear energy under the Red-Green government since 2014. Spain has moved from freezing (since 1983, renewed 1994) to reactor capacity upgrading and specific reactors' licence renewal (i.e. lifetime extension) after 2004 to ending the moratorium for new construction and general lifetime extension. Switzerland has moved from freezing nuclear energy for ten years (resulting from a 1990 initiative) to rejuvenating nuclear energy with the government plan to build two new reactors in the 2000s to phasing out in 2011, just after Fukushima. Belgium moved away from its pro-nuclear course first with a long moratorium period just after the Three Mile Island accident. The moratorium gave way to inconsequential expansion plans, and was reinstalled after Chernobyl and several times renewed before a nuclear energy phase-out was decided in 2003. Yet Belgium granted lifetime extensions for the existing reactors in 2013 and 2015 and thus has bought itself more time to decide its energy future. The Netherlands stopped nuclear energy expansion after Chernobyl and in 1993 decided to close its two nuclear plants by 2003. However, it granted one ten-year and one twenty-year lifetime extension in the 2000s to the single remaining reactor. Provided no further lifetime extension or building of new plants occur this makes 2033 the end-date of nuclear energy in the Netherlands.

Belgium, the Netherlands, and Spain currently seem to be waiting—at least as some actors are concerned—for an open window of opportunity for another period of nuclear expansion, or, at least, the replacement of ageing reactors. In some cases, specific plans for a nuclear rejuvenating had been prepared but held back as a consequence of Fukushima, low oil and gas prices, and low economic growth.

Notwithstanding the differences between the countries in this group, for the study of policy reversals it is important that they all made considerable investments in nuclear energy. While it is obvious that political actors associated with steering the country on the nuclear power track may find it politically costly to reverse their own decisions, sunk costs make a policy reversal a difficult and often politically risky move even for parties not involved in the original decisions. Political decisions producing stranded investment typically burden the economy and cause direct or indirect negative effects for the government budget. This, in turn, may undermine the viability of other goals cherished by the relevant actors such as economic growth or public spending in other areas. For all these reasons reversals of advanced nuclear energy policy programmes are typically contested and decisions may not be taken as final by the losers as long as they can technically be re-reversed.

Why do this group's countries have such complex histories of nuclear energy policy? We begin by highlighting the importance of what we dubbed the 'natural enemies' of nuclear energy in Chapter 4 in these countries. Street protest against nuclear energy was particularly important in Germany, the Netherlands, Spain, and Switzerland. It helped to eliminate particular controversial nuclear energy projects from the agenda, such as the German reprocessing plant in Wackersdorf, the three-country fast-breeder project in Kalkar, the Lemoniz reactor in the Basque region of Spain, and the planned reactor Kaiseraugst in Switzerland. Yet political protest did not derail the countries' nuclear energy policy in a broader perspective. We have discussed the development of public opinion in these countries in greater detail in Chapter 4, finding relatively large shares of citizens who oppose nuclear energy but considerable differences over time and between countries (see Figure 4.1). For several of the countries of group 3, nuclear energy policy was out of tune with public opinion for long periods. As we have seen in this chapter's previous section, decision-makers were also quite immune to massive short-term moves of public opinion. We may exempt public opinion changes that are related to the three major reactor accidents—Three Mile Island and, in particular, Chernobyl and Fukushima.

While public opinion is an important parameter in representative democracies, it only impacts directly on policy outcome if the referendum mode is invoked. This has been the case in Austria (1978), Sweden (1980), Italy (1987, 2011), and Switzerland (several times). The referendum mode can be invoked bottom-up in Italy and Switzerland but only top-down in the other countries. The country chapters have shown that even when the people have decided this is rarely the final word. In Austria, the nuclear energy structures were maintained and for most of a decade attempts were made by the government and industry to reverse the referendum outcome. In Sweden the three referendum options produced an outcome that gave the elites much freedom in formulating the new nuclear energy policy and to reverse it several times thereafter. In Italy the 1987 referendum rejecting nuclear energy was observed but probably only because the winning side was represented in government. The 2011 government-induced referendum to revive nuclear energy in Italy turned into a political debacle due to the Fukushima accident. The outcome was respected (and the Berlusconi cabinet did not survive it long) but if the Constitutional Court had not prevented it, the government would have backtracked from holding a referendum and waited for a better opportunity. In Switzerland both nuclear energy opponents and supporters demonstrated repeatedly that they are able to enforce a referendum. Referendum outcomes had been on both sides and were observed, as it is typical for Switzerland. At the same time, each referendum result for the losing side was only the starting point to work towards its revision. In the context of Fukushima, no referendum was held but the government anticipated further rounds of direct-democratic decision-making and decided to phase out nuclear energy.

In the absence of direct-democratic decision-making, issue-specific public opinion is one of many inputs to the representative channel. To become effective, it depends on political parties formulating alternative positions, competing on these in elections and acting upon their stated policy preferences between elections. Following Tavits (2007), we have distinguished parties with principled and those with pragmatic positions (i.e. ones that can be traded) on a specific policy issue. We have identified the Green party family as the one with a principled (and negative) attitude towards nuclear energy and have assumed that all other parties will take pragmatic positions on that issue. However, in Switzerland (Social Democrats), Italy (Radical Party), and Spain (Communists, United Left)—similar to some of the group 2 countries discussed above—the nuclear energy issue has been taken on in a principled way by other parties even before Green parties emerged on the national political scene.

Other parties have also turned against nuclear energy but have more pragmatic issue positions such as the Dutch, Swedish, and German Social Democrats, the Socialists in Italy, Spain, and Flanders. Some of the parties turning away from nuclear energy early on are non-Socialist parties such as the Swedish Centre Party and the Austrian Freedom Party and People's Party. What these parties have in common is that their turning against nuclear energy occurred due to genuine concerns of *some* intra-party actors *and* strategic party positioning. These parties have either responded to a strategic dilemma or tried to exploit a strategic opportunity. The strategic dilemma typically is a large share of issue-inconsistent voters in the (potential) party electorate who may decide to vote for another party, typically one already positioned against nuclear energy such as a Green or Radical Left party in the case of mainstream left parties. A move from a pro- to an anti-nuclear position resulting from a strategic dilemma, of course, means that it also involves the risk of losing voters who are in favour of nuclear energy. Similarly, the borderline between responding to a dilemma and trying to exploit a strategic opportunity often is fluid.

In Germany, the SPD's repositioning on the nuclear energy issue was removing the single most important roadblock on the way to a Red-Green alliance and hence a credible alternative to the seemingly permanent government coalition of the CDU/CSU-FDP. The Austrian Freedom Party, the Swedish Centre Party, and the Italian PSI tried to reach out to new 'post-materialist' voters, the Austrian People's Party—itself split over the issue—hoped to use it as a lever for breaking the Social Democratic majority and returning to cabinet.

Other parties also have changed their issue position on nuclear energy or, at least, have become more flexible in its interpretation. The Swedish Liberals, originally pro-nuclear, supported earlier phase-out in 1991 but returned to the pro-nuclear energy camp already in 1997. Despite a long history of taking a stance against nuclear energy the Dutch D66 supported lifetime extensions in the 2000s. In contrast, the Swiss CVP, after years of reluctant support for nuclear energy, tipped the balance in favour of phasing out after Fukushima. The Flemish Liberals and the German FDP have taken more ambivalent positions over the years and maintained flexibility to adjust their nuclear energy positions to context.

Context is of general importance here. On the one hand, it means the hard facts of energy and, more recently, also climate policy. Abandoning nuclear energy in most cases simply amounts to a major challenge in terms of providing sufficient energy supply without unduly increasing energy security, climate policy, and budgetary problems. On the other hand, it refers to the political opportunity structures of the parties: their chances to appeal to voters, to build coalitions, and to implement party policies. As we have seen, parties with pragmatic issue positions are willing to trade the nuclear energy issue as long as they expect to benefit overall.

Party behaviour, be it principled or pragmatic, is related to nuclear energy policy decision-making in many ways that can be summarized in three major patterns. One is the classic *programme-election-policy mode*, with parties competing on a platform that includes the relevant policy reversal. The party or parties winning the elections then form the government and implement the policy (Dalton et al. 2011). The second pattern is that a policy reversal results from *coalition bargaining*, that is, some parties are strongly committed to nuclear energy policy reversal and use their leverage in coalition negotiations to make their more pragmatic partners accept this position. The third pattern is a *reversal by an incumbent government as a reaction to external pressure or events* as it reckons that policy consistency will be punished electorally and may lead to losing government office.

The first country of group 3 to make a nuclear energy policy reversal was Austria. Notwithstanding some agenda-setting by the anti-nuclear movement, the issue eventually was a high politics game between the then three parties in parliament. Within a few years, nuclear energy and the first ready-to-start reactor Zwentendorf moved from all-party consensus to the Social Democrats' exclusive project—with the two opposition parties trying to use the issue for their electoral and coalitional benefits. Although the Social Democrats remained steadfast on nuclear energy itself, they chose the referendum option—hoping that would allow them to win the referendum in 1978 and to keep their electoral alliance intact for the next election in 1979. They were wrong on nuclear energy, and quickly outlawed its use after the lost referendum. As the Social Democrats opted for a procedural solution, this is a special case of a party changing its policy in government. The story continued for almost a decade as the losers tried to reverse the decision. It was Chernobyl that put a final end to the attempts at reviving nuclear energy in Austria.

In Belgium the first major change in the country's nuclear energy programme was a moratorium enforced in 1979 as a spontaneous reaction of the government to the Three Mile Island accident that was renewed after Chernobyl and thereafter. These were classic issue avoidance decisions of governments not in urgent need to move. The next move was the 2003 phase-out decision, a coalition concession to the Greens in their first-time government participation. The lifetime extensions of 2013 and 2015 were the product of another coalition, without Greens but with the pro-nuclear Christian Democrats, Liberals, and Flemish nationalists.

In Sweden the first major nuclear energy policy reversal, the decision to phase out by the year 2010, resulted from the 1980 referendum. The referendum had been called in a joint initiative of opposition and government parties to resolve the issue that had plagued both the Social Democrats, contributing to their 1976 defeat, and the non-Socialist governments in office since 1976. Subsequent policy reversals had a clear party profile and followed the programme-election-policy mode. The 1991 pushing forward of the phasing-out date pitted the then anti-nuclear parties—Social Democrats, Centre, and Liberals—against the others in a parliamentary vote called by the Social Democratic government. Speeding up this process further in the late 1990s resulted from the issue realignment of parties. The Left Party had replaced the Liberal Party in the anti-nuclear alliance while the Liberals now had returned to the pro-nuclear side. The next party to change position was the Centre Party. It joined the non-Socialist government with the Conservatives and Liberals, assuming office in 2006, already as a pro-nuclear party. This government granted lifetime extensions and allowed the renewal of worn-out reactors on existing sites. The final policy reversal came with the Red-Green alliance taking office in 2014 and is more of a stealthy nature as the government employs market mechanisms to terminate nuclear energy.

In Spain the first nuclear energy policy reversal was the 1984 moratorium by the Socialist (PSOE) government and it was confirmed in 1994 still by the same government. In initiating the moratorium, the PSOE reacted to its electoral competitors of the Radical Left and a public opinion largely negative towards nuclear energy. As the PSOE had vaguely promised 'ordered suspension' of nuclear energy in its electoral manifesto of 1982 this reversal follows the programme-election-policy mode. The same applies to the reversal made by the conservative Partido Popular (PP) by expanding the capacities of existing reactors between 1998 and 2003. The next major nuclear energy decision was made the PSOE that had returned to government in 2004 after it had promised to phase out in 2000. However, once in office it rather continued the PP's strategy of maintaining nuclear energy by renewing the licences (i.e. extending the lifetime) of existing reactors that otherwise would have been closed down between 2011 and 2018. This direction was continued with the PP returning to office in 2011 that was followed by lifting the moratorium for new construction. While the PP's policy reversal follows the programme-election-policy mode, the one before made by the PSOE was a change of course by an incumbent government party. Rather than responding to issue-specific pressure from public opinion, second-order elections, or protest behaviour the PSOE seems to have weighed the short-term costs and problems resulting from nuclear exit that would have further reduced its capacity to fight the economic crisis. In other words, it has traded its nuclear energy policy goal against socio-economic goals closer to the heart of the party.

The Netherlands entered a period of debate of nuclear energy already in 1981, responding to public criticism and little support for plans to expand nuclear energy. This debate failed to produce a societal consensus and right after Chernobyl was followed by a review of the country's nuclear programme. The expansion plans dating from the mid-1970s were officially cancelled when the first formal and major policy reversal took place: the CDA-PvdA government's decision to phase out nuclear energy and to switch off its two nuclear power plants by 2003. This was a decision in the coalition mode: the CDA at that time was not a strongly pro-nuclear party and the PvdA wanted to terminate nuclear energy as soon as possible. Reacting to a court decision, the following CDA-VVD-D66 coalition decided in 2003 to extend the lifetime of the only remaining plant to 2013. The same government in 2006 decided to further extend its lifetime to 2033. These decisions were triggered by an external event, a court decision, but were largely in line with what the larger parties had stated in their electoral manifestos (although a concession needed to be extracted from D66).

In Germany the first major reversal of nuclear energy policy was the phase-out decision of 2001. It was made by the Red-Green coalition and corresponded to the parties' pre-electoral promises (though the Greens would have preferred to have a more radical break). This decision was partially reversed in 2011, by extending the lifetime of reactors, by the CDU/CSU-FDP coalition, again in line with what these parties had announced before the election. Both reversals thus follow the programme-election-policy mode. The final policy reversal followed swiftly, when the CDU/CSU-FDP government returned to a phase-out policy similar to the one the Red-Green coalition had left behind. In this case the government reacted to Fukushima-influenced signals from public opinion and regional elections.

Switzerland in several ways is a special case. The permanent coalition of all major parties, the toleration of individual cabinet parties departing from the government course, and direct-democratic bottom-up processes have, in a way, limited the impact of nuclear energy on party competition. Direct-democratic decision-making has directly or indirectly steered Swiss nuclear energy policy. The government's decision in 2011 to phase out nuclear energy rests on the conclusion that a stop-and-go policy as it may result from further rounds of direct-democratic decision-making is not compatible with making long-term decisions on major investments and ensuring the country's energy supply.

Bringing the analysis of group 3 countries to a conclusion, the nuclear energy issue has been party-politicized after initial agenda setting by other actors, mostly anti-nuclear movements. While Green parties played a key role in this process in Germany and Belgium, the spectrum of political parties taking positions against nuclear energy is broader and ranges from the radical left to the mainstream-right. Notwithstanding true concern of individual actors within mainstream parties about the dangers of nuclear energy, these parties typically thought to improve their position in party competition by making this move. The mainstream parties of the left abandoned the post-war pro-nuclear energy consensus mostly because of being pressured by internal opposition, party electorates with large shares of issue-inconsistent voters, and the need to find allies for government coalitions. However, Green and left parties have no monopoly of turning against nuclear energy. Other parties have shown remarkable flexibility in adapting their positions when their traditional pro-nuclear positions turned into a liability and threatened their office gaols. Actual nuclear energy policy reversals have their individual stories that can be summarized in three broad patterns: the classic programme-election-policy mode (such as the German Red-Green phase-out), where a policy reversal is carried out by election winners according to their programme, the coalition mode, when it is a concession made to forge a government coalition (such as the Belgian phase-out decision in 2003), and finally incumbent governments reacting to external pressure or events that seem to undermine their chances of holding on to government office (such as the U-turn of the German government under Chancellor Merkel after the Fukushima accident).

12.3.4 Group 4: Non-Reversal Countries Continuing on the Nuclear Energy Track

The countries in this group are Finland, France, and the United Kingdom.[7] These three countries never made the decision to abandon nuclear energy. However,

---

[7] While France is covered in detail in Chapter 6, the other two countries are discussed in this chapter's Appendix.

France recently has decided to put a cap on the total number of its reactors and all countries have gone through periods with a de facto freeze on nuclear energy. Although there are considerable differences between these three countries, nuclear energy is important in the energy mix in each case. Moreover, these countries are currently planning and building new nuclear energy production facilities.

France and the UK were early in developing nuclear energy, building a first wave of reactors already in the 1950s. Nevertheless, the size and relevance of nuclear energy is quite different in these countries. Clearly, France is most committed to it, having expanded its nuclear energy programme in several major waves. In contrast, in the UK the process of nuclear energy build-up had been de facto stopped in the 1980s due to the large-scale production of North Sea oil and gas since the mid-1970s. Britain turned to nuclear energy renewal only in the 2000s when its fleet of nuclear reactors was ageing and the oil and gas revenues dwindling.

Why have the three countries maintained their commitment to nuclear energy? We begin by highlighting the importance of what we dubbed the 'natural enemies' of nuclear energy in Chapter 4 and discuss the factors that have figured prominently in the episodes leading to nuclear energy reversal in group 3 countries.

Street protest against nuclear energy was prominent in France in the 1970s and early 1980s (Nelkin and Pollak 1982) and also noticeable in the UK in these decades (Chapter 4). To the best of our information, it was largely absent in Finland (Kitschelt 1988: 221). Similarly, public opinion on nuclear energy has been much more critical in the UK (Figure 12.3) and, in particular, France (Chapter 6), with large shares of the electorates evaluating nuclear energy critically. Yet even in Finland, more than a third of the electorate opposed nuclear energy in 2008 (Chapter 4).

In none of this group's countries have the citizens been asked to vote in a referendum on nuclear energy. As already noted, in the absence of direct-democratic decision-making, issue-specific public opinion is just one of many inputs to the representative channel. To become effective, it depends on political parties formulating alternative positions, competing on these in elections, the issue having high salience, and the parties acting upon their positions between elections.

Turning to party-political agents who politicise nuclear energy, Green parties, the archetypical expression of anti-nuclear energy positions, exist in all three countries. Yet in Britain the first-past-the-post electoral system has prevented their electoral breakthrough. In France the two-round majoritarian system had a similar protective effect from Green competition until the 1990s. Only after having demonstrated their viability in European and regional elections under PR rules, did the French Greens enter the national parliament in 1997. The Finnish Greens were represented in parliament since 1987 as one of nine or ten parliamentary parties, typically being the largest of the smaller ones.

Before the breakthrough of the Greens, the only other party-political opponent to nuclear energy in France was a tiny radical left party that merged with the Socialists in 1974. In Britain, the Liberal Democrats began to compete on this issue in 1992 by adopting a phase-out nuclear energy position. In all three countries all major parties had been involved, at least in some way, in developing the nuclear energy programmes. Such involvement, however, does not preclude later position change.

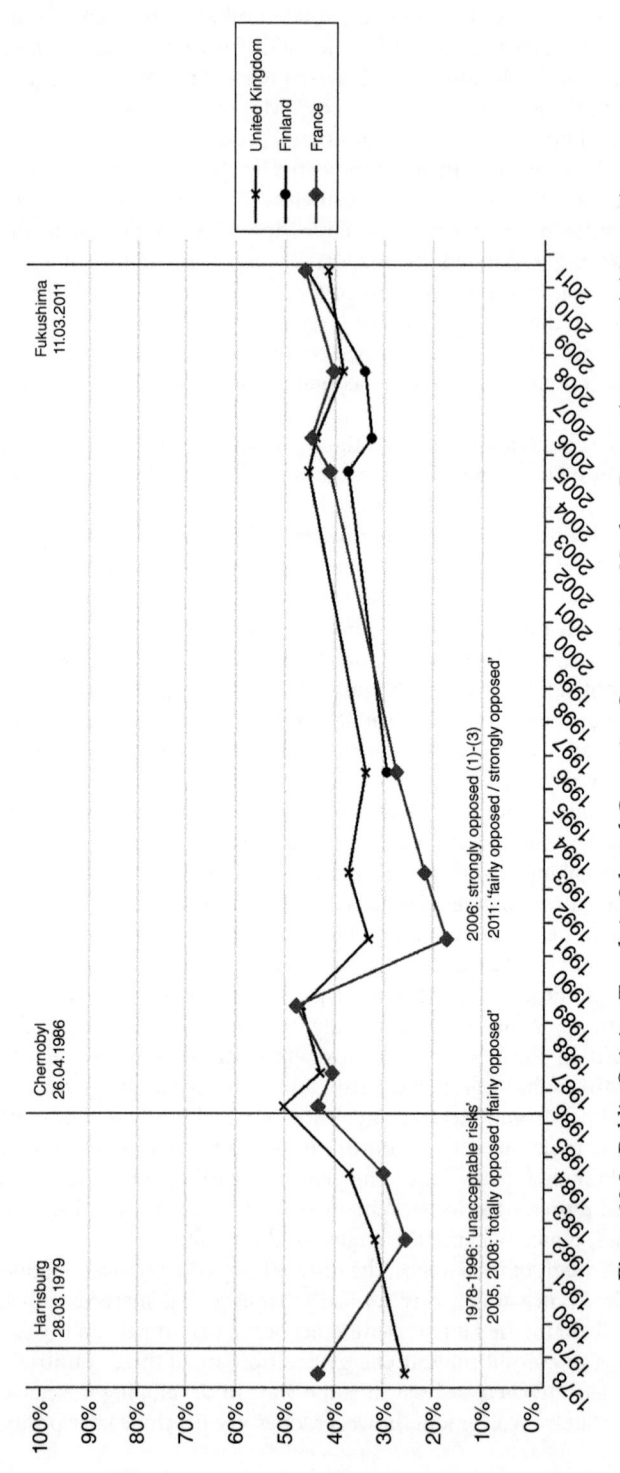

Figure 12.3. Public Opinion Trends in Selected Countries: Opposition to Nuclear Energy (1978–2011) (Group 4)

Note: EB 75.1 was conducted before Fukushima.

Sources: Eurobarometer 10A, 17, 22, 26, 28, 31A, 35.0, 39.1, 46.0, 63.2, 65.3, 69.1, 75.1.

In Britain and France, the electorates of most parties were split over the issue. The rational strategy for the major parties was to keep it off the agenda to the best of their abilities. Of the mainstream parties those of the left have been the most likely ones to abandon the post-war pro-nuclear energy consensus. Typically, they have more issue-inconsistent (potential) voters, suffer from intra-organizational conflict over this issue, and are often need to reach out to Green or radical left parties as allies in the electoral and parliamentary arenas. This is also true for the French Socialists, British Labour, and the Social Democrats in Finland. We have indeed observed a repositioning on the nuclear energy issue in the cases of the French Socialists and the British Labour Party when these parties were in opposition.

As shown in Chapter 6, the French Socialists began a limited retreat from nuclear energy already in the late 1970s, at that time trying to find a balance between appealing to voters with a critical attitude towards nuclear energy and the pro-nuclear Communists whom they needed as allies in the electoral and parliamentary arenas. After the Green breakthrough they signed a cooperation agreement with the Greens, committing to a moratorium on the building of new reactors and the cancellation of particularly controversial projects. In the presidential elections of 2007 and 2012 their presidential candidates, Ségolène Royal and Francois Hollande, respectively, promised to reduce the share of nuclear energy and to cancel particularly controversial projects. In Britain, Labour stepwise retreated from nuclear energy and in 1992 demanded a phase-out at the end of the projected lifetime of the existing reactors. In so doing, they built bridges to both important segments of the electorate and the Liberal Democratic partner required in the electoral and presumably parliamentary arenas. In contrast to their British and French brethren, the Finnish Social Democrats have not experienced a long period out of government office since the 1970s. Although suffering from intra-party opposition regarding its nuclear energy policy, they remained on a pro-nuclear energy course. In so doing, they maximized their eligibility as coalition partner of the other mainstream parties and did not compromise their socio-economic policy goals. The Finnish Social Democrats thus continue to give support to Kitschelt's (1986) observation that mainstream-left parties in government are likely to follow a nuclear energy policy different from those in opposition.

The differences between these mainstream-left parties, however, vanish when we look at actual government policy. On closer inspection, the French Socialists' concessions to the anti-nuclear side in the 1980s and 1990s, with the exception of the cancellation of individual reactor projects, were compatible with the long-term development of the country's nuclear energy programme. This applies to the short period of reviewing the programme under Mitterrand and the de facto freezing under PM Jospin (setting in when an expansion programme had just been completed), and even the programme's recent capping under President Hollande may not yield outcomes very different from what a conservative government might be able to do (as there are several other limiting factors such as the existing fleet's ageing and lack of qualified personnel: Schneider and Froggatt 2015: 144–8). Once in office, the British Labour Party made a more radical break with what it had announced in opposition. Rather than phasing out the ageing reactor fleet, it turned to renewal, making reference to climate change and energy security considerations. Obviously, all these mainstream-left parties have pragmatic positions on the nuclear energy issue. Quite simply, their traditional socio-economic goals are much more important to them than nuclear energy policy. None of them would be willing to jeopardize these traditional goals for the benefit of nuclear retreat. Still, in the British and French cases, some concessions were required to keep anti-nuclear voters on board and win the support of the Liberal Democrats and Greens that was considered essential for winning government office.

In a nutshell, nuclear energy policy in group 4 countries was subject to similar challenges as elsewhere but no reversal was made. In Britain and France the pro-nuclear post-war consensus benefited from the major parties' being shielded from Green competitors by the majoritarian electoral systems. After the Green breakthrough in France and the Liberal Democrats turning against nuclear energy in Britain the mainstream-left parties in opposition made anti-nuclear concessions to the extent required for winning government office. Yet, as for the mainstream-right parties, the traditional socio-economic party goals remained their central concerns not to be compromised by the costs of an ambitioned policy of replacing nuclear energy. In Britain, once in office the Labour Party switched from phasing out to renewing the country's reactor fleet, thereby in a way completing the party's general policy reorientation under PM Tony Blair. In France, also the sheer size of the nuclear energy programme would have made a speedy nuclear exit virtually impossible. Anti-nuclear policy concessions of the Socialists in office have led to adaptations of the country's nuclear energy policy but not full reversal. The political situation is different in Finland, as the Greens did not take on the role of an essential ally of the mainstream-left party. Indeed, the Social Democrats spent only short periods in opposition, always with a clear perspective of returning to office soon in another (pro-nuclear) multi-party cabinet. The Social Democrats thus could continue to privilege their traditional socio-economic policy goals rather than compromising these by demanding a costly reversal in nuclear energy policy. In such context, even cabinet participation of the Greens was possible without derailing Finland's nuclear energy policy.

12.4 STATISTICAL ANALYSIS

We now subject our cases to statistical analysis. This attempt to detect quantitative regularities and relationships complements the causal reasoning based on the in-depth analysis of cases. In a structural model, we test selected hypotheses with regard to the major and minor policy reversals we identified in the chapters and in the additional case analyses as having occurred in the 1945–2013 period (see Appendix). We include seventeen Western European countries in our analysis, focusing on the time periods where nuclear energy was a relevant policy issue. Table 12.1 provides the details. Excluded states are Andorra, Cyprus, Iceland, and Malta. These countries are small in terms of geography, population, and economy and never attempted to develop nuclear energy programmes. Focusing on Western Europe reduces time and country-specific selection bias and works towards the causal homogeneity assumption being met.

Table 12.1. Observation Window and Number of Cabinets until 2013

Country	Observation Window	Number of Cabinets
Austria	1955–1999	21
Belgium	1952–2013	26
Denmark	1955–1985	18
Finland	1962–2013	26
France	1945–2013	43
Germany	1955–2013	23
Greece	1974–1981	4
Ireland	1968–1999	13
Italy	1946–1990	34
Luxembourg	1972–1977	2
Netherlands	1955–2013	24
Norway	1945–1978	15
Portugal	1975–1986	8
Spain	1977–2013	12
Sweden	1947–2013	29
Switzerland	1945–2013	19
UK	1946–2013	22

Our cases are year-cabinet combinations. A cabinet is defined by the same electoral period, party composition, and the identity of the Prime Minister (http://www.erdda.se). Hence a new cabinet is triggered by any of the following events: a parliamentary election, a change in the cabinet's party composition, and a replacement of the Prime Minister.

The observation window begins with the government decision to go nuclear (as logically no policy reversal can occur before). We exit countries whenever the nuclear energy issue seems to be settled in a negative way, ruling out this form of energy production and having a broad political consensus that the issue is settled once and for all. Hence the basic criterion of inclusion in the sample is the theoretical possibility to decide negatively on a nuclear energy programme (policy reversal). For that reason a nuclear energy programme has to be started, at least in an active planning manner. We do not, however, require that the countries included at one point must have been 'active' in terms of actually producing nuclear energy.

Relying on these definitions we assembled all major and minor reversals directed against the use of nuclear energy in Table 12.2. Minor reversals are defined as stopping only the further expansion of an existing nuclear energy programme while major reversals are operationally defined as changing a state's nuclear energy policy by at least one step towards the negative pole on our joint policy scale (ranging from −5 to +5).[8]

---

[8] Note that as soon as we observe a de facto ending of a country's nuclear energy programme (e.g. stopping of all preparatory measures to start an industrial nuclear energy programme, phasing out, or even outlawing nuclear energy) we remove these countries from the pool of being at risk for a further reversal. This was the case for Austria in 1999, Denmark in 1985, Greece in 1981, Ireland 1999, Italy in 1990, Luxembourg in 1977, Norway in 1978, and Portugal 1986. The underlying logic of this approach is that those countries at a certain moment crossed a threshold where further reversals are theoretically

Table 12.2. Overview of Minor and Major Nuclear Energy (NE) Policy Reversals in Western Europe 1945–2013

Country	Reversal Year	Description	Major or Minor Reversal
Austria	1978	Ruling out NE after referendum	Major
	1999	NE ban in Constitution	Major
Belgium	1976	Moratorium in effect for 6 years	Minor
	1988	Moratorium on construction of NPP until 1999	Minor
	2003	Phase-out translated into law	Major
	2011	Confirmation of phase-out decision	Minor
Denmark	1985	NE Ban-Law by parliament	Major
Finland	1986	Parliament against expansion of NE program	Minor
	1993	Parliament against expansion of NE program	Minor
France	1981	Cancellation of construction Plogoff plant	Minor
	1998	Abandoning of Superphénix project	Major
Germany	1982	Sharp shortening of budget on NE	Minor
	1989	Abandoning of Wackersdorf reprocessing project	Minor
	1991	Halt on fast breeder reactor	Minor
	2001	Phase-out decision	Major
	2011	Confirmation of phase-out decision	Major
Greece	1981	Papandreou anti-nuclear decision	Major
Ireland	1982	Decision to stop all nuclear planning activities	Major
	1999	NE Ban-Law by parliament	Major
Italy	1988	Referendum decision against NE: Shut down Trino and Latina plants	Major
	1990	Closure of remaining plants Montalto di Castro	Major
Luxembourg	1977	Decision against Remschen plant based on Luxembourg territory	Major
Netherlands	1994	Decision to phase-out by 2003	Major
Norway	1978	Norwegian all party turn against NE	Major
Portugal	1986	Government decision to stop all NE planning activities	Major
Spain	1984	Moratorium on NE, stop on some construction activities	Major
	1994	Moratorium on NE confirmed and stop of all remaining construction activities	Major
Sweden	1970	Decision to limit Swedish NE plants to max. 11	Minor
	1977	Law enacted to toughen start-up of new reactors	Minor
	1980	Referendum and parliament decision to phase-out NE within 30 years	Major
	1987	Restrictions on NE research, phase-out by late 1990s	Major
	1999	Closure of Barsebäck plant I	Minor
	2005	Closure of Barsebäck plant II + research reactor Studsvik	Minor
Switzerland	1989	Kaiseraugst project abandoned	Major
	1990	10 year moratorium	Major
	2011	Phase-out decision of NE until 2034	Major
UK	1989	Decision to freeze nuclear program at current status	Major

Source: Own data collection.

In Table 12.3 we provide the operational definition of all our variables and the sources. Table 12.4 presents the results of our multivariate statistical models, distinguishing results for all reversals and major reversals only. As Table 12.3 illustrates, there are thirty-five reversals in the period 1945–2013. Only considering major reversals the number decreases to twenty-four. In either specification, it is a small number of events and hence the quantitative results have to be viewed with some caution. Due to the rare events property of our sample we also use rare events models (routines and results are electronically available from Oxford University Press and the editors) that support the conclusions from the models presented here. As we are using time-variant covariates and cannot assume that residuals are uncorrelated with these covariates, we rely on a panel model with country-fixed effects (see Wooldridge 2002) and the explicit modelling of time effects (see Carter and Signorino 2010).[9] As Finland had no major reversal, it drops out in the major reversals-only model.

In a first approach we inserted an indicator variable 'Disaster' in order to find its partial effect on reversal. However, it turned out that we had to differentiate between the effects of Harrisburg (Three Mile Island), Chernobyl, and Fukushima, in order to detect the respective relevance of these three major disasters in the history of industrial nuclear energy production. The Three Mile Island accident had immense negative repercussions for the nuclear energy programme in the US, yet it is evident that it did not really put into question nuclear energy in Western European countries. Only the Chernobyl accident, causing radioactive fallout and considerable contamination outside the Soviet Union, and the Fukushima disaster triggered a serious political reconsideration of nuclear energy production in Western Europe. Focusing exclusively on major reversals, Fukushima is indeed another historical turning point in the history of nuclear energy. It induced major countries despite being heavily dependent on nuclear energy to venture its gradual abandonment.

Our modelling of time shows that the propensity to reversals first increases over time, approaching a maximum and then continues with a slight dampening in later years as indicated by the quadratic term. Thus, there is a general trend that is not captured by our time-varying predictor variables. Hence the time polynomial helps to avoid omitted variable effects.

With regard to the economic factors we discussed in Chapter 2 we included the dependence on external resources (import dependency) and the contribution of nuclear energy to electricity production. Import dependency, just as in the bivariate scatter plots in Chapter 3, does not reveal a statistically significant relationship with policy reversals in any of the models. High reliance on nuclear

---

implausible. Admittedly, the Italian attempt of 2011 to return to nuclear energy violates this coding. However, given the complete withdrawal of this country from nuclear energy after the 1988 referendum, a different decision would have been post-hoc. The case is also substantively different from Austria, where our coding reflects that the conflict continued for years after the referendum and the outlawing of nuclear energy.

[9] Note that we conducted multiple robustness checks with regard to the statistical model and model specifications which are available upon request. The same applies to our dataset and routines. As random effects models and rare events logit models lead to similar results, we present only the results of the in our view most appropriate modelling approach.

Table 12.3. Operationalization of the Variables

Variable Label	Coding Description	Source
Dependent Variables		
All Reversals	Dummy variable which is coded 1 if there was a minor or major reversal during cabinet period t.	Book chapters and Appendix
Major Reversals	Dummy variable which is coded 1 if there was a major reversal during cabinet period t.	Book chapters and Appendix
Independent Variables		
Harrisburg	Dummy variable, which is coded 1 if a cabinet is in office during the accident or within a timespan of 2.5 years after the accident (28.03.1979).	General knowledge
Chernobyl	Dummy variable, which is coded 1 if a cabinet is in office during the accident or within a timespan of 2.5 years after the accident (26.04.1986).	General knowledge
Fukushima	Dummy variable, which is coded 1 if a cabinet is in office during the accident or within a timespan of 2.5 years after the accident (11.03.2011).	General knowledge
Government	Seat-weighted positioning of current cabinet towards nuclear energy. Pro Nuclear Energy was coded 0, Contra Nuclear Energy was coded 1. Positions weighted by the seats of all government parties. Range of variable is between 0 (totally in favour of NE) to 1 (totally against NE).	Comparative Manifesto Project Party manifestos for nuclear position Parlgov.org for parties cabinet seats
U-Turn Any Party	Dummy variable, which is coded 1 if any party in the run up to elections t in country A changed its position from pro nuclear to anti nuclear.	Comparative Manifesto Project Party manifestos for nuclear position Parlgov.org. And-Elections.eu
Share Green Parties	Variable, that measures the vote-share of all Green parties in a country during a cabinet tenure.	
Strength Regional Units	Variable, that measures competencies of countries sub-units (states, Länder, Kantone, etc.) vis-à-vis central government. This assessment is based on the Regional Authority Index that theoretically ranges from 0 (no competencies at all) to 100 (maximum competencies).	Hooghe et al. (2008, 2016)
Disproportionality	Variable, that measure how disproportional national legislative elections are. This assessment is based on the Gallagher index.	ElectionIndices (2015)
Share Electricity	Variable, that measures the nuclear share concerning overall electricity production.	IAEA
Energy Import Dependency	Imports of energy in % of overall energy use.	Worldbank, extended by Extrapolation
Time Linear	Count variable, that takes on values from 0 to 14 for all 5-year periods between 1945 and 2015. Coded as follows: 1945–9=1, 1950–4=2, 1955–9=3,..., 2010–5=14.	Own
Time quadratic	Quadratic term of count variable.	Own

Table 12.4. Fixed Effects Logit Model of Nuclear Policy Reversals (Against Nuclear Energy) in Western Europe 1945–2013

Dependent Variable	Nuclear Energy Policy Reversal—all		Nuclear Energy Policy Reversals—major ones only	
Independent Variables	Logit-Coeff.	SE	Logit-Coeff.	SE
Harrisburg	0.072	0.821	−0.049	1.231
Chernobyl	1.604**	0.603	1.455*	0.722
Fukushima	2.259+	1.394	5.918*	2.495
Positioning Government	1.984+	1.077	4.157**	1.465
U-Turn any Party	−0.113	0.681	−0.053	0.785
Share Green Parties	0.004	0.127	−0.013	0.172
Strength Regional Units	0.027	0.090	0.073	0.152
Disproportionality	0.085	0.116	0.207	0.172
Nuclear Share Electricity	−4.862+	3.019	−4.231	5.099
Energy Import Dependency	−0.033	0.032	−0.036	0.039
Time linear	2.807**	1.093	4.447*	2.077
Time quadratic	−0.157**	0.061	−0.266*	0.119
Country Fixed Effects	yes		yes	
N	339 (17 countries)		313 (16 countries)	
LR Chi^2				
Log-Pseudolikelihood	56.37		54.88	
	−57.51		−32.51	

+p <0.10, *p <0.05; **p <0.01, ***p < 0.001

energy in electricity production leads to refraining from reversals in general. However, if we restrict the model to major reversals this relationship is no longer statistically significant.

With regard to political process and institutional factors the models included five variables. The strength of regional units (regionalization index) and the disproportionality of the electoral system variables are indicators capturing the openness of a political system for new parties representing anti-nuclear attitudes. While these variables originate from earlier attempts at explaining the success of anti-nuclear movements (Kitschelt 1986; Midttun and Rucht 1994) our model for the first time includes time-varying measures for both variables. We clearly see that these institutional variables do not exert an influence on policy reversals. This refutes our expectations. The same applies to the size and power of Green parties in a specific cabinet period.

We also control for the fact that a relevant party signalled a U-turn in its nuclear energy policy in the manifesto for the election immediately preceding a cabinet's office term. This variable indicates that the nuclear energy issue has been contested between the parties competing for public office. Again, the analysis shows that such position-taking of major parties is not sufficient for inducing a reversal. Rather it is cabinet composition that exercises a significant effect towards a nuclear policy reversal. The more pronounced the anti-nuclear stance of cabinet parties and the higher their combined seat shares, the larger the tendency of the cabinet to move away from nuclear energy. Policy reversals thus result from parties with anti-nuclear positions being in governments. This is the archetypical programme-election-policy mechanism that we should expect in party democracies. Naturally this is compatible with the institutional openness argument. It appears that parties are strategically adapting to the resulting competitive situation.

Given the pattern of the other variables this demonstrates that the logic of party competition and representative government is at work here as outlined in Chapter 2: parties having taken positions against nuclear energy and then assuming government office implement their positions. The strongest mechanism to introduce anti-nuclear policy change in Western Europe thus has been the classic one of parties contesting elections by presenting alternative policies and alternation in government office.

While Green parties occasionally have been part of winning and policy-reversing alliances, their involvement in government alone is neither a necessary nor a sufficient cause for reversals as most were made without a Green party in government. As we have seen, even the indirect effect of Greens, as measured by their strength in elections, does not exercise a statistically significant influence on anti-nuclear policy change in Western Europe.

The strong effects of Chernobyl and Fukushima do not relate to any specific mechanism. For one they have helped bring to office parties committed to anti-nuclear policy change. They have also made parties sincerely rethink their positions on nuclear energy or make U-turns for opportunistic reasons. Finally, they have also influenced referendum outcomes.

A statistical analysis such as the one presented here can help in distinguishing the more important from the less important factors. It cannot account for all the (sequential) complexities of the cases entered into the analysis. This is why we have chosen a mixed approach in the present volume and we refer back to the qualitative studies for the more indirect ways other factors have influenced the trajectories of nuclear energy in Western Europe.

12.5 CONCLUSION AND OUTLOOK

In this chapter we have been trying to understand the factors that have driven national decisions on nuclear energy and that account for the West European countries' different energy policy trajectories. In so doing, we have been following a three-track strategy, concentrating exclusively on our seven case-study countries as a first step. We have then extended the scope of our analysis to cover all of Western Europe and have subjected the national nuclear energy trajectories to qualitative comparative analysis and, in the final step, to quantitative analysis.

The seven case-study countries include some of the most complex cases of nuclear energy policy trajectories. The outlined reversals were typically hotly contested and quite often only the beginning of a process aiming at or leading to another policy reversal in the opposite direction or important policy adaptations. The in-depth information of the country chapters has allowed us to evaluate our catalogue of hypotheses derived from the literature in Chapter 2 (see section 12.2).

On a more general level we find the greatest common factor leading to nuclear energy policy changes in the competition of the established parties. Movement politics and street protest clearly have contributed much to make nuclear energy, which back in the 1950s and 1960s was generally considered an element of welcomed technological progress, a contested political issue. Yet only few policy reversals, typically confined to individual reactor projects, can be directly related to the activities of the protest movement. The party-political offspring of the anti-nuclear (and other) protest movement(s), Green parties, have been more consequential in terms of nuclear energy policy. Green government participation is behind the most important exit from nuclear energy, the German one of 2001, and it led to policy adaptations in France and currently even a capping of this country's nuclear energy programme. Overall, Green parties and parties of the radical left that pre-empted much of the Green agenda in some countries, have been more important in terms of changing the competitive environment for the established parties, in particular of the mainstream left. However, the case-study countries also show that issue entrepreneurship in the nuclear energy domain was not confined to Green and leftist parties but was a strategy also followed by some mainstream parties of the centre-right. Overall, mainstream parties have a record of having been supportive of nuclear energy as part and parcel of twentieth-century technological progress and as a means to support economic growth. Typically, these parties broke with their pro-nuclear tradition when they reckoned that such a move would substantially improve their competitiveness, in particular when this was related to the prospect of winning or maintaining government office. Mainstream parties turning against nuclear energy when in government typically were confronted with a vital opposition that challenged the government on the nuclear energy issue. In making these moves, mainstream parties typically reacted to having among their potential electorates relatively large shares of what we called issue-inconsistent voters.

As factors external to the decision-making processes the major nuclear energy accidents—Three Mile Island, and, in particular, Chernobyl and Fukushima—had great impact all over Western Europe. The accidents triggered or were important for policy reversals against nuclear energy. A country's amount of dependency on and investment in nuclear energy effectively worked in the opposite direction, in particular by limiting the short-term ambitions of anti-nuclear decision-making (resulting in long phasing-out periods) and by providing a window of opportunity for re-reversal when the context and/or the majority constellation changed.

Extending our analysis to all of Western Europe (in section 12.3) meant widening the range of nuclear energy trajectories. Except the least populated and mostly geographically small states (group 1), all countries at some point planned for the use of nuclear energy. With the exception of Finland, the countries that were late in the process of realizing nuclear energy plans, typically aiming for the first reactors to be built in the 1970s, already met the resistance of the emerging anti-nuclear movement and faced large shares of citizens who were sceptical or negative about nuclear energy. The party-centred politicization of the issue was quick to occur. At that time the potential of the nuclear energy issue to break existing electoral ties was already known. With the exception of Portugal, the early exit countries (group 2) largely shared the expectation that they soon would tap alternative energy resources (oil, gas, lignite). Given this prospect, the lack of sizeable sunk costs, and the political risks associated with steering a pro-nuclear course, government parties of different colours abandoned the nuclear energy track. Although the issue has occasionally returned as an item of discussion in some of the countries no serious attempt was made to reverse the decision to abstain from nuclear energy.

The other countries (groups 3 and 4) had started earlier or proceeded more forcefully in developing nuclear energy. They all had made major investments therein when the nuclear energy issue became politicized mostly by the protest movement and issue entrepreneurs among politicians from established parties. Green parties and parties of the radical left were the most likely parties to give anti-nuclear positions a permanent voice in the political debate. Most often conservative and economically liberal parties constituted the opposite pole while parties of the mainstream left were torn between competing with Green and radical left parties by taking a position against nuclear energy and remaining faithful to the post-war course of supporting nuclear energy and giving preference to the traditional economic and social policy goals of their core voters (Kitschelt 1986). Yet, as we have seen, the dominant pattern does not hold in each case as mainstream parties of the centre-right have championed anti-nuclear position-taking in Sweden and Austria and Social Democrats have turned against nuclear energy even before the emergence of the Greens in Switzerland. Most important, however, mainstream political parties of both the left and right have been remarkably flexible in taking positions and making decisions on nuclear energy. For these parties nuclear energy is not an identity issue or principled issue but has to be considered in the context and within the hierarchy of party goals (Müller and Strøm 1999). While the specifics differ between countries and situations, overall mainstream parties have tended to give preference to their office goals and have adapted their nuclear energy issue position accordingly. When government office was not at stake, mainstream parties have tended to privilege their traditional party policy goals.

The main difference between those countries that at some point decided to abandon nuclear energy even after making major investments and those that remained on the nuclear energy track is that the parties of the mainstream left in the latter countries (group 4) were less pressured to make an exit from nuclear energy. To be sure, the parties of the mainstream left in Britain and France moved in the exit direction while in opposition but then proved more positive towards nuclear energy when in government. The Finnish Social Democrats, in contrast, neither suffered through long stretches of opposition periods nor could have credibly improved their chances to return or remain in government by adopting an exit strategy from nuclear energy.

In its third and final step our analysis has been quantitative, focusing exclusively on important decisions that have changed the policy status quo towards the *direction* of exit from nuclear energy (section 12.4). Our statistical analysis identifies the relative strength of government parties that have taken position against nuclear energy as the main factor driving public policy decisions that curb, reduce, or abolish nuclear energy production. Although such linkage between pre-electoral announcements and government policy is normatively important, this finding might be considered rather trivial. Yet it gains relevance by comparing it to the earlier movement-focused literature which—implicitly or explicitly—related policy outcome in the nuclear energy domain exclusively to the efforts of movements and public opinion.

As can be seen from, for instance, the examples of Finland, Spain, and the UK, there is no genuine Social Democratic positioning against nuclear energy in Europe in the post-Chernobyl period. At the same time parties of the centre-right have adopted a broad range of different nuclear energy policy positions under specific conditions. Nuclear energy does not belong to the mainstream parties' core issue portfolio where positions can be directly derived from their ideology and historical mission. Rather, the parties take them strategically, considering how they can serve their main party goals in the given historical situation, while the complexity of the nuclear energy issue and its changing context provide ample possibilities for justifying moves between different positions.

Strategic party position-taking nevertheless is a challenging endeavour. It also needs to anticipate the impact of electoral formula and the capacity of government to implement the chosen positions. We thus do not conclude that institutional openness—measured by the proportionality of the electoral system and by the possibility to influence national policy agendas via regional and federal channels—is irrelevant.

Overall, our analyses demonstrate that nuclear energy policy is not the outcome of technocratic decision-making or the result of a confrontation between a pro-growth cartel of the established parties and economic interests on the one side and the anti-nuclear movement, its party-political manifestation, and critical citizens on the other. Rather the issue has become incorporated in the competition the mainstream parties wage among themselves. While movement politics can influence the issue's salience and mass attitudes, mainstream parties have proved remarkably flexible in adapting their positions and policy-making if government office—the main prize of politics—was at stake.

12.5.1 Outlook: What Future for Nuclear Energy in Western Europe?

While globally countries such as China, India, South Korea, Russia, and several Eastern European countries are unperturbedly following the nuclear energy path, and even post-Fukushima Japan decided to continue with nuclear energy, the Western European region constitutes a special case that requires specific answers. As we have seen, nuclear energy was rejected early on or later abandoned by about half of Western European states (some of which are currently in the stage of phasing out). Will the countries currently still committed to nuclear energy follow their neighbours, will there be a permanent bifurcation of Western Europe between countries with and without nuclear energy, or will countries currently on an exit strategy return to the pro-nuclear camp and rejuvenate nuclear energy? Before providing necessarily speculative answers to these questions we briefly highlight which factors will influence the decision-making and what are some of the major issues at stake.

Economic Aspects

As Schneider and Frogatt (2015) argued in their *World Nuclear Industry Status Report*, nuclear power will survive globally only if it is able to prove its economic sustainability. Even pro-nuclear commentators agree that the very economic conditions of nuclear energy currently are a major obstacle for this technology to survive. This reflects the fact that there are serious competing energy carriers (especially cheap fossils and expanding renewables) on the market. The abundance of cheap shale gas has made the US reluctant to follow through with its announced plan of nuclear energy renewal (see Chapter 1) and the consistently low world market prices for conventionally produced oil and gas constitute a very difficult economic environment for nuclear energy world-wide. Supporters of nuclear energy therefore are currently stressing some economic aspects of nuclear energy—the extremely high front-end costs and immense uncertainties with regard to the slow returns on investments, increased costs for tightened safety requirements, and the successive internalization of previously externalized costs for decommissioning and waste management.[10] Even large multinational energy companies in Western Europe seem unable to absorb the market uncertainties. Therefore, the European Commission and the UK have recently argued that nuclear energy constitutes an essential long-term public infrastructure that the state should provide by guaranteeing returns for such high-risk investment. Energy companies in European countries but also the US are already using this argument vis-à-vis their national governments, threatening to withdraw investment and even to close large-scale fossil-based plants.

Yet the very aim of the European Union has been the liberalization of markets. This contradiction may lead to a renewed debate about the role of the state in regulating and providing energy structures. To the extent that market intervention requires EU resources,[11] a built-in conflict is that countries without nuclear ambitions are forced to contribute. The heterogeneity of nuclear energy policies in the EU thus constitutes a latent cleavage that may lead to open conflict in European energy policies.

Nuclear energy in Western Europe traditionally has not been just about producing electricity but also about an important engineering industry. It would be an irony of history if it turned out that the European Generation III EPR reactor developed with massive support from the EURATOM programme cannot be built at competitive prices, as the delays and cost overruns of the reactor projects in

---

[10] For this topic see the IPCC report, Bruckner et al. (2014), for a comparative description of the state of waste management regulation, see Brunnengräber et al. (2015).

[11] Commissioner Miguel Arias Cañete declared in mid-2015 before the European Nuclear Safety Regulators Group that the Commission will continue its funding of fission technology and that nuclear energy will be part of the European Strategic Energy Technology Plan (SET-Plan) adopted in Feb. 2015. The Commission provided a Nuclear Illustrative Programme (PINC) in April 2016. A major goal is to contribute to Generation IV reactors (i.e. small-sized reactors). As the incoming European Commission agreed on a European Fund for Strategic Investments (EFSI) over €315 billion, the nuclear energy industries are waiting in the wings, and have built up a series of groups and initiatives: The European Sustainable Nuclear Industrial Initiative (ESNII), Nuclear Cogeneration Industrial Initiative, NUGENIA: Nuclear Generation II&III Association.

France (Flamanville) and Finland (Olkiluoto) seem to indicate. The UK and Finland, like several East European countries, therefore are considering Russian and Chinese bids. If the 'French Nuclear Model falters',[12] the *raison d'être* of the EURATOM treaty would disappear. If Europe is not able to implement its own reactor technology but has to rely on Chinese and Russian reactor types or financing, this would be a major disaster for the European Union cooperation in industrial and energy policy. It would also be a major setback for nuclear energy in Western Europe. The question here will be whether the European nuclear industry with EDF as the largest firm will be too big to fail, or rather fail due to bigness.

Energy (Supply) Security

Nuclear energy has traditionally been promoted as a technology that would help countries to ensure energy supply even in international crisis situations constraining oil and gas imports. Currently, many of Western Europe's traditional sources of imports are considered insecure (Chapter 1). Political unrest has severely reduced imports from Iraq and Libya in recent years. There is also fear that Russia may hold back from providing energy to exercise political pressure, in particular on the Eastern European countries. Its role in ensuring energy security will continue to boost nuclear energy from a technocratic perspective. Yet politically it is often difficult to succeed with a long-term policy designed to minimize risk, in particular when oil and gas prices are low despite political turmoil in the Middle East and when the risk of nuclear accidents can be held up against the risk of potential supply problems.

Climate Policy

The occurrence of human-caused climate change has been accepted even by the US administration. The targets of the EU in its Roadmap 2050 are a 40 per cent reduction in greenhouse gas emissions compared to 1990 levels.[13] The EU considers nuclear energy a 'decarbonization option' in the provision of energy. Accordingly, the fifth report of the Intergovernmental Panel on Climate Change (IPCC) in 2014 (Bruckner et al. 2014) continues to view nuclear energy as a potential component of climate change mitigation. Specifically, the report states 'that no single mitigation option in energy supply will be sufficient to hold the increase in global average temperature change below 2°C above pre-industrial levels. A combination of some, but not necessarily all of the options' would be required (Bruckner et al. 2014: 569). In this context one particular challenge is the provision of sufficient electricity base-load without nuclear energy.

Whether a transition towards decarbonization will be possible without nuclear fission is a crucial question to be answered in the next decades. Countries within the European Union have obviously quite different expectations on what

---

[12] See <http://www.nytimes.com/2015/05/08/business/energy-environment/france-nuclear-energy-areva.html>.
[13] See <http://ec.europa.eu/energy/en/topics/energy-strategy/2030-ene>.

constitutes a workable strategy. The UK, France, Finland, and the majority of Eastern European countries are not willing to exclude nuclear energy from their portfolio. Rather they push towards the implementation of the new generation of reactors collectively co-developed under the EURATOM regime. Other countries such as Belgium, the Netherlands, Spain, or Sweden currently seem to be in a waiting position. Yet even if Germany's exceptional path proves successful in the next two decades, other countries are unlikely to follow quickly due to path dependency.

Political Rationales

In the end it is political actors who make the decisions and they do so by following their own rationales. Clearly, the factors discussed in this book will have considerable weight in their decision-making on the overall question of the use of nuclear energy. Yet, as we have seen, for most political parties office concerns come first, in particular when the winning or maintaining of government office is a realistic option that can be credibly influenced by the party's nuclear energy policy course. While it is impossible to foresee all contingencies that will prevail in future situations of decision-making, we reason that the prospects for a revival of nuclear energy in nuclear exit countries are rather gloomy. The situation may be different in countries currently in a waiting position. However, highly proportional electoral systems and multiple regional access points may also load the dice against nuclear energy there. As in the past, the survival of nuclear energy is most likely under political institutions that shield the traditional parties from competition with niche parties and allow them to focus on their traditional concerns.

APPENDIX: OTHER EUROPEAN COUNTRIES—AN ANALYTICAL RECONSTRUCTION

Paul W. Thurner, Wolfgang C. Müller, and Christian Schulze

Here we present short analyses of country cases not covered by individual chapters in this volume. These cases, however, figure in the comparative Chapters 3 and, to some extent, 4 and are included alongside those covered by individual chapters in our Conclusion. The aim of these short analyses is to describe the trajectory nuclear energy has taken in the individual countries, paying special attention to the analytic categories and variables of this volume. The countries are ordered by group and alphabetically within each group.

Early Withdrawers from Nuclear Energy Plans

The countries in this group are Denmark, Greece, Ireland, Luxembourg, Norway, and Portugal.

Denmark

Denmark, whose physicist Nils Bohr was a key person in the research on nuclear fission, very early started to develop the scientific preconditions for a nuclear energy programme.[14] It signed a bilateral agreement with the US in 1955 on research cooperation, but no agreement on the delivery of a power reactor (see Drogan 2011). Three research reactors were built already by the end of the 1950s, and preparatory legislation for the industrial use of nuclear energy was provided in 1962 with the Nuclear Installation Act. Lund and Breinholt (1979: 85–6) argue that the decision to produce a Danish reactor was also nourished by the hope of having access to their own uranium reserves in Greenland— which did not come about. The same applies to the development of a heavy water reactor of Danish design. The project was abandoned in 1965. The following joint venture for the co-development of a Swedish heavy water reactor proved also to be an impasse and was abandoned in 1970.

In 1973, when the decentralized electric utilities were faced with increasing demand and the oil crisis hit Denmark, one of the producer companies (ELSAM) announced it would build a reactor. A first attempt at passing an energy report that envisaged the use of nuclear energy by the Liberal minority government in 1974 failed due to the high fragmentation of the parliament since the 1973 election. The succeeding Social Democratic minority government provided the first Danish Energy programme in 1976. It proposed the building of five reactors. Yet the Social Democratic Party was faced with a massive mobilization of anti-nuclear protest especially by the Organization for Information about Atomic Power. This organization cleverly played a postponement game in the 1974 debate by proposing a reflection phase of three years.

Having been confronted with the fierce anti-nuclear Left Socialist Party (Venstresocialisterne), a new leftist party created already in 1967, and the Socialist People's Party also taking position against nuclear energy, the Social Democrats included a reservation in its Energy Programme that the nuclear energy part would come into effect only conditionally on a special law for the building of reactors to be passed later. With that reservation the Energy Programme was passed in parliament in 1976. Making this concession was necessary, as one third of the opposition would have been able to call for a referendum (see Lund and Breinholt 1979: 99 for this argument) against the Act. Such a move might have precluded the implementation of the reactor programme for years. This shows that another institutional feature, namely the thresholds for holding referendums, impacts the openness of political systems to extra-parliamentary pressures.

Given the mobilization and the increasingly hostile public opinion—more than one-third of the electorate considered nuclear power to bear unacceptable risks already in 1978 (see Figure 12.1)—the Social Democratic Prime Minister, recalling the Common Market referendum that had spit the party deeply, wanted to avoid any further split. Finally, in opposition the Social Democratic Party performed a programmatic U-turn and initiated a parliamentary vote against the governing party in 1984 not to implement nuclear power. The resulting Act prohibiting nuclear energy in Denmark in 1985 is the current legal status quo (Figure 12.A1).

Denmark is obviously a very open system in terms of the highly proportional electoral system, but also with regard to the possibility of facultative referendums. Thus, movements like the activist Organization for Information about Atomic Power as well as the existing leftist competitors campaigning on nuclear energy constituted a serious electoral threat for the minority government of the Social Democratic party. That the Green party appeared only late on and its performance remained poor is certainly due to the crowding of

---

[14] See Andersen (1990), Nathan (1981), Nielsen et al. (1999). The most detailed description of the early period is provided by Lund and Breinholt (1979).

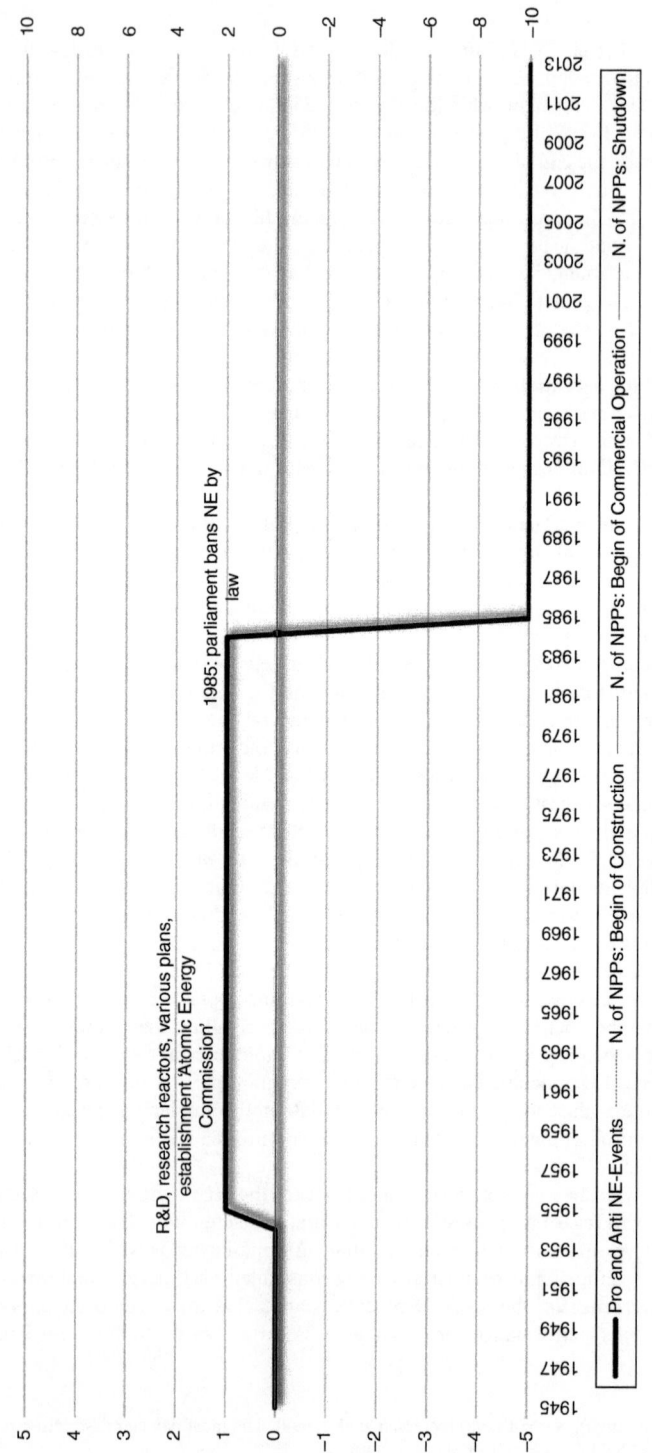

Figure 12.A1. Nuclear Energy Policy Development in Denmark, 1945–2013

— Pro and Anti NE-Events ⸺ N. of NPPs: Begin of Construction ⸺ N. of NPPs: Begin of Commercial Operation ⸺ N. of NPPs: Shutdown

R&D, research reactors, various plans, establishment 'Atomic Energy Commission'

1985: parliament bans NE by law

left-libertarian parties and the absorption of the issue by an already existing leftist party competing on this issue.

In terms of the economic consequences of abandoning nuclear energy, sunk investment costs were rather low in the Danish case. More fundamentally, one might additionally ask why the Danish government was so late in starting to consider the implementation of a nuclear programme. It seems that the country's perceived prospect of exploiting indigenous resources for energy production prevented early state intervention and further steps going beyond building research reactors. Note that oil production in Denmark began back in 1972, whereas the production of natural gas began in 1984 (see IEA 2011a). Thus, an alternative energy carrier was available.

Ireland

In contrast to Denmark and Norway, Ireland never had research reactors. This mirrors the fact that their post-war governments never planned or had the economic resources and technological opportunities to invest into the development of nuclear energy. Irish initiatives to build an industrial reactor date back to 1968 (see Dalby 1984; Baker 1988; Leonard 2008) when the Electricity Supply Board advanced this option. The government reacted by adopting the Nuclear Energy Act in 1971 and established the Nuclear Energy Board (NEB) in 1973. The Ministry of Transport and Power mandated the NEB as the responsible regulatory authority to provide advice on the examination of Carnsore Point, County Wexford, as a site for a nuclear power station. In September 1974 the Electricity Supply Board NEB applied for planning permission. As in other countries, this assessment led to strong local anti-nuclear movements. The Fianna Fáil single-party government (1969–73) supported this project—as all other Irish parties did at that time. However, this government was replaced in 1973 by a Fine Gail-Labour Party coalition that remained inactive on this project during its term in office.

Fianna Fáil regained power in 1977 and proactively supported the further development of nuclear plants. In the Green Paper on energy in Ireland, the government and especially its Minister for Energy took a clear position in favour of constructing one or two reactors. The local opposition culminated in the 1978 anti-nuclear Carnsore festival (see Baker 1988; Leonard 2008). In the 1978 Eurobarometer (see Figure 12.1), more than one-third of the electorate considered nuclear power as bearing unacceptable risks. During this crucial situation, the Three Mile Island accident of March 1979 occurred. By the end of 1979, the pro-nuclear minister O'Malley was replaced. In anticipation of the repositioning of its main competitor, Fine Gail, Fianna Fáil adjusted its position on nuclear energy: in 1979, the government decided to build a power station based on coal.

In order to understand the rather quick adjustment of the parties, one has to note that Ireland began off-shore exploration for oil in 1971, leading in 1973 to the discovery of the Kinsale Head gas field, with the gas production starting in 1979 (IEA 2012). This indicates that Ireland had a politically attractive alternative to the strategy of 'going nuclear' in energy policy at that time. As there were no major sunk costs on nuclear energy, the parties easily adjusted towards anti-nuclear positions: Fine Gael and the Labour Party did so already in their 1981 manifestos. The Labour Party repeated this position in 1982. Finally, all major parties explicitly took an anti-nuclear position in their 1987 manifestos. This consensus is also reflected in the rather indirect, politically completely uncontroversial prohibition of nuclear energy in the course of the adjustment of the Irish electricity regulation to the European Union liberalization of the electricity markets (see Electricity Regulation Act 1999, section 18(6)) (Figure 12.A2).

The heavy reliance on gas, however, turned out to be an impasse in the Irish case. The proven gas reserves diminished quickly and production has decreased steadily since the mid-1990s. As a consequence, Ireland is heavily dependent on imports of fossil fuels (90 per

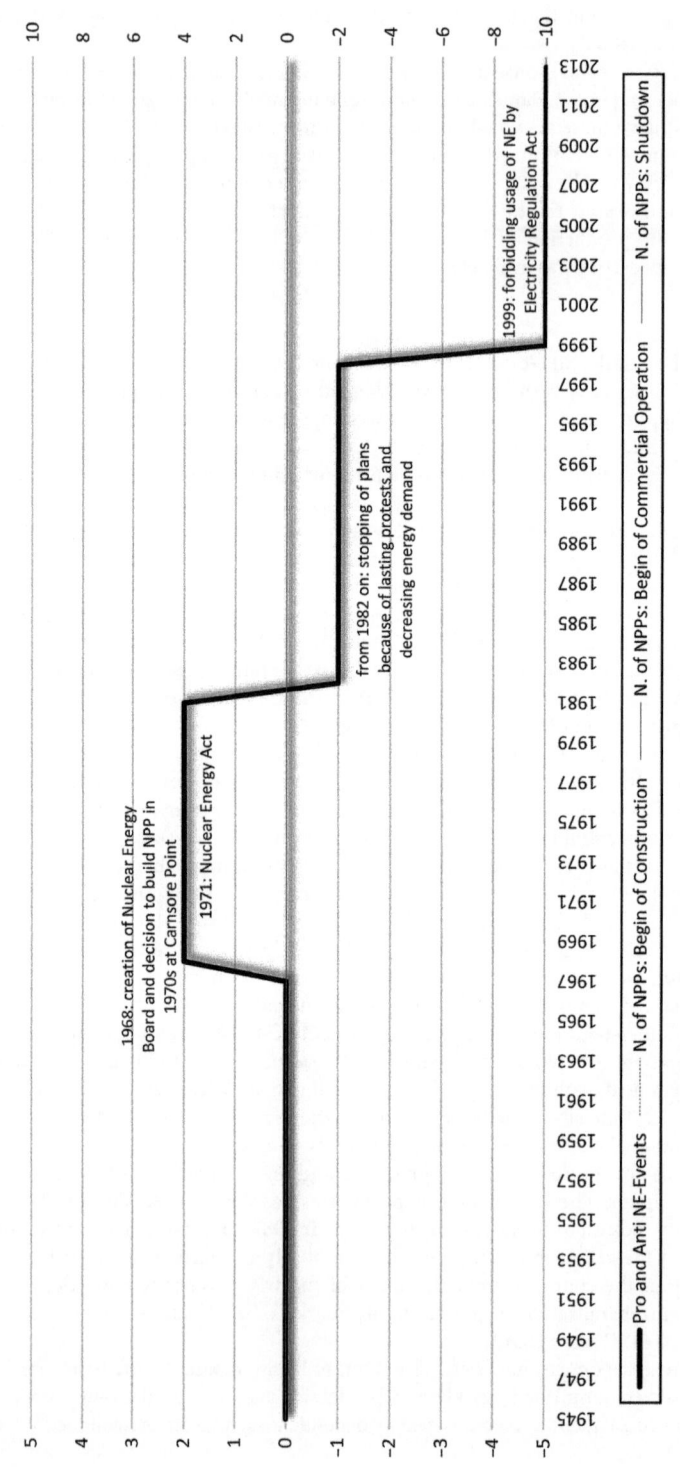

Figure 12.A2. Nuclear Energy Policy Development in Ireland, 1945–2013

cent of its gas, and 100 of its oil in 2006) and more recently it has received electricity inflows from the UK as it has been connected to the British grid since 2012.

In 2006, the government commissioned a report by Forfás, a policy advisory board for enterprise, trade, science, technology, and innovation, to assess the necessity to reconsider the nuclear power option in order to guarantee energy security. As a result of this, the 2007 White Paper reaffirmed the commitment of the Irish government not to consider the nuclear option again. A *Green Paper on Energy Policy in Ireland* (of May 2014) reconsidered the issue of introducing nuclear energy. It concluded that it may not be the right time to consider the economic and technical implications of 'going nuclear' or 'to test public acceptance' but also mentioned that it might be worth reconsidering the issue once smaller 'generation IV' reactors become available in the future.

At least one interesting observation from the Irish case is worth keeping in mind: just as in Luxembourg (see below), a conservative-centre party withdrew its initial support for nuclear energy after heavy anti-nuclear mobilization and an electoral disaster.

Luxembourg

Luxembourg was a co-founder of the EURATOM treaty in 1957 that may be considered as a European counterpart to the US-led Atoms for Peace programme in the mid-1950s (see Drogan 2015). The early international cooperation in energy matters is the more understandable as Luxembourg has a population below 0.5 million. The support of the establishment of a Europe-wide nuclear energy industry was therefore a reasonable strategy in this case. Luxembourg did not invest in domestic nuclear programmes or research reactors. Whereas coal contributed up to 25 per cent of total energy consumption until the mid-1970s, the importance of this energy carrier declined dramatically thereafter. The country is meanwhile nearly completely dependent on external resources and relies on fossil fuels to a greater extent than any other EU country. More than half of its electricity demand has been imported since the early 1970s (see IEA 2008).

There was an episode in the past, however, when Luxembourg seemed on the nuclear energy track. In 1973 its government—a Christian-liberal coalition of the CSV and DP led by long-term Prime Minister Pierre Werner (CSV)—signed an agreement with the German RWE to build a reactor on Luxembourg territory to reduce the country's dependence on energy imports (see Tauer 2013). This project was supported by the German Federal government and by all Luxembourg parties, with the exception of the Communist Party. Germany even consented to integrate the reactor into the German fuel and waste system. The project attracted local protest and induced the creation of an anti-nuclear movement. Although the issue was not prominent in the 1974 election campaign, it is likely to have contributed to the dramatic losses the CSV, the party that had dominated the post-war period, experienced in this landslide election. The CSV-led government was replaced by a coalition of the Luxembourg Socialist Workers' Party (LSAP) with the DP. Note that in both governments Marcel Mart took the Ministry for the Economy, Middle Classes, Tourism, Transport, and Energy. He was a fervent proponent of the reactor project in both governments. In September 1977, Marcel Mart left the ministry for a post at the European Court of Auditors. In December 1977, the LSAP opted for a moratorium on the nuclear energy project that is generally considered its end (Figure 12.A3).

The next general elections were held on June 1979, followed by another coalition government of the CSV and DP—the party combination that had put nuclear energy on the agenda—again under PM Werner. Yet the nuclear energy issue did not reappear on the government agenda. A pro-nuclear strategy might have undermined the CSV's attempts at renewal and reaching out to younger segments in the electorate. Clearly, the Swedish elections in 1976, the Austrian referendum in 1978, and the Three Mile Island accident in March 1979 had shifted the odds against nuclear energy also in Luxembourg.

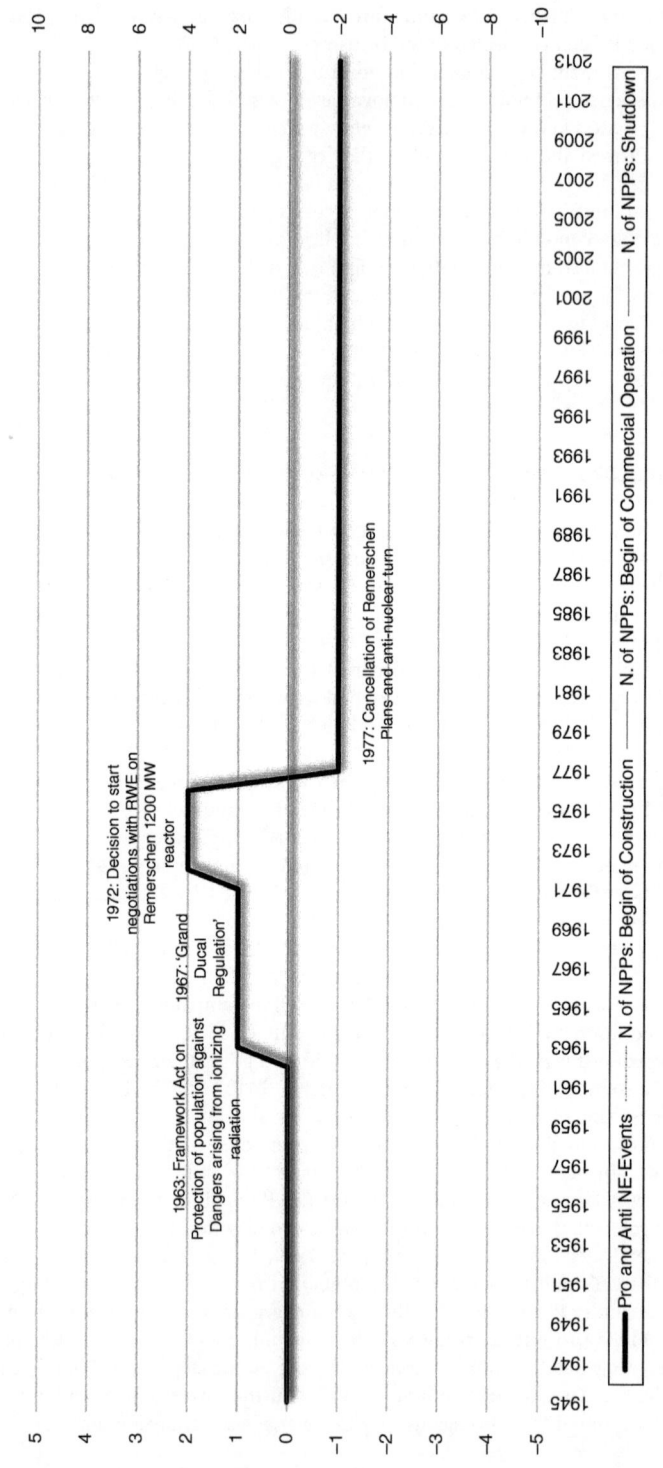

Figure 12.A3. Nuclear Energy Policy Development in Luxembourg, 1945–2013

Norway

The nuclear energy history of Norway is very similar to that of Denmark (see Andersen 1980; Aardal 1990; Knutsen 1997). The country was early in taking initial steps to make nuclear energy a part of its energy mix. Norway is the only Scandinavian country to sign a bilateral cooperation agreement on research with the United States and on the building of power reactors (in June 1957). Until the beginning of 1970s, all political parties supported the plan of using nuclear power. The first of four research reactors was already operative in 1951. The political debate on the issue was even weaker than in Denmark:

> An important aspect of the Norwegian energy debate is, however, that nuclear power has never been much of an issue (. . .). In contrast, environment protest in Norway has not 'benefited' from public reactions against nuclear power. (. . .) It may sound like a paradox, but in Norway the development of what is perhaps the cleanest and safest of all forms of energy, hydroelectric power, has been the focus of environmental protest. (Aardal 1990: 148)

Knutsen (1997: 240), however, refers to a lively debate in 1973 provoked by the announcement of concrete construction plans by the Norwegian Water Resources and Electricity Board with one of the several reactors to be placed near Oslo. Whereas the pro-growth Labour government after this year's election still took a pro-nuclear stance, it consented to establish a committee to assess the safety of nuclear energy. This delaying strategy is understandable if one takes into account that throughout the 1970s the Labour party formed minority governments. Even if a parliamentary majority of the pro-growth Labour party and the Conservative party were in favour of using nuclear energy, they were faced with a large majority of the public opinion refusing nuclear energy (see Knutsen 1997: 240), a repositioning of the Centre Party (proposing a ten-year moratorium), and the accenting of environmental issues by the Liberal party as well as the Socialist Left party. Note that, in the words of Knutsen (1997: 248), 'the Socialist Left party is the Norwegian green and left-libertarian party'. Knutsen also highlights that the Norwegian Labour party wanted to avoid the experience of Swedish Labour losing power in the 1976 election with the nuclear energy issue playing some role. The Norwegian Labour party repositioned itself in 1978 by stating as a government party that Norway should not build reactors (see Knutsen 1997: 241). This can be considered the definite decision to renounce nuclear energy in Norway (Figure 12.A4).

Why did all parties adjust to environmental concerns so easily and so quickly? Just as in the case of Denmark, the repositioning of the Labour party is not surprising. According to the IEAs Energy Profile (2011b), Norway is the 'the third-largest exporter of energy in the world, after Russia and Saudi Arabia'. The country always had abundance of hydropower for low-carbon production of electricity. Note that the production of oil began in 1971, the respective licensing dating from 1965. Thus, there was obviously no perceived need for this energy-rich country to follow the nuclear energy track that by the mid-1970s had turned out to be politically risky.

Despite a fervent anti-nuclear public opinion, more recently (2013), the country allowed thorium reactors to be constructed and tested. As the Thorium Report Committee, commissioned by the Labour-Socialist Left-Centre government in 2007 states, Norway is ranked fourth in world-wide thorium resources that can be used in nuclear fission reactors. The official government reaction to the report was to stress that it had no intention to build nuclear power plants. Even conservative politicians see no need for thorium-based commercial production of energy in Norway but rather consider the raw material and the technology as assets for exports.

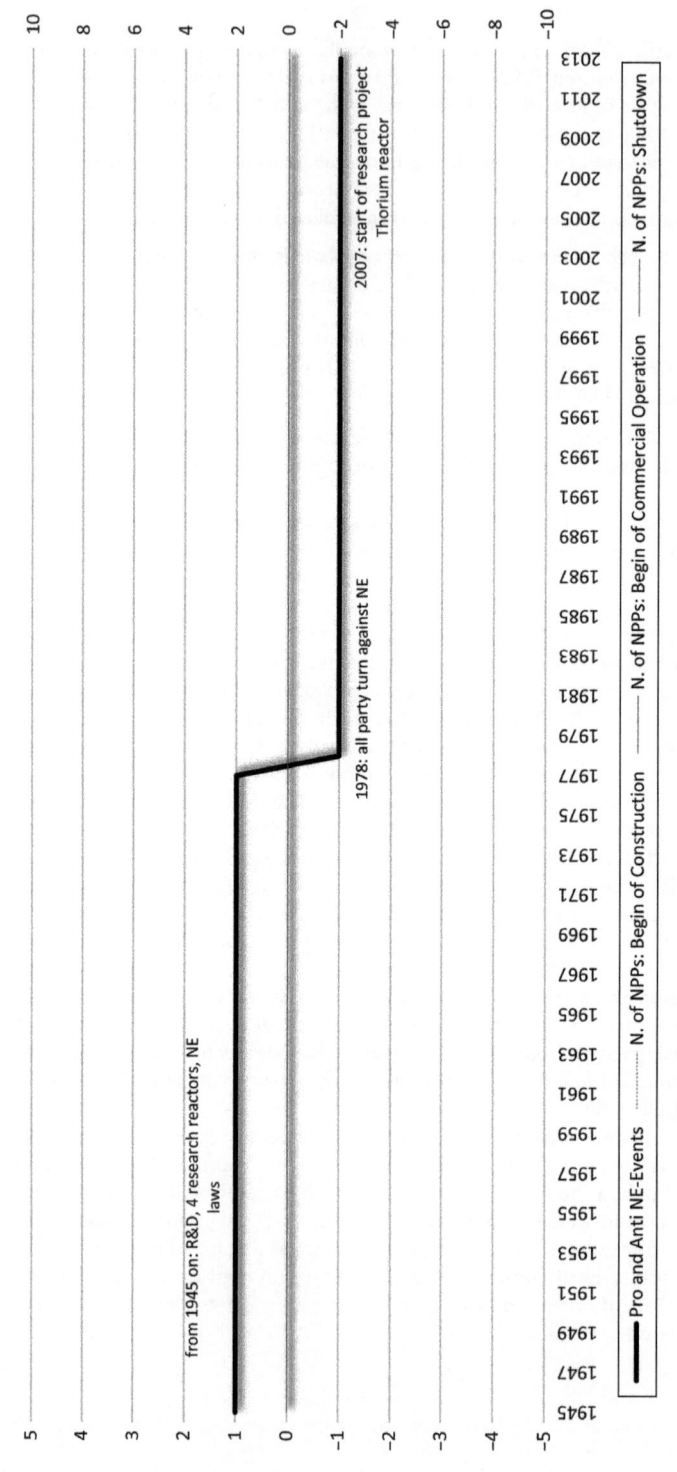

Figure 12.A4. Nuclear Energy Policy Development in Norway, 1945–2013

Portugal

The history of nuclear energy in Portugal goes back to its authoritarian regime. Preparations for nuclear research began in the early 1950s.[15] Portugal signed a bilateral agreement with the US in July 1955 on research cooperation, but not on energy production. It resulted in a still active research reactor that become critical already in 1961. Regulation of uranium mining began in 1950, and mining started early due to the interest of the US. That interest, however, ebbed already in the early 1960s (see Gaspar 2010). As the last IAEA country report on Portugal in 2009 indicates, decree laws for the licensing process of nuclear power stations are from 1969 and 1972. However, no licensing process was carried out and the country remained without nuclear energy (Figure 12.A5). In a nutshell the energy situation of Portugal can be characterized as being highly dependent on oil and gas imports (see Chapter 3): more than 80 per cent since the 1990s.

Portugal had planned for beginning the construction of nuclear power plants in the 1960s but the implementation of these plans was delayed. A major reason may have been Portugal's strained budget situation resulting from its very costly involvement in the decolonialization wars of the 1960s and 1970s (Angola 1961–75, Guinea-Bissau 1962–74, Mozambique 1965–74).[16] Given these constraints, opportunity costs of investing in nuclear research were obviously considered too high by the Salazar regime. Nevertheless, there were initiatives by the electricity monopolist Electricidade de Portugal[17] in 1972 to start construction of a first reactor in the early 1970s and to build another four reactors in the 1980s. The turmoil of the overturn of the authoritarian regime by the 'Carnation Revolution' of April 1974—the beginning of the Third Wave of Democratization[18]—did not prevent the new regime from deciding to build a reactor at Ferrel in 1976.

Strong local protest against preparatory works for the construction of the Ferrel reactor in 1976 led to the creation of national anti-nuclear and environmental movements. The effectiveness of this mobilization may have been nurtured by the experience of nearby Spanish reactors (Almaraz 1 and 2). Mobilization efforts persisted and culminated in 1978 (Delicado 2013: 194). According to Delicado (2013) there were parliamentary discussions until the end of the 1970s. Coalition governments consisting of the PSD and CDS (January 1980–June 1983) and of the PS and PSD (June 1983–November 1985) continued to propose National Energy Programmes in 1982 and 1984, respectively, that still included plans for the construction of nuclear power plants. It was in 1986—after the Chernobyl disaster—that the government definitely stopped nuclear plans (Delicado 2013). Note that PM Aníbal Cavaco Silva at that time led a PSD minority government backed by only 29.8 per cent of the voters, in cohabitation with Socialist President Mario Soares. Later pro-nuclear private initiatives were rejected under subsequent Socialist governments in 2005 and 2010. Public opinion is clearly anti-nuclear as compared to the EU average (see Figure 12.2), but anti-nuclear attitudes increased to a lesser extent than in the other non-nuclear countries.

Why this trajectory? Portugal had clearly nuclear energy ambitions, but cooperation with the US and UK did not intensify as in Spain (see Gaspar 2010), and the country's financial situation did not allow an independent nuclear energy programme in the 1960s.

---

[15] For the early period see Gaspar (2010) and Delicado (2013); for a historical account see da Costa Oliveira (2005). There is also a country report by the OECD Nuclear Energy Agency (2009).

[16] Due to high deficits, trade imbalances, high prices of energy, and unemployment, the country requested two economic support programmes in 1977/8 and 1983 financed by the IMF.

[17] EDP was a state-controlled electricity monopoly. In 1960, electricity-producing companies merged into the Companhia Portuguesa de Electricidade. After the Portuguese dictatorship was overthrown in the 1974 revolution, the left government nationalized Portugal's power generation and transmission infrastructure and renamed it Electricidade de Portugal.

[18] This pioneer role is especially accentuated by Linz and Stepan (1996) in their assessment of the success of transitions.

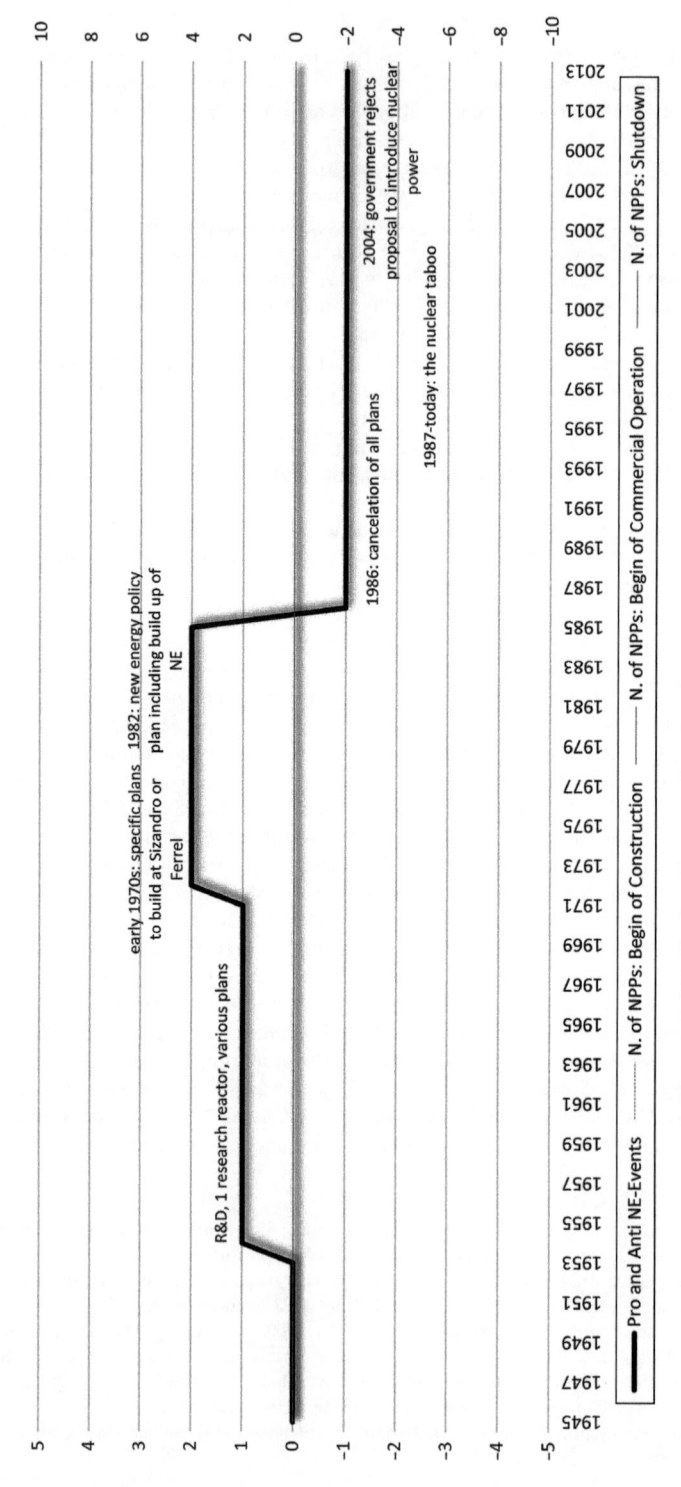

Figure 12.A5. Nuclear Energy Policy Development in Portugal, 1945–2013

The 1974 revolution was followed by political instability in the early years, and ongoing military presidencies (until as late as 1986) (Amorim Neto 2003). According to Linz and Stepan (1996: 124) democratic consolidation and implementation of economic reforms began only in 1982 with constitutional reform. Attempts to build a reactor in 1976 were undermined not only by grassroots movements but also by the origin of these plans in the authoritarian regime.

Our investigation of the electoral manifestos of major parties indicate that for the key political actors the nuclear energy option was not explicitly excluded: there are only very few relevant passages, meaning that the parties remained largely silent on this issue. The PSD (Partido Social Democrata), a left-centre party until the early 1980s then moving successively to the right and becoming a liberal party, stated in its 1983 manifesto: 'Prepare the necessary conditions to the public debate and decision of the National Assembly on the energy plan' and 'options of electric energy production by nuclear means'.

Greece

Greece, another transition country, originally had clear nuclear energy ambitions. Still under the monarchy, Konstantinos Karamanlis, the leader of the conservative National Radical Union, initiated during his premiership (1955–66) the construction of the Greek Research Reactor (GRR-1) running until 2004. The construction of further three research reactors was planned in this period. Tympas et al. (2013) show that only after the military dictatorship (1967–74) did plans to build an industrial reactor become relevant. In 1976, the Public Power Company put forward an initiative for a ten-year nuclear power investment programme. In 1979, under the conservative Prime Minister Karamanlis, the purchase of a 1000 MW reactor from the Soviet Union was discussed in the media.[19] However, following the electoral victory of PASOK under its leader Andreas Papandreou in 1981, no further advance of this programme was made.

The intervening event was heavy earthquakes in February and March 1981. As Tympas et al. (2013: 177) show, earlier geological arguments by anti-nuclear scientists and movements became decisive thereafter. The parliamentary elections in October 1981 were proverbial earthquake elections, with heavy losses for the Conservatives, and the PASOK winning the election. Since then, a reactor was no longer an option. The Chernobyl accident was also relevant in tying Greece to a position of rejecting nuclear energy as the fallout strongly affected Greece and caused much public concern. Even before that, according to the first Eurobarometer available for Greece, in 1982, 42 per cent of the respondents considered nuclear power bearing an 'unacceptable risk' whereas only around 18 per cent considered it a worthwhile option (see Figure 12.1).

Notwithstanding the weight of these political arguments there are also structural parameters leading to a heavy path dependency in Greek energy policies. Note that Greece has the highest carbon-oriented energy mix in the IEA. It relies heavily on oil and on domestic lignite resources. Greece ranks fifth in terms of lignite resources world-wide and this type of brown coal provides about one-third of Greek's total energy consumption. More importantly, more than 90 per cent of lignite is used for electricity production. Lignite production, electricity production, transmission, and distribution are owned by a public sector quasi-monopolist established in 1959 (under PM Karamanlis) until today, even though Greece has announced that it will transpose the EU directives on the liberalization of energy markets (see IEA 2011c). These structural parameters—high endowment with coal in combination with a public monopolist—naturally would not lead us to expect a centrist

---

[19] According to Tympas (personal communication) it is unclear which type of power plant was actually discussed in Moscow. The ambivalence potentially provided Greece with leverage with regard to its negotiations with NATO and the EC at that time.

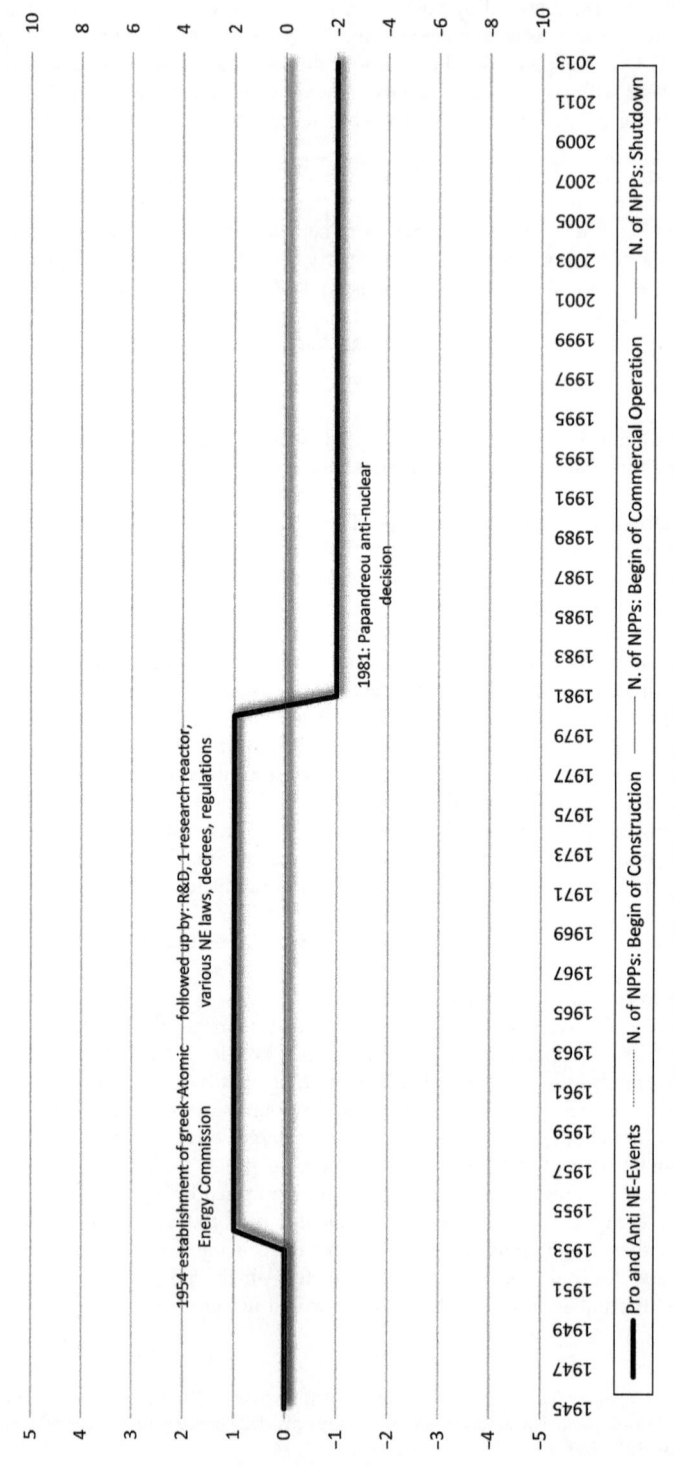

Figure 12.A6. Nuclear Energy Policy Development in Greece, 1945–2013

Socialist party like PASOK to implement the nuclear energy plans inherited from its conservative predecessors in government against public opinion so late on the Western European time bar of the nuclear energy age.

Nuclear Energy Policy Reversal Countries

The countries in this group are Austria, Belgium, Germany, Italy, Switzerland, Sweden, and Spain. All but Belgium and Spain are covered in individual chapters in this volume.

Belgium

Belgium currently has seven nuclear power reactors producing more than 40,000 GW and half of the country's electricity demand in 2013. In the first post-war decades the country followed the typical Western European nuclear energy path. Based on early cooperation with the US it was building research reactors in the 1950s and 1960. It was then planning for industrial nuclear energy production in the early 1960s, and building nuclear power plants in the late 1960s and 1970s.[20] The first plants went operational in 1974. Four more reactors were commissioned from 1973 in the context of the first oil crisis. These reactors were connected to the grid by the mid-1980s, bringing Belgium's nuclear reactor fleet to today's total of seven. Belgium for many years covered almost the entire nuclear fuel cycle and for the years 1967–91 aimed for a fast-breeder reactor in a joint venture with Germany and the Netherlands in Kalkar—a project that was eventually stopped by Germany (see Chapter 7). The Belgian capital is also involved in the French nuclear energy programme, specifically in the Chooz nuclear power plant close to the Belgian boarder that produces for the Belgian market.

Politically, the choice of nuclear energy was not contested initially but protest began to emerge in the 1970s. Fuelled by the Three Mile Island accident it caused a first six-year moratorium in 1979. Belgium was early in the institutionalization of anti-nuclear mobilization in Green parties (the Flemish AGALEV, later renamed Groen! and Groen, respectively, and the Walloon Ecolo) which have been represented in parliament since 1981 (as a consequence anti-nuclear street protest virtually disappeared).

In terms of reacting to nuclear events, the governments of the day have continued to be responsive. Thus plans for nuclear expansion came to a halt with the Chernobyl disaster of 1986. In 1988 the government called a moratorium on the construction of nuclear plants in Belgium that was renewed by successive governments.

A more radical break came in 1999 with the new government consisting of the Liberals (VLD and MR), Socialists (SP.A and PS), and, for the first time, the Greens (Groen! and Ecolo), one of the few Belgian cabinets without the Christian Democrats. When taking office, the government announced the plan to end nuclear energy production in Belgium by prohibiting the building of new reactors and limiting the lifetime of the existing ones to forty years. It also introduced a moratorium on reprocessing. However, the parliamentary enactment of the nuclear energy phase-out did not happen before January 2003. In-between a government commission and foreign experts appointed by the government recommended the opposite. Still, the law enacted in 2004 prohibited the building of further nuclear power plants and limited the lifetime of the existing ones to forty years. By implication this would have meant the phasing out of all Belgian reactors between 2015 and 2025. However, the phase-out law allowed the government to depart from the phase-out plan if Belgium's security supply was threatened and provided such action was recommended by the Gas and Electricity Regulatory Commission (Figure 12.A7).

---

[20] This country profile draws on the country reports of the IEA (2009), IAEA (updated 2014), and the WNA (updated June 2015), the Wikipedia entry 'Nuclear energy in Belgium' (last modified 10 Sept. 2014), the manifestos of the Belgian parties, newspaper articles, and Chapter 4 of this volume.

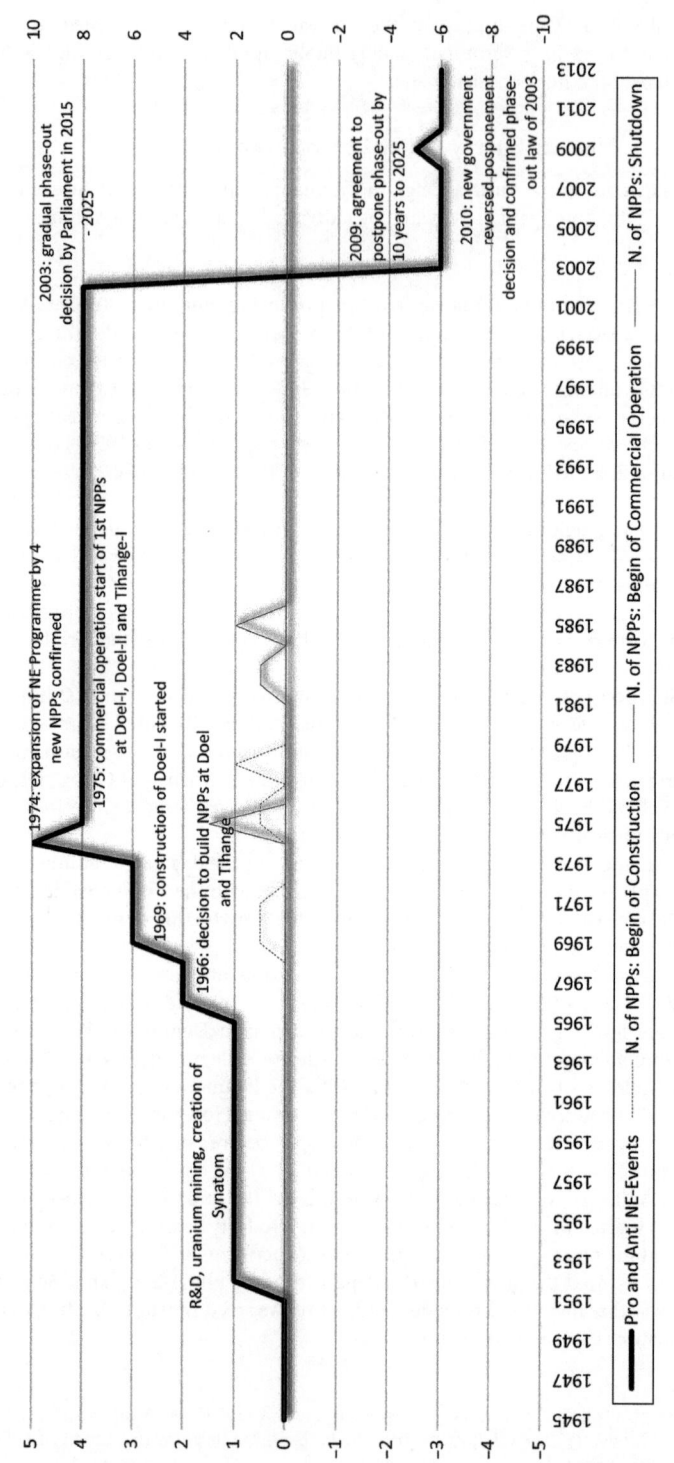

Figure 12.A7. Nuclear Energy Policy Development in Belgium, 1945–2013

The Greens did not participate in subsequent governments. In the years following the phase-out decision concerns were prominent in the domestic energy debate about Belgium not reaching its emission targets to conform to the Kyoto Protocols and about the consequences the removal of nuclear electricity production would have on the domestic energy prices and energy security. Most government-commissioned studies recommended the adaptation of the phase-out plan (Kunsch and Friesewinkel 2014). The first government after the phase-out decision, Verhofstadt II (2003-7), did not try to reverse it. There was also no reactor to be shut down in its term or shortly thereafter. A short-lived government of the three major political camps in Belgium—Christian Democrats, Socialists, and Liberals—under the Christian Democratic Prime Minister Yves Leterme initiated a nuclear policy reversal consisting of lifetime extensions for the existing reactors combined with heavily taxing the extra profits of the providers in 2008. Due to a political crisis over the issue of state reform and cabinet change these plans could not be realized before the 2010 elections. The record long government formation process, taking 541 days, brought the new government comprising again the three major political camps into office in December 2011—that is, only after the Fukushima accident had occurred. As a consequence the new government under Prime Minister Elio di Rupo (francophone Socialists) initially shelved the proposal for lifetime extensions. Yet in 2012, while confirming the phasing-out decision, it also initiated a change of its timetable: in December 2013 parliament allowed a life extension for one reactor (Tihange 1) that would have stopped operation 2015 under the old law. At the same time the government's decree power in case of endangered supply security was scrapped. The next government, a centre-right coalition of the Flemish nationalists (N-VA), the Flemish Christian Democrats (CD&V), and the Liberals under Prime Minister Charles Michel (N-VA) continued the policy of lifetime extensions. In June 2015 the Belgian parliament legislated to grant the two soon-to-be-switched-off reactors, Doel 1 and 2, a lifetime extension until 2025. This implies that none of the country's seven reactors will stop production before 2025. These three reactors will then have a projected total lifetime of fifty years while the remaining four ones are still on a forty-year track until scheduled shutdown. This suggests that there might be potential for further lifetime extensions in the future. The policy development as outlined here clearly is strongly influenced by the country's strong dependence on nuclear energy.

Belgian nuclear energy policy is a product of party politics. Early parliamentary entry of the Greens has institutionalized one principled opponent of nuclear energy among the contenders in electoral politics. The Belgian electorate has remained fairly critical towards nuclear energy (with 30 to 40 per cent holding critical attitudes towards nuclear energy 1976-2011) (see Figure 12.A8) and the electorates of the major parties have always displayed some issue-inconsistency (see Figure 12.A8 and 12.A9). There are also only small margins between the major parties' electoral strength, a fact that may potentially make parties particularly responsive to public opinion also given the very proportional electoral system. Yet the nuclear energy issue has never been particularly relevant in domestic electoral and party politics.

In terms of the traditional parties' programmatic commitment to nuclear energy we observe a trend to become silent or negative on this issue in their electoral manifestos. While the Christian Democrats and Liberals have become mostly silent, the Flemish Socialists (sp.a) turned negative in 1981, that is, the year of the Green breakthrough to parliamentary representation. They first committed to freezing (in 1981), then to downsizing (in 1987), and finally to fully phasing out nuclear energy (in 2010). There is a kind of bifurcation between Flanders (modern industry and more postmodern value culture) and Wallonia (heavy industry and more materialist value culture), however (see also Barbé 2009). The Christian Democrats (CD&V) and Socialists (PS) of Wallonia have remained more openly committed to nuclear energy for most of the time, with the Socialists turning

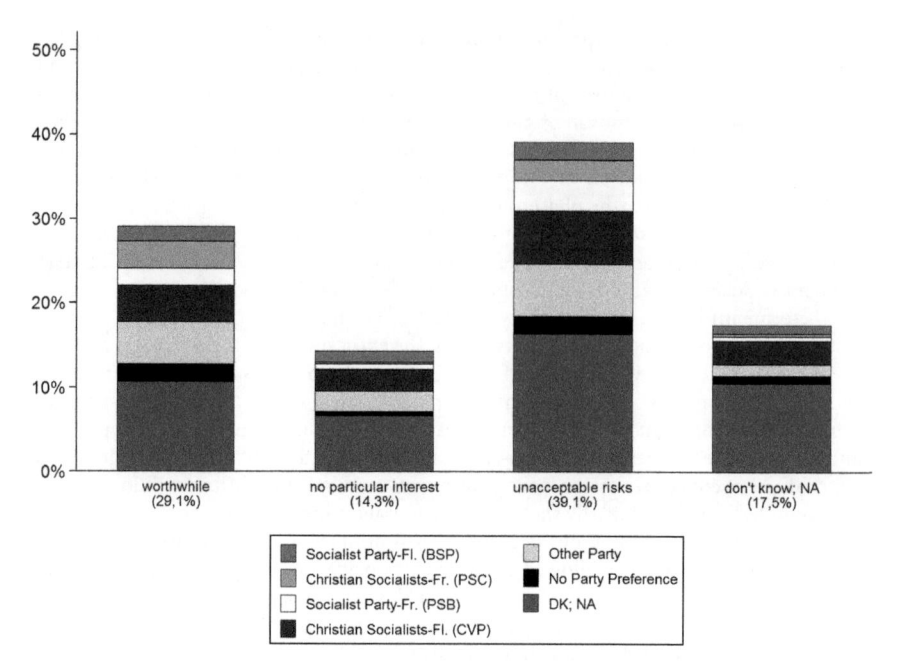

Figure 12.A8. Attitudes on Nuclear Energy among Belgian Party Voters in 1978 (First Available EB)
Source: EB 10A.

negative to nuclear phase-out, however, only late and moderately (in 2014). The strongest supporters of nuclear energy have always been the Christian Democratic parties and the Liberals from Wallonia, with the Flemish Liberals being divided and more erratic in position-taking.

To summarize the Belgian story, we see nuclear energy policy and policy reversals in particular largely driven by party competition. First, the emerging competition of the Greens is likely to have influenced the position-taking of the Socialists (sp.a). Second, changes in the party composition of the government have preceded policy reversals, the direction of which was influenced by the positions taken by the participating parties. Yet the parties have been quite pragmatic in making decision, taking into consideration Belgium's strong dependence on nuclear energy.

Spain

Spain has currently seven nuclear units at five sites, contributing about 20 per cent to electricity production in 2013.[21] This share has continuously declined since 1990 where it contributed 35.9 per cent.[22] Two reactors have been shut down, one in July 1990 (under a government of the Conservative PPE), and one in April 2006 (under a government of the Socialist PSOE). A PSOE government enacted a ten-year moratorium in 1983 and another one confirmed it in 1994. No new reactors have been commissioned since then.

---

[21] See Caro et al. (1995), Ordonez and Sanchez (1996), Bechberger (2009), Sánchez-Vázquez (2010), and Sánchez-Vázquez and Menéndez-Navarro (2015).

[22] For a detailed presentation of (nuclear) energy policies in Spain see IEA (2013, 2015).

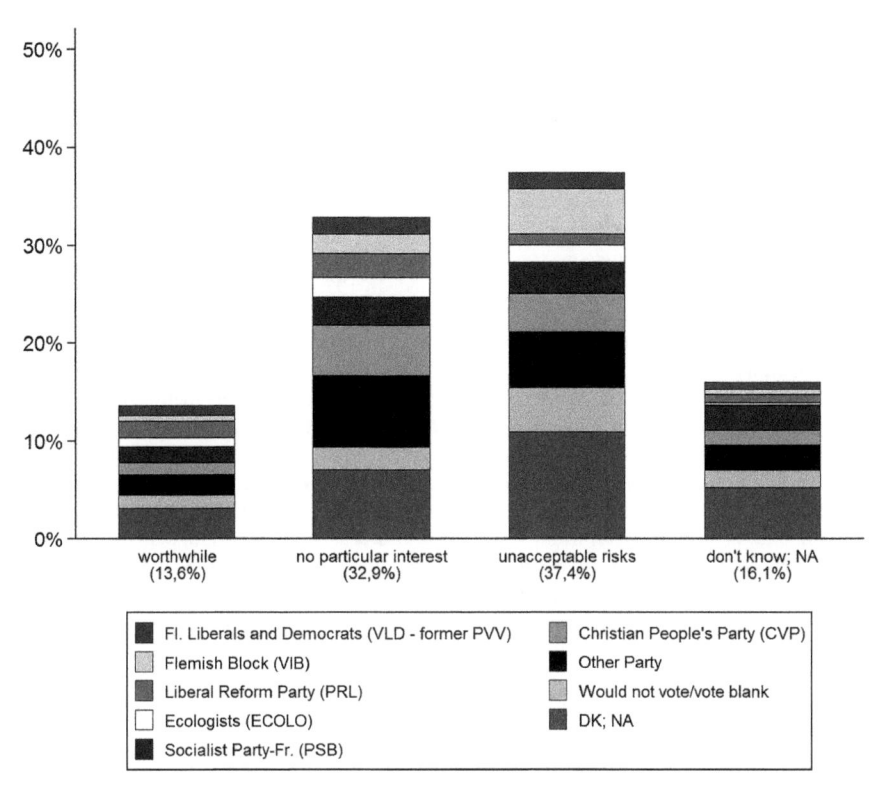

Figure 12.A9. Attitudes on Nuclear Energy among Belgian Party Voters in 1996
Source: EB 46.0.

Spain already started to develop a nuclear programme by the end of the Second World War (i.e. before the Atoms for Peace initiative). As in many other countries the initial intention was a dual one (military and industrial).[23] The US signed a bilateral agreement with the Franco regime on both nuclear research and a power reactor in July 1955. Note that this was beyond what happened in the cases of Portugal and Greece where the US agreed only on research cooperation. The bilateral agreement was extended in August 1957 over a ten-year period and the sale of uranium. Both push and pull factors have been relevant in this case: the Franco regime clearly followed a military objective at least in the early period (Presas i Puig 2005). One major reason beyond dominant business considerations in the US was the endowment of Spain with uranium reserves, just as in the cases of Belgium and Portugal. Economic reforms by the end of the 1950, initiated by Spanish technocrats and supported by the US and IMF, led to enormous economic growth in the 1960s. Many of the Spanish reactors that are still operational were actually planned and built during this period. There was neither a state agency in charge of the nuclear energy programme (as in Italy and France), nor a monopolist electricity provider (as in Greece or Portugal). Rather the energy sector was deregulated and private actors competed also in the

---

[23] See the ambivalent perception of the US administration with regard to the economic viability of nuclear energy production at that time, as illustrated by Drogan (2011).

nuclear energy sub-sector. In contrast with Portugal, the country was not burdened with decolonialization wars and the transition to democracy was less turbulent (see Linz and Stepan 1996: Chapter 6).

The construction of industrial reactors begun in the 1960s (1964, 1966, 1968) and grid connections were made in 1968, 1971, and 1972, respectively. The start of construction of a second wave was in 1973 (two reactors), the wave continued in 1974 (two reactors) and 1975 (two reactors). Grid connections followed in 1981, 1983 (two reactors), 1984, 1987, and 1988. According to Bechberger (2009) there were sixteen licence requests in the 1963–76 period, eight of which were approved. In sum, thirty-seven licences were requested in Spain, ten of which were approved and realized. In 1975, as a result of the 1973 energy crisis, the first Nuclear Energy Plan called for the building of eleven more reactors. Under the new democratic regime, more specifically, under the minority government of the Union of the Democratic Center (UCD), two reactors were licensed (Trillo I and Vandellos II) with the reactors connected to the grid in 1988. The Socialist government coming into power in 1982 cancelled four reactors under construction in 1984. There were shutdowns of two reactors in 1990 (Vandellos I) and 2006 (José Cabrera), respectively (i.e. one each by a conservative (Partido Popular, PP) and socialist (PSOE) government). Yet, given the small capacities of these reactors, both shutdowns have been considered mainly as symbolic acts.

Anti-nuclear protest began in the early 1970s and peaked after 1977/8, being fuelled by the government's first and second Nuclear Energy Plans of 1975 and 1978 that aimed for a substantial expansion of nuclear power (Sánchez-Vázquez and Menéndez-Navarro 2015). Already the first of the UDC minority cabinets at the beginning of democratic period terminated several projects. Facing local and regional mobilization and a highly regionalized political system, the whole spectrum of parties became responsive, despite the PP and its predecessor, the UCD, clearly preferring the nuclear path. Anti-nuclear protests were very effective, and even violent in the case of the unfinished Lemoniz reactor in the Basque region. Altogether twenty-seven licence requests were not granted and the Nuclear Energy Plan of 1978 was only approved by parliament in 1979 (Sánchez-Vázquez and Menéndez-Navarro 2015: 84). Although the sequence of events suggests that anti-nuclear protests have indeed been effective, other factors such as overestimated demand and underestimated construction costs are also relevant.

Whereas all parties were supportive of the nuclear course during the transition phase, as can be seen in the Moncloa pact signed in 1978,[24] the left parties quickly repositioned. The PSOE followed a strategy of ambivalence and postponement of decisions, whereas its leftist competitors—the United Left and the Communist Party—requested a referendum already in 1979, especially in the affected regions. The PSOE, in contrast, asked for a careful parliamentary discussion in its electoral manifesto. The United Left gained more than 10 per cent and twenty-three parliamentary seats, thus impeding the PSOE (30.5 per cent, 121 seats) from becoming the majority party in 1979. In order to attract potential voters from the anti-nuclear (new) radical left, the PSOE in the 1982 election declared an 'ordered suspension' of the nuclear programme.[25] Due to its broad appeal to the centre, the PSOE absorbed much of the former UCD electorate, while its nuclear repositioning contributed to reducing the electoral appeal of the anti-nuclear United Left and PCE (which were reduced from twenty-three to a mere four seats in 1982). The actual implementation of the moratorium in 1984 implied that the construction of four reactors was terminated, several

---

[24] The Moncloa pact was a political pact between all political parties. On nuclear energy see Chapter 9; 'Política energética y estatuto de la empresa pública' explicitly envisaged continuity with regard to nuclear energy.
[25] See Electoral Manifest 1982.

licences were withdrawn, and the new reactor construction prohibited by law. At the same time a forty-year maximum operational life of reactors was fixed.

Yet under the same PSOE government the building of more reactors was completed and the reactors were connected to the grid (i.e. in 1983 (two reactors), 1984, 1987, and 1988). The moratorium was affirmed in 1994 again by a PSOE government. Under the subsequent PPE government the capacity of the existing reactors was expanded (in 1998, 2002, 2003). More surprisingly, the 2004–11 PSOE government allowed licence renewals, a decision that contradicted its earlier promises to phase out. The incoming PP government in 2011 removed the moratorium and parliament confirmed reactor lifetime fixed at forty years (Figure 12.A10).

Whereas the United Left and the Communist Party in the June 1986 election demanded a moratorium also for the plants still under construction, the PSOE just played 'continuation' by stressing its concern for a maximum of reactor safety. Again, this position-taking was helpful for the PSOE to hold on to power (184 seats) and to keep down its leftist competitor United Left (winning seven seats). It is all the more remarkable when considering that the Chernobyl disaster had just occurred that April. Note, however, that Spain was not as affected by nuclear fallout as many other countries (e.g. Germany, Austria, Finland, Sweden, and Greece). Still, the PSOE's policy of maintaining nuclear energy fed into the reincrease of its leftist competitor United Left in the elections from 1989 to 1996 (when the PSOE lost government office). The 1996 electoral manifestos of the left parties as well as of the PP were very extensive on nuclear energy. The PSOE explicitly promoted the continuation of international cooperation in the development of nuclear energy, whereas the United Left demanded the immediate closure of first-generation reactors and a full phase-out until 2003. In opposition, the PSOE then promised for the 2000 election an ordered decommissioning and phase-out of nuclear energy—just as the German Social Democrats had done for the 1998 election (followed by the 'ordered phasing out' decided by the new Red-Green government in 2000). Just like the German Greens, the United Left requested an immediate closure of the first-generation reactors and a phase-out of the others until 2005.

Back in government, the PSOE in the period 2004–11 did not keep its earlier promises to phase out. Although the PSOE government closed one reactor in 2006, it also extended the reactors' run-times and allowed their upgrading. Similar to the strategy followed by the German Chancellor Gerhard Schröder, PM José Luis Rodríguez Zapatero initiated a round table on the future of nuclear energy in 2005, aiming for national consensus (Bechberger 2009). The conclusions of these round table talks, however, remained open to a future use of nuclear energy due to its continuous relevance for energy security in Spain. Subsequently, the PSOE minority government more and more took a pro-nuclear stance. For instance, it relied on the Partido Popular to pass the Nuclear Energy Law in 2007 that included the reduction of liabilities (Molina and Sanz 2011: 10; Field 2014, 2016). It renewed licences for a ten-year extension for Almaraz 1 and 2 in 2010 and decided 70 MWe uprates of these reactors in January 2011. In February 2011, the Sustainable Energy Act amended the previous Nuclear Energy Act, giving the government the power to determine lifetime extensions and the extent to which nuclear energy shall contribute to electricity production, as long as safety standards are guaranteed. This far-reaching amendment reversed the forty-year operating life rule that would have implied the closure of the remaining eight reactors between 2011 and 2018. Shortly thereafter, lifetime extensions were decided for Vandellos 2 in 2010, and for Cofrentes and Asco 1 and 2 in 2011 just before the elections in November 2011. Together with Tony Blair's U-turn this appears to be the most intriguing pro-nuclear reversal of a party's nuclear energy policy in Western Europe over the entire period.

These pro-nuclear reversals right after the Fukushima disaster indicate a second major U-turn of the PSOE that lost the election in November 2011. What are the reasons for these two reversals of the PSOE's nuclear energy policy? We argue that several factors played together differently in the different periods. The careful strategic position-taking of the PSOE, as can be seen from its manifestos, has its background in the distribution of policy

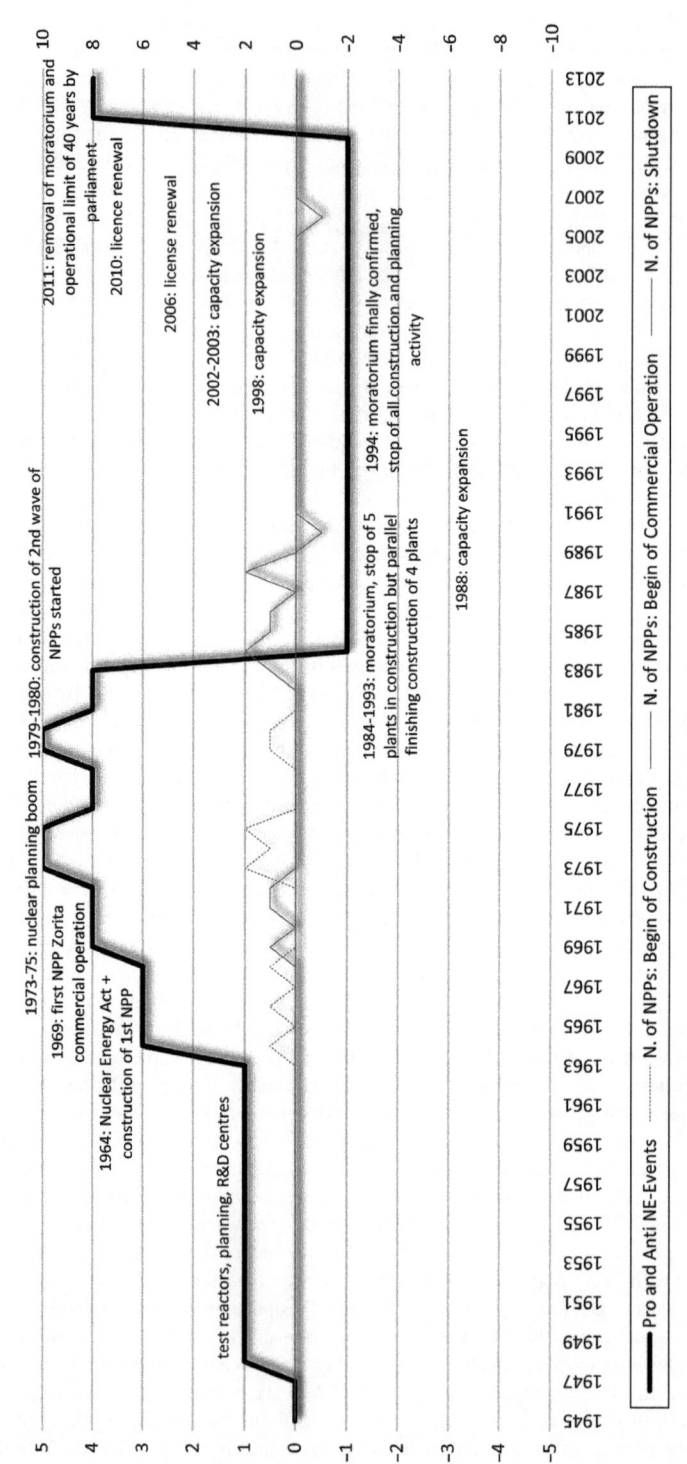

Figure 12.A10. Nuclear Energy Policy Development in Spain, 1945–2013

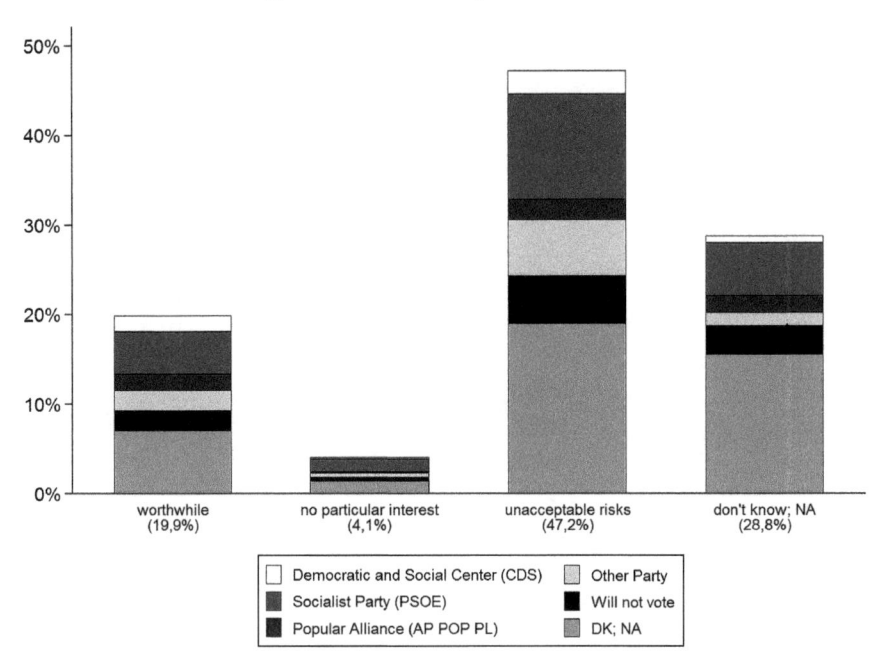

Figure 12.A11. Attitudes on Nuclear Energy among Spanish Party Voters in 1986
Source: EB 26.

preferences of the electorate. In one of the earliest surveys in 1983 (Molina and Sanz 2011) roughly one-third of the electorate was undecided, one-third was for, and one-third against nuclear energy. From there, public opinion moved quickly. As Figure 12.A11 shows, already in 1986 nearly 50 per cent of the Spanish electorate were against nuclear energy. Given the high salience of the issue and in order to succeed electorally, the PSOE either had to adjust and/or to influence the distribution of preferences. Nevertheless, the party had to be careful because at least in 1986 still nearly 5 per cent of the PSOE-leaning voters considered nuclear energy worthwhile (see Figure 12.A11). This indicates a heterogeneous preference structure of its electoral base. The PSOE thus had to monitor carefully the development of anti-nuclear protest and to be strategic in its position-taking in order to hold on to its parliamentary majority or at least to remain strong and flexible enough to form viable minority governments (see Field 2009, 2016). The pre-existence of left-to-PSOE parties taking up the nuclear issue was important for preventing a Green party from becoming successful in Spain.

The opinion structure changed considerably by 1996 (Figure 12.A12) and the shares of those refusing nuclear energy increased to one of the highest in Europe (around 71 per cent in 2005 see Figure 12.A11). The share of nuclear sceptics fell below 50 per cent in 2006, but increased again to 64 per cent by 2011. The PSOE's U-turn in this period thus must have reasons different from the ones behind its first one. The failure in 2005 of the German Red-Green government with their most prominent phase-out policy and its replacement by a grand coalition of the CDU/CSU-SPD may have been considered by the PSOE as a sign of failure to effectively steer a large economy with an anti-nuclear policy. In particular, however, the economic crisis was looming large in Spain already in 2007. This was not

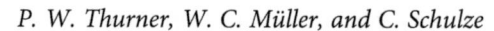

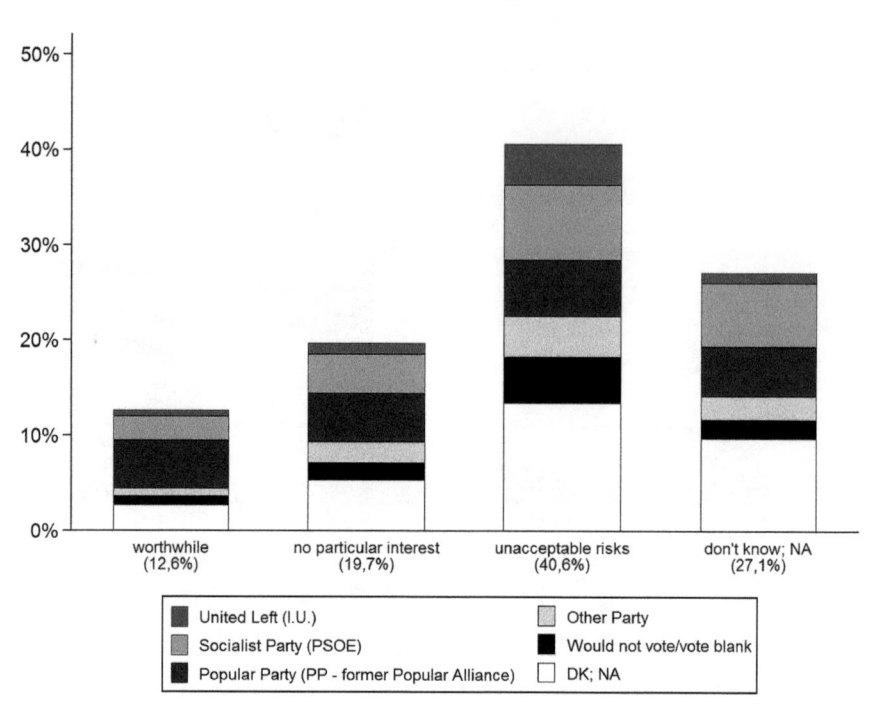

Figure 12.A12. Attitudes on Nuclear Energy among Spanish Party Voters in 1996
Source: EB 46.0.

the situation to risk further downturn by turmoil on the energy market that might result from switching off reactors earlier than technically necessary.

A major impact on the repositioning after 2004 is the increasing reliance of the PSOE minority cabinet on a broader basis for its anti-crisis policies since 2007. This could explain, why the PSOE government began to oscillate in its position-taking in 2007 and to enact pro-nuclear policies in 2010/11. In contrast, the PPE stuck more or less to its original positions in the 1982 election, considering nuclear energy as a base-load power with renewables being complementary energy carriers while at the same time very much downsizing its salience in the manifestos.

The 2015 and 2016 elections could be a watershed election in Spain's energy policy: as of 2016, most reactors' projected lifetime—gradually extended over the years—will end in the early 2020s. Given the countries' import dependency (around 80 per cent since 2005) and the long planning periods of nuclear energy, the new minority government has either to opt for the building of new reactors or accept a de facto phase-out within a few years. In this case, the country would have to implement a rapid energy turn just as in Germany. Given that nuclear energy continues to contribute about 20 per cent to electricity production, this would require a major effort. Heavy reliance on fossil fuels until today—around 72 per cent of total primary energy supply (see IEA 2015)—despite Spain's pioneering role in renewables (wind and solar contribute one-quarter to electricity production in 2014)—should aggravate the situation. Alternatively, Spain may join the international trend in granting its reactors another round of lifetime extensions beyond the forty-year mark and thus push the major decision further into the future.

Appendix: Other European Countries 347

Non-Reversal Countries

This group includes Finland, France (covered in Chapter 6), and the United Kingdom.

Finland

After having conducted preparatory studies and settled nuclear energy legislation in the 1950s, Finland's commitment to an industrial nuclear energy programme dates back to the late 1960s.[26] On the initiative of the private industry, the government decided the order of two Soviet-type reactors in 1969 and 1971, both constructed at Loviisa in 1971–7 and connected to the grid in 1979 and 1981, respectively.[27] A second order by private companies included two further Swedish reactors at Olkiluto, constructed in 1974–8 and 1975–80, respectively. This testifies to a very quick construction after a late entry. As the decision-making and implementation process was smooth, the Finnish case contradicts the argument that nuclear latecomers in the 1970s soon run into difficulties due to anti-nuclear movements (see e.g. Flam 1994; Midttun and Rucht 1994). However, nuclear energy did not take an entirely smooth development as private sector initiatives for further reactors submitted to parliament by government in 1986 and 1993 were voted down. The next initiative for a fifth reactor, Olkiluto III, came in 1998, a positive parliament decision was made in 2002, and construction (of a generation III European Pressurized Reactor (EPR) by a French-German consortium under the lead of AREVA) started in 2005 (with grid connection originally envisaged for 2009). Note that in 2001, the parliament decided the construction of the first nuclear waste disposal world-wide and in 2006–7 the early reactors' lifetime of was extended. In 2010, the parliament accepted government proposals for two more reactors. Due to modifications in the design of one reactor to be constructed by a Russian company using Russian technology, this decision had to be reaffirmed by parliament in December 2014. In 2010 a decision-in-principle opened a window of opportunity to begin the construction of the second reactor (Olkiluto IV) that, however, elapsed due to extreme delay and cost overrun of the Olkiluto III reactor (Figure 12.A13).

Overall, Finland resembles the UK and French cases by continuing on the nuclear energy path even after Fukushima and despite considerable problems with the most recent reactor project. Such steadfast policy-making in an extreme multi-party system is extraordinary given the comparative evidence. In attempts at explaining such behaviour the literature has made reference to weak protest movements (Rüdig 1990; Kolb 2008), effective lobbying and consensual elite discourse (Kojo and Litmanen 2009), or to favourable public opinion. While all these factors are probably relevant, they alone cannot account for the Finnish nuclear energy policies.

We propose a somewhat different rationale for the understanding of this country's nuclear energy trajectory that is analytically interesting in many aspects. First, the status of a politically neutral country sharing a long border with the Soviet Union was the reason why the country did not buy US reactor technology already in the 1950s. In contrast to the other neutral countries, Austria and Sweden, Finland did not even have a bilateral cooperation agreement with the US (which would have collided with the 'Agreement of Friendship, Cooperation, and Mutual Assistance' with the Soviet Union from 1948). Finland in the post-war period followed the Paasikivi-Kekkonen line of avoiding any policy, and even government compositions, that might have had disturbing effects on the country's relationship with the Soviet Union.

---

[26] See IAEA Finland 2013: 16. To our knowledge there are no comprehensive political science case studies on Finland's nuclear energy policies so far. For a study focusing on recent aspects see Kojo and Litmanen (2009).

[27] Bärs (1979) and Vehmas (2009) provide some details on the early years.

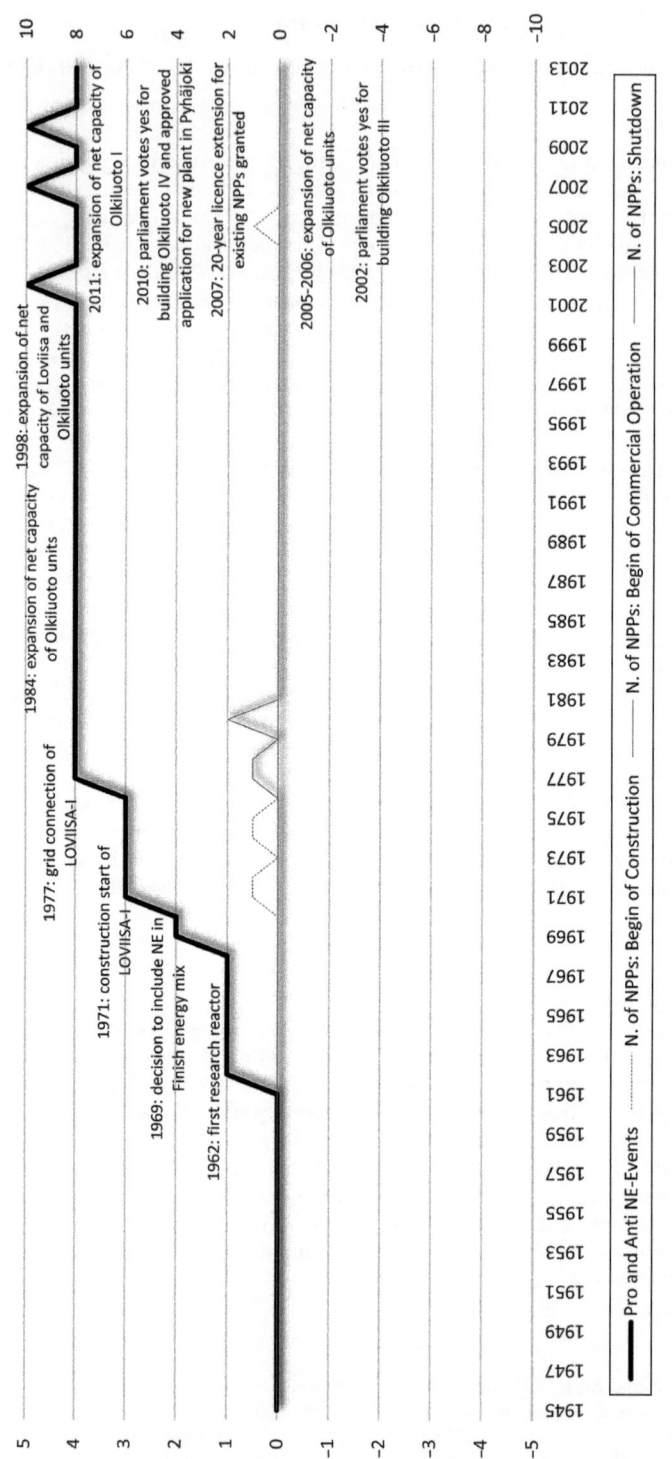

Figure 12.A13. Nuclear Energy Policy Development in Finland, 1945–2013

The initiative to set up a nuclear industrial programme came from the energy-hungry forest and heavy industries that urged President Urho Kekkonen (Agrarian Party, the later Centre Party (KESK)) in 1968 to develop an alternative energy base for the rapidly growing economy. Industrial expansion tied together Finland's long-standing coalition between the Agrarians and Social Democrats (the Communists participated until 1982). The Communist party (later Left Alliance) and the Social Democratic party were strongly pro-nuclear. In order to appease the Soviets, in a 'package deal' the government ordered two reactors from the Soviet Union while private industry ordered two more reactors from Sweden.

Despite the extremely fragmented party system, party competition was not very intense in the decades putting Finland on the nuclear energy track. One reason for this was the towering figure of President Kekkonen (1956–81) who during his twenty-five years in office dominated government formation (Arter 1981; Nousiainen 2000).

Our content analysis of all electoral manifestos of the main parties shows that parties have been more or less silent on nuclear energy:[28] The Left alliance (formerly SKDL in 1970, meanwhile reduced to a splinter group) acclaimed the order of Soviet nuclear reactors. In the 2011 election, the party took a stand against nuclear energy. A small passage on nuclear energy can be found in the Social Democratic party's 1979 manifesto: 'Nuclear power plants' safety and environmental requirements have to be tightened up'. The Social Democrats' 2011 manifesto concisely stated:

> Finland depends on imports of energy resources. The share of energy resources in Finland is only 30 per cent.... Domesticly, Finland only possesses renewable energies like water, wind and solar. Thanks to these, and thanks to nuclear power, today 60 per cent of electricity is produced with*out* greenhouse emission. This energy is an indispensable input for the production in the Finnish economy.

The Centre party (until 1965 the Agrarian Union), that is the party of Kekkonen, only in 1987 had a small note on nuclear energy: 'We have to implement a decentralized electricity production as an alternative to nuclear energy by using as basic fuel peat in the central and northern parts, and gas in the southern part of Finland'. The Centre party MPs had been split in the parliamentary vote on the fifth reactor in 2002.[29]

The National Coalition party (KOK), Finland's Conservative party, is the only party unambiguously legitimating and demanding nuclear energy, but it did so for the first time only in its 1999 manifesto: 'Additional nuclear power construction is to be welcomed as part of a comprehensive energy policy. Its basic elements are the security of energy supply at competitive prices, as well as controlling and reducing the energy sector's climate impact'. The party remained steadfast on the nuclear energy issue. In 2007 it stated: 'Construction of nuclear power is justified. It is an emission-free and non-polluting form of energy'. And it demanded 'additional nuclear power to guarantee that households' electricity bills remain reasonable'.

The Green League contested its first election in 1991. In their manifesto for this election the Greens promise to terminate nuclear energy by the year 2000. Their manifesto in 1995, the year when the first Green Minister was included in a national government world-wide,

---

[28] This is also the conclusion of Bärs (1979) focusing more on party manifestos in the 1970s: only few parties had energy programmes or referred to nuclear energy. The Social Democratic Party in its 1974 energy programme considered nuclear energy as the only viable strategy of providing the country with sufficient amounts of energy. The Centre Party in 1976 indicates that security should have top priority and waste management has to be solved first. The Liberal Party in its environmental programme in 1975 requests that the number of reactors should be restricted to the planned one. This is analogous to the National Coalition Party.

[29] See Unto Hämäläinen, 'More Power from Parliament', *Helsinki Times*, 12 Feb. 2002 <http://www2.hs.fi/english/archive/news.asp?id=20020212IE9>.

the so-called 'rainbow coalition', states very briefly that taxing electricity prices would reduce the demand, that additional nuclear energy plants should not be built, and that gas should be a substitute carrier. In the 1999 manifesto the nuclear energy issue is not mentioned. The rainbow coalition including the Greens continued—but the Greens left the coalition in 2002 due to the legislative decision to build a fifth reactor (Olkiluto III) (Sundberg and Wilhelmsson 2008). Still, the moderate tone continued in the Greens' 2007 and 2011 manifestos: they contain no calls for phase-out or for plant closures. However, the party which was part of the incumbent centre-right-Green government, campaigned in 2011 that it would not participate in any coalition giving licences for new reactors. The Greens did not leave the government in 2010 when parliament decided in July (during the turmoil of PM Matti Vanhanen's resignation from his government and party offices) the construction of two further reactors. The Green League was again part of the next coalition government in 2011—and left in 2014 after the parliament's renewed approval of a nuclear power reactor that had originally been approved in 2010 but was now to be built with Russian reactor technology.

Why this comparatively moderate tone of the 'natural enemy' of nuclear energy? Why the near absence of nuclear energy in the manifestos of the relevant parties? Is it the consensual political culture of the Finns? Perhaps the constitutional clause that allowed a parliamentary minority of one-third of the MPs to postpone decision-making until the next parliamentary term needs to be considered here. This clause that was in force until the constitutional reform of 2000 provided government architects with an incentive to build oversized coalitions (Nousiainen 2000: 269) and parties with an incentive to remain ambiguous on issues that may have led to their exclusion from government. The interplay between the de facto requirement of super-majorities and a semi-presidential system may have contributed to the moderation of the parties despite a very low entrance hurdle to parliament and a highly fragmented party system.[30] Given the President's considerable influence on government formation, in particular during the Kekkonen period, parties had no incentive for taking positions conflicting with those of the President or following other centrifugal strategies.

The Finnish Social Democratic party (SDP), the strongest party in the period when the construction of reactors was decided and implemented, and the strongest party in the rainbow coalition after the 1995 elections, in contrast to other Social Democratic parties in Western Europe, did not consider alternatives to nuclear energy. Whereas the German Red-Green coalition enacted the phase-out of nuclear energy in 2002, the Finnish cabinet under PM Paavo Lipponen (SDP), after the renewal of the rainbow coalition in 1999, initiated the building of a new reactor in 2002. Lipponen received only a narrow backing from the parliament (107 yes to 92 no votes). By this decision Finland became the first European country in more than a decade to build a new nuclear reactor. The Green League left the coalition and internal divisions appeared in the SDP. Lipponen survived politically and remained party leader until 2005 even beyond his party's defeat in the 2003 elections. The Finnish Social Democratic party did not change its position until today: 'We approve the construction of additional nuclear power plants as part of the diversification of Finnish energy sources' (http://www.sdp.fi/en/our-values, June 2015). Note that the Finnish Social Democrats have not experienced a long period out of government office since the 1970s. They continue to give support to Kitschelt's (1986) early observation that mainstream-left parties in government are likely to follow a nuclear energy policy different from those in opposition.

---

[30] Thus, we argue that a real parliamentarization and fierce party competition should be seen only after the constitutional reform in 2000—with some delay because parties have to learn the opportunities of the new system. Meanwhile parliamentary majority formation seems to be accepted, as is demonstrated by the decision in 2014 where 102 MPs voted against an opposition bloc of 98.

Further governmental proposals for a fifth reactor in 1986 and 1993 were not voted on or voted down in parliament. Only in 2010 was an initiative to build two more reactors supported by the government consisting of the Centre party, National Coalition party, Swedish People's party, and Green League. Note that the Green League had opposed this so-called decision-in-principle but had opted to remain in cabinet despite having been outvoted on that issue. As the voters punished the Greens in the 2011 election, the party's condition for re-entering the government was that no new permits for the construction of further nuclear power facilities would be granted. The Greens' exit from government was rewarded—they gained five parliamentary seats in 2014. Nevertheless, the Finnish case contradicts our hypothesis in Chapters 2 and 4 according to which the involvement of Green parties in government reduce, delay, or end the use of nuclear energy. The Finnish case offers itself for a detailed crucial case study, under which conditions central positions of a government party do not impact on the cabinet's policy. One answer could be that the governmental decision to build new reactors in 2002, 2010, and 2014, respectively, were always taken at the end of the legislative period. Another would be to refer to the lack of explicitness of the Greens in their manifestos. In other words, they did not credibly commit to making a government policy of nuclear exit a condition of government participation.

As can be seen from Figure 12.A14, public opinion on nuclear energy in Finland is the least negative in Western Europe. Proponents and rejecters are more or less evenly split across responses in 1996. One exception is the National Coalition where the proponents clearly predominate.

Finland's parliamentarization (as formalized by the 2000 constitutional reform) and less consensual decision-making in the Finnish parliament are leading to incentives to politicize the nuclear energy issue more than in the past. Nevertheless, the main parties' positions are

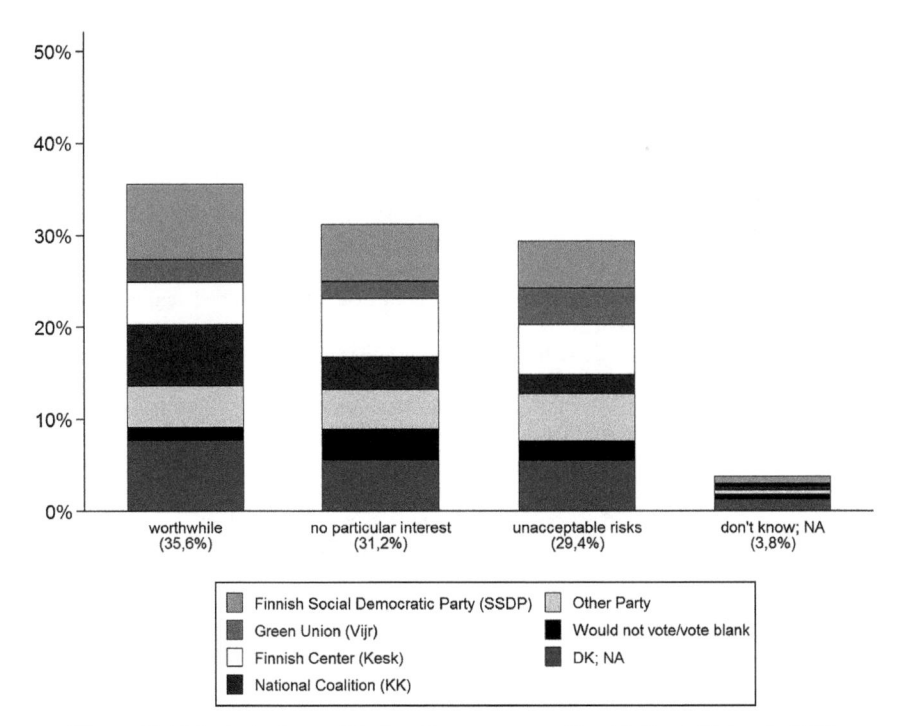

Figure 12.A14. Attitudes on Nuclear Energy among Finnish Party Voters in 1996

Source: EB 46.0.

still supportive, including the Social Democratic Party despite internal divisions since 2000. Increasingly detrimental factors for nuclear energy, however, are the enormous delay in the building of the Olkiluto III reactor and the extreme cost overruns. Due to these delays, the decision-in-principle to build Olkiluto IV after the completion of Olkiluto III expired (it had originally been projected for 2010 but in 2015 the new date was 2018). The government programme of the coalition government of the Centre party, True Finns, and National Coalition taking office in 2015 does not mention nuclear energy but puts great store on the further expansion of renewables.

However, the structural background conditions of Finland are favourable to nuclear energy: the country's energy import dependency is extremely high (see Chapter 3). Not only because the country produces neither oil nor gas, and therefore had to import 77.8 per cent of total energy supply in 2011. The really surprising fact is that, despite the high contribution of nuclear energy to domesticly produced electricity (more than 40 per cent in the early 1980s, 31.6 per cent in 2011) the country imports another 17 per cent in 2011 of its total electricity from Russia and the Nordic Power Exchange Market (see IEA country profile 2013: 89). The reason behind this is the cold climate and the energy-intense economy: Finland has the second highest per capita energy and electricity consumption among the countries of the IEA. Finland is also a high performer in renewables, meaning mostly the use of solid biofuels (i.e. wood).

United Kingdom

The UK has currently sixteen reactors contributing 18 per cent of electricity production. There has been a continuous decline of the role of nuclear energy since the 1990s where it contributed about 25–30 per cent (see IEA 2014). Twenty-six reactors have been permanently shut down. With the exception of the Sizewell reactor connected to the grid in 1995, all existing reactors are expected to be closed down by 2023 at the latest, when reaching the end of their projected lifetimes.

Britain's nuclear power programme was initiated already in 1955, and expanded in the 1960s and 1970s under both Conservatives and Labour governments (Figure 12.A15). According to the IAEA (2015: 41–56), construction of twenty reactors was started in the 1950s, eighteen in the 1960s, six in the 1970s, five in the 1980s, and none in the 1990s. The de facto stop in investing in nuclear energy has to be seen in context with the discovery of large-sized oil and gas fields in the North Sea beginning in the mid-1960s. Oil and gas production started in the mid-1970s and soon turned Britain from a net-importer of energy to a net-exporter. In the boom years investment in nuclear energy seemed neither necessary nor the most rewarding strategy.

A detailed analysis of all party manifestos shows that the nuclear energy issue was not very salient for the three most important parties—Conservatives, Labour, Liberals—with two exceptions: the euphoric 1955 manifesto of the Conservative party (spending 235 words on nuclear energy), and the quite ambivalent manifesto (freezing at current state of expansion but continuation of research including fast-breeder technology) of the Liberal party in 1987 (191 words). In its 1955 electoral manifesto the Labour party wrote: 'Atomic energy and other new inventions can bring dramatic increases in productivity and therefore in wealth and leisure'. This view was widely shared still in the late 1960s (see, for instance, the 1966 manifesto of the Liberal party).

The gradual politicisation of the nuclear energy issue began in the 1970s. Anti-nuclear movements were quite forceful in terms of mobilizing street protest in the 1970s. However, the first past the post electoral system prevented the establishment of a Green party in parliament and the other parties were not very responsive to the movement's concerns. Rüdig (1990, 1994) even considered the British anti-nuclear movement as a low-profile failure. This characterization may be too harsh and driven by the policy outcome as public opinion moved towards a near majority refusing nuclear energy from 1978 to 1986

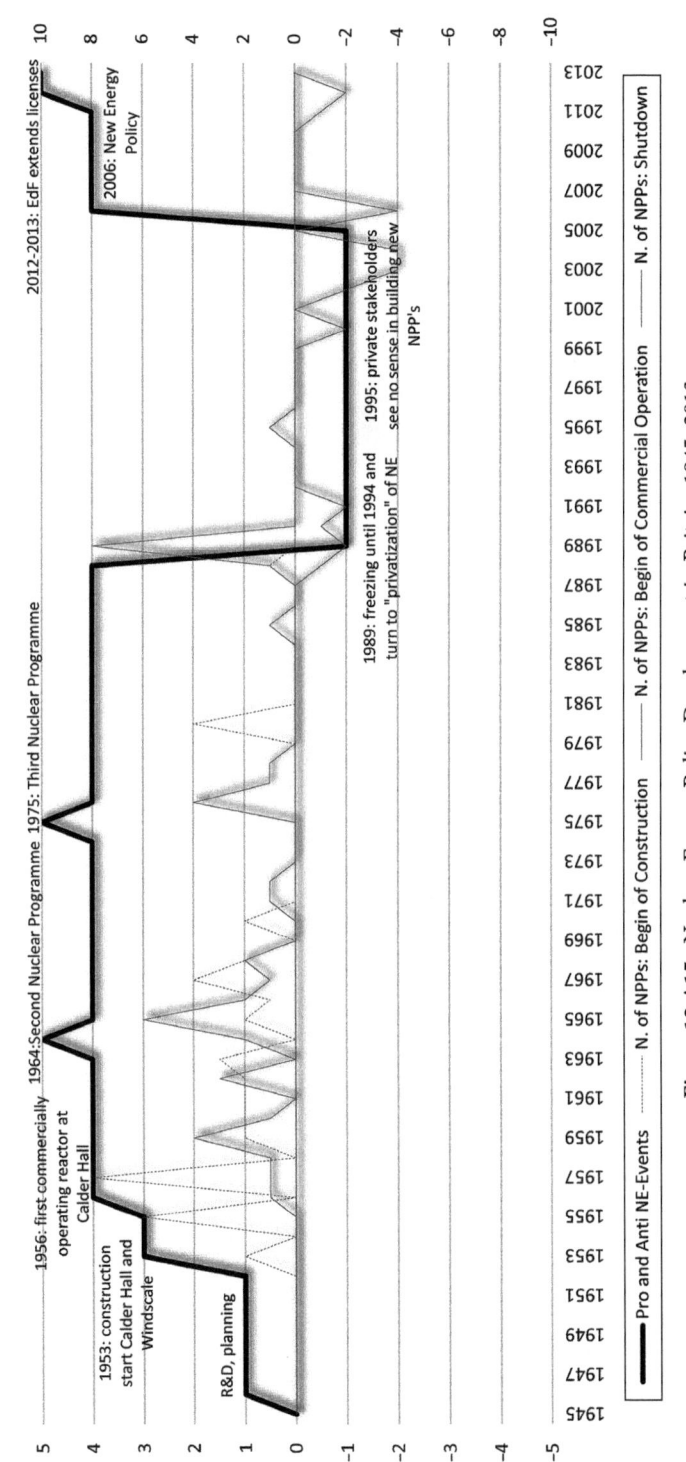

Figure 12.A15. Nuclear Energy Policy Development in Britain, 1945–2013

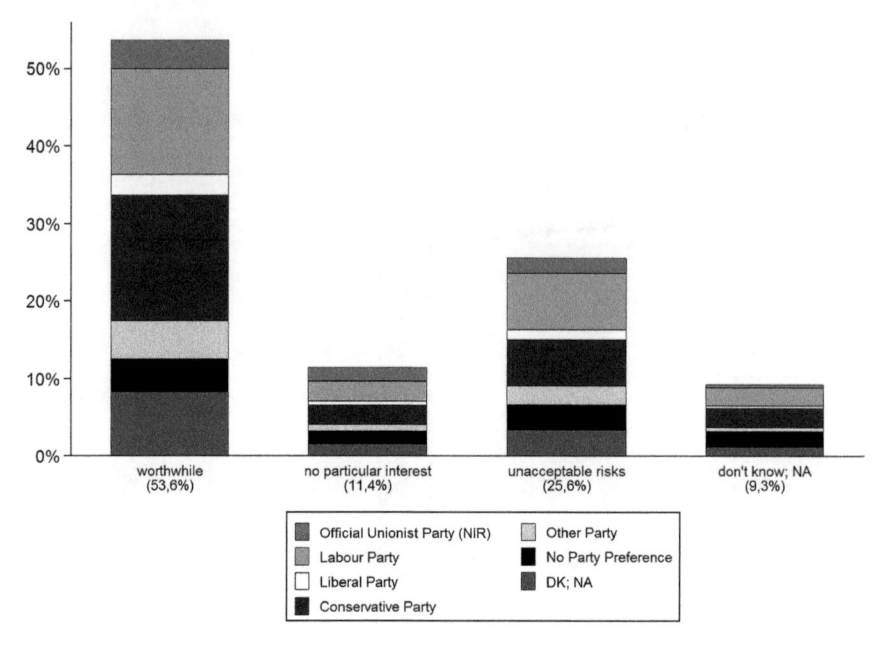

Figure 12.A16. Attitudes on Nuclear Energy among British Party Voters in 1978
Source: EB 10A.

(Figures 12.A16 and 12.A17). Such a gap between public opinion and policy outcome is not exceptional in comparative perspective. What is exceptional is the continuous reduction of that gap that followed over the next years. Accordingly, the Labour party adjusted to public opinion in its manifesto in 1983: 'There are also important savings to be made by cancelling the present government's massive expenditure programmes on Trident and on PWR nuclear reactors. Stop Sizewell and scrap the Tory PWR programme. The need for a continuing nuclear programme based on the British AGR (Advanced Gas-cooled Reactor) will be reassessed when we come to office'.

Labour thus resisted the massive extension of the nuclear energy programme the Conservatives planned, and rejected the new Sizewell reactor project in particular. However, the Labour manifesto remained silent with regard to the already existing large fleet of nuclear power plants.

In the 1987 campaign (i.e. at a time, where the German SPD already requested a phase-out of nuclear energy after Chernobyl) Labour addressed the nuclear energy issue more comprehensively: 'Labour will initiate a major energy conservation programme and ensure that Britain develops the full potential of its coal, oil and gas resources, whilst gradually diminishing Britain's dependence upon nuclear energy'. The manifesto continued: 'We will not proceed with the building of the proposed Pressurised Water Reactor at Sizewell. We share national concern about the problem of nuclear waste. We will ensure a safe future for Sellafield and develop a new strategy for the monitoring, storage and disposal of nuclear waste'. And: 'Stop radio-active discharges into our seas and oppose the dumping of nuclear waste at sea'. Why this subtle, very reserved, and clearly ambivalent declarations?

We refer to Figure 12.A16 showing the amounts of party adherents across different categories of issues attitudes. Note that we use here as reference point the whole sample for the calculation of percentages in order to be able to assess electorally relevant segments. The first Eurobarometer available for the UK in 1978 revealed that 13.7 per cent consider

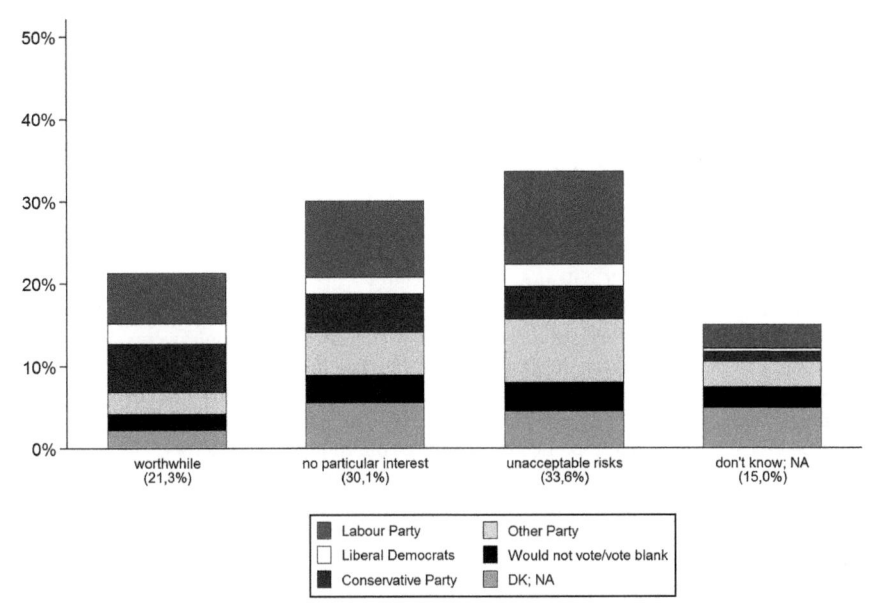

Figure 12.A17. Attitudes on Nuclear Energy among British Party Voters in 1996
Source: EB 46.0.

nuclear energy worthwhile against 7.3 per cent considering it 'unacceptable due to its risks'. Whereas the relationship was 2:1 in the case of Labour, it was 3:1 in case of the Conservatives. More than 8 per cent of the sample considered nuclear energy 'worthwhile' but did not yet know which party to vote for. Although the British parties thus faced a strategic dilemma with regard to the nuclear energy issue it was a minor one as the electoral system protected them against a Green party and the issue was not very salient.

As we have already seen, the Liberals, a party appealing to voter segments that are susceptible to vote for Green parties in other countries, was most responsive to anti-nuclear concerns. In the 1987 elections the Liberals also switched position and took a stand against the building of Sizewell, but continued to promote the development of the fast-breeder technology—nine years after the German FDP in North-Rhine-Westphalia had positioned itself against the completion of the fast-breeder reactor Kalkar. In 1992, the Liberals eventually took a fully fledged anti-nuclear position, demanding a phase-out until 'at the latest by the year 2020 (and earlier if feasible)'.

In their 1992 manifesto, after having been out of government for thirteen years, Labour demanded a phase-out: 'We will not invest in new nuclear power stations, continue with those in the planning process or extend the lives of existing nuclear stations beyond their safe life span. Britain's dependence on nuclear power will therefore steadily diminish. We will use the most modern technology to deal with the problems of decommissioning and nuclear waste'.

The Sizewell reactor went operational in 1995. Nuclear energy had a low profile in the 1997 elections although this election was relatively close to the Chernobyl accident. The topic was not even mentioned by the Conservatives. Labour simply and shortly stated: 'We see no economic case for the building of any new nuclear power stations'. The Liberals in their fifty-eight-word statement made another step in calling for a shift of research to decommissioning and nuclear waste management.

This election returned Labour under Tony Blair to government office. Although the election eventually turned out a landslide in Labour's favour, that had not been clear beforehand. Labour and Liberals had pre-electoral cooperation and mutual support arrangements in several constituencies and the option of Labour-Liberal coalition government was considered in the run-up to the election. Figure 12.A16 indicates according to the 1996 Eurobarometer that Labour was ahead, that voters' rejection of nuclear energy had increased, but also that all parties' electorates continued to be quite heterogeneously composed with regard to the nuclear energy issue.

As a governing party the Labour party prepared its return to nuclear energy already in 2001 by stating that: 'Coal and nuclear energy currently play important roles in ensuring diversity in our sources of electricity generation'. It also highlighted that 'BNFL[31] is an important employer and major exporter'. The Liberals were meanwhile committed to phasing out, however without specifying the exact date: 'We will decommission and not replace nuclear power stations as they reach the end of their safe operating lives'.

In 2006, Labour eventually explicit endorsed the building of new reactors. This had been foreshadowed by its 2005 manifesto: 'We have a major programme to promote renewable energy, as part of a strategy of having a mix of energy sources from nuclear power stations to clean coal to micro-generators'. This mixed strategy has to be read against the steady but smooth increase in anti-nuclear attitudes until 2004. At the same time Britain had reached its peak in oil and gas production in 1999 and suffered a major decline thereafter, turned into being a net-importer of oil and gas after years of exporting.[32] Tony Blair framed his support for nuclear energy as a solution to dependence on energy imports as well as to climate change.

A government White Paper of January 2008 recommended building as much nuclear energy capacity as possible to contribute to the de-carbonization of energy production, envisaging the installation of up to 16 GW (see IEA 2014: 16). As Elliot (2013) has shown, the UK reactions to the Fukushima disaster were 'muted'. The government expressed incomprehension about the behaviour of the German government, and corroborated the British position to go forward with nuclear power. In 2011, the government provided a list of eight potential sites where nuclear facilities already existed (see IEA 2014: 19). World Nuclear Energy provides details of bids by different consortia that include inter alia EDF Energy, GE-Hitachi, ROSATOM, as well as Chinese companies. In October 2014, the European Commission approved UK plans to subsidize the construction and operation of a new reactor at Hinkley Point and considered them to be in line with EU state aid rules. Due to action taken by the Austrian government that is supported by Luxembourg and several providers of alternative energy this decision is currently (in 2015) under review with the European Court of Justice. Provided the plan is implemented, it may turn out to be the starting point for a new period of reactor building in the UK with projected grid connection in 2032. Another challenge on the way is construction itself given that the ERP III+ projects Olkiluoto (Finland) and Flamanville (France) are very much delayed and costs multiplied.

---

[31] British Nuclear Fuels until 2005 was the government-owned nuclear energy and fuels company.
[32] British oil production fell from close to 140 million tonnes in 1999 to less than 80 million tonnes in 2005 and continued to fall to slightly more than 40 million tonnes in 2013. Projections see a flattening out of this development until 2012. The curve of gas production has taken a similar shape. See UKCS Oil and Gas Production Projections, <www.gov.uk/government/uploads/system/uploads/attachment_data/file/503852/OGA_production_projections_-_February_2016.pdf>.

REFERENCES

Aardal, Bernt (1990). 'Green Politics: A Norwegian Experience.' *Scandinavian Political Studies*, 13(2): 147–62.
Amorim Neto, Octavio (2003). 'Portugal: Changing Patterns of Delegation and Accountability under the President's Watchful Eye', in Kaare Strøm, Wolfgang C. Müller, and Torbjörn Bergman (eds), *Delegation and Accountability in Parliamentary Democracies*. Oxford: Oxford University Press, 552–72.
Andersen, Jørgen Goul (1990). 'Denmark: Environmental Conflict and the "Greening" of the Labor Movement.' *Scandinavian Political Studies*, 13(2): 185–210.
Andersen, Svein S. (1980). 'Conflict over New Technology: The Case of Nuclear Power Planning in Norway 1972–74.' *Acta Sociologica*, 23(4): 297–310.
Arter, David (1981). 'Kekkonen's Finland: Enlightened Despotism or Consensual Democracy?' *West European Politics*, 4(3): 219–34.
Baker, Susan (1988). 'The Nuclear Power Issue in Ireland: The Role of the Irish Anti-Nuclear Movement.' *Irish Political Studies*, 3: 3–17.
Barbé, Luc (2009). 'Energy Policy and the Nuclear Sector in Belgium', in Lutz Mez, Mycel Schneider, and Steve Thomas (eds), *International Perspectives on Energy Policy and the Role of Nuclear Power*. Brentwood: Multi-Science Publishing, 223–35.
Bärs, Brun (1979). 'Finnland: Atomkraft zwischen den Blöcken', in Lutz Mez (ed.), *Der Atomkonflikt: Atomindustrie, Atompolitik und Anti-Atom-Bewegung im internationalen Vergleich*. Berlin: Olle & Wolter, 118–30.
Bechberger, Mischa (2009). 'Nuclear Power in Spain: From Energy Autarchy and Military Dreams via Moratorium and Phase out to a Nuclear Renaissance?', in Lutz Mez, Mycle Schneider, and Steve D. Thomas (eds), *International Perspectives on Energy Policy and the Role of Nuclear Power*. Brentwood: Multi-Science Publishing, 351–70.
Bruckner T., I. A. Bashmakov, Y. Mulugetta, H. Chum, A. de la Vega Navarro, J. Edmonds, A. Faaij, B. Fungtammasan, A. Garg, E. Hertwich, D. Honnery, D. Infield, M. Kainuma, S. Khennas, S. Kim, H. B. Nimir, K. Riahi, N. Strachan, R. Wiser, and X. Zhang (2014). 'Energy Systems', in O. Edenhofer, R. Pichs-Madruga, Y. Sokona, E. Farahani, S. Kadner, K. Seyboth, A. Adler, I. Baum, S. Brunner, P. Eickemeier, B. Kriemann, J. Savolainen, S. Schlömer, C. von Stechow, T. Zwickel, and J. C. Minx (eds), *Climate Change 2014: Mitigation of Climate Change. Contribution of Working Group III to the Fifth Assessment Report of the Intergovernmental Panel on Climate Change*. Cambridge: Cambridge University Press, 511–97.
Brunnengräber, Achim, Maria Di Nucci, Rosaria Isidoro Losada, Ana Maria, Lutz Mez, and Miranda A. Schreurs (eds) (2015). *Nuclear Waste Governance: An International Comparison*. Wiesbaden: Springer.
Caro, Rafael, Manuel López Rodríguez, and Francisco Vighi (1995). *Historia Nuclear de España*. Madrid: Sociedad Nuclear Española.
Carter, David B., and Curtis S. Signorino (2010). 'Back to the Future: Modeling Time Dependence in Binary Data.' *Political Analysis*, 18(3): 271–92.
da Costa Oliveira, Jaime (2005). *O Reactor Nuclear Português: Fonte de Conhecimento*. Santarém: Editora O Mirante.
Dahl, Robert A. (2000). *On Democracy*. New Haven: Yale University Press.
Dalby, Simon (1984). 'The Nuclear Syndrome.' *Dawn Train* (Dublin/Belfast), 3: 3–24.
Dalton, Russel J., David M. Farrell, and Ian McAllister (2011). *Political Parties and Democratic Linkage: How Parties Organize Democracy*. Oxford: Oxford University Press.
Delicado, Ana (2013). 'Scientists, Environmentalists and the Nuclear Debate: Individual Activism and Collective Action', in Ana Delicado (ed.), *Associations and Other Groups in Science: An Historical and Contemporary Perspective*. Newcastle: Cambridge Scholars Publishing, 189–208.

Drogan, Mara (2011). *Atoms for Peace: US Foreign Policy and the Globalization of Nuclear Technology, 1953–1960*. Dissertation. Albany, NY: State University of New York.

Drogan, Mara (2015). 'The Nuclear Imperative: Atoms for Peace and the Development of U.S. Policy on Exporting Nuclear Power, 1953–1955.' *Diplomatic History* (first published online: 18 Sept. 2015 doi:10.1093/dh/dhv049).

ElectionIndices. www.tcd.id/Political_Science/staff/michael_gallagher/ElSystems/Docts/ElectionIndices.pdf

Elliot, David (2013). *Fukushima. Impacts and Implications*. Basingstoke: Palgrave Macmillan.

Field, Bonnie N. (2009). 'Minority Government and Legislative Politics in a Multilevel State: Spain under Zapatero.' *South European Society and Politics*, 14(4): 417–34.

Field, Bonnie N. (2014). 'Minority Parliamentary Government and Multilevel Politics: Spain's System of Mutual Back Scratching.' *Comparative Politics*, 46(3): 293–312.

Field, Bonnie N. (2016). *Why Minority Governments Work: Multilevel Territorial Politics in Spain*. Basingstoke: Palgrave Macmillan.

Flam, Helena (ed.) (1994). *States and Anti-Nuclear Movements*. Edinburgh: Edinburgh University Press.

Gaspar, Júlia (2010). 'The Two Iberian Nuclear Programmes: Post-War Scientific Endeavours in a Comparative Approach (1948–1973).' Paper presented at the 7th STEP Meeting, Galway, 17–20 June.

Hooghe, Liesbeth, Gary Marks and Arjan Schakel (2008). 'Measuring Regional Authority.' *Regional and Federal Studies*, 18(2–3): 111–20.

Hooghe, Liesbet, Gary Marks, Arjan H. Schakel, Sara Niedzwiecki, Sandra Chapman Osterkatz, and Sarah Shair- Rosenfield (2016). *Measuring Regional Authority: A Postfunctionalist Theory of Governance, Vol.I.* Oxford: Oxford University Press.

IAEA (2015). *Nuclear Power Reactors in the World*. Reference Data Series No. 2. 2015 edn. Vienna: IAEA.

IEA (2008). *Energy Policies of IEA Countries: Luxembourg 2008 Review*. Paris: IEA.

IEA (2009). *Energy Policies of IEA Countries: Belgium 2009 Review*. Paris: IEA.

IEA (2011a). *Energy Policies of IEA Countries: Denmark 2011 Review*. Paris: IEA.

IEA (2011b). *Energy Policies of IEA Countries: Norway 2011 Review*. Paris: IEA.

IEA (2011c). *Energy Policies of IEA Countries: Greece 2011 Review*. Paris: IEA.

IEA (2012). *Energy Policies of IEA Countries: Ireland 2012 Review*. Paris: IEA.

IEA (2013). *Energy Policies of IEA Countries: Finland 2013 Review*. Paris: IEA.

IEA (2014). *Energy Policies of IEA Countries: The United Kingdom 2014 Review*. Paris: IEA.

IEA (2015). *Energy Policies of IEA Countries: Spain 2015 Review*. Paris: IEA.

Kitschelt, Herbert P. (1986). 'Political Opportunity Structures and Political Protest: Anti-Nuclear Movements in Four Democracies.' *British Journal of Political Science*, 16(1): 57–85.

Kitschelt, Herbert P. (1988). 'Left-Libertarian Parties: Explaining Innovation in Competitive Party Systems.' *World Politics*, 40(2): 194–234.

Knutsen, Oddbjørn (1997). 'From Old Politics to New Politics: Environmentalism as a Party Cleavage', in Kaare Strøm and Lars Svåsand (eds), *Challenges to Political Parties: The Case of Norway*. Ann Arbor: University of Michigan Press, 229–62.

Kojo, Matti, and Tapio Litmanen (2009). *The Renewal of Nuclear Power in Finland*. New York: Palgrave Macmillan.

Kolb, Felix (2008). *Protest and Opportunities: The Political Outcomes of Social Movements*. Frankfurt am Main: Campus.

Kunsch, Pierre L., and Jean Friesewinkel (2014). 'Nuclear Energy Policy in Belgium After Fukushima.' *Energy Policy*, 66: 462–74.

Leonard, Liam (2008). *The Environmental Movement in Ireland*. Dordrecht and London: Springer.

Linz, Juan J., and Alfred Stepan (1996). *Problems of Democratic Transition and Consolidation*. Baltimore: John Hopkins University Press.
Lund, Anne, and Finn Breinholt (1979). 'Dänemark – "Atomkraft – Nein Danke": Wie man Atomkraft erfolgreich verhindern kann', in Lutz Mez (ed.), *Der Atomkonflikt: Atomindustrie, Atompolitik und Anti-Atom-Bewegung im internationalen Vergleich*. Berlin: Olle & Wolter, 83–100.
Manin, Bernard, Adam Prezeworski, and Susan C. Stokes (1999). 'Elections and Representation', in Adam Prezeworski, Susan C. Stokes, and Bernard Manin (eds), *Democracy, Accountability, and Representation*. Cambridge: Cambridge University Press, 29–54.
Midttun, Atle, and Dieter Rucht (1994). 'Comparing Policy Outcomes of Conflicts over Nuclear Power: Description and Explanation', in Helena Flam (ed.), *States and Anti-Nuclear Movements*. Edinburgh: Edinburgh University Press, 383–415.
Molina, Ignacio, and Alberto Sanz (2011). 'The Politics of Nuclear Energy Policy in Spain.' Unpublished manuscript, Department of Political Science and International Relations, Universidad Autónoma de Madrid.
Müller, Wolfgang C., and Kaare Strøm (eds) (1999). *Policy, Office, or Votes? How Political Parties in Western Europe Make Hard Decisions*. Cambridge: Cambridge University Press.
Nathan, Ove (1981). 'Denmark: Power Options Still Open.' *Bulletin of the Atomic Scientists*, 37(3): 29–33.
Nelkin, Dorothy, and Michael Pollak (1982). *The Atom Besieged: Antinuclear Movements in France and Germany*. Cambridge, MA: MIT Press.
Nielsen, Henry, Keld Nielsen, Felmming Peterson, and Hans Siggaard (1999). 'Risø and the Attempts to Introduce Nuclear Power into Denmark.' *Centaurus*, 41(1–2): 64–92.
Nousiainen, Jaako (2000). 'Finland: The Consolidation of Parliamentary Governance', in Wolfgang C. Müller and Kaare Strøm (eds), *Coalition Governments in Western Europe*. Oxford: Oxford University Press, 264–99.
OECD Nuclear Energy Agency (2009). *Energy Policies of IEA Countries: Portugal. 2009 Review*. Paris and Washington, DC: OECD Publications and Information Center.
Ordóñez, Javier, and Sánchez Ron, José Manuel (1996). 'Nuclear Energy in Spain: From Hiroshima to the Sixties', in Paul Forman, Sánchez Ron, and José Manuel (eds), *National Military Establishments and the Advancement of Science and Technology*. Studies in 20th Century History. Dordrecht and Boston: Kluwer Academic Publishers, 185–213.
Presas i Puig, Albert (2005). 'Science on the Periphery: The Spanish Reception of Nuclear Energy. An Attempt at Modernity?' *Minerva*, 43(2): 197–218.
Richardson, Jeremy J. (ed.) (1982). *Policy Styles in Western Europe*. London: Francis Pinter.
Riker, William H. (1962). *The Theory of Political Coalitions*. New Haven: Yale University Press.
Rüdig, Wolfgang (1990). *Anti-Nuclear Movements: A World Survey of Opposition to Nuclear Energy*. Harlow: Longman.
Rüdig, Wolfgang (1994). 'Maintaining a Low Profile: The Anti-Nuclear Movement and the British State', in Helena Flam (ed.), *States and Anti-Nuclear Movements*. Edinburgh: Edinburgh University Press, 70–100.
Sabatier, Paul A. (1998). 'The Advocacy Coalition Framework: Revisions and Relevance for Europe.' *Journal of European Public Policy*, 5(1): 98–130.
Sánchez-Vázquez, Luis (2010). *La legitimación de la energía nuclear en España: El Fórum Atómico Español*. Granada: University of Granada.
Sánchez-Vázquez, Luis, and Alfredo Menéndez-Navarro (2015). 'Nuclear Energy in the Public Sphere: Anti-Nuclear Movements vs. Industrial Lobbies in Spain (1962–1979).' *Minerva*, 53(1): 69–88.
Schneider, Mycle, and Antony Froggatt (2015). *The World Nuclear Industry Status Report 2015*. Paris: Mycle Schneider Consulting.

Soroka, Stuart N., and Christopher Wlezien (2010). *Degrees of Democracy: Politics, Public Opinion, and Policy*. Cambridge: Cambridge University Press.

Sundberg, Jan, and Niklas Wilhelmsson (2008). 'Moving from Movement to Government: The Transformation of the Finnish Greens', in Kris Deschouwer (ed.), *New Parties in Government*. London: Routledge, 121–36.

Tauer, Sandra (2013). 'Kampfplatz Remerschen: Das Projekt eines Atomkraftwerks in Luxembourg aus Sicht deutscher und französischer Archive.' *Forum*, 327: 60–3.

Tavits, Margit (2007). 'Principle vs. Pragmatism: Policy Shifts and Political Competition.' *American Journal of Political Science*, 51(1): 218–29.

Thurner, Paul W. (1998). *Wählen als rationale Entscheidung: Die Modellierung von Politikreaktionen im Mehrparteiensystem*. Munich: Oldenbourg.

Thurner, Paul W. (2000). 'The Empirical Application of the Spatial Theory of Voting in Multiparty Systems with Random Utility Models.' *Electoral Studies*, 19(4): 493–517.

Thurner, Paul W. (2010). '"Issue-Unentschiedene" und "Issue-Inkonsistente" als Targetpopulationen? Das Beispiel Kernenergie (1987–2005)', in Thorsten Faas, Kai Arzheimer, and Sigrid Roßteutscher (eds), *Information-Wahrnehmung-Emotion: Politische Psychologie in der Wahl-und Einstellungsforschung*. Wiesbaden: VS Verlag, 333–53.

Tympas, Aristotle, Stathis Arapostathis, Katerina Vlantoni, and Yiannis Garyfallos (2013). 'Border-Crossing Electrons: Critical Energy Flows to and from Greece', in Per Högselius, Anique Hommels, Arne Kaijser, and Erik van der Vleuten (eds), *The Making of Europe's Critical Infrastructures: Common Connections and Shared Vulnerabilities*. Bassingstoke: Palgrave-Macmillan, 157–83.

Vehmas, Jarmo (2009). 'The Role of Nuclear Power in Finnish Energy and Climate Policies', in Lutz Mez, Mycle Schneider, and Steve D. Thomas (eds), *International Perspectives on Energy Policy and the Role of Nuclear Power*. Brentwood: Multi-Science Publishing, 37–54.

Wooldridge, Jeffrey (2002). *Econometric Analysis of Cross Section and Panel Data*. Cambridge, MA: MIT Press.

APPENDIX

Policy Scales for a Country's Nuclear Energy Policy

Pro-nuclear decisions are shown in Table A.1.

Table A.1. Pro-Nuclear Decisions

Code	Label	Description	Example
0	'State of nature'	None of the following decisions taken	Most countries in the early 1950s
1	Preconditions	Establishing the preconditions for a nuclear energy programme: building up research capacity, research reactors, establishing government institutions with specific tasks	France 1945 creation of Commissariat à l'Energie Atomique (CEA) Germany 1955 founding Federal Ministry for Atomic Issues (Bundesministerium für Atomfragen) Italy 1952 National Committee for Nuclear Research (Comitato Nazionale per le Ricerche Nucleari CNRN).
2	Decision to go nuclear	Government decision, parliamentary decision, or, if left to the private sector, decision of industry (e.g. founding of firms/firm divisions with purpose of building nuclear capacity) (whatever comes first)	France 1952 decision to go nuclear approved by parliament Italy 1955 electricity producing companies set up the Società Elettronucleare Italiana (Italian Electronuclear Company, Selni) Austria 1969 parliamentary resolution supporting plan to go nuclear
3	Building	Building of the first commercial nuclear plant(s) (including test runs): date construction started AND Building of first nuclear plant after a preceding phasing-out decision: date construction started	Italy 1958 Latina plant: construction started Germany 1962 Grundremmingen plant: construction started Austria 1972 Zwentendorf plant: construction started
4	Commercial operation	Connection of first plant to the grid for commercial purposes	France 1959 Marcould G2 Italy 1964 Latina
5	Expansion	Binding decision (not just White Paper, etc.) of expanding nuclear capacity beyond first step of planning (code 3) and commercial operation (code 4): planning and building new plants, replacing older stations by more powerful new ones, extending the lifetime of existing stations, . . . [Not recording each of the years where a decision was implemented but only the years of new decisions]	France 1964 Messmer Plan Italy 1966 CIPE approves the construction of a new nuclear power plant

Anti-nuclear decisions are shown in Tables A.2 and A.3. The scale relates to nuclear energy programmes, not individual power stations. That means we code the overall effects. Any expansion programme may shut down individual power stations (because they are unsafe, have reached their projected end of life, or are no longer efficient). When this happens but the total MW nuclear energy will be increased we code 5 (Expansion).

Table A.2. Anti-Nuclear Decisions 1

Code	Label	Description	Example
−1	Freezing	'Enough is enough'. Delay moratorium, stop expansion moratorium ('no more nuclear energy than we currently have') Including not connecting already built capacity to the grid (NB economic costs may be higher than with some forms of downsizing)	France 1981 time for debate under new Socialist government (no new projects started) = delay moratorium Germany 1987 decision not to build reprocessing plant Wackersdorf NL 1981 start of government-organized national debate on nuclear energy = reorientation towards freezing
−2	Downsizing	Goal: 'We want less nuclear energy', including the deliberate terminating of research programmes or the closing down of prominent research institutes (for the goal stated)	Germany/Netherlands ???? not connecting the fast-breeder reactor Kalkar France 1998 closing down of Superphénix
−3	Gradual shutdown	Goal: 'Zero nuclear power tomorrow', code changes of original phasing-out plan as follows: Lifetime extension: Move up 0.5 (−2.5) Lifetime shortening: Move down 0.5 (−3.5)	Germany 2001 phasing-out decision under Red-Green government
−4	Immediate shutdown	Goal: 'Zero nuclear power today'	Italy 1987 discontinuing supply of Trino plant
−5	Forbid	Nuclear energy production forbidden by law	Austria 1978 ban on nuclear energy

Table A.3. Anti-Nuclear Decisions 2

—	Avoidance of decision	No new entry
—	Decision not to go nuclear (from 0, 1, or 2)	No new entry

Position-taking on nuclear energy in party manifestos is shown in Table A.4.

Table A.4. Position-Taking on Nuclear Energy in Party Manifestos

Code	Label	Description	Example
—	No statement about nuclear energy	No text on nuclear energy production (perhaps there is text on the nationalization of the nuclear industry, etc.: we do not code that)	
2	Unconditional support	Unqualified commitment to nuclear energy (to be found at heyday of belief in technological progress)	France PC 1973: 'it is by the implementation of a big nuclear programme that the satisfaction of the needs will be possible on the long run in the respect of national independence'
			NL parties of the extreme right PVV (Wilders) LPF (Fortune) 2000s: We should build nuclear power stations
1	Weak, conditional support		Italian Communists 1979: Limited and controlled use of nuclear energy...
0	No commitment		NL CDA 1980s: the expansion of nuclear energy production cannot be excluded
			Germany FDP 1976
-1	Freezing		I Socialist Party 1987: We should finish the existing building programme but not begin a new one
			NL D'66 2006: No new plants should be built but existing plants can still play a role...
-2	Downsizing		France PS 2007: 'We will decrease the part of nuclear by increasing the part of renewable energy from 20% to 50% (...)'.
-3	Gradual or immediate shutdown, exit		Italy Socialist Party 1987: We should replace nuclear energy with renewable energies
			Germany SPD 1998
-4	Forbidding		

Index

Accidents *see* Chernobyl accident;
    Fukushima accident; Three Mile
    Island accident
Austria
  see also **European Union (EU)**
  comparative case study analysis 302–8
  concluding remarks 120–2
  evolution of public opinion over time 71
  Green Party
    coalition politics 128
    comparative development 85–8
    electoral rise 127
    first running in national election 104, 113
    regional development 89
    relationship with movements and
      institutional openness 90–2
  impact of ban on electricity industry and
    other institutions 101–3
  policy development 99–101
  protest movements
    relationship with wider political
      context 80–3
    strength and development 75–9
  relevance of nuclear power in national
    politics 98–9
  statistical analysis 312–18
  voter attitudes and party competition
    current attitudes to nuclear
      energy 114–19
    institutional and party system
      background 103–11
    post-referendum attitudes 111–14

Belgium
  see also **European Union (EU)**
  analytical reconstruction 337–40
  comparative case study analysis 302–8
  evolution of public opinion over time 70–1
  protest movements
    relationship with wider political
      context 80–3
    strength and development 75–9
  recent national developments 9
  statistical analysis 312–18
Business communities
  Austria 102–3, 109–12
  political economy of electricity sector 39–40
  Switzerland 266, 273, 280
  United States 341

CDA (Netherlands)
  coalition politics 224–5
  party positions 222–4
  perceived party positions 225–31

CDU/CSU (Germany)
  permissive consensus until mid-
    1970s 159–60
  position-taking in electoral
    manifestos 176–9
  re-phasing in and re-phasing out 166–8
  stopping the fast-breeder reactor
    (FBR) 163
  stopping the Wackersdorf reprocessing
    plant 164
  voter preferences 174–6
Centre Party (Sweden) 240–4
Chernobyl accident
  accentuation of differences between
    systems 67–8
  cause of policy change 34
  dampening effect 22
  Dutch response 224–5
  effect on decision-making 13
  impact on French voting preferences 145
  impact on Italian nationalization
    policy 188–9, 198
  impact on public opinion
    France 141
    Germany 174
    Sweden 246
    Western Europe 70–1
  reminder of dangers 1
  Swedish policy response 242
  Swiss policy response 266–7
  underlying hypothesis 295–6
China
  assistance for Romania 7
  French market penetration 130–1
  Global Nuclear Energy Partnership 4
  recent national developments 6
Christian Democrats (Sweden)
  position-taking 241–4
  support for nuclear energy 249–51
Christian Socialist Party (Switzerland)
  275, 284
Climate change policy
  see also CO_2 reduction
  EU initiative 5
  France 143, 311
  G8 summit 4
  Germany 166
  government goals 31
  impact of Chernobyl 115
  Italy 289
  major challenges from policy change 305
  Netherlands 217–19
  Sweden 243, 256
  United Kingdom 356

CO₂ reduction
  argument for renaissance of nuclear
    energy 11
  Austria 116
  EU commitments 41
  Germany 158, 178–9
  Netherlands 223
  new evidence causing policy change 33
  Poland 55
  policy impacts 25
  Sweden 267, 278
Coalition politics
  Austria 113, 115, 128
  France 128, 151–2
  Germany
    phasing out nuclear energy 164–6
    pro-nuclear parties 172
    re-phasing in and re-phasing out 166–8
    role of Green Party 172–3
    stopping the fast-breeder reactor
      (FBR) 163
    stopping the Wackersdorf reprocessing
      plant 164
  Italy
    important variable 205–6
    party positioning on nationalization in
      1960s 193
    post-1994 era 192
    regionalization in 1970s 193–6
    relaunch of nuclear energy policy 203–5
    reversal of policy following
      Chernobyl 196–200
  Switzerland
    pro-ecology coalition 271, 274–6
    pro-growth coalition 271, 273–4
  underlying hypothesis 292–4
  United Kingdom 9
Communists (France)
  coalition agreement to stop
    Superphénix 128
  electoral and coalition strategies 147–52
  party positioning on nuclear power
    issue 135–9
  voter preferences 144–6
Comparative case study analysis
  see also **Statistical analysis**
  abstainers 299
  early complete withdrawal 299–302, 324–7
  non-reversal countries 308–12
  overview 298–9
  policy reversals 302–8, 337–46
Competitiveness *see* **Economic competitiveness**
CVP (Switzerland)
  opposition to nuclear energy 275
  party scales 272–3
Cyprus 55–6, 61, 62, 299, 312

DC (Italy)
  party positioning on nationalization in
    1960s 193
  position-taking in Electoral manifestos 213
  post-war governments 192
  regionalization in 1970s 193–6
  reversal of policy following
    Chernobyl 196–200
Denmark
  see also **European Union (EU)**
  analytical reconstruction 325–7
  comparative case study analysis 299–302
  evolution of public opinion over time 71
  import dependency 55
  statistical analysis 312–18

Economic competitiveness
  argument for renaissance of nuclear
    energy 11
  French electricity production 131, 135, 139
  Italian doubts about nuclear energy 187
  need for long-term planning 47
Electoral salience
  France 135, 141–4
  Germany 176
  impact of movement politics 321
  Italy 195, 205–6, 213
  Netherlands 233
  relationship with protest 76
  Spain 345
  Sweden 256, 277, 283
  underlying hypothesis 29, 288
Energy policy
  see also **Climate change policy**
  common underlying problems 11–13
  comparative case study analysis
    abstainers 299
    early complete withdrawal 299–302,
      324–7
    non-reversal countries 308–12, 347–56
    overview 298–9
    policy reversals 302–8, 337–46
  concluding remarks 42, 318–21
  development within individual countries
    Austria 99–101
    France 127–9, 153
    Germany 160–8
    Italy 185–90
    Netherlands 215–19
    Sweden 236–8
    Switzerland 261–71
  framework for change in EU
    costs inflicted by opponents on
      government policy 32
    EU integration 40–2
    institutions 37–40
    new evidence for external developments
      and events 32–4
    party and government goals 30–2
    path dependence 34–6
    public opinion 28–9
    responsive parties 29–30
  impact on of Green parties policy
    choices 68–9
  obstacles to revival of nuclear energy

availability of fuel 14
economic arguments 13-14
long-term concerns 15
proliferation of nuclear weapons 15
scarcity of qualified personnel 14-15
policy reversals
  see also **Policy reversals**
  dimensions which allow second order variations 25-7
  'first' and 'second' order changes distinguished 26-7
  meaning and scope 24-5
  role of politics 27
policy scales 361-3
statistical analysis 312-18
value of quantitative approaches 21-4
European Union (EU)
  contribution of NPPs to gross inland consumption 56-7
  differences chosen by comparable countries 60
  energy mix of countries 56-60
  evolution of public opinion over time 72-3
  external energy dependency 54-6
  framework for policy change
    costs inflicted by opponents on government policy 32
    EU integration 40-2
    institutions 37-40
    new evidence for external developments and events 32-4
    party and government goals 30-2
    path dependence 34-6
    public opinion 28-9
    responsive parties 29-30
  French conflicts with competition policy 131
  future prospects for nuclear energy in Western Europe
    climate policy 323-4
    energy security 323
    political rationales 324
    special answers for special case 321-3
  key comparative facts
    contribution of nuclear to overall electricity generation 49-52
    development of NPPs over time 52-4
  recent intiatives 5
  recent national developments
    differing approaches within Western Europe 8-10
    enthusiasm of new Member States 7-8
External energy dependency
  effect of diminishing resources 48
  European Union 54-7, 59-60, 61-3
  evolution of public opinion over time 74
  Finland 352
  future prospects for Western Europe 323
  importance to policy debate 47
  Italy 183, 184, 203
  relationship with consumption 184

  relationship with policy reversal 315-19
  underlying hypothesis 295

FDP (Germany) 159-60
  position-taking in electoral manifestos 176-9
  stopping the Wackersdorf reprocessing plant 164
  voter preferences 174-6
FDP (Switzerland)
  opposition to nuclear energy 275
  party scales 272
Federal systems
  Austria 119
  Germany 158-9, 163, 165, 168-73
  Green party development 89
  indicator of openness 91
  Luxembourg 91
  power divisions 39
  Switzerland 260-5
Finland
  see also **European Union (EU)**
  analytical reconstruction 347-52
  comparative case study analysis 308-12
  statistical analysis 312-18
FLI (Italy) 204
Forum for Nuclear Cooperation 5
FPÖ (Austria)
  concluding remarks 120-2
  current attitudes to nuclear energy 114-19
  institutional and party system background 103-11
  post-referendum attitudes 111-14
France
  see also **European Union (EU)**
  absence of major political cleavage 134
  central role of state and government 130
  Communists
    coalition agreement to stop Superphénix 128
    electoral and coalition strategies 147-52
    party positioning on nuclear power issue 135-9
    voter preferences 144-6
  comparative case study analysis 308-12
  concluding remarks 152
  conflicts with EU competition policy 131
  effect of new laws after 2006 133
  enduring committment to nuclear energy 125
  evolution of public opinion over time 70-1
  Gaullists
    electoral and coalition strategies 147-52
    party positioning on nuclear power issue 135-9
    voter preferences 144-6
Global Nuclear Energy Partnership 4
government decrees 133
Green Party
  absence of major political cleavage 134

France (cont.)
    coalition agreement to stop
        Superphénix 128
    comparative development 85–8
    electoral and coalition strategies 147–52
    party positioning on nuclear power
        issue 135–9
    voter preferences 144–6
  institutions
    absence of democratic debate 133
    Commission for Atomic Energy
        (CEA) 127–8, 130
    Institute of Radioprotection and Nuclear
        Safety 131–2
  main events 1945–2015 154
  main topic of agenda since 1950s 126–7
  massive development of nuclear
    energy 125–6
  parliamentary voting 132
  parties' electoral and coalition
    strategies 147–52
  party positioning on nuclear power
    issue 135–9
    absence of parliamentary challenges 135
    Gaulists 135–9
    Socialist Party 134
  policy development 127–9, 153
  'policy of champions' 130–1
  protest movements
    relationship with wider political
        context 80–3
    strength and development 75–9
  public opinion
    absence of majority support for nuclear
        energy 139–40
    impact of nuclear accidents 141
    varying public salience 141–4
  response to Fukushima 8
  scientific community
    links with nuclear energy 129
    public appeals against nuclear
        energy 129–30
  Socialists
    coalition agreement to stop
        Superphénix 128
    electoral and coalition strategies
        147–52
    party positioning on nuclear power
        issue 135–9
    voter preferences 144–6
  statistical analysis 312–18
  support for state-owned industry 126
  voter preferences 144–6
Fukushima accident
  accentuation of differences between
    systems 67–8
  cause of policy change 34
  effect on decision-making 13
  end of nuclear energy in Germany 167
  France's response 8
  impact on French voting preferences 145
  impact on public opinion in Western
    Europe 70–3
  Japan's response 6–7
  overall impact on nuclear build-up 9–10
  reminder of dangers 1
  Swiss policy response 269–71
  underlying hypothesis 295–6

Gaullists
  electoral and coalition strategies 147–52
  voter preferences 144–6
Generation IV International Forum (GIF) 4
Germany
  see also European Union (EU)
  CDU/CSU
    permissive consensus until mid-
        1970s 159–60
    position-taking in electoral
        manifestos 176–9
    re-phasing in and re-phasing out 166–8
    stopping the fast-breeder reactor
        (FBR) 163
    stopping the Wackersdorf reprocessing
        plant 164
    voter preferences 174–6
  centralized oversight 169–70
  comparative case study analysis 302–8
  concluding remarks 179–81
  energy as part of public services 168
  evolution of public opinion over time 70–1
  FDP
    permissive consensus until mid-
        1970s 159–60
    position-taking in electoral
        manifestos 176–9
    stopping the fast-breeder reactor
        (FBR) 163
    stopping the Wackersdorf reprocessing
        plant 164
    voter preferences 174–6
  Green Party
    comparative development 85–8
    institutionalization 171–3
    phasing out nuclear energy 164–6
    position-taking in electoral
        manifestos 177–9
    regional development 89
    relationship with movements and
        institutional openness 90–2
  ministerial involvement 169
  overview
    current energy mix 158–9
    nuclear energy as conflicting issue 157
    pre- and post-1985 history
        contrasted 157–7
  path dependence 168–9
  policy development
    phasing out nuclear energy 164–6
    re-phasing in and re-phasing out
        166–8
    reduction of research subsidies 160–2

stopping the fast-breeder reactor
    (FBR) 162-3
  stopping the Wackersdorf reprocessing
    plant 163-4
policy reversals
  changes in public opinion 173-6
  institutionalization of Green
    Party 171-3
  key question 159
  movements and protests 170
  phasing out nuclear energy 164-6
  pre- and post-1985 history
    contrasted 157
  re-phasing in and re-phasing out 166-8
  reduction of research subsidies 160-2
  series of policy modifications and
    adjustments 170-1
  stopping the fast-breeder reactor
    (FBR) 162-3
  stopping the Wackersdorf reprocessing
    plant 163-4
position-taking in electoral
  manifestos 176-9
protest movements
  relationship with wider political
    context 80-3
  strength and development 75-9
public opinion 173-6
recent national developments 9
SPD
  permissive consensus until mid-
    1970s 159-60
  phasing out nuclear energy 164-6
  position-taking in electoral
    manifestos 176-9
  re-phasing in and re-phasing out 166-8
  stopping the fast-breeder reactor
    (FBR) 163
  stopping the Wackersdorf reprocessing
    plant 164
  voter preferences 174-6
statistical analysis 312-18
Global Nuclear Energy Partnership 4-5
Government involvement
  framework for policy change in EU
    costs inflicted by opponents on
      government policy 32
    government goals 30-2
  France
    central role of state and government 130
    implementation of decisions by
      decree 133
  Germany
    centralized oversight 169-70
    energy as part of public services 168
    ministerial involvement 169
    path dependence 168-9
  Italy
    impact of centralized decision-
      making 187-8
    Ministry of the Environment role 192

nationalization 186-7
reversal of policy following
  Chernobyl 188-9
Sweden 236-8
Switzerland
  federal initiatives 264-5
  importance of federal structure 260-2
  intensified legislative action 267-8
Greece
  analytical reconstruction 335-7
  comparative case study analysis 299-302
  evolution of public opinion over time 71
  import dependency 55
  recent national developments 9
Green parties
  Austria
    see also **FPÖ (Austria)**
    coalition politics 128
    electoral rise 127
    first running in national election 104, 113
  classification 84-5
  comparative development 85-8
  France
    absence of major political cleavage 134
    coalition agreement to stop
      Superphénix 128
    comparative development 85-8
    electoral and coalition strategies 147-52
    party positioning on nuclear power
      issue 135-9
    voter preferences 144-6
  Germany
    comparative development 85-8
    institutionalization 171-3
    phasing out nuclear energy 164-6
    position-taking in electoral
      manifestos 177-9
    regional development 89
    relationship with movements and
      institutional openness 90-2
  impact on policy choices 68-9
  institutionalization 84
  regional development 89
  relationship with movements and
    institutional openness 90-2
  relationship with political openness 67-8
  relationship with public opinion 65-7
  statistical analysis 312-18
  Sweden
    policy development 238
    response to Fukushima 269
  Switzerland
    coalition politics 275
    comparative development 85-8
    limited role 283-4
    regional development 89
    relationship with movements and
      institutional openness 90-2
  underlying hypothesis 292

Harrisburg see **Three Mile Island accident**

Index

Iceland 299, 312
IdV (Italy) 203
Import dependency *see* **External energy dependency**
India
  ambitious plans 6
  French market penetration 130–1
  large number of commercial reactors 9, 22
  nuclear waste disposal 106
Institutions
  Austria - impact of ban on electricity industry and other institutions 101–3
  federal systems
    Austria 119
    Germany 158–9, 163, 165, 168–73
    Green party development 89
    indicator of openness 91
    Luxembourg 91
    power divisions 39
    Switzerland 260–5
  France
    absence of democratic debate 133
    Commission for Atomic Energy (CEA) 127–8, 130
    Institute of Radioprotection and Nuclear Safety 131–2
  Germany
    centralized oversight 169–70
    ministerial involvement 169
    path dependence 168–9
  imput structures
    see also federal systems *above*
    electoral systems 37–8
    representative and direct democracies 37
  Italy
    important variable 205
    Inter-ministerial Committee on Economic Planning/nl(CIPE) 191
    market operators 191
    Ministry of the Environment 192
    State–Regions Conference 192
  Netherlands
    environmental groups and organizations 221
    universities and institutes 221–2
  openness of political systems 67
  output structures
    political economy of electrical sector 39–40
    vertical power divisions 39
  relationship with movements parties and institutional openness 90–2
  state structure 67
  Sweden 239–40
International Framework for Nuclear Energy Cooperation 4–5
International learning 12–13
Investment
  Austria 104
  cost-benefit outcomes for EU 41–2
  France 129, 149
  Germany 165–6
  Italy 199, 206
  Netherlands 218, 221
  obstacle to revival of nuclear energy 14
  relevance 8
  'stranded cost' 35
  Sweden 244, 254
  underlying hypothesis 296–7
  United States 6
Ireland
  see also **European Union (EU)**
  analytical reconstruction 327–9
  comparative case study analysis 299–302
  statistical analysis 312–18
Issue entrepreneurs
  institutionalization as Green Parties 84
  Italian PSI
    comparison with PdL 291
    exception to general rule 288
  new political actors 23
  politicization of nuclear energy 320
  strategy followed by mainstream parties 319
  Swedish Centre Party
    exception to general rule 288
Issue-inconsistency
  Austria 104, 108, 108–11
  Belgium 339
  defined 30
  France 147
  Germany 174–5
  impact on policy change 290–2
  Italy 184, 201, 201–5, 205
  Netherlands 225, 227, 230
  Switzerland 272
  underlying hypothesis 290–2
Italy
  see also **European Union (EU)**
  comparative case study analysis 302–8
  evolution of public opinion over time 71
  explanations for policy 206
  historical shifts 183–4
  institutions
    important variable 205
    Inter-ministerial Committee on Economic Planning/nl(CIPE) 191
    market operators 191
    Ministry of the Environment 192
    State–Regions Conference 192
  market operators 191
  parties 192
  party competition
    important variable 205
    nationalization in 1960s 193
    regionalization in 1970s 193–6
    relaunch of nuclear energy policy 203–5
    reversal of policy following Chernobyl 196–200
  policy development
    early regulation 185–6
    graph 1945–2013 212

impact of centralized decision-
making 187–8
nationalization 186–7
relaunch and new regulatory
framework 190
reversal of policy following
Chernobyl 188–9
ventures during 1960s 185
policy reversals
historical shifts 183–4
impact of Chernobyl 188–9
relaunch and new regulatory
framework 190
reversal of policy following
Chernobyl 188–9
policy variables 205–6
position-taking in Electoral manifestos 213
protest movements
relationship with wider political
context 80–3
strength and development 75–9
public opinion
1978–89 196
1991–2011 200–2
important variable 205
Raw Data for a Nuclear Energy Policy
Scale 207–11
recent national developments 9
statistical analysis 312–18

Japan
Global Nuclear Energy Partnership 4
recent national developments 6
response to Fukushima 6–7

Left Party (Sweden)
position-taking 240–4
support for nuclear energy 249–51
Liberal Party (Sweden)
position-taking 241–4
support for nuclear energy 249–51
Luxembourg
see also **European Union (EU)**
analytical reconstruction 329–30
comparative case study analysis 299–302
federal openness 91
nuclear energy consumption 61
statistical analysis 312–18

Malta 55–6, 61–3, 299, 312
see also **European Union (EU)**
Movements
Austria 104–6
France
failure to influence policy 127
government response 138
importance 149, 152
Germany
cause of policy reversals 170
stopping the fast-breeder reactor
(FBR) 162

stopping the Wackersdorf reprocessing
plant 164
importance 75
Italy
cause of delays 188
explanations for policy 205
regionalization in 1970s 194
mobilization of resistance 299
'natural enemies' of nuclear energy 92–3
Netherlands 216, 221
relationship with parties and institutional
openness 90–2
relationship with public opinion 65–7
relationship with wider political
context 80–3
strength and development 75–9
Sweden 240, 255
Switzerland
concluding remarks 282–3
constitution as national actor 264
critical events 259–60
failures of 1980s 266
framing of debate 278
impact of Chernobyl 266–7
impact of radical wing 265–6
impact on policy change 262
policy milestones 263
popular initiatives in 2001 268
position of the Swiss Social
Democrats 274–5
roots of pro-ecology coalition 274
MSI (Italy) 193

Nationalization see **Government
involvement**
'Negative feedback' 34
Netherlands
see also **European Union (EU)**
coalition politics 224–5
comparative case study analysis 302–8
concluding remarks 231–3
evolution of public opinion over time 70–1
Green Party
comparative development 85–8
industry views 221
institutions
environmental groups and
organizations 221
universities and institutes 221–2
overview 215
party competition 225–31
party positions 222–4
perceived party positions 225–32
policy development 215–19, 220
professionalism 221
protest movements
relationship with wider political
context 80–3
strength and development 75–9
recent national developments 9
statistical analysis 312–18

NL (Italy) 203
Norway
  analytical reconstruction 331–2
  comparative case study analysis
    299–302
  statistical analysis 312–18
Nuclear accidents *see* Chernobyl accident;
    Fukushima accident; Three Mile
    Island accident
Nuclear energy *see also* Energy policy
  concluding remarks 318–21
  future prospects for Western Europe
    climate policy 323–4
    energy security 323
    political rationales 324
    special answers for special case 321–3
  post-war belief in progress 3
  return to the political agenda
    development of Generation IV
      reactors 4
    early protests 3
    Generation IV International Forum
      (GIF) 4
    global initiatives 4–5
    national initiatives 5–10
    new bifurcation of policy 10
    period of stagnation and decline 4
    regional initiatives 5
    'renaissance' from late 1990s
      onwards 3–4
Nuclear renaissance
  broad international trend 10–11
  current changes 24
  France 143
  Italy 183, 190, 203
  late 1990s return to nuclear energy 3
  protest mobilization 79, 83
  public opinion 71
  short-term obstacles 13
Nuclear weapons
  Austria 116
  France 127
  Germany 169
  no connection with nuclear energy
    expansion 21
  obstacles to revival of nuclear energy 15
  Sweden 235

Openness of political systems 67
ÖVP 103–11
ÖVP (Austria)
  concluding remarks 120–2
  current attitudes to nuclear energy
    114–19
  institutional and party system
    background 103–11
  post-referendum attitudes 111–14

Parties
  see also Party competition
  Austria

  institutional and party system
    background 103–11
  relevance of nuclear power in national
    politics 98–9
framework for policy change in EU
  party goals 30–2
  responsive parties 29–30
France
  absence of major political cleavage 134
  coalition agreement to stop
    Superphénix 128
  electoral and coalition strategies 147–52
  positioning on nuclear power
    issue 134–9
Germany
  permissive consensus until mid-
    1970s 159–60
  phasing out nuclear energy 164–6
  position-taking in electoral
    manifestos 176–9
  re-phasing in and re-phasing out
    166–8
  stopping the fast-breeder reactor
    (FBR) 163
  stopping the Wackersdorf reprocessing
    plant 164
Green parties
  classification 84–5
  comparative development 85–8
  impact on policy choices 68–9
  institutionalization 84
  'natural enemies' of nuclear energy
    92–3
  regional development 89
  relationship with movements and
    institutional openness 90–2
  relationship with political
    openness 67–8
  relationship with public opinion 65–7
Italy 192
Netherlands 222–4
position-taking
Switzerland 272–3
underlying hypothesis 287–8
Party competition
  see also Parties
  Austria
    banning of nuclear energy 98
    current attitudes to nuclear
      energy 114–19
    institutional and party system
      background 103–11
    post-referendum attitudes 111–14
    voter attitudes 103–19
  classic electoral systems 38
  Germany 176–9
  Green party development 85, 87
  Italy
    important variable 205
    nationalization in 1960s 193
    regionalization in 1970s 193–6

relaunch of nuclear energy policy
    203–5
reversal of policy following
    Chernobyl 196–200
Netherlands 225–31
relevance 2
Sweden 240–4
underlying hypothesis 294–5
vertical power divisions 39
Path dependence
Austria 122
cause of policy change 34–6
Germany 168–9
PCI (Italy)
party positioning on nationalization in
    1960s 193
position-taking in Electoral manifestos 213
post-war governments 192
regionalization in 1970s 193–6
PD (Italy) 203–5
PdL (Italy) 203
Phase-out
Germany
    reversal I 164–6
    reversals II and III 166–8
Japan 6
Sweden 24, 236–7, 242–8, 251, 257–8
Switzerland 263, 270
underlying hypothesis 35–6
PLI (Italy) 193
position-taking in Electoral manifestos 213
reversal of policy following
    Chernobyl 196–200
Policy see **Energy policy**
Policy reversals
see also individual countries
comparative case study analysis 302–8
concluding remarks 318–21
dimensions which allow second order
    variations
    comprehensiveness of programme 25
    magnitude of programme 25
    procedural measures 25–6
    quality of programme 25
    time-related changes 26
'first' and 'second' order changes
    distinguished 26–7
framework for change in EU
    costs inflicted by opponents on
        government policy 32
    EU integration 40–2
    institutions 37–40
    new evidence for external developments
        and events 32–4
    party and government goals 30–2
    path dependence 34–6
    public opinion 28–9
    responsive parties 29–30
meaning and scope 24–5
statistical analysis 312–18
Political parties see **Parties**

Portugal
see also **European Union (EU)**
analytical reconstruction 333–5
comparative case study analysis 299–302
import dependency 55
nuclear revival dynamics 9
recent national developments 9
statistical analysis 312–18
Position-taking see **Party competition**
PRI (Italy)
position-taking in Electoral manifestos 213
regionalization in 1970s 193–6
reversal of policy following
    Chernobyl 196–200
Protests
see also **Movements**
France in 1970s 128
Germany 163–4, 170
    role of Green Party 172
massive citizen protests of 1970s 3
relationship with wider political
    context 80–3
strength and development 75–9
Sweden 240
PSDI (Italy)
position-taking in Electoral manifestos 213
regionalization in 1970s 193–6
reversal of policy following
    Chernobyl 196–200
PSI (Italy)
party positioning on nationalization in
    1960s 193
position-taking in Electoral manifestos 213
post-war governments 192
regionalization in 1970s 193–6
reversal of policy following
    Chernobyl 196–200
Public opinion
Austria
    relevance of nuclear power in national
        politics 98–9
classic electoral systems 38
evolution in specific countries 70–4
framework for policy change in EU 28–9
France
    absence of majority support for nuclear
        energy 139–40
    impact of nuclear accidents 141
    varying public salience 141–4
Germany 173–6
impact on nuclear energy 67–8
Italy
    1978–89 196
    1991–2011 200–2
    important variable 205
'natural enemies' of nuclear energy 92–3
'negative feedback' from accidents 34
Netherlands 225–31
relationship with formation of new
    parties 65–7
relevance 2

374 Index

Public opinion (*cont.*)
  Sweden
    on nuclear power 245–51
    on official nuclear policy 251–4
  Switzerland 278–81
  underlying hypothesis 28–90
PvdA (Netherlands)
  coalition politics 225
  party positions 222–4
  perceived party positions 225–31

Renaissance *see* Nuclear renaissance
Russia
  first atomic reactor 3
  Global Nuclear Energy Partnership 4

Salience *see* Electoral salience
Security of energy supply
  argument for renaissance of nuclear energy 11–12
  EU commitments 41
  Finland 349
  Germany 169
  policy impacts 25
Social Democrats (Sweden)
  position-taking 241–4
  support for nuclear energy 249–51
Social Democrats (Switzerland) 274–5
Socialists (France)
  coalition agreement to stop Superphénix 128
  electoral and coalition strategies 147–52
  party positioning on nuclear power issue 135–9
  voter preferences 144–6
Soviet Union 3
SP (Switzerland) 272
Spain
  see also European Union (EU)
  analytical reconstruction 340–7
  comparative case study analysis 302–8
  protest movements
    relationship with wider political context 80–3
    strength and development 75–9
  recent national developments 9
  statistical analysis 312–18
SPD (Germany)
  permissive consensus until mid-1970s 159–60
  phasing out nuclear energy 164–6
  position-taking in electoral manifestos 176–9
  re-phasing in and re-phasing out 166–8
  stopping the Wackersdorf reprocessing plant 164
  voter preferences 174–6
SPÖ (Austria)
  concluding remarks 120–2
  current attitudes to nuclear energy 114–19

institutional and party system background 103–11
post-referendum attitudes 111–14
State involvement *see* Government involvement
Statistical analysis 312–18
  see also Comparative case study analysis
Surveys
  Austria 105, 108–10, 113–14
  Chernobyl effect 71
  few national surveys on issue salience 288, 290
  France 139, 144, 146
  Germany 171, 173–4
  identification of general trends 92–3
  Italy 196, 200, 204
  measuring public opinion 69
  mobilization of resistance 299
  Netherlands 225–7, 230
  Sweden 246–8, 251
  Switzerland 278–82
  voter preferences 345
SVP (Switzerland)
  party scales 272
  support for nuclear energy 275
Sweden
  see also European Union (EU)
  comparative case study analysis 302–8
  concluding remarks 254–7
  current reliance on nuclear energy 235
  early politicization of energy 235
  government involvement 236–8
  Green parties
    comparative development 85–8
    policy development 238
    response to Fukushima 269
  party competition 240–4
  policy development 236–8
  protest movements
    relationship with wider political context 80–3
    strength and development 75–9
  public opinion
    on nuclear power 245–51
    on official nuclear policy 251–4
  recent national developments 9
  statistical analysis 312–18
  voter opinions 244–5
Switzerland
  see also European Union (EU)
  business community 272–3
  comparative case study analysis 302–8
  concluding remarks 282–4
  critical junctures in nuclear policy 259–60
  current reliance on nuclear energy 259
  federal structure 260–2
  Green Party
    coalition politics 275
    comparative development 85–8
    limited role 283–4

regional development 89
relationship with movements and
 institutional openness 90–2
importance of direct democracy 260
liberalization of electricity 273–4
movements
 concluding remarks 282–3
 constitution as national actor 264
 critical events 259–60
 failures of 1980s 266
 framing of debate 278
 impact of Chernobyl 266–7
 impact of radical wing 265–6
 impact on policy change 262
 policy milestones 263
 popular initiatives in 2001 268
 position of the Swiss Social
  Democrats 274–5
 relationship with wider political
  context 80–3
 roots of pro-ecology coalition 274
 strength and development 75–9
parties 272–3
policy development
 1945–2013 261
 ambitious programme from 1960s
  264
 extended impasse 265–6
 federal involvement 264–5
 intensified legislative action 267–8
 policy milestones 263
 regulatory framework 262–4
 response to Chernobyl disaster 266–7
 response to Fukushima 269–71
 third turning point 268–9
policy reversals 282–4
political competition 276–82
pro-ecology coalition 271, 274–6
pro-growth coalition 271, 273–4
public opinion 278–81
recent national developments 9
statistical analysis 312–18

Technological progress
 argument for renaissance of nuclear
  energy 12
 Austria 110
 French energy policy 127
 Germany 158
 movement politics 319
 position-taking 363
 post-war belief in progress 3
Three Mile Island accident
 accentuation of differences between
  systems 67–8
 cause of policy change 34
 effect on decision-making 13
 impact on public opinion
  Austria 111
  France 141
  Germany 173

 Sweden 245–6
 Western Europe 70–1
Swedish policy response 241
underlying hypothesis 295–6

UdC (Italy) 203
UDF (France) 137
United Kingdom
 see also **European Union (EU)**
 analytical reconstruction 352–6
 change of course under Labour in 2008 8
 comparative case study analysis 308–12
 economic arguments against nuclear
  energy 14
 effect of diminishing resources 48
 first atomic reactor 3
 green light for construction programme by
  Coalition Government 9
 protest movements
  relationship with wider political
   context 80–3
  strength and development 75–9
 statistical analysis 312–18
United States
 economic arguments against nuclear
  energy 13–14
 French market penetration 130–1
 Global Nuclear Energy Partnership 4
 post-war belief in progress 3
 protest movements
  relationship with wider political
   context 80–3
  strength and development 75–9
 recent national developments 5–6

Voter attitudes
 see also **Electoral salience; Public opinion**
 issue-inconsistency
  Belgium 339
  defined 30
  France 147
  Germany 174–5
  impact on policy change 290–2
  Italy 201, 205
  Netherlands 225–31
  Switzerland 280–1
Voter opinions 254
 see also **Electoral salience; Public opinion**
 Sweden 244–5
Voter preferences
 see also **Electoral salience**
 Austria
  current attitudes to nuclear energy
   114–19
  post-referendum attitudes 111–14
 France 144–6
 Germany 174–6
 impact on responsive parties 29
 importance 28
 institutional imput 37–8
 policy choices 30–1

VVD (Netherlands)
  coalition politics 224–5
  party positions 222–4
  perceived party positions 225–31

Waste disposal
  argument for renaissance of nuclear energy 11

Austria 106, 116
Finland 347
France 133
Germany 166, 171, 177
Italy 186
long-term costs 15
Sweden 260, 267, 271, 276
Weapons *see* **Nuclear weapons**